Curriculum
LEADERSHIP

This book is dedicated to Dr. Allan A. Glatthorn,
Distinguished Professor of Education (Emeritus) at
East Carolina University, Greenville, North Carolina.
During his 55 years in education, he has served as a teacher,
principal, supervisor, and professor. He has authored more than
20 books in the fields of curriculum and instruction and consulted
with more than 200 school districts, assisting them in developing and
implementing their curricula. As coauthors of Curriculum Leadership:
Development and Implementation, *we hope this book will continue to provide*
completeness in curriculum thought, theory, development, and implementation.

—Floyd Boschee
—Bruce M. Whitehead

Curriculum
LEADERSHIP
Development and Implementation

Allan A. Glatthorn
East Carolina University

Floyd Boschee
The University of South Dakota

Bruce M. Whitehead
Missoula School District #4, Montana

SAGE Publications
Thousand Oaks ■ London ■ New Delhi

For information:

Sage Publications, Inc.
2455 Teller Road
Thousand Oaks, California 91320
E-mail: order@sagepub.com

Sage Publications Ltd.
1 Oliver's Yard
55 City Road
London EC1Y 1SP
United Kingdom

Sage Publications India Pvt. Ltd.
B-42, Panchsheel Enclave
Post Box 4109
New Delhi 110 017 India

Printed in the United States of America

Library of Congress Cataloging-in-Publication Data

Glatthorn, Allan A., 1924–
Curriculum leadership: Development and implementation / Allan A. Glatthorn, Floyd Boschee, Bruce M. Whitehead.
    p. cm.
Includes bibliographical references and index.
ISBN 978-1-4129-0426-1 (cloth)
  1. Curriculum planning—United States. 2. Educational leadership—United States. I. Boschee, Floyd. II. Whitehead, Bruce M. III. Title.
LB2806.15.G57 2006
375′.001—dc22   2005007119

This book is printed on acid-free paper.

        07   08   09   10   9   8   7   6   5   4   3

Acquisitions Editor:	Diane McDaniel
Editorial Assistant:	Erica Carroll
Production Editor:	Laureen Shea
Copy Editor:	Kristin Bergstad
Typesetter:	C&M Digitals (P) Ltd.
Proofreader:	Taryn Bigelow
Indexer:	Teri Greenberg
Cover Designer:	Janet Foulger

CONTENTS

PREFACE

This book is intended for those presently functioning as curriculum leaders and those preparing for such roles. Its central intent is to provide such readers with the knowledge and the skills needed to exercise leadership in curriculum at several levels and in many roles. To that end, it begins by exploring the foundations of the field so that decisions are made from a broad perspective and with a deep knowledge. The aim of this important book is to prepare prospective curriculum leaders to meet the challenges of today's changing globally connected classroom. Becoming an effective curriculum leader requires being totally committed to an important idea, having unwavering faith in the process, and understanding and promoting the value of positive change.

DEVELOPING CURRICULUM LEADERSHIP

It is crucial that our new leaders have the knowledge to apply curricula solutions that are working in one school with the changes that are needed in another—that they be able to understand problems and link similar innovations together to amplify their impact in education. It is through hard work, commitment, an inquiring mind, and the ability to learn from experiences, as noted in this text, that future curriculum leaders will be able to go from a local to a global understanding.

The challenge for the new leaders will be difficult, but the satisfaction is worth the effort. This book is designed to be an invitation for those in leadership to assume an active role in curriculum development. It is organized around the following questions:

- Is this a new idea?
- What is the quality of thinking as well as the quality of leadership that is being tested?
- Are we being creative in our approach?
- Have we learned from the past?
- What is the impact of changing curriculum, and will it spread and be shared by other leaders?

These are just a few of the important questions that must be addressed.

FEATURES OF THE TEXT

Several special features make *Curriculum Leadership: Development and Implementation* more accessible to you. Each chapter begins with **Keys to Leadership**, and includes **Chapter Overview**, **Chapter Terms**, and a section on practical **Applications**. Each chapter also contains a reflective **Case Study** as well as a **Challenge** to the reader with **Key Issues/Questions**. Scattered throughout each chapter are innovative **Curriculum Tips**. The book also provides a plethora of ideas and strategies that address present and future professional curricula needs.

Keys to Leadership

Keys to Leadership provide a series of informative strategies that relate to special understandings needed by future curriculum leaders. Each leadership key gives a practical and insightful view into the world of what works in the area of curriculum leadership.

Chapter Overview

The Chapter Overview provides an understanding of what is covered in the chapter as well as a cognitive set for chapter content. The overview also gives the reader the major concepts covered in the chapter as well as the organization of the chapter. As such, it represents a quick reference to chapter content.

Chapter Terms

Important terms used throughout the chapter are listed for easy reference. This gives the reader a quick and easy way to check on key definitions and understanding throughout the chapter.

Applications

This feature encourages the reader to stop at the end of each chapter to think carefully and reflect on the issues being presented. The applications are designed to help identify and analyze beliefs about the curriculum process. Each application deals with an important or controversial concept that provides thought-provoking exercises pertinent to the subject under discussion. These reflect features that reinforce the content, examine contentious topics, and challenge readers to explore their own ideas and beliefs.

Web Links and References

A series of Web links and references are noted throughout the book. These references are designed to encourage readers to explore links to Web sites where they can learn more about the curriculum process by researching issues, learning more about current curriculum applications and looking at practical applications of the material being presented in the text. These links may change over time, but they will initially help the reader gain an understanding and perspective about current curriculum issues and questions posed.

Case Study

This feature gives the reader an opportunity to spend additional time investigating controversial issues and topics that affect education today. Each issue or topic highlighted has been chosen because of its direct impact on schooling and its potential for impacting curriculum leadership.

The Challenge

At the end of each Case Study, the authors pose a Challenge to the reader. This segment is meant to provide a thought-provoking exercise that stimulates discussion and promotes self-understanding.

Key Issues/Questions

A series of meaningful and personalized questions that relate to ideas and content within the case study are provided to stimulate discussion. These thought-provoking questions help the reader analyze and develop deeper insights into the issues and concepts being discussed.

ORGANIZATION OF THE TEXT

In **Part 1**, the first chapter establishes the central concepts used through the work, explaining the general concept of curriculum and explicating its essential elements; the goal of this chapter is to provide the reader with a set of conceptual ideas. Chapter 2 reviews the past 100-plus years of curriculum history, so that decision makers can see the problems and solutions of the present from an informed historical perspective. Chapter 3 reviews several types of curriculum theory, because good theory provides deeper insight into the complex relationships involved in all curriculum work. Chapter 4 examines the politics of curriculum work—the way that power and influence affect curriculum decision making at the federal, state, and local levels.

Part 2 focuses on processes. The general goal of this part is to help the reader acquire the skills needed to bring about major curricular change. This part begins with an overview of the curriculum-planning process. Chapters 5, 6, 7, and 8 deal with the specific processes involved in improving and developing the three levels of curricula—programs of study, fields of study, and courses and units of study.

Part 3 of the book addresses management of curriculum. If curricula are to be truly effective, they must be managed well. Chapter 9 shows explicit ways in which the leader can supervise instructional processes and the selection and use of materials—the "supported" and the "taught" curriculum—to use the constructs employed throughout this work. Chapter 10 tells what is known about effective curriculum implementation and recommends specific processes for implementing curricula effectively. Chapter 11 provides a rationale for and explains the processes used in aligning the curriculum—ensuring that the written, the taught, the tested, and the learned curricula are brought into closer alignment. The last chapter in this part, Chapter 12, reviews several models for evaluating the curriculum and makes specific suggestions for developing and implementing a comprehensive evaluation plan.

The book closes with **Part 4** on curricular trends. Chapter 13 examines trends in the subject fields; Chapter 14 presents trends across the curriculum, including the use of computers; and Chapter 15 appropriately concludes with a focus on trends linking individualizing the curriculum and the needs of special students.

ANCILLARY MATERIAL FOR THE INSTRUCTOR

Appendix A

Appendix A displays the famous Management and Monitoring Matrix, which has proven to be one of the most useful and effective curriculum planning tools over the past decade. This unique matrix allows curriculum leaders to easily set Indicators of Success, leadership roles, activities, and a calendar of events to expedite a shared vision of curriculum change. The Management and Monitoring Matrix has also proven highly successful in aiding curriculum leaders during the process of writing grant applications.

Appendix B

This segment provides a step-by-step approach to developing a philosophy and rationale statement for a school's English and Language Arts program. With this addendum, curriculum leaders have at their fingertips a tried and true example of how to develop an entire subject area or discipline.

Appendix C

This important section provides a practical and detailed step-by-step approach on how to construct a scope and sequence for a program, program goals, objectives for the program goals, learning outcomes for the objectives, and authentic tasks for the learning outcomes (practical and results-centered) for students. Critical to the process is an example of a program's philosophy and rationale statement.

FUTURE CHALLENGE

Curriculum Leadership: Development and Implementation is an exceptional and an important textbook that allows for a better understanding of what future curriculum leaders will need if they are to address the educational challenges before them in curriculum development and implementation.

The overriding aim of curriculum leadership is to improve the opportunity for *all* children of whatever background in our public schools so that the borders between school and the independent sectors will be blurred. Curriculum leaders and educators need to constantly look for ways to achieve excellence in our schools. Like many other professionals, they must understand that changes in society require them not only to improve their performance, but to substantially redefine education's mission as well. Curriculum leaders and educators cannot continue to use their equivalent of the Model-T Ford for curriculum development and implementation. Education for *all* children requires the delivery capacity of a supersonic jet, a postindustrial information-age model, if we are to educate youth for the workplace and for social cohesion in the 21st century.

The recent education reform movements, stimulated by the No Child Left Behind Act, cannot be seen in isolation. These are part of a tightly knit package that is redrawing the educational landscape. The reforms, ranging from public schooling of 4-year-olds to federal funding of private schools, to accountability and results aimed at raising academic achievement for all students and improving the performance of poorly performing schools, were designed to generate excellence in education. The excellence movement is foundering and, at best, has brought on an alienation that pervades the nation's public schools.

Effective curriculum leadership can be the supersonic jet model for our schoolchildren, who will grow up in a world where nearly all of them will be brain workers, not manual workers. As curriculum leaders and educators, we are on the frontline of this change, and we have the responsibility to show that we can develop and implement curriculum without acrimony and resentment.

ACKNOWLEDGMENTS

Several colleagues and students have assisted us by recommending sources, locating and supplying materials, and reviewing portions of the manuscript. We especially wish to acknowledge the assistance received from the following graduate students in the School of Education, Division of Educational Administration, at The University of South Dakota: Jason Alons, Brian Corlett, Donavan G. DeBoer, Beth Dykstra, Tim Frederick, Robert Hirsch, Jerry Joachim, Sheryl Knutson, Preston Kooima, Dean Kueter, Joe Meyer, and Ronda Zinter.

The authors express their appreciation for the invaluable assistance given them by Marlene Jacobson in preparing the manuscript. Her editing and constructive reviews provided counsel throughout the project. In addition, we are grateful for the assistance we received from Ryan Sevening for his work, which added clarity to the manuscript.

The authors would also like to thank the staff at Sage who helped bring this textbook to life. Diane McDaniel has done a masterful job of keeping it on track and deserves special thanks. Her leadership will always be remembered and appreciated. Appreciation also is extended to professional colleagues at other colleges and universities who served as reviewers: Chris Zirkle, The Ohio State University; Kristine Reed, The University of South Dakota; Cynthia Chapel, Lincoln University; Phil McKnight, University of Kansas; Charles Lamb, Texas A&M University; Allen H. Seed, University of Memphis; Mary C. Clement, Berry College; Andrew L. Hunt, University of Arkansas at Little Rock; Robert Ferrera, Notre Dame de Namur University; David L. Grey, University of South Alabama; and Barbara Gonzalez-Pino, The University of Texas at San Antonio. Their insights were not only helpful but also encouraging and constructive. Finally, we wish to acknowledge the continuing and supportive help received from our wives and colleagues, Barbara Glatthorn, Marlys Ann Boschee, and Charlotte Whitehead.

Part 1

Foundations of Curriculum

Chapter 1

THE NATURE OF CURRICULUM

The intent of this introductory chapter is essentially to provide the reader with a general overview of the curriculum field and a set of concepts for analyzing that field. To accomplish these related goals, the discussion that follows focuses on these outcomes: defining the concept of curriculum, examining the several types of curricula, describing the contrasting nature of curriculum components, and analyzing the hidden curriculum. In this manner, some fundamental concepts essential for understanding the comprehensive field of curriculum can be established at the outset. Questions addressed in this chapter include the following:

- What is curriculum and why is it important?
- What are the types and components of curricula and how have they changed over the years?
- What are mastery, organic, and enrichment curricula, and what roles do they play in the development of curriculum?
- Why is knowledge of the "hidden curriculum" important to curriculum leaders?

Key to Leadership

Curriculum leaders should review and monitor curriculum policies to make sure that the policies align with curricular goals and that they support student learning.

THE CONCEPT OF CURRICULUM

In a sense, the task of defining the concept of curriculum is perhaps the most difficult of all, for the term *curriculum* has been used with quite different meanings ever since the field took form. *Curriculum,* however, can be defined as prescriptive, descriptive, or both. "Prescriptive definitions provide us with what 'ought' to happen, and they more often than not take the form of a plan, an intended program, or some kind of expert opinion about what needs to take place in the course of study" (Ellis, 2004, p. 4). Analogous to prescriptive curricula are medical prescriptions that patients have filled by pharmacists; we do not know how many are actually followed. "The best guess is that most are not" (Ellis, 2004, p. 4). This is parallel to the prescribed curriculum for schools where the teacher, like the patient, ultimately decides whether the prescription will be followed. In essence, "the developer proposes, but the teacher disposes" (Ellis, 2004, p. 4).

To understand the nature and extent of curriculum diversity, it might be useful at this juncture to examine the prescriptive and descriptive definitions offered by some of the past and present leaders in the field. The prescriptive definitions in the list below, which are arranged chronologically, have been chosen simply for their representativeness.

- Curriculum is a continuous reconstruction, moving from the child's present experience out into that represented by the organized bodies of truth that we call studies . . . the various studies . . . are themselves experience—they are that of the race. (John Dewey, 1902, pp. 11–12)
- Curriculum is the entire range of experiences, both directed and undirected, concerned in unfolding the abilities of the individual; or it is the series of consciously directed training experiences that the schools use for completing and perfecting the unfoldment. (Franklin Bobbitt, 1918, p. 43)
- [The curriculum is] a succession of experiences and enterprises having a maximum life-likeness for the learner . . . giving the learner that development most helpful in meeting and controlling life situations. (Harold O. Rugg, 1927, p. 8)
- The curriculum is composed of all the experiences children have under the guidance of teachers. . . . Thus, curriculum considered as a field of study represents no strictly limited body of content, but rather a process or procedure. (Hollis Caswell in Caswell & Campbell, 1935, pp. 66, 70)
- [The curriculum is] all the learning experiences planned and directed by the school to attain its educational goals. (Ralph Tyler, 1957, p. 79)
- A curriculum usually contains a statement of aims and of specific objectives; it indicates some selection and organization of content; it either implies or manifests certain patterns of learning and teaching. . . . Finally, it includes a program of evaluation of the outcomes. (Hilda Taba, 1962, p. 11)
- Curriculum is a sequence of content units arranged in such a way that the learning of each unit may be accomplished as a single act, provided the capabilities described by specified prior units (in the sequence) have already been mastered by the learner. (Robert Gagne, 1967, p. 23)
- [Curriculum is] all planned learning outcomes for which the school is responsible. . . . Curriculum refers to the desired consequences of instruction. (James Popham & Eva Baker, 1970, p. 48)
- The word *curriculum* means output of the curriculum-development process that is intended for use in planning instruction. (Michael Schiro, 1978, p. 28)
- Curriculum is a plan for providing sets of learning opportunities for persons to be educated. (J. Galen Saylor & William M. Alexander in Saylor, Alexander, & Lewis, 1981, p. 8)
- The curriculum is not a tangible product, but the actual day-to-day interactions of students, teachers, knowledge, and milieu. (Catherine Cornbleth, 1990)

- [Curriculum] refers to a written plan outlining what students will be taught (a course of study). Curriculum may refer to all the courses offered at a given school, or all the courses offered at a school in a particular area of study. (J. L. McBrien & R. Brandt, 1997)
- Curriculum is a prescribed body of knowledge and methods by which it might be communicated. (Alan Block, 1998)

The descriptive definitions of *curriculum* displayed below go beyond the prescriptive terms as it forces thought about the curriculum, "not merely in terms of how things ought to be . . . but how things are in real classrooms" (Ellis, 2004, p. 5). Another term that could be used to define the descriptive curriculum is *experience*. The experienced curriculum provides "glimpses" of the curriculum in action. Several examples of descriptive definitions of curriculum are listed below:

- All the experiences children have under the guidance of teachers. (Hollis Caswell & Doak Campbell, 1935)
- Those learnings each child selects, accepts, and incorporates into himself to act with, on, and upon, in subsequent experiences. (Thomas Hopkins, 1941)
- All experiences of the child for which the school accepts responsibility. (W. B. Ragan, 1960)
- The set of actual experiences and perceptions of the experiences that each individual learner has of his or her program of education. (Glen Hass, 1987)
- The reconstruction of knowledge and experience that enables the learner to grow in exercising intelligent control of subsequent knowledge and experience. (Daniel Tanner & Laurel Tanner, 1995)

The definitions above for prescriptive and descriptive curricula vary primarily in their breadth and emphasis.

It would seem that a useful definition of *curriculum* should meet two criteria: It should reflect the general understanding of the term as used by educators; and it should be useful to educators in making operational distinctions.

Curriculum Tip

The following definition of curriculum is offered and will be used in this work: The curriculum is the plans made for guiding learning in the schools, usually represented in retrievable documents of several levels of generality, and the actualization of those plans in the classroom, as experienced by the learners and as recorded by an observer; those experiences take place in a learning environment that also influences what is learned.

Several points in this definition need to be emphasized. First, it suggests that the term *curriculum* includes both the plans made for learning and the actual learning experiences provided.

Limiting the term to the plans made for learning is not enough, because, as will be discussed below, those plans are often ignored or modified. Second, the phrase "retrievable documents" is sufficiently broad in its denotation to include curricula stored in computer software or shared on the Internet. Also, those documents, as will be more fully explained below, are of several levels of specificity: Some, such as curricular policy statements, are very general in their formulation; others, such as daily lesson plans, are quite specific. Third, the definition notes two key dimensions of actualized curriculum: the curriculum as experienced by the learner and that which might be observed by a disinterested observer. Finally, the experienced curriculum takes place in an environment that influences and impinges upon learning, constituting what is usually termed the *hidden curriculum*.

Although the definition, for the sake of brevity, does not deal explicitly with the relationship between curriculum and instruction, an implicit relationship does exist. Instruction is viewed here as an aspect of curriculum, and its function and importance change throughout the several types of curricula. First, in the written curriculum, when the curriculum is a set of documents that guide planning, instruction is only one relatively minor aspect of the curriculum. Those retrievable documents used in planning for learning typically specify five components: a rationale for the curriculum; the aims, objectives, and content for achieving those objectives; instructional methods; learning materials and resources; and tests or assessment methods.

Instruction is a component of the planned curriculum and is usually seen as less important than the aims, objectives, and content at the actualized level; when the planned or written curriculum is actually delivered, instruction takes on a new importance. The supervisor or administrator observing the curriculum as the total learning experiences of a classroom seems to focus on instruction—how the teacher is teaching.

THE TYPES OF CURRICULA

The definition stipulated above suggests that there is a major difference between the planned curriculum and actualized curriculum. Yet even these distinctions are not sufficiently precise to encompass the several different types of curricula. Goodlad (Goodlad & Associates, 1979) was perhaps the first to suggest several key distinctions. As he analyzed curricula, he determined that there were five different forms of curriculum planning. The *ideological curriculum* is the ideal curriculum as construed by scholars and teachers—a curriculum of ideas intended to reflect funded knowledge. The *formal curriculum* is that officially approved by state and local school boards—the sanctioned curriculum that represents society's interests. The *perceived curriculum* is the curriculum of the mind—what teachers, parents, and others think the curriculum to be. The *operational curriculum* is the observed curriculum of what actually goes on hour after hour in the classroom. Finally, the *experiential curriculum* is what the learners actually experience.

While those distinctions in general seem important, the terms are perhaps a bit cumbersome and the classifications are not entirely useful to curriculum workers. It seems to be more useful in the present context to use the following concepts with some slightly different denotations: *the recommended curriculum, the written curriculum, the supported curriculum, the taught curriculum, the tested curriculum,* and *the learned curriculum.* Four of these curricula—*the written, the supported, the taught,* and *the tested*—are considered components of the intentional curriculum. The intentional curriculum is the set of learnings that the school system consciously intends, in contradistinction to the hidden curriculum, which by and large is not a product of conscious intention.

The Recommended Curriculum

The recommended curriculum is the curriculum that is recommended by individual scholars, professional associations, and reform commissions; it also encompasses the curriculum requirements of policy-making groups, such as federal and state governments. Similar to Goodlad's "ideological curriculum," it is a curriculum that stresses "oughtness," identifying the skills and concepts that ought to be emphasized, according to the perceptions and value systems for the sources.

Curriculum Tip

Recommended curricula are typically formulated at a rather high level of generality; they are most often presented as policy recommendations, lists of goals, suggested graduation requirements, and general recommendations about the content and sequence of a field of study, such as mathematics.

Several influences seem to play key roles in the shaping of recommended curricula. First, societal trends seem to have a strong influence on policymakers. The prevailing conservative mood of the 1980s in the United States and the concern about competing with Japan were undoubtedly factors that influenced many of the reform reports of that period. Second, advancements in technology also play a role. The widespread use of technology in the nation's schools has influenced several of the professional associations to include aspects of technology across the curriculum in their recommendations. Advancing excellence in technological literacy in our schools is vital because

> citizens of today must have a basic understanding of how technology affects their world and how they coexist with technology. Attaining technological literacy is as fundamentally important to students as developing knowledge and abilities in the traditional core subject areas. Students need and deserve the opportunity to attain technological literacy through the educational process. (Dugger & Nichols, 2003, pp. 316–317)

Professional associations and individuals also seem to have an impact. First, the professional associations representing the several disciplines, such as the National Council of Teachers of Mathematics, and those that represent school administrators, such as the National Association for Secondary School Principals, have been active in producing recommended curricula. Also, there seems to be a network of opinion shapers in the profession, who through their writing and consulting have a strong impact on recommended curricula as they attempt to translate the latest research into recommendations for content and methodology. Also, as will be discussed in Chapter 4, federal and state legislation and court decrees play a significant part. Public Law 94-142, requiring the "least restrictive environment" for handicapped pupils, and Public Law 107-110 H.R.1, as well as the No Child Left Behind Act (NCLB), charter schools, home schooling, school choice, and vouchers have had a profound influence on all those developing recommended curricula for these groups of learners.

Over the past several years, national educational organizations have launched a series of ambitious projects to define voluntary standards for science, mathematics, art, music, foreign languages, social studies, English language arts, and other subjects. These efforts have served as catalysts in a wide-ranging national conversation about the needs of students and the instructional approaches of their teachers. This also adds to the national dialogue by presenting the consensus that exists among thousands of educators about what all students in K–12 schools should know and be able to do in the various subject fields. The authors endorse the act of defining standards by the national organizations because it invites further reflection and conversation about the goals of public schooling. Those recommended curricula serve some useful functions. First, as recommendations about policies and requirements, they identify important boundaries, emphases, and endpoints for curriculum planning: All high school students should study one semester of computer science. Second, they promote equity and excellence for all students: learning how to learn; equal access to resources; adequate staffing; and safe, well-equipped schools. Finally, as we reviewed the standards set forth by the various learned societies, it was concluded that curriculum specialists and teachers should consider the following points:

- Standards are not a national curriculum.
- Standards are an attempt to define what students should be able to know and do.
- The standards are informed by the latest theory and research regarding the various curricula.
- Standards are field based; they build on past successes of teachers and students.
- Standards can be met through a variety of teaching styles and strategies.
- The standards project emphasizes that *all* students can learn and achieve at high levels if their background, needs, and interest are considered.
- Standards should be a source of professional conversation and critique about what to do and how to do it.
- Teachers are members of a professional community, and a variety of professional organizations are available to support teacher growth.
- The literacy demands of the 21st century will require students to construct meaning with a variety of tools and texts. (Wilhelm, 1996, pp. 2–13)

The recommended curriculum by the learned societies raises the sights of curriculum workers and teachers by suggesting what the curriculum ideally might become.

Since the late 1980s, raising standards in the core curriculum subjects has gained momentum in states and districts across the country. States have begun to use academic standards to make clear what students should learn and what teachers should teach. The recommended curricula by the learned societies will help curriculum coordinators and teachers make decisions about developing their instructional programs.

The Written Curriculum

Generally similar to Goodlad's "formal curriculum," the written curriculum seems intended primarily to ensure that the educational goals of the system are being accomplished;

it is a curriculum of control. Typically, the written curriculum is much more specific and comprehensive than the recommended curriculum, indicating a rationale that supports the curriculum, the general goals to be accomplished, the specific objectives to be mastered, the sequence in which those objectives should be studied, and the kinds of learning activities that should be used. Note, however, that Glatthorn (1980) questions such comprehensiveness; he recommends that the written curriculum should be delivered to teachers as a loose-leaf notebook, containing only a scope-and-sequence chart, a review of the research, a list of course objectives, and a brief list of materials to be used. This simpler format, he believes, would make the written curriculum more likely to be used.

Curriculum Tip

The written curriculum is the curriculum embodied in approved state and district curriculum guides.

Written curricula are both generic and site specific, to use two concepts proposed by Walker (1979): Generic curricula are those written for use in various educational settings. During the 1960s, numerous generic curricula were produced by federally funded research and development laboratories; now, more typically, they are produced by a state curriculum office and intended for use throughout the state, with some local leeway provided. Site-specific written curricula are those developed for a specific site, usually for a local school district or even for a particular school.

Site-specific written curricula are influenced by several different sources. First, as will be explained more fully in Chapter 4, federal and state legislation and court directives play a role. The passage of PL 94-142 with its requirement that schools provide the "least restrictive environment" for handicapped learners undoubtedly precipitated much local curriculum work to help teachers work toward "inclusion." The textbooks and standardized tests in use in the district seem to influence decisions about the inclusion and placement of content. The expectations of vocal parent and community groups seem to have at least a constraining influence on what can be done.

In general, however, the guides seem to reflect the preferences and practices of a local group of elites: a director of curriculum, a supervisor of that subject area, a principal with a strong interest in curriculum, and a small group of experienced teachers used to playing a leadership role. They, in turn, seem most influenced by the practice of "lighthouse" districts: There is much well-intentioned plagiarizing going on as they meet during the summer to produce the new guide.

The chief functions of written curricula seem to be three: mediating, standardizing, and controlling. They first mediate between the ideals of the recommended curriculum and the realities of the classroom; in this sense they often represent a useful compromise between what the experts think should be taught and what teachers believe can be taught. They also mediate between the expectations of administrators and the preferences of teachers. The best of them represent a negotiated consensus of administrative and classroom leaders.

They also play an important role in standardizing the curriculum, especially in larger districts. Often they are produced as a result of directives from a superintendent who is concerned that students in School A are studying a social studies curriculum or using a reading series quite different from those in Schools B and C.

Standardizing and centralizing curriculum is often used by district and school administrators as management tools to control what is taught. This control function seems to be perceived differently by administrators and teachers. Administrators believe that controlling the curriculum is an important management responsibility; they point to the research on school effectiveness that seems to indicate that in schools with higher pupil achievement there is a principal actively monitoring the curriculum to ensure that the written curriculum is being delivered. Waters, Marzano, and McNulty (2003), in *Balanced Leadership: What 30 Years of Research Tells Us About the Effect of Leadership on Student Achievement*, compiled more than three decades of research on the effects of instruction and schooling on student achievement and found a substantial relationship between leadership and student achievement (see Exhibit 1.1). The results of this study have provided practitioners with specific guidance on the curricular, instructional, and school practices that, when applied appropriately, can result in increased achievement.

However, as Walcott (1977) discovered in his ethnographic study of a district monitoring plan, most teachers view such attempts to control the curriculum as intrusive and counterproductive and will work hard to subvert such plans.

Predictably, written curricula, especially site-specific ones, are of uneven quality. The best of them seem to represent a useful synthesis of recommended curricula and local practice; they seem well conceptualized, carefully developed, and easy to use. Too many, however, lack those qualities. Careful reviews of a large number of such curriculum guides reveal that they suffer from some common faults: The objectives are often not related to the stated goals; instructional activities are not directly related to the objectives; the activities do not reflect the best current knowledge about teaching and learning; and the guides are generally cumbersome and difficult to use.

The Supported Curriculum

The supported curriculum is the curriculum as reflected in and shaped by the resources allocated to support or deliver the curriculum. Four kinds of resources seem to be most critical here: the time allocated to a given subject at a particular level of schooling (How much time should we allocate to social studies in Grade 5?); the time allocated by the classroom teacher within that overall subject allocation to particular aspects of the curriculum (How much time shall I allocate to the first unit on the explorers?); personnel allocations as reflected in and resulting from class-size decisions (How many teachers of physical education do we need in the middle school if we let PE classes increase to an average of 35?); and the textbooks and other learning materials provided for use in the classroom (Can we get by with those old basals for one more year?).

The patterns of influence bearing upon the supported curriculum seem rather complex. First, the state seems to exercise a strong influence on the supported curriculum. State curriculum guidelines often specify minimum time allocation, and some state-approved lists of basic texts restrict the choice of textbooks to a relatively small number.

The local school board, under the leadership of its superintendent, seems to play a key role. In many districts, boards will adopt curriculum policies specifying minimum time allocations to the several subjects, will approve district-purchased texts, and will make major budget

Exhibit 1.1   Principal Leadership Responsibilities

Responsibilities	The extent to which the principal . . .
Culture	establishes a set of standard operating procedures and routines
Discipline	protects teachers from issues and influences that would detract from their teaching time on focus
Resources	provides teachers with material and professional development necessary for the successful execution of their roles
Curriculum, instruction assessment	is directly involved in the design and implementation of curriculum, instruction, and assessment practices
Focus	establishes clear goals and keeps those goals at the forefront of the school's attention
Knowledge of curriculum, instruction assessment	is knowledgeable about current curriculum, instruction, and assessment practices
Contingent rewards	recognizes and rewards individual accomplishments
Communication	establishes strong lines of communication with teachers and among students
Outreach	is an advocate and spokesperson for the school to all stakeholders
Input	demonstrates an awareness of the personal aspects of teachers and staff
Affirmation	recognizes and celebrates school accomplishments and acknowledges failure
Relationship	demonstrates an awareness of the personal aspects of teachers and staff
Change agent	is willing to and actively challenges the status quo
Optimizer	inspires and leads new and challenging innovations
Ideals/beliefs	communicates and operates from strong ideals and beliefs about schooling
Monitors/evaluates	monitors the effectiveness of school practices and their impact on student learning
Flexibility	adapts leadership behavior to the needs of the current situation and is comfortable with dissent
Situational awareness	is aware of the details and undercurrents in the running of the school and uses this information to address current and potential problems
Intellectual stimulation	ensures that faculty and staff are aware of the most current theories and practices and makes the discussion of these a regular aspect of the school's culture

decisions that impact strongly on the personnel and material support provided. At the school level, principals also seem to have a major influence. They usually have some discretion in the allocation of funds for texts and other learning materials. They often are given some latitude in their requests for additional staff. The school master schedule is the major means for translating school priorities into decisions about curricular support.

Of course, the teacher plays a crucial role. Elementary teachers exercise a great deal of influence in determining how much time is allocated to particular subjects, despite the attempts of principals to limit such autonomy. All teachers have much autonomy about how time is allocated to given units or aspects of the curriculum.

Obviously the supported curriculum needs to be examined. The data are clear that several aspects of the supported curriculum have a major bearing upon what and how much is learned. First, time seems to be an important factor. In her review of the research, Stallings (1980) concludes that "the body of knowledge emanating from the research on teaching in the 1970s suggests that teachers should allocate more time to academic subjects, keeping in mind ability levels, and students should be kept engaged in the tasks" (p. 12).

Berliner (1984) cites some examples of the dramatic differences in the way time is allocated in elementary school classrooms. One fifth-grade teacher devoted only 68 minutes a day to reading and language arts; another teacher, 137 minutes. Karweit (1983), however, questions one aspect of this concern for time. In a review of the research on time-on-task, Karweit noted that "by a variety of criteria for the importance of an effect, the most outstanding finding relating the effects of time-on-task to learning is that the effects are as small as they are" (p. 46).

Second, does class size make a difference?

In a study of 20,000 fourth- and eighth-graders in 182 school districts across the country, the Educational Testing Services Policy Information Center found that fourth-graders from classes of 20 students or less scored higher on the National Assessment of Educational Progress (NAEP) than did their peers in larger classes. (Chambers, 1999, pp. 1–2)

Several studies have been conducted regarding class size. The results reveal the following conclusions: The Tennessee class size experiment demonstrated that students learn better when class sizes are reduced (Mosteller, 1995; Finn & Achilles, 1990). Achilles (1997) has shown that a ratio of 15 students per class, especially in the first grade, has the greatest effect on student achievement. Farber and Finn (2000) found that fourth graders who had experienced small classes through the third grade were more engaged in learning than those who had experienced [larger] classes with teacher aides (Danielson, 2002).

A doctoral study titled *Serendipitous Policy Implications From Class-Size-Initiated Inquiry: IAQ?* found different behavior patterns between teachers who had small classes (15–17) and regular classes (20–28). The findings revealed that as the day wore on, teachers in regular classes became irritable, edgy, and tired. "They wiped their eyes, sat down, and slowed or regimented instruction, often neglecting students' indiscipline, lassitude, and off-task misbehavior. All [teachers] seemed hassled" (Achilles, Finn, Prout, & Bobbett, 2001, p. 2). In contrast, teachers with small classes "remained full of energy all day. Time-on-task stayed high and constant with students remaining well behaved, engaged, and energetic. Student and teacher behavior were reciprocal, but positive" (Achilles et al., 2001, p. 2). Another factor that the study revealed was carbon dioxide (CO_2) levels. "CO_2 is related to the number of persons in a space, is cumulative, and causes drowsiness and lethargy that may influence teaching and learning. Class size and time of day seemed to be key variables" (p. 2).

Finally, the quality of the textbook and other learning resources as an aspect of the supported curriculum seems to play a central role. After noting that the textbook constitutes the basis of many teacher lectures and that seatwork with worksheets represents as much as two thirds of the time in elementary classrooms, Doyle (1983) noted several deficiencies of textbooks that researchers have discovered. For example, many textbooks present information in a confusing manner; the instructional procedures in the teacher's manual are often unnecessarily complicated for students; textbooks provide little explanation and direct instruction, but a great deal of practice and assessment material; and the overlap of textbooks and standardized tests is very low. Allington (2002) noted that "many students in Grades 5–12 struggle to learn from content-area textbooks that don't match their reading levels" (p. 16). As Chall (as cited in Allington, 2002) noted, the demands of reading increase dramatically for students in fourth grade as their learning begins to rely more on textbooks. For example, "the vocabulary for fourth graders is less conversational and less familiar, with more specialized, technical terms (delta, plateau, and basin) and abstract ideas (democracy, freedom, civilization)." In essence, "the syntax of texts becomes more complex and demanding" (pp. 16–17). Also, "the reasoning about information in textbooks shifts, with a greater emphasis on inferential thinking and prior knowledge. (For example, what stance is the author taking on industrial polluters? Is there another stance that others might take?)" (p. 17). As Baumann and Duffy (as cited in Allington, 2002) indicate,

> Schools have typically exacerbated the problem by relying on a single-source curriculum design—purchasing multiple copies of the same science and social studies textbooks for every student. This one-size-fits-all approach works well if we want to sort students into academic tracks. It fails miserably if our goal is high academic achievement for all students. (p. 17)

It should be noted that elementary school reading series contain several flaws: Stories written for use in the primary grades do not give enough insight into characters' goals, motives, and feelings; many of the so-called stories do not actually tell a story; textbooks lack a logical structure, often emphasizing a trivial detail rather than a fundamental principle. Harder textbooks, unfortunately, have captured the attention of educators and policymakers who want to raise academic achievement. Allington (2002) parallels the harder textbooks to one's own experience, for example, building a Web site. "Do you reject many of the books because they are too easy? Do you say to yourself, 'Gosh, only 11 words on this page I can't pronounce—not hard enough for me!'" (p. 18). With that thought, there needs to be a rethinking of what curriculum and instruction should look like.

Carol Ann Tomlinson (as cited in Tomlinson et al., 2002), noted curriculum author, indicates that the supported curriculum can also involve the use of flexible options and the formation of a parallel curriculum model. She notes in her book, *The Parallel Curriculum,* that parallels can be used to develop or support curriculum for individuals, small groups, and entire classes. The term *parallel* indicates several formats through which educators can approach curriculum design in the same subject or discipline. Tomlinson refers to the four parallels as: Core Curriculum, Curriculum and Connections, Curriculum of Practice, and Curriculum of Identity. These parallel processes can be deductive or inductive and can be used as a catalyst to discover student abilities and interests or in response to student abilities and interests. Tomlinson believes that these parallels act as support for thematic study and help connect content that might otherwise seem disjointed to learners. Using her model, a teacher might establish a definition of change, identify key principles related to change, and introduce students to key skills as well as specify standards that need to be covered. Tomlinson's parallel model for curriculum development is only one of the many approaches that can be used to help support curriculum.

The supported curriculum plays a central role at several stages of the curriculum cycle. First, in developing curricula, educators should give specific attention to the supported curriculum, paying special attention to time allocations and the materials of instruction. Second, in implementing the curriculum, administrators should be sure that adequate support is provided. Next, as Chapter 11 indicates, those involved in aligning the curriculum should assess to what extent there is a good fit between the written, the supported, and the taught curricula. Finally, any comprehensive evaluation of the curriculum should assess the supported curriculum, because deficiencies in support will probably be a major factor in student achievement.

The Taught Curriculum

The extent to which there is consonance between the written curriculum and the taught curriculum seems to vary considerably. At one extreme are those school systems that claim to have achieved a high degree of consonance between the two by implementing curriculum alignment projects. At the other extreme are schools where a state of curricular anarchy exists: Each teacher develops his or her own curriculum, with all sorts of disparate activities going on across the school.

Curriculum Tip

The taught curriculum is the delivered curriculum, a curriculum that an observer would see in action as the teacher taught.

How does the taught curriculum, regardless of its fit with the written curriculum, become established? The question is a complex and an important one that can best be answered by synthesizing several studies of teachers' thinking, planning, and decision making.

Thus, teachers' decisions about the curriculum are a product of many interacting variables. Rather than being mindless choices or acts of willful rebellion, those decisions instead seem to represent the teacher's considered judgment about what compromises will be best for that teacher and a particular class.

The Tested Curriculum

The tested curriculum is that set of learnings that are assessed in teacher-made classroom tests, in district developed curriculum-referenced tests, and in standardized tests. To what extent are these several types of tests related to the taught curriculum? The answers seem to vary. First, teacher-made tests tend not to correspond closely with what was taught. In general, teachers are not highly skilled test developers and tend to be somewhat selective in what they include in unit examinations. For the most part, their tests concentrate on assessing students' comprehension and memory of objective information, and their attempts to measure understanding of concepts result in multiple-choice items that really assess students' guessing ability.

The evidence on the congruence between curriculum-referenced tests and instruction suggests a somewhat different picture. In districts using curriculum-referenced tests as a means of monitoring teacher compliance, the test seems to drive instruction. The result is a closer fit. Yet here the congruence is not reassuring to those who value higher-order learning. An examination of a curriculum-referenced test used in a large district's alignment project indicated that the test items were concerned almost exclusively with such low-level objectives as punctuating sentences correctly, spelling words correctly, and identifying the parts of speech.

Finally, the research on standardized tests suggests that there is not a good fit between widely used standardized tests and what most teachers teach. Currently, teachers are using online-based programs to provide testing as well as data analysis of student strengths and weaknesses as they relate to state and national standards. Online testing programs provide pre- and posttests and analysis charts, as well as possible teaching strategies in order to address specific areas of need.

The consequences of such mismatches are serious. First, as Berliner (1984) points out, the research suggests that achievement is lower in schools where there is not a close fit between what is taught and what is tested. Second, students are put at a disadvantage when the teaching and testing do not match. Their grades and scores would probably not be a valid measure of what they had learned. Finally, there may be serious legal consequences when poorly fitting tests are used to make decisions about promotion and graduation. The courts have ruled that when tests are used for purposes that may deny constitutional guarantees of equal protection or due process (as in retention or denial of graduation), schools must provide evidence that those tests assess skills and concepts actually taught in the classroom.

Curriculum Tip

Components of the curriculum determine the fit between what is taught and what is learned.

It might be useful at this juncture to note again that the four curricula discussed above—*the written, the supported, the taught,* and *the tested*—might be seen as constituting the intentional curriculum, which comprises that set of learning experiences that the school system consciously intends for its students.

The Learned Curriculum

The term *learned curriculum* is used here to denote all the changes in values, perceptions, and behavior that occur as a result of school experiences. As such, it includes what the student understands, learns, and retains from both the intentional curriculum and the hidden curriculum. The discussion here focuses on what is learned from the intentional curriculum; the last part of the chapter analyzes what is learned from the hidden curriculum.

What, then, do students learn and retain from the intentional curriculum? Obviously, the answer varies with the student, the teacher, and the curriculum. However, there are some subtle transformations, especially between the taught curriculum and the learned curriculum, that occur in most classrooms, regardless of the specific conditions. (The discussion that follows draws primarily from Doyle's 1983 review of the research on academic work.)

To begin with, the students seem especially sensitive to the accountability system at work in the classroom and take seriously only that for which they are held accountable. Regardless of what objectives the teacher announces or what the teacher emphasizes, the students seem to assess the importance of classroom transactions in relation to their value in that accountability system: "Will this be on the test?"

In order to achieve success in that accountability-oriented classroom, the students invent strategies for managing ambiguity and reducing risk. They will restrict the output they provide teachers, giving vague and limited answers to minimize the risk of making public mistakes. They also attempt to increase the explicitness of a teacher's instructions, asking the teacher for more examples, hints, or rephrasing of the question. Furthermore, they pressure teachers to simplify curriculum complexity, strongly resisting any curriculum that forces them to think, inquire, and discover.

In sum, students learn what is assessed and remember those learnings as discrete answers to questions; their learning is somewhat disorganized and unconnected.

COMPONENTS OF THE CURRICULUM

Although several texts in the field seem to treat curriculum development as if it were one undifferentiated process, the realities are quite different. The concept subsumes several distinct entities that might best be described as components of the curriculum. They are as follows. Each of these will be analyzed briefly below and then discussed more fully in the chapters that follow.

Curricular Policies

The term *curricular policies,* as used here, designates the set of rules, criteria, and guidelines intended to control curriculum development and implementation. As Kirst (1983) notes, there are macropolicies, such as a board policy on courses required in high school, and micropolicies, such as a set of recommendations for a curriculum unit in mathematics. Policy making, as he notes, is essentially the "authoritative allocation of competing values" (p. 282). Thus, as a board makes a policy requiring 3 years of science in the high school curriculum, but does not require any study of art, it is perhaps unwittingly according a higher value to science as a way of knowing than it does to aesthetics. Saylor, Alexander, and Lewis (1981) make a useful distinction between de jure policy making (as implemented in court decisions, state legislative acts, and local agency regulations) and de facto policy making (as carried out by community networks, testing bureaus, accrediting associations, and advisory boards).

Curriculum Tip

Educators, administrators, and teachers are well advised to reexamine policies affecting curriculum and the accepted practices at their schools.

The decisions that a school makes regarding established policies and practices can affect students enormously. For example, teachers' instructional decisions influence students' feelings about (and success with) the curriculum, but the policies and practices in both classrooms and in the entire school provide the context for teacher-student interactions around instruction (Danielson, 2002).

Schools have multiple policies and practices that can and do affect curriculum development. Some policies are deliberately set in place while others evolve with time.

Curricular Goals

Curricular goals are the general, long-term educational outcomes that the school system expects to achieve through its curriculum. Three critical elements are included in this definition. First, goals are stated much more generally than objectives. Thus, one goal for English language arts might be: "Learn to communicate ideas through writing and speaking." One objective for fifth-grade language arts would be much more specific: "Write a letter, with appropriate business-letter form, suggesting a community improvement." Second, goals are long-term, not short-term outcomes. The school system hopes that after 12 years of formal schooling, its students will have achieved the goals that the system has set for itself.

Finally, curricular goals are those outcomes that the school system hopes to achieve through its curriculum. Here it is important to make a distinction between educational goals and curricular goals. Educational goals are the long-term outcomes that the school system expects to accomplish through the entire educational process over which it has control.

How do curricular policies and curricular goals interrelate? In a sense, the policies establish the rules of the game ("take 3 years of health education") and the goals set the targets ("at the end of those 3 years, you will adopt constructive health habits"). In this sense, they should determine in a rational system the form and content of all the other components that follow. As will be evident throughout this work, however, educational organizations are usually not very rational. Typically, policies are not related to goals, and goals are not related to fields and programs of study.

Fields of Study

A field of study is an organized and clearly demarcated set of learning experiences typically offered over a multiyear period. In most school curricula, such fields of study are equivalent to the standard school subjects: English language arts, mathematics, social studies, science, and so on. At the college level, fields are more narrowly defined: thus, students pursue majors in history, or anthropology, or sociology—not "social studies."

Programs of Study

A program of study is the total set of learning experiences offered by a school for a particular group of learners, usually over a multiyear period and typically encompassing several fields of study. The program of study is often described in a policy statement that delineates which subjects are required and which are electives, with corresponding time allocations and credits. Here, for example, is a typical program of studies for an elementary school:

Reading and language arts: 8 hours a week

Social studies: 3 hours

Mathematics: 4 hours

Art: 1 hour

Music: 1 hour

Health and physical education: 1 hour

At the college level, a student's program of studies includes all the courses he or she will take or has taken.

Courses of Study

A course of study is a subset of both a program of study and a field of study. It is a set of organized learning experiences, within a field of study, offered over a specified period of time (such as a year, a semester, or a quarter) for which the student ordinarily receives academic credit. The course of study is usually given a title and a grade level or numerical designation. Thus, "third-grade science" and "English II" are courses of study. At the college level, courses of study seem to be the most salient component for both students and faculty: "I'm taking Economics I this term"; "I'm offering Elizabethan Literature this quarter."

Units of Study

A unit is a subset of a course of study. It is an organized set of related learning experiences offered as part of a course of study, usually lasting from 1 to 3 weeks. Many units are organized around a single overarching concept, such as "Mythical Creatures" or "The Nature of Conflict." Not all teachers think about units as they plan. Many high school teachers simply aggregate lessons: "I'll have a spelling lesson tomorrow and a grammar lesson on the next day." As college instructors conceptualize their courses, they often seem to think about a sequence of lectures rather than a unit of study.

Robert Marzano (as cited in Marzano, Pickering, & Pollock, 2001), noted author and researcher, believes that when developing units of study at any level it is best to view the process as a series of phases. The planning phases of unit development include the following:

- At the *beginning* of a unit, include strategies for setting learning goals.
- *During* a unit, include strategies
    - for monitoring progress toward learning goals
    - for introducing new knowledge
    - for practicing, reviewing, and applying knowledge
- At the *end* of a unit, include strategies for helping students determine how well they have achieved their goals.

Marzano's intent is for teachers to systematically utilize strategies that work. These are best-practice approaches. Basically, teachers should present students with the components and sub-components of the unit process and then structure tasks to emphasize a specific component or subcomponent.

Lessons

A lesson is a set of related learning experiences typically lasting for 20 to 60 minutes, focusing on a relatively small number of objectives. Ordinarily a lesson is a subset of a unit, although, as noted above, the unit level is sometimes omitted by teachers while planning for instruction.

These distinctions among the several components of curriculum have an importance that transcends the need for conceptual clarity. Each seems to involve some rather different planning processes. Thus, to speak generally about "curriculum planning," without differentiating between planning a program of studies and planning a course of studies, is to make a rather serious mistake.

Improving and enhancing lessons based on current brain research and curriculum design is becoming a critical component in the search for best practices. With that in mind, Marzano et al. (2001) identified nine categories of strategies that have a strong effect on student achievement. They are as follows:

- Identifying similarities and differences
- Summarizing and note taking
- Reinforcing effort and providing recognition
- Homework and practice
- Nonlinguistic representations
- Cooperative learning
- Setting objectives and providing feedback
- Generating and testing hypotheses
- Questions, cues, and advance organizers

As can be seen from analyzing Marzano et al.'s nine strategies, students need a fair amount of guidance when learning complex processes. Classroom teachers therefore need to realize that curriculum planning should emphasize metacognitive control of all processes. These processes are similar to skills in that they often produce some form of product or new understanding.

THE MASTERY, THE ORGANIC, AND THE ENRICHMENT CURRICULA

One additional classification system first proposed by Glatthorn (1980) has proved useful, especially in developing and improving fields of study.

Curriculum Tip

Curriculum leaders should distinguish between the three types of learning in each field of study. The three types of learning are mastery, organic, and enrichment.

The three types of learning result from the following analytical steps. First, divide the learnings in that field between those that are basic and those that are enrichment. Basic learnings are those that, in the views of knowledgeable educators, are essential for all students (all, in this use, refers to the top 90% of learners, excluding the least able and those with serious learning disabilities). Enrichment learnings are the knowledge and skills that are interesting and enriching, but are not considered essential: they are simply "nice to know." Thus, in fifth-grade social studies, curriculum workers might decide that the early settling of the Vikings in Iceland would be interesting enrichment content.

Once the first division between basic and enrichment is made, then further divide the basic learnings into those that require structure and those that do not require structure. Structured learning, as the term is used here, has four characteristics:

1. Sequencing

2. Planning

3. Measurable outcomes

4. Clearly delineated content

Nonstructured learning, on the other hand, includes all those skills, knowledge, and attitudes that can be mastered without such careful sequencing, planning, testing, and delineation.

These two analytical steps yield the three types of curricula depicted in Exhibit 1.2: mastery, organic, and enrichment. Mastery learnings are those that are both basic and structured. An example of a mastery objective for language arts, Grade 2, is the following:

Use a capital letter for the first word in a sentence.

Organic learnings, however, are those that are basic, but do not require structuring. They are the learnings that develop day by day, rather naturally, as the result of numerous interactions and exchanges. They tend not to be the focus of specific learnings. They are just as important as the mastery outcomes (if not more so), but they do not require sequencing, pacing, and articulation. Here is an example of organic learning for language arts, Grade 2:

Listen courteously while others speak.

The teacher might emphasize that learning on every occasion, not devote a specific lesson to it. And enrichment learnings, as noted above, are those learnings that simply extend the curriculum; they are not considered basic.

This tripartite division is more than an interesting intellectual exercise. It has significant implications for curriculum development. In general, district curriculum guides and scope-and-sequence charts should focus solely on the mastery elements. The nurturing of organic components can be enhanced through effective staff development; such outcomes do not need to be explicated fully and carefully in guides. The enrichment components can be included in a supplement for those teachers who want to share enrichment activities.

Curriculum-referenced tests should focus only on mastery elements; organic elements should not be tested. One district that ignored this important distinction wasted a great deal

Exhibit 1.2   The Three Types of Curricula

	Basic	Enrichment
Structured	Mastery	
		Enrichment
Nonstructured	Organic	

of time trying to develop a test for courteous listening before it was forced to give up in frustration. The distinction also has implications for the purchase of texts: Textbooks should focus on the mastery objectives; the teacher can nurture the organic without the aid of textbooks.

Finally, the distinction helps resolve the issue of district versus teacher control. In general, the district should determine the mastery curriculum, to the extent of specifying objectives. The district emphasizes the important outcomes, but gives the teacher great latitude of choice in nurturing them. In addition, the enrichment curriculum is the teacher's own: Here the teacher can add whatever content he or she feels might be of interest to the students.

In addition to the discussion of basic versus organic structure of curriculum, it is also important that teachers be aware of brain research and how students learn. According to Patricia Wolfe (2001), an educational author and consultant, learning is a process of building neural networks. She notes that children construct networks in the cortex of the brain that contain information about an unbelievable variety of concepts. She lists three levels of learning: Concrete Experience, Representational or Symbolic Learning, and Abstract Learning.

Concrete Learning, according to Wolfe, is pretty much what the word implies. It is a combination of repeated experiences and visualizations that allow the brain to store, network, and recall when necessary.

The second level, Representational or Symbolic Learning, is based on the brain linking and cross-referencing information. All sensory data are linked through association and become part of memory. With concrete experiences available, sensory data can be "activated" when remembered. Without the concrete experience, the representation or symbol may have little meaning, no matter how much someone explains it to the student.

The third level, Abstract Learning, involves the brain using only abstract information, primarily words and numbers. With a strong neural network formed both by concrete experience and representations, it is possible for children to visualize in their "mind's eye." An understanding of terms, sets, and similarities depends on a child's developmental age and on a teacher's ability to give sufficient examples that relate to the student's experiences. It is also important for the teacher to involve students in experiences that make the abstract concepts understandable.

Curriculum Tip

The key to enriching curriculum is to involve students in real-life problem-solving scenarios.

Using real-life problem-solving scenarios assists in the process of developing the strongest brain networks that will be formed by actual experience. As a result, most schools are now using critical-thinking and problem-solving skills and strategies as a major part of the curriculum-development process.

THE HIDDEN CURRICULUM

The hidden curriculum, which is sometimes called the "unstudied curriculum" or the "implicit curriculum," might best be defined in the following manner:

> Those aspects of schooling, other than the intentional curriculum, that seem to produce changes in student values, perceptions, and behaviors.

As the definition suggests, students learn a great deal in school from sources other than the intentional curriculum. Although the term *hidden curriculum* is often used with negative connotations, those learnings can be both desirable and undesirable from the viewpoint of one aspiring to optimal human development. In examining the specific nature of the hidden curriculum, it seems useful at this point to distinguish between what might be termed the constants—those aspects of schooling that seem more or less impervious to change—and the variables—those aspects that seem susceptible to reform.

Curriculum Tip

Hidden curriculum might be seen as those aspects of the learned curriculum that lie outside the boundaries of the school's intentional efforts.

The Constants of the Hidden Curriculum

Certain important aspects of the hidden curriculum are so intrinsic to the nature of schools as a cultural institution that they might be seen as constants. The depiction of those constants presented below has been influenced by a close reading of several authors: curricular reconceptualists such as Apple (1979), Pinar (1978), and Giroux (1979); sociologists such as Dreeben (1968); and educational researchers such as Jackson (1968) and Goodlad (1984). One of the constants of the hidden curriculum is the ideology of the larger society, which permeates every aspect of schooling. Thus, schools in the United States inevitably reflect the ideology of democratic capitalism.

A key component of the school as an organization is the classroom, where the most salient aspects of the hidden curriculum come into play. The classroom is a crowded place, where issues of control often become dominant. Control is achieved through the differential use of power; the teacher uses several kinds of power to control the selection of content, the methods of learning, movement in the classroom, and the flow of classroom discourse. Control also is achieved by the skillful use of accountability measures; teachers spend much time evaluating and giving evaluative feedback. In such a classroom, students unconsciously learn the skills and traits required by the larger society; they learn how to be punctual, clean, docile, and conforming. They learn how to stand in line, take their turn, and wait. Even though the above features of the hidden curriculum are presented here as constants relatively impervious to change, it is important for curriculum leaders to be aware of their subtle and pervasive influence.

The Variables of the Hidden Curriculum

Several other important aspects of the hidden curriculum can be more readily changed by educators. The most significant of these can be classified into three categories: organizational variables, social-system variables, and culture variables.

Organizational Variables

The term *organizational variables* is used here to designate all those decisions about how teachers will be assigned and students grouped for instruction. Here, four issues seem worthy of attention: team teaching, promotion and retention policies, ability grouping, and curriculum tracking. The evidence on the effects of team teaching on student achievement is somewhat inconclusive. Even though many school systems during the 1980s were implementing "promotional gates" policies that promoted students solely on the basis of achievement, several syntheses of the research indicate that social promotion results in better attitudes toward school, better self-image, and improved achievement.

Grouping practices in the schools have often been attacked by critics as one of the most baleful aspects of the hidden curriculum. Here the indictment of Giroux and Penna (1979) is perhaps typical:

> The pedagogical foundation for democratic processes in the classroom can be established by eliminating the pernicious practice of "tracking" students. This tradition in schools of grouping students according to "abilities" and perceived performance is of dubious instructional value. (p. 223)

Two problems surface with such an indictment. The first is that the authors seem to ignore a rather important distinction made by Rosenbaum (1980) between ability grouping—sorting students into ability-based groups for instruction (such as high, average, and low ability)—and curriculum grouping: sorting students into such curricular tracks as vocational, general, and college preparatory. The other, more serious problem is that the empirical evidence available does not support their assertions.

The practice of curriculum grouping or tracking, in which students follow a predetermined career-oriented program, such as college preparatory or vocational, seems to be a more complex matter. Here Rosenbaum's (1980) review of the research seems most enlightening. He first notes that there is no clear finding from the research on whether ability or social class is the primary determiner of track placement. According to several studies, the guidance counselor plays a key role in track selections. Many students, according to Rosenbaum, are in curricular tracks that are inconsistent with career choices. The lack of congruence is complicated by the fact that curricular tracking is relatively stable, and there is more movement from college preparatory to general and vocational than the other way around.

The chief problem with curriculum tracking, according to researchers, is the lack of challenge in the general curriculum. Secada (1992) concluded that tracking or ability grouping generally benefited only those students placed in high-end groups while having a detrimental effect on students placed in low-end groups. Evidence of other negative results exists due to tracking students based on ability.

- Minorities and low-income students are disproportionately represented. (Century, 1994)
- Experiences in mathematics and science differ between minorities and low-income students compared to their more advantaged white peers during elementary school. (Oakes, Ormseth, Bell, & Camp, 1990)
- Students in low-ability tracks tend to receive lower-quality instruction. (Secada, 1992)
- Students in lower-ability tracks have difficulty in moving up to higher-ability tracks. (Century, 1994)

Another option in ability tracking is between-class grouping. Students participating in this arrangement find themselves grouped at different ability levels for each subject, depending upon their ability in that subject area. Secada (1992) finds the negative results plaguing full-time grouping also to be a problem here.

Most researchers agree that grouping is beneficial for gifted students. Advocates of grouping and opponents alike maintain the necessity to continue grouping gifted students together and that any reforms introduced to tracking in a school not necessarily affect gifted and talented programs (Century, 1994). Nevertheless, high-end grouping practices must include regular entry evaluations for students to ensure that these gifted tracks are open to all.

A better alternative to tracking would be the regular use of cooperative learning groups. Cooperative learning groups within a heterogeneous classroom have been shown to result in higher achievement, little or no psychological harm to the students, and reduced segregation (Slavin, 1987). Students also gain experience in individual accountability and responsibility, as well as acquiring skills in working with others.

The weight of the research evidence suggests educational leaders interested in improving the organizational variables of the hidden curriculum might focus their attention on promotion policies and curriculum tracking as the key variables. They should ensure the general curriculum is neither dull nor trivial.

Other organizational variables might include class size, breakfast and lunch, noncategorical special help, special programs like Reading Recovery, better libraries and better access to books, better assessment, as well as extended day and after-school programs (Cunningham & Allington, 1994).

Much discussion takes place as to the impact of class size on curriculum planning and implementation. Many authors and researchers believe that smaller class sizes facilitate better teaching and more personalized instruction. Some authors and researchers do not. The key is that smaller class size may facilitate, but does not necessarily ensure, better teaching and learning. Most individuals do agree, however, that class size does affect how the curriculum is delivered and thus the curriculum's nature can be implicit.

Breakfast and lunch may lie outside the boundary of curriculum, but they still may have an important impact on planning. For example, classes have to be scheduled around these activities, especially if the breakfast- and lunchroom is located in the gymnasium. Children having to eat late or not having proper nutrition may also influence when and how the curriculum is delivered.

Noncategorical special help has a substantial and yet hidden impact on a school's schedule in that staff may have to adjust classes in order to compensate for students' being out of the room. Teachers also have to adjust their classroom organization to accommodate students' arriving back into a classroom after receiving special help in another setting.

Special programs such as Reading Recovery and Read Well are now important components of the classroom after the passage of the NCLB Act in 2002. The hidden aspect of these special phonics-based programs is that primary teachers must now schedule their units and lessons around these intensive reading programs to accommodate high-risk children. There is little doubt about the impact of these special programs on how the curriculum in the classroom is being delivered.

Schools with better libraries and/or that provide students with better access to books may have an advantage over schools that do not. Getting reading and informational materials to students in a timely matter can be a key to learning. Albeit hidden, the ability of a teacher to have access to books and materials will make a big difference on how that teacher will teach.

Assessment and *accountability* are becoming bywords with the advent of the No Child Left Behind Act. Although perhaps not obvious to some, assessment and data analysis are now becoming major determiners of what is taught, when it is taught, and how it is taught. Entire curricula are being changed based on the collection of assessment data and student test scores.

Although the impact of assessment is not totally understood or noticed, extended days and after-school programs appear to be having a major impact on curriculum planning and implementation. Teachers are now being paid extra for extended days to complete in-service and staff development requirements. Additional staff development opportunities often mean that teachers will be learning new material and trying different approaches in their classrooms. The impact of this change on curriculum may be hidden to some, but is often immeasurable in scope.

Social-System Variables

The term *social system* as an aspect of school climate was first used by Tagiuri (1968) to refer to the social dimension concerned with the patterned relationships of persons and groups in the school. Anderson's (1982) review of the research on school climate indicated several social-system factors associated with positive student attitude and achievement. Several of these had to do with administrator-teacher relationships: The principal was actively involved in instruction; there was good rapport and communication between administrators and teachers; teachers shared in the decision-making process; and there were good relationships among teachers. Others were related to teacher-student relationships: Teacher-student interactions in general were positive and constructive; students shared in decision making; and there were extensive opportunities for student participation in activities. Obviously, all these factors can be influenced through effective leadership by both administrators and teachers.

Curriculum Tip

Social and economic issues can affect aspects of the hidden curriculum.

Social- and economic-related programs such as Head Start and Even Start are designed to assist economically challenged preschool children. Head Start is a federal program that has been around since the 1960s. Some school districts are designing their school operation to have Head Start on campus. This allows a good transition for the Head Start children to matriculate into a kindergarten program. Having Head Start onsite in a school district also enhances opportunities for staff development as well as offers a way to improve staff relations. Head Start teachers and administrators have an opportunity to plan their curricula so that it threads unnoticed into the district curriculum. Onsite Head Start teachers are thus better able to understand the goals and objectives of the school district and are better able to correlate their program with district primary teachers.

Even Start is a family literacy program that includes preschool children and their parents. Both children and parents go to school. Parents work to complete their high school education or receive adult literacy instruction. The implicit aspect of this program is that children are provided with an enriched preschool curriculum. Parents also learn more about parenting, including ways to involve their children in reading and writing (Cunningham & Allington, 1994).

Another social aspect of curriculum that may be hidden is the involvement of parents and community. Although parents may not directly create a change in curriculum, their approval or disapproval can have a tremendous impact on how a school is operated, what is taught, and how it is taught. An example might be the involvement of parents at the primary level and their support of technology. When parents are in the school at the primary level and see the impact that technology is having on their child, they often become major supporters of educational technology. This support is generated in the passage of special levies and bonds that affect the use of technology at all grade levels—even high school.

The involvement of the community can also have an impact on curriculum development in much the same way. If members of the community feel positive about what is happening in their schools, they are much more apt to support the schools financially. This financial support might include more staff, improved facilities, materials, and/or staff development. The connection to the curriculum may not be readily apparent or even hidden to some, but it is definitely a major factor in the success of the school.

Culture Variables

Tagiuri (1968) defined *culture variables* as the social dimensions concerned with belief systems, values, cognitive structures, and meaning. According to Anderson's (1982) review, several key factors here play an important role in the hidden curriculum. All of the following are associated with either improved achievement or improved attitude:

1. The school has clear goals that are understood by all; those goals are supported by a strong consensus among administrators and teachers.

2. Administrators and teachers have high expectations for each other, and both groups are strongly committed to the importance of student achievement.

3. Administrators and teachers have high expectations for students, and these high expectations are translated into an emphasis on academics.

4. Rewards and praise are publicly given for student achievement; rewards and punishments are administered in a fair and consistent manner.

5. The school emphasizes cooperation and group competition, rather than individual competition.

6. Students value academic achievement; peer norms support the value of such achievement.

These aspects of the hidden curriculum also can be influenced by administrators and teachers working together.

To summarize, then, the hidden curriculum is seen here as both constant and variable aspects of schooling (other than the intentional curriculum) that produce changes in the student. The constants—the ideology of the larger society, the way in which certain knowledge is deemed important or unimportant, and the power relationships that seem necessary in large bureaucratic institutions—seem unlikely to change. However, the variables—those aspects of the organizational structure, the social systems, and the culture of the school that can be influenced—require the systematic attention of curriculum leaders.

In reviewing the intended and hidden curriculum, a coming together of the two can be observed. Exhibit 1.3 illustrates how the intentional curriculum and the hidden curriculum extend into the learned curriculum.

CHAPTER OVERVIEW

This introductory chapter provides a general overview of the curriculum field and a set of concepts for analyzing that field. The chapter defines the concept of curriculum, examines the several types of curricula, describes the contrasting nature of curriculum components, and analyzes the hidden curriculum to provide some fundamental concepts essential for understanding the comprehensive field of curriculum. The chapter includes the topics of what curriculum is and why it is important; the types and components of curricula and how they have changed over the years; what mastery, organic, and enrichment curricula are and the roles they play in the development of curriculum; and why knowledge of the "hidden curriculum" is important to curriculum leaders.

Exhibit 1.3   Relationships of Types of Curricula

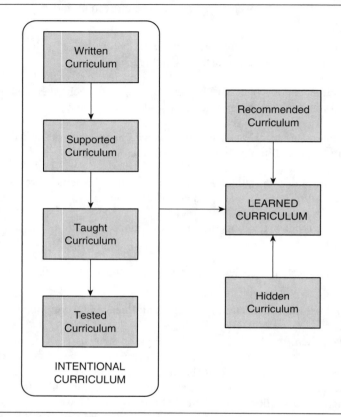

SOURCE: Developed by Mark A. Baron, Chairperson, Division of Educational Administration, School of Education, The University of South Dakota. Used with permission.

CHAPTER TERMS

Recommended Curriculum	Field of Study
Written Curriculum	Program of Study
Supported Curriculum	Courses of Study
Taught Curriculum	Units of Study
Tested Curriculum	Lessons
Learned Curriculum	Mastery Curriculum
Intentional Curriculum	Organic Curriculum
Hidden Curriculum	Enrichment Curriculum

APPLICATIONS

1. By reviewing the definitions given here and by reflecting on your own use of the term, write your own definition of *curriculum.*

2. Some educators have suggested that the profession should use simpler definitions for *curriculum* and *instruction:* curriculum is what is taught; instruction is how it is taught. Do these definitions seem to suffice, from your perspective?

3. Some leaders have argued for a very close fit between the written and the taught curriculum, suggesting that teachers should teach only what is in the prescribed curriculum. Others have suggested that some slippage is desirable—that teachers should have some autonomy and latitude, as long as they cover the essentials. What is your own position on this issue?

4. Although most curriculum texts do not make the distinctions noted here between programs of study, fields of study, and courses of study, those distinctions do seem to matter. To test this hypothesis, do the following: (1) List the steps you would follow in designing a program of studies for one level of schooling, such as elementary or middle school; (2) List the steps you would follow in designing a field of study, such as social studies, K–12.

5. It has been suggested here that the "constants" of the hidden curriculum are not easily changed. Others would argue that they should be changed if we truly desire democratic and humanistic schools. As a school leader, would you attempt to change any of those "constants," or would you give more attention to the "variables"?

6. Outline a change strategy you would use in attempting to improve the "culture" variables that seem to be associated with improved attitude and achievement.

CASE STUDY

Dr. John Summers was hired to be the curriculum director to enhance the teaching and learning process for the Dover School District. Dr. Summers was the superintendent's choice for the position because he was highly qualified in the area of curriculum development, and his performance at a somewhat smaller school district with 5,000 students, in a neighboring state, was outstanding. The district John came from was known for its high academic achievement, which was attributed to a well-planned curriculum supported by the principals and teachers.

In contrast, the Dover School District was in curriculum disarray, and student achievement was low when compared to statewide achievement scores. As Dr. Summers soon discovered, some teachers in the Dover School District construed the curriculum as ideal because it met their standards. They also felt that if something was being taught, a curriculum existed. The principals in the district, however, felt that a planned curriculum was vital for the district, but they were unable to generate the necessary leadership to bridge the gap between theory and practice.

THE CHALLENGE

Analyze the nature and concepts of curriculum in this chapter. As curriculum director of the Dover School District, how should Dr. Summers bridge the gap between curriculum theory and practice?

Key Issues/Questions

1. To what extent do you believe a written curriculum for the various disciplines plays a role in this case?

2. To what extent do you believe the supported, tested, and learned curricula for the various disciplines play a role in improving the intentional curriculum?

3. Do you think there is any hope of changing the teachers' attitude? If so, how would you attempt to do this? If not, why?

4. Do you feel that the intentional curriculum is prescriptive or descriptive, or a combination of both? Why?

5. What roles do the recommended curriculum and hidden curriculum play in developing the intentional curriculum?

6. In planning curricula, mastery curriculum should require from 60% to 75% of the time available. Do you agree that Dr. Summers should place an emphasis on mastery curriculum? Why?

REFERENCES

Achilles, C. M. (1997, October). Small classes, big possibilities. *The School Administrator, 54*(9), 6–15.

Achilles, C. M., Finn, J. D., Prout, J., & Bobbett, G. C. (2001, February 18). *Serendipitous policy implications from class-size-initiated inquiry: IAQ?* Paper presented at the meeting, Conference-Within-a-Conference, of the American Association of School Administrators (AASA), Orlando, FL.

Allington, R. L. (2002). You can't learn much from books you can't read. *Educational Leadership, 60*(3), 16–19.

Anderson, C. S. (1982). The search for school climate: A review of the research. *Review of Educational Research, 52,* 368–420.

Apple, M. W. (1979, Winter). On analyzing hegemony. *The Journal of Curriculum Theorizing, 1,* 10–43.

Berliner, D. C. (1984). The half-full glass: A review of research on teaching. In P. L. Hosford (Ed.), *Using what we know about teaching.* Alexandria, VA: Association for Supervision and Curriculum Development.

Block, A. (1998). Curriculum as affichiste: Popular culture and identity. In W. Pinar (Ed.), *Curriculum: Toward new identities* (pp. 325–341). New York: Garland.

Bobbitt, F. (1918). *The curriculum.* Boston: Houghton Mifflin.

Caswell, H. L., & Campbell, D. S. (1935). *Curriculum development.* New York: American Book Co.

Century, J. (1994). *Making sense of the literature on equity in education. Draft one: ". . . A think piece. . . ."* Newton, MA: Educational Development Center, Inc., Statewide Systemic Initiative Equity Leadership Institute.

Chambers, L. (1999, September). Sizing up the effects of class size. *Changing Schools, 8,* 1–2.

Cornbleth, C. (1990). *Curriculum in context.* New York: Falmer.

Cunningham, P., & Allington, R. (1994). *Classrooms that work.* New York: HarperCollins College.

Danielson, C. (2002). *Enhancing student achievement: A framework for school improvement.* Alexandria, VA: Association for Supervision and Curriculum Development.

Dewey, J. (1902). *The child and the curriculum.* Chicago: University of Chicago Press.

Doyle, W. (1983). Academic work. *Review of Educational Research, 53,* 159–199.

Dreeben, R. (1968). *On what is learned in schools.* Reading, MA: Addison-Wesley.

Dugger, W. E., Jr., & Nichols, C. (2003, December). Advancing excellence in technological literacy. *Phi Delta Kappan, 85,* 316–317.

Ellis, A. K. (2004). *Exemplars of curriculum theory.* Larchmont, NY: Eye on Education.

Farber, S., & Finn, J. (2000, April). *The effect of small classes on student engagement.* Paper presented at the annual AREA meeting in New Orleans, LA.

Finn, J., & Achilles, C. (1990). Answers and questions about class size: A statewide experiment. *American Educational Research Journal, 27,* 557–577.

Gagne, R. W. (1967). Curriculum research and the promotion of learning. In R. W. Tyler, R. M. Gagne, & M. Scriven (Eds.), *Perspectives of curricular evaluation.* Chicago: Rand McNally.

Giroux, H. A. (1979). Toward a new sociology of curriculum. *Educational Leadership, 37,* 248–253.

Giroux, H. A., & Penna, A. N. (1979). Social education in the classroom: The dynamics of the hidden curriculum. In H. A. Giroux, A. N. Penna, & W. F. Pinar (Eds.), *Curriculum and instruction* (pp. 209–230). Berkeley, CA: McCutchan.

Glatthorn, A. A. (1980). *A guide for developing an English curriculum for the eighties.* Urbana, IL: NCTE.

Goodlad, J. I. (1984). *A place called school: Prospects for the future.* New York: McGraw-Hill.

Goodlad, J. I., & Associates. (1979). *Curriculum inquiry: The study of curriculum practice.* New York: McGraw-Hill.

Hass, G. (1987). *Curriculum planning: A new approach* (5th ed.). Boston: Allyn & Bacon.

Hopkins, L. T. (1941). *Interaction: The democratic process.* Boston: D. C. Heath.

Jackson, P. (1968). *Life in classrooms.* New York: Holt, Rinehart & Winston.

Karweit, N. C. (1983). *Time-on-task: A research review.* Baltimore, MD: Johns Hopkins University, Center for Social Organization of Schools.

Kirst, M. W. (1983). Policy implications of individual differences and the common curriculum. In G. D. Fenstermacher & J. I. Goodlad (Eds.), *Individual differences and the common curriculum* (Eighty-Second Yearbook of the National Society for the Study of Education: Part I, pp. 282–299). Chicago: University of Chicago Press.

Marzano, R., Pickering, D., & Pollock, J. (2001). *Classroom instruction that works: Research-based strategies for increasing student achievement.* Alexandria, VA: Association for Supervision and Curriculum Development.

McBrien, J. L., & Brandt, R. (Eds.). (1997). *The language of learning: A guide to educational terms.* Alexandria, VA: Association for Supervision and Curriculum Development.

Mosteller, F. (1995). The Tennessee study of class size in the early school grades. *Future of Children, 5(2),* 113–127.

Oakes, J., Ormseth, T., Bell, R., & Camp, P. (1990, July). *Multiplying inequalities: The effects of race, social class, and tracking on opportunities to learn mathematics and science.* Santa Monica, CA: RAND.

Pinar, W. F. (1978). The reconceptualization of curriculum studies. *Journal of Curriculum Studies, 10*(3), 205–214.

Popham, W. J., & Baker, E. I. (1970). *Systematic instruction.* Englewood Cliffs, NJ: Prentice Hall.

Ragan, W. B. (1960). *Modern elementary curriculum* (Rev. ed.). New York: Henry Holt.

Rosenbaum, J. E. (1980). Social implications of educational grouping. In D. C. Berliner (Ed.), *Review of research in education* (Vol. 8, pp. 361–404), Washington, DC: AERA.

Rugg, H. O. (Ed.). (1927). Curriculum-making: Past and present. In C. Davis (1927). *Our evolving high school curriculum* (p. 8). Yonkers-on-Hudson, New York: World Book.

Saylor, J. G., Alexander, W. M., & Lewis, A. J. (1981). *Curriculum planning for better teaching and learning* (4th ed.). New York: Holt, Rinehart & Winston.

Schiro, M. (1978). *Curriculum for better schools: The great ideological debate.* Englewood Cliffs, NJ: Educational Technology Publications.

Secada, W. (1992). Race, ethnicity, social class, language, and achievement in mathematics. In D. Grouws (Ed.), *Handbook of research on mathematics teaching and learning.* Reston, VA: National Council of Teachers of Mathematics.

Slavin, R. E. (1987, Summer). Ability grouping and its alternatives: Must we track? *American Educator, 11*(2), 32–36, 47–48.

Stallings, J. (1980, December). Allocated learning time revisited or beyond time on task. *Educational Researcher, 9*(4), 11–16.

Taba, H. (1962). *Curriculum development: Theory and practice.* New York: Harcourt Brace Jovanovich.

Tagiuri, R. (1968). The concept of organizational climate. In R. Tagiuri & G. H. Litwin (Eds.), *Organizational climate: Exploration of a concept.* Boston: Harvard University, Graduate School of Business Administration.

Tanner, D., & Tanner, L. (1995). *Curriculum development: Theory and practice* (3rd ed.). New York: Merrill.

Tomlinson, C. A., Burns, D., Renzulli, J. S., Kaplan, S. N., Leppien, J., & Purcell, J. (2002). *The parallel curriculum: A design to develop high potential and challenge high-ability learners.* Thousand Oaks, CA: Corwin.

Tyler, R. W. (1957). The curriculum then and now. In *Proceedings of the 1956 Invitational Conference on Testing Problems.* Princeton, NJ: Educational Testing Service.

Walcott, H. F. (1977). *Teacher vs. technocrats.* Eugene: University of Oregon, Center for Educational Policy and Management.

Walker, D. (1979). Approaches to curriculum development. In J. Schaffarzick & G. Sykes (Eds.), *Value conflicts and curriculum issues: Lessons from research and experience* (pp. 263–290). Berkeley, CA: McCutchan.

Waters, T., Marzano, R. J., & McNulty, B. (2003). *Balanced leadership: What 30 years of research tells us about the effect of leadership on student achievement* (Working paper). Aurora, CO: McREL.

Wilhelm, J. D. (1996). *Standards in practice, grades 6–8.* Urbana, IL: National Council of Teachers of English.

Wolfe, P. (2001). *Brain matters: Translating research into classroom practice* (pp. 135–138). Alexandria, VA: Association for Supervision and Curriculum Development.

Chapter 2

CURRICULUM HISTORY
The Perspective of the Past

Understanding the history of curriculum development is useful for both scholars and practitioners. It results in a deeper awareness of the extent to which curricular changes are often influenced by and are a manifestation of larger social forces. It also offers a broader perspective from which to view so-called innovations and reforms, which often seem to reverberate with echoes of the past.

This understanding seems especially facilitated by a careful analysis of the past 110 years of that history. Such a demarcation results in a closer focus on the major developments affecting American schools, while still providing the broader perspective that is so essential. Those developments perhaps can be better grasped if analyzed as parts of specific periods of history. Of course, an obvious fallacy occurs in delineating such periods. Historical periods become an artifact of the historian's analysis: People do not live and events do not occur in neat chronological packages called "periods." Given that caution, an analysis of that century plus a decade of curriculum history seems to suggest that there were eight distinct eras, each with its own distinguishing features. This framework is therefore suggested as a way of examining the past century plus a decade of curriculum theory and practice:

Date	Period
1890–1916	Academic Scientism
1917–1940	Progressive Functionalism
1941–1956	Developmental Conformism
1957–1967	Scholarly Structuralism
1968–1974	Romantic Radicalism
1975–1989	Privatistic Conservatism
1990–1999	Technological Constructionism
2000–Present	New Privatistic Conservatism

Although the verity of the eight eras may be accepted by most individuals, it follows that any attempt to understand or instigate educational reform would be based on an inquiry of what has occurred in the past. As described by Sarason (1990),

> The significance of the historical stance is not only in what it tells us about the manifestations of a particular problem over time, or what one learns about the efficacy of remedial actions, but also in what one learns about the system quality—that is, the features of the system in which the problem arises and recurs, or remains constant but unremarked until it is seen [again] as destabilizing the system. (p. 34)

Sarason also concluded that "one can write human history as a saga of the inability to recognize the obvious" (p. 146). Also, "public schools cannot exist as cocoons, isolated from a changing environment and climate" (Goens & Clover, 1991, p. 3). Questions addressed in this chapter include:

- What were the periods of Academic Scientism, Progressive Functionalism, Developmental Conformism, Scholarly Structuralism, Romantic Radicalism, Privatistic Conservatism, Technological Constructionism, and New Privatistic Conservatism and why was each important in the development of curriculum?
- What were some of the predominant trends that transcended each major period of curriculum development?

Key to Leadership

In reviewing curriculum history, two general observations should be made. The first is to note the pace of change. The second is to note the rhythms and directions of that change.

ACADEMIC SCIENTISM

The term used here to identify the period from 1890 to 1916, Academic Scientism, derives from the two influences that seemed to predominate: the academic and the scientific. The academic influence was the result of systematic and somewhat effective efforts of the colleges to shape the curriculum for basic education; the scientific influence resulted from the attempts of educational theorists to use newly developed scientific knowledge in making decisions about the mission of the school and the content of the curriculum.

Curriculum Tip

There is a direct relationship between curriculum of the past and curriculum today.

The Temper of the Times

The educational trends of this period can perhaps best be discerned if viewed against the backdrop of societal changes. The turn of the century was characterized, first of all, by the post–Civil War growth of industry and the development of urban areas, both stimulated primarily by the rapid growth of railroads.

The second distinguishing feature of the era was the impact of popular journalism. The linotype machine was introduced in 1890, the price of newspapers dropped to one cent, and the number of newspapers doubled. Magazines were also reaching larger audiences. Finally, it was a time when new immigrant waves were reaching these shores. The volume of immigrants increased, and their places of origin changed markedly. Whereas prior to the 1890s, immigrants came chiefly from the Western European countries, during the turn-of-the-century decades, they were more likely to come from the Eastern European countries.

The Predominant Trends

As noted above, the major educational influences of the period were both academic and scientific. The man who most clearly represented the academic influence of the colleges was Charles W. Eliot, president of Harvard University. In a perhaps immodest fashion, Eliot saw the entire curriculum as his purview, making specific recommendations for elementary, secondary, and higher education.

In essence, Eliot's position was that a sound academic curriculum was best for all students, regardless of their college aspirations.

The scientific influence was perhaps stronger, even though less direct. One interesting sign of this scientific influence was the change of one of the major educational organizations: What had once been the Herbart Society changed its name in 1900 to the National Society for the Scientific Study of Education.

The scientific perspective seemed to influence educational thinkers in three important ways. First, science provided intellectual support for a rational and meliorist worldview, a view widely held by the educational thinkers of the period. Problems could be solved by the rational application of scientific processes: All that was needed was more knowledge and the ability to apply that knowledge.

Second, science provided a content focus for the curriculum. Flexner (1916) was one of several theoreticians who argued for the primacy of science. In his view, the central purpose of the school was to prepare children to cope in the real world—and that preparation would best be accomplished through a study of the physical and social world.

Finally, science provided a means for improving the schools. Scientific knowledge about the child yielded insights, proponents argued, about the desired nature of the curriculum—about what children could learn. Scientific knowledge also offered a rationale for the optimal methods of teaching.

The Exemplary Leaders

The major thrusts of this period were probably best represented by the careers and contributions of two educational leaders: G. Stanley Hall and Francis W. Parker.

G. Stanley Hall

G. Stanley Hall (1904, 1969) was an eminent psychologist who provided scientific support to the child-centered educators of the day. While earlier developmentalists had argued for the study of the child as the basis for curricular decision making, it was Hall who provided the charismatic leadership for the movement. As a social Darwinian, he believed in evolutionary social change, not radical transformation. The essential task of the school was to support this gradual change through the nurturing of the gifted, providing the gifted child with the opportunity to grow through individualized activities.

Francis W. Parker

Francis W. Parker seemed to have had even more influence than G. Stanley Hall; in fact, John Dewey (1964) himself called Parker "the father of progressive education." Parker is significant for his contributions to both pedagogy and curriculum development. The pedagogical methods he advocated could perhaps best be described as natural, child-centered methods.

His contributions to curriculum theory were similarly comprehensive. In his *Talks on Pedagogics* (Parker, 1894), he argued for a child-centered curriculum that builds upon what the child instinctively knows.

In contrast to Hall's essentially conservative orientation, Parker was in almost every respect a progressive who believed that the common school was the key to human advancement. In a chapter in his pedagogic work, he anticipated at least the rhetoric of more current social reformers: "This mingling, fusing, and blending [of children from all social classes] give personal power, and make the public school a tremendous force for the upbuilding of democracy" (p. 421).

The Major Publications

The major publications of the Academic Scientism period were perhaps the reports of two committees established by the NEA: the Committee of Ten, appointed to make recommendations for the high school curriculum; and the Committee of Fifteen, for the elementary curriculum.

The Committee of Ten

Although many educators cite the work of the Committee of Ten as an example of the attempt of colleges to dominate the curriculum, the committee was appointed by the NEA at the request of members. There was so much variation in college preparatory curricula in schools across the country that school administrators themselves desired more uniformity.

The major recommendation of the committee report (National Education Association [NEA], 1893) was that four separate programs of study be offered to high school students: classical, Latin-scientific, modern languages, and English. In essence, the Committee of Ten said to the profession and to the public, "A sound academic curriculum is the best preparation for life—for all students."

The Committee of Fifteen

The other committee appointed by the NEA at almost the same time was given the charge of making recommendations for elementary curriculum and instruction. Eliot had some influence with this committee, which accepted two of his recommendations: that the number of elementary grades be reduced from ten to eight; and that algebra be substituted for arithmetic in Grades 7 and 8. However, it rejected his recommendation that the time devoted to grammar and arithmetic be reduced so that the program could be diversified and enriched (the committee's recommendations were reported in the NEA's 1895 report).

In its curriculum recommendations, the Committee of Fifteen advocated a rather conservative approach. Grammar, literature, arithmetic, geography, and history were seen as the central subjects for training the mind, and clear separation of those subjects was essential. The following subjects were to be taught every year, from first to eighth: reading, English grammar (except in the eighth year), geography, natural science and hygiene, general history, physical culture, vocal music, and drawing. Handwriting was to be taught in the first 6 years, and spelling lists, in Grades 4, 5, and 6. Latin was to be introduced in the eighth year, and manual training (for boys) and sewing and cooking (for girls) in the seventh and eighth. In mathematics, arithmetic was to be studied in the first through the sixth years, followed by algebra in the seventh and eighth.

In addition to the required oral lessons in general history for all grades, U.S. history was to be taught in the seventh year and the first half of the eighth; the Constitution was to be taught in the second half of the eighth year. Thus, a pupil in the fourth year would be studying 11 separate "branches" or subjects: reading, handwriting, spelling lists, English grammar, arithmetic, geography, natural science and hygiene, general history, physical culture, vocal music, and drawing.

The ultimate impact of the Committee of Fifteen report was to sustain a somewhat fragmented and subject-centered curriculum.

PROGRESSIVE FUNCTIONALISM

The era of Progressive Functionalism, which lasted approximately from 1917 to 1940, was characterized by the confluence of two seemingly disparate views: the progressive, child-centered orientation of the followers of John Dewey and the functional orientation of curriculum scientists.

The Temper of the Times

The decade of the 1920s was a time of seemingly unbridled optimism and growth in this country. Houses were being built at a record-making pace. By 1929, there were more than 26 million cars registered: one car for every five people.

All that optimism and growth was tragically destroyed in the Depression and the very slow recovery that followed. The human suffering of that period is difficult to exaggerate. At one point it was estimated that 28% of the population was without any income at all. Many school systems simply shut down because there was no money to pay teachers.

The international picture was no less depressing, for the 1930s was the decade marking the rise of Hitler in Germany and Stalin in the Soviet Union, both of whom were ultimately responsible for the mass genocide carried out in both nations. Confronted with the global rapacity of the dictators in Germany, Italy, the Soviet Union, and Japan, the Western democratic governments seemed for many years to be confused and impotent.

The Predominant Trends

As noted above, the term given this era derives from two forces—progressivism and functionalism—that, while seemingly antithetical in principle, often combined to influence both curriculum and instruction.

Progressivism in Education

It is obviously difficult in the brief space available to summarize a movement so complex and so often misunderstood as progressive education. Whereas in the prior decade the dominating influence of the curriculum was the academic subject, for progressive educators it was the child. The child-centered curriculum was based upon a somewhat romantic and perhaps even naive view of child development: The child is innately curious and creative, with a thirst for learning and a need for self-expression. Such a view has clear implications for both the process and the content of the curriculum. In using a curriculum-development process, child-centered curriculum workers begin by determining the child's interests, assured that any desired content can be linked with those interests.

The content of the curriculum is similarly influenced. The arts are emphasized, because the nurturing of creativity is paramount. Subjects that have little immediate appeal to the child, such as mathematics and grammar, tend to be slighted.

Functionalism

Functionalism is the term given here to the educational theory of those whom Kliebard (1985) calls "the social efficiency educators," who argued essentially that the curriculum should be derived from an analysis of the important functions or activities of adult life. As a curriculum theory, it was clearly influenced by two significant ideas current at the time. It reflected the concern for efficiency at the heart of the "scientific management" of Frederick Taylor (1911) and his followers. Taylor argued that any task could be analyzed for optimal efficiency by observing skilled workers, studying the operations they carried out, determining the time required, and eliminating wasted motion. Similarly, education could be made more efficient by analyzing learning tasks. It was also avowedly influenced by the stimulus-response learning theory of Edward Thorndike that supported the importance of successful practice.

The Exemplary Leaders

Two figures seem to stand out in retrospect: John Dewey and Franklin Bobbitt. Although they espoused diametrically contrary views of the curriculum in particular, they both seemed to exert a strong influence on their contemporaries.

John Dewey

In a sense, of course, it is fallacious to identify Dewey as a leader of this period alone, because his career as a philosopher and an educator spanned the eras of both Academic Scientism and Progressive Functionalism (Dewey, 1964).

Dewey's (1900) beliefs about the relationship of school and society are, of course, fundamental to his theories of the curriculum and are best understood at the outset. For Dewey, democracy was the ideal society, and he believed that the society can prevail only as it enables diverse groups to form common interests, to interact freely, and to achieve a mutual adaptation. Dewey (1916) pointed out in his book, *Democracy and Education*, that such a society needed schools for more than the superficial reason of producing an educated electorate.

It was this concern for the social nature of schooling and learning, of course, that led him to place so much emphasis upon experience. Yet he did not advocate a mindless activity-centered curriculum in which any activity is considered worthwhile as long as it is perceived by the learners as interesting and relevant. In *Experience and Education*, Dewey (1938) noted that experience and education cannot be directly equated; some experiences are "mis-educative," to use his term. Desirable learning experiences had to meet certain stringent criteria: They had to be democratic and humane, they had to be growth-enhancing, they had to arouse curiosity and strengthen initiative, and they must enable the individual to create meaning.

Franklin Bobbitt

Franklin Bobbitt was the other curriculum theorist who seemed to exert a profound influence on the schools of his time, and who still seems to affect indirectly even those who are not familiar with his work. The curriculum, in his view, was whatever was needed to process the raw material (the child) into the finished product (the model adult). He summarized in this early work the curriculum process as he saw it in the following manner:

1. We need first to draw up in detail for each social or vocational class of students in our charge a list of all of the abilities and aspects of personality for the training of which the school is responsible.

2. Next we need to determine scales of measurement in terms of which of these many different aspects of the personality can be measured.

3. We must determine the amount of training that is socially desirable for each of these different abilities and state these amounts in terms of the scales of measurement.

4. We must have progressive standards of attainment for each stage of advance in the normal development of each ability in question. When these four sets of things are at hand for each differentiated social or vocational class, then we shall have for the first time a scientific curriculum for education worthy of our present age of science.

(Bobbitt, 1913, p. 49)

Thus, while both Dewey and Bobbitt espoused a social meliorist view of the purpose of schooling, they differed sharply in their conception of the curriculum. From Dewey's (1902) perspective, the developing child was the beginning point for curriculum development; from

Bobbitt's, the model adult was the starting point. Furthermore, while Dewey embraced an experience-centered program in which learnings emerged somewhat organically and informally from social interactions, Bobbitt seemed more concerned with a precise scientific matching of activity with outcome.

The Major Publications

Obviously, the writings of both Dewey and Bobbitt had an important influence on educational leaders of the times. However, two other works might be seen to have had a more direct impact: the *Cardinal Principles of Secondary Education* and *The Foundation of Curriculum Making (The Twenty-Sixth Yearbook of the National Society for the Study of Education)*. While quite different in both their genesis and their intended audience, the two publications were surprisingly similar in their major emphases.

The Cardinal Principles of Secondary Education

In 1913, the National Education Association, perceiving a need to reconcile some important differences about the nature of secondary education, appointed the Commission on the Reorganization of Secondary Education. After 5 years of deliberation, the commission (1918) published its recommendations.

The seven cardinal principles emerged, therefore, from this rationale: health, command of fundamental processes (reading, writing, arithmetic, oral and written expression), worthy home membership, vocation, citizenship, worthy use of leisure time, and ethical character. These principles were seen as closely interrelated, not as separate goals. In achieving those goals, schools were encouraged to construct programs of study around three elements: constants (required courses), curriculum variables (specialized subjects chosen in relation to the student's goals), and free electives (subjects chosen to develop the special interests of the student).

In addition to providing a useful framework for the secondary school curriculum, the commission accomplished two other important goals. It attempted somewhat successfully to free the secondary schools from the domination of the colleges, and it articulated forcefully a rationale for the comprehensive high school. In the commission's view, the American high school should serve the needs of all youth, not just the college-bound.

The Twenty-Sixth Yearbook

In the midst of all the ferment resulting from the attempts to reshape the schools, the National Society of Education (Rugg, 1927) decided to bring together in two volumes the thinking of all the major experts in the field—as the preface noted, "making a special effort to bring together, and as far as possible to unify or to reconcile, the varying and often seemingly divergent or even antagonistic philosophies of the curriculum that were being espoused by leading authorities" (p. 6). It is obviously difficult to summarize adequately these two volumes produced by men whom Tyler (1971) calls "pioneering leaders in curriculum development" (p. 28).

DEVELOPMENTAL CONFORMISM

The next period of educational history—the era of Developmental Conformism (1941–1956)—might be seen as a transition period, with the nation first embroiled in a cataclysmic war and then recovering from it to find a "cold war" on its hands.

The Temper of the Times

This period, of course, was in many ways a turbulent time. It was, first of all, a time of international conflict and tension. The United States entered World War II in 1941, and by 1945 the Allies had defeated the Axis nations. However, only 3 years after the war ended, tensions between the United States and the Soviet Union became critical with the Soviet blockade of Western Berlin—tensions that were to affect the nation for the next four decades.

It was also a time of racial unrest. For most of the period, this was a strongly segregated society, with deep-seated racial and ethnic biases. The U.S. Supreme Court outlawed school segregation in 1954, and in 1955 Rosa Parks refused to give her seat to a white man on a bus in Montgomery, Alabama.

Finally, it was the dawning of the atomic age. As several observers noted, the atom bomb profoundly changed the way the average person felt and thought about the world.

Most of the American people seemed to react to this societal turbulence by attempting to live lives of quiet conformity. As presidents, both Truman and Eisenhower seemed able to assure the American people that, despite these signs of unrest, the nation was essentially sound and its future was bright.

The Predominant Trends

Here again, two trends are singled out as shaping educational efforts: the interest in the developmental abilities and needs of youth, and a concern with conformity as an educational goal.

The Developmental Theorists

It was, first of all, a period marked by rather intensive interest in the educational implications of child and adolescent development. As noted above, Dewey had long been concerned with delineating and responding to the stages of growth in children and youth.

As will be discussed below, Piaget's work was just becoming known by educators who perhaps sensed its importance but could not yet discern fully its implications. Yet, it was the theories and research of Havighurst (1972) that during this period seemed to make the most immediate difference to educators. Havighurst conceptualized need as a "developmental task," which he defined as

a task which arises at or about a certain period in the life of the individual, successful achievement of which leads to his happiness and to success with later tasks, while failure leads to unhappiness in the individual, disapproval by society, and difficulty with later tasks. (p. 2)

The importance of these developmental tasks for curriculum can be seen at once by examining just a few of the tasks that Havighurst identified for childhood and adolescence. Consider these examples:

Early Childhood

1. Getting ready to read

2. Learning to distinguish right from wrong

3. Learning sex differences and sexual modesty

4. Learning to talk

Middle Childhood

1. Learning physical skills necessary for games

2. Learning to get along with age-mates

3. Learning an appropriate masculine or feminine social role

4. Developing fundamental skills in reading, writing, and calculating

Adolescence

1. Accepting one's physique and using the body effectively

2. Preparing for marriage and family life

3. Preparing for an economic career

4. Desiring and achieving socially responsible behavior

5. Developing intellectual skills and concepts necessary for civic competence

Conformity as an Educational Goal

Implicit in the conceptualization and language of Havighurst's developmental tasks is a strong sense of conforming to the status quo. Consider, for example, such tasks as these: "learning an appropriate masculine or feminine role"; "accepting one's physique"; "desiring and achieving socially responsible behaviors"; "accepting and adjusting to the physiological changes of middle age." It is perhaps not unfair to say that such a strong emphasis upon conformity was both a reflection of and a contribution to a prevailing educational view that held that one of the important responsibilities of the schools was to help children and youth conform to existing societal norms.

A second assumption was that the curriculum should emphasize functional outcomes— practical skills and knowledge that had immediate value for the student.

A concomitant assumption was that the disciplines themselves were not important as organizing bases for the curricula. Instead, schools were encouraged to develop "core curricula" that would minimize subject-matter distinctions and integrate learnings around major themes and issues. As Oliver (1977) notes, the primary objective of the core curriculum is "to develop unified studies based upon the common needs of the learners and organized without restriction by subject matter" (p. 246). Here, for example, are some of the "centers of experience" that Van Til, Vars, and Lounsbury (1961) recommend for structuring a core program: making and keeping friends, coming to terms with my body, money-magic or madness, meet your new school.

The recurring theme throughout much of this literature is that this is a good society that simply must be maintained. Also, the attempt to make education more relevant too often produced curricula that trivialized learning and overemphasized the needs of the present. Finally, in too many cases it provided a curricular excuse for tracking systems that imprisoned children from poor families into low-level programs that were banal and unimaginative and denied them the opportunity to pursue academic studies needed for success in college.

The Exemplary Leaders

Two curriculum theorists seem to have been important in this period: Ralph Tyler and Hollis Caswell. Although, like most exemplary leaders, their careers spanned several of the periods demarcated here, it seems most appropriate to examine their work within the framework of the period presently under discussion.

Ralph Tyler

Tyler first gained professional attention through his participation as research director of the Eight-Year Study sponsored by the Progressive Education Association to evaluate and systematize the efforts of progressive schools to free their curricula from the domination of the colleges. The curriculum results of the study were summarized by Giles, McCutchen, and Zechiel (1942), who noted that curriculum development and evaluation involved attention to four basic issues: identifying objectives, selecting the means for attaining those objectives, organizing those means, and evaluating the outcomes. It seems apparent that their work influenced Tyler in his preparation of the syllabus for the graduate course he was offering at the University of Chicago. It is this syllabus for "Education 305" (Tyler, 1950) that presents and explicates what has become known as the "Tyler rationale."

In the syllabus, Tyler noted that the first question that must be answered in developing any curriculum is, "What educational purposes should the school seek to attain?" These educational objectives can first be identified by examining three sources: studies of the learners themselves, studies of contemporary life outside of school, and suggestions from subject specialists.

The second question is, "How can learning experiences be selected that are likely to be useful in attaining these experiences?" Here he argued for several general principles that should guide curriculum workers in selecting objectives.

The third question is, "How can learning experiences be organized for effective instruction?" In making determinations about the organization of experiences, the curriculum developer should consider three criteria: continuity, sequence, and integration.

The final question is, "How can the effectiveness of learning experiences be evaluated?" Valid and reliable curriculum-based tests should be developed and the results used to improve the curriculum.

Tyler's publication has had a lasting impact on curriculum leaders. By 1985, more than 100,000 copies of the syllabus had been purchased. It made a significant contribution by systematizing in a sequential manner, and curriculum workers seemed to value its clearness, its comprehensiveness, and its simplicity.

Hollis Caswell

Caswell was one of the first to understand the importance of staff development as a necessary foundation for curriculum work. To that end, he developed excellent study materials and bibliographies helping teachers perceive the larger issues of child development and curriculum ends and using those materials in educating the teachers of Florida and other states who were working with him in a comprehensive curriculum-revision project.

Second, he put into practice on a major scale the widespread belief teachers should be involved in curriculum development. In developing state curriculum for Virginia, he involved ten thousand Virginia teachers studying and discussing curricular issues.

Third, he developed a useful set of organizing structures that integrate the three determiners of curricula—child interests, social meaning, and subject matter. He began by reviewing what was known about child development in order to identify important child interests.

The Major Publications

Two quite different publications are singled out here for attention: one by the distinguished Swiss psychologist Jean Piaget, and one by a somewhat anonymous committee of American educators.

The Psychology of Intelligence

Because Piaget's publishing career spans several decades during which many seminal publications were produced, it is obviously difficult to select one work as most important. However, his 1950 book, *The Psychology of Intelligence*, seems to have been especially influential because it was one of the earliest to present in a systematic manner his comprehensive view of the nature of intelligence and the child's developmental stages.

Thus the developmental stages he identified are organized around this essential principle. Four such stages are usually discussed in the extensive literature on Piaget: sensorimotor, pre-operational, concrete operations, and formal operations. While these stages, in his view, are invariant in their sequence, they are also hierarchically related: Early stages are integrated into later ones.

The sensorimotor stage, which begins with conception and lasts until about age 2, is a pre-verbal period in which the child relies upon sensorimotor information to adapt to the environment and to acquire new behaviors. The child begins with simple reflex actions, then makes responses modified by experience.

During the next stage, the preoperational, which lasts until about age 6 or 7, language and symbolic thought have their beginnings. The learner reconstructs the developments of the sensorimotor stage, integrating prior knowledge into the new intellectual structures.

During the stage of concrete operations, between ages 7 and 11, the child develops the cognitive ability to classify, order, and handle numbers, spatial operations, and all the operations of classes and relations. In a sense, the concrete operations are similar to those of the prior stage, except for the fact that the child is able to use representational thought instead of direct action on the object. In this stage, the child seems to have a well-integrated cognitive system by means of which he or she can act upon the environment. However, the child is still able to deal effectively in a cognitive sense only with concrete objects, not with symbolic representations of those objects.

During the final stage of formal operations, the adolescent can think about both the real and the possible. Educators who first learned of the Piagetian stages in the late 1950s and early 1960s were initially impressed with the research data supporting this stage theory.

More recently, however, other researchers have been more concerned with conducting research to verify or challenge Piaget's stage theory. After reviewing all the pertinent research, Gelman and Baillargeon (1983) reach this conclusion:

> In our opinion there is little evidence to support the idea of major stages in cognitive development of the type described by Piaget. Over and over again the evidence is that the preoperational child has more competence than expected. (p. 214)

In substance, the report was essentially an argument for Developmental Conformism.

SCHOLARLY STRUCTURALISM

The Temper of the Times

In retrospect, the era of Scholarly Structuralism (1957–1967) seems to have been an interesting period of history. First, it was a time when the factors producing the turbulence of the previous period seemed to gather in strength. International tensions continued unabated.

The major event in education was the launching of Sputnik in 1957—an event that dramatized the need for strong programs in science and mathematics in American schools. Under the prodding of President Johnson, Congress responded with massive allocations of federal aid.

The Predominant Trends

The period under consideration was an interesting one from an educational perspective. This was the first time in American educational history that academic scholars decided that they had a key role to play in the development of specific curricula. Largely supported by federal funds channeled through the National Science Foundation, those scholars produced numerous curricula for every major discipline in both elementary and secondary education.

The Exemplary Leaders

During this interesting time, two curriculum theorists seem to have made major impacts—Jerome Bruner and Joseph Schwab.

Jerome Bruner

Bruner (1960) sets forth rather cogently in this volume, *The Process of Education*, a comprehensive rationale for Scholarly Structuralism. First, school curricula must be primarily concerned with effecting and facilitating the transfer of learning. Because school time is limited, educators must find the most efficient means of using the limited time available.

Understanding broad principles was especially important in the latter part of the twentieth century. Bruner argued increased scientific knowledge was able to clarify those structures in a way that perhaps was not possible before. The explosion of knowledge made it impossible for the student to learn everything. Therefore, learning the structures of a discipline resulted in a kind of curricular parsimony.

Joseph Schwab

Schwab's (1969, 1971, 1973, 1978, 1983) writings on curriculum span a period of at least 20 years and have proved to be rather influential in the field of curriculum theory. Like Bruner, Schwab was early concerned with the structure of the disciplines; yet it seems fair to say that his writings on the matter demonstrate a complexity and sophistication missing from the Bruner work.

Rather than insisting that there is only one way of understanding the world, Schwab argues for a "permissive eclecticism," which enables the inquirer to use any valid approach to understand natural and human phenomena. He noted that few disciplines have a single structure and that the scientists in a field are too diverse in their preferences to be unanimous about one right mode of attack.

Schwab's later writings on curriculum seem much more concerned with process and much less concerned with the structure of the disciplines. The outcome, he hoped, would be incremental change, and the process would be an eclectic one, drawing from several bodies of knowledge and from several perspectives.

The Major Publications

Two publications seem worthy of note: the Conant Report and the Physical Science Study Committee (PSSC) curriculum project. One looked back; the other seemed to look ahead.

The Conant Report

In 1959, James Bryant Conant, former president of Harvard University, authored *The American High School Today*. The book instigated the "Conant Report" by purporting the following curricular recommendations that were quite specific and somewhat conventional:

1. All students should be required to complete 4 years of English, 3 years of social studies, 1 year of mathematics, and 1 year of science.

2. Academically talented students should be required to take 3 additional years of mathematics, 4 years of one foreign language, and 2 additional years of science. If they wished, a second foreign language could be added.

3. All students should be required to take a senior course in America problems, as part of their social studies requirement. In this course, students, heterogeneously grouped, would have free and open discussions of controversial issues.

Because the nation seemed to be searching for a new direction for its schools, the above recommendations were endorsed by most educators of the time. Principals and their faculties used the report as a set of criteria to judge their schools and changed their programs to bring them into line with Conant's recommendations.

PSSC Physics

This major curriculum project of the late 1950s and early 1960s (Physical Science Study Committee, 1961) claimed to involve students in discovery and inquiry as the basic pedagogical methods for identifying the structure of physics. Students "did physics" as physicists did, at least to the extent of their ability to do so. Although the implementation of the new course was supported by numerous federally funded teacher-training institutes, the developers had made a significant attempt to develop a "teacher-proof" curriculum that attempted to control all aspects of the instructional process.

ROMANTIC RADICALISM

The era of Romantic Radicalism (1968–1974) seemed to many observers to be a time of national fragmentation and upheaval, one in which the fabric of the society was stretched to its breaking point.

The Temper of the Times

It was, first of all, a time of rampant violence. It was also a time when youth seemed to be in the saddle. Popular writers trumpeted the glories of being young. A strongly vocal "counterculture" developed, espousing the virtues of drug-induced hallucinogenic visions, rock music, and spontaneous "openness" in all relationships—and at the same time rejecting the "bourgeois" values of work, punctuality, and bodily cleanliness.

The Predominant Trends

This period was obviously a time of experimentation in an attempt to develop child-centered schools and programs. The experimentation took three related but different forms: alternative schools, open classrooms, and elective programs.

Alternative Schools

The alternative schools were perhaps the most radical of all. While in later years alternative schools often seemed to be very similar to the conventional schools, at the outset their faculties worked hard to make them different. Although these alternative schools ranged from completely unstructured "free schools" to mildly experimental schools that seemed different in only superficial ways, they did share certain characteristics (see Glatthorn, 1975, for a fuller account of the schools and their programs).

First, they were strongly teacher-centered: Teachers often administered the schools without a principal, teachers determined the curriculum, and teachers offered many of the supportive services provided by specialists in the conventional schools. Second, the schools were in a real sense child-centered: Curricula were shaped in response to the needs and interests of the children, and learning activities were selected primarily on the basis of their appeal to the children and parents. The most radical schools simply ignored the whole issue of evaluation;

teachers in the more conventional alternative schools wrote anecdotal reports, basing their evaluations on students' self-assessments. Finally, of course, they were "schools of choice": Students elected to attend the alternative, rather than being assigned to it.

Open Classrooms

The open classroom was perhaps an attempt on the part of the educational establishment to respond to the mood of the times. Largely influenced by developments in the best British primary schools, the open classroom movement in the United States was to a great extent a revitalization of a moribund progressivism. Although the term *open classroom* was often simply an ill-defined slogan, there were certain important characteristics. There was, first of all, an emphasis upon a rich learning environment. Teachers in the open classroom typically began by provisioning the classroom with stimulating learning materials and activities— centers of interest that would immediately appeal to the child and at the same time help the child learn. Children were free to move from center to center, to work together, and to engage each other in discussion. Thus, there was little concern for order in the conventional sense of that term: The best discipline was the self-discipline that came from learning on one's own.

Elective Programs

The elective programs were perhaps an attempt on the part of secondary schools to capture the vitality and excitement of the open classroom, which to a great extent had been limited to the primary grades. The basic concept of the elective program was a relatively simple one: Instead of a student taking "English, Grade 10," the student should be able to choose from a variety of short-term courses, such as "Women in Literature," "The Romance of Sports," and "War and Peace." In this sense, of course, such "electives" are different in organizational function from a subject such as music, which students elect to study or not to study.

The Exemplary Leaders

It is perhaps symbolic that the two figures selected as representing this exciting period of innovation and experimentation were not educators in the conventional sense of that term. Carl Rogers was a psychologist, and John Holt was perhaps a professional gadfly.

Carl Rogers

Rogers was a psychologist whose name came to be used to identify a school of counseling psychology: A Rogerian counselor is one who attempts to enter into the client's world, adopt the client's frame of reference, and listen empathically without advising.

Although Rogers (1969) worked with several college and school faculties who were interested in a Rogerian approach to organizational revitalization, his chief contribution seems to have been his ability to articulate clearly and to practice effectively what open educators and free school advocates could only haltingly express and imperfectly implement.

John Holt

If Rogers was a counselor who did not believe in advising, then Holt might be characterized as a teacher who did not believe in teaching. In a sense, of course, he is selected here as a representative figure of an influential group that included such other disenchanted teachers as Jonathan Kozol, James Herndon, and Herbert Kohl.

While it might seem surprising to identify a radical teacher as a major curriculum figure, Holt is selected because he and his associates represent a period of time when curriculum making itself was called into question. In Holt's (1964) view, the teacher was the curriculum. From his perspective, the schools did not need scope-and-sequence charts, clearly articulated objectives, or specified learning activities. The schools needed, instead, exciting and imaginative teachers who could provision a stimulating learning environment and who could involve learners in meaningful learning experiences.

The Major Publications

Two publications are selected here for quite different reasons: One heralded the promise of open education; the other marked the end of federal involvement in curriculum making.

Crisis in the Classroom

In Ravitch's (1983) view, this book "projected open education into the public limelight as nothing previously had been done" (p. 245). Its author, Charles Silberman (1970), was an experienced journalist who had been commissioned by the Carnegie Corporation to conduct a study of teacher education. Silberman, however, realized that a more important story was breaking—open education might be the one movement that would revolutionize education.

The answer, of course, was open education. Silberman was a highly skilled writer who knew how to personalize the dry stuff of educational change. He presented fascinating portraits of educators who seemed to be making a difference, and his own conviction made his message seem even more authentic.

Man: A Course of Study

This curriculum project (Curriculum Development Associates, 1972), usually identified by the acronym MACOS (Man: A Course of Study), had been developed at the Education Development Center with financial support from the National Science Foundation. As a social studies course designed for fifth- or sixth graders, MACOS seemed, in many ways, to represent the best of federally supported curriculum work. It drew heavily from Brunerian curriculum theory, taking pains to provide interesting "discovery" experiences that would help young children understand some of the basic structures of the social sciences.

PRIVATISTIC CONSERVATISM

The Temper of the Times

The period of Privatistic Conservatism (1975–1989) is generally recognized as the time when a strongly conservative philosophy permeated the national consciousness. It seemed that the American people were tired of violence, of experimentation, and of protest—and yearned for peace, stability, and traditional values.

It was also a time of increased religiosity. Fundamentalist groups especially became more active in the political arena, advancing their own candidates and giving large amounts of financial support to candidates who supported their agenda. Their agenda was concerned primarily with so-called family issues: elimination of abortion, restriction of the rights of homosexuals, and a return of Bible reading and prayer to the public schools. Interestingly enough, the resurgence of religiosity in this country seemed paralleled by an increase in religious fanaticism abroad.

This period was also a time when the information age fully arrived. More than 98% of American households owned one or more television sets—and most of those were color models.

Finally, it was a period of widespread immigration, especially of Hispanics and Asians. For the decade 1971–1980, more than 44% of all immigrants were from South American or Central American nations; and more than 35% were from Asian countries.

The Predominant Trends

As noted above, this period seems to have been a time when a conservative view of both the society and its schools held sway. Those espousing such a conservative educational view essentially argued that the chief function of the school was to transmit the culture and to prepare students for their roles in a technological society; in accomplishing such a mission, the curriculum should emphasize the scholarly disciplines, should be characterized by intellectual rigor, and should be closely monitored for its effectiveness. Emanating from this broadly conservative view of the school and its curriculum were several specific trends.

School Effectiveness and School Reform

The first significant development was a broad-based research effort to identify the key elements in effective schools, with a concomitant attempt to translate those elements into a plan for reforming the schools. Following some groundbreaking research, one of the most useful was performed by Purkey and Smith (1983) who, after reviewing, critiquing, and synthesizing all the research, were able to identify the key factors shown in Exhibit 2.1.

A More Rigorous Curriculum

Central to this reform effort was an emphasis on "curriculum rigor." In general, this slogan seemed most useful simply as a rallying cry for those who believed that a more academically challenging curriculum would best serve the needs of American youth. The most common expressions of this concern for curricular rigor were state laws and district policies mandating additional graduation requirements.

The Critical Thinking Movement

This concern for a new rigor in the curriculum also took the form of widespread interest in teaching critical thinking. Most of those in the forefront of the movement argued for the importance of critical thinking by stressing the need for better thinking in a technologically oriented information age. Typical of these arguments was the conclusion reached by the Education Commission of the States (1982). After analyzing the needs of the society in an information age, the commission concluded in a special report that these were the "basics of tomorrow": evaluation and analysis skills, critical thinking, problem-solving strategies, organization and reference skills, synthesis, application, creativity, decision making given incomplete information, and communication skills.

Exhibit 2.1   Key Factors in Effective Schools

Organizational and Structural Variables

1. The leadership and staff of the school have considerable autonomy in determining the means they will use to improve academic performance.

2. The principal plays an active role as an instructional leader.

3. The staff remains relatively stable in order to maintain and promote further success.

4. The elementary curriculum focuses on basic and complex skills, with sufficient time provided and close coordination across grade levels and across disciplines; the secondary curriculum includes a planned and purposeful program without too many electives.

5. There is schoolwide staff development closely related to the instructional program of the school.

6. There is active parent involvement and support.

7. The school recognizes academic success, through symbols and ceremonies.

8. A greater portion of the day is devoted to academic subjects, with effective use made of academic time and with active involvement of students.

9. There is district support for school-based efforts.

Process Variables

1. There are collaborative planning and collegial relationships.

2. There is a pervasive sense of community.

3. Clear goals and high expectations are commonly shared.

4. There is order and discipline, with clear and reasonable rules fairly and consistently enforced.

SOURCE: Adapted from Purkey and Smith (1983).

Accountability

Allied with the concern for more rigor in the curriculum was a demand that teachers and students be held more accountable. First, school districts seemed eagerly to embrace several programs that attempted to hold teachers more accountable for teaching and testing the prescribed curriculum. Such programs were usually identified as "curriculum alignment projects." Although they varied in detail, they attempted to align the written and the taught curriculum, usually by monitoring what was taught, and the written and the tested curriculum, ordinarily by matching the test with the instructional objectives.

These conservative responses noted some undesirable side effects: increased pressure on less able students, resulting in an unfavorable climate for growth; and the overemphasis on the knowledge-transmission function, resulting from mandates and competency tests.

Charter Schools

The birth of charter schools started in the late 1980s in the state of Minnesota. Charter schools were publicly funded, publicly controlled, and privately run. They were usually required to adhere to fewer district rules than regular public schools, and, subsequently, became a part of the "school choice movement." School choice referred to a school district allowing parents to decide how to run their school. The underlying philosophy of school choice appeared to be that parents would have the right to choose how their children were educated and how their schools were administered. Once underway, experiential information on whether charter schools improved education was, at best, slim and tentative. Murphy and Shiffman (2002), however, analyzed the empirical evidence gathered over a period of time to determine the impact of charters—both on individual charter communities and on the larger educational system. They concluded that "by and large, the picture that emerges from the data . . . compiled was disappointing to charter purists—those who hold that the central goal of charters is to overhaul the extant system of education in the United States" (p. 216). Further, "the data on student achievement and school accountability . . . are not nearly as positive as charter advocates had hypothesized" (p. 216). To this day, charter schools have yet to throw off the kind of illumination hoped for by founders of the charter movement.

Vouchers

Historians credit Adam Smith for giving birth to the voucher system in 1778 when he argued that parents are in the best position to decide how their children should be educated and that the state should give parents the money to hire suitable teachers. The intent of the voucher/choice schema was to provide opportunities, supported by tax monies, to target populations. Advocates of the voucher/choice concept believed that competition improves the marketplace and enhances educational effectiveness. Adversaries of the voucher/choice concept for public school, however, argued that:

- Choice is a notion that flies in the face of the basic mission of American public education
- Choice is a means to circumvent laws, governing due process, religious activities, and desegregation
- Choice is a means to express personal biases and to construct and reform society through political/religious beliefs
- Choice lowers the quality of some schools, and lessened enrollments can threaten equal educational opportunity for the majority of the students
- The focus ought to be on improving schools rather than directing funds from one school district to another.

(Boschee & Hunt, 1990, p. 75)

In the 1980s, states that endorsed the voucher/choice concept with varied and different requirements included Alaska, Arizona, California, Florida, Iowa, Louisiana, Massachusetts, Missouri, New York, Vermont, Virginia, Washington, and Wisconsin. Taking issue with where people stand on educational choice and vouchers, Boschee and Hunt (1990), in an article in the *NASSP Bulletin*, wrote that

> people take sides without really knowing what impact the concepts will have on the economies of daily life in a competitive marketplace; the organization and regulation of educational systems related to teaching, learning, and financial accountability;

professional employment; cultural, social-psychological, and racial issues; parental choice; the state and federal laws; and values. (p. 86)

Having said that, they developed an instrument titled "Pros/Cons of Voucher/Choice" to help people determine whether they really endorsed the concept, were neutral, or were opposed. The instrument addressed seven areas, including Regulation Versus Deregulation; Effectiveness/Efficiency of Schooling; Legal/Constitutional Issues; Roles: Local, State, Regional, Federal, Student, Teacher, Parent; Accountability/Instability Factors; Society, Values, and Schooling; and Research on Schooling. (The instrument and score key are published in the March 1990 *NASSP Bulletin*.)

The National Education Goals

In 1989, the President of the United States, George H. W. Bush, and the nation's 50 governors came together for a historic summit on one of the most important issues affecting America's future: the education of our nation's children. Born of an urgent realization that America's future prosperity was at stake, the first Education Summit, cochaired by Governor Carroll Campbell and then-Governor Bill Clinton, produced six ambitious goals for the nation's performance in education:
By the year 2000,

1. All children in America will start school ready to learn.

2. The high school graduation rate will increase to at least 90 percent.

3. American students will leave grades four, eight and twelve having demonstrated competency over challenging subject matter including English, mathematics, science, history, and geography, and every school in America will ensure that all students learn to use their minds well, so that they may be prepared for responsible citizenship, further learning, and productive employment in our modern economy.

4. United States students will be first in the world in mathematics and science achievement.

5. Every adult American will be literate and will possess the knowledge and skills necessary to compete in a global economy and exercise the rights and responsibilities of citizenship.

6. Every school in America will be free of drugs and violence and will offer a disciplined environment conducive to learning.

(Archived Information, n.d.)

With the passage of Goals 2000 legislation in 1994, the U.S. Congress added to Goal Three the subjects of foreign languages, civics and government, economics, and the arts and added two additional goals:
By the year 2000,

1. The nation's teaching force will have access to programs for the continued improvement of their professional skills and the opportunity to acquire the knowledge and skills needed to instruct and prepare all American students for the next century.

2. Every school will promote partnerships that will increase parental involvement and participation in promoting the social, emotional, and academic growth of children.

(Archived Information, n.d.)

Knudsen and Morrissette (1998) made an analysis and critique of Goals 2000 and concluded that "although a gallant effort, Goals 2000 will be remembered as a reform movement that funneled millions, perhaps billions, of dollars into American public schools with little to show in return" (n.p.). The concept for Goals 2000 lacked agreement. It was a vision that did not reach the grassroots level. It can be argued that America was built from the grassroots level, and it appeared that American public education needed to be built from the grassroots level.

The Exemplary Leaders

Two figures stand out in this period for their pervasive influence: Benjamin Bloom and John Goodlad. Each in his own way made major contributions and influenced both research and practice.

Benjamin Bloom

Bloom was a psychologist and Professor of Education at the University of Chicago. He first attracted widespread attention from the profession with the publication of what quickly became known as "Bloom's taxonomy" (see Bloom, 1956).

While his work on the taxonomy was obviously influential, Bloom's theory of and research on mastery learning had perhaps an even greater impact. In discussing his work on mastery learning, it is important to make a sharp distinction between three understandings of "mastery learning": what he himself has advocated, how his students have applied his ideas in developing curricula, and what some publishers have done in commercializing mastery learning.

Despite the fact that some have distorted his theory, Bloom made a major contribution to curriculum—one whose effects will probably endure for some time.

John I. Goodlad

Goodlad is another leading figure in the curriculum field whose career spans several periods. For more than 25 years he conducted research, organized centers of educational change, and taught graduate courses in the field, publishing more than 20 books and some 200 articles. Educators tended to perceive him as a curriculum leader who understood schools, who had a clear vision of what those schools could become, and who had some tested ideas for helping them achieve their goals.

His analysis of the content of that balanced curriculum yielded a rather discouraging picture. By observing classes, interviewing teachers and students, analyzing texts and tests, and examining curriculum guides, he and his research team concluded that in all the academic areas—English language arts, mathematics, social studies, and science—the emphasis was on teaching basic skills and facts. Almost no attention in any grade was given to inquiry, critical thinking, or problem solving. The picture was especially dismal in lower-track classes.

The Major Publications

In 1983, nine national "school reform" reports were issued—so many that several educational publications saw fit to publish "scorecards" and "readers' guides" to help the profession make sense of the reform literature. Two of these reports seemed especially influential.

A Nation at Risk

This publication was produced by the National Commission on Excellence in Education (1983), appointed in 1981 by the then Secretary of Education, Terrel H. Bell. The report presented what it termed the "indicators of risk," carefully selected statistics purporting to demonstrate the gravity of the risk and to warrant the dramatic language.

Perhaps because the language was so dramatic, the picture portrayed so dismal, and the recommendations so clear and simple, *A Nation at Risk* seemed to have a pervasive and widespread impact, especially on the public. It became the subject of television and radio broadcasts, it was discussed at parent and citizen meetings across the nation, and legislators often made reference to it as they drafted their own reform legislation. In retrospect, perhaps, the chief value of *A Nation at Risk* is that it dramatized the issue of educational reform and moved such reform into the arena of public debate.

High School

This book by Ernest Boyer (1983), while not getting the media attention of *A Nation at Risk,* was received much more favorably by educators and thus probably had a more pervasive impact. It was the result of a 2-year study of the American high school funded by the Carnegie Foundation for the Advancement of Teaching. The research staff reviewed the literature, consulted with numerous educational leaders, and spent 20 days in each of 15 high schools. While the study lacked perhaps the breadth and comprehensiveness of the Goodlad study, it resulted in some recommendations that in many ways seemed more useful to the profession.

Several features of the Boyer report made it seem especially useful. First, it presented a balanced view of the achievement of American schools, eschewing the inflammatory rhetoric of *A Nation at Risk*. Second, it drew upon solid research, but used the research in an illuminating and interesting manner, because the book was intended to reach a large audience. Next, it offered specific recommendations about the quality of the core curriculum that provided useful guidelines for local curriculum leaders. Finally, its recommendations for required service made great sense at a time when, according to some commentators, American youth seemed self-centered and materialistic.

The Charter Schools Decade

This book on charter schools provides a thorough explanation of the charter schools phenomenon. Now well into its second decade, the charter schools movement has not been scrutinized carefully; it has enjoyed largely positive press generated by its advocates and occasionally some bitter criticism by opponents. The author, Anne Turnbaugh Lockwood (2004), also examines problems and obstacles that charter schools need to overcome in order to succeed, and she gives a glimpse of what the next decade holds for charter schools.

TECHNOLOGICAL CONSTRUCTIONISM

The Temper of the Times

The era of Technological Constructionism (1990–1999) can be viewed as a time when the net was cast more widely. Along with digital opportunity, it was an era when state content standards came into being, the "school choice" movement was given an intellectual boost, voucher legislation allowed students to attend religious schools at taxpayers' expense, students being home schooled increased from 10,000 in the 1970s to nearly 1,000,000 in the 1990s, and Goals 2000 was adopted.

The decade also saw increased prosperity for Americans as the Dow Jones and NASDAQ stock markets reached all-time highs. Due to the prevalence of computers and Internet use, "Dot-commies" became a new type of upper-middle class. With that, 82% of the population had completed high school compared to 41% in 1960. Education subject guides appeared on the World Wide Web, and the Elementary and Secondary Education Act provided assistance to disadvantaged students or students with limited proficiency in English, as well as to improve instruction in math, science, and drug use prevention. The nation also experienced extreme violence in the form of school shootings; according to the National School Safety Center, 255 school-associated violent deaths occurred during this decade ("School House Hype," 2000).

The appointment of Lamar Alexander, a prominent former governor from Tennessee, as Secretary of Education brought the Department of Education closer to the president. Another former governor, Richard Riley, succeeded Alexander when Bill Clinton began his first term as president in 1993. During Riley's 8-year term, the longest of any previous secretary, he weathered congressional attacks on the Department of Education. Nonetheless, he initiated substantive policies (e.g., higher standards, accountability, and increased investments) that helped to establish education as the key policy issue in the 2000 presidential election.

Predominant Trends

This period followed an era, the 1980s, when the nation struggled mightily to improve public education. A report from InfoMedia (1993) titled *Educational Reform: A National Perspective* indicated that "ten years have passed since the hoopla surrounding *A Nation at Risk*. Ten years of speechmaking and of handwringing" (p. 3).

Computers

The stability of the core tool and the keystone of the educational system, the printed textbook yielded significant ground to the astonishing storage and retrieval capacities of the computer. A new educational future was no longer inhibited and shaped by the exigencies of print-/textbook-based education. It was during this era that we experienced the first stages of humankind's third major, massive change in the way to communicate with each other and with future generations yet unborn. In the same manner that the alphabet and movable type changed everything about work and living in the decades after they were invented, the invention of the computer did change, and will continue to change, our lives and our children's lives dramatically.

The new technologies enabled a person with a computer and a phone line or cable in the remotest part of any state to connect to the equivalent of a million libraries worldwide. The use of an Internet browser and search engine allowed people to acquire within seconds the exact information they needed. Those same tools allowed those people to organize and analyze huge quantities of acquired information to use in solving problems and creating new opportunities. These technologies also enabled people to share information with one other person or with many millions of people worldwide (Whitehead, Jensen, & Boschee, 2003).

It was also during this decade that federal money was made available so that the country could go from a "digital divide" to a "digital opportunity" status. In 1994, President Clinton and Vice President Gore bridged the digital divide by setting the goal of connecting every classroom and library to the Internet. In 1996, President Clinton unveiled his Technology Literacy Challenge—and made a major commitment of resources to (a) connect every classroom to the Internet; (b) expand access to modern, multimedia computers; (c) make high-quality educational software an integral part of the curriculum; and (d) enable teachers to integrate technology effectively into their instruction. The funding for educational technology was increased by more than 3,000%—from 23 million dollars to 777 million dollars in a 6-year period (White House Office of the Press Secretary, 2000).

The Standards-Based Movement

The decade of the 1990s ushered in state educational standards. All the states, with the exception of Iowa, have adopted academic standards. Iowa requires each school district to develop its own standards. Although the research on the value of state standards is fairly new, and much of it is still in progress, the findings, according to Jones (2000), offer the following unfaltering guidelines (excerpts are taken from the article)[1]:

1. **Make academic standards everybody's business**. Everybody—students, parents, teachers, business, everybody—needs to know what the standards are and why they're important. Research shows that when students and teachers better understand what is expected of them, they perform better.

2. **Focus, focus, focus**. Each state's standards are different, but they all have one thing in common: They're not perfect. Some state standards are so vague that teachers aren't sure what they mean. Others are so specific and so numerous that it's impossible to cover everything in the 13 years between kindergarten and high school graduation. Robert Marzano, senior fellow at the Mid-continent Regional Laboratory (McREL) in Aurora, Colorado, studied the standards around the country and found it would take 23 years of schooling to cover all of the benchmarks. "Teachers can't teach it all . . . and kids couldn't possibly learn it all."

3. **Make standards-based decisions.** If you want standards to work, researchers say, you have to work on standards. The simplistic-sounding advice means each decision, each program, each new hire should be examined with an eye toward its impact on helping students meet standards. Researchers say school districts should put their money where their standards are. If a district wants to improve students' performance in math, for instance, it should hire more qualified math teachers.

4. **Invest in teachers**. Numerous studies have identified the importance of teachers' credentials in determining students' academic achievement. . . . Teacher quality is so important that some researchers are beginning to suspect that low student achievement often seen in low-income communities just might reflect the fact that the least qualified teachers are often assigned to schools in those communities.

5. **Demand helpful assessments that align with the curriculum**. If you want the curriculum to be taken seriously, you have to do something about assessments. In cases where there's concern about alignment between the test and the standards, districts ought to raise that with the state, and not assume that everything will work itself out. There can be real consequences if there's not good alignment.

6. **Approach accountability cautiously.** Most researchers recommend using test results and other standards-based data to make decisions about everything from textbooks to teachers.

7. **When students are in trouble, intervene.** Researchers have long touted the benefits of early intervention. Studies show . . . that a few weeks of one-on-one tutoring aimed at teaching first-graders to decode words can save many children from special education. (pp. 27–31)

With the development of state educational standards, and if public education is to be improved, teachers will require better training and staff development. Moreover, curriculum, instructional materials, and parental attitudes will have to change. Rick Melmer, South Dakota Secretary of Education, said that "in today's era of accountability, it is important to have clear standards to guide the curriculum and instruction in classrooms across the state" (South Dakota Department of Education, 2004).

Long overdue is the linking of high school and college standards. School administrators around the country have begun to modify their curricula so that students going to college succeed academically. David T. Conley, who directed the 3-year study assessing what college freshmen need to know to succeed academically, stated that "as things are, state standards are developed without reference to college standards" (Potter, 2003, p. A31).

The Exemplary Leaders

Three figures stand out in this period of change: Elliot W. Eisner, Robert J. Marzano, and Joseph S. Renzulli. Each of these individuals contributed his own special influence to the field of curriculum development.

Elliot W. Eisner

Eisner is a Professor of Education and Art at Stanford University. He is widely considered a leading theorist on art education. Eisner has won wide recognition for his work internationally. Among his many awards is the Palmer O. Johnson Award from the American Educational Research Association. He has been a John Simon Guggenheim Fellow and a Fulbright Scholar, and has served as the President of the National Art Education Association, the International Society for Education Through Art, the American Educational Research Association, and the John Dewey Society (Provenzo, 2003).

Eisner works primarily in three fields: arts education, curriculum studies, and qualitative research methodology (identifying practical uses of critical qualitative methods from the arts in school settings and teaching processes). His research interests have focused on the development of aesthetic intelligence and on the use of methods from the arts to study and improve educational practice. Originally trained as a painter, Eisner teaches ways in which schools might improve by using the processes of the arts in all their programs. He is considered one of the foremost leaders in the field of arts in education.

Robert J. Marzano

Marzano is a Senior Fellow at Mid-continent Research for Education and Learning (McREL) Institute in Aurora, Colorado. He is largely noted for translating research and theory into classroom practices. He heads a team of authors who developed *Dimensions in Learning* as well as *Tactics for Thinking*. Most recently, he is noted for his efforts in addressing standards. He has developed programs and practices used in K–12 classrooms that translate current research and theory in cognition into instructional methods. Marzano has authored 18 books and more than 150 articles (Marzano, Pickering, & Pollock, 2001).

Joseph S. Renzulli

A Professor of Educational Psychology at the University of Connecticut, Renzulli also serves as director of the National Research Center on the Gifted and Talented. His research has focused on the identification and development of creativity and giftedness in young people and on organizational models and curricular strategies for total school improvement. He is a Fellow in the American Psychological Association and was a consultant to the White House Task Force on Education of the Gifted and Talented. He was recently designated a Board of Trustees Distinguished Professor at the University of Connecticut (Tomlinson et al., 2001).

The Major Publications

Educators at this time began focusing on individualized instruction, technology, and data analysis. Although there were many outstanding works during this period of time, two publications are obvious for their pioneering and innovative approaches.

Classrooms That Work

Patricia Cunningham and Richard Allington's (1994) publication, *Classrooms That Work: They Can Read and Write,* compiled some of the best strategies that work effectively in classrooms. The book was one of the first to put an analytical emphasis on classroom instruction and focus on successful practices in schools from both research and a teacher point of view. It is a positive resource containing practical ideas, activities, and organizational strategies. Five major components are noted in the book: engagement in real reading and writing, supported comprehension activities, supported writing activities, decoding and spelling activities, and knowledge-building activities. These components best describe the critical components of a balanced classroom program.

Data Analysis

The book *Data Analysis: For Comprehensive Schoolwide Improvement* by Victoria Bernhardt (1998) had a vast impact on state officials, school district administrators, and teachers. As a result, it continues to have a major role on the school improvement process nationally. It was written to help educators learn how to deal with data that will inform them of where they are, where they want to be, and how to get there. Bernhardt explained why data make the difference in quality school improvement. Also, depending on what data make the difference and how they are gathered, analyzed, and whether properly used, they make a difference in meeting the needs of every student in school. This book took data from schools and demonstrated how powerful data analyses emerge logically. It shows how to gain answers to questions to understand current and future impacts.

NEW PRIVATISTIC CONSERVATISM

The Temper of the Times

Educational reform has become one of the most divisive issues in America, especially in the 21st century. Concerns about our educational system are reverberating at the national, state, and local levels. A heated debate involving American education has raged in the press over time, but more since the passage of the No Child Left Behind Act. Politicians, business leaders, educators, and parents are just some of the diverse groups of people engaged in the educational reform controversy. The intensity of the issues is accentuated by proponents across the political spectrum.

In addition to the educational issues for America's public schools to start the new century, Hardy (2004) reminds us that "over the past four years, the American electorate has been dealt a series of body blows, each capable of altering the political landscape" (p. 2). "The voting system broke down in a presidential election. A booming economy faltered, punctuated by revelation of one of the worst business scandals in U.S. history. And the country endured a devastating attack on its own soil" (p. 2). These events revealed a nation almost evenly divided politically, and farther apart in political values. The question looms: Where does that leave education?

Predominant Trends

According to Thomas Lickona (1993), author of *The Return of Character Education*, there appears to be concern over the moral condition of American society, and it is this moral decline that is prompting school reform. Lickona believes that the problem lies with a breakdown in the family structure, an increase in divorce and sexual promiscuity, as well as an increase in the amount of violent activity seen on TV and in the movies. This situation is translating into a perception that there is a deterioration of civility in everyday life that needs to be addressed by schools and teachers.

An attempt to address this situation occurred in the 1970s, but it was in the form of values clarification. The values clarification movement stressed the importance of individual rights and focused on not imposing values upon students; it permeated school curriculum throughout the 1970s and the 1980s. This began to change, however, in the early 1990s with a new movement away from values clarification and toward the development of "good student character," which developed into a "character counts" curriculum for elementary and middle school students.

Lickona indicated that the move away from values clarification is largely due to a groundswell of interest in character education. It was a backlash and reaction to the decline of the family and an increase in crime throughout the United States. Its supporters desired to infuse the teaching of ethical values into the school curriculum and believed that schools need to promote morality by teaching the young, directly and indirectly, such values as respect, responsibility, trustworthiness, fairness, caring, and civic virtue.

Lickona (1993, pp. 5–6) noted that a comprehensive approach to character education called upon the individual teacher to do the following:

- *Act as caregiver, model, and mentor,* treating students with love and respect, setting a good example, supporting positive social behavior, and correcting hurtful actions through one-on-one guidance and whole-class discussion.
- *Create a moral community,* helping students know one another as persons, respect and care about one another, and feel valued membership in, and responsibility to, the group.
- *Practice moral discipline,* using the creation and enforcement of rules as opportunities to foster moral reasoning, voluntary compliance with rules, and a respect for others.
- *Create a democratic classroom environment,* involving students in decision making and the responsibility for making the classroom a good place to be and learn.
- *Teach values through the curriculum,* using the ethically rich content of academic subjects (such as literature, history, and science), as well as outstanding programs.
- *Use cooperative learning* to develop students' appreciation of others, perspective taking, and ability to work with others toward common goals.
- *Create a positive moral culture in the school,* developing a schoolwide ethos (through leadership of the principal, discipline, a schoolwide sense of community, meaningful student government, a moral community among adults, and making time for moral concerns) that supports and amplifies the values taught in classrooms.

Whether character education will take hold and/or continue to be viable in American schools remains to be seen. There has certainly been a trend in this direction during the early part of the 21st century. Factors that will determine its success will be the level of support from the community, the role of religion, and future leaders in education.

School Vouchers

With the advent of a new Republican administration in 2001, educational reform moved away from technological structuralism and returned to a more privatistic and conservative nature. This is especially the case with President George W. Bush's endorsement of vouchers.

One of the predominant trends, according to Joseph Bast (as cited in Bast, Harmer, & Dewey, 1997), has been the interest in school vouchers. He acknowledged that a Nobel Prize winner, Milton Friedman, proposed ending the traditional model of schooling by giving parents tax-financed certificates or vouchers to pay tuition at schools, public or private, to which they chose to send their children. It was emphasized that school vouchers were to be considered a type of government grant that provides school tuition that can be used at both public and private schools and that could become a way to increase the option of school choice for low-income families. The concept behind school vouchers continues to focus on giving parents a wider choice of educational institutions and approaches.

The school voucher program is controversial at best in that many individuals believe that such a program, if broadly applied, can destroy the American public education system. There is also debate over constitutional church-state issues when vouchers (if and when) are used to allow students to attend religious schools. This continues to be a controversial issue, even though a federal court held that when a voucher system resulted in almost all recipients attending religious schools instead of public schools, the system violated the Constitution.

Cook (2004) provided a sample of the voucher programs implemented or attempted at some cities and states:

- Milwaukee started in the 1990–1991 school year and served 12,950 students who attended 102 private and religious schools. Enrollment in the voucher program was capped at 15% of the public school population, or about 15,000 students. The cost exceeds 76 million dollars.
- Cleveland started in the 1996–1997 school year and served 5,200 students in 50 private and religious schools in 2002–2003. The program is limited to K–3 students who live within the Cleveland school district; however, once a student qualifies, he or she can continue to receive a voucher through 10th grade. The Ohio legislature expanded the program in 2003 by 1,000 students and increased the funding for private schools by 44%.
- Colorado was scheduled to begin in the fall of 2004; however, a district judge's ruling halted the implementation. This ruling is being appealed by the state.
- Florida started the program in the 1999–2000 academic school year. The A+ Opportunity Scholarships supported 663 students, the McKay Scholarship program supported 12,200 students, and Corporate Income Tax Scholarship supported between 14,000 and 16,000 students. The corporate tax credits provide $3,500 worth of vouchers to students from low-income families. These scholarship programs have been heavily criticized due to reports of financial corruption, lack of state oversight, and lax or nonexistent academic standards. For example, "the Department of Education provided tax credits to a Muslim school in Tampa that has been linked to terrorist activity" (Cook, 2004, p. 14).
- Washington, D.C., was tentatively scheduled to start the voucher program in fall 2004 if approved by Congress. A minimum of 1,700 K–12 public school students would be served in the nation's capital. The 13-million dollar program would be the first federally funded program that was approved by one vote in the U.S. House of Representatives, but stalled in the Senate until a 2004 December vote that put the starting time in jeopardy.

Home Schooling

According to Janet Sugameli (2003), a Metro Detroit freelance writer, there are no accurate figures for the number of home-schooling families because homeschoolers are generally not required to register with states. The National Home Education Research Institute estimates that nearly two million school-age children are being home schooled throughout the country. Although many parents say their choice is related to their religious affiliations, many home-schooling parents note that the ability to customize their children's education is a significant factor.

Sugameli notes that a number of parents decide to home school because it is easier to offer a tailored curriculum that no classroom teacher with 30 students can offer. She states that stay-at-home parents can purchase curriculum packages and modify them to fit the needs of their children. In addition, a home-schooling parent can move at a different pace than a traditional classroom teacher, who often has to stay at a pace suitable for the majority of students. Sugameli indicates that there is a great deal of flexibility in the system of home schooling and that some older students can even attend community colleges to get more intense subjects.

Sugameli has found in her research that some parents have indicated that they home school because private religious schools are often expensive, have larger class sizes, and may not focus on a religion of choice. She goes on to note that with many new resources, like Web sites and support groups, home schooling is becoming more mainstream. In addition, Sugameli found that homeschoolers often get together for parent-organized field trips in addition to extracurricular activities such as dance classes, sports, choir, art classes, and other offerings (for information about home schools, go to the National Center for Home Education Web site, supported by the Home School Legal Defense Association at www.hslda.org).

No Child Left Behind Act

The biggest public school story in the 21st century thus far was the 1,100-page No Child Left Behind Act. At first a Congressional coalition formed around the ambitious federal education bill; however, that unity dissolved as Democrats blamed Republicans for withholding funding, and Republicans criticized Democrats for abandoning school reform.

President George W. Bush signed the No Child Left Behind Act (NCLB) into law in January 2002. NCLB requires all schools to make Adequate Yearly Progress (AYP) to ensure that all students are "proficient" in state standards by 2014. It calls for all students to be proficient in both mathematics and English language arts. Failure to make Adequate Yearly Progress results in severe financial sanctions for Title I schools, beginning with providing transportation funds for open enrollment and supplemental services for students, and could potentially lead to closing a school. Often 20% of district Title 1 funds must be set aside to pay for the open enrollment and supplemental service cost of students in schools that have failed to make the required progress. For schools that do not receive Title 1 funding, failure to make Adequate Yearly Progress could be used as a criterion for determining state-level sanctions.

In addition, local education agencies (LEA), including school districts, county offices of education, and direct-funded charter schools, are required to meet Adequate Yearly Progress. There are other aspects of NCLB too extensive to note here, but it should be mentioned that the intent of the act is to make schools accountable for student academic progress. The No Child Left Behind Act has continued to be highly controversial with vocal supporters and critics since its implementation. What the law requires is considered by some as one of the greatest challenges that education leaders have ever had to face. According to Vince Ferrandino (2003), Executive Director of the National Association of Elementary School Principals (NAESP), the intent of NCLB is to reinforce the work and to

- [set high standards and] set high expectations for all students, regardless of race, ethnicity, family, background, or disability
- get all students to grade level or higher

- emphasize reading and mathematics
- report test results separately for all different groups
- identify students most in need of assistance
- require a state to set specific goals for student achievement
- require that schools make Adequate Yearly Progress
- require that every classroom have a highly qualified teacher
- have paraprofessionals in Title 1 meet new requirements (see p. 3)

Even opponents to NCLB agree that it has brought schools to focus on weaknesses and to elicit ideas and partnerships to address issues of academic progress effectively. Few disagree that the act forces school administrators to dialogue strategies with teachers, parents, and community leaders. It is through this process that NCLB will, it is hoped, build mutual understanding and provide some collaborative solutions for the future of education.

Gerald Bracy (2003), in the "13th Bracy Report" for Phi Delta Kappa, referred to NCLB as "a weapon of mass destruction targeted at the public schools in a campaign of shock and awe" (pp. 148–149). States across the nation are taking opposition to the law. For example, in a rebuke to NCLB, the Utah House voted to prohibit the state's education authorities from using local money to comply with the president's signature education law ("Utah House Rebukes Bush," 2004).

The Exemplary Leaders

Two major figures stand out during this unusual time of direct government involvement in individualized and differentiated learning, assessment, and school improvement. Never before has the federal government been so involved in making sure that schools apply standards and are accountable.

Linda Darling-Hammond

Darling-Hammond is a Charles E. Ducommun Professor of Education at Stanford University School of Education. She also served as executive director of the National Commission on Teaching and America's Future, which produced the 1996 widely cited blueprint for education reform: *What Matters Most: Teaching for America's Future*. Darling-Hammond's research, teaching, and policy work focus on teaching and teacher education, school restructuring, and educational equity. She has been active in the development of standards for teaching, and served as a two-term member of the National Board for Professional Teaching Standards and as chair of the Interstate New Teacher Assessment and Support Consortium (INTASC) committee that drafted model standards for licensing beginning teachers. She is author of *The Right to Learn, A License to Teach*, and *Professional Development Schools: Schools for Developing a Profession*, along with 6 other books and more than 200 book chapters, journal articles, and monographs on education.

Darling-Hammond has served as the faculty sponsor for Stanford's Teacher Education Program (STEP). As a leader in the charge for enhanced teacher education and teacher preparedness, she has been instrumental in redesigning programs to better prepare teachers to teach diverse learners in the context of challenging new subject matter standards (Glass, 2003).

It is evident that Darling-Hammond has made a major contribution to education and continues to work on issues of education policy and practice, including school reform, authentic assessment, professional development schools, and educational research.

Carol Ann Tomlinson

Tomlinson is a noted author whose work in the area of differentiated instruction is well known internationally. She is an Associate Professor of Educational Leadership, Foundations and Policy at Curry School of Education, University of Virginia. Her work has had a tremendous impact on the school improvement process. Her books include information on curriculum and instruction for advanced learners and struggling learners, effective instruction in heterogeneous settings, and bridging the fields of general education and gifted education. She is the author of more than 100 articles, book chapters, and books. One of her best-known books is *The Differentiated Classroom: Responding to the Needs of All Learners*. Many school officials are turning to her work in their efforts to individualize classrooms and comply with the No Child Left Behind Act.

The Major Publications

No Child Left Behind Act

With the passage of the No Child Left Behind Act (2001), schools are continuing to turn to ways to enhance student achievement, align standards, and learn more about the brain and how children learn. There are three authors, Charlotte Danielson, Patricia Wolfe, and Michael Fullan, whose works have dramatically helped build a foundation in these areas.

Enhancing Student Achievement

The book *Enhancing Student Achievement: A Framework for School Improvement* by Charlotte Danielson (2002) is fast becoming one of the most important books in education. Danielson's framework stresses the importance of aligning state and national standards and determining a means of assessing the school program as a whole. When educators learn to "put it all together" to improve their schools, they will be bringing their entire expertise to bear on providing a first-rate education to all children (Danielson, 2002).

Brain Matters

Brain Matters: Translating Research Into Classroom Practice by Patricia Wolfe (2001) has had a significant impact on classroom instructional strategies. Much of the research in this field confirms what experienced educators already know. Wolfe's book helps to functionally understand the brain and how it operates. This allows teachers to critically analyze the vast amount of neuroscientific information arriving in the classroom daily. The book is divided into three parts. Part I is a mini-textbook on brain-imaging techniques and the anatomy and physiology of the brain. Part II introduces a model of how the brain processes information, and explores some of the implications of this process for classroom practice. Part III presents examples of teaching strategies that match how the brain learns best: through projects, simulations, visuals, music writing, and mnemonics.

Leading in a Culture of Change

Michael Fullan is the Dean of the Ontario Institute for Studies in Education at the University of Toronto. An innovator and leader in teacher education, he has developed a number of partnerships designed to bring about major school improvement and educational reform. His powerful and pioneering book, *Leading in a Culture of Change* (2001), integrates theory, research, case studies, and anecdotes to flesh out the dynamics of effective leadership in this new privatistic era. He identifies and elaborates on five components of leadership that can affect sustainable and systemic change. The five components are: moral purpose, understanding change, relationship building, knowledge creation, sharing, and coherence making. Fullan notes that in an increasingly complex and fast-changing world it is crucial that we cultivate leadership at all levels of organization, business, and education.

SUMMARY: A CENTURY OF CURRICULUM TRENDS IN RETROSPECT

In reviewing this century of curriculum history, two general observations might be made. The first is to note the pace of change. Observe that the first five periods become increasingly shorter, lasting 27 years, 24 years, 16 years, 11 years, and 7 years, respectively. The sixth and seventh periods—Privatistic Conservatism and Technological Constructionism—lasted about a decade each. The latest period, New Privatistic Conservatism, seems to be gaining in momentum and is showing no early signs of ending. With this exception noted, it would seem that futurists who have commented on the rapid pace of change in today's society are probably correct. One, therefore, might predict that future trends in curriculum will be relatively short-lived.

The second observation is to note the rhythms and directions of that change. Here it might be useful to search for the best metaphor describing those rhythms and directions. Currently, when most educators speak about the general directions of the curriculum past and present, they seize initially on the metaphor of the pendulum, which suggests short swings between extreme positions. Or they talk of cycles, a more abstract figure that suggests longer periods of recurring tendencies. Neither metaphor seems to portray the past century plus of curriculum history. Instead, it might be more appropriate and more insightful to speak of separate streams that continue to flow—at times swollen, at times almost dry; at times separate, at times joining.

In identifying such streams in our curricular history, some useful terms are proposed by Eisner and Vallance (1974), who delineated five orientations in the curriculum: cognitive processes (help children acquire the basic skills and learn how to think); academic rationalism (foster intellectual growth in the subjects most worthy of study); personal relevance (emphasize the primacy of personal meaning); social adaptation and reconstruction (derive educational aims from an analysis of the society); and curriculum as technology (operationalize curricular outcomes by technological analysis of the observable behaviors sought).

The eight curricular orientations are thus seen as streams that have always been present during this past century of curricular history. Exhibit 2.2 shows how these streams seem to have ebbed and flowed throughout the separate periods. It reflects how their strength has varied and how, during a given period, one or two have predominated. It suggests that the strength of a

Exhibit 2.2   The Streams of Curricular History

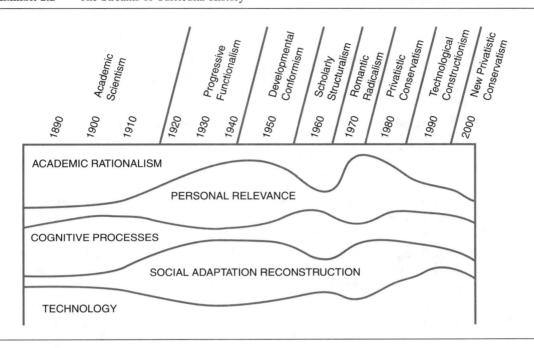

given orientation at a particular period of time seems to have resulted from powerful social forces impinging upon the curriculum. It also makes clear that educators in general have typically espoused a pragmatic eclecticism, one in which all eight streams have at least some part to play.

CHAPTER OVERVIEW

This chapter provides a useful understanding of the history of curriculum development for scholars and practitioners. The chapter provides a careful analysis of the past 110 years of curriculum development history. A historical understanding results in a deeper awareness of the extent to which curricular changes are often influenced by and are a manifestation of larger social forces. Chapter 2 offers an expansive perspective from which to view so-called innovations and reforms. This chapter focuses on the major developments affecting American schools, and provides an essential broader perspective. Specifically, the chapter addresses the periods of Academic Scientism, Progressive Functionalism, Developmental Conformism, Scholarly Structuralism, Romantic Radicalism, Privatistic Conservatism, Technological Constructionism, and New Privatistic Conservatism and why each was important in the development of curriculum. Finally, some of the predominant trends that transcended each major period of curriculum development are identified.

CHAPTER TERMS

Academic Scientism

Progressive Functionalism

Developmental Conformism

Scholarly Structuralism

Romantic Radicalism

Privatistic Conservatism

Technological Constructionism

New Privatistic Conservatism

Committee of Ten

Committee of Fifteen

APPLICATIONS

1. Based upon what you have learned about the history of curriculum and what you observe happening now, when do you think the period of New Privatistic Conservatism will end, and what type of period will succeed it?

2. Some have argued that there are really no new ideas in education and that all so-called innovations are simply a refurbishing of old ideas. Based upon your knowledge of curriculum history, would you agree or disagree?

3. Most nationally disseminated reports recommending educational reform have very little impact. How, then, do you explain the seemingly profound impact made by the reform reports of the 1990s and the early years of the 21st century?

4. Charter schools, school vouchers, and home schooling movements are becoming commonplace in American education. How do you feel about each of these practices, and do you believe that they will continue in the future? Why or why not?

5. The No Child Left Behind Act of 2001 (NCLB) has had a major impact on how schools plan and implement curriculum as well as on how students are assessed. What aspects of NCLB do you feel have been advantageous to the school improvement process? What aspects, if any, do you feel have been detrimental? Why or why not?

CASE STUDY

The new elementary school principal, Dr. Susan Davenport, was hired to replace Dr. Robert Edwards, who left the Dover School District for a professorship at a university in the same town. When she was hired, the superintendent told her that he expected the principal to get the school's staff on board to bring the curriculum into compliance with district, state, and federal standards.

With the superintendent's edict to bring the staff on board so that the standards could be met, Dr. Davenport felt that information was needed about the diverse faculty at Washington Elementary School. She arranged a meeting with the previous principal to get some insights about the faculty at the school. Dr. Edwards was pleased to meet with Susan and share some information about the teachers.

In describing the six fourth-grade faculty at Washington Elementary School, Dr. Edwards made reference to Mr. Anderson, who was a 40-year veteran at the school. He noted that

Anderson is very conservative in nature and a blend of Academic Scientism and Progressive Functionalism. He also does not believe in individualizing or having students work in groups. Another teacher, Mrs. Ferrell, is less conservative than Mr. Anderson; however, she is not a big fan of technology and focuses on the social aspects of the child, a type of Developmental Conformism.

Mrs. Bardwell, a close friend of Mrs. Ferrell, is a far more structured teacher who has the desks lined up in rows. She does focus on fundamentals, but uses an inquiry approach to teaching at times, especially in science. Dr. Edwards felt that Bardwell fit nicely into the era of Scholarly Structuralism—curriculum should be focused on discipline-based principles, concepts, and inquiry processes. Tammy Rabine, another fourth-grade teacher, Dr. Edwards notes, is right out of the Romantic Radicalism period. She is an exciting and imaginative teacher, but does not follow the district curriculum scope and sequence and is not interested in clear and articulated objectives. Her philosophy is that learning is about student discovery and student self-esteem. In contrast, Tammy's colleague, Jack Duringer, is very much into critical thinking and the development of an academically challenged curriculum. He is also a stickler for assessment and accountability, as well as technology, which places him in the Privatistic Conservatism and Technological Constructionism eras.

Juanita Sanchez, the last fourth-grade teacher that Dr. Edwards talked about, has taught for 2 years and is a wiz with technology. Because she is interested in cultural diversity, she believes in teaching values through the curriculum. She is a strong proponent of standards for teaching and assessment and could well fit the Technological Constructionism and the New Privastistic Conservatism eras.

THE CHALLENGE

Analyze the behavior of the fourth-grade teachers in this case. How can the new principal get the thinking of the fourth-grade faculty and others to work together to bring the curriculum into compliance with district, state, and federal standards?

Key Issues/Questions

1. Judging from your own experience, do you sense it was ethical for Dr. Edwards to discuss his former teachers with the new principal? Why or why not?

2. Curricular changes are often influenced by and are manifestations of larger social forces. What societal changes are influencing curricular changes today?

3. Is it possible to bring a school facing the problem of unsatisfactory levels of student achievement to meet the current standards set by the district, state government, and federal government with a diverse faculty? Why or why not?

4. One of the major problems of this school was the lack of incentive to change, a situation not unique to Washington Elementary School. Tradition and goal ambiguity tended to make this school sluggish. How can the new principal initiate change efforts and find ways of providing help instead of "managing" school-level programs?

5. How might the principal use the diversity of faculty as strength to improve the teaching and learning process?

NOTE

1. Reprinted with permission from *American School Board Journal*, September 2000. Copyright 2000 National School Boards Association. All rights reserved.

REFERENCES

Archived information. (n.d.). *Goals 2000: Educate America act* (H.R. 1804: One Hundred Third Congress). Retrieved April 11, 2005, from http://www.ed.gov/legislation/GOALS2000/TheAct/intro.html

Bast, J., Harmer, D., & Dewey, D. (1997, March). *Vouchers and educational freedom: A debate.* Retrieved February 7, 2004, from http://www.cato.org/pubs/pas/pa-269.html

Bernhardt, V. L. (1998). *Data analysis: For comprehensive schoolwide improvement.* Larchmont, NY: Eye on Education.

Bloom, B. S. (Ed.). (1956). *Taxonomy of educational objectives: The classification of educational goals: Handbook 1. Cognitive domains.* New York: McKay.

Bobbitt, F. (1913). *The supervision of city schools* (Twelfth Yearbook of the National Society for the Study of Education, Part I). Chicago: University of Chicago Press.

Boschee, F., & Hunt, M. M. (1990). Educational choice and vouchers—Where do you stand? *NASSP Bulletin, 74*(524), 75–86.

Boyer, E. L. (1983). *High school: A report on secondary education in America.* New York: Harper & Row.

Bracy, G. W. (2003). The 13th Bracey report on the condition of public education. *Phi Delta Kappan, 85,* 148–149.

Bruner, J. S. (1960). *The process of education.* Cambridge, MA: Harvard University Press.

Commission on the Reorganization of Secondary Education. (1918). *Cardinal principles of secondary education.* Washington, DC: Government Printing Office.

Conant, J. B. (1959). *The American high school today.* New York: McGraw-Hill.

Cook, G. (2004, January). Vouchers, choice & controversy. *American School Board Journal, 191*(1).

Cunningham, P. M., & Allington, R. L. (1994). *Classrooms that work: They can read and write.* New York: HarperCollins.

Curriculum Development Associates. (1972). *Man: A course of study.* Washington, DC: Author.

Danielson, C. (2002). *Enhancing student achievement: A framework for school improvement.* Alexandria, VA: Association for Supervision and Curriculum Development.

Dewey, J. (1900). *The school and society.* Chicago: University of Chicago Press.

Dewey, J. (1902). *The child and the curriculum.* Chicago: University of Chicago Press.

Dewey, J. (1916). *Democracy and education.* New York: Macmillan.

Dewey, J. (1938). *Experience and education.* New York: Macmillan.

Dewey, J. (1964). In *John Dewey on education: Selected writings* (R. Archambaust, Ed.). New York: Random House.

Education Commission of the States. (1982). *The information society: Are high school graduates ready?* Denver, CO: Author.

Eisner, E. W., & Vallance, E. (1974). *Conflicting conceptions of curriculum.* Berkeley, CA: McCutchan.

Ferrandino, V. (2003, July 25). *A practical guide to talking with your community: Talking points on No Child Left Behind* [Newsletter to NAESP members]. Alexandria, VA: National Association of Elementary School Principals.

Flexner, A. (1916). The modern school. *American Review of Reviews, 8,* 465–474.

Fullan, M. (2001). *Leading in a culture of change.* San Francisco: Jossey-Bass.

Gelman, R., & Baillargeon, R. (1983). A review of some Piagetian concepts. In P. H. Mussen (Ed.), *Handbook of child psychology* (Vol. 3, pp. 167–230). New York: John Wiley.

Giles, H. H., McCutchen, S. P., & Zechiel, A. N. (1942). *Exploring the curriculum.* New York: Harper.

Glass, G. V. (Ed.). (2003). *Education policy analysis archives.* Retrieved February 7, 2004, from http://epaa.asu.edu/epaa/board/darling-hammond.html

Glatthorn, A. A. (1975). *Alternatives in education: Schools and programs.* New York: Dodd, Mead.

Goens, G. A., & Clover, A. (1991). *Mastering school reform.* Boston: Allyn & Bacon.

Hall, G. S. (1904). The natural activities of children as determining the industries in early education. *National Education Association Journal of Proceedings and Addresses,* 443–444.

Hall, G. S. (1969). *Adolescence.* New York: Arno Press and The New York Times. (Original work published 1904)

Hardy, L. (2004, March). A nation divided. *Education Vital Signs 2004* (An ASBJ Special Report), 2–6.

Havighurst, R. J. (1972). *Developmental tasks and education* (3rd ed.). New York: David McKay.

Holt, J. (1964). *How children fail.* New York: Pitman.

InfoMedia, Inc. (1993). *Educational reform: A national perspective.* Ellenton, FL: Author.

Jones, R. (2000, September). Making standards work: Researchers report effective strategies for implementing standards. *American School Board Journal, 187*(9), 27–31.

Kliebard, H. M. (1985). What happened to American schooling in the first part of the twentieth century? In E. Eisner (Ed.), *Learning and teaching the ways of knowing* (pp. 1–22). Chicago: University of Chicago Press.

Knudsen, L. R., & Morrissette, P. J. (1998, May 12). Goals 2000: An analysis and critique. *International Electronic Journal for Leadership in Learning, 2*(4). Retrieved February 7, 2004, from http://www.ucalgary.ca/~iejll/volume2/knudsen2_html

Lickona, T. (1993, November). The return of character education. *Educational Leadership, 51*(3), 6–11.

Lockwood, A. T. (2004). *The charter schools decade.* Lanham, MD: Scarecrow Education.

Marzano, R. J., Pickering, D. J., & Pollock, J. (2001). *Classroom instruction that works: Research-based strategies for increasing student achievement.* Aurora, CO: McREL.

Murphy, J., & Shiffman, C. D. (2002). *Understanding and assessing the charter school movement.* New York: Teachers College Press.

National Commission on Excellence in Education. (1983). *A nation at risk: The imperative for educational reform.* Washington, DC: Government Printing Office.

National Education Association. (1893). *Report of the Committee on Secondary School Studies.* Washington, DC: Government Printing Office.

National Education Association. (1895). *Report of the Committee of Fifteen.* New York: Arno Press and The New York Times. (Original work published 1895)

Oliver, A. I. (1977). *Curriculum improvement: A guide to problems, principles, and process* (2nd ed.). New York: Harper & Row.

Parker, F. W. (1894). *Talks on pedagogics.* New York: E. L. Kellogg.

Physical Science Study Committee. (1961). *PSSC physics: Teacher's resource book and guide.* Boston: D. C. Heath.

Piaget, J. (1950). *The psychology of intelligence.* New York: Harcourt.

Potter, W. (2003, May 2). Report seeks to align state standards for high schools and colleges. *Chronicle of Higher Education, 49*(34), p. A31.

Provenzo, E. F. (2003). *Contemporary educational thought.* University of Miami School of Education. Retrieved December 21, 2004, from http://www.education.miami.edu/ep/contemporaryed/home.html and http://www.education.miami.edu/ep/contemporaryed/Eliott_Eisner/eliott_eisner.html

Purkey, S. C., & Smith, M. S. (1983). Effective schools: A review. *Elementary School Journal, 83,* 426–452.

Ravitch, D. (1983). *The troubled crusade: American education 1945–1980.* New York: Basic Books.

Rogers, C. (1969). *Freedom to learn: A view of what education might become.* Columbus, OH: Merrill.

Rugg, H. O. (Ed.). (1927). *The foundation of curriculum-making* (Twenty-Sixth Yearbook of the National Society for the Study of Education, Part II). Bloomington, IL: Public School Publishing.

Sarason, S. B. (1990). *The predictable failure of educational reform.* San Francisco: Jossey-Bass.

School house hype: Two years later. (2000). *Center on Juvenile and Criminal Justice.* Retrieved March 3, 2005, from http://www.cjcj.org/pubs/schoolhouse/shh2.html

Schwab, J. T. (1969). The practical: A language for curriculum. *School Review, 78,* 1–23.

Schwab, J. T. (1971). The practical: Arts of eclectic. *School Review, 79,* 493–542.

Schwab, J. T. (1973). The practical 3: Translation into curriculum. *School Review, 81,* 501–522.

Schwab, J. T. (1978). Education and the structure of the disciplines. In I. Westbury & N. J. Wilkof (Eds.), *Science, curriculum, and liberal education: Selected essays of Joseph T. Schwab* (pp. 229–270). Chicago: University of Chicago Press.

Schwab, J. T. (1983). The practical 4: Something for curriculum professors to do. *Curriculum Inquiry, 13,* 239–265.

Silberman, C. (1970). *Crisis in the classroom.* New York: Random House.

South Dakota Department of Education. (2004). *SD board of education adopts revised reading and communication standards: Schools to use for 04–05 school year.* Retrieved February 13, 2004, from http://www.state.sd.us/deca/release/readingandcomnstandards0405.htm

Sugameli, J. (2003). Home schooling wins converts: Parents like being able to tailor lessons to kids' strengths. *Home School Legal Defense Association.* Retrieved February 8, 2004, from http://www.hslda.org/docs/link.asp?URL=http%3A%2F%2Fwww%2Edetnews%2Ecom%2F2004%2Fschools%2F0402%2F02%2Fc05%2D52339%2Ehtm

Taylor, F. W. (1911). *The principles of scientific management.* New York: Harper and Bros.

Tomlinson, C. A., et al. (2001). *The parallel curriculum: A design to develop high potential and challenge high-ability learners.* Thousand Oaks, CA: Corwin.

Tyler, R. W. (1950). *Basic principles of curriculum and instruction.* Chicago: University of Chicago Press.

Tyler, R. W. (1971). Curriculum development in the twenties and thirties. In R. M. McClure (Ed.), *The curriculum: Retrospect and prospects* (pp. 26–44). Chicago: University of Chicago Press.

Utah House rebukes Bush with vote on school law. (2004). *New York Times.* Retrieved February 11, 2004, from http://www.nytimes.com/2004/02/11/national/11UTAH.html?th=&pagewanted=print&pos

Van Til, W., Vars, G. F., & Lounsbury, J. H. (1961). *Junior high years.* Indianapolis, IN: Bobbs-Merrill.

White House Office of the Press Secretary. (2000). *The president's new market trip: From digital divide to digital opportunity.* Retrieved February 9, 2004, from http://clinton4.nara.gov/textonly/WH/New/New_Markets-0004/20000417-7.html

Whitehead, B. M., Jensen, D. F. N., & Boschee, F. (2003). *Planning for technology: A guide for school administrators, technology coordinators, and curriculum leaders.* Thousand Oaks, CA: Corwin.

Wolfe, P. (2001). *Brain matters: Translating research into classroom practice.* Alexandria: VA: Association for Supervision and Curriculum Development.

Chapter 3

CURRICULUM THEORY

While curriculum theory is usually esteemed by scholars in the field as an important component of curriculum studies, it seems to be held in low regard by most practitioners, who often dismiss it as completely unrelated to their day-to-day work. Although that impatience with the theoretical is quite understandable, the view advanced in this chapter is that sound theory can be of value to both the scholar and the practitioner. At its best, curriculum theory can provide a set of conceptual tools for analyzing curriculum proposals, for illuminating practice, and for guiding reform.

Melding theory and the reality of school curriculum together is an important step in the educational planning process. Not all curriculum theories translate smoothly into real-world practice. Educators have found it difficult to use theoretical approaches to make continual analyses, reevaluations, and revisions of curriculum in light of such fields as informational technology and the sociology of knowledge. It is a daunting task to undertake the complexity of curriculum design given race, class, economic conditions, and cultural diversity—not to mention the continual changes evolving with technological advances in education. It is therefore essential to develop a fundamental understanding of curriculum theory by providing the tools necessary when analyzing curriculum proposals, illuminating practice, and guiding reform. Questions addressed in this chapter include the following:

- What is the nature and function of curriculum theory?
- Why is it important to meld the theory and reality of school curriculum together as part of the planning process?
- What is the role of leadership in the development of curriculum theory?
- What are the major classifications of curriculum theory?
- How has technology been a catalyst for curriculum change?

Key to Leadership

Successful leaders realize that curriculum seems to be changing even more to meet today's needs and realities. There seems to be little doubt that technology is serving as the catalyst for that change.

THE NATURE AND FUNCTION OF CURRICULUM THEORY

The concept of schooling and education has long been associated with the idea of curriculum and curriculum theory. With no definitive comprehensive theory that covers the field, a great deal of argument and discussion occurs in the field as to what curriculum theory is and what it is not.

To understand the concept of theory, it is essential to understand the nature of theory in general. Much disagreement exists among philosophers of science. On the one hand, some espouse what has come to be known as the Received View of scientific theory. According to this view, science consists of bold theories that outpace the facts. Scientists continually attempt to falsify these theories, but can never prove them true. Many subtleties of the received view of scientific theory are still found in contemporary literature in psychology (Acton, 2003).

Historically, the Received View holds that a theory is a formalized, deductively connected bundle of laws that are applicable in specifiable ways to their observable manifestations. In the Received View, a small number of concepts are selected as bases for the theory; axioms are introduced that specify the fundamental relationships among those concepts; and definitions are provided, specifying the remaining concepts of the theory in terms of the basic ones.

As Atkins (1982) notes, several criticisms of the Received View exist, even in its revised formulation. First, Suppe (1974) criticized it for its narrowness in requiring axiomatization, noting that several scientific theories are not and cannot be axiomated profitably. He argued instead for a broader view of theory that emphasizes the dynamic nature of all sound theory. Other critics, such as Hanson (1958) attacked the Received View for its posture of value-neutrality; as Hanson and others have pointed out, every aspect of theory development is value laden. Scientists do not observe objectively; their observations are profoundly influenced by their worldviews and their values. Popper (1962) rejected the assumption of the Received View that scientific theories can be observationally verified; in his view, theories are conjectures that, although not verifiable, can be submitted to severe tests of falsifiability.

Those who reject the positivist assumptions of the Received View tend to be classified as either realists or instrumentalists, as Atkins notes. Realists see science as a rational and empirical endeavor, concerned primarily with explanatory and predictive outcomes: Thus, in the view of realists, theory is a description of those structures that generate observable phenomena. In addition, the primary feature of scientific theory is the explanation of how underlying structures and mechanisms work to generate the phenomena being studied (Keat & Urry, 1975). Instrumentalists, on the other hand, concentrate on the function the theory performs: In this view, a theory is a tool of inquiry, rather than a picture or map of the world. In this sense, then, a theory is not judged in terms of its truth or falsity; instead, it is assessed on the basis of the quality of predictions it demonstrates (Kaplan, 1964).

Thus, current philosophers of science tend to take a more open view of the nature of theory, and it is this more open view that seems especially useful in a field such as education, where theory development seems still to be in a somewhat primitive stage. For the purposes of this chapter, therefore, this broader definition of curriculum theory is stipulated:

A curriculum theory is a set of related educational concepts that affords a systematic and illuminating perspective of curricular phenomena.

What are the functions of curriculum theory? Most philosophers of science argue that theory has only three legitimate purposes: to describe, to explain, and to predict. A review of curricular theory, however, suggests that many of those theories serve two additional functions. Some theorists, like Michael Apple, seem most concerned with providing educators with a critical perspective on the society and its schools. While Apple and others who share his viewpoint are concerned with describing and explaining curricular phenomena, their stance is an openly critical one. Some theorists, such as Ralph Tyler, seem most concerned with guiding practice. While Tyler and others whom he has influenced attempt to describe and explain, the primary intent of their work is to help educators make more reasoned choices.

Educational experiences are selected based on their likelihood of attaining the educational goals. After educational experiences are selected, they are organized in a logical manner, with the intent of obtaining the maximum cumulative effect. The curriculum is then improved and refined by a process of evaluation. According to Tyler, curriculum development should be viewed as a cycle: The quality and impact of curricula functions are to be monitored by carefully observing the outcomes, and data from these observations are to be used to fine-tune the curricula (Burks, 1998).

The extent to which a particular theory is able to discharge its functions effectively seems to be influenced by the complexity and maturity of that theory. Here Faix's (1964) classification of the stages of theory development seems useful.

Basic theory, Stage 1, is an early speculative stage, in which a theory has not yet been correlated with empirical data. Basic theory sets up untested hypotheses, involves few variables, and employs concepts that are not systematically refined and classified. Basic theory provides only descriptive explanations and directions for more meaningful theory. Glatthorn's (1980) analysis of the curriculum into mastery, organic, and enrichment elements might be described as a basic theory.

Middle-range theory, Stage 2, includes hypotheses that have been empirically tested. An effort has been made to eliminate unlikely variables and relations by the use of models and testing. Experimental laws and generalizations result, and theory can be used to illuminate, predict, and control events. Goodlad's (1979) delineation of what he calls a "conceptual system" for guiding inquiry and practice is a good example of a middle-range theory.

General theory, Stage 3, is a general theoretical system or an inclusive conceptual scheme for explaining an entire universe of inquiry. General theory attempts to integrate the substantive knowledge produced from middle-range theories. Beauchamp's articulation of a comprehensive theory of curriculum might be seen as an attempt to present a general theory, although some would criticize the shallowness of its empirical foundation (Beauchamp, 1981).

LEADERSHIP IN CURRICULUM THEORY

The need for leadership and theoretical planning in school curriculum is a common thread running through education on a global level. Today's school administrators currently face one of the most challenging and exciting times in educational history. New curriculum leaders will need to be familiar with a broad spectrum of curriculum theory ranging from behavioral to critical. Leaders will need to fully understand the "mirrored" relationship between theory and practice and how each can be used to mold and define the other.

The role of leadership in reviewing the relationship between theory and practice will be a crucial element in the future success or failure of curriculum change and how it impacts schools. It is therefore paramount for communities to encourage and recognize successful leaders who demonstrate an ability to make a difference in teaching and learning. No set rules or formulas exist for leaders to follow, only general guidelines, ideas, and generalities. In this age of technological reform, it is crucial that effective leaders formulate an understanding of curriculum theory if they are truly to evoke educational change in the future. Exercising leadership in these areas helps deepen a comprehension of "what works" and "the why" of curricula development.

Leaders also need to be aware of the cyclical nature of curriculum theory. This is especially true when reviewing needs analysis, methodologies, evaluation, processes, and assessment procedures. Areas of review for curriculum leaders of the future should include the following:

- Historical development of curriculum studies
- Current theory and practice in the field
- Macro and micro dimensions in curriculum
- Ethos and cultural considerations
- Process of curriculum change
- Impact of technology on curriculum
- Models and processes of instructional design
- Models and processes of developing learning strategies
- Identification and implementation of appropriate teaching methods
- Models and techniques of assessment and the evaluation process
- Staff development needs
- Practical application of curriculum design and product for student work programs

Quality leadership means having a thorough understanding of curriculum and being able to change administrative roles and responsibilities when needed to meet the new challenges of curriculum design. It is an art to know how and when to be flexible and yet at the same time to be able to make important curriculum decisions. It is an art to be able to change administratively by shifting from a focus on the system to a focus on the learner. Such shifts in leadership style allow teachers to have more input on curriculum changes that will allow for the greatest impact on learning. Having educational leaders who understand the curriculum review process, are supportive of change, and are willing to formulate new instructional strategies is a definite key to the success of schools in the future.

CLASSIFYING CURRICULUM THEORIES

Numerous attempts have been made to classify curriculum theories in terms of maturity and complexity as well as attempts at categorization. McNeil (1985) sets up what seems to be an unilluminating dichotomy: soft curricularists and hard curricularists. Soft curricularists, in his view, are those such as William Pinar and other reconceptualists who draw from the "soft" fields of religion, philosophy, and literary criticism; hard curricularists, such as Decker Walker and Mauritz Johnson, follow a rational approach and rely on empirical data. The difficulty with such a dichotomy seems obvious. It results in a grouping together of such disparate theorists as Elliot Eisner and Henry Giroux as "soft curricularists" simply because they draw from similar research perspectives.

A tripartite classification proposed by Pinar seems equally unsatisfactory: In his formulation, all curriculum theorists can be classified as traditionalists, conceptual empiricists, or reconceptualists. Traditionalists, in his formulation, are those such as Ralph Tyler who are concerned with the most efficient means of transmitting a fixed body of knowledge in order to impart the cultural heritage and keep the existing society functioning (Pinar, 1978).

Traditionalists like Tyler view curriculum as notions of class, teacher, course, units, lessons, and so forth. For example, Hirsch (1995), in one of his many books, *What Your Fifth Grader Needs to Know: Fundamentals of Good Fifth-Grade Education,* reveals his commitment to the concept of basic knowledge and cultural literacy in school curricula. He founded the core knowledge series to promote excellence and fairness in early education. Proponents of formal education are generally very interested in the concept of schooling that emphasizes basic knowledge and a definitive structure of instruction that involves the classics. Common themes of formal education proponents might include the development of a syllabus, transmittal of data and knowledge via lecture, formulation of goals and objectives, assessment, and a focus on an end product.

Theorists who espouse an informal education reveal an entirely different perspective on how curriculum should be designed and implemented. Informal proponents such as conceptual empiricists and reconceptualists view education more as an existential experience. Conceptual empiricists, such as Robert Gagne, are those who derive their research methodologies from the physical sciences in attempting to produce generalizations that will enable educators to control and predict what happens in schools. The reconceptualists (a label Gagne applies to his own work) emphasize subjectivity, existential experience, and the art of interpretation in order to reveal the class conflict and the unequal power relationships existing in the larger society. The basic difficulty with this tripartite formulation is that it mixes in a confusing fashion the theorists' research methodologies and their political stances as bases for categorizing theorists. Other theorists such as Elliot Eisner (1985) are equally informal in their approach and seem to be more interested in predicting what will happen in schools. Eisner, as a proponent of informal education, has been a leader in curriculum revision and new approaches for many years.

For example, one of the most widely cited classifications of curriculum theories is proposed by Eisner and Vallance (1974) in their *Conflicting Conceptions of Curriculum.* As they survey the field, they find five different conceptions of or orientations to the curriculum. A "cognitive-process" approach is concerned primarily with the development of intellectual operations and is less concerned with specific content. The "curriculum-as-technology" orientation conceptualizes the function of curriculum as finding the most efficient means of accomplishing predetermined ends. "Self-actualization" sees curriculum as a consummative experience designed to produce personal growth. "Social reconstruction-relevance" emphasizes societal needs over individual needs. Theorists with this orientation tend to believe that the primary role of the school is to relate to the larger society, with either an adaptive or a reformist stance. Finally, "academic rationalism" emphasizes the importance of the standard disciplines in helping the young participate in the Western cultural tradition.

While the Eisner and Vallance system seems to make more useful distinctions than either a dichotomy or tripartite system, it does seem to err in including "technology" as a basic orientation of the curriculum. All of the other four seem to designate the major sources for determining curriculum content—the cognitive processes, the person, the society, and the subject. A technological orientation is, on the other hand, concerned primarily with advocating one process for developing a curriculum—a process that could be used with any of the other four types.

The basic error of all three formulations (McNeil; Pinar; Eisner & Vallance) is that they do not sort out curricular theories in terms of their primary orientation or emphasis. Here, Huenecke's (1982) analysis of the domains of curricular inquiry seems most productive. She postulates three different types of curricular theorizing: structural, generic, and substantive. Structural theories, which she claims have dominated the first 50 years of the field, focus on identifying elements in curriculum and their interrelationships, as well as the structure of decision making. Generic theories center their interests on the outcomes of curriculum, concentrating on the assumptions, beliefs, and perceived truths underlying curriculum decisions. Sometimes referred to as critical theories, they tend to be highly critical of past and present conceptions of curriculum. They seek to liberate the individual from the constraints of society, using political and sociological frameworks to examine issues of power, control, and influences. The substantive theories speculate about what subject matter or content is most desirable, what knowledge is of the most worth.

While Huenecke's typology seems very useful, it seems to err in omitting one major domain—those theories such as Schwab's that are concerned primarily with the processes of curricular decision making (Schwab, 1970). While Huenecke would probably argue that Schwab's work is primarily structural in its emphasis, the distinction between structure and process seems to be one worth maintaining.

It therefore seems most useful to divide curriculum theories into the following four categories, based upon their domains of inquiry.

Structure-oriented theories are concerned primarily with analyzing the components of the curriculum and their interrelationships. Structure-oriented theories tend to be descriptive and explanatory in intent.

Value-oriented theories are concerned primarily with analyzing the values and assumptions of curriculum makers and their products. Value-oriented theories tend to be critical in nature.

Content-oriented theories are concerned primarily with determining the content of the curriculum. Content-oriented theories tend to be prescriptive in nature.

Process-oriented theories are concerned primarily with describing how curricula are developed or recommending how they should be developed. Some process-oriented theories are descriptive in nature; others are more prescriptive.

The rest of this chapter will use this categorization system for examining several major curriculum theorists.

STRUCTURE-ORIENTED THEORIES

As indicated above, structure-oriented theorists of curriculum are concerned with the components of the curriculum and their interrelationships. Primarily analytical in their approach, they seek to describe and explain how curricular components interact within an educational environment. Structure-oriented theories examine questions such as the following:

1. What are the essential concepts of the curriculum field and how may they most usefully be defined? For example, what does the term *curriculum* mean?

2. What are the levels of curriculum decision making and what forces seem to operate at each of those levels? For example, how do classroom teachers make decisions about the curriculum?

3. How may the curriculum field be most validly analyzed into its component parts? For example, how does a program of study differ from a field of study?

4. What principles seem to govern issues of content selection, organization, and sequencing? For example, how can curricular elements be articulated?

In seeking answers to such questions, structure-oriented theorists tend to rely upon empirical research, using both quantitative and qualitative methodologies to inquire into curricular phenomena.

Structure-oriented theorists seem to operate at what might be termed either a macrolevel or a microlevel. Macrolevel theorists attempt to develop global theories that describe and explain the larger elements of curricular structure.

Here it is necessary to turn to the work of microlevel theorists who seem more concerned with describing and explaining curricular phenomena as they occur at the institutional instructional levels. George Posner seems most representative of the microlevel theorists. Over the course of several years, he has identified and analyzed several microelements of curricular structure. Typical of his theoretical work is an article coauthored with Kenneth Strike in which they present and explicate a "categorization scheme for principles of sequencing content" (Posner & Strike, 1976). By bringing to bear some useful epistemological distinctions and by analyzing the curriculum literature, Posner and Strike are able to identify five major types of content sequence.

The first principle for sequencing content they call "world related"—the content structure reflects the empirical relationships among events, people, and things. Subtypes here include sequences based on spatial relations, temporal relations, and physical attributes. The second principle is "concept related," in which sequences reflect the organization of the conceptual world. Thus one subtype of concept-related sequences is "logical prerequisite"—when it is logically necessary to understand the first concept in order to understand the second. "Inquiry-related" sequences are those that sequence the curriculum in relation to a particular method of inquiry, such as Dewey's analysis of the problem-solving process. "Learning-related" sequences draw from knowledge of the psychology of learning in making decisions about sequence; thus sequencing decisions based upon such assumptions as "begin with content of intrinsic interest" or "start with the easiest skills" are learning related in nature. The final principle, "utilization related," sequences learning in relation to three possible contexts for utilization—social, personal, and career.

As Posner and Strike point out, these categories can be considered as a set of concepts that should be useful to the curriculum developer, the curriculum evaluator, and the curriculum researcher.

VALUE-ORIENTED THEORIES

Value-oriented theorists seem to be primarily engaged in what might be termed "educational consciousness-raising," attempting to sensitize educators to the values issues that lie at the hearts of both the hidden and the stated curricula. Their intent is primarily a critical one; thus they sometimes have been identified as "critical theorists." Because many have argued the need for reconceptualizing the field of curriculum, they often are labeled as reconceptualists.

In their inquiries, value-oriented theorists tend to examine issues such as the following:

1. In what ways do the schools replicate the power differentials in the larger society?

2. What is the nature of a truly liberated individual, and how does schooling inhibit such liberation?

3. How do schools consciously or unwittingly mold children and youth to fit into societal roles predetermined by race and class?

4. As curriculum leaders determine what constitutes legitimate knowledge, how do such decisions reflect their class biases and serve to inhibit the full development of children and youth?

5. In what ways does the schools' treatment of controversial issues tend to minimize and conceal the conflicts endemic to the society?

In examining these issues, most value-oriented theorists draw eclectically from several inquiry methodologies, such as psychoanalysis, philosophical inquiry, historical analysis, and political theory.

The Major Value-Oriented Theorists

Because many critical theorists seem to focus on the person, and many others on the sociopolitical milieu, it seems appropriate to select for examination one person-oriented theorist, James Macdonald, and one milieu-oriented theorist, Michael Apple.

James Macdonald

For a period of almost two decades, James Macdonald seemed to serve as a respected gadfly for the curriculum profession, challenging educators to question their assumptions, to aspire to more worthy goals, and to reconceptualize the enterprise of curriculum making. A prolific writer, his work is so multifaceted that it is difficult to summarize.

Basic to all his work is his view of the human condition. Central to that human condition is a search for transcendence, the struggle of the individual to actualize the whole self. Much influenced toward the end of his career by the writings of Carl Jung, Macdonald (1974) used almost mystical metaphors in "A Transcendental Developmental Ideology of Education" to speak of this journey toward transcendence as the primary concern of all humans.

Although Macdonald has been criticized for being too mystical and vague, the cumulative effect of his work has been to challenge curriculum leaders to rethink their basic assumptions and to reconceptualize their field.

Michael Apple

Michael Apple is a critical theorist who seems to be concerned primarily with the relationship between the society and the school. Central to Apple's critique of the society and its schools is his use of the concept of *hegemony*.

One crucial way in which this cultural hegemony influences educators is in their perception of science. In this telling critique of what might be termed "educational pseudoscientism," Apple (1975) notes that almost all educators rely upon a narrow and strict view of science, one that values only rationality and empirical data in the service of predictability and control and that ignores the close relationship between science and art, science and myth.

CONTENT-ORIENTED THEORIES

Content-oriented theorists are concerned primarily with specifying the major sources that should influence the selection and organization of the curriculum content. For the most part, their theories can be classified in terms of their views as to which source should predominate: child-centered theories, knowledge-centered theories, or society-centered theories.

Child-Centered Curricula

Those who espouse child-centered curricula argue that the child is the beginning point, the determiner, and the shaper of the curriculum. Although the developing child will at some point acquire knowledge of subject matter, the disciplines are seen as only one type of learning. While the child develops in and is influenced by a social environment, the needs of the society are not considered paramount; that society will best be served by the kind of mature and autonomous individual that child-centered curricula attempt to develop. As Francis Parker (1894) expressed it many decades ago, "The centre of all movement in education is the child."

During the past three decades, three major child-centered curriculum movements have occurred: affective education, open education, and developmental education.

Affective Education

The affective education movement emphasized the feelings and values of the child. While cognitive development was considered important, it was seen only as an adjunct to affective growth. Thus, curriculum leaders were concerned primarily with identifying teaching and learning activities that would help the child understand and express feelings and discern and clarify values. For example, Brown (1975), who advocated "confluent education" (a curriculum approach that attempted to synthesize physical, emotional, and intellectual growth), recommended a "fantasy body trip" as a learning activity. Students are asked to close their eyes and "move into themselves"; each person is asked to concentrate on different parts of the body, beginning with the toes, then all participants share their experiences.

Open Education

As previously noted, open education was a child-centered curriculum movement that emphasized the social and cognitive development of the child through informal exploration, activity, and discovery. Here the "whole child" was considered the beginning point and focus of curriculum work. As Lillian Weber (1971), one of the foremost exponents of open education, stated,

These questions about children seem uppermost in developing plans for the classroom, for plans were not made from the vantage point of a syllabus of demand which a child had to meet, but with relevance to children in the most immediate way. A plan fitted itself to the child. (p. 169)

In fitting the plans to the child, the teacher provisioned a rich learning environment, one that emphasized the use of concrete and interactive materials organized in "learning centers."

The school day was not compartmentalized into subject periods, such as "language arts" and "mathematics." Instead, children experienced an "integrated day"; they were encouraged to solve problems that required the development of several skills and the acquisition of many kinds of knowledge.

Developmental Education

Developmental education, as the term is used here, refers to any curriculum theory that stresses the developmental stages of child growth as the primary determiners of placement and sequence.

Some current curriculum leaders use a Piagetian framework in selecting, placing, and structuring appropriate learning experiences. For example, Brooks (1986) describes how the teachers in the Shoreham-Wading River (New York) schools first receive extensive training in the theory and research on cognitive development. They then learn how to assess their students' cognitive development by using a variety of formal and informal measures. Finally, they are taught specific strategies for modifying and adapting predetermined curricula to match students' cognitive levels.

In the developmental perspective, curricula tend to be seen as instruments for facilitating child development. Certain general outcomes are postulated. The child's present developmental level is assessed. Then learning activities and content are selected that will challenge the student enough to produce growth, but without overwhelming the student with impossible demands. In all developmental curricula, the teacher is seen primarily as an adapter of curricula, one who learns to modify predetermined content to fit the developmental needs and capabilities of the learner.

While it seems useful to consider the child's development in selecting and placing content, no conclusive evidence exists that developmental curricula are more effective than those not embodying such a perspective.

Knowledge-Centered Curricula

Those leaders who advocate a knowledge-centered approach argue essentially that the disciplines or bodies of knowledge should be the primary determiners of what is taught. While they acknowledge that child-development research should affect decisions about placement, they pay greater attention to the structure of the disciplines or the nature of knowledge, even in matters of sequence. While they admit that the child lives and grows in a social world, they see the society as playing only a very minor role in developing curricula. In general, curricula based upon a knowledge-centered approach might be divided into two groups: "structures-of-the-disciplines" curricula and "ways-of-knowing" curricula.

Structures of the Disciplines

Two major attempts have been made to reform the curriculum so that it places greater emphasis upon the subjects. During the period from 1890 to 1910, the concern of curriculum leaders was to standardize the school curriculum and to bring it into closer alignment with college requirements. During the period from 1958 to 1970, the curriculum-reform movement emphasized the updating of curriculum content by emphasizing the structures of the disciplines.

Ways of Knowing

This approach to the curriculum is of rather recent vintage. As Eisner (1985) notes, it grows out of several emerging research lines: cognitive science, human creativity, brain functioning, and conceptions of intelligence and knowledge. While Vallance (1985) sees this interest in ways of knowing as producing a radically different "curriculum map" that is quite distinct from the traditional disciplines, its emphasis upon knowledge and knowing seems to warrant placing it in the broader category of knowledge-centered approaches.

Briefly, those espousing such a view argue that there are multiple ways of knowing, not just one or two. Further, these multiple ways of knowing should be given greater attention in the school's curriculum.

Society-Centered Curricula

Several curriculum theorists agree that the social order should be the starting point and the primary determiner of the curriculum. They differ sharply among themselves, however, about the stance the schools should take toward the existing social order; accordingly, they can best be understood by categorizing them on the basis of this factor: the conformists, the reformers, the futurists, and the radicals.

The Conformists

The conformists believe that the existing order is a good one—the best of all possible worlds. While problems obviously exist in that social order, in the eyes of the conformists those problems are of lesser consequence and can be handled by mature adults. Accordingly, the essential task of the curriculum is to indoctrinate the young: help them understand the history of this society, teach them to value it, and educate them to function successfully in it. Curriculum workers with a conformist intent begin curriculum development by identifying the needs of the existing society and its institutions; curriculum objectives are derived from those needs. The teacher is usually expected to serve as an advocate for the free-enterprise system, helping students understand why it is so much better than competing systems.

Curricula with a conformist thrust have been advocated in almost every period of curriculum history. Bobbitt (1918), in his basic work *The Curriculum,* argued for a social point of view, defining the curriculum as "that series of things which children and youth must do and experience by way of developing abilities to do the things well that make up the affairs of adult life; and to be in all respects what adults should be." In the eyes of many critics, the career education movement of the 1970s had a conformist thrust: Bowers (1977) saw its purpose as "designed to socialize students to accept the present organization of work and technology as the taken-for-granted reality." William Bennett, Secretary of Education during Reagan's second term, advocated a brand of citizenship education that had clearly a conformist intent.

The Reformers

Those classified as reformers see the society as essentially sound in its democratic structure, but want to effect major reforms in the social order. The major vehicle is the curriculum: Courses should be developed that will sensitize students to emerging social issues and give students the intellectual tools they need to solve social problems. Thus, curriculum workers should begin the task of curriculum development by identifying social problems. Those social problems—such as racism, sexism, and environmental pollution—then become the center of classroom activity. The teacher is expected to play an active role in identifying the problems, in "raising the consciousness" of the young, and in helping students take actions to bring about the needed reforms.

The reformers seem most vocal during times of social unrest. During the 1930s, Counts (1932) challenged the schools to take a more active role in achieving his vision of a more liberal society: The title of his book—*Dare the School Build a New Social Order?*—conveys the tone of his work. During the late 1960s and early 1970s, liberal educators advocated curricula that would be responsive to what they perceived as a "cultural revolution." For example, Purpel and Belanger (1972) called for a curriculum that would institutionalize compassion and increase students' sense of social responsibility.

The Futurists

Rather than being attuned to the present problems of the society, futurists look to the coming age. They analyze present developments, extrapolate from available data, and posit alternative scenarios. They highlight the choices people have in shaping this coming age and encourage the schools to give students the tools to create a better future for them. In a sense, they might be described as reformers intent on solving the problems of the year 2020. In their view, the school curricula should have such a futurist orientation, focusing on the developments likely to occur and involving students in thinking about the choices they have and the consequences of the choices they make. Rapidly advancing and clear-cut new technologies will force schools to change rapidly. Gradual improvements of the educational process will not suffice. The education system of today will be completely transformed by 2020. Many factors will promote this change. The most important are the following:

- New management models from business will be applied to the educational system.
- Parents and students will promote change in the system.
- Private companies will play a larger role in the education process.
- Technology will influence the education landscape.

(imagitrends, n.d.)

Our schools thrive on information. In the ever-changing world filled with new technology, our teachers and students require the right information, from the right sources, today.

Having direct access to industry information gives the competitive edge needed to succeed. Student performance can be improved when the enhancement of teaching and learning using technology is adopted as the norm ("Why Technology," 2003).

The Radicals

Those who regard the society as critically flawed espouse curricula that would expose those flaws and empower the young to effect radical changes. Typically, reasoning from a neo-Marxist perspective, they believe the problems of the age are only symptoms of the pervasive structural inequities inherent in a technological capitalistic system. As a consequence, they want to reach the masses by revolutionizing education by "deschooling" the educational process.

One of the leading exponents of such an approach is Paulo Freire (1970), the Brazilian educator whose *Pedagogy of the Oppressed* made a significant impact on radical educators in this country. In Freire's view, the goal of education is *conscientization,* a process of enlightening the masses about the inequities inherent in their sociocultural reality and giving them the tools to make radical changes in that social order that restricts their freedom. He makes the process explicit in explaining how he teaches reading. Adults learn to read by identifying words with power—words such as *love* and *person* that have pragmatic value in communicating with others in the community. They create their own texts that express their perceptions of the world they live in and the world they want. They learn to read in order to become aware of the dehumanizing aspects of their lives, but they are helped to understand that learning to read will not guarantee them the jobs they need.

PROCESS-ORIENTED THEORIES

Over the past two decades, when curriculum theory seems to have reached its maturity as a systematic field of inquiry, several attempts have been made to develop conceptual systems for classifying curricular processes and products (see, e.g., Eisner & Vallance, 1974; Gay, 1980; Schiro, 1978). However, most of these categorization schemes are deficient on two grounds. First, they badly confuse what have been described above as value-oriented, content-oriented, and process-oriented theories. Second, they seem to give only scant attention to the curriculum-development process advocated by the theorist under consideration. Most suggest that there is some correspondence between the value or content orientation of the theory and the type of process espoused, although such connections do not seem apparent. Thus, one of Gay's "conceptual models of the curriculum-planning process" is what she terms the "*experimental model*" (Eisner & Vallance, 1974). Her description of the experiential model suggests that it gives predominant weight to the needs of the child as a determiner of content, is vaguely liberal in its value orientation, and emphasizes a planning process that she describes with such terms as *organic, evolving, situational,* and *inquiry-centered,* but she does not provide much detail about the specifics of the planning process.

Thus, if we are asking about alternative planning models, we will have to turn to sources other than these widely known classification schemes. One source that offers some promise is Short's (1983) article, "The Forms and Use of Alternative Curriculum Development Strategies."

His work seems to build upon previous efforts, it reflects a comprehensive knowledge of both the prescriptive and descriptive literature, and it seems to offer the greatest promise for analyzing and generating alternative systems.

Short's article has two explicit goals. One is to analyze what is known about the forms and use of alternative strategies of curriculum development, and the other is to organize this knowledge in a way that permits one to assess the policy implications of choosing and using one or the other of these strategies.

A System for Examining Curricular Processes

It would seem more pragmatic to both scholars and practitioners to have available for their use a systematic means for examining curricular processes. Such an analytic system should have the following characteristics: It would include all the process elements that the research would suggest are important, thus enabling curriculum researchers to make useful distinctions between sets of recommended and implemented processes; it would be open-ended in form, thus enabling practitioners to become aware of a comprehensive set of alternatives; and it would emphasize description and analysis, not evaluation, enabling both scholars and practitioners to reach their independent conclusions about desirability.

The set of descriptors presented in Exhibit 3.1 represents an initial attempt to formulate such an analytic system. Certain caveats should be noted here. First, the descriptors have been drawn from a preliminary analysis of the literature and the authors' personal experiences, but that analysis has not at this point been completely systematic and rigorous. Second, while there has been some initial success in using it to discriminate between development strategies that on the surface seem quite similar, it needs much more extensive testing and refinement. It is thus presented here as an initial formulation that invites criticism and improvement.

The first descriptor focuses on the participants in the process. As Short indicates, their competence and their perspective are so important that we need to have such information. The second descriptor is concerned with the general tenor of the discussions. A monologic discussion is one in which only one person participates or makes decisions, such as a college instructor developing a new course independently. In a participatory discussion, one individual clearly is in control, but makes a genuine effort to solicit the input of others. A dialogic discussion is one in which there is much open discussion in an attempt to achieve consensus on key issues.

The third descriptor identifies those elements that influence curriculum decision making, even though they may not be explicitly referred to in the final document. As Exhibit 3.2 indicates, several factors variously impact upon curriculum decisions. Thus, nursing educators who have been observed developing courses seemed most conscious of the requirements of accrediting bodies. On the other hand, teachers in a large urban district seemed chiefly concerned about "accountability procedures."

The fourth descriptor is concerned with the starting point for the substantive deliberations. As indicated in Exhibit 3.3, several curricular elements are in this formulation, any one of which might conceivably be a starting point. The obvious intent here is to challenge the conventional wisdom that curriculum development must begin with a clear statement of objectives. As indicated in Exhibit 3.4, the fifth descriptor is concerned with those elements emphasized and the sequence in which they are considered.

The sixth descriptor focuses on the organizing structures of the course—the structural elements that give the course shape. Four structural components are included: the general structure and movement of the course itself, the units, the lessons, and the lesson components.

Exhibit 3.1   An Analytic System for Examining the Curriculum Process

---

1. What groups or constituencies should be represented in the developmental sessions?

2. What type of participation structure is recommended for the sessions—monologic, participatory, dialogic?

3. What shaping factors should receive significant consideration throughout the process?

4. Which curriculum element should be used as the starting point in the substantive deliberations?

5. Which curriculum elements should receive significant consideration—and in what sequence should such consideration occur?

6. Which organizing structures should receive significant consideration—and in what order: course structure, units, lessons, lesson components?

7. Should the progression from element to element or from structure to structure be predominantly linear or recursive?

8. What curriculum images and metaphors seem to influence the process?

9. What general type of problem-solving approach should be used throughout the process—technological, rational, intuitive, negotiating?

10. What recommendations are made about the form and content of the curriculum product?

11. What recommendations are made for implementing the curriculum product?

12. What recommendations are made for assessing the curriculum product?

13. What criteria should participants use to assess the quality and effectiveness of the process?

14. To what extent should developers be sensitive to the political aspects of curriculum development?

The seventh descriptor examines the progression of the discussion. A linear progression would move sequentially from element to element or from structure to structure; a recursive discussion would move back and forth in some systematic fashion. The eighth descriptor asks the researcher to be sensitive to the curricular images and metaphors that seem to influence the process. Does the developer seem to conceptualize a curriculum as a mosaic or a patchwork quilt, as a journey or series of travel experiences, as a set of steps moving from the basement to the top floor? The obvious point, of course, is that such images and metaphors reveal the pervasive belief systems of the developers with respect to that field of study—and such belief systems subtly but profoundly influence their decision making.

The ninth descriptor examines the type of problem-solving process at work. Contrary to what some deliberative theorists assert, it seems in many respects that all curriculum making is a type of problem solving. Four types of problem-solving processes have been recommended by theorists: technological, rational, intuitive, and negotiating. A technological approach to curriculum problem solving argues for a tightly controlled process assessing needs, deriving goals from those needs, performing a task analysis to identify learning objectives, determining the sequential or hierarchical relationship among the objectives, specifying instructional activities, and identifying evaluation procedures.

Exhibit 3.2   Shaping Factors in Curricular Deliberations

1. The developers: their espoused and practiced values; their knowledge and competence
2. The students: their values, abilities, goals, learning styles
3. The teachers: their values, knowledge, teaching styles, concerns
4. The organization: its ethos and structure
5. The administrators of that organization: their values and expectations
6. External individuals and groups (parents, employers, pressure groups): their values and expectations
7. Accrediting bodies: their requirements and recommendations
8. Scholars in the field: their recommendations, their reports of research; their perceptions of the structure of that discipline
9. The community and the larger society: what is required to maintain or change the social order
10. Other courses in that field of study, courses taken previously and subsequently
11. Courses in other fields that students are likely to take concurrent with the course being developed: their contents, impacts, and requirements
12. The schedule for the course: number of meetings, length of meetings, frequency
13. Accountability procedures: examinations, "curricular audits"

Exhibit 3.3   Curricular Elements

1. Rationale, philosophy, or statement of espoused values
2. Institutional goals or aims
3. Knowledge outcomes for the course, the units, the lessons: concepts, factual knowledge
4. Skill or process outcomes for the course, the units, the lessons
5. Affective outcomes for the course, the units, the lessons: values, attitudes
6. Content choices: elements of subject matter selected for their intrinsic worth (literary or artistic works, periods of history, important individuals, significant events, etc.)
7. Organizing elements: themes, recurring concepts, structures of linkage:
   a. Those used to link this course with courses previously or subsequently studied
   b. Those used to link this course with other courses studied concurrently
   c. Those used to link units in this course with each other
   d. Those used to organize units and relate lessons in a unit to each other
8. Teaching/learning activities
9. Instructional materials and media
10. Time allocations
11. Methods for assessing student learning

Exhibit 3.4   Analysis of Doll's (1986) Curriculum-Development Process

1. Groups represented: teachers, pupils, administrators, supervisors, school board, lay community

2. Participation structure: participatory

3. Shaping factors: organizational ethos; pupil needs; teachers' values, knowledge, teaching style, concerns

4. Starting point: institutional goals

5. Elements considered: goals, course objectives, evaluation means, type of design, learning content, interunit linkages, interlesson linkages

6. Organizing structures: not specified

7. Progression: linear

8. Images and metaphor: not used

9. Problem-solving approach: rational

10. Form and content of product: no specific recommendations

11. Implementation recommendations: no specific recommendations

12. Recommendations for evaluating product: extensive formative and summative assessments

13. Criteria in assessing process: eleven specific criteria offered

14. Political sensitivity: limited

A rational approach to curriculum problem solving describes the somewhat looser but still logical approach advocated by Schwab and others: Deliberators collect and examine pertinent data, formulate the curriculum problem, generate alternative solutions, and evaluate those solutions in order to determine which is best.

In an intuitive approach, participants are encouraged to rely upon their intuition and tacit knowledge, like Schon's "reflective practitioners" who make wise choices but cannot explain how they make those choices (Schon, 1983). Moreover in some processes, the problem solving is more like a negotiating exchange in which bargaining and trading and making compromises seem to be the predominant activities.

The tenth descriptor examines the decisions about the form and content of the final product. Again, there might be much variation here. For example, Glatthorn recommends that the final product should be a loose-leaf notebook that contains only a summary of pertinent research and a list of the required and testable objectives (Glatthorn, 1980). Teachers using the notebook thus have much latitude in how they organize the objectives and which methods and materials they use.

The eleventh and twelfth descriptors are concerned with the future—what plans are made for implementing and for testing the product? The thirteenth descriptor examines the criteria that the participants seem chiefly to rely upon in assessing the quality of their work, and the last descriptor examines the extent to which the process is sensitive to the political aspects of curriculum work.

Exhibit 3.5   Analysis of Glatthorn's (1986) Curriculum-Development Process

1. Groups represented: teachers

2. Participation structure: dialogic

3. Shaping factors: students, teachers, administrators, scholars, other courses, schedule

4. Starting point: knowledge and skill outcomes for course; starting point for unit planning varies

5. Elements considered: knowledge and skill outcomes for units and lessons, unit themes, teaching/learning activities, instructional materials and media, time allocations, student assessment

6. Organizing structures: units, lessons

7. Progression: recursive

8. Images and metaphors: not used

9. Problem-solving approach: intuitive

10. Form and content of product: open-ended "scenarios"

11. Implementation recommendations: no specific recommendations

12. Recommendations for evaluating product: emphasis on quality of learning experiences

13. Criteria in assessing process: none provided

14. Political sensitivity: extensive

If such an analytic system is at all valid, then it suggests, of course, that the Tyler rationale is not the only system for developing curricula; in fact, the system has been used in initial trials to analyze the significant differences between several distinct models of curriculum development. Exhibit 3.4 shows how the descriptors were used to analyze Doll's (1986) process, and Exhibit 3.5 shows how they describe the "naturalistic" process reviewed in Chapter 8 of this work.

Alternative Curriculum Approaches

Glatthorn's four curriculum categories still hold up to scrutiny today and continue to help provide a road map for curriculum theory. Nonetheless, Mark Smith (1996, 2000), author of "Curriculum Theory and Practice" in the *Encyclopaedia of Informal Education,* developed his own categories for understanding curriculum development. Smith's approaches are listed as follows:

- *Transmission of Information:* Curriculum as a body of knowledge to be transmitted via a syllabus
- *End Product:* Curriculum as an attempt to achieve certain ends (products)
- *Process:* Curriculum as a process
- *Praxis:* Curriculum as praxis (action that is committed)

Exhibit 3.6   Elements of Curriculum Theory and Practice

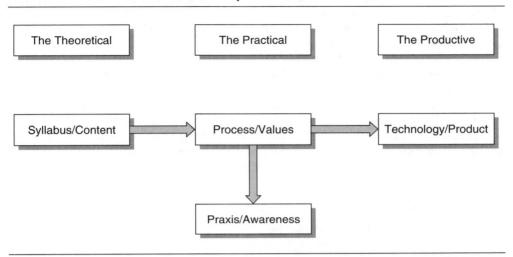

SOURCE: Adapted from Smith, M. K. (1996, 2000). Curriculum theory and practice, *The encyclopaedia of informal education,* www.infed.org/biblio/b-curric.htm. Last updated: 30 January 2005.

Smith's categories reflect and synthesize the essence of curriculum theory into four easily understood approaches. With this in mind, the authors have taken the liberty of combining Smith's ideas into a figure that also includes categories noted by Glatthorn. Exhibit 3.6 is modified to reveal some clear links between Glatthorn and Smith. Areas of consideration include the body of knowledge and content to be transmitted, the process and value models to be conveyed, the focus on an end product, and the practical and technical deliberation. Most interestingly, Smith's categories mirror elements of Aristotle's characterization of the productive.

When reviewing the model using ideas from Smith and Glatthorn, it is important to note change results from several different perspectives. The model blends together the substantive nature of curriculum theory as well as the development of awareness and understanding. Below, we expand upon and compare the similarities between Smith's categories of transmitter of knowledge, end product, process, and praxis as they relate to Glatthorn's typology of structure-oriented theories, value-oriented theories, content-oriented theories, and process-oriented theories.

Curriculum as Transmission of Information

Smith views curriculum as a body of knowledge to be transmitted and equates it with the use of a syllabus. Some theorists believe that an overemphasis on the use of a syllabus as the sole foundation of curriculum is a dependence on content as well as an overdependence on a particular way of organizing a body of knowledge, content, and/or subjects.

The syllabus and transmitter-of-knowledge approach seems to follow closely with Glatthorn's *structured-oriented theories.* Structure-oriented theorists generally wish to transmit the body of knowledge, but tend to rely upon empirical research, using both quantitative and qualitative methodologies to inquire into curricular phenomena.

For example, macro structural theorists are now more globally oriented and use technology to transmit information about curriculum. The use of e-mail and the Internet is becoming a larger part of developing curriculum at this level. Educators are using the World Wide Web to share curriculum designs and syllabi. Larger, global forces of polity, economics, common cultures, and classics are becoming points of interest and are more evident when transmitting and sharing basic information. The transmitter-of-knowledge approach is often determined and manipulated to agree with the local interests, values, needs, and wants of the controlling agency, such as a state government educational agency, community, or school.

Curriculum as End Product

A second fundamental aspect of Smith's curriculum theory is that of *achieving an end product.* Goals and objectives become the common focus of theorists using this approach. Educators using this approach are less concerned with how curriculum is taught than what the end product is, and what the goals and objectives are that are used to achieve that product or result—for example, a science report, multimedia math project, piece of literature, poetry, or a speech. This follows with the concept of expanding and explaining curriculum. Themes often center on preparing the student for life, developing abilities, attitudes, habits, and appreciations. The focus of curriculum is generally that of systemic study, needs assessment, training, implementation, and evaluation with an emphasis on students' producing tangible results that reflect their potential.

End product approaches seem to follow closely with Glatthorn's *content-oriented theories.* As mentioned previously, content-oriented theorists are often concerned with determining and specifying the major sources as well as the details that influence the selection and organization of curriculum content.

Proponents of product-based curriculum usually focus on the following:

- *Real Problems*—real and relevant to the student and the activity,
- *Real Audiences*—utilising an "audience" that is appropriate for the product, which could include another student or group of students, a teacher (not necessarily the class teacher), an assembly, a mentor, a community or specific interest group,
- *Real Deadlines*—encouraging time management skills and realistic planning,
- *Transformations*—involving original manipulation of information rather than regurgitation, and
- *Appropriate Evaluation*—with the product and the process of its development being both self-evaluated and evaluated by the product's audience using previously established "real world" criteria that are appropriate for such products.

(Farmer, 1996)

An example of a product-based approach is Understanding by Design. Understanding by Design proponents Grant Wiggins and Jay McTighe (2005) noted that this approach often looks at instruction from a "results" orientation. They believe that Understanding by Design is a recursive process, not a prescriptive program. It targets achievement through a "backward design" process that focuses on assessment first and relevant instructional activities last. The design also uses a spiral of learning where students use and reconsider ideas and skills versus a linear scope and sequence. Individuals using the Understanding by Design approach have a tendency to view curriculum in terms of desired "performances of understanding" and then "plan backwards" to identify needed concepts and skills.

Researchers who espouse product-based curriculum commonly place an emphasis on case studies. Case studies help curriculum designers focus on the realities of classroom life. Teachers have long been aware of the increasing gap between the principles of education taught in university pre-service programs and the classroom. The current burgeoning interest in educational case methods is testimony to the promise of case-based teaching as a way of bridging that gap and of easing the novice teacher's entry into the classroom. A case study holds attributes of both theory and practice, enabling teachers and students alike to examine real-life situations under a laboratory microscope. Case studies provide a piece of controllable reality, more vivid and contextual than a textbook discussion, yet more disciplined and manageable than observing or doing work in the world itself (Wiggins & McTighe, 2005).

Curriculum as Process

A third fundamental aspect of current curriculum theory noted by Smith focuses on *curriculum as process*. Viewing curriculum as process places the emphasis on the interaction among teacher, student, parent, and knowledge rather than on a syllabus and/or on an end product. The focus is on what is actually taking place in the classroom as well as the learning process itself. Critical thinking, listening, and communication are important components of process curriculum. Often an emphasis is placed on thinking about planning, justifications of procedures, and actual interventions, as well as providing feedback and changes during the curriculum process.

One of the earlier curriculum planning approaches involved the *instructional design process*. The instructional design process, often referred to as ISD, emerged from psychology laboratories and helped establish the first systematic approach to the development of instructional materials and teaching strategies. Instructional design is the systematic development of instructional specifications using learning and instructional theory to ensure the quality of instruction. It is the entire process of analysis of learning needs and goals and the development of a delivery system to meet those needs. It includes development of instructional materials and activities, and tryout and evaluation of all instruction and learner activities (Shulman, 2003). Robert Gagne's (1985) *The Conditions of Learning and Theory of Instruction* and *Principles of Instructional Design* (Gagne, Briggs, & Wager, 1992) describe this approach. Gagne (as cited in Willwerth, 2003) once said,

> To know, to understand, to gain insight into, and so on are not useful as descriptions of relatively observable behavior; nor are their intended meanings easily agreed upon by individuals. . . . The action verbs which are used in the construction of the behavioral objectives for Science: A Process Approach are: identify, construct, name, order, describe, demonstrate, state a rule, apply a rule. (n.p.)

The instructional design process continues to be an important part of the planning, implementation, and evaluation of curriculum.

Allan Glatthorn's concept of *value-oriented theorists* relates well to Smith's process and end product approach. It is primarily engaged in what might be termed "educational consciousness-raising," attempting to sensitize educators to the values and issues that lie at the heart of the stated curriculum. Advances in technology and the World Wide Web have provided value-oriented theorists with a global platform to access electronically to share information on social reform, culture, and economics.

Value-oriented theorists draw heavily and eclectically from several inquiry methodologies, such as psychoanalysis, philosophical inquiry, historical analysis, and political theory. For example, A. N. Maheshwari (2003), chairperson of the National Council for Teacher Education, states,

> As the world enters the Information Age another dimension to value education concerns information itself. This is to do with the nature of information. (¶ 4)
>
> Information is received by human beings through five senses—the senses of seeing, hearing, touch, taste and smell. Information as any one of us receives it is value neutral. Information of seeing is carried by ElectroMagnetic waves, which consist of vibrations of electric and magnetic fields. These vibrations when received by our eyes are transmitted as signals to the brain. The response of brain to information that is received by it is determined by its sub-conscious mind. (¶ 5)

"Therefore," according to Maheshwari, "teachers of the future will have to provide learning experiences for holistic development of mind, body intellect and emotions" (¶ 7), and this will require value-oriented teacher education. Maheshwari goes on to state, "There are two challenges that may have to be faced in providing value orientation to teacher education—stability and change. Stability demands preservation of culture and change demands technology" (¶ 10).

Curriculum as Praxis/Awareness

The fourth aspect of Smith's curriculum model is *praxis*. Praxis models deal primarily with practical deliberation and differentiated curriculum. Through the use of technological advances, curriculum leaders can now access a body of knowledge, formulate content that is interdisciplinary, and provide a process of electronic communication that helps cut across cultural, economic, and social boundaries worldwide. The praxis concept encourages the student and teacher to reach a higher level of awareness through curriculum differentiation and with the use of technology to speed up the process.

Curriculum differentiation is a broad term referring to the need to tailor teaching environments and practices to create appropriately different learning experiences for different students. Keirouz (as cited in Maheshwari, 2003) suggests the following procedures for enhancing differentiation:

- Deleting already mastered material from existing curriculum
- Adding new content, process, or product expectations to existing curriculum
- Extending existing curriculum to provide enrichment activities
- Providing course work for able students at an earlier age than usual
- Writing new units or courses that meet the needs of gifted students

The focus here is to create a differentiated learning environment that encourages students to engage their abilities to the greatest extent possible, including taking risks and building knowledge and skills, in what they perceive as a safe, flexible environment. In that regard, a differentiated learning environment should

1. assess students before a unit of instruction to determine what they already know.

2. adjust the core curriculum by content (below to above grade level), process (concrete to abstract), and product (simple to complex).

3. provide assignments tailored for students of different levels of achievement.

4. have HIGH expectations for ALL students.

5. provide educational experiences which extend, replace, or supplement standard curriculum.

6. structure class assignments so they require high levels of critical thinking and allow for a range of responses.

7. have students participate in respectful work.

8. have students and teachers collaborate in learning.

9. put students in situations where they don't know the answer–often.

10. differ the pace of instruction.

11. provide a blend of whole class, group, and independent learning.

> (Principles of Differentiation, n.d. Used with
> permission from the Manteno C.U.S.D. #5, Manteno, Illinois.)

Differentiated curriculum in enriched learning environments follows closely with a constructivist philosophy and focuses on making meaning of one's environment and becoming aware of the interaction between the enacted curriculum and the experienced curriculum. For example, Seymour Papert (1993) uses the term *constructionism* to brand his favored approach to learning. He states,

> Constructionism is built on the assumption that children will do best by finding ("fishing") for themselves the specific knowledge they need. Organized or informal education can help most by making sure they are supported morally, psychologically, materially, and intellectually in their efforts. As such, the goal is to teach in such a way as to produce the most learning for the least teaching. (¶ 4)

Constructionism differs from constructivism in that it looks more closely than other educational-isms at the idea of mental construction. It attaches special importance to the role of constructions in the world as a support for those in the head, thereby becoming less of a purely mentalist doctrine. As examples of constructionist learning activities, Papert refers, amongst others, to measuring quantities while making a cake, building LEGO or working with the computer programming language LOGO developed specifically . . . for educational use. (¶ 5) As scientists study learning, they are realizing that a constructivist model reflects their best understanding of the brain's natural way of making sense of the world (Papert, 1993). Some educators in the field, however, become confused as to who are constructivists and who are behaviorists. In a behaviorist class, one focuses on the answers desired and tries to shape the responses until they resemble a prototype. In a constructivist classroom, students continually try out ideas and practice for themselves to see where the ideas will work and where they prove to be inadequate (Abbot & Ryan, 1999).

Constructivists and differentiated instruction does, however, require that teachers study differences in understanding, learning modalities, and interests. This can be a problem in that it requires a great deal of time as well as requires the complexity of keeping track of different approaches (Perkins, 1999). Critics of differentiated instruction and constructivist approaches also note that is too permissive and that it lacks rigor. The concern is that the teacher may cast aside the information, facts, and basic skills embedded in the curriculum (Scherer, 1999). There is an additional fear concerning how it will fare with a continuing emphasis on curriculum based on standards and high-stakes testing. With the advent of state and national assessments and a focus on the alignment of standards, some constructivists are concerned that students are losing out on special instructional practices that foster meaningful learning (Brooks & Brooks, 1999).

Conflicts between constructivists and those who favor high-stakes testing may be softened by the advent of technology. Advances in technology may hold the promise of providing a means to ameliorate the situation by allowing students to have an active, social, and creative learning environment as well as enable educators to align the curriculum to state and national standards and assessments.

Through actual practice and activities in the classroom, students will be able to negotiate problems and analyze strategies on a case-by-case, situation-by-situation basis. This approach not only allows for description and explanation, but also emphasizes prediction and problem solving at higher levels. It is a curriculum that makes teachers and students more introspective on a global level and allows teachers and students to see through each other's eyes. Learning involves exploration and is based on reflection, exploration, and physical experience. The praxis model becomes more activity- and metacognitively centered and more personal in nature, allowing the development of real-life experiences to unfold. A greater chance exists for the dynamic interaction and reflection between student and teacher that drives the learning process. With the assistance of technological advances, a teacher today can be more involved in the process and better able to capture the coveted "teachable moment."

CURRICULUM AS CHANGE

Curriculum, whether it is hidden or apparent, seems to be changing even more to meet today's needs and realities. Current instructional design based on brain research is becoming more common. Brain research completed by D'Arcangelo revealed that the brain changes physiologically as a result of experience and that an individual's environment may determine to a large extent the functioning ability of the brain (Brooks & Brooks, 1999). Work in the field of brain research is helping to suggest strategies for teachers in the classroom. Research is helping teachers know how students learn and how students receive, process, and interpret information (Caulfield, Kidd, & Kocher, 2000). The importance of a student's emotional intelligence is also being considered. Daniel Goleman's *Emotional Intelligence* and Joseph LeDoux's *The Emotional Brain* are books that have advanced our understanding of the role of emotions in learning. In addition, Howard Gardner's work in multiple intelligences and the dimensions of learning reveals that human intelligence encompasses a far wider and more universal set of competencies than a single general intelligence (Given, 2000). Bransford, Brown, and Cocking (2001), in *How People Learn: Brain, Mind, Experience, and School,* note that it is important for students to organize their knowledge around important ideas and concepts—that students "learn how to see" a problem like an expert and understand the "Why?" and "When?" as well as the "What?" and "How?" They state that it is important that students integrate their new knowledge with existing knowledge (constructivism) and for students to monitor their learning and problem solving (metacognition) (Caulfield et al., 2000).

With the advent of more innovative ideas and with the advancement of technology, curriculum is becoming more comprehensive and differential in nature. It is forcing change in order to meet new challenges and changes. Educational content and teaching-learning materials now appear to be more functional, diversified, and operational in nature. An increased emphasis is placed on relevance, flexibility, needs, and speed. Demographics, population, health, nutrition, and environment are becoming dominant factors in what appears to be a value-oriented instructional design process focused on the global community.

A case can be made that the very nature of educational structure and educational methodologies is undergoing a significant change. The World Wide Web, computer-assisted instruction, programmed instruction, educational technologies, multimedia capability, and distance education are changing the face of educational curriculum worldwide. Electronic media on a global level appear to be evolving their own pedagogical methodologies and strategies. These advancements in technology are leading to a multitude of approaches that are blending a milieu of curriculum that caters to the needs of interested, disinterested, and remedial learners worldwide.

Technology as Catalyst of Curriculum Change

Little doubt is evidenced that technology is serving as the catalyst for change. The advent of new media, such as the Internet and hypermedia, has brought about not only technological innovations, but also provides new ways of approaching learning and instruction. Douglas Leigh (2003), a specialist on instructional systems at Pepperdine University, notes that theorists such as Thomas Duffy and Seymour Papert are suggesting a model whereby sociocultural and cognitive issues regarding the design of learning environments can be supported by computer tools. Future designers will be able to focus on one aspect of learning or instruction as well as act as consultants or subject matter experts, whether internal or external to the organization. Technology advancements will therefore allow practitioners to oversee the development of instructional projects on a broad scale rather than just narrow their efforts exclusively on assessment, analysis, design, development, implementation, evaluation, or continuous improvement (Bransford et al., 2001).

The use of technology also promotes investigative skills, makes learning more exciting, provides opportunities to apply knowledge, and prepares students for an increasingly technologically advanced world. Through a type of diffusion theory and process, technology is changing how we think of curriculum and how we think of education (Leigh, 2003). It is important to note that the emphasis is on developing ways to use technology in the curriculum, not just adding a new curriculum area. Disciplines can remain, but with a focus on activities and cooperative learning. Technical advances are allowing teachers to move the focus of curriculum to thematic units that emphasize an interdisciplinary approach, an integrated learning approach, and encourage effective habits of the mind. According to Hirsch (as cited in *Unit Curriculum Theory,* 2003),

> To give all children a chance to take advantage of the new technology means not only seeing to it that they have access to the technology, but also ensuring that they possess the knowledge necessary for them to make effective use of it. (¶ 4)

With technology making such vast, sweeping changes in curriculum worldwide, it is crucial to emphasize that the underlying foundation for educational change is to meet the needs of students at whatever age on a global level. Access to technology and the use of cooperative learning via the use of technology in classrooms is becoming more commonplace as a way not only to advance a body of knowledge, but to access knowledge with blinding speed electronically. Teachers globally are finding that the use of computer clusters with a 1:5 ratio of computers to students in classrooms can aid in the development of cooperative learning strategies. The use of cooperative learning strategies has been directly linked to an increase in student achievement (Hirsch, 2000). As a result, the concept of using technology with cooperative learning strategies as a curriculum strategy is gaining even more acceptance. An article on discussing curriculum theory on WebQuest indicates that when students work and study together cooperatively, they appear to learn more quickly (Whitehead, Jensen, & Boschee, 2003). Towns and Grant also found that cooperative learning helped students develop "meaningful strategies" in order to synthesize other concepts in the classroom (*Unit Curriculum Theory,* 2003). Developing new strategies and meeting students' needs globally is a key to success.

As part of that global change process, further advances in technology are now utilizing the cooperative learning and differentiated curriculum strategies and combining them with the use of wireless handheld computing devices. Currently a movement is toward low-cost, portable handheld devices for student use that can be connected through global networks and tailored for specific tasks or applications. Some classroom teachers now have the capability of communicating and exchanging information worldwide with students via classroom workstations and district servers. When viewing the potential of technology in the classroom of tomorrow, Howard Gardner probably said it best: "I believe that the computer revolution is already changing how students acquire and use information; if our schools do not rise to their technological opportunity and challenge, they risk becoming completely anachronistic" (Scherer, 1999, p. 16).

THE THEORETICAL CLASSROOM OF THE FUTURE

When reviewing possible scenarios of the theoretical classroom of the future, Barbara Means (2001), the director of the Learning and Technology Program at SRI International, probably expressed it best when she described a science class of the future in an article for the Association for Supervision and Curriculum Development's publication, *Educational Leadership.* Means envisions students in a middle school classroom of tomorrow monitoring local haze using a sun photometer to measure attenuation of sunlight caused by haze, smoke, and smog. Seven small groups of students take their photometer reading at their school's softball field each day at noon, and the readings are automatically sent to their handheld wireless MathPads. The information from the MathPads is transferred to a share board computer at the school. When the students return, the teacher begins a class review and discussion of the data on a wall-sized display. According to Dr. Means, the middle school teacher or students plot each of the group's readings on a graph showing measurements over the past 6 months and discuss distinction between accuracy and precision.

The middle school teacher then introduces the next assignment involving data analysis. Small groups of students investigate haze data from their own and other schools using the Internet to go online to the Haze Project database. The teacher reminds the students of the contents of the database and strategies for navigating to the Web site. Students are asked comprehension questions to ensure that they are interpreting and understanding the data tables correctly. The middle school teacher can make on-the-spot evaluations of student learning via electronic assessment software and Web-based evaluation programs that are aligned with state and national standards.

Middle school students participating in the project are asked to explore the data archive before deciding on a research question. Information will be noted in articles on the Haze Project's online student journal. The technology supports access to similar data sets and conferencing with others involved in the project. Students can choose to collaborate with students locally, statewide, nationally, or internationally at other schools via e-mail and real-time online discussions using software that allows them to share and manipulate data graphs.

This type of classroom-of-tomorrow scenario is actually being piloted in experimental classrooms today. The increasing availability of and accessibility to Web-based alternative learning creates all types of theoretical constructs. Technology invites innovation and allows us to envision future curriculum design in many new and different dimensions. The implications of technology for curriculum theory seem to be limitless. The implications of new theoretical constructs embracing technology to change education globally are staggering.

CONCLUSION

The nature of curriculum theory appears to be a culmination of functions and approaches, whether they are hidden or apparent and/or whether they are old or new. Curriculum theorists are becoming more aware that curriculum can be both the description of what happens in the classroom and what actually happens in the classroom—and why not? Future theorists can help describe, explain, and predict the teaching and learning process. They can also help provide the constructs necessary for analyzing proposals, illuminating practice, and guiding reform. In addition, they can help in developing strategies to transmit knowledge via a syllabus, focus on an end product, state and demonstrate a process of learning, as well as provide praxis by fostering a more dynamic milieu in the technological global classroom of the future. More important, they can provide dynamic models of teaching and learning that can elicit educational change worldwide. The key, then, is for future curriculum theorists to elicit an educational change via technology on a global scale that will allow us to develop new and meaningful ways of improving awareness and understanding throughout the world.

CHAPTER OVERVIEW

Chapter 3 explains that sound theory can be of value to both the scholar and the practitioner because curriculum theory can provide a set of conceptual tools for analyzing curriculum proposals, for illuminating practice, and for guiding reform. This chapter shows how melding theory and the reality of school curriculum is an important step in the educational planning process. Because it is difficult to use theoretical approaches to make continual analyses, reevaluations, and revisions of curriculum, especially in such fields as informational technology and the sociology of knowledge, this chapter explains the necessity of developing a fundamental understanding of curriculum theory by providing the tools necessary when analyzing curriculum proposals, illuminating practice, and guiding reform. This chapter addresses the nature and function of curriculum theory. It also addresses why it is important to meld the theory and reality of school curriculum together as part of the planning process. This chapter explains the role of leadership in the development of curriculum theory and the major classifications of curriculum theory. Finally, it addresses how technology has been a catalyst for curriculum change.

CHAPTER TERMS

Curriculum Theory	Open Education
Traditionalists	Developmental Education
Conceptual Empiricists	Knowledge-Centered Curricula
Reconceptualists	Ways of Knowing
Structure-Oriented Theories	Society-Centered Curricula
Value-Oriented Theories	Conformists
Content-Oriented Theories	Reformers
Process-Oriented Theories	Futurists
Child-Centered Curriculum	Radicals
Affective Education	

APPLICATIONS

1. As noted in this chapter, much debate occurs in the field about the value of curriculum theory. As you understand the nature of curriculum theory, how much professional value does it seem to have for you?

2. Most of the theoretical work in the field would be subsumed under the headings of value-centered and content-centered theories. How do you explain the fact that structure and process matters have received much less attention from curriculum theorists?

3. Several experts who have analyzed process theories claim that all attempts to develop new process approaches turn out to be simply variations of the Tyler rationale. To what extent do you agree with this assessment?

4. Use the proposed descriptive system to analyze any article or book that describes a curriculum-development process.

5. As noted in this chapter, very little work has been done in applying ways-of-knowing approaches to curriculum development projects. What do you think a school curriculum would look like, in general, if it attempted to embody a ways-of-knowing approach to the curriculum?

6. Looking at your school system, how have advancements in technology changed the roles of the education process?

CASE STUDY

Bruce Novac has been a PK–5 elementary school principal in the Dover School District for the past 2 years. This is the beginning of his third year and the year in the district in which he will be up for tenure. He has a meeting scheduled with the school superintendent, Dr. Robert Kerr, and the curriculum director, Dr. Karla Johnson, to review test score data of the third-grade students in his school. The results revealed that the third-grade students' scores were well below state and federal guidelines for proficiency. In fact, second-grade students had higher achievement scores than the third-grade students in his school.

Mr. Novac was told by the two central office administrators that his theory of curriculum implementation was not working. In fact, what he was doing was held in low regard by the teachers in his school. In a panic, Novac begins to search for some answers on curriculum theories espoused by authors of curriculum textbooks and in educational journals. His focus is captured by structure-oriented, value-oriented, content-oriented, and process-oriented curriculum theories, which he hopes will provide answers to the third-grade low-achievement dilemma in his school.

THE CHALLENGE

Student achievement is often thought to be the result of curriculum theory that teachers support. How can Mr. Novac educate and motivate the third-grade teachers to integrate sound curriculum theory into their day-to-day work with students?

Key Issues/Questions

1. What are your impressions of the superintendent and curriculum director? Did they adequately address Mr. Novac's responsibilities in this incident? Why or why not?

2. What are your impressions of the third-grade teachers in this elementary school in the Dover School District?

3. If the principal meets with the third-grade teachers, what should be discussed?

4. What are some possible reasons why third-grade students in Mr. Novac's school are low achievers?

5. What are some theoretical curriculum approaches that Principal Novac might use to increase student achievement scores? Identify the strategies and explain why you think they might be effective.

REFERENCES

Abbot, J., & Ryan, T. (1999). Constructing knowledge, reconstructing schooling. *Educational Leadership, 57*(3), 66–69.

Acton, G. S. (2003). *Scientific method and psychological theory.* Retrieved March 8, 2003, from http://www.personalityresearch.org/courses/method/syllabus.html

Apple, M. W. (1975). Scientific interests and the nature of educational institutions. In W. Pinar (Ed.), *Curriculum theorizing: For reconceptualists* (pp. 120–130). Berkeley, CA: McCutchan.

Atkins, E. S. (1982). *Curriculum theorizing as a scientific pursuit: A framework for analysis.* Unpublished doctoral dissertation, University of Pennsylvania.

Beauchamp, G. A. (1981). *Curriculum theory* (4th ed.). Itasca, IL: Peacock.

Bobbitt, F. (1918). *The curriculum.* Boston: Riverside Press.

Bowers, C. A. (1977, September). Emergent ideological characteristics of educational policy. *Teachers College Record, 76,* 1.

Bransford, J., Brown, A. L., & Cocking, R. R. (2001). *How people learn: Brain, mind, experience, and school.* Washington, DC: National Academy Press.

Brooks, M. (1986, April). *Curriculum development from a constructivist perspective.* Paper presented at the annual meeting of the American Educational Research Association, San Francisco.

Brooks, M., & Brooks, J. (1999). The courage to be a constructivist. *Educational Leadership, 57*(3), 18–24.

Brown, G. I. (1975). Examples of lessons, units, and course outlines in confluent education. In G. I. Brown (Ed.), *The live classroom* (pp. 231–295). New York: Viking.

Burks, R. (1998). *A review and comparison of Ralph W. Tyler's basic principles of curriculum. Curriculum and instruction.* Retrieved March 8, 2003, from http://www.randallburks.com/critique.htm

Caulfield, J., Kidd, S., & Kocher, T. (2000). Brain-based instruction in action. *Educational Leadership, 58*(3), 62–65.

Counts, G. S. (1932). *Dare the school build a new social order?* New York: Day.

Definitions of instructional design. (2003). Adapted from Training and Instructional Design. Applied Research Laboratory, Penn State University. Retrieved February 24, 2004, from http://www.umich.edu/~ed626/define.html

Doll, R. C. (1986). *Curriculum improvement: Decision making and process* (6th ed.). Boston: Allyn & Bacon.

Eisner, E. (Ed.). (1985). *Learning and teaching the ways of knowing* (Eighty-Fourth Yearbook of the National Society for the Study of Education, Part II). Chicago: University of Chicago Press.

Eisner, E. W., & Vallance, E. (Eds.). (1974). *Conflicting conceptions of curriculum.* Berkeley, CA: McCutchan.

Faix, T. L. (1964). *Structural-functional analysis as a conceptual system for curriculum theory and research: A theoretical study.* Unpublished doctoral dissertation, University of Wisconsin, Madison.

Farmer, D. (1996, January). *Curriculum differentiation: An overview of the research into the curriculum differentiation educational strategy.* Retrieved April 5, 2005, from http://www.austega.com/gifted/provisions/curdifferent.htm

Freire, P. (1970). *Pedagogy of the oppressed.* New York: Herder and Herder.

Gagne, R. (1985). *The conditions of learning and theory of instruction* (4th ed.). New York: Holt, Rinehart & Winston.

Gagne, R., Briggs, L., & Wager, W. (1992). *Principles of instructional design* (4th ed.). Fort Worth, TX: HBJ College.

Gay, G. (1980). Conceptual models of the curriculum planning process. In A. W. Foshay (Ed.), *Considered action for curriculum improvement* (pp. 120–143). Alexandria, VA: Association for Supervision and Curriculum Development.

Given, B. (2000). Theaters of the mind. *Educational Leadership, 58*(3), 72–75.

Glatthorn, A. A. (1980). *A guide for designing an English curriculum for the eighties.* Urbana, IL: National Council of Teachers of English.

Glatthorn, A. A. (1986). Analysis of Glatthorn's (1986) curriculum-development process. In Glatthorn, A. A. (1987). *Curriculum leadership* (p. 120). New York: HarperCollins.

Goodlad, J. I. (Ed.). (1979). *Curriculum inquiry: The study of curriculum practice.* New York: McGraw-Hill.

Hanson, N. R. (1958). *Patterns of discovery.* Cambridge, UK: Cambridge University Press.

Hirsch, E. D., Jr. (1995). *What your fifth grader needs to know: Fundamentals of good fifth-grade education.* Los Alamitos, CA: Delta Publishing.

Hirsch, E. D., Jr. (2000, Spring). "You can always look it up" or can you? *American Educator: The Professional Journal of the American Federation of Educators 24*(1), 4–9.

Huenecke, D. (1982). What is curricular theorizing? What are its implications for practice? *Educational Leadership, 39,* 290–294.

imagitrends. (2000). *Future primary educational structure.* Retrieved April 5, 2005, from http://pages .prodigy.net/imagiweb/reports/file00/oct1.htm

Kaplan, A. (1964). *The conduct of inquiry: Methodology for behavioral science.* San Francisco: Chandler.

Keat, R., & Urry, J. (1975). *Social theory as science.* London: Routledge & Kegan Paul.

Leigh, D. (2003). *A brief history of instructional design.* Retrieved March 8, 2004, from the International Society for Performance Improvement Web site: http://www.pignc-ispi.com/ articles/education/brief%20history.htm

Macdonald, J. B. (1974). A transcendental developmental ideology of education. In W. Pinar (Ed.), *Heightened conscience, cultural revolution, and curriculum theory.* Berkeley, CA: McCutchan.

Maheshwari, A. N. (2003). *Value orientation in teacher education.* Retrieved March 1, 2003, from http://www.geocities.com/Athens/Parthenon/2686/value.htm

McNeil, J. D. (1985). *Curriculum: A comprehensive introduction* (3rd ed.). Boston: Little, Brown.

Means, B. (2001). Technology use in tomorrow's schools. *Educational Leadership, 58*(4), 57–61.

Papert, S. (1993). *The children's machine: Rethinking school in the age of the computer.* New York: Basic Books. Retrieved March 9, 2004, from http://www.stemnet.nf.ca/~elmurphy/emurphy/papert.html

Parker, F. W. (1894). *Talks on pedagogics.* New York: E. L. Kellogg.

Perkins, D. (1999). The many faces of constructivism. *Educational Leadership, 57*(3), 6–11.

Pinar, W. F. (1978). The reconceptualization of curriculum studies. *Journal of Curriculum Studies, 10,* 205–214.

Popper, K. R. (1962). *Conjectures and refutations.* New York: Basic Books.

Posner, G. J., & Strike, K. A. (1976). A categorization scheme for principles of sequencing content. *Review of Educational Research, 46,* 665–690.

Principles of differentiation. (n.d.). Retrieved March 23, 2005, from http://www.manteno.k12.il.us/ curriculumdiff/principles.htm

Purpel, D. E., & Belanger, M. (1972). Toward a humanistic curriculum theory. In D. E. Purpel & M. Belanger (Eds.), *Curriculum and the cultural revolution* (pp. 64–74). Berkeley, CA: McCutchan.

Scherer, M. (1999). The understanding pathway: A conversation with Howard Gardner. *Educational Leadership, 57*(3), 12–16.

Schiro, M. (1978). *Curriculum for better schools: The great ideological debate.* Englewood Cliffs, NJ: Educational Technology.

Schon, D. A. (1983). *The reflective practitioner: How professionals think in action.* New York: Basic Books.

Schwab, J. (1970). *The practical: A language for curriculum.* Washington, DC: National Education Association.

Short, E. C. (1983). The forms and use of alternative curriculum development strategies: Policy implications. *Curriculum Inquiry, 13,* 45–64.

Shulman, J. (2003). *Institute for case development.* WestEd Inc. Retrieved March 2, 2004, from http://www.wested.org/cs/we/view/pj/173

Smith, M. K. (1996, 2000). Curriculum theory and practice. *The encyclopaedia of informal education.* Retrieved February 20, 2003, from http://www.infed.org/biblio/b-curric.htm

Suppe, F. (Ed.). (1974). *The structures of scientific theories.* Urbana: University of Illinois Press.

Unit curriculum theory. (2003). Retrieved February 19, 2004, from http://www.dade.k12.fl.us/ohes/bratcher Mol/webquestcurriculumtheory.html

Vallance, E. (1985). Ways of knowing and curricular conceptions: Implications for program planning. In E. Eisner (Ed.), *Learning and teaching the ways of knowing* (pp. 199–217). Chicago: University of Chicago Press.

Weber, L. (1971). *The English infant school and informal education.* Englewood Cliffs, NJ: Prentice Hall.

Whitehead, B. M., Jensen, D. F. N., & Boschee, F. (2003). *Planning for technology: A guide for school administrators, technology coordinators, and curriculum leaders.* Thousand Oaks CA: Corwin.

Why technology. (2003). Retrieved January 10, 2004, from http://www.nsba.org/sbot/toolkit/whytech.html

Wiggins, G., & McTighe, J. (2005). *Understanding by design* (expanded 2nd. ed.). Alexandria, VA: Association for Supervision and Curriculum Development.

Willwerth, D. (2003). *Heuristics and curriculum theory.* (Originally cited in Schiro, M. [1978]. *Curriculum for better schools: The great ideological debate* [pp. 7–16]. Englewood Cliffs, NJ: Educational Technology Publications.) Retrieved March 1, 2004, from http://www2.bc.edu/~evansec/curriculum/index.html

Chapter 4

THE POLITICS OF CURRICULUM

What actually is taught in the classroom results from a confluence of several often conflicting factors. Federal and state governments, professional organizations, local school boards, textbook publishers, accrediting organizations, parent and community groups, school administrators, and classroom teachers all seem to make a difference. Those conflicting influences seem to change in their strength from time to time, and their particular impact upon a given classroom is often difficult to trace. However, any curriculum leader who wishes to develop or improve curricula needs to understand the politics of curriculum, the way those organizations and individuals attempt to influence what is taught in the schools. For example, many reform books have been on the market, like John Holt's *How Children Fail* (1964) and Ivan Illich's *Deschooling Society* (1972). Jonathan Kozol's *Savage Inequalities: Children in America's Schools* (1991) and Grace Llewellyn's *Teenage Liberation Handbook: How to Quit School and Get a Real Life and Education* (1997) are also examples of reform books that are still popular. As a result, this chapter presents an overview of the way influences are brought to bear and then examines in greater detail those agencies that seem to have the greatest influence. Questions addressed in this chapter include the following:

- What has been the role of the federal government in curriculum development, and how has this changed over the years?
- What is the general role of state governments in curriculum development today? How has this changed over the years?
- What are the roles of educational organizations, courts, educational leaders, and classroom teachers on current curriculum development?

Key to Leadership

Curriculum leaders are now realizing that we have entered a political era of global knowledge exchange and application.

AN OVERVIEW OF THE CURRICULUM-INFLUENCE PROCESS

In understanding how several groups and individuals influence curriculum policy and curriculum development, it is important at the outset to realize that such influences do not take place in a vacuum. They occur in a complex social and cultural environment—an environment that significantly determines which belief systems and practices will gain the widest audience. Here Schon (1971) is most illuminating. As he sees it, ideas "in good currency" flow into the mainstream, mediated by certain roles. "New ideas incompatible with the prevailing conceptions are suppressed within the social system," but kept alive by people in vanguard roles until a crisis occurs. At that time those new ideas might be released and spread by information networks and the mass media. Before they are accepted, however, these new ideas become issues in power struggles. As Schon sees it, only a limited number of "slots" are available for new ideas, because these new ideas are attached to advocates competing for power positions. In this manner, inquiry around the ideas becomes politicized. Those that have the most powerful support become legitimated by approval from powerful people. Only then can the new ideas become public policy.

Curriculum Tip

This struggle for power in the curriculum-making process seems to occur most sharply at the federal, state, and local district levels and differentially affects the recommended, the written, and the taught curricula.

The end of the 1970s signaled a dramatic change in the form and purpose of public schools. From an economical standpoint, individual income and state financial resources were falling and costs were spiraling upward. School enrollments were declining with parents moving their children into private schools or into the suburbs. Financial problems of public schools, especially large urban public schools, continued to be a problem. Budgets reflected a drop in local support from 60% to 30% while the role of the state increased. Federal government educational assistance continued at around 10%. With an increase in state contributions to education, the role of politics intensified.

At the same time that states were gaining a firmer foothold in education, Ronald Reagan was elected to the presidency. This began a new era of conservative government at the federal level. Between a decline of enrollment and rising costs, school boards were in difficulty and began to take a more conservative stand. The code phrase of the conservative movement became, "Back to the Basics," and accountability became the norm.

At the federal level, the struggle for power occurs chiefly behind the scenes, as several influence groups and individuals attempt to persuade members of both the executive and legislative branches. Bell (1986) describes how the decision not to abolish the Department of Education during President Reagan's second term came about as the result of such behind-the-scenes maneuvering. First, the platform-drafting committee for the 1984 Republican

National Convention decided to ignore pressures to abolish the department that came mainly from individuals whom Bell calls movement conservatives, "ideologues of the far right." As Bell points out, key members of the platform committee were House Republicans running for office in 1984. They had read *A Nation at Risk,* they had sensed the grassroots interest in education, and they did not want to be perceived by voters as being anti-education. Although the "movement conservatives" continued to attempt to persuade Reagan to exert leadership on the issue, Reagan was, in Bell's view, a pragmatist with different priorities. He cared deeply about tuition tax credits, vouchers, and prayer in the schools, but he saw the fate of the Department of Education as a matter of lesser consequence. Knowing there was no broad-based support to abolish the department and not caring enough to spend his political capital in fighting the battle, Reagan quietly put the proposal on the back burner and never again raised the matter with Bell.

Lobbying groups can play an important role in this hidden power struggle at the federal level. Levine and Wexler (1981) document clearly how the Council for Exceptional Children and other interest groups representing the handicapped played a determining role in the passage of Public Law 94-142, the most important national legislation affecting the handicapped. These lobbyists had developed close relationships with the staff and members of the Congressional education committees, had formed close alliances with leaders in the Bureau of Education for the Handicapped, and spoke authoritatively at every Congressional hearing on the bill.

The same picture of policy being made in a highly charged and politicized environment with much behind-the-scenes lobbying is seen at the state level. A case in point is the way Pennsylvania adopted its new curriculum regulations. In 1981, a forward-looking secretary of education proposed a radical restructuring of the state's curriculum regulations, replacing lists of required courses with the specification of student competencies that could be developed in a variety of ways. For 2 years these changes were discussed and debated by lobbyists (chiefly those from professional organizations), by the state board of education, and by department of education officials. No action was taken; state legislators were indifferent. One legislative leader expressed it this way:

> The reaction of the legislature when they were talking about these learning outcomes— the competency-based curriculum proposal—was pretty much a hands-off thing. They realized it was an issue they didn't want to get involved in. . . . Then all the reports came out in the intervening time, and there was a kind of a rush to judgment to see who was going to address this serious problem . . . all of a sudden the national environment was "let's do these things," and so everyone wanted to have their stamp on them. (Lynch, 1986, p. 74)

The governor published his own recommendations for "turning the tide," the House passed legislation mandating increased curriculum rigor and an emphasis upon traditional subjects (not competencies), the Senate passed a resolution directing the state board of education to take action, and the state board adopted revised curriculum regulations—all within 6 months' time.

In such a politicized environment at the state level, numerous groups and individuals have a differential impact. In her study of policy making in one of the eastern states, Marshall (1985) identified 15 influence groups. The strongest of those include the governor and his or her executive staff, the chief state school officer, individual members of the state legislature, the legislature as a whole, the legislative staff, and education interest groups. Those with moderate influence are the teachers' association, the state board of education, and the administrators' organization. The courts, the federal government, the school boards' association, noneducator groups, and researchers had much less influence.

It was during this time that an attempt was made to introduce "international" achievement testing as a measure of excellence. There was concern that United States children were somehow behind the children in other countries. Berliner and Biddle's (1997) book, *The Manufactured Crisis,* soon put this argument to rest by noting that the top 10% of children in countries like Germany were being compared to the upper 50% of American children. Berliner and Biddle contended that America's best and brightest children could compete with Europe's top children on any testing measure.

At the local level, there is the same interplay of conflicting and coalescing influences; only the key actors are different. As the local school board sets general curriculum policy, it too is sensitive to prevailing trends in the society; in this context, it makes general decisions that have been strongly influenced by the superintendent, who is responding to his or her own perception of the larger educational scene and local needs. At the same time, local pressure groups, often acting in concert with nationally organized lobbies, will attempt to influence the board's curriculum policy as it involves such specific controversial issues as sex education, evolution, creationism, and values education.

Once general policy has been determined at the district level, key decisions are made about the written curriculum by curriculum leaders, school administrators, and teachers. At the district level, the assistant superintendent for curriculum and instruction and several subject-matter supervisors usually provide leadership in developing and improving a field of study, such as mathematics K–12. Typically, the assistant superintendent or a supervisor will appoint a committee made up of representatives of the major constituencies: a principal, a team leader or department chair, two to five teachers, and perhaps a token parent. In making decisions about the scope and sequence of that field, the committee typically uses a variety of professional sources: It consults state guidelines, checks standardized tests, reviews available texts, confers with consultants, reviews guides from other districts and from professional associations, and surveys classroom teachers. When conflicts arise in their deliberations, the committee members typically resolve them through political processes—negotiating, compromising, and deferring to the most powerful. At this stage, external pressure groups seem to have little influence, although the committee will usually make decisions based upon its own assessment of the community's "zone of tolerance."

The picture changes somewhat at the school level. In elementary schools, the principal seems to play a key role in determining curricular priorities and in monitoring the curriculum. If conflict arises, it will usually occur between the principal and a small group of teachers who are jealous of their curricular autonomy. At the secondary level, the principal will usually delegate that responsibility to a team leader or department chair, because subject-matter expertise is more important at this level. In secondary schools, curricular battles are usually waged between departments as they compete for scarce resources.

Then the classroom door closes, and the teacher becomes the curriculum. The teacher makes decisions based upon a somewhat unconscious response to several sources: the district guide, the textbook, curriculum-referenced and standardized tests, the teacher's knowledge of and perception of the subject matter, and the teacher's assessment of pupil interest and readiness.

Thus, at different levels of curriculum decision making, the major sources of influence vary considerably, yet at every level the process seems to be a highly politicized one in which issues of power and control are resolved in curriculum decision making. At this juncture, a closer examination of certain key elements might be useful.

THE ROLE OF THE FEDERAL GOVERNMENT

Since 1970, in the United States, the business sector has been invading schools with the objective of replacing public schools with something else. As early as the first Nixon administration (1968–1972), the federal government promoted "performance contracts" to enable business to complete with schools for tax dollars. More recently, the George W. Bush administration has promoted testing and vouchers as a means of discrediting public schools and opening up a $389 billion "market." An additional $261 billion worth of opportunity at the postsecondary and higher education level provides an irresistible target for "takeover" (Wiles & Lundt, 2004).

The discussion below, therefore, examines that role in the three most recent periods discussed in Chapter 2 of this work: Scholarly Structuralism, 1957–1967; Romantic Radicalism, 1968–1974; and Privatistic Conservatism, 1975–1989. Prior to 1957, there was almost no federal involvement in curriculum; before the 1950s, as Kliebard (1979) notes, the activities of the federal government in education were limited to convening prestigious groups, creating professional societies, and disseminating the recommendations of prominent individuals.

Curriculum Tip

In examining the role of the federal government in influencing the school curriculum, it is useful to bring to bear a historical perspective, because patterns of influence have changed over the past few decades.

1957–1967: Scholarly Structuralism

This was the period of the national frenzy to "catch up with the Russians." Largely instigated by the launching of Sputnik, it was a time of intensive and extensive federal intervention in curriculum. During this period, education seemed to be dominated by what Atkin and House (1981) call a "technological" perspective. Educational leaders were convinced that rational, technological approaches could solve the schools' problems. Teaching was seen as a technological endeavor: The essential skills of teaching could be identified and taught through a step-by-step approach. Curriculum development similarly was viewed as a rational technological enterprise: The right content could be identified by the scholars and then delivered in tested packages. Even the change process was seen from this perspective: The agricultural model of conducting research and disseminating its results through "change agents" was viewed as the only proper means for changing the schools.

The primary intervention strategy adopted by the federal government was the development and dissemination of generic curricula. To use the constructs explicated in Chapter 1, the developers of the "alphabet-soup curricula" attempted to fuse the recommended, the written, and the taught curricula; they sincerely believed that their idealistic recommendations would be embodied into district curriculum guides and that teachers would willingly and faithfully implement what they had produced.

The developers of these generic curricula seemed most concerned with course content: The National Science Foundation developed and supported the "Course Content Improvement Program," which in turn strongly influenced a similar program adopted by the U.S. Office of Education, called the "Curriculum Improvement Program." In the view of these leaders, curriculum and content were synonymous. That content, in their view, should be determined only by the scholars in the disciplines—not by "educationists." It was the scholars alone who understood the structures of the disciplines, who could identify the critical concepts, and who knew how to organize and sequence that content.

Once the scholars had developed these ideal curricula, the dissemination effort began. Large-scale publicity efforts were undertaken: Articles appeared in the professional journals touting the high quality of the products, and sessions were held at the major professional conferences advocating the adoption of the materials. Teachers were trained in summer institutes with rather generous stipends provided. More than 30 regional laboratories were funded to aid in the development and dissemination efforts, and the curriculum was translated into marketable packages—either textbooks produced by commercial entities or sold by the developers themselves.

Initially these federally funded generic curricula seemed successful. The materials produced were significantly different from what had been developed before, especially in science and mathematics. Even the conventional textbooks produced by mainline publishing houses included concepts introduced by the scholarly curriculum projects. Early users, the most committed and knowledgeable of teachers, seemed enthusiastic.

However, resistance to these federal efforts to transform the curriculum through direct intervention began to increase at the end of this period. First of all, concern surfaced about what some termed the *federal curriculum,* a fear that these federally supported curriculum projects would reduce local curricular autonomy. Others pointed out, of course, that in some fields, at least, the effect was quite the opposite. Until Project Social Studies came along, there was in effect a nationally standardized curriculum in social studies—a curriculum that was limited almost solely to recurring courses in U.S. history, a little geography in elementary schools, and a smattering of civics in junior high schools and "Problems of Democracy" in senior high schools. Project Social Studies offered more alternatives: Schools could now teach economics, anthropology, and sociology, using materials that had a scholarly cachet.

Objections also mounted as to the specifics of the content. Many teachers complained that the materials were too difficult for their students. Parents and lay critics argued that the "basics" were being slighted: Not enough attention was paid to computational skills in the mathematics curriculum projects or to spelling and grammar in the English curricula. There were also numerous protests about the values issues embedded in many of the social studies and science curricula; many individuals and organizations felt that these nationally disseminated projects espoused values they considered too liberal and permissive. As noted in Chapter 2, these complaints reached a crescendo in the bitter controversy over *Man: A Course of Study* (MACOS; Curriculum Development Associates, 1972).

Finally, it was obvious that these so-called teacher-proof curricula were doomed to fail, because they were put in the hands of "curriculum-proof" teachers. The developers of these curricula seemed totally oblivious to the nature of schools as organizations and to the complexities of classroom life. They somewhat naively believed that their curricula would be adopted uniformly and implemented as designed. They foolishly expected teachers to acquire, internalize, and use teaching strategies that were radically different from those they already used and that were quite demanding in their complexity.

1968–1974: Romantic Radicalism

During this period, the national agenda changed. While international issues such as the war in Vietnam continued to dominate the headlines, at the grassroots level people seemed more concerned with their own individual freedoms. It was a time when "rights," not responsibilities, was the dominant slogan: Black people, handicapped individuals, homosexuals, women, and nonnative groups all asserted their rights to liberation and to greater power.

In this 7-year period, educational thinking at the policy-making level seemed to be dominated by what Atkin and House call a political perspective, in contradistinction to the technological perspective that had dominated the previous period. A political perspective views educational reform essentially as a political process. The legitimacy of several conflicting views is recognized. Decisions are made primarily through a process of compromise and negotiation.

It was this political perspective that seemed to influence both Congress and the several federal agencies empowered to enforce compliance with federal legislation. Their intervention strategy seemed to be a "carrot-and-stick" approach: Develop specific policies mandating changes in the operation of schools and offer financial rewards to those who comply. Their impact on school curricula is best seen perhaps in an analysis of their response to pressures from two groups: those insisting on the need for bilingual education and those arguing for the educational rights of the handicapped.

Bilingual Education

As Ravitch (1983) points out, the demand for bilingual education seemed to result from a surge of new ethnocentrism that argued for ethnicity as a basis for public policy. Initially, the demand seemed modest enough. As Ravitch notes, those advocating bilingual education in the Congressional hearings of 1967 desired funding only for demonstration projects that would meet the special educational needs of Hispanic children; in their view, the aim of bilingual education was to help the Hispanic child master the English language. The Bilingual Education Act of 1968, which ultimately became Title VII of the Elementary and Secondary Education Act, covered not just Hispanic children, but all children of limited English-speaking ability, especially those from low-income families. The act was intentionally vague in key particulars: Bilingual education was not defined, and the purpose of the act was never made explicit.

Although the act itself did not require districts to provide bilingual programs, in 1970 the Office of Civil Rights (OCR) informed every school district with more than 5% "national origin-minority group children" that it had to take "affirmative steps" to rectify the language deficiency of such children or be in violation of Title VI of the Civil Rights Act. The OCR guidelines were sustained and supported by the Supreme Court in its *Lau v. Nichols* decision, which directed the schools to create special language programs for "non–English-speaking children," to correct what it called "language deficiency."

Also in 1974, Congress renewed and extended the 1968 act, making several important changes in response to pressures from lobbying groups representing ethnic minorities. First, the provisions of the act covered all children, not just those from low-income homes. Instead of being primarily concerned with teaching these children how to speak English, the act recognized the importance of maintaining the native language and cultural heritage. As Ravitch notes, the 1974 act was a landmark in that it marked the first time the Congress had dictated a specific pedagogical approach to local districts.

What had started out as a modest demonstration program to aid Hispanic students had become a mammoth program that funded the teaching of 68 languages, including 7 Eskimo languages and a score of Native American languages.

Educating the Handicapped

In many ways, federal intervention in the education of the handicapped seemed to parallel its activities on behalf of nonnative children. What began as a relatively small effort became a major establishment supported with federal funds. Prior to 1965, there seemed to be almost no concerted effort to secure federal funds to aid the education of the handicapped. The leaders of organizations such as the National Association for Retarded Citizens and the Council for Exceptional Children, however, viewing the success of the civil rights movement, began to coordinate their lobbying efforts. Their efforts quickly paid off: In 1966, Congress established a Bureau of Education for the Handicapped, within the Office of Education, and in 1970 passed new legislation increasing the amount of aid for the education of the handicapped and expanding the definition of the term to include the learning disabled and the socially and emotionally disturbed.

Two important court decisions provided strong impetus for further efforts. In 1971 the federal courts issued a consent decree requiring Pennsylvania to provide a free public education to all exceptional children between the ages of 6 and 21; and in 1972 the federal court in the District of Columbia held that every school-age child in the district had to be provided with a "free and suitable publicly supported education regardless of the degree of a child's mental, physical, or emotional disability or impairment" (*Mills v. Board of Education,* 1972).

Congress then responded by enacting the Rehabilitation Act of 1973, including Section 504, which Ravitch terms "the handicapped person's equivalent of Title VI of the Civil Rights Act of 1964" (p. 307). The enactment of that legislation was quickly followed by the passage in 1975 of Public Law 94-142. In many ways this particular law was the most prescriptive educational legislation ever passed by Congress. The law not only required that every child receive an Individualized Educational Program (IEP), but it even specified the content of these plans. They had to include a statement of present levels of performance, a statement of annual goals and short-term objectives, a statement of the educational services to be provided, and the extent to which the child will be able to participate in regular programs. Projected dates for initiation and duration, objective criteria and evaluation procedures, and schedules also determined whether the objectives were being achieved. Finally, the law required the mainstreaming of the handicapped: Such children were to be educated with the nonhandicapped "to the maximum extent appropriate."

Whereas the development of generic content-oriented courses did not seem to make a lasting impact, the carrot-and-stick approach of passing and enforcing legislation had a pervasive impact, to the extent that many educational leaders of the time expressed grave concern about the intrusion of the federal government and the courts into matters that they believed were better left to local control.

1975–1989: Privatistic Conservatism

This period, of course, was dominated by President Ronald Reagan, who was elected on a conservative platform and who used his considerable leadership skills to implement that platform. As perceived by Terrel H. Bell (1986), then Secretary of Education, Reagan had in mind six goals relating to education: substantially reduce federal spending, strengthen local and state control, maintain a limited federal role in assisting states in carrying out their educational responsibilities, expand parental choice, reduce federal judicial activity in education, and abolish the Department of Education.

Certain of the Reagan administration's initiatives had clear implications for curriculum. In order to strengthen the state role in education and to provide equitable services for private-school students, Congress adopted under Reagan's prodding a program to award block grants to the states: Chapter 2 of the Education Consolidation and Improvement Act of 1981 consolidated more than 30 categorical programs into a single block grant to each state. An initial study by Hertling (1986) of the effects of this block-grant program indicated that, in general, the Chapter 2 money had been used to support computer-based education, curriculum development, staff development, and pilot development of new programs. Although inner-city districts tended to lose the largest amount of money under the block-grant approach, 75% of the districts gained funds under Chapter 2 and per-pupil spending for nonpublic schools increased.

Much of this curriculum development undertaken by the states seems to have responded to Secretary of Education William J. Bennett's agenda of "choice, content, character, and citizenship." In his initial distribution of more than $2.5 million in discretionary grants to 34 organizations, Bennett made 11 awards to organizations desiring to develop materials in character education and seven to those interested in strengthening the academic content of the curriculum.

The most controversial of Bennett's initiatives was his attempt to modify the federal government's approach to bilingual education. He proposed several changes in the regulations governing the distribution of bilingual education funds: Allow districts to increase the English-language component of bilingual programs, encourage them to mainstream limited-English-proficiency students more rapidly, and require districts to assume increased financial responsibility for the programs. His proposals were hailed by many who criticized the practice of teaching such students in their native language and attacked by those who saw the new proposals as jeopardizing the educational rights and opportunities of such students.

1990–1999: Technological Constructionism

Throughout much of the 1990s, conservatives would address their concerns with education via teacher certification (National Board certification), standards-based curriculum (America's Choice), as well as other similar programs. The standards-based and technological reform movement continued to gain support at the national, state, and local levels. This was especially true with regard to having chief state officers (politically elected state commissioners of education) disseminate and enforce tests and measures of educational competency. With more interest focused on standards and student achievement, the U.S. Department of Education and Congress began looking at more effective ways to close the achievement gap between students in wealthy and poor communities.

It was during this time that Jonathan Kozol's (1991) publication of *Savage Inequalities* exposed the gross disparities existing between public school districts serving the poorest of the poor and the most affluent sectors of American society. Kozol's work shed light on overlapping inequalities emergent in public education. Such disparities merely reflected the growing gap between rich and poor exacerbated by the Reaganomics of the previous decade (*History of Education,* 2003).

On March 26, 1994, President Clinton's Goals 2000: Educate America Act, was passed by the U.S. Congress. This bill was intended to

> improve learning and teaching by providing a national framework for education reform; to promote the research, consensus building, and systemic changes needed to ensure equitable educational opportunities and high levels of educational achievement for all American students; . . . [and] to promote the development and adoption of a voluntary national system of skill standards and certifications. (History of Education, 2003, para. 1)

Part A of the legislation outlined national goals for education, to be achieved by the year 2000. The goals were organized in eight categories: (1) school readiness; (2) school completion; (3) student achievement and citizenship (including access to physical and health education); (4) teacher education and professional development; (5) mathematics and science; (6) adult literacy and lifelong learning; (7) safe, disciplined, and drug-free schools; and (8) school and home partnership.

The Goals 2000 Technology Plan, built upon local, state, and regional initiatives in technology and telecommunications was a major part of the technological constructionism reform movement. Goals 2000 included such programs as the Star Schools project as well as the growing demand for and use of the Internet. The planning and implementation efforts of the Goals 2000 Technology Plan greatly helped the enhancement of telecommunications in education.

To help schools and communities, especially those with high concentrations of poor children, meet higher education standards, Congress and the U.S. Department of Education in 1997 also developed the Comprehensive School Reform Demonstration (CSRD) program (Partnerships 1990–2000: Ten Years of Supporting Education, 2003). The CSRD program was designed to give schools more flexible funding to adopt research-based models that focused on improving the whole school, not just specific students or subject areas. CSRD grants created a wave of interest among schools and districts, all seeking to improve teaching and learning and to meet higher education standards. The grants allowed schools to choose among a new and wider range of research-based models, many of which provided both strategies and technical assistance for school improvement and student achievement.

More and more communities began to realize the pressing needs and challenges of public schools as the nation increased its focus on new education reform strategies. School systems were being asked to aim higher academically and do more for students and families, but many lacked the resources (financial, human, and administrative) needed to accomplish these ambitious goals. In light of this situation, partnerships emerged as a powerful strategy for strengthening and improving schools. For many communities, meeting higher education standards and special education needs was often dependent on finding more resources to apply to the task.

For example, new legislation in the 1990s restructured IDEA (Individuals with Disabilities Education Act) into four parts: Part A, General Provisions; Part B, Assistance for Education of All Children with Disabilities; Part C, Infants and Toddlers with Disabilities; and Part D, National Activities to Improve Education of Children with Disabilities (Summary of the Individuals with Disabilities Education Act [IDEA], 2003). Affirmative action programs were also becoming more prevalent during this time of technological constructionism. A new focus on children's rights and school safety emerged following the aftermath of such tragedies as the Columbine High School shooting. A move toward home schooling was on the rise as well.

School leaders searched for new ways to use local resources to meet education goals and current challenges. Building on new coalitions of schools and communities forced a move away from individualism and toward partnerships at the end of the century. With the assistance of university and college programs, schools began providing much-needed training and professional development to teachers. In addition, partnerships with small and large businesses emerged to help school officials learn how better to leverage their human and financial resources. Through successful collaborations with community agencies, public schools started blending resources and offering a continuum of comprehensive and preventive services. A transition to a new more federal conservative privatistic movement could be seen in the offing.

2000–Present: New Privatistic Conservatism

With a new privatistic conservative agenda, a focus continues on making all students perform alike. Competency testing and standardizing the curriculum became the norm. It is as if an interest in students and their emotional state had been pushed to the background overnight. With a new move to standardization and testing, the "education industry" quickly became a major financial entity. Elementary and secondary schools alone account for the expenditure of $389 billion. Corporate and business education ($65 billion), government education ($42 billion), vocational training ($23 billion), and consumer learning ($21 billion) quantify the scale of the educational industry (Wiles & Lundt, 2004).

During the Republican administration in 2001, educational reform moved away from technological constructionism and returned to a more privatistic and conservative nature. This is especially the case with President George W. Bush's move toward charter schools, vouchers, and tax credits. Supporters for charter schools, vouchers, and tax credits believed that the government should not be in the business of running schools. State-funded vouchers should pay for privately run education at private schools, parochial schools, charter schools, home schooling, or whatever schools parents choose. "Charter schools" were generally considered publicly funded and publicly controlled schools that were privately run. They were usually required to adhere to fewer district rules than regular public schools. "Vouchers," on the other hand, were considered by the Republican administration as a means of implementing school choice— parents were to be given a "voucher" by the school district, which entitled them to choose their public school or private school ("Parents Choose Schools via Vouchers," 2003). This same movement was initially called the School Choice Movement. "School Choice" referred to a school district allowing parents to decide in which school within the district to enroll their children. The underlying philosophy of school choice appeared to be that parents should have the right to choose how their children were educated, regardless of income level. The political issue became whether to allow the choice to include private schools, parochial schools, and home schooling at taxpayer expense ("Parents Choose Schools via Vouchers," 2003).

Another aspect of the new privatistic conservative approach linked vouchers and charter schools to a move toward standards, assessment, and accountability of public schools. This came with the passage of President George W. Bush's No Child Left Behind Act in 2001. According to the 2003 Education Commission of the States, the No Child Left Behind Act (NCLB) and the revised Elementary and Secondary Education Act are blends of new requirements, incentives, and resources, and they pose significant challenges for states. The law sets deadlines for states to expand the scope and frequency of student testing, revamp their accountability systems, and guarantee that every teacher is qualified in his or her subject area. NCLB requires states to make demonstrable annual progress in raising the percentage of students' proficiency in reading and math, and in narrowing the test-score gap between advantaged and disadvantaged students.

According to Jay Mathews, *Washington Post* staff writer, NCLB is an ambitious law and forces states to move faster and further to improve the achievement of every student. Mathews (2003) states, "Rarely has such a gulf existed between the authors of a major piece of federal legislation and its executors—in this case, the 90,000 public schools across the country" (p. A12).

Something must change. The focus on annual yearly progress, narrow standards, and NCLB's political grip on education cannot reflect the shared vision that is needed for the future. According to authors Jon Wiles and John Lundt (2004), we have entered an era of global knowledge exchange and application and yet schools have not been able to make the conversion. They note that in order for our schools even to begin to respond to the kind of political paradigm shift needed, they would first have to develop the following:

- New avenues for learning and communicating would have to be designed.
- Standardization of the curriculum would have to be de-emphasized.
- Human differences and capabilities would have to be acknowledged.
- New facilities would have to be envisioned and constructed.
- Huge sums of start-up capital for technology would have to be expended.
- Large investments in technological training would have to be allocated.
- A new kind of teacher would have to recruited.
- Teachers and students would have to be networked and allowed freedom.
- Knowledge would have to be valued for its application, not acquisition.

To appreciate the difficulty of administrating the above changes, one only needs to review a 2003 study of facilities, "Modernizing Our Schools," by the National Education Association. This organization estimated that to repair, renovate, and install modern technology in existing schools would cost $322 billion. This figure is approximately ten times what the 50 states are currently spending. School facilities in America have been largely ignored since the inflationary period of the 1980s (Wiles & Lundt, 2004).

Education reform, therefore, continues to be a major problem facing political administrations seeking to limit the role of the federal government in education in the coming years. States and localities continue to grapple with ways to improve their education systems. Whatever the outcome, the reform process presents difficult challenges to this new privatistic conservative movement. At present, it appears that standards-based teaching and high-stakes testing are going to be with educators for a while. Time will tell whether teaching to the standards will succeed or if the standards approach will die under its own weight. While schools are still expected to teach students to read, write, and compute, they are also expected to meet an ever-increasing number of responsibilities related to societal demands (Gilman & Gilman, 2003).

STATE ROLE IN CURRICULUM

When examining the role of the states in curriculum, two problems present themselves. The first is the fact that the states differ significantly in the extent to which they are centralized, retaining authority at the state level, or decentralized, delegating authority to the local districts.

The second difficulty is that the patterns of state influence have shifted with time. While education is identified by the United States Constitution as a state responsibility, in years past the states often chose to delegate that authority, at least in curricular matters, to local districts.

Curriculum Tip

Forty-nine of the 50 states have adopted state standards.

What has caused such an increase in the influence of the states? Doyle and Hartle (1985) posit several reasons: the increased quality and competence of state governments, the concern over school quality stimulated by reports of declining SAT scores and by the reform publications, a growing body of research on school effectiveness, an insistent public demand to make schools more accountable, and a conviction that high-quality education would ensure economic growth.

While these problems of differences persist from state to state with variations over time, some constants prevail about the nature of the states' influence over curricula. In general, most states have adopted policies and procedures regulating the following matters:

1. Specifying time requirements for the school year, for the school day, and for particular subjects

2. Mandating specific subjects, such as English and mathematics, and requiring instruction in such specific areas as alcohol and drug abuse, driver safety, and the American economic system

3. Setting graduation requirements

4. Developing programs for such special groups as the handicapped and those for whom English is a second language

5. Mandating procedures for the adoption of textbooks and other instructional materials

6. Specifying the scope and sequence of topics to be covered in various subjects and grades

7. Mandating a testing program at specific grades in certain critical areas

The last three matters listed—the adoption of textbooks, the scope and sequence of the curriculum, and the testing program—perhaps deserve some careful attention here. First, according to Van Geel (1979), 20 states have strong textbook-adoption laws. Perhaps the strongest and most restrictive of these are found in Texas. In Texas, the state periodically adopts a small number of approved textbooks in a given field, such as secondary English grammar and composition. School districts that select their texts from that approved list receive those texts without charge from the state textbook depository. If a district wishes to adopt a text not on the approved list, then it must use its own funds. Obviously, in a time of limited educational funding, few districts bother to adopt books other than those on the approved list.

Because teachers rely greatly on the textbook in making their own curricular choices, strong adoption laws like those of Texas have the effect of standardizing the curriculum. In a sense, the state controls the curriculum by selecting the texts, and the issue of textbook quality becomes a major curriculum concern in such states. This issue was dramatized in 1985 when William Honig, commissioner of education for the state of California, announced that the state board of education had rejected all the science books recommended by its committee because none of those books adequately dealt with the subject of evolution.

In dealing with the scope and sequence of the curriculum, most state offices of education seem to be at an intermediate position between centralization and decentralization. The predominant pattern is for a given subject-matter office, such as the Division of Mathematics Education, to develop and disseminate general guidelines, not to prescribe specific content and placement. These general guidelines, often called "frameworks," typically indicate the goals to be achieved in that subject area, summarize present theory and research dealing with that subject, and recommend two or three alternative curricular patterns for achieving the goals. Local districts can then use the state frameworks in developing their own more specific curricula.

THE ROLE OF PROFESSIONAL ORGANIZATIONS

At the national level, such influence takes three forms. First, as noted above, professional groups such as the Council for Exceptional Children and the National Education Association are at times highly effective in lobbying for or against curriculum-related legislation. Second, several professional organizations, such as the National Council of Teachers of Mathematics, attempt to influence the written curriculum by publishing curricular guidelines or model scope-and-sequence charts. These professional publications seem to be effective in reaching only a limited audience of subject-matter curriculum specialists. School administrators and classroom teachers for the most part do not give them much attention: They are usually perceived as too "idealistic," insensitive to the realities of the classroom. Finally, they attempt to influence local practice by sponsoring institutes and workshops in which new programs and approaches are explained and demonstrated. Such show-and-tell sessions seem to have an impact upon participants; they return to their schools often eager to share what they have learned.

Curriculum Tip

Professional organizations exercise their influence at the national, state, and local levels.

At the state level, the professional organizations that seem most influential are those with large memberships and strong lobbyists—the teachers' and administrators' associations that fight to protect the interests of their constituencies. In many states, the state teachers' association is so active politically that it can be the determining factor in close elections and thus has significant influence with both office holders and candidates. At the local level, professional associations' attempts to influence curricula have been curtailed with the passing of the No Child Left Behind Act (NCLB). Many states are following explicit directives from their state boards of education or legislatures. Also, because the Education Commission of the States began tracking states' progress toward meeting the components of NCLB, local school districts across the nation, and especially teachers, are less influential in determining curriculum than in the past (Christie, 2005).

THE COURTS

Increasingly, the courts seem to have played an active role in curriculum. Both federal and state courts have become so active in this area that some educators now speak of the "court-ordered curriculum."

Consequent to several decisions by the federal courts, Van Geel (1979) examined school programs and points programs that might be termed constitutionally required. Based on his analysis of the major decisions by federal courts in the area of curriculum and program, certain salient features of such a required program emerge. First, it must be secular, but not militantly secular. The schools cannot establish a religion of secularism. Second, English may be the chief language of instruction, as long as non–English-speaking students are assisted in learning it. Third, the program must be minimally adequate for all students, even those with serious limitations of ability and capacity. Antiquated notions of sex roles may not be imposed on students by segregating them for instruction in such courses as industrial arts and home economics. Instructional materials and courses may be politically biased in favor of the free-enterprise system, but teachers and students who hold views favoring some other system of government may not be excluded from the school. As Van Geel notes, the courts in general have determined that students have a constitutional right to receive information and ideas, no matter how distasteful those ideas might seem to the local community.

State courts have taken positions similar to those supported by the federal courts. Several state courts have held that state plans for the financing of education may be unconstitutional if they result in significant differences among local districts in the level of expenditures for education; such differences, the courts have held, violate the equal-protection clause of state constitutions. As Van Geel (1979) notes, a doctrine of a "state-created right to an education" is emerging from the decisions of state courts that will have profound implications for school programs: Education is no longer seen as a privilege, but as a right for all. He also points out that as state legislatures become more active in adopting complex and often ambiguous educational codes, state courts will have increased influence as they resolve issues of the rights, duties, and discretionary authority allocated by those codes.

LOCAL EDUCATIONAL LEADERS

At the local district level, central office administrators and building principals seem to play key roles in influencing curriculum. First, the typical school superintendent perceives himself or herself as relatively weak in the curriculum area and appoints a generalist as an assistant superintendent for curriculum and instruction, who then serves as the district leader in the area of curriculum. Several factors complicate the assistant superintendent's role. First, such individuals are usually assigned an array of responsibilities that always seem to have a higher day-to-day priority—meeting with unhappy parents, conferring with principals about the budget, planning an in-service program. Second, the assistant superintendent for curriculum in even some larger districts is expected to supervise the curriculum with little or no staff support; districts faced with budget problems typically begin to reduce personnel by reducing the size of the central office supervisory staff. Finally, the emphasis on the school as the locus of educational improvement has created confusion in the minds of many assistant superintendents about the importance of their roles in curriculum development and improvement. Despite such complicating factors, the assistant superintendent for curriculum and instruction in most districts is the sole individual exercising general supervision over the entire curriculum.

As noted above, the role of the principal in curriculum leadership seems to vary with the level of schooling. Despite the conventional wisdom that all principals should act as instructional leaders, growing evidence supports that the most effective elementary and secondary principals are quite different in this respect (see, e.g., Firestone & Herriott, 1982; Glatthorn & Newberg, 1984). Elementary principals in the most effective schools tend to take very active roles in curriculum leadership. They play the central role in articulating educational goals and curricular priorities, in influencing teacher perceptions about curricular emphases and approaches, in helping teachers use test results, and in aligning the curriculum. At the secondary level (especially in larger schools), however, the effective principal is more likely to delegate these roles to department heads, whose subject-matter expertise enables them to influence the curricular decision making of secondary teachers.

THE CLASSROOM TEACHER

As discussed in Chapter 1, to a great extent the teacher is the curriculum. As Connelly and Ben-Peretz (1980) note, teachers do not neutrally implement curricula; they adapt, translate, and modify given programs and develop their own. In doing so, they seem to be responding to both internal and external pressures.

The Internal Pressures

First, the teacher needs to satisfy some strong personal needs. In one major study (MacDonald & Leithwood, 1982), teachers indicated that the four strongest rewards, from their perspective, were affiliation, independence, usefulness, and achievement. To begin with, in making curricular decisions, they felt a strong need for affiliation with students—a feeling that they were responding to students' interests, were sensitive to student concerns, and were generating student enthusiasm. Second, they needed a sense of autonomy and independence, a conviction that they had the power to make important decisions. Third, they needed to feel that they were useful—that students needed them, that they were important in the organization. Finally, teachers have a strong need for achievement, a need to feel that they are efficacious in achieving important learning outcomes and helping students succeed. Another major study (Leithwood, Ross, & Montgomery, 1982) found some other strong internal factors besides these: the teachers' past experience ("what works") and the teachers' attitudes and interests.

Professional motivations are also very strong. Here Doyle's (1986) continuing research is most illuminating. Based upon his studies, he finds that teachers are primarily concerned with classroom management, in order to make classroom life more predictable and thus more controllable. The decisions they make about curriculum and instruction are designed to achieve those goals. They standardize the curriculum, reducing or eliminating elements of novelty. They simplify the curriculum, modifying complex elements so that they are easily managed. They routinize instruction in order to reduce the time needed for planning.

The External Pressures

Besides responding to these personal and professional needs, the teacher is also susceptible to numerous external pressures. As Floden and his colleagues (Floden, Porter, Schmidt, Freeman, & Schwille, 1980) note, these sources are multiple and all seem to have some discernible influence on teachers: Their research suggests that teachers are quite malleable when these pressures are brought to bear.

Which external influences are strongest? The conventional wisdom holds that the textbook is the major determiner, but two major studies question this conventional wisdom (Leithwood et al., 1982; Floden et al., 1980). In both these studies, the external factors that teachers reported as being most influential were district curriculum objectives and test results. Other factors, of course, are variably influential: the values and priorities of colleagues; the requirements of administrators; the interests of students; the expectations of parents; and government legislation such as the No Child Left Behind Act, school choice, and vouchers. In fact, it must seem at times to the teachers that they are power brokers, attempting to negotiate several conflicting claims.

The bottom line is that there will have to be major changes in our educational system to accommodate societal and political pressures in this new global age. According to authors Jon Wiles and John Lundt (2004), the future of education in the United States will require five things in order to construct it: (1) a rationale for learning, (2) a learning place, (3) learning mediums, (4) validation of learning, and (5) informed teachers. By contrast, the new vision of education should promise the following:

1. Instead of linear learning, it promises multimedia convergent learning.

2. Instead of instruction, it promises construction and discovery.

3. Instead of teacher-centeredness, it promises student-centeredness.

4. Instead of memorization, it promises exploration and navigation.

5. Instead of place-bound learning, it promises learning anywhere, anytime.

6. Instead of promoting learning as work, it promises learning as natural and motivating.

7. Instead of the teacher as transmitter, it promises the teacher as a facilitator.

The rationale for learning in the past has been politically dominated by the desire of government and educators to have students acquire content or knowledge. The new rationale will have to be that of students' developing a value of knowing as well as requiring a belief that learning is a continuous process that is defined by individual needs and experiences. The key to improving education is having a *shared vision* of teaching and learning.

CHAPTER OVERVIEW

Federal and state governments, professional organizations, local school boards, textbook publishers, accrediting organizations, parent and community groups, school administrators, and classroom teachers all pose conflicting influences that seem to change in their strength from time to time, and in their particular impact upon a given classroom. This chapter provides curriculum leaders who wish to develop or improve curricula an understanding of the politics of curriculum and the way organizations and individuals attempt to influence what is taught in the schools. This chapter presents an overview of the way influences are brought to bear and then examines in greater detail those agencies that seem to have the greatest influence. This chapter addresses the role of the federal government in curriculum development and how it has changed over the years. Chapter 4 gives an overview of the general role of state governments in curriculum development today and how this has changed over the years. Finally, this chapter explains the roles of educational organizations, courts, educational leaders, and classroom teachers on current curriculum development.

CHAPTER TERMS

Scholarly Structuralism

Romantic Radicalism

Privatistic Conservatism

Technological Constructionism

New Privatistic Conservatism

APPLICATIONS

1. Some experts have argued that the difficulty of finding sufficient fiscal resources will shortly reduce state activity in the curriculum field. If that development does occur, and if the federal government continues to take a less active role, which sources of influence do you believe will increase in power?

2. Based on what you now know about the sources of curriculum influence, what advice would you give a superintendent who posed this question to you: "Does our district really need central office curriculum specialists?"

3. Some analysts have reached this conclusion: "All curriculum making is essentially a political process." Would you agree or disagree? Prepare a well-thought-out response to the question.

4. As the conclusion in Application 3 suggests, the federal government has for the most part abandoned the change strategy of funding the development of exemplary generic

curricula. Some have argued that such abandonment was premature—that given greater insight into the change process, such a strategy might be effective. Consider two related issues: Under what circumstances would you recommend that this strategy be reintroduced? What modifications in the approach would you recommend?

5. What advice would you give this fourth-grade teacher: "My principal and the district science supervisor do not agree about what I should emphasize in teaching science. The principal wants me to spend more time on practical applications; the supervisor, on science processes."

6. The biggest public school story in 2002 and 2003 was the No Child Left Behind Act. How has this legislation affected the written curriculum in your school district?

7. Various individuals and/or groups influence curriculum in our states. Complete the chart below to identify the relative influence that you feel individuals or groups have on curriculum.

Perceptions Regarding Curriculum Influence in Your State

The chart below is designed to explore your perceptions regarding the relative influence exerted by various individuals and groups on the curriculum process within the state in which you work. Please identify the state in which you work and rate the relative influence you feel that each individual or group within the state exerts by placing a check ✓ in the most appropriate columns in the chart below.

	Level of Influence				
State:	None	Little	Some	Great	Don't Know
1. Governor					
2. State Department of Education					
3. State Board of Education					
4. Chief State School Officer					
5. State and Local Courts					
6. State Legislature					
7. Local Board of Education					
8. Local Superintendent					
9. Local Principal(s)					
10. Local Teachers					

	Level of Influence				
State:	None	Little	Some	Great	Don't Know
11. Local Community Members					
12. State Administrators' Organization(s)					
13. State Teachers' Association(s)					
14. State Special Interest Groups					
15. Local Teachers' Organization(s)					
16. National Professional (Subject-Area) Organizations					
17. Federal Government					
18. Other:					

CASE STUDY

Richard F. Elmore (1997) in the article "The Politics of Education Reform" wrote that "U.S. elementary and secondary education is a vast and extraordinarily complex enterprise that seems to defy simple generalizations. However, the two central imperatives of U.S. educational governance are dispersed control and political pluralism" (p. 1). He believes that control of education is not decentralized in the United States and that "local control of schools is largely inaccurate and outmoded, especially in the light of the direction education reform has taken in the past decade" (p. 2). In essence, "the idea of political pluralism is more straightforward. It captures a fundamental principle of U.S. politics—that political decisions and actions are the result of competing groups with different resources and capacities vying for influence" (p. 2).

According to Elmore, "the story of U.S. education reform since the 1980s is worthy of either a Gilbert and Sullivan operetta or theater of the absurd, depending upon your tastes" (p. 2). Consider the following, which called for major educational reform: *A Nation at Risk* in 1983, Goals 2000 in 1989, and the No Child Left Behind Act in 2001. Intermittent interventions resembled a "horse trade—greater flexibility and less regulation for schools and school systems in return for tangible evidence of results, reckoned mostly in terms of student achievement" (p. 2). Subsequently, "control of education . . . is only local when schools and school systems appear to be doing the right thing; when they're not, they are fair game for elected officials, at whatever level of government, with a political interest in their performance" (p. 3).

THE CHALLENGE

How can educators, especially curriculum specialists looking for the cutting edge of curriculum and instructional practice, deal with the virtual blizzard of leading-edge advice on curriculum and pedagogy?

Key Issues/Questions

1. Various groups compete for resources and thus require school districts to prioritize their needs to gain political influence and resources. How do politics influence what is included or excluded in curriculum and determine what is funded?

2. What measures can a school district take to leverage resources to enable the district to achieve higher curriculum standards?

3. If the federal government allocates 6% of a district's budget, but mandates a specified curriculum, how do you justify the discrepancy?

4. What questions should curriculum leaders ask before addressing state and federal mandates and embarking on a course of major change within their school districts?

5. What role does politics play in the development of state and national education regulations?

6. What are the differences between internal political pressures and external political pressures?

REFERENCES

Atkin, J. M., & House, E. R. (1981). The federal role in curriculum development, 1950–80. *Educational Evaluation and Policy Analysis, 3*(5), 5–36.

Bell, T. H. (1986). Educational policy development in the Reagan administration. *Phi Delta Kappan, 67,* 487–493.

Berliner, D. C., & Biddle, B. J. (1997). *The manufactured crisis: Myths, fraud, and the attack on America's public schools.* White Plains, NY: Longman.

Christie, K. (2005, January). Stateline: Providing the facts. *Phi Delta Kappan, 86,* 341–342.

Connelly, F. M., & Ben-Peretz, M. (1980). Teachers' roles in the using and doing of research and curricula development. *Curricular Studies, 12,* 95–107.

Curriculum Development Associates. (1972). *Man: A course of study.* Washington, DC: Author.

Doyle, D. P., & Hartle, T. W. (1985). Leadership in education: Governors, legislators and teachers. *Phi Delta Kappan, 66,* 21–28.

Doyle, W. (1986). Classroom organization and management. In M. C. Wittrock (Ed.), *Handbook of research on teaching* (3rd ed., pp. 392–431). New York: Macmillan.

Elmore, R. F. (1997, Fall). The politics of education reform [Electronic version]. *Issues in Science and Technology Online,* 1–3.

Firestone, W. A., & Herriott, R. E. (1982, December). Prescriptions for effective elementary schools don't fit secondary schools. *Educational Leadership, 40,* 51–53.

Floden, R. E., Porter, A. C., Schmidt, W. J., Freeman, D. J., & Schwille, J. R. (1980). *Responses to curriculum pressures: A policy capturing study of teacher decisions about content.* East Lansing, MI: Institute for Research on Teaching.

Gilman, D. A., & Gilman, R. A. (2003, November/December). Standard-based teaching overcoming the side effects. *Principal, 83*(2), 44–48.

Glatthorn, A. A., & Newberg, N. A. (1984, February). A team approach to instructional leadership. *Educational Leadership, 41,* 60–63.

Hertling, J. (1986, March 12). Block grants found to achieve gains. *Education Week,* p. 8.

History of education: Selected moments of the 20th century. (2003). Retrieved November 20, 2004, from http://fcis.oise.utoronto.ca/~daniel_schugurensky/assignment1/1994goals2000.html

Holt, J. (1964). *How children fail.* New York: Dell.

Illich, I. (1972). *Deschooling society.* New York: Harper and Row.

Kliebard, H. M. (1979). Systematic curriculum development, 1890–1959. In J. Schaffarzick & G. Sykes (Eds.), *Value conflicts and curriculum issues* (pp. 197–236). Berkeley, CA: McCutchan.

Kozol, J. (1991). *Savage inequalities: Children in America's schools.* New York: Crown.

Lau v. Nichols, 414 U.S. 563 (1974).

Leithwood, K. A., Ross, J. A., & Montgomery, D. J. (1982). An investigation of teachers' curriculum decision-making. In K. A. Leithwood (Ed.), *Studies in curriculum decision-making* (pp. 14–46). Toronto: Ontario Institute for Studies in Education.

Levine, E. L., & Wexler, E. M. (1981). *P.L. 94-142: An act of Congress.* New York: Macmillan.

Llewellyn, G. (1991). *Teenage liberation handbook: How to quit school and get a real life and education.* Eugene, OR: Lowery House.

Lynch, K. L. (1986). *School finance policy formulation in Pennsylvania: A case study.* Unpublished doctoral dissertation, University of Pennsylvania.

MacDonald, R. A., & Leithwood, K. A. (1982). Toward an explanation of the influences on teacher curriculum decisions. In K. A. Leithwood (Ed.), *Studies in curricular decision making* (pp. 35–51). Toronto: Ontario Institute for Studies in Education.

Marshall, C. (1985, March). *Policymakers' assumptive worlds: Informal structures in state education policymaking.* Paper presented at the meeting of the American Educational Research Association, Chicago.

Mathews. J. (2003). *To educators, "no child" goals out of reach.* Retrieved September 16, 2004, from http://www.washingtonpost.com/ac2/wp-dyn/A15836-2003Sep15?language=printer

Mills v. Board of Education, 348 F. Supp. 866 (D.D.C. 1972).

Parents choose schools via vouchers. (2003). Retrieved May 3, 2004, from http://www.issues2000.org/VoteMatch/q10.asp

Partnerships 1990–2000: Ten years of supporting education. (2003). Retrieved November 20, 2003, from http://www.napehq.org/d.pdf

Ravitch, D. (1983). *The troubled crusade: American education 1945–80.* New York: Basic Books.

Schon, D. A. (1971). *Beyond the stable state.* New York: Random House.

Summary of the Individuals with Disabilities Education Act (IDEA). (2003). Retrieved November 20, 2004, from http://edworkforce.house.gov/issues/108th/education/idea/idea.htm

Van Geel, T. (1979). The new law of the curriculum. In J. Schaffarzick & G. Sykes (Eds.), *Value conflicts and curriculum issues* (pp. 25–72). Berkeley, CA: McCutchan.

Wiles, J., & Lundt, J. (2004). *Leaving school: Finding education.* St. Augustine, FL: Matanzas Press.

Part 2

Curriculum Processes

Chapter 5

CURRICULUM PLANNING

The specific details of the curriculum-planning process are determined by the level and nature of curriculum work; designing a field of studies, improving a program of studies, and developing a course of study involve quite different processes, as the following chapters indicate. Nevertheless, some general planning processes are useful in all curriculum work. This chapter describes a general planning model as well as focuses on the following questions:

- What is a goal-based model of curriculum planning and how does one determine the locus of planning decisions and organizational structures that are needed?
- How can we identify and allocate leadership functions as well as align goals with curricular fields?
- How do we organize, evaluate, change, and provide curriculum resources?

Before answering these questions in detail, it might be useful at the outset to define curriculum planning: *Curriculum planning* is the specification and sequencing of major decisions to be made in the future with regard to the curriculum.

Key to Leadership

Successful curriculum leaders know that a goal-based model of curriculum planning provides organizing strategies to determine the locus of control in decision making and what organizational structures are needed.

A GOAL-BASED MODEL OF CURRICULUM PLANNING

Although several planning models are available to educators, one that seems very effective for curriculum planning is the *goal-based model* described on the next page. Exhibit 5.1 lists and briefly explains all the steps in the model. The rest of this chapter then explains the steps in the model more fully.

Exhibit 5.1   A Goal-Based Curriculum Planning Model

Organize for Planning

1. Determine the locus of planning decisions: differentiate between district and school planning responsibilities.

2. Determine the organizational structures needed to facilitate planning, and set up those structures.

3. Identify leadership functions and allocate those functions appropriately.

Establish the Planning Framework

1. Align the district's educational goals with appropriate curricular fields.

2. Develop a curriculum database.

3. Develop a planning calendar based upon leaders' assessments of organizational priorities.

Carry Out Specific Planning Activities

1. Conduct needs assessment in high-productivity areas by using standardized tests, curriculum-referenced tests, and other measures and data sources; use assessment results to determine the need for curriculum development or improvement.

2. Organize task forces to carry out development or improvement projects, and monitor the work of the task forces.

3. Evaluate development or improvement projects.

4. Make necessary organizational changes and provisions for effective implementation.

5. Secure resources needed for new or revised curricula.

6. Provide staff development needed for effective implementation.

The model begins with three organizing strategies. First, the leaders distinguish between district- and school-based responsibilities to clarify the locus of decision making. They then decide what organizational structures are needed, appointing the needed advisory groups and task forces. Finally, they allocate specific leadership functions to district and school staff.

With those organizational moves accomplished, leaders take steps to establish a framework for planning. First, leaders align the broad educational goals of the district with the several fields of study, so that each field of study has a clear set of curricular goals for which it is responsible. Then the district develops a computerized knowledge base for curriculum, systematizing the information needed for good curriculum work. Leaders then assess general district priorities and develop a 5-year planning calendar, showing the major events and foci of the curriculum-improvement process.

With the framework established, the specific planning activities are undertaken. With the goals thus stipulated, a needs assessment is conducted, using standardized and curriculum-referenced tests and other appropriate measures, as well as the data stored in the knowledge base. Task forces are appointed to carry out the development and improvement projects suggested by the needs assessment. Their work is evaluated, and appropriate plans are made to implement the new or revised programs effectively.

This goal-based model has several features that recommend it. It is goal-based, ensuring that curriculum revisions are made with general outcomes clearly in mind. It emphasizes feasibility: It assists the district in undertaking only priority projects that leaders believe can be accomplished effectively. It is systematic: Planning decisions are cast in a rational framework that emphasizes orderly progression.

Curriculum Tip

Sharing common goals is key to making curriculum changes in a classroom, school, or district.

Leading change and implementing a goal-based approach often go hand in hand. The key to success in both is a thorough, inclusive curriculum-planning process. The process described and tools provided in this book will assist you in leading change and help guide you through the curriculum-planning process.

DETERMINE THE LOCUS OF PLANNING DECISIONS

Curriculum planning obviously occurs at several levels: at the federal level, when policy decisions and their implementation are planned; at the state level, when state offices of education plan for major changes in graduation requirements; at the district level, when the district plans to revise a field of study; at the school level, when the school revises its program of studies or adds a new course; and at the classroom level, when the teacher plans a unit of study. Because most of the important alterable decisions are made at the district and school levels, the discussion that follows focuses on these two critical levels of planning.

The central question is the balance between district-based and school-based curricular decision making. On the one hand, there are those who argue for strong district control. Fenwick English (1980), for example, acknowledges only two levels of curriculum management, the state and the district. In his curriculum-management system, district policies and curriculum documents completely control what occurs at the school and classroom levels. His views seem to be shared by the leaders of many large school districts, who have attempted in recent years to standardize the curriculum throughout the entire district. For example, curriculum guides issued by the Vermillion School District #13.1, Vermillion, South Dakota, in 2004 not only specified what was to be taught and what materials were to be used, but even indicated when it was to be taught. Here is a sample entry from the district's secondary mathematics curriculum guide (Vermillion School District, 2004):

Grade 7: September 24–October 19. Whole numbers. 3.5 weeks.

The rationale for such standardization speaks in terms of achievement, equity, and efficiency. The first argument is that standardized curricula will result in higher achievement, although no evidence exists to support such a claim. The second is that standardization ensures equity: Every student gets the same curriculum, regardless of school and teacher assignment. Critics would point out that equity does not equal uniformity. The final argument is that the standardized curriculum is more efficient and thus more economical: The district can offer the same type of staff development, order large quantities of the same texts, and develop a single set of curriculum-referenced tests. This claim of efficiency is probably a reasonable one; the issue is whether other considerations are more important.

On the other hand, some argue just as persuasively for school-based curriculum development. Gass (1979) suggests two major reasons for encouraging school-based curriculum development: Schools are clamoring for autonomy, and there is some evidence that centrally developed curricula have been less successful than expected and often are not implemented as planned. Also, as Zmuda, Kuklis, and Kline (2004) note, teachers desire to have a more active role in curriculum development—and it is more likely that school-based processes will provide for such active participation. Additional support for school-based curricula could be inferred from the large body of school-effectiveness research, which generally suggests that the school, not the district, is the primary unit for improvement (e.g., see Joyce, 1986). However, several reservations might be noted about granting schools too much curricular autonomy. The resulting collection of different curricula would be difficult to coordinate and manage; the process would result in much inefficiency and duplication of effort; and quality might be adversely affected, because the school-based curriculum team would probably not have as many resources as district teams.

Because no conclusive research exists on this issue, it would seem wise for each local district to resolve the matter through a clear analysis of the options, weighing such factors as the size of the district, the competence of district and school leaders, and the degree of heterogeneity throughout the district. The major issues involved here, as listed in Exhibit 5.2, should be discussed and resolved by the superintendent and the district leadership team; those decisions can then be used as policy guidelines for future curriculum planning.

One of the areas most affected by the school-based versus the district-based approach to curriculum planning is the area of technology. In order to assess the impact of technology use on students and staff, it is important to establish achievable outcomes for the use of technology. In developing curricular outcomes, it is wise to consult local, state, or national technology use standards. Districts or states that have no adopted standards should consider reviewing International Society for Technology in Education (ISTE) standards at http://www.iste.org.

DETERMINE THE ORGANIZATIONAL STRUCTURES NEEDED

With those district and school delineations made, the district leadership team should next determine which organizational structures are needed to provide ongoing curriculum leadership. Many school districts seem to err here by appointing too many standing curriculum committees. Such a mistake results in a cumbersome bureaucratic structure that only complicates curriculum planning. It is more desirable to have a simple and flexible organizational structure that can provide the continuity required and also respond quickly to changing needs. An examination of both the research and reports of effective practice suggest that the following structures would accomplish those goals.

Exhibit 5.2 Issues in District/School Curriculum Decision Making

---

1. May the school modify district goals so that those goals are more appropriate for the students of that school?

2. May the school reconceptualize and reorganize fields of study, using such approaches as interdisciplinary courses and "broad-fields" curricula?

3. May the school develop its own instructional objectives or modify district objectives, as long as those objectives are consonant with district goals?

4. May the school recommend which instructional processes and activities are to be used?

5. May the school make its own recommendations about the pacing of instruction?

6. May the school develop and select its own tests for evaluating student achievement?

7. May the school select its own instructional materials, as long as the materials meet district guidelines?

8. May the school evaluate its own program of studies and make needed changes, including the addition or elimination of specific courses?

District Curriculum Advisory Council

The District Curriculum Advisory Council is a standing committee, with members appointed by the superintendent of schools. Its membership will vary with the size of the school district. The following members or constituencies should be represented:

- The school superintendent or assistant superintendent
- The school district curriculum directors or supervisors
- Secondary school principals
- Elementary school principals
- Teachers
- Parents and other community representatives
- Secondary school students

The advisory council, as its name suggests, serves in an advisory capacity only, recommending to the superintendent what problems require systematic attention and what processes might be used to solve those problems. Typically it would meet four times during the school year to identify problems, review planning calendars, receive evaluation reports, and review curriculum proposals. Its members would serve for a stated period of time; a rotating 3-year term of office would ensure both continuity and fresh ideas.

Larger districts may wish to establish a separate community advisory council composed of parents and representatives of the business and professional community. Most superintendents, however, seem to feel that such separate councils complicate the work of the curriculum advisory group and may even attempt to usurp certain board functions.

School Curriculum Advisory Council

Each school should also have a standing advisory group, especially if individual schools are to have a large measure of curricular autonomy. Its members should be nominated by the faculty and appointed by the principal. The school advisory council would include the principal, subject-matter specialists or grade-level leaders, teachers, and parents. Students from upper grade levels might also be included. One of the teachers and one of the parents on the school advisory council should represent the school on the district council to ensure good communication between the two advisory groups. The school advisory council advises the principal on school-based curricular issues, in a manner similar to the district advisory council. Its members would also serve for a specified term, like those on the district council.

In smaller school districts, there might not be a need for separate school councils; the district council could be composed so that it had representatives from each school. In either case, these standing groups provide the continuity required for effective planning.

Curriculum Task Forces

In addition to these two standing committees, the superintendent would appoint a number of task forces to deal with any major issues that might need attention. These task forces would be seen as working groups, numbering from perhaps 6 to 12 members, depending upon the nature of the problem. Members would be appointed on the basis of the technical skills required for the job; at the same time, the superintendent should be sure that the membership is generally representative of the types of professional roles that exist in the district. Thus, most task forces would include a curriculum specialist, a principal, and several knowledgeable teachers. If a task force needed additional technical assistance, it would request approval from the superintendent to secure a qualified consultant.

Each task force would be given a specific problem to solve, a deadline for developing and implementing the solution, and the resources required to do the job. Ordinarily, a task force would continue in existence only until the problem had been solved. These temporary ad hoc groups give the school system the flexibility it needs and in this sense complement the standing bodies.

An example might be the formation of a technology task force committee. A technology task force committee can be made up of administrators, teachers, parents, and community members. At least six of the members of this larger committee can be asked to form a special steering committee.

Curriculum Planning Tip

Giving the task force a special title is an important part of the process. Some school districts call their Task Force Council "The Vision Alive Committee."

This select committee can assist with the development of the district's vision and curricula mission statements as well as assist with the development of guidelines for technological infrastructure. The committee can also help to formulate guidelines for equipment use and programs designed to enhance communication and technological awareness. This type of task force committee is representative of how a school district special committee might be organized. Developing an effective task force or select committee can be a crucial part of the process of curriculum planning.

IDENTIFY AND ALLOCATE LEADERSHIP FUNCTIONS

During the period from 1980 to 2003, a somewhat common pattern of curriculum staffing developed in larger districts across the nation. Typically, an assistant superintendent for curriculum and instruction was expected to provide systemwide leadership. The central office staff also included several subject-matter coordinators, who usually were responsible for coordinating the curriculum from K–12 in a designated content area. At the school level, the building principal was expected to provide leadership; in larger secondary schools the curriculum responsibility was usually delegated to an assistant principal for curriculum and instruction. In large elementary schools, either grade-level leaders or teacher specialists, especially in reading and mathematics, assisted the principal. All high school–level department chairs were appointed to provide subject matter leadership. Some middle school principals relied upon grade-level team leaders; others used department heads.

In recent years, this prevailing pattern has been seriously altered. Three factors seem to be at work here. The first, of course, is money. Many districts, forced to economize by tax caps, considered central office staff the most expendable and dismissed all central office curriculum supervisors. The second factor is dissatisfaction with the prevailing pattern. Much of this dissatisfaction focused on the performance of district coordinators and school department heads; in many cases, they seemed not to be providing the leadership needed. The final factor is the widespread conviction, supported by some research, that the principal should be the instructional leader. If that is the case, then, it is reasoned, district coordinators and department heads are not needed.

These interacting forces seem to have decimated the ranks of curriculum leadership and, in many districts, have led to a state of uncertainty and confusion in which no curricular leadership exists. A busy assistant superintendent, suffering from role overload, attempts to respond to curricular crises, and building principals, overwhelmed by administrative responsibilities, wonder what it means to provide curriculum leadership.

The response to this crisis, it would seem, would not be to return to the previous pattern and simply hire additional personnel to fill these old positions. A more useful answer is to analyze the leadership functions required at both the district and school levels, allocate these functions to those best able to perform them, and then decide what additional staff, if any, are needed—in some cases, creating new kinds of positions. This specification and allocation process can begin by having the district curriculum advisory council develop a form like the one shown in Exhibit 5.3. It lists all the leadership functions relating to curriculum, organizing them into four categories based upon the level and the focus of the responsibility. The intention here is to describe these functions as clearly as possible, because too many curriculum workers have only a vague understanding of their responsibilities.

The advisory council should first review the form to ensure that it includes all the functions they consider important and that it uses language that communicates clearly to the educators in that district. At that point, the superintendent or the assistant superintendent, with input from central office staff and the building principals, should take over the complex and sensitive task of reallocating and reassigning those functions for maximum effectiveness. The leaders should

Exhibit 5.3   Functions of Curriculum Leadership

Function	Now	Assign	New
At the district level—for all areas of the curriculum			
1. Articulate district curriculum goals and priorities.	**Supt.**	**Supt.**	
2. Chair district advisory council.	**Supt.**	**Asst.**	
3. Develop and monitor curriculum budget.	**Supt.**	**Supt.**	
4. Develop and implement plans to evaluate curricula and use evaluative data.			**Dir. of Curr.**
5. Identify and prioritize curricular problems to be solved.			
6. Develop curriculum planning calendar.			
7. Appoint task forces and review their reports, proposals, and products.			
8. Develop and monitor processes for materials selection and evaluation.			
9. Plan districtwide staff-development programs required by curricular changes.			
10. Represent district on curricular matters in relationships with state and intermediate unit curriculum offices.			
11. Evaluate district-level curriculum staff.			
12. Develop general district guideline for aligning curricula at the school level.			
At the district level—for special areas of the curriculum			
1. Develop and implement plans to evaluate curriculum, as specified in district planning calendar.			
2. Use evaluative data to identify specific curricular problems, and develop proposals to remedy them.			
3. Evaluate articulation of the curriculum between elementary and middle schools and between middle and high schools.			
4. Provide leadership in developing and improving K–12 curriculum materials in that special area.			
5. Implement district guidelines in selecting and evaluating texts and other instructional materials.			
6. Provide leadership in implementing K–12 staff-development programs for that specific area.			
At the school level—for all areas of the curriculum			
1. Implement plans to monitor and align the curriculum.			
2. Evaluate curricula at the school level and use evaluative data to identify school-level problems.			
3. Ensure that important skills that cut across the disciplines are appropriately taught and reinforced in those disciplines.			
4. Monitor coordination of the curriculum between those content areas where close coordination is important.			
5. Develop school-based budget for curriculum needs, reflecting school priorities.			
At the school level—for special areas of the curriculum			
1. Supervise teachers with respect to curriculum implementation.			
2. Assist teachers in developing instructional plans based upon curriculum guides.			
3. Implement school-based staff development required by curriculum change.			
4. Select instructional materials.			
5. Help teachers use student-evaluation results to make needed modifications in curriculum.			

first analyze which individuals in the district are presently responsible for those functions, entering role designations in the "Now" column. In many instances, they will indicate that no one is presently performing those functions.

After assessing how effectively those functions are being performed and how equitably they are distributed, they should next determine where changes should be made in present assignments, entering those decisions in the "Assign" column. The entries in this column yield a clear picture of which functions can best be discharged by reassigning them to present role incumbents. In some cases, however, it will be apparent that a new role is needed: Several important functions are not being performed successfully, and no one among the present staff is available and competent to assume those critical functions. The allocation of functions to a newly conceived role is reflected by placing the new role title in the "New" column. The first few entries on the form have been completed to show how the form can be used to record and analyze those decisions.

The preliminary decisions are first reviewed by central office staff and school principals and then by the district advisory council, in order to secure their input and keep them informed. The final allocations then become the basis for reconceptualizing present roles and creating any new positions needed. This process thus enables a local district to develop its own staffing pattern, one that reflects its special needs and resources.

Leadership and planning appear to be common threads invariably found in the curricula design of any successful K–12 program. Today's school administrators face one of the most challenging and exciting times in the educational history of this nation. The changes in curriculum that schools are being asked to accommodate can be both academically threatening and liberating for teachers and administrators.

In order to exercise the level of leadership required to ensure the successful integration of planning into the curriculum, principals, curriculum coordinators, and superintendents must reach clear answers to four basic questions:

- What is required to make the improvements we wish to see in the student-centered learning environments of our schools?
- Why do we want to commit a great deal of time and money to a curriculum initiative for change? How are our motives focused on improving student learning?
- Who is the best person to lead the curriculum initiative we are considering?
- Who will be best suited to assess and maintain the quality of curricular programs after the initial stages of implementation are completed?

The ability of the school administrator to shift leadership styles can provide a supportive climate for broad-based discussions between administrators and teachers. Such discussions can also build a platform for shared decision making when opportunities are appropriate. Involving teachers in curricular deliberations may well take a good deal of courage on the part of the administrator, but that courage enables real benefits for student learning.

ALIGN EDUCATIONAL GOALS WITH CURRICULAR FIELDS

Determining the goals for each field of study remains the key step in the goal-based model. Several methods are available to accomplish this task. This chapter explains one method for allocating goals to curriculum fields as an aspect of the planning process; the next chapter explains a somewhat different process for aligning and assessing the several fields for goal conformance as part of the program-improvement process.

1. Specify district educational goals. An educational goal is a general long-term outcome to be accomplished through the total educational program. Most states have developed lists of such goals to be used in all school districts. For example, the Nebraska Department of Education specifies that "for a school building or school district to meet federal accountability, each group of students must meet all target goals for reading, mathematics, writing, high school graduation rate, assessment quality, and student participation" (Christensen, 2004). The state goal for proficiency has a starting point between 61% and 66%, while other states have proficiency goals ranging from 14% to 80%. School districts that have the freedom and wish to develop their own goal statements might well consult Goodlad's (2004) book titled *A Place Called School.* This work includes an excellent set of goal statements that he developed after reviewing a large number of state and district statements. Two other excellent sources are the Association for Supervision and Curriculum Development (ASCD) publication, *A Blueprint for Increasing Student Achievement* (Rettig, McCullough, Santos, & Watson, 2003) and the *Phi Delta Kappan* article, "Responding Effectively to Test-Based Accountability" (Hamilton & Stecher, 2004).

2. Determine which of the educational goals should be accomplished primarily through the courses of study. Many educational leaders neglect this important step; they assume that every educational goal is a curricular goal. Thus, Pennsylvania educators, noting that the state board specifies the development of self-esteem as an educational goal, mistakenly assume that they need to develop courses and units in self-esteem. Many educational goals, like this one, can better be accomplished through other means such as instructional methods or programs, the organizational climate, the activity program, or through the guidance program.

For this reason, the leadership team and school faculties should carefully analyze each educational goal and make a preliminary determination of whether that goal will be accomplished primarily through organized courses of study or through some other means. In this manner, they identify a shorter list of curriculum goals—those general long-term outcomes that are to be accomplished primarily through the organized curriculum. Advisory councils should review their tentative decisions. The input from those groups should then be used to make any needed modifications so that the resulting list represents a broad consensus.

3. Allocate the curricular goals to the several fields of study. Once the curricular goals have been identified, the leadership team, with faculty input, should allocate those goals to appropriate fields of study. A system like this one seems to work.

This is a "top-down" process—one that begins with the district's educational goals and ends with curricular goals for each field. The process can be reversed: Each field can develop its own list of curricular goals, and these can be synthesized into one comprehensive district list. The outcome, not the process, is important: Each field should have a clear list of curricular goals.

Curriculum Tip

A good example of a "top-down" process is the alignment of technology goals into curricular fields.

A school district technology task force often establishes district-level technology goals, but the teachers at a grade level or subject area generally align these goals with their lessons. Teachers often use this template to create a more detailed plan for how they are going to incorporate technology into their individual classrooms. Once created, this document can be shared with the principal and a school-site technology support person.

Technology Planning Goals:

- To improve the quality and effectiveness of teaching and learning with the assistance of technology-based resources
- To promote the inclusion of staff, parents, students, and community in the planning process
- To ensure that technology resources are aligned with district curricula programs and planning
- To facilitate integration of technology with the instructional program in the manner consistent with the district's curriculum ("Overview: School Technology Use Planning," 2004)

DEVELOP A CURRICULUM DATABASE

A second key aspect of the planning framework is development of a comprehensive curriculum database. The argument here is that good curriculum work requires extensive knowledge about resources, inputs, and constraints. To that end, each district should develop a computerized knowledge base that can be used in assessing needs and developing curricula. What should be included? The temptation is to collect too much information, just because it is available or seems interesting. It makes more sense to collect and organize only that information likely to be used. Exhibit 5.4 lists the kinds of information that seem most essential in the needs-assessment process; as will be explained in Chapter 8, a shorter list of information needs can be useful in the course-planning process.

Such information stored in a computerized data bank will greatly facilitate the work of the several task forces. Consider, for example, how the data bank would be used by a task force appointed to develop a new course for middle school students in "Personal Well-Being" that would combine health and physical education. They would first get comprehensive data about the students likely to take the course, in order to become aware of students' needs, limitations, and capacities: "About 15% of the students will have limited English proficiency; we may need a separate section or special materials for them." Next, they would get data on student participation in extracurricular activities and note that very few students participate in activities that require a high level of physical exercise: "We should include a unit that deals explicitly with the value of and opportunities for in-school aerobics activities." They then would retrieve information about other professional resources available—state curriculum guides, guides from other districts, banks of learning objectives: "A nearby district has just started a pilot program similar to the one we're planning; let's see how it's going." Then they would take a look at faculty data: "The teachers we plan to use do not seem to have an up-to-date knowledge of nutrition; we had better plan some special staff development here and beef up the teacher's guide for that unit." Finally, they would examine community resources: "The hospital dietitian has offered to share her media on good nutrition for the young." For the task force, the curriculum database is invaluable.

Exhibit 5.4   Information for Curriculum Database

Community Resources
1. People with knowledge, expertise, and influence
2. Organizations and places useful as resources

Students
1. Date of birth, sex, and ethnic identity
2. Eligibility for federal or state assistance programs
3. Parents' occupations and marital status
4. Verbal and mathematical abilities and IQ score
5. Talents, skills, and special interests
6. School achievement: standardized test scores and curriculum-referenced test scores
7. English proficiency; native language if other than English
8. Limitations: physical, emotional, and learning disabilities
9. Learning styles and cognitive levels
10. School record: subjects studied, grades, and attendance
11. Career and educational plans
12. Extracurricular activities
13. Community activities

Faculty
1. Subjects and grades certified to teach
2. Present assignment
3. Special interests and competencies
4. Recent professional development: courses, workshops, etc.

School
1. Courses offered and enrollments
2. Extracurricular activities and student participation

Other Resources
1. State curriculum guides
2. Curriculum guides from other districts
3. Other sources of learning objectives
4. Professional materials and resources for teachers

Having a curriculum database team can be very beneficial in aiding the process. The team would have the task of translating national and state content standards into academic performance indicators from pre-kindergarten to Grade 12, which can then be adopted as official achievement targets for the district. Next, the district would develop yearlong curriculum maps for each subject and grade level that sequence the topics, process, skills, and materials needed to master the performance indicators (March & Peters, 2002).

Following implementation and assessment of the performance indicators, ADAM (Academic Data Analysis and Management, an electronic system for data management that enables teachers to monitor student mastery) can help a district connect data from each student's classroom performance with other measures of student learning (e.g., state test scores, standardized test scores, academic intervention history, prior letter grades, and attendance; March & Peters, 2002).

Developing an effective data analysis program to improve curriculum is therefore a vitally important component. When planning change, school leaders will find that a technology database and a system of data analysis can be used to facilitate systemic curriculum changes regarding issues between teachers and administrative personnel, between administrators and parents, and among administrators within the same district or throughout a region. For example, databases in the area of curriculum can be used to: determine professional development interests and needs, develop a background of skills and usage, and identify individuals willing to share ideas and techniques as well as to inventory the type and level of materials and resources used in the classroom. Conducting an in-depth analysis of your curricular needs is, therefore, a crucial part of any program.

DEVELOP A PLANNING CALENDAR

One of the central leadership functions is to develop and monitor the district's curriculum-planning calendar, a master that assists district leaders in making systematic plans for curriculum evaluation and development.

As Exhibit 5.5 suggests, the planning calendar should include the six steps listed as "specific planning activities" in Exhibit 5.1. Note that a distinction is made between major and other fields, simply to assist in the planning process, not to depreciate the importance of such areas as art and industrial arts. Provision is also made for evaluating the several programs of study. Note that, in this example, the district has chosen to do a needs assessment each year of one major and one other field and one program level. With such a schedule, the district would be able in a 5-year period to assess all major fields, five other fields, and every program level.

The superintendent and the district leadership team should begin by tentatively mapping out a 5-year plan that would indicate year by year the major projects to be undertaken. They should make these decisions based upon their own analysis of district needs and their own priorities for improvement. The decision about how many projects should be initiated will, of course, be influenced by their perception of district needs and resources. A large school district with well-staffed curriculum and evaluation offices could obviously plan for many more projects than a smaller district with an overextended staff. A newly appointed superintendent given a mandate by the board to improve the curriculum would want to plan for a more ambitious and comprehensive development program than a superintendent who has been presiding for several years over a district that seems to be making excellent progress.

Exhibit 5.5   Curriculum-Planning Calendar

Major Projects	2005–2006	2006–2007	2007–2008
1. Needs assessment, major fields	Lang. arts	Math	Science
2. Needs assessment, other fields	Ind. arts	Art	
3. Needs assessment, programs	**Middle**	**Elem.**	**High**
4. Task forces appointed, at work		Lang. arts Ind. arts	Math Art
5. Evaluate projects		Lang. arts Ind. arts	Math Art
6. Organizational provisions		Lang. arts Ind. arts	Math Art
7. Resources selected and provided		Lang. arts Ind. arts	Math Art
8. Staff development			Lang. arts Ind. arts

Those tentative decisions should be reviewed by district and school administrators and supervisors and then be shared with the district advisory council for its input before a final form of the calendar is developed. The final form of the calendar can then be used by leaders to develop budget requests, appoint task forces, and monitor their progress.

Curriculum Tip

The planning calendar should mark important reference points for the planning committee to reach in order to keep the project on schedule.

Administrators and curriculum committee members must work closely together to construct a practical calendar for any curriculum project. Realistic target dates are a key ingredient, and committee members should be included as this is really the only way to ensure a workable schedule of events. In this respect, it is important to remember that committee members are usually chosen because they know how to get tasks done, and they are also the ones who usually have the best idea of how long it will take to accomplish these tasks.

CONDUCT NEEDS ASSESSMENT

The next major step in the model is to conduct a needs assessment. The term *needs assessment* seems to be used often in the profession without much understanding of what is involved. Here Kaufman's (1982) definition seems most useful: A needs assessment is a process of identifying

Exhibit 5.6   Establishing a Data-Driven School Culture Checklist

---

What does the district want to know?

Where to look:

- Current district goals.
- Patterns in data.
- Upcoming district decisions.
- Questions raised by teachers, administrators, or the community.

How will the district find out?

What to do:

- Form data team.
- Conduct inventory of data currently compiled in the district and determine format (electronic or paper)
- Assess technological capacity of the district to manage and analyze data.
- Determine the extent to which personnel in the district have time, skills, and willingness to engage in data-driven projects.
- Identify indicators of input, process, and outcome variables related to goals.
- Determine which additional data are reasonable to collect.
- Train staff to collect and use data.
- Analyze and disaggregate data.

What does the district do next?

How to proceed:

- Establish benchmarks and measure progress toward goals over time.
- Develop action or school improvement plans.
- Communicate findings.

SOURCE: Noyce, P., Perda, D., & Traver, R. (2000, February). Creating data-driven schools. *Educational Leadership*, 57(5), pp. 52–57. Used with permission.

gaps between what is and what should be. In his comprehensive review, he identifies and analyzes 17 needs-assessment models. His analysis of these 17 models leads him to conclude that they share several major shortcomings: They focus on internal elements, ignoring the societal impact and payoffs; they shy away from empirical data, relying too much on people's perceptions; they place too much emphasis on such "middle-level" concerns as learner characteristics, methods, and test scores, slighting long-term outcomes; most are really status surveys and thus give too much attention to "what is"; and most are not sufficiently comprehensive, limiting attention to only a few components (see Exhibit 5.6).

To deal with these deficiencies, Kaufman advocates a rather complex and sophisticated model that would use multiple data about inputs, processes, products, outputs, and outcomes and would be sensitive to both the internal organization and the external society. The major drawback of the model he advocates is that it would seem to be too complicated, time-consuming, and expensive for most districts to implement.

A simpler needs-assessment model that avoids many of the pitfalls noted in Kaufman's review could be built upon several of the elements explained in this chapter and in Chapter 12 (note that this section explains the needs-assessment process in developing a field of study; the next chapter explains how to assess needs in improving a program of studies). First, the district would develop a comprehensive curriculum database, as noted above. This would provide information about what Kaufman and others call the two major "inputs"—the teachers and the learners. Next, the district would develop for each field a clear set of curricular goals, using the processes described above. These specify the ends to be accomplished. Then the district would evaluate selected fields of study, assessing the major components of the field explained in Chapter 1: the written curriculum, the supported curriculum, the taught curriculum, the tested curriculum, and the learned curriculum. Thus, if a district is concerned with assessing curricular needs in a single field of study, the process is a rather straightforward one.

On the other hand, if a district wishes to make a needs assessment that focuses on a general curriculum goal (not a single field), then the process is slightly more complex. This process is explained below, using as an example the general goal of "enhancing creativity."

The process begins with a vague sense of deficiency. Some individual or group asks, "Are we doing all we can in the curriculum to enhance creativity?" (Note that the question focuses on the curriculum; if a broader assessment of an educational goal is desired, then other components, such as the guidance and activity programs, would also be included.) A task force is appointed to answer the question; it begins its work by identifying those fields of study that emphasize or contribute to this goal. In this case, it would be likely that these fields would make such a claim: English language arts, home economics, art, music, science.

The task force would then proceed to examine the written curriculum in those fields: Do the written guides give sufficient and explicit attention to the goal of enhancing creativity? They then would turn to the supported curriculum, examining budgets, schedules, and materials: Does the district provide sufficient funds for creative materials? Do texts and other instructional materials emphasize creativity in their approach and content? Are these fields of study allocated sufficient time to include creative activities?

They would then consider the more complicated matter of the taught curriculum. Here they would focus on two critical issues: Do teachers actually teach those units in the written guide that were designed to enhance creativity? Do the teachers teach in a manner that fosters creative thinking? Obviously these questions would require evaluators to observe a representative sample of classrooms.

The tested curriculum would next warrant scrutiny: Do curriculum-referenced and teacher-made tests make adequate provisions for assessing creativity? Finally, they would attend to the learned curriculum: Are the students actually learning to think creatively and to produce creative works? This question could be answered through several data sources: results from tests of creativity; results from surveys of teachers, parents, and students; and an evaluation of a representative sample of student creative products.

The results of these several processes would then be used to determine which elements of the curriculum need strengthening or to suggest that perhaps a new course should be added to the curriculum.

As can be seen, a curriculum needs assessment format can be used for a series of multilevel purposes. Through the use of a needs assessment program, the district curriculum specialist along with staff members can examine curriculum goals and objectives in order to best identify instructional opportunities. Information derived from a quality needs assessment program can be used to infuse change directly into the classroom. The result is a major improvement in the teaching and learning process and a major improvement in the learning environment. Effective curriculum planning, therefore, should always include some type of needs assessment. It is through the development of quality needs assessment programs that administrators, curriculum leaders, and teachers can best facilitate systemic educational change and reform in our schools and in our classrooms.

ORGANIZE, EVALUATE, CHANGE, PROVIDE RESOURCES

The next steps in the planning process involve development and implementation strategies more fully explained in subsequent chapters. After determining whether to strengthen existing elements or add new ones, the leaders appoint another task force to take over the responsibility of developing the recommended solution. The original task force's work is evaluated by expert review and systematic field testing. Any necessary organizational elements are changed, such as the school schedule, teacher assignments, or grouping practices. Then plans are made to secure the necessary material resources required by the new or improved program.

Curriculum Tip

It is critical to avoid implementing change for change's sake.

Implementing change without regard for how resources and materials will be integrated into the curriculum has usually not been successful. It is important to make sure that the curriculum process is based on curricular goals and available resources. Available resources include not only materials, but also the capacity to provide training and staff development. The curriculum planning committee along with administration should decide, based on their goals and resources, the extent to which staff development will be infused into the daily operation of the curriculum, classroom, or school.

The entire school system must be evaluated in the curriculum-planning process. Legislation increasingly requires that schools establish objectives, develop plans, drive instruction, and prescribe assessment. Evaluating curriculum systemwide is based on the premise that school systems must set objectives and provide the means for administrator and teacher performance to enable students to meet those objectives. Decisions to guide school personnel performance need to be provided by board of education policy. "While an individual school may be accountable for a segment of a student's education, the school system is accountable for the total education of the student" (Frase, English, & Posten, 2000, p. 7).

PROVIDE STAFF DEVELOPMENT

One of the most effective means of ensuring successful implementation of new curricula is to integrate effective staff-development programs with any major curricular change. Many curriculum projects of excellent quality have not been implemented successfully because they were not supported with the right kind of staff development. The discussion that follows focuses on the planning of staff-development programs as they relate to the general curriculum-planning process; Chapter 9 examines staff development as a means of supervising the taught curriculum, and Chapter 10 offers detailed suggestions for using staff development during the implementation stage.

Curriculum Tip

The strength of a staff development model relies not only on the model's guiding principles, but also on its flexible implementation.

One of the major planning issues is the timing of staff development as it relates to curricular change. Although there are many variations in the specifics of this issue, we will address three general models that have been used successfully: Staff development precedes and leads to curricular change; staff development follows and supports curricular change; and community-based learning provides for the needs of the community.

In the first model, staff-development sessions are held prior to any major curriculum change. The intent here is to update teachers' knowledge about new developments in the field, to give them the skills they need for writing curriculum and instructional materials, and to provide an opportunity for them to exchange and try out such materials. In general, this is the planning model used in the highly successful National Writing Project (see Keech, Stahlecker, Thomas, & Watson, 1979, for a comprehensive evaluation of this approach). James Gray, the individual chiefly responsible for the Bay Area Writing Project, the precursor of the National Writing Project, explicitly rejected curriculum change as the major intervention strategy. His knowledge of the research on the change process led him and his colleagues to begin with a highly effective staff-development model that showed teachers new ways of teaching writing. As teachers explored the new process approach and developed instructional materials, they began gradually to change the curriculum.

The chief advantage of this approach is that it tends to result in a teacher-produced curriculum of high quality. The teachers involved in the staff-development program become local experts who have a better understanding of the field, and the materials they produce have usually stood the test of rigorous trials in the classrooms. The chief drawback to this model is that it can result in piecemeal change; the curriculum becomes a collection of interesting exercises and lacks an integrating conceptual framework.

In the second model, staff-development sessions are held subsequent to the curriculum change. The new curriculum is developed, then those who developed the curriculum identify the new knowledge, skills, and attitudes required for successful implementation. Those new learnings then become the basis for a series of staff-development programs offered immediately prior to the introduction of the new program and during its implementation stage. This essentially is the model used in most curriculum-development and implementation projects. A very effective use of this model is reported by Romberg and Price (1983) in their account of the Curriculum Review Project of the Berea (Ohio) public schools. One of the factors that seemed to account for the success of this project was that the developers were sensitive to the culture of the local schools and made a specific attempt to change the beliefs and traditions of the teacher implementers.

The chief advantage of this model is the close fit between curricular change and staff development. If planned carefully, the staff-development program equips the teachers with the skills they need to implement the new curriculum. The chief drawback is that it can place the teacher in a passive role: "Here is your new curriculum, and this is how you teach it."

The third model, *community-based learning,* is a broad framework that includes service-learning, experiential learning, school-to-work, youth apprenticeship, lifelong learning, and other types of learning experiences that are beneficial to the local community. A problem with these individual approaches is that each focuses on only a portion of the learning outcomes that potentially can be achieved through community-based learning. For example, service-learning concentrates on learning emerging from service provided to meet important needs—such as cleaning up our rivers—in a particular community, while school-to-work generally focuses only on preparing youth for employment (Owens & Wang, 1996).

Community-based learning may be better described as the broad set of teaching/learning strategies that enable youth and adults to learn what they want to learn from any segment of the community. This definition provides for learners of all ages to identify what they wish to learn and opens up an unlimited set of resources to support them. By *community,* we are including the schools, formal and informal institutions in one's neighborhood, and the entire world through such resources as the Internet (Owens & Wang, 1996).

Principles of community-based learning relate to the changing nature of society, the learner, the learning processes, and sources of learning. These principles have been articulated and refined over a 5-year period by participants in a summer seminar organized by the Northwest Regional Educational Laboratory and focused on future directions in work-relevant education (Owens & Wang, 1996).

While the principles of staff development models provide a firm pedagogical foundation, each model requires somewhat different schedules and support arrangements. Each model should be somewhat responsive to the needs and challenges of different teachers, schools, and school systems.

CHAPTER OVERVIEW

Curriculum planning is the specification and sequencing of major decisions to be made in the future with regard to the curriculum. Some general planning processes are useful in all curriculum work. A goal-based model of curriculum planning provides organizing strategies to determine the locus of control in decision making and what organizational structures are needed, and enables a targeted allocation of functions to staff. Curriculum planning provides a district with the opportunity to identify and allocate leadership functions and align goals with curricular fields. Curriculum planning also entails organizing, evaluating, changing, and providing curriculum resources as an integrated process. Long-range curriculum planning combined with strong leadership, a shared vision, and a successful staff development model can be powerful tools to support student learning and increase staff productivity. It remains, therefore, vitally important that educational leaders realize the importance of implementing and enforcing a successful curriculum plan. By doing so, our future educational leaders will help ensure that all teachers will be able to teach and that all students will be able to learn.

CHAPTER TERMS

Curriculum Planning   Needs Assessment

Goal-Based Model   Community-Based Learning

APPLICATIONS

1. Some specialists argue for a simpler planning model, one that would require less time and fewer resources. If you wanted to simplify this goal-based model, how would you do so? Indicate the specific steps that would occur in your simplified model.

2. In the school district about which you are most knowledgeable, would you recommend a separate community advisory council, rather than appointing representatives to a general council? Explain the reasons behind your decision to set up a separate council or to appoint a general one.

3. In the school district you know best, how would you balance the need for school autonomy? Use the questions in Exhibit 5.2 as guidelines for resolving this issue.

4. How would you allocate leadership functions in that same district? Use the form shown in Exhibit 5.3 to answer this question, indicating how you think functions should be allocated.

5. Develop a planning calendar you would use in a district you know well. Use the form shown in Exhibit 5.5.

6. Some experts in the field have recommended a more complex needs-assessment model, one that would make extensive use of such measures and processes as parent interviews, community surveys, student interviews, and futures forecasting techniques. If you were in a district leadership position, would you recommend using one of these more complex processes instead of the more sharply focused model described here? Justify your answer.

7. How will No Child Left Behind influence assessment methods of curriculum? What changes in the NCLB Act would you advocate to improve the overall effectiveness of the law in public schools?

8. Will No Child Left Behind influence "enhancing creativity" through not developing enriched curriculum? How will NCLB's emphasis on testing change what is taught in public schools and how will NCLB impact the teaching of the arts?

CASE STUDY

A Kentucky school district superintendent appoints David Tiebucker, local businessman, to the district's curriculum committee. The businessman is viewed as an influential person who can get things done in the community—an individual who is called a "Mover and Shaker."

"Thanks for being able to attend our meeting, Mr. Tiebucker," says Principal Leonard Powers.

"Glad to be here. What are some things you want to do with curriculum?" he asks.

"Well, we were just discussing some options—but the concern is that a number of committee members don't have a good understanding of what is needed. That means that we should develop an extensive needs-assessment component as well as draft some surveys as part of the process."

"I understand," says the businessman. "Education is changing pretty rapidly these days. I happen to be on the boards of several banks here in town—perhaps I can bring a business as well as community perspective to some of the questions on some of the needs assessment surveys."

"That would be great!" says the superintendent enthusiastically.

Principal Leonard Powers can feel the excitement in the room. "We really appreciate your help, Mr. Tiebucker," he says smiling. "We want to involve the community in our decision-making process. I'll talk to the superintendent and begin setting up a meeting and check on surveys as soon as possible. This will make it a lot easier for the committee to have a better understanding of how our community feels about the school and about our curriculum."

THE CHALLENGE

Reaching out to the community and developing a school-to-community connection is becoming a vital component of the curriculum-planning process. What are some possible criteria that Principal Powers can use to select other community members who are similar to Mr. Tiebucker and who can lend their expertise to his school?

Key Issues/Questions

1. In planning curricula most administrators agree that determining the locus of planning is crucial. To what extent should Principal Leonard Powers involve community member David Tiebucker?

2. Do you think the decision to involve businessman David Tiebucker in the curriculum-planning process should have been made by the district superintendent? Why or why not?

3. What are some other strategies that the district superintendent and/or Principal Powers can use to involve more community members in the curriculum-planning process?

4. Do you think there might have been any resistance from staff or teachers unions in having community members like David Tiebucker on the Curriculum Advisory Council? Why or why not?

5. How might a businessman like David Tiebucker help in developing a curriculum planning calendar?

6. What roles might David Tiebucker play in organizing, evaluating, and providing resources for curriculum programs?

REFERENCES

Christensen, D. (2004). *2002–2003 state of the school report: A report on Nebraska public schools* [Electronic version]. Lincoln, NE: Department of Education.

English, F. W. (1980). *Improving curriculum management in the schools.* Washington, DC: Council for Basic Education.

Frase, L. E., English, F., & Posten, W. K. (2000). *The curriculum management audit: Improving school quality.* Lanham, MD: Scarecrow.

Gass, J. R. (Ed.). (1979). *School-based curriculum development.* Paris: Centre for Educational Research and Innovation.

Goodlad, J. I. (2004). *A place called school.* New York: McGraw-Hill.

Hamilton, L., & Stecher, B. (2004). Responding effectively to test-based accountability. *Phi Delta Kappan, 85,* 578–583.

Joyce, B. R. (1986). *Improving America's schools.* New York: Longman.

Kaufman, R. A. (1982). Needs assessment. In F. W. English (Ed.), *Fundamental curriculum decisions* (pp. 53–67). Alexandria, VA: Association for Supervision and Curriculum Development.

Keech, C., Stahlecker, J., Thomas, S., & Watson, P. (1979). *National Writing Project evaluation report.* Berkeley, CA: University Press Books.

March, J. K., & Peters, K. H. (2002). Curriculum development and instructional design in the effective schools process [Electronic version]. *Phi Delta Kappan, 83,* 2.

Noyce, P., Perda, D., & Traver, R. (2000, February). Creating data-driven schools. *Educational Leadership, 57*(5), 52–57.

Overview: School technology use planning. (2004). *WestED Bulletin.* International Society for Technology in Education (ITA WestEd). Retrieved June 14, 2004, from http://www.wested.org/techplan/pdfs/TPGUIDE.PDF

Owens, T. R., & Wang, C. (1996, January). *Community-based learning: A foundation for meaningful educational reform* (Topical Synthesis #8). Portland, OR: Northwest Regional Laboratory. Retrieved April 5, 2005, from http://www.eric.ed.gov/ERICDocs/data/ericdocs2/content_storage_01/0000000b/80/27/04/b4.pdf

Rettig, M. D., McCullough, L. L., Santos, K., & Watson, C. (2003). A blueprint for increasing student achievement. *Educational Leadership, 61*(3), 71–75.

Romberg, T. A., & Price, G. G. (1983). Curriculum implementation and staff development as cultural change. In G. A. Griffin (Ed.), *Staff development* (pp. 154–184). (Eighty-Second Yearbook of the National Society for the Study of Education, Part II). Chicago: University of Chicago Press.

Vermillion School District #13.1. (2004). *Lessons for standardized curriculum: Mathematics, Grades 7–12.* Author.

Zmuda, A., Kuklis, R., & Kline, E. (2004). *Transforming schools: Creating a culture of continuous improvement.* Alexandria, VA: Association for Supervision and Curriculum Development.

Chapter 6

IMPROVING THE PROGRAM OF STUDIES

$\mathbf{A}$s explained earlier, the program of studies is the total set of organized learning experiences at a given level of schooling—all the courses offered at the elementary, middle, or high school level. From time to time, it is useful for educational leaders to implement a systematic process to assess and to improve the program of studies offered at one or more of these levels. This chapter suggests such a process, after reviewing some recent attempts to reconceptualize programs of study. It should be noted here that the chapter focuses on improving an existing program, rather than developing a completely new program, because few educators have the opportunity to develop new programs of study. With that in mind, this chapter addresses the following questions:

- What basic attempts have been made in the past to reconceptualize programs of study?
- What can current curriculum leaders do to best improve programs of study?

Key to Leadership

Successful curriculum leaders know that improving school studies should involve the interaction of teachers, students, and instructional materials with an integrated knowledge base.

RECONCEPTUALIZING PROGRAMS OF STUDY

Before discussing the assessment and improvement strategies, it might be useful to examine briefly some widespread attempts to reconceptualize schools' programs of study. Those attempts have mostly been motivated by dissatisfaction with the discipline-based curriculum, which uses the standard disciplines as the fields or organizing centers of learning. There are those who argue that the traditional disciplines, such as science and mathematics, are rigid boxes that fragment knowledge unduly (see Cawelti, 1982, for a statement of this position).

As a consequence, there have been several attempts to break away from the standard academic disciplines as ways of organizing knowledge. Such attempts have a long history. In fact, one of the by-products of the progressive era was widespread interest in developing a curricular mode that transcended or ignored the traditional disciplines. One of the most pervasive models of this period was the core curriculum movement, which flourished in the 1940s and still persists as a curricular model for many middle schools. In one widely disseminated model of the core curriculum, the ninth-grade student would have two periods a day of learning experiences related to personal interests, three periods a day of "common learnings" (one continuous course that would help students develop life competencies), and one period of health and physical education (Educational Policies Commission, 1952). The organizing center of the common-learnings course was not the disciplines, but the needs of youth.

Some of the basic principles of the core curriculum still influence current attempts to reconceptualize the curriculum. While there are many possible ways of categorizing those attempts, most can be classified as attempts either to develop interdisciplinary courses or to achieve a total restructuring of the program of studies.

Interdisciplinary Courses

Interdisciplinary courses are courses of study that either integrate content from two or more disciplines (such as English and social studies) or ignore the disciplines totally when organizing learning experiences. Integrated approaches often take the form of "humanities" courses that include content from literature, history, art, and music. Such humanities courses can be organized in terms of cultural epochs ("The Renaissance"), area studies ("American Studies"), ethnic identity ("The Black Experience"), or themes ("The Utopian Vision"). While such courses include material from several disciplines, there is still a strong sense of the disciplines' informing the decisions about content and sequence. At the elementary level, while not concerned with "humanities courses," innovative teachers have always developed interdisciplinary units, such as "Our Animal Friends," that draw from such subject areas as language arts, social studies, science, and art.

Courses or units that ignore or transcend the disciplines are almost always thematically structured. Thus, a team of teachers might develop a course in "The Nature of Conflict," which would embody concepts from literature, biology, anthropology, philosophy, and psychology. The planning focuses on key concepts and skills, with no regard for their disciplinary sources. Or an elementary team might cooperatively develop an integrated unit on "Families First," which would integrate content from social studies, reading, and language arts.

Interdisciplinary courses of both types can be offered either as a substitute for the standard required courses ("take American Studies instead of junior English and American history") or as enrichment electives ("take our new humanities course in addition to junior English and American history").

The research on interdisciplinary courses has been neither extensive nor deep. However, the few well-designed studies available suggest that such interdisciplinary courses are as effective as the standard courses in teaching basic skills (see Vars, 1978, for a review of such studies).

Restructured Programs of Study

Reformers who have been critical of the standard discipline-based curriculum have expressed impatience with modest attempts to reform it by adding interdisciplinary courses. They have advocated instead a total restructuring of the curriculum, arguing that only a completely fresh reconceptualization can bring about meaningful change. Typical of such advocates is Mortimer Adler (1982), creator of the *Paideia* proposal. Adler recommends that the school curriculum be perceived as "three columns of learning"—column one, the acquisition of organized knowledge (language, literature, fine arts, mathematics, natural science, history, geography, and social studies); column two, the development of intellectual skills (reading, writing, speaking, listening, calculating, problem solving, observing, measuring, estimating, and exercising critical judgment); and column three, the enlarged understanding of ideas and values (through discussion of books and other works of art and involvement in artistic activities).

Despite the attractiveness of such proposals, most educators believe that the disciplines will persist. One reason for such persistence, of course, is the force of tradition: Curricula have been discipline based for several hundred years, and such time-honored educational traditions are difficult to change. There are the practical arguments: Teachers are trained and certified in the disciplines, and textbooks are written for the disciplines. With the implementation of the No Child Left Behind (NCLB) Act of 2001, those who advocate continuing the emphasis on the disciplines gained national support. The NCLB Act emphasizes the use of "Highly Qualified Teachers" in each school. The NCLB Act requires "new teachers" to have full state certification, a bachelor's degree, and a state test. In lieu of the state test, middle school and high school teachers could meet the requirement by having a major in the content area or having a graduate degree in the content area. For experienced teachers, the NCLB Act again requires the three basic parts for meeting the criteria as a Highly Qualified Teacher with the option of substituting subject-specific requirements for the state test. School districts will be very cautious in their hiring practices because poor results in the standardized tests will require more and more accountability by schools. Districts who hire teachers outside their major field of study would be hard pressed to explain to the constituents why their children were not given a Highly Qualified Teacher. This trend will keep the disciplines as the driving force for programs of study.

Finally, there is an intellectual basis for continuing discipline-based curricula. As several writers have pointed out, each discipline has its own special way of knowing its own syntax of inquiry; consequently, they assert, attempts to ignore the disciplines might produce students who do not know how to think mathematically or artistically (see Schwab, 1962, for an especially cogent statement of this position).

IMPROVING THE PROGRAM OF STUDIES

While it is unlikely that there will be widespread interest in these total reconceptualizations, there is a continuing concern for improving the program of studies. Some of that concern results from external pressures. Accrediting bodies, such as the Middle States Association of Secondary Schools, are scheduled to conduct an evaluation. The federal government, under the auspices of NCLB and state departments of education, continues to issue new requirements for all schools. Local school boards decide to increase graduation requirements, or the superintendent asks each principal to determine where reductions in the instructional budget might be made with the least damage to the educational program. In a sense, all these mandates are external demands for assessing and improving the program of studies. While such externally mandated reviews are useful and necessary, they are no substitute for an internally motivated assessment that responds to the special concerns of those directly involved with that school—its administrators and faculty. This section, therefore, explains a process that a school district can use on a systematic basis to assess and improve the program of studies in its schools.

Improving Low-Performing Schools

Many schools are facing major challenges in making school improvement changes as mandated by such programs as the No Child Left Behind Act (NCLB) of 2001. According to University of Montana Research Professor Conrad W. Snyder (2004), this situation is particularly a problem for many schools trying to achieve AYP or annual yearly progress as per NCLB regulations. Low-performing schools with a large number of nonproficient and novice students are now facing several formidable tasks: to change and improve their curriculum process, streamline their political institutions, and reform their education systems. Schooling, in these settings, is often dominated by memorization and lecture. In addition, educators are confronting serious problems such as low salaries; uncomfortable or unsuitable classroom conditions; and lack of books, apathetic teachers, and disinterested students. All too often, students only memorize, without having to think and develop knowledge on their own.

Curriculum Tip

Two major factors for school improvement are cooperation and buy-in of state and local educational agencies and the development of some type of specialized district curriculum team.

For any project involving curriculum improvement to succeed, several factors need to be addressed. One is the cooperation and buy-in of state and local educational agencies. Another is the development of some type of specialized district curriculum team that is dedicated to combining the best of the school's current curriculum with enhancements based on modern approaches to knowledge development, curriculum design, and teacher education. The development of a Curriculum Development Team (CDT) is an example of how some school districts are helping to improve the program of studies.

A model CDT is often made up of approximately six CDT members who are highly interested in helping schools to improve curricular programs. If the model is to be successful, team members selected must be creative, innovative, contemporary, and visionary. All participants on the team should have prior experience in teaching and in writing instructional materials. School districts can recruit a combination of specialists and educators as well as a member of the community for this important committee.

A major purpose of the CDT is to provide briefings on the status of curriculum within the district. It is best if these briefings and meetings are held with organizations working in the education arena, the state educational agency, teachers, students, and so forth. Members of the CDT can then visit various schools and begin the process of assessing all relevant documents.

An early goal of any curriculum team is to visit selected schools, interview teachers and students, and review materials. This is necessary to conduct preliminary needs assessments. Schools selected for participation in the CDT process should have a means of providing data collection and Internet accessibility. Having access to digitized survey data will be important when noting differences between teaching methods, student involvement, and the like, at schools where only traditional teaching methods are utilized. It is best if CDT members are linked via interactive Internet connections to maintain communication throughout the process.

After data have been collected and analyzed by the CDT, the role of the committee is to select specific topics or subtopics for which curriculum materials and accompanying units in the teacher's manual can be developed or enhanced. The CDT then has the ability to send different examples of textbooks, supplemental materials, visual aids, curriculum guides, teacher's manuals, video media, evaluation forms, and more to individual schools and to individual teachers.

Topics to be covered might include examples of other school curriculum, contemporary approaches to knowledge development, new approaches to curriculum design and development, evaluation and assessment, and educational leadership, as well as hands-on training in computers and Internet use, and new technologies for classrooms. Interviews with students, teachers, and administrators can be arranged throughout the process. Meetings and interviews with specialists in state agencies and other educational organizations can be organized as well.

The process for developing a draft of curricular materials and a teacher's manual is primarily the responsibility of the committee. CDT members can meet with each selected school's principal and teacher(s) to review new concepts and programs to be introduced. They can also reaffirm CDT's readiness to provide support throughout the school year and emphasize its need for feedback, and they can reaffirm that CDT members will regularly visit the schools to talk with teachers and "sit in" on classes to view progress, reaction, interaction, receptivity, and so forth. Information collected and shared with participating schools and individuals is often invaluable. Intensive interactions among all members often lead to strong mentoring relationships and personal ties between the individual administrators and teachers. These ties can be sustained throughout the project, and into future years as well, assisted by communications via the Internet.

Common Findings at Low-Performing Schools

In many low-performing schools, especially in many large public urban schools, CDT committees are finding that the most common form of instruction is the development of declarative knowledge, facts, and concepts. Trained teachers and relevant curriculum materials serve as the key resources for knowledge development of this kind. Memorization is an enabling goal so that the information is useful in the development and application of procedural knowledge. Without effective teachers and materials, students have no external framework to structure the activities of their schooling experience, and given the wealth of information in textbooks and other learning materials, the most obvious way to learn facts is to memorize them through rote practice. This limits the development of procedural knowledge and devotes instruction to factual memory.

More effective methods, such as those labeled "elaboration," can be used to enhance memorization and help the student develop semantic or graphic representations of information so that more mental links enable efficient recall, or analogical thought. The links also help provide clues for application with knowledge already acquired at other times, thus increasing the complexity of the schemas that engage the world and laying the groundwork for the development of procedural knowledge. A trained teacher, a textbook, and other instructional materials can present declarative information in ways that aid the process of memorization and encourage application, but they can also assist in the development of dynamic knowledge.

Developing Dynamic Knowledge

Dynamic knowledge refers to metacognitive strategies, cognitive processes, thinking skills, and content-area procedural knowledge. In dynamic knowledge, curricula and teachers no longer serve solely as static knowledge options, but assist in the development of a knowledge base that is student centered and enhances effective thinking on the part of the individual learner. Lessons are comprehensively planned and developed, and both the teacher and the materials become key resources in the instructional strategy menu to build the cognitive base for greater student understanding and application.

Curriculum Tip

A goal of curriculum planning is to increase the knowledge and levels of understanding that students take from the instructional events embedded in learning and instructional materials.

Developing Learner Interaction and Curriculum Integration

Improving school studies involves the interaction of teachers, students, and instructional materials with an integrated knowledge base, an extended understanding of that knowledge in the ability to use the knowledge meaningfully, and the proper development of attitudes, perceptions, and effective habits of cognition that enable complex reasoning and effective applications of that reasoning. These processes are embedded in declarative knowledge, but enable the student to extend that base and operate successfully in an increasingly complex world where learning is a lifelong endeavor. The problem is that dynamic knowledge is often absent from education in low-performing schools. Many teachers require their students simply to repeat verbatim the lessons assigned. The key to effective thinking about problems of history, civics, and government (including law and constitution) is the development of deep understanding, in terms of both declarative and procedural knowledge.

The goal is not to define intelligence in terms of the apprehension of truths or fact in these areas, but to explicate instead the apprehension of truths in terms of intelligence. Under this type of approach, students develop the capacity to find and organize facts, and to exploit them in application. Understanding, then, is more than mere knowledge.

Operationalizing Change and Reform

When curriculum questions are operationalized in an effective package, the roles of a teacher, textbook, and other instructional materials are changed from the articulated, comprehensive curriculum framework to an outline of possibilities. Both the teacher and the materials are more of a resource and reference book that lies in the background of the instructional program. Lecturing teachers and printed materials, by their very nature, provide linear presentations, and due to the inherent development limitations, both time and finance, they reflect the sequential perspective of one or a few people (and not that of the student). For this reason, a lot is not covered in textbooks and other materials that are part of a content area. A successful classroom can add the richness that is needed to build deeper understanding and encourage effective habits of the mind by including important and uncovered aspects as an intentional part of the instructional strategy.

Developing the Assessment Agenda

The first step is to develop the assessment agenda. District administrators, school administrators, key faculty members, and parent leaders should meet to discuss these issues:

- How often should program assessment be undertaken?
- Which program-assessment issues should be addressed?
- What levels of schooling should be examined?
- What resources are available?

These questions should be answered, of course, by weighing assessment priorities ("Are we most concerned with our middle school?"), by noting any forthcoming external reviews ("When is the high school scheduled for its next accreditation visit?"), and by reflecting on the importance of program assessment ("How much time and effort should we really be putting into this process?").

One of the key components of the assessment agenda is the set of assessment issues. The five major issues that might be considered are listed briefly here and then discussed at length in the following sections:

1. Goal-curriculum alignment: To what extent does the program of studies reflect and respond to the school district's goals?

2. Curriculum correlation: To what extent do learning experiences in the various subjects correlate with each other at a given grade level?

3. Resource allocation: To what extent does the district's allocation of resources to the program of studies reflect district priorities and provide for equity of opportunity?

4. Learner needs: To what extent does the program of studies respond to present and future needs of the students?

5. Constituent satisfaction: To what extent are teachers, students, and parents satisfied with the program of studies?

The decisions about the assessment agenda can be formalized in a program-assessment calendar, such as the one shown in Exhibit 6.1.

Exhibit 6.1   Program-Assessment Calendar

Year	Level	Assessment Issues
2004–2005	Middle schools	Goal-curriculum alignment Resource allocation Learner needs
2005–2006	Elementary schools	Goal-curriculum alignment Resource allocation Constituent satisfaction
2006–2007	High schools	Goal-curriculum alignment Resource allocation Curriculum correlation

Using Standards and Outcome Statements

Practically speaking, this approach involves turning content standards and outcome statements into question form, and then designing assignments and assessments that evoke possible answers. Only by framing our teaching around valued questions and worthy performances can we overcome activity-based and coverage-oriented instruction and the resulting rote learning that produces formulaic answers and surface-level knowledge. The benefit of a modern curriculum development training model is that it serves as the core of the content coverage for topics while tending to uncover concerns. Reinterpreting textbook information within the same instructional objectives will add to instructional effectiveness by taking students into the realm of cognitive understanding. The curriculum materials and teacher's manual will help structure learning episodes that include both declarative and procedural knowledge and that enable students to think thoroughly and deeply about enduring and changing schemas. What is learned in the classroom will relate to life and enhance individual students' understanding of their world. Interactive learning and the incorporation of standards, outcome statements, and databased forms of assessment will give students the ability to think for themselves and generate a better understanding of how what has been learned relates to their lives.

Aligning District Goals and the Curriculum

In the previous chapter, the process of aligning goals with specific fields of study was explained as a critical step in the goal-based planning model. This chapter suggests a slightly different procedure to use when the focus is on improving a program of studies.

The first step is to identify the school's curriculum goals—those educational goals to which the curriculum is expected to make a major contribution. As indicated in Chapter 5, too often educators assume that all educational goals are curriculum goals. Such an assumption ignores the fact that some goals might best be met through noncurricular means. Consider this goal, one found in many goal statements: *The student will develop a positive self-image.*

Exhibit 6.2   Identification of Curriculum Goals

To the Faculty: Listed below are the educational goals of the school. In your opinion, to which of these educational goals should the school's curriculum make a major contribution? Write the letter C after each educational goal to which you think the curriculum should make a major contribution. We should note here that not all these educational goals necessarily have to be curriculum goals. Some goals, for example, might be achieved primarily through the extracurricular program, with the curriculum making only a minor contribution.

1. Develop a positive self-image.   _____

2. Value own ethnic identity and accept
   people of other ethnic groups.   _____

In general, the research suggests (see, e.g., Brookover & Erickson, 1975) that self-image is chiefly affected by the expectations of others, such as peers, parents, and teachers, and by the role one chooses for oneself. Because the curriculum makes only a relatively minor contribution, this educational goal probably should not be identified as a curriculum goal.

One useful way of making such a determination is to survey the faculty, using a form such as the one shown in Exhibit 6.2. Rather than simply distributing and collecting the forms without discussion, it makes more sense to provide time at a faculty meeting for a general discussion of the issues, to let teachers meet in small groups for fuller discussion, and then to ask them to complete the survey after such analysis and reflection. After the surveys have been completed, the faculty should meet again to discuss the results in an attempt to achieve a consensus. In general, any educational goal that at least half the faculty believes should be met primarily through the curriculum should be considered a curriculum goal for the school.

The next step is to determine to what extent and in what subjects these curriculum goals are being met. The objective here is to develop a matrix that shows in graphic form each goal and the contributions of each subject, grade by grade.

Part of such a matrix is shown in Exhibit 6.3 to illustrate the format and content desired here. The curriculum goals are listed down the left-hand side. Across the top are the required subjects offered by the school (note that only required subjects are listed; because not all students take electives, the contributions of electives should not be assessed here). Each subject column is further subdivided into grade levels, because it is important to analyze grade-level progression. The entries note major curriculum units, which make a major contribution to each goal.

How can the data for this matrix best be obtained? Two ways are possible. One method is to do a goal analysis of the curriculum guides for all major subjects. A member of the leadership team can go through a guide systematically, entering in the matrix the titles of units that relate to a particular goal and listing any units that do not seem directly related to any of the goals. One drawback to this process is that the matrix reflects only what is in the written guides, not what is actually taught. For that reason, districts may prefer to build the matrix by surveying teachers. The form can be a simple one, with these directions:

Exhibit 6.3   Curriculum Goals and Subject Contributions

Goal	Grade 4	Grade 5
Think critically and solve problems	Solving personal problems	Solving school problems

Listed above is a sample of our school's curriculum goals. Consider each goal. If you teach a unit of study that relates directly to or makes a major contribution to that goal, enter the title of the unit. Please keep in mind that we are trying to identify only major units of the curriculum that make major contributions; therefore, you should not note any incidental attention you give to this goal.

Because the objective is to get valid data from individual teachers, individuals should probably complete this survey without consultation or discussion with colleagues. Teachers working in groups often claim to be teaching a particular unit because they sense pressure from colleagues to be doing so.

The results collated in the matrix should then be reviewed by the leadership team, keeping these questions in mind:

1. Is each curriculum goal adequately addressed in at least one of our required subjects? This question examines the basic goal-curriculum relationship to ensure that every goal is dealt with in at least one subject.

2. Are complex curriculum goals reinforced appropriately in two or more subjects? This question is concerned with reinforcement across the curriculum. A complex goal, such as the development of critical thinking, should appear as a focus in several subject areas.

3. Is each goal appropriately developed and reinforced from grade to grade? This question examines the developmental sequence from grade to grade to be sure that each goal is sufficiently reinforced.

4. Are we avoiding unnecessary duplication and overlap from subject to subject and from grade to grade? This question focuses on the particular units to be sure that unnecessary duplication is avoided.

5. Does each required subject seem to be making an adequate contribution to the curriculum goals of the school? This question focuses on a given subject and examines its contributions to all the goals.

The results of the alignment process can lead to several responses. One response is to reconsider the set of curriculum goals. If it turns out that a curriculum goal is not adequately treated in at least one of the required subjects, then perhaps that goal might better be assigned to some other aspect of the educational program, such as the activity program. A second response is to add a new required course or sequence of courses specifically designed to address a particular goal. Thus, if it appears that critical thinking is not sufficiently stressed in any of the subjects, a required course could be developed that students would have to take at some point in their program. The third response to a perceived deficiency—and perhaps the most effective—would be to determine with teachers in each department how they could develop new units in their courses that would specifically relate to goals not receiving adequate treatment.

Curriculum Tip

Correlating curricula is a process of aligning the contents of two or more subjects.

Correlating Curricula

Correlation of curriculum is most essential in schools with a departmentalized structure. An elementary teacher in a self-contained classroom is probably able to achieve whatever correlation is necessary without special intervention. In the same way, a group of teachers working closely together in an interdisciplinary team are probably able in their own way to effect the correlation they consider desirable. In departmentalized schools, however, teachers in each subject often go their own separate way, so that what is taught in one subject has no relationship to what is taught in the rest of the program.

Some good reasons exist for a closely correlated curriculum, as long as the integrity of individual disciplines is not violated. Teachers in one subject can call upon and develop the skills students have learned in another discipline, without having to take the time to teach those skills themselves. So the chemistry teachers know that they can expect students to be able to handle quadratic equations. Important skills that transcend a given discipline, such as retrieving and evaluating information, can be reinforced from subject to subject without excessive repetition. The sense of isolation that seems endemic to departmentalized teaching can be reduced as teachers discuss their curricula and develop correlated units of study. Consequently, students begin to see more clearly how their learning is related.

There are some obvious drawbacks, however, to excessive or misdirected correlation. In some cases, misdirected efforts to correlate can impose unduly restrictive constraints upon teachers. Consider, for example, the problems in trying to correlate American history and American literature. The period of the American Revolution is vitally important in American history, deserving intensive treatment from a historical perspective, but the literature of that period is considered by most experts to be insignificant as literature and merits only brief consideration. A second drawback is that some attempts to impose correlation can result in a situation where one is perceived as a "service" subject that exists chiefly to serve the needs of other disciplines. English often suffers this fate: "That's the English teacher's job" is the common cry across the disciplines.

For these reasons, a problem-solving approach to correlation is emphasized, where school leaders work with classroom teachers in determining subject by subject how much correlation is needed. The process begins with a survey, using a form such as that shown in Exhibit 6.4. Notice that it first asks about five general sets of skills and concepts that seem to have applicability across

Exhibit 6.4   Curriculum-Correlation Analysis

Department/Team

Directions: Our school has decided to undertake a study of curriculum correlation to determine how what is taught in the various subjects can be mutually reinforcing. Consider the subject you teach and answer the following questions based upon your knowledge of your own subject.

1. What library/study skills do you think your students should have in order to perform more successfully in your subject?

   Grade 10 _____

   Grade 11 _____

   Grade 12 _____

2. What special reading skills (other than comprehension skills) do you think your students should have?

   Grade 10 _____

   Grade 11 _____

   Grade 12 _____

3. What academic writing skills do you think your students should have?

   Grade 10 _____

   Grade 11 _____

   Grade 12 _____

4. What mathematics skills do you think your students should have?

   Grade 10 _____

   Grade 11 _____

   Grade 12 _____

5. What knowledge of English grammar (parts of speech, parts of the sentence) do you think your students should have?

   Grade 10 _____

   Grade 11 _____

   Grade 12 _____

6. List below any units of study you presently teach that you think could profitably be correlated with units in other subjects, or any new units with a correlated approach that you might be interested in developing.

   Grade 10 _____

   Grade 11 _____

   Grade 12 _____

the curriculum: library and study skills; reading skills other than basic comprehension; academic writing skills, such as summarizing an article; mathematics skills; and English grammar. The data from this section of the survey can be collated and shared with the faculty to help them determine how to proceed.

These data will usually indicate two sorts of problems in correlation. One problem occurs when one or more departments indicate that the curriculum requires the intensive development of one of the basic skills. Suppose it happens, for example, that several departments indicate that their students should know certain basic library skills. There are essentially three options available to administrators. One would be to develop a new course that would teach the required skills; such a new course would serve the needs of all departments. A second option would be to ask one department (in this case reading/language arts) to assume primary responsibility, with each department then adding its own special content. The third option would be to decide that each department should teach in its own way the library skills its students need. A fuller discussion of these options as they relate to academic writing and critical thinking is presented in Chapter 14.

In some cases, the problem is misalignment of content: The ninth-grade science curriculum requires a mathematics skill that the mathematics curriculum places in tenth grade. In such instances, the two departments should confer to determine which adjustment seems more feasible—to change the science curriculum so that the skill is not required until the later grade, or to change the mathematics curriculum so that the skill is taught in the earlier grade.

In the same manner, the responses to the last question, dealing with the possibilities of developing correlated units, can be shared with the appropriate departments or teams to see if such units might be cooperatively planned. It might happen, for example, that the mathematics teachers, learning about a unit in logical thinking taught by the English teachers, would suggest a correlated unit that would include an analysis of valid and invalid uses of statistics in reasoning.

Thus correlation is achieved through a problem-solving process of determining need, assessing the options, and making decisions that seem best for the students.

Analyzing Resources Allocated to Curricula

The third process for assessing and improving the program of studies is to analyze the resources allocated to the several curricula. The resource allocation analysis provides data relevant to these related issues:

- Does the school's allocation of resources reflect its educational priorities? The assumption here is that the manner in which resources are allocated should reflect the system's priorities.
- Does the school's allocation of resources seem adequate for achieving the outcomes desired? If certain important educational outcomes are desired, then those classes will need adequate time, appropriate staffing, and suitable class size.
- Does the allocation of resources seem to be cost-effective? This question essentially examines the relationship between the number of students served and the resources required to serve them.
- Is the allocation of resources equitable? This question is concerned with whether the needs of all students are being met in an equitable fashion. In too many instances, less-able students receive less than their share.

Exhibit 6.5   Analysis of Curriculum Resources

Subject	Required or Elective	Enrollment	Number of Sections	Faculty Assigned	Minutes per Week
Art	Elective	250	14	1.0	80
Phys. Ed.	Required	1,500	50	6.0	120
Russian	Elective	36	3	0.6	200

The examples shown in Exhibit 6.5 illustrate the types of data that might be analyzed in answering those questions. Obviously, additional data could be included, such as classroom space, instructional costs, noninstructional costs, and overhead and indirect costs. However, that additional information would contribute only some refinements to the basic data presented in Exhibit 6.5 and therefore might be omitted without harm to the analysis.

A special note might be made about the importance of analyzing time allocations. Several studies (see, e.g., Stallings, 1980) indicate quite clearly that the time allocated to a particular area of the curriculum is directly related to student achievement in that area. One useful standard for assessing time allocations has been provided by John Goodlad (2004). After reviewing the time allocations in the numerous schools he studied and assessing his own extensive experience in curriculum development, he concluded that the following allocations would be desirable for the three upper grades of elementary school: language arts, 1.5 hours a day; mathematics, 1 hour a day; social studies, 2.5 hours a week; science, 2.5 hours a week; health and physical education, 2.5 hours a week; arts, 3.5 hours a week. In many states, of course, minimum time allocations are stated in the school code; where the district has some flexibility, however, allocations should be closely examined.

In examining those data in relationship to the questions noted above, the leadership team might decide that certain reallocations would strengthen the overall program. Such reallocations might take several forms: increasing or decreasing time allotments, increasing or decreasing section size, increasing or decreasing the number of teachers assigned.

Curriculum Tip

In the current world of technology and education, data analysis is fast becoming one of the most important aspects of assessment and of improving programs of study.

Importance of Data Analysis in Assessment

Victoria L. Bernhardt (1998), in her book *Data Analysis for Comprehensive Schoolwide Improvement*, helps school leaders learn how to deal with curricular data that will inform them of where they are, where they want to be, and how to get there. Her pioneering work reveals that data analysis is a major help in identifying and uncovering powerful curriculum solutions to some of our schools' biggest problems. Data analysis, however, has not always been well received in the study of school improvement. Some of the reasons that schools may not use data regularly include the following:

- Work culture does not focus on data
- Gathering data is difficult and often perceived as a waste of time
- Teachers are trained to be subject oriented, not data oriented
- Data are often not used systematically

Supporters of data analysis, however, note that data collection and analysis provide curriculum leaders with the power to make good decisions, work intelligently, work effectively and efficiently, change in better ways, understand the impact of hard work, help prepare for the future, and know how to make work benefit children. The collection of data can make a major difference in school reform by

- Replacing hunches and hypotheses with facts concerning changes that are needed
- Identifying root causes of problems
- Assessing needs to target curriculum services and issues
- Determining if goals are accomplished

The key is that schools gather data correctly and use the data appropriately. According to Lynn Olson (2004), writer for *Education Week,* officials should inventory the data currently stored by their district, assess the quality of that information, and estimate the cost of correcting or "cleaning" the data. Schools also need to evaluate their data and analytical needs, and must weigh how much outside or third-party help they require to set up the system, including inventorying the initial data, cleaning the data, merging data sets, and housing the data over time. Districts also need to consider how long it will take to get the system up and running, as well as its cost. Olson goes on to state that schools and districts would be well advised to contact other schools using the software, query them thoroughly, and visit as many as possible to get practical feedback on the types of products and levels of services each vendor offers.

Assessing Learner Needs

One of the most important analyses of the program of studies involves the extent to which the curriculum seems to respond to both present and future needs of the learners. However, to argue for the importance of such an analysis is not to assert that learner needs must always be the primary determiner of curriculum. As explained in Chapter 3, other sources might be just as or more important, depending upon the orientation of curriculum planners. Yet even curricula that have been influenced primarily by other sources should give some attention to present learner needs if they are to be successful in eliciting student interest. In addition, all curricular orientations seem to accept the importance of preparing students for the future, even though they construe that preparation differently.

If such an assessment is therefore important, it must be done carefully and conscientiously; it should not be perceived as a meaningless exercise undertaken just to satisfy administrators or some external group. The process should begin by involving the faculty in a systematic study that results in an explicit statement of present and future learner needs. How this is done will obviously vary with the local situation; however, the process explained below is one that should work well in most systems.

Begin by setting up a small task force or committee composed of one district administrator, one or more school administrators, and several key faculty members. Their first task should be to develop a tentative draft of present learner needs. Two points should be stressed about this needs analysis. First, it should focus on the developmental needs of the age group enrolled in that school, not on the needs of all children and youth. The assumption is that the district's goals speak to the broader needs of all students; the needs analysis is concerned solely with the age group served by that school. Second, it should be concerned primarily with those needs that might best be served through the curriculum, because the emphasis is on assessing the educational program, not other aspects of schooling.

The task force should use two general sources of information: publications and people. First, task force members should undertake a systematic examination of current publications dealing with that age group. For each age level—the children in elementary schools, the preadolescents, early adolescents in middle schools, and the youth in high schools—numerous sources synthesize the research on the psychological, physical, social, and intellectual needs of that population. The task force would be wiser, perhaps, to limit themselves to a careful study of a smaller number of the best sources (perhaps no more than five or six), rather than attempting a comprehensive survey. They should also use whatever expert advice they can get from both district personnel (such as school nurses, counselors, social workers, and psychologists) as well as from professionals in the community.

Their draft report might take the form of the one shown in Exhibit 6.6. This document synthesizes the most current and reliable information about middle school learners. Observe that it first states the need and then suggests a curricular response.

Their second major task is to identify future needs of the learners. Here, the intent is not to play the role of futurist and attempt to develop elaborate scenarios about the 21st century. Instead, the goal is to identify rather predictable features of the next 20 years that should influence the kind of education provided for today's students. Here, the task force can turn to two types of documents for assistance. First, there were several commission reports written during early 2000 that both examined the present performance of schools and addressed specifically the issue of future curricular needs. Two that seem worth checking are the National Science Board report, *U.S. Losing Ground in Science Education* (Ashton, 2004) and the Education Commission of the States (American Association of Colleges for Teacher Education [AACTE], 2004) study, *No Child Left Behind.* Second, several reports are available that look more broadly at the issue of planning for the future. While some of these seem unduly speculative, one that seems especially worthwhile is the Secretary's Commission on Achieving Necessary Skills (SCANS) report (Northwest Mississippi Community College, 2004), which defines competencies.

Improving the Program of Studies

This section of the draft report might take the form shown in Exhibit 6.7. Again, a future development is indicated and then a curricular response is suggested. The draft report on present and future needs should then be analyzed and discussed by the faculty, meeting in small groups, with perhaps a member of the task force leading each group. Out of these discussions should emerge a final draft reflecting a faculty consensus. That process results in a final

Exhibit 6.6   Adolescent Needs and Curricular Responses

The research suggests that young adolescents have these needs:	Their program of studies therefore should probably respond in these ways:
1. Understanding the physical changes occurring and the special nutritional needs that result	1. Health education units and science units emphasizing that these changes are normal and stressing importance of good nutrition
2. Developing greater physical coordination in a nonthreatening environment	2. Physical education experiences that build coordination without overemphasizing competition
3. Increasing level of cognitive development, moving from semiformal to formal operations	3. Units in all appropriate subjects that include a mix of concrete and abstract learnings
4. Becoming more supplicated in their political reasoning	4. Units in social studies that help them examine complexities of current political issues
5. Increasing level of moral development	5. Units in social studies, science, and English that help them examine complex moral issues
6. Developing clear sense of personal identity	6. Units in English that explore issues of personal identity and self-awareness
7. Maintaining balance between growing sense of autonomy and continuing need for peer approval	7. Units in social studies that explore the nature of peer influence from a sociological perspective

document that can then be used in assessing the programs of study. The process obviously is a time-consuming one, but the commitment of large amounts of time seems warranted. Not only will the faculty have produced a highly useful document, but teachers will also have had an opportunity to analyze and discuss some very critical issues.

How can this document be used in assessing the program of studies? Two processes might be considered. The first is a mapping of what may be called the "needs-responsive curriculum"—those aspects of the curriculum that specifically respond to the needs that have been identified. A form similar to the one shown in Exhibit 6.8 should be distributed to departments or teams of teachers, who should meet in small groups to discuss the questions and respond to the survey. The results can then be reviewed by the leadership team to determine areas of strength and weakness.

It might be useful here to distinguish between the goal-curriculum alignment process and the mapping of the needs-responsive curriculum. Goals are usually very general statements that apply to all levels of schooling and are ordinarily produced at the state or district level. The goal-curriculum alignment process attempts to align larger curriculum entities, such as units of study, with these very general outcomes. The statement of needs is produced at the

Exhibit 6.7   The Future and the Curriculum

The experts predict that the future will be marked by these developments:	The curriculum should probably respond in these ways:
1. The world becomes a "global village."	1. Units in social studies and English that increase students' awareness of national interdependence; foreign language study made available to all students.
2. New immigrant groups continue to arrive in this country in large numbers.	2. Units in English and social studies that emphasize our immigrant past and the contributions of immigrants.
3. The information age arrives: a glut of information made available by computers.	3. Units in all appropriate subjects on information retrieval, evaluation, and application.
4. Television becomes increasingly dominant as a medium of communication and entertainment.	4. Units in English that emphasize critical viewing.
5. The family continues to change; more family instability, more one-parent families.	5. Units in social studies that put such changes in perspective.
6. The technology continues to change, with the job market changing frequently and unpredictably.	6. Units in English and social studies that emphasize career-mobility skill, rather than examining particular careers.

Exhibit 6.8   The Needs-Responsive Curriculum

Directions: The following curriculum characteristics have been suggested by our analysis of our students' present and future needs. Consider each characteristic. If you feel that the curriculum in your subject in some way reflects that characteristic, then indicate specifically how it does.

Department: English language arts

A needs-responsive curriculum should have these characteristics:	Our curriculum reflects these characteristics in these ways:
1. Helps students develop a global perspective	1. Students read some contemporary literature written by European and Asian writers.

school level and focuses on the more specific needs of a given age level, and the mapping process seeks detailed evidence of how a given curriculum responds to those needs. Because the alignment and mapping processes are somewhat similar in approach, however, it might be desirable to use only one, not both, during a given assessment project.

The other process for assessing the needs-responsive curriculum takes an entirely different approach. Each homeroom or adviser-room teacher is asked to identify three students from that homeroom and conduct an in-depth interview with them to ascertain the students' perceptions of how well the program of studies responds to the needs identified. If the homeroom group is heterogeneous in abilities, the teacher should choose one student from each ability level. The interview might open with a statement of this sort:

> The teachers in our school have been thinking about students your age and the kinds of things they should be learning. We'd like to find out from some of our students how they feel about what they are learning. You've been selected because I think you have some good ideas about what you're studying. I'm going to read a statement about what our faculty believes you should be learning. I would then like you to answer in two ways. First, tell me if you agree that those things are important to learn. Then tell me in which subjects, if any, you are learning those things.

The teacher, of course, should caution students not to be critical of particular teachers, because the intent is not to evaluate teachers, but to examine the program of studies.

Each teacher should then be asked to prepare a written summary of results of the interviews. Time should also be provided for small groups of homeroom advisers to meet together to discuss their findings. The written summaries should be reviewed by the leadership team to identify specific ways in which the program of studies does not seem sufficiently responsive to learner needs.

Both these processes will have identified certain needs-based deficiencies in the existing program of studies. The leadership team can then decide how to respond to those deficiencies. One response, obviously, is to determine that a particular need should not be addressed in the curriculum. Upon further reflection, the leaders might determine that a particular need can better be satisfied through some other educational means or through some other agency. The more likely response is to suggest to appropriate teams or departments that they spend more time deciding how they could make the curricula more responsive. Thus, if it is apparent that none of the school's courses is concerned with, for example, the need to develop a global perspective, several departments might be asked to examine how their curricula might be suitably modified. The social studies, English, music, art, and family and consumer science (formerly home economics) departments would need to be involved in this instance.

Curriculum Tip

The curriculum leadership team should decide which groups should be surveyed, and whether the total population or only a sample should be included.

Assessing Constituent Satisfaction

The last assessment process involves measuring constituent satisfaction; *constituent* is used here as an umbrella term that includes students, teachers, and parents as constituents whom the curriculum serves. This is not to suggest that all groups need to be surveyed, especially at the elementary level. Measures of pupil perceptions tend not to yield valid results. Curriculum leaders might decide to survey all teachers, a stratified sample of 20% of the students, and all parents.

Ordinarily, the survey should focus on the entire program of studies, not on individual subjects or the instructional processes; a faculty committee should be charged with the responsibility of developing the specific items to be included. The items shown in Exhibit 6.9 suggest types of items that might make up the survey. Observe that the survey shown in Exhibit 6.9 attempts to assess satisfaction with several dimensions of the program of studies: present relevance, future value, interest, the required/elective balance, difficulty and challenge, subject correlation, curricular equity. These seem to be the aspects where constituent satisfaction is most salient.

The results of these surveys require careful analysis before steps are taken to improve the program of studies.

The leadership team should examine the data with these questions in mind:

1. Do major discrepancies exist in the extent to which teachers, parents, and students seem satisfied with the program of studies? If so, what do those discrepancies mean?

2. Where general dissatisfaction is expressed with some dimension of the program of studies, what changes might best be made?

It should be stressed here that constituent satisfaction is only one standard by which a program of studies should be assessed. The leadership team and the faculty should use one or more of the measures discussed above to supplement this particular analysis.

Taken together, then, these five assessment processes can yield some highly useful data that the leadership team and the faculty can use in improving the program of studies.

CHAPTER OVERVIEW

Educational leaders periodically need to implement a systematic process to assess and to improve each program of studies. The process usually involves improving an existing program rather than investing in developing new programs of study. Value is gained from examining past attempts to reconceptualize programs of study. Curriculum leaders can improve existing programs of study by developing an assessment agenda, aligning district goals and the curriculum, correlating curricula, analyzing resources allocated to curricula, and finally assessing constituent satisfaction.

CHAPTER TERMS

Discipline-Based Curriculum	Dynamic Knowledge
Core Curriculum Movement	Standard and Outcome Statements
Interdisciplinary Courses	Correlating Curricula
Curriculum-Development Team	

Exhibit 6.9   Student Survey

To the Student: Below you will find several statements about the subjects you are studying this year. Consider each statement and decide how much you agree with it. Circle one of these responses to show how much you agree or disagree with that statement:

> SA = strongly agree   D = disagree
> A = agree   SD = strongly disagree
> ? = uncertain

Remember also to read the question at the end of this survey.

Statement	*Your Response*
1. I am learning things that seem useful to me now.	SA A ? D SD
2. I am learning things that will be helpful to me in the future.	SA A ? D SD
3. I am learning things that seem interesting to me.	SA A ? D SD
4. I think I should have a chance to take more electives.	SA A ? D SD
5. The things I am studying seem much too difficult for me.	SA A ? D SD
6. The courses I am taking make me think and develop my abilities.	SA A ? D SD
7. The courses I am taking seem connected with each other; what I learn in one course ties in with what I learn in the other courses.	SA A ? D SD
8. The bright students in our school have better courses than students who are not so bright.	SA A ? D SD

Is there some course not offered by our school that you would like to see offered? If so, list it below. You may list more than one course if you wish.

_____   _____

_____   _____

_____   _____

APPLICATIONS

1. Compare a process from this chapter with a process recommended by one of the accrediting bodies. What do you perceive to be the advantages and disadvantages of each? List at least two advantages and two disadvantages. What local factors might affect the one you would recommend to a school district?

2. Some argue that speculating about the future is a futile pursuit, because the future is so unpredictable. Many also point out that if we teach students how to think, how to communicate, how to read, and how to solve problems, there is no need to worry about the future. How would you respond to such arguments? What are some specific recommendations you would give curriculum leaders when speculating about future educational events?

3. Try your hand at reconceptualizing the curriculum. Choose a level of schooling you know best (elementary, middle, high). Identify the way you would organize learning (using some of the disciplines, if you wish) and indicate what percentage of time would be devoted to each broad field.

4. Develop a detailed program-assessment calendar for a school that you know. Include the following: the program-assessment issues to be analyzed, the individuals primarily responsible, and the dates by which the final assessments should be made.

5. What implications do you see the No Child Left Behind Act of 2001 having for curriculum development?

6. Because the standards and regulations of NCLB are the driving force in the creation of state standards, and these standards will be tested for school accountability, what impact will this have regarding schools' flexibility in curriculum?

CASE STUDY

A Pennsylvania principal talks to her fifth-grade teacher about ways to teach difficult material that will help improve student achievement.

"Ron, I know that you use a lot of high-level math curriculum in your classroom and your student test scores are always high. Is there a way we can use some of your strategies with other fifth-grade teachers?" asks Susan Neal, principal of Cecilia Hazelton Intermediate School. "I had a few of the other fifth-grade teachers in my office and they are very upset about the standards and what is expected. They think the material is too difficult. As you know, many of our students are far below the math proficiency standard set by the state. I sure hope that you can help me with this problem."

"I'll be glad to help," says Ron. "I'm in the process of meeting with our fifth-grade teaching team this afternoon. I know that they're concerned, but I can share what I'm doing on the Web that improves students' scores in the area of Number Sense and Operations. The teachers have been pretty frustrated with student test results in that area. For example, our textbooks emphasize Standard Rounding while the test items call for Front Ending."

"That sounds like just what we need," notes Principal Neal. "I'm sure that the teachers will respond better to your suggestions rather than just hearing from me all the time."

THE CHALLENGE

Developing an active Web site for each grade level as a way to improve programs of studies is becoming an important component of the school curriculum. Analyze this process and propose other strategies that Principal Susan Neal could use to get more teachers involved in building grade-level and/or classroom Web sites.

Key Issues/Questions

1. Judging from your own experience, how do you feel about Ron's classroom Web site approach being used to help develop interdisciplinary courses?

2. Restructuring curriculum may involve a great deal of resistance. What types of problems might Principal Susan Neal experience when she proposes that all teachers should be developing their own classroom Web sites?

3. What are some ways that Principal Neal can use technology and Web site development to enhance program assessment?

4. How do you think the parents of Cecilia Hazelton Intermediate School will react to their children's work and grades being posted on the Internet? How might Principal Neal deal with this concern?

5. How can Principal Susan Neal use Ron's Web site approach to help develop and assess constituent satisfaction of her school?

REFERENCES

Adler, M. J. (1982). *The Paideia proposal: An educational manifesto*. New York: Macmillan.

American Association of Colleges for Teacher Education. (2004, December 30). No Child Left Behind (NCLB) research [Electronic version]. *AACTE Education Policy Clearinghouse*. Retrieved December 30, 2004, from http://www.edpolicy.org/research/nclb/index.php

Ashton, A. (2004, May 5). Report: U.S. losing ground in science education. *USA Today*. Retrieved December 28, 2004, from http://www.usatoday.com/news/education/2004-05-05-sciteach_x.htm

Bernhardt, V. L. (1998). *Data analysis for comprehensive schoolwide improvement*. New York: Eye on Education.

Brookover, W. B., & Erickson, E. L. (1975). *Sociology of education*. Homewood, IL: Dorsey.

Cawelti, G. (1982). Redefining general education for the American high school. *Educational Leadership, 39*, 570–572.

Educational Policies Commission. (1952). *Education for all American youth—A further look*. Washington, DC: National Education Association.

Goodlad, J. I. (2004). *A place called school*. New York: McGraw-Hill.

Northwest Mississippi Community College (NWCC). (2004, October). *NWCC SCANS committee monthly minutes.* Retrieved December 30, 2004, from http://www.northwestms.edu/administration/scans.html

Olson, L. (2004). Researchers sort out data-analysis software. *Education Week, 23*(18), p. 6.

Schwab, J. T. (1962). The concept of the structure of a discipline. *Educational Record, 43,* 197–201.

Snyder, C. W. (2004). *Calendar of activities/itinerary narrative.* An unpublished paper completed for the University of Montana International Studies Program.

Stallings, J. (1980). Allocated academic learning time revisited, or beyond time on task. *Educational Researcher, 9,* 11–16.

Vars, G. F. (1978). *Bibliography of research on the effectiveness of block-time, core, and interdisciplinary team teaching programs.* Kent, OH: Kent State University.

Chapter 7

IMPROVING A FIELD OF STUDY

When a school district decides to improve a field of study, it usually is concerned with strengthening one subject area, such as English language arts, across several grade levels. Such a decision typically emerges from an awareness of a deficiency: Poor articulation exists between the various levels of schooling, teachers are no longer using existing guides, or the present curriculum has become outdated. This chapter describes a process for effecting such improvements, after noting some attempts to reconceptualize fields of study. Questions addressed in this chapter include the following:

- What basic attempts have been made in the past to reconceptualize fields of study?
- What can current curriculum leaders do to best improve fields of study?

Key to Leadership

School district leaders need and deserve accurate measures that align with standards and produce timely results.

RECONCEPTUALIZING FIELDS OF STUDY

Whereas attempts to reconceptualize programs of study usually are concerned with proposals for minimizing the rigid demarcations between the disciplines, those involving fields of study ordinarily focus on eliminating the rigidity imposed by graded curricula. Proponents of such approaches argue that curricula organized by grade level (Grade 10 English, Grade 6 mathematics) militate against individualization and result in "batch processing" that ignores individual differences. They argue for curricula that are not bound to grade levels, but that instead facilitate individual progress.

The idea of minimizing the importance of grade levels in designing curricula is not new, of course. As early as 1919, Carleton Washburne, working in the Winnetka (Illinois) schools, developed an individualized program that emphasized self-paced progress. The pupils worked as long as they needed on self-instructional and self-correcting materials, progressing to subsequent units on the basis of teacher-administered tests (see Washburne & Marland, 1963, for a fuller discussion).

While several current models for a nongraded curriculum are available, most seem to be varieties of two basic ones: the diagnostic-prescriptive model and the elective model.

Diagnostic-Prescriptive Models

Diagnostic-prescriptive models of the curriculum begin by structuring the field of study as a series of sequential nongraded levels of learning. The diagnostic-prescriptive approach is also labeled as an approach to instruction of students on an individual basis, with attention to strengths or weaknesses, followed by teaching prescriptives to remediate the weaknesses and develop strengths. Thus, elementary mathematics might be organized into 18 levels instead of six grades. Each level, in turn, comprises several sequential modules or units. Thus, in Level 3 mathematics, 16 modules might be arranged in a developmental sequence so that Module 2 builds on Module 1 and leads to Module 3. The curriculum is thus conceptualized as a linear series of tightly sequenced learning experiences, ordered without respect to grade level. The student moves through this linear sequence at an individualized pace. The teacher diagnoses the student's present level of achievement, prescribes the appropriate placement ("begin with Module 4, Level 3"), and monitors the student's progress through a series of formative and summative tests.

How effective are the diagnostic-prescriptive models? The answer is difficult to determine, because it is almost impossible to sort out the effects of the curricular structure itself from those of the instructional system. A review of several so-called individualized programs indicates that they seem to be superior at the college level (Bangert, Kulik, & Kulik, 1983). However, recent studies by Jim Ysseldyke and Steven P. Tardrew (2003) show implementing a computer-based math management system with a school's existing curriculum improved scores in a short time. The difference in gains in just one semester for students in Grades 3–10 ranged from 7 percentile points in Grade 6 to 14 percentile points in Grades 3 and 5.

Elective Models

Elective models are quite different in concept from diagnostic-prescriptive models. Whereas developers of diagnostic prescriptive models conceptualize the curriculum as a linearly ordered sequence, those advocating elective models view the curriculum as a multipath network. The contrast is illustrated in Exhibit 7.1. The elective curriculum is usually delivered as an array of mini-courses typically lasting 6, 9, 12, or 18 weeks (see Oliver, 1978, for a useful description of the various elective options). Because those mini-courses usually are offered to students from several grade levels, they achieve nongrading in their own way.

The content of a given elective course is usually determined by an individual teacher or a team of teachers who draw upon their own special interests and perceptions of student interest. Thus, an English department might offer electives with titles such as the following:

The Black Experience

Hispanic Literature

The Dialects of the South

Exhibit 7.1   Individualized and Elective Systems Contrasted

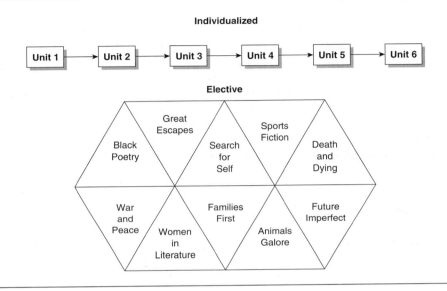

Conflict: Literature of Battle

Looking at Television With a Critical Eye

Communicating With Computers

Utopias, Real and Imagined

The research on the effectiveness of the elective model is even less conclusive than assessing the diagnostic-prescriptive models. Although several writers blamed the elective program for the "educational crisis" of the early 1980s, no hard evidence supports such a conclusion (see Copperman, 1978, for one such attack). In fact, only a handful of studies even attempted to assess electives systematically. Hillocks's (1972) study of English electives is one of those few. After reviewing more than 100 such programs, he concluded on a rather optimistic note:

> Given the time to study, plan, and evaluate their work, English teachers, with their newly awakened sense of professional dignity, may manage to revolutionize the teaching of English. . . . For that reason alone, elective programs will have been worth the effort. (p. 123)

While most objective observers tend to agree that electives were often poorly designed, the issue of whether well-designed programs could be as effective as the standard curriculum must still be considered unresolved.

What of the future of diagnostic-prescriptive and elective models? First, the diagnostic-prescriptive model has been enhanced in the past few years, mainly because of the extensive use of computers in the classroom. The computer facilitates diagnosis, prescription, and assessment.

Therefore, computer-based programs help the teacher modify curriculum for each student's individual needs. An example of this is Accelerated Math by Renaissance Learning. Implementation of Accelerated Math resulted in improved performance for students at multiple points on the ability/disability spectrum. Accelerated Math has a significant effect in all respects for students who are gifted and talented, low achieving, English language learners, and for students in the Title I programs (Ysseldyke & Tardrew, 2003). The elective model at this time seems to have been a short-lived fad; its openness and lack of structure are considered suspect by those concerned with standards and rigor. Most leaders in the field seem to take for granted that the graded curriculum will persist because it is so deeply entrenched in the ways in which schools are organized, teachers are assigned, students are grouped, and materials are written. However, the process described below for improving the field of study can be applied in a way that will permit nongrading, if local administrators and teachers decide that such an option is desirable.

IMPROVING THE FIELD OF STUDY

The process described below is a teacher-centered process that relies on teacher input; a rationale for such an approach is presented in the next section. It is only one of many ways that a field of study might be improved; however, it has been used successfully by several school districts and seems to achieve the results desired without requiring excessive time or money. The phases in the process include the following:

1. Establish project parameters
2. Orient for mastery
3. Map the desired curriculum
4. Refine the map
5. Develop curriculum materials
6. Suggest time allocations
7. Select and develop tests
8. Select instructional materials
9. Provide for staff development

Each of these aforementioned steps will be explained in detail in the sections following the rationale. Although the English language arts curriculum is used for most of the examples, the process has worked equally well with several other fields of study.

Curriculum Tip

Teacher-centered planning should reflect either the formal, perceived, or operational curriculum.

A RATIONALE FOR A TEACHER-CENTERED PROCESS

This teacher-centered process has been developed as a solution to a problem perhaps first identified by Goodlad (1977). As discussed in Chapter 1, his studies of school curricula indicate that there are in fact five different curricula that exist almost as separate entities: the *ideal* curriculum (in this work termed the *recommended* curriculum), that set of recommendations proposed by the scholars and experts in the field; the *formal* curriculum (identified in this work as the *written* curriculum), the curriculum embodied in the school district's curriculum guides; the *perceived* curriculum (in this work called the *taught* curriculum), the curriculum that the teachers believe they are teaching; the *operational* curriculum, which an observer would observe; and the *experiential* curriculum (in this work called the *learned* curriculum), the curriculum that students are learning.

According to Goodlad, the ideal curriculum rarely influences either the written or the taught curriculum: The written curriculum often is completely ignored by the classroom teacher, the teacher and an observer do not agree as to what the teacher actually taught, and students do not learn all that the teacher attempts to teach. His conclusions have been supported by several subsequent studies focusing on the teacher as curriculum maker (see, e.g., Cusick, 1983). Those studies present this general picture: Classroom teachers (especially secondary teachers) in making decisions about what to teach rely primarily on their knowledge of the subject, their teaching experience, and their perceptions of their students, giving only cursory attention to the district curriculum guide. In studies by Homan (as cited in Schmidt, 2004) of fifth graders and high school algebra students, teachers who were engaged in curriculum planning, had strong classroom management skills, and were able to teach the curriculum they planned with specific teaching strategies produced the highest achievement among their students.

A process is needed that will at least bring the recommended, the written, and the taught curricula into closer alignment. The recommended curriculum should not be ignored: What teachers teach should reflect the best current knowledge about that subject, tempered by the realities of the classroom. Moreover, the written and the taught curricula should be more congruent. Each teacher doing what he or she wants to do can result in curricular anarchy.

The process described below attempts to accomplish these objectives. It begins with the teachers' determining what they think should be taught. It reviews their decisions in light of the best current knowledge, and it produces written guides that reflect that synthesis of the recommended and the taught. Observe that this improvement process, therefore, is not concerned primarily with improving the written materials; it is concerned with the much larger issue of improving teaching and learning in that field throughout the district. When discussing curriculum that is recommended, written, and taught, it is best perhaps to view the process of improving curriculum as a series of steps.

Curriculum Tip

Curriculum plans are often set up as content matrices, and the lessons or units are described in terms of key content.

According to University of Montana Research Professor Conrad W. Snyder (2004), the first step in determining the development of a desirable curriculum for schools entails identifying and specifying understanding that is enduring and needed, and what is important to know and what would be good to be familiar with (for students to encounter). This information may already exist in the curriculum created by a state educational agency or local school district, but it needs to be checked for comprehensiveness and expansiveness. Four criteria are often used to sort content listings and begin the development of generative questions around which the instructional events of materials can operate:

- To what extent does the idea, topic, or process represent a big idea that has enduring value beyond the classroom in everyday life and reality?
- To what extent does the idea, topic, or process reside at the heart of the discipline?
- To what extent does the idea, topic, or process require coverage through other instructional events in the classroom, extending the textbook?
- To what extent does the idea, topic, or process offer potential for engaging students, keeping their attention, and encouraging their interest in the topic?

In the second step, it is important to develop each unit framed around the enduring understandings and essential questions. Once a unit is established, then the question to ask is, What evidence exists to accept this as an understanding? The design criteria or filters at this point for the assessments are: (1) Validity, (2) Reliability, (3) Sufficiency, (4) Authenticity, (5) Feasibility, and (6) Friendliness. These criteria are instructional events, with the difference that the student produces all the required responses in order to diagnose or check the status of the student in the areas of importance. Standard measurement criteria apply, but we make allowances because the effects are only remediation, which probably doesn't hurt as continuing thoughtful practice. The better the evidence, however, the better the decisions made for instructional strategies. Quality of measurement is an essential feature of quality instruction.

It is here that one should introduce technology in order to enhance the process, enable continuous connection among the educational colleagues, and allow substantive work to be ongoing and sustainable. Several technologies that can be utilized are: Microsoft's Live Meeting (software for online/Internet meetings), and Comprehensive Performance Assessment devices (assessment software). Both of these are available online, the operational costs are low, and these technologies enable continuing dialogue and frequent contact. Online editing and review routines also enable interchange and interaction within the curriculum-development process. The curriculum is available for update and revision without expensive printing and publishing requirements, and the distribution of materials can be carried out efficiently.

In the third step, it is important to attend to research-based teaching strategies to implement an intended curriculum. These strategies are guides to effective approaches; the problem with modern instructional design for school improvement lies in the level of teacher training and practicing expertise. The ideal project requires a teaching cadre that is trained in modern approaches to knowledge development and the corresponding teaching methods. Teachers do not always know how to use instructional material to provide a rich classroom learning experience. This requires considerable expertise. Therefore, it is important to combine the curriculum in understandable terms with the structure of more didactic approaches (i.e., improving on the direct instruction methods already in place) with structured instructions to teachers in the newer teaching strategies. At first, teachers may find this restrictive, because every step in the process is standardized and fixed. As inquiry methods are explored, there should be adequate structure to assist the lesser-trained and unsophisticated teachers. This occurs in the third step, planning of the teaching strategies. In typical curriculum development, the teacher is given only the barest of instructions, and the final enactments are creative products of the teacher, not the designer. In the approach to teacher education under this project, the designer would provide complete strategic scaffolding for teacher enactments. Student instructional materials, whether textbooks or otherwise, will reflect an inquiry approach, but the teacher's guide will spell out the specific instructional events and behaviors. Because many teachers have not been trained in modern technological methods, they have no examples from their own school or that they learned during training at their previous university or college to fall back on. Various teacher manuals developed by current curriculum publishing companies should help in providing teachers with some new ideas and strategies that can be used as beginning building blocks.

Preparation of curricular materials and teacher's manuals seeking to combine the best parts of a district's current curriculum with modern approaches will require many steps to complete. Each step needs to be negotiated in terms of progress and effectiveness as the process continues from initial selection of curriculum development team members to review of existing materials and methods, to training, preparation of first and final drafts, pilot testing, and evaluation. Each step also constitutes professional development on the part of the team members themselves. The steps we envision are as follows (based on Snyder, 2004):

1. Study local school district's curriculum. The local school district may have special needs and emphases different from those of other schools, so it is important to be sure that these are given attention and appreciation in the design process.

2. Select certain topics or subtopics in the school's curriculum and match with both state and federal standards to ascertain areas of coverage and uncoverage.

3. Merge these plans to look for emphases and gaps.

4. Identify text and other printed material from a wide range of sources to serve as exemplars of good instructional content and approaches in terms of the selected essential questions.

5. Review of content by teachers in consultation with team members. Create collaborative teams to work through development details, using interactive international video and special curriculum links to provide for simultaneous connection to the materials.

6. Enhance materials and write the text for selected curriculum portions and teacher manual.

7. Identify educational assessments from a wide range of sources.

8. Study assessments provided by state educational agencies at relevant grade levels that have proven to be effective guides to instruction.

9. Compare/contrast the school's assessment material to other assessment material. Enhance and rewrite using various methods for demonstration, and creating an item bank of assessments for reference.

10. Prepare initial drafts of written materials; obtain feedback from other curriculum members, trainers, and mentors; revise and prepare final draft versions.

11. Select pilot test and assessment sites in the school district (with current classes) to ascertain level of difficulty and usefulness of responses.

12. Check to see that material exists for those areas where deficits are apparent in the current school district instructional program. (Use a small sample evaluation.)

13. Create pictures/illustration used in the curriculum subtopics. Identify new pictures or retain old ones as appropriate. Work again with the collaborative teams.

14. Identify other media resources needed for each topic.

15. Create enhancement and revision materials using multimedia materials. Pictures and media will be drawn from many sources of materials and resources.

16. Develop student and teacher assessment instruments for pilot tests: evaluate and incorporate feedback into preparation of final versions; print and distribute school district sample copies of curriculum and teacher's manual as required.

These are some of the important steps noted by Snyder (2004) to help initialize change and enhance the overall school improvement process.[1]

Curriculum Tip

Defining the scope of a project and setting budget parameters is crucial to the success of curriculum planning.

Establish Project Parameters

The first task is to define the scope of the project. In addition to providing for the necessary budget support, administrators need to answer several questions.

What Grade Levels Will Be Included?

The usual answer here is to improve the entire field, from kindergarten to Grade 12. However, other options might be considered: Improve elementary, and then add middle and high school levels; improve the middle and then add elementary and high; improve the high school and then build backwards to middle and elementary.

Which Ability Levels Will Be Included?

If the schools group by ability levels, then the district has to decide whether it will produce a different guide for each level or produce one basic guide that will then be supplemented with other materials. The mastery-curriculum theory posits a curriculum that can be mastered by most students. It makes more sense to produce one basic mastery guide, which is then supplemented with special materials for more able students.

Who Will Direct the Improvement Project?

Nearly all districts have found that a small task force is most efficient and effective. It should include one district administrator, one or two school administrators, the district supervisor for that field, at least one teacher-leader from each level to be included, and one parent representative. The task force should probably be led by one of the district administrators or the district supervisor.

How Much Time Will Be Needed?

Although the answer will vary with the size of the district, the scope of the project, and the resources available, most districts have found that one school year is sufficient for the entire project.

Orient for Mastery

Once the project parameters are set, the process begins with an orientation for all teachers who will be affected by the improvement program. The project leader should prepare materials summarizing the project and stressing two basic features: the improvement program will rely heavily on teacher input; and the improvement program will focus on the mastery curriculum only. As explained in Chapter 1, the mastery curriculum is that part of a field of study that meets two criteria: It is considered essential for all students; and it requires careful structuring and organization for optimal learning. District curriculum efforts should focus on the mastery curriculum; the organic curriculum and the enrichment curriculum can be strengthened at the school level, chiefly through staff development.

Map the Desired Curriculum

With that orientation accomplished, the next phase is mapping the desired curriculum, or finding out what teachers think *should* be taught in that field of study at their grade level. Note that the intent is to determine what teachers believe should be taught, not what they actually teach. Although several experts (see English, 1980, e.g.) advocate mapping to determine what teachers actually teach, several studies indicate quite clearly that teachers in effect know better than they teach. For a variety of reasons, they do not teach what they think should be taught: They lack materials, they believe they are constrained by administrators' or parents' preferences, and they are not sure that colleagues would approve (see Lieberman & Miller, 1984, for an excellent picture of the conflicts teachers experience in making decisions about classrooms and curricula). Therefore, it seems desirable to find out what they think they should be teaching, rather than simply formalizing the unnecessary compromises they have made. The process attempts to tap the classroom teacher's perception of the "ideal," as well as that of the scholars.

The best way to map the desired curriculum is to survey the teachers grade by grade. The survey instrument is a crucial element here, because the content and structure of the instrument will very much affect the kinds of data elicited. An expert in the field (either someone from the district or an external consultant) should develop a draft of the form by considering several crucial issues (Exhibit 7.2 shows a portion of a form used to map the social studies curriculum in a suburban school district):

- What elements of the mastery curriculum will be mapped? The objective is to elicit only essential information, not to clutter up the process with unnecessary detail. English teachers, for example, might decide that they do not want to get specific data about punctuation or usage items, because those matters are extensively covered in most English textbooks.
- What strands will be used for the mapping process? The strands are the elements that make up a given field of study—the divisions of that field. Any given field of study could be analyzed differently in terms of its strands. Some, for example, would argue that English language arts comprises only three strands: language, literature, and composition. The objective is to identify strands that make sense to the teachers—to conceptualize the field as they do, not as the experts do.

Exhibit 7.2   Mapping the Social Studies Curriculum: Skills

The Experts Recommend That . . .

1. Skill development is an important aspect of social studies goals. A skill is the ability to do something well—"knowing how."

2. Social studies skills are best developed through sequential instruction and practice, from kindergarten through Grade 12.

3. The social studies curriculum should emphasize the important skills of *acquiring information:* reading skills, study skills, reference and information searching skills, and the use of the computer in acquiring information.

4. The social studies curriculum should emphasize the skills of *organizing and using information:* critical thinking and decision-making skills.

5. The social studies curriculum should emphasize the skills needed for effective *interpersonal relationships and social participation:* personal skills, group skills, and social and political participation skills.

What information-acquiring skills do you think should be taught for mastery at your grade level?

1.

2.

3.

What information-organizing skills do you think should be taught at your grade level?

1.

2.

3.

What interpersonal and social skills do you think should be taught at your grade level?

1.

2.

3.

- How detailed should the mapping data be? Some who use mapping prefer to get very detailed data—long lists of specific objectives. Extensive experience with mapping suggests that more general data at this stage of the process are desirable. The specific objectives can be produced at a later stage of the process.
- Will the survey form include a summary of the recommendations of experts, so that teachers can make more informed decisions? One advantage of including such information is that the process of completing the mapping form also serves to educate teachers about recommended practice. A remaining concern is that summaries might influence teachers to recommend content they would probably not really want to include. Someone who knows the teachers well should make this decision.

That draft of the survey form should be tested with a small group of teachers to be sure that the directions are clear, that the strands seem appropriate, and that the structure of the form will elicit the kinds of information desired.

Teachers should then have an opportunity to complete the form during an in-service day or a faculty meeting. They should be notified in advance about the mapping process in case they wish to bring along textbooks, lesson plan books, or existing curriculum guides. Should the teachers complete the form together in small teams, or should they work alone? Either approach can be used. The team approach provokes good discussion; the individual approach prevents assertive teachers from dominating too much. The principal should make the decision, because he or she probably best understands faculty work habits.

The returns should then be collated on a large scope-and-sequence chart, which shows the strands, the grade levels, and the teachers' responses. Exhibit 7.3 shows a portion of such a chart. Note in this example that the chart also shows responses school by school, because such information can help leaders identify special staff-development needs.

Exhibit 7.3   Results of the Mapping Process: Grade 7 English

The following chart shows how the English language arts teachers in our three middle schools responded in indicating where they believe the parts of speech should be taught for mastery. The tallies indicate the number of teachers so responding for each part of speech.

Grammar: Parts of Speech		
North	*South*	*Central*
Noun-2	Noun-3	Do not wish to teach parts of speech in Grade 7
Verb-2	Verb-3	
Adjective-2	Adjective-3	
Adverb-2	Adverb-3	
	Determiner-3	
	Conjunction-3	
	Pronoun-3	
	Preposition-3	

> **Curriculum Tip**
>
> Teachers should have an opportunity to critique curriculum revisions.

Refine the Map

The next phase of the process is refining the map—reviewing the first version of the scope-and-sequence chart and making the necessary modifications. Here the advice of an expert in the field might be needed, unless there are local leaders who have a deep and current knowledge of that field. The results should be reviewed with these questions in mind:

1. What important skills and concepts have been omitted and should be included? Have the teachers ignored some important recommendations of the experts?

2. What less-important content has been included that might be dropped in order to reduce the overall content load? Have teachers tried to accomplish too much?

3. What skills and concepts seem to be misplaced by level and might better be taught at some lower or higher level? Does placement reflect current knowledge about cognitive development?

4. Where is there unnecessary duplication and repetition? Should some concepts and skills be taught for mastery at more than one grade level?

5. Does each strand show a desirable development from grade to grade? Is there good progression in relation to difficulty and complexity?

6. Is there good balance from grade to grade? Are some grades overloaded?

7. Does the scope-and-sequence chart respond adequately to state and district mandates concerning student competencies?

It is this phase especially where the influence of the ideal curriculum is paramount: The recommendations of the teachers are checked against the best judgment of the scholars and the experts.

The results of that critique are then reflected in a revised scope-and-sequence chart, which should be distributed to all administrators and classroom teachers involved. If a majority of the teachers object to the inclusion or placement of any specific item, then that item should be changed to reflect majority wishes. The intent is to develop a consensus curriculum, one that teachers will support.

Develop Curriculum Materials

The revised scope-and-sequence chart shows the grade-level placement of the major skills and concepts, strand by strand. The task force now needs to resolve this important issue: What curriculum materials are needed to help teachers implement the improved curriculum?

Three likely options are available for the curriculum materials: a curriculum guide, a curriculum-objectives notebook, and a curriculum-scenario book.

The standard *curriculum guide,* described in detail in Chapter 8, is perhaps used most often by districts. Its main components are the specific learning objectives and the activities suggested for each objective. If it is decided that a standard curriculum guide is needed, then a team of teachers should first use the general skills and concepts identified in the scope-and-sequence chart to develop the specific objectives. Thus, if the scope-and-sequence chart includes "nouns" as a concept in the grammar strand for Grade 8, then the team might develop this list of objectives:

1. Define *noun.*

2. Identify nouns in sentences.

3. Define *concrete* and *abstract nouns.*

4. Identify concrete and abstract nouns in sentences.

5. Use concrete and abstract nouns appropriately in sentences.

6. Define *proper* and *common nouns.*

7. Identify proper and common nouns in sentences.

8. Use proper nouns in sentences, capitalizing correctly.

That list of specific objectives is developed by analyzing the general skill or concept and determining what specific knowledge would be most appropriate for a given grade level. For each objective or set of objectives, the team would then identify the necessary learning activities.

The distinguishing feature of the curriculum guide is its comprehensiveness. It ordinarily covers every grade level. It not only details objectives and activities, but also contains a statement of the philosophy, suggestions for evaluation, and lists of materials.

The second option is to produce a *curriculum-objectives notebook.* The curriculum notebook is a loose-leaf notebook that contains the following: a summary of the research on how to teach a given subject, a copy of the scope-and-sequence chart in reduced form, and a list of the objectives for those grade levels taught by the teacher to whom the guide is issued. Thus, a seventh-grade teacher would have a copy of the seventh-grade objectives only. The objectives are developed through the process described above.

The distinguishing features of the curriculum-objectives notebook are its simplicity and flexibility. Only the essentials are included for only the grade level needed. Learning activities are not suggested; it is assumed that teachers can develop their own activities or be trained how to use varied educational activities from staff-development programs. An important message is implied by this format: "Achieve these mastery objectives in any reasonable way you wish." The flexibility is of two sorts. First, the loose-leaf format makes it easy for teachers to add, delete, and modify. They are encouraged to make the notebook their own: to include their own learning materials, to insert their lesson plans, to add professional articles they find useful. The second type of flexibility results from listing only the objectives. Teachers thus have a great deal of freedom both in how they organize those objectives for teaching and in how they teach. If some teachers wish to teach integrated units, they may; if some wish to focus on discrete skills, they may do so.

The *curriculum-scenario book* is the term given here to describe a collection of learning scenarios. The team takes each general concept or skill and asks, "What mix of learning activities, learning materials, and learning objectives can result in quality learning experiences?" Thus the team working on the concept *noun* might produce these scenarios, among others:

1. Have students read the section from Helen Keller's autobiography where she first learns that things have names. Introduce the concept of nouns as names. Discuss the importance of naming as an aspect of using language. Discuss as well the danger of reification—of believing that whatever is named, is real.

2. Have students write noun poems—poems made of lists of very specific nouns. Discuss the importance of specificity. Ask students to think about the usefulness of general nouns. Advanced students may be interested in the "abstraction ladder" of the general semanticists.

Notice that the scenarios emphasize the holistic nature of the learning experience; the objectives are there, but they are implicit and do not dictate what occurs. In addition to the learning scenarios, the scenario book would also include a copy of the scope-and-sequence chart and a summary of the research.

Which of these three choices is best? The answer depends on the needs of the system and the maturity and competence of the teachers. The curriculum guide probably best serves the needs of a school district in which administrative control is important and in which teacher experience is limited. The curriculum notebook is perhaps best in a district wishing to give mature and competent teachers a great deal of freedom while still emphasizing the importance of the mastery learning objectives. The scenario book perhaps best serves the needs of those districts whose leaders feel they can be more concerned with the quality of the learning experiences and less concerned with the specification of objectives.

Curriculum Tip

Time allocated to a particular area of the curriculum often relates directly to student achievement in that area.

Suggest Time Allocations

At some point in the improvement process, the leadership team should suggest time allocations to be used in teaching that subject. As noted previously, several studies (see Stallings, 1980) indicate that the time allocated to a particular area of the curriculum is related to achievement in that area. If 40% of the time in English is devoted to the study of grammar and 10% to writing, then achievement in grammar will be sharply ahead of achievement in writing.

Time allocations can be set several ways. One method uses the several strands as the basis for establishing time allocations at a district level. The curriculum-improvement task force reviews the recommendations of experts, reflects on district curricular goals, and recommends time allocations for each strand of the curriculum. These recommendations are made part of the final curriculum report.

A variation of this method relies more upon teacher input about time and strands and sets allocations level by level. A district supervisor poses the question to all teachers in the district who teach that subject at a given level of schooling: "As you think about the students in our middle schools, what percentage of time do you think we should allocate to each strand of this curriculum?" The supervisor helps the teachers agree on time allocations that reflect their perceptions and at the same time are responsive to district priorities. Here is how one group of middle school social studies teachers answered the question:

History: 50%

Map and study skills: 20%

Geography: 15%

Civics: 10%

Other: 5%

A third method focuses on unit planning at the school level. At every grade level in each school, teachers are asked to submit at the start of every marking period a unit-planning proposal, indicating for each unit the unit objective, the important concepts and skills emphasized, and the number of instructional periods allocated. The principal reviews these plans and discusses with the teachers any proposals that seem to reflect unwise allocations of time.

A fourth method relies upon staff development. Rather than specifying district guidelines or checking on unit plans, a member of the leadership team uses staff-development sessions to raise with the teachers issues of time allocation and achievement, to encourage teachers to discuss openly with each other how they allocate time, and to assist teachers in making decisions about time that reflect their knowledge of the learners and the district's curricular priorities.

Obviously, these methods can be used together, because in effect they complement each other.

Select and Develop Tests

The testing aspect of curriculum improvement involves both selection of the appropriate standardized tests and development of curriculum-based tests. First, the task force should consult with measurement specialists in the district to select standardized tests that adequately reflect the improved curriculum. This is an important consideration, because performance on standardized tests is often used as a measure of school success. While the issue is most critical in reading and mathematics, it also needs careful consideration in any area of the curriculum where standardized tests are used.

Curriculum-based or curriculum-referenced tests are also needed. These are locally developed examinations that are based solely on the district's curriculum. They can be used both to assess student achievement and to ensure that teachers are implementing the mastery curriculum. If teachers know that their students will be tested on specific content, they are more likely to emphasize that content.

How many curriculum-based tests are needed at each grade level? The answer seems to vary with the district and the level. The Pittsburgh Public Schools have developed a comprehensive program of curriculum-based tests (called Monitoring Achievement in Pittsburgh) that tests all students once at each grade level (see Rifugiato & Wilson, 1983, for a fuller discussion of this program). In many high schools, curriculum-based tests are administered as semester and final examinations.

Because these tests are often used as measures of student progress, school success, and even teacher performance, it is essential that they be developed with the utmost care, to ensure reliability and validity. The advice of measurement specialists will be required, and every form of the tests should be used in pilot studies before the tests are administered throughout the district.

Curriculum Tip

Computerized testing can provide quick and accurate measures that can be aligned with state and national standards.

Computerized Testing

School districts need and deserve accurate measures that align with standards and produce timely results. Districts also need scores that have meaningful references, for example:

- Norms for public accountability
- Curriculum references to focus instruction
- Prior scores to assess growth individually and collectively
- Benchmarks to measure yearly adequate progress

The Northwest Evaluation Association (NWEA; Olson, 2004) is one of a few organizations providing computerized achievement-level tests, aligned with local curriculum and state standards that provide accurate information about academic performance. The computerized adapted tests combine the benefit of technology with the integrity of level tests. Those tests draw from a bank of more than 15,000 calibrated test items. When students use the computerized adaptive test, the difficulty of the test is adjusted to the student's performance. The difficulty of each question is based on how well the student has answered the questions up to that point. As the student answers correctly, the questions become more difficult. If the student answers incorrectly, the questions become easier. Each student then receives a personalized test. Schools using NWEA's Measures of Academic Progress (MAP) system find that it reduces test anxiety and is very accurate. Students can stop at any point and go to lunch or recess and come back to start where they left off.

When a student completes the computerized adaptive test, the MAP system reports the student's score on the screen, allowing for immediate feedback. A student's score should show growth from year to year, and can be correlated longitudinally to scores from previous years. NWEA prepares tests for the district around local standards and curriculum or an already prepared state version. Within 24 hours, test administrators can download information about students and classes to a local server and print them off for individual teachers or parents.

Administrative printouts can also be obtained for data analysis purposes. Teachers can assess individual students at any time throughout the year to obtain gains made in certain areas. Curriculum and teaching strategies can be altered, depending on immediate feedback. This type of computerized adaptive test has proven to be one of the fastest and easiest ways to assess student learning and learner needs.

Select Instructional Materials

The improved curriculum will probably require new instructional materials. The task force should develop guidelines for evaluating materials, pointing out any special features that the improved curriculum might require ("All language arts texts must give special attention to the composing process."). An instructional materials committee should then use those guidelines in reviewing and selecting materials that will provide the best support for teachers implementing the improved curriculum.

It should be stressed here that the textbooks should serve the curriculum, not dictate it. In too many instances, districts reverse the process. They purchase a basic text and then use the publisher's scope-and-sequence chart as the basis of their own curriculum. The folly of such an approach is apparent to anyone who understands how school textbooks are designed. To sell well, they must appeal to a mass market; as a consequence, textbook authors often include content that they know is inappropriate, for no other reason than because they believe the market demands it. Thus, almost every elementary language arts series includes a great deal of grammar, even though most experts in the field believe that such content is totally inappropriate at the elementary level.

Curriculum Tip

Staff development is the key to successful curriculum implementation.

Provide for Staff Development

Consider two major issues in planning for staff development: timing and content. Because resources are limited, staff-development sessions must be held at a time when they will be most effective. As explained in Chapter 5, two approaches seem to be successful in the timing of staff development. One approach begins with and emphasizes staff development. The teachers in a given field of study meet for several sessions to review the research, to reflect on the recommendations of experts, to exchange ideas about teaching that subject, and to develop and share materials. The materials they produce—units of study, sample lessons, and student learning materials—in a sense become the improved curriculum. All that is needed is some work at the end to systematize and formalize what they have produced. Many new composition curricula, for example, have been developed in this way.

The second approach provides staff development at the crucial implementation stage. Once the improved project has been completed, instructional leaders conduct a series of staff-development sessions to help teachers understand the new program, to assist teachers in

Exhibit 7.4   Summary of Research on Effective Staff Development

---

Duration

1. The program should be ongoing and continuous.

Management

1. The principal should participate actively but should not dominate.
2. Teachers and administrators should plan the program jointly.
3. There should be regular project meetings in which participants review progress and discuss substantive concerns.

Content

1. The program should provide a necessary theoretical base for the new skills.
2. The program should give primary attention to the specific skills teachers believe they need.
3. The content should be timely, directly related to job needs.

Learning Activities

1. The program should make extensive use of hands-on activities and demonstrations of new skills.
2. The program should provide for the trial of those new skills in simulated or real settings.
3. The program should make it possible for teachers to get structured feedback about their use of those skills.
4. The program should provide opportunities for observation in other classrooms and schools.

Site

1. The program should be school-based, not university-based.

Instructors

1. Local teachers should be the instructors, with minimal use of outside consultants.

---

acquiring the new skills they will need, and to work with teachers in fleshing out the details of the improved program. In this manner, the staff development is seen as supportive of the curriculum. Either of these approaches can work well. The important consideration is to provide good staff development at a time when teachers seem to need it.

What is good staff development? Over the past decade, numerous research studies showed results that yield a clear picture of what staff development should be. Those results are summarized in Exhibit 7.4. While it may not be possible for a district to offer staff-development programs that meet all those guidelines, they should be given serious consideration whenever staff-development programs are planned (the guidelines have been synthesized from the following reviews of the research: Berman & McLaughlin, 1978; Joyce & Showers, 1980; Lawrence, 1979).

These nine steps taken together can help a district improve any field of study. Obviously they are time-consuming, but there are no shortcuts to educational quality.

Setting Staff Development as Priority

The key to providing staff in-service is to make staff development a priority from the onset (Whitehead, Jenson, & Boschee, 2003). For example, being able to integrate multimedia technology as a tool along with the traditional resources is now one of the essential elements of any classroom curriculum experience. Instituting the appropriate professional development for faculty, staff, and students is critical to the success of linking technology to the curriculum. It is essential to remember that computer technology is a tool and like any educational tool, teachers need to be trained in its appropriate use.

Curriculum Tip

It is the creation of a vision, formation of a sound plan, and the implementation of the plan at a local level that will determine the success or failure of any quality staff-development program.

Creative Staff-Development Strategies

A creative and innovative use of physical and human resources for staff development at the local level is going to make the real difference as to whether curriculum change will be successful. Most schools have been fortunate to have a number of educators and community members who have used this sense of creativity and innovation to provide quality staff development in their schools. A partial list of creative staff in-service ideas that have proven successful with limited resources include the following:

The Rule of Three

Teachers and staff are encouraged to help each other before going to a principal, supervisor, curriculum leader, or technology coordinator. *The simple rule is: Ask three and then me.* This little rule helps take pressure off of supervisors and coordinators and improves staff development and cooperation. Teachers can also use the rule with their students. If students ask three other students for help before going to the teacher, the teacher will have more time for curriculum-related instruction.

Early-Out Time for Students

Numerous schools have found ways to adjust schedules and provide one hour of planning and/or in-service time for teachers while maintaining state requirements for student contact time. Teachers have agreed to start earlier and end later each day as well as give up some recess time in order to develop a one-hour block of time per week for in-service and planning.

A key is to make sure that at least one early out per month is devoted to in-service. It is also important to make sure that state requirements for student contact time are met.

Sending Pairs of Individuals to Workshops and Seminars

A minimum of two individuals should attend workshops, seminars, and conferences. Teachers feel more comfortable working and training in a cooperative and supportive environment. Having at least two teachers (preferably from the same grade level) obtain the same in-service background is a tremendous way to increase the success of the curricular programs. Many programs have failed because only one teacher received the training and did not have the time or energy to carry the program through all of the implementation stages.

Substitute Rotation

School leaders have developed blocks of time by having a set of substitutes rotate through the schedule. For example, a set of five substitutes could release five teachers in the morning while the same five substitutes could release another set of teachers in the afternoon. Because this procedure diminishes regular teacher/student contact time, it is recommended that it should be used sparingly. It is beneficial when scheduling a special consultant for a certain period of time.

Free Consulting Services

Innovative school districts have collaborated to obtain the services of a free national consultant during a textbook adoption process. Some textbook companies are often happy to provide consultants without obligation on the hopes that their book series or materials will be selected. Naturally, some publishers do not provide such services. It is up to the creative administrator to contact publishing companies for possible services. A key here is to work with company representatives and collaborate with several adjoining school districts to justify the cost of bringing a consultant into a certain area.

Schedule Adjustment

Creative school leaders have found ways to adjust and align scheduled prep-times—such as music, art, library, and physical education classes—in order to provide in-service to new teachers. For example, it is beneficial to align an experienced teacher's prep-times with a new teacher's so they can visit and share ideas. The experienced teacher can assist and model effective uses of technology during these times.

College and University Pre-Service Programs

Higher education is always looking for ways to extend learning on campus as well as beyond campus. Recent restructuring efforts have led to major changes in pre-service and student teaching programs. Additional core classes now address curricular change as well as professional leadership projects. An innovative program now being used by a number of universities includes the use of online staff-development opportunities. Another involves the development of a collaborative master's degree in Educational Leadership to be delivered via interactive video from regional sites.

School/University/College Partnerships

Both college and university faculty are always looking for ways to integrate their students into local schools, whether they are small or large. Many schools are using college and university students to help in-service faculty on technological innovations and/or model teaching strategies involving technology in the classroom. Local school faculty members learn new ideas, and the university student receives a grade and credit for the experience.

Curriculum and Technology Cooperatives

More small and rural school districts are now realizing the benefits of developing cooperatives. What cannot be achieved singly can be achieved through a collaboration of resources. School districts have banded together and have hired curriculum and technical coordinators who can provide the training and staff development needed at a local level. Some school district cooperatives have joined with colleges and universities to provide credit to experienced teachers acting as instructors, as well as credit for participants.

Community Resources

Both small and large school districts across the country have found valuable resource people within their communities. Individual community members who have a great deal of technical experience can provide both equipment and knowledge to school districts. Many individuals in the private sector are especially good at providing in-service in the area of word processing, electronic mail, satellite, multimedia, cable, and other technical applications. The key is that school leaders seek out and involve community members who can make these types of contributions in the area of technology to the district.

Management Planning Matrix

The Management Planning Matrix has been one of the most successful tools used by school leaders in designing effective staff-development programs in the country. The Northwest Regional Educational Laboratory in Portland, Oregon, has developed a Management Planning Matrix that can be used to plan, implement, and evaluate an effective staff-development program. The matrix design encourages planners not only to develop technology staff-development goals, but also to formulate measurable indicators of successful in-service. The matrix also forces planners to detail activities, leadership roles, and to set implementation and evaluation dates (Whitehead et al., 2003; see also Appendix A, Management and Monitoring Matrix, in this volume).

It is therefore apparent that staff development is becoming an increasingly integral and critical part of our schools. Our nation's schools cannot address the problem of educational equity without first talking about substantial teacher preparation linking technology, pedagogy, and curriculum development. If teachers are to make the most effective use of new teaching strategies and technology applications available for classrooms, then state leaders will have to focus on providing adequate funding for staff development. Currently, many school districts are investing thousands of dollars in technological equipment and software, but very little toward in-service programs. It is now time to establish an equitable balance between technology and staff development.

CHAPTER OVERVIEW

This chapter describes a process for reconceptualizing fields of study and emphasizes that staff development is becoming an increasingly integral and critical part of our schools. The chapter illustrates how basic attempts have been made in the past to reconceptualize fields of study, and it outlines what current curriculum leaders can do to best improve fields of study. School districts usually decide to improve a field of study by strengthening one subject area over several grade levels. The decision to reconceptualize a field of study typically emerges from an awareness of a deficiency, such as when poor articulation across the various levels of schooling exists, when teachers are no longer using existing guides, or when the present curriculum for a particular field of study has become outdated. Substantial teacher preparation is necessary to improve a field of study so that teachers are equipped to make the most effective use of technology, pedagogy, and curriculum development in our nation's classrooms.

CHAPTER TERMS

Diagnostic-Prescriptive Model

Elective Model

Recommended (Ideal) Curriculum

Written (Formal) Curriculum

Taught (Perceived) Curriculum

Operational Curriculum

Learned (Experiential) Curriculum

Curriculum Guide

Curriculum-Objectives Notebook

Curriculum-Scenario Book

APPLICATIONS

1. If you wanted to develop a series of elective English courses for high school students, how could you ensure that all students would develop their reading and writing skills, regardless of the electives they chose?

2. Design a mapping form for a subject you know well. In designing the form, consider the issues presented in this chapter's discussion of such forms.

3. Develop a detailed planning schedule that you could follow in improving a field of study in a local school district. Note strengths and weaknesses of the planning schedule and why you chose this approach.

4. How do you account for the fact that the ideal curricula of the scholars and experts have had such little impact on the written or the taught curriculum? As an administrator, how would you counteract this problem?

5. Suppose you are part of a Grade 5 team of teachers. You decide that you would like to give the pupils some choices about the social studies content by offering elective units. How would you ensure that all pupils mastered the requisite skills, regardless of the content emphasis? How would you incorporate technology to achieve this goal?

CASE STUDY

The following case study is an example of how an Ohio principal is able to use curriculum mapping in order to improve the school curriculum.

"We have a situation whereby the fourth-grade teachers are not teaching the basic skills in science," says Principal Art Mandel. "The fourth-grade teachers are so busy teaching areas of personal interest that they are not addressing basic skills. The students, as a result, are not doing as well as they should on their standards-based test."

Susan Gibbons, a fourth-grade teacher, listens and nods her head in agreement. "Yes, you are right," she says. "Martha and Bob do have a rather eclectic approach to teaching and have been teaching that way for years."

Principal Mandel is frustrated. "How are we going to get our curriculum scope and sequence on track?" he asks.

"Well," says Gibbons, smiling. "Why don't you arrange for some staff development on curriculum mapping? That way, Martha and Bob can see how the fourth-grade curriculum either aligns or doesn't align with other district schools as well as with state standards. Once they visibly see that their programs are not in alignment, they will hopefully be more understanding as to why they need to make a change."

"That sounds like a great idea," says Principal Mandel approvingly. "I'll contact the district office as well as the local university to see if we can get some help in setting up an in-service on curriculum mapping."

THE CHALLENGE

Formulating strategies to improve fields of study and enhance staff development is a major goal for many school administrators. What can Principal Mandel do to get more teachers like Susan Gibbons involved in using technology effectively in their classrooms?

Key Issues/Questions

1. What are your impressions of how Principal Art Mandel handled the situation involving Martha—a technology-reluctant teacher at his school?

2. Do you feel that Principal Mandel might have used or manipulated teacher Susan Gibbons to solve his problem?

3. How do you think other teachers will react when they find out that Susan Gibbons received a new computer laptop and they didn't? What should be discussed?

4. What are some other possible ways that Principal Mandel can use the coordination and rescheduling of teacher prep-periods—such as music, art, physical education, and library—to enhance staff development and improve fields of study at his school?

5. How would you feel about Principal Mandel asking Susan Gibbons and Martha to attend a technology-related curriculum conference together? Do you think this would be useful? Why or why not?

NOTE

1. Snyder, C. W. (2004). *Calendar of activities/itinerary narrative.* An unpublished paper completed for the University of Montana International Studies Program. Used with permission.

REFERENCES

Bangert, R. L., Kulik, J. A., & Kulik, C. C. (1983). Individualized systems of instruction in secondary schools. *Review of Educational Research, 53,* 143–158.

Berman, P., & McLaughlin, M. W. (1978). Federal programs supporting educational change. In *Implementing and sustaining innovations* (R-1589, No. 8, HEW). Washington, DC: U.S. Office of Education.

Copperman, P. (1978). *The literacy hoax.* New York: William Morrow.

Cusick, P. A. (1983). *The egalitarian ideal and the American high school: Studies of three schools.* New York: Longman.

English, F. W. (1980). Curriculum mapping. *Educational Leadership, 37,* 558–559.

Goodlad, J. I. (1977). What goes on in our schools. *Educational Researcher, 6,* 3–6.

Hillocks, G., Jr. (1972). *Alternatives in English: A critical appraisal of elective programs.* Urbana, IL: National Council of Teachers of English.

Joyce, B. R., & Showers, B. (1980). Improving inservice training: The messages of research. *Educational Leadership, 37,* 390–392.

Lawrence, G. (1979). *Patterns of effective inservice education: A state of the art summary of research on materials and procedures for changing teacher behaviors in inservice education.* Tallahassee: Florida Department of Education.

Lieberman, A., & Miller, L. (1984). *Teachers, their world, and their work: Implications for school improvement.* Alexandria, VA: Association for Supervision and Curriculum Development.

Oliver, A. I. (1978). *Maximizing mini-courses: A practical guide to a curriculum alternative.* New York: Teachers College Press.

Olson, L. (2004). Researchers sort out data-analysis software. *Education Week, 23*(18), p. 6.

Rifugiato, F. J., & Wilson, H. A. (1983). *A guide to the MAP project.* Pittsburgh, PA: Pittsburgh School District.

Schmidt, B. W. (2004, June 21). District's new leader plans better learning. *Argus Leader,* p. A2.

Snyder, C. W. (2004). *Calendar of activities/itinerary narrative.* An unpublished paper completed for the University of Montana International Studies Program.

Stallings, J. (1980). Allocated academic learning time revisited, or beyond time on task. *Educational Researcher, 9,* 11–16.

Washburne, C. W., & Marland, S. P., Jr. (1963). *Winnetka: The history and significance of an educational experiment.* Englewood Cliffs, NJ: Prentice Hall.

Whitehead, B., Jenson, D. F. N., & Boschee, F. (2003). *Planning for technology: A guide for school administrators, technology coordinators and curriculum leaders.* Thousand Oaks, CA: Corwin.

Ysseldyke, J. E., & Tardrew, S. P. (2003). *Differentiating math instruction: A large-scale study of accelerated math: Final report.* Wisconsin Rapids, WI: Renaissance Learning, Inc. Retrieved March 23, 2005, from http://research.renlearn.com/research/139.asp

Chapter 8

PROCESSES FOR DEVELOPING NEW COURSES AND UNITS

From time to time, administrators, supervisors, or teachers will decide that a new course is needed. In some cases, they will determine that an existing course should be completely redeveloped with a fresh perspective: "Let's rewrite our American history course—the old course just isn't working anymore." In some instances, they will see the need for a new course to fill a gap newly perceived in the existing program: "We need a course in Career Planning." Elementary teachers will also often sense the need for a new integrated unit. This chapter explains how to develop a new course or unit using two contrasting processes: the standard *technological* process, and what is termed here a *naturalistic* process. The intent is not to suggest that one process is better than the other, but only to contrast two divergent processes that might be used in different subject areas, at different grade levels. The following questions will be addressed in this chapter:

- What is the technological process of curriculum planning?
- What is the naturalistic process of curriculum planning?
- How can curriculum leaders develop new courses that involve both the technological and naturalistic processes of curriculum planning?

Key to Leadership

Successful curriculum leaders realize that curriculum planning should drive technology rather than technology drive curriculum.

THE TECHNOLOGICAL PROCESS
OF CURRICULUM PLANNING

Curriculum Tip

The term *technological process* describes any curriculum development model that emphasizes the importance of defining terminal learning objectives early in the process and then identifies the steps needed to accomplish those objectives.

While the technological process has many variations, it tends to be a rational, systematic, ends-oriented model. Its basic principles were perhaps most clearly articulated by Tyler (1949), and its details are probably most clearly explained in manuals written for industrial training (see, e.g., Mager & Beach, 1967). Its systematic nature and its efficiency make it the preferred process in most industrial and military training. While details of the process will vary from specialist to specialist, in general it moves in an orderly sequence through certain specified steps (for a useful explication of the technological process, see Wulf & Schave, 1984):

1. Determine the course parameters—a rationale for the course, its general goals, and its probable time schedule.

2. Assess the needs of the learners.

3. On the basis of those needs and the goals previously specified, identify the course objectives, the terminal outcomes desired.

4. Determine the optimal sequence for those course objectives and cluster related objectives into unified learning experiences.

5. For each objective, identify learning activities that will enable the learners to achieve those objectives.

6. Select instructional materials that will support the learning activities.

7. Identify methods by which the attainment of those objectives will be assessed.

8. Systematize all these decisions in a curriculum guide.

(Wulf & Schave, 1984, cited in Glatthorn, 1987, p. 198)

It should be noted that the steps identified above are usually followed in that sequence; the most competent technological developers use them in a recursive, iterative fashion and do not apply them in a mechanistic, unthinking manner.

Each of these steps will be described in detail below, using as an example a course for high school students in career planning.

Curriculum Tip

A statement of principles guiding curriculum development and an argument for any new course is an important step in developing parameters of curriculum projects.

Determine Course Parameters

The first step is to determine course parameters by establishing a rationale for the course—a statement of the principles guiding the developers and an argument for the course. With the rationale established, the curriculum specialist then makes a determination about the goals of the course—the general outcomes desired (the term *curriculum specialist* is used here to designate any administrator or supervisor with responsibility for and training in curriculum development; he or she may organize a team of colleagues to assist in the process). A course goal is a very general statement of the intended outcomes; typically, a one-semester course would have no more than three goals. Thus, the goal for the career course might be stated in this fashion:

This course will help students develop their career-planning skills.

A new integrated unit for fourth grade might have this as its goal:

This unit will help the pupils understand that there are many different kinds of careers and that each career has value to the society.

With the course or unit goal established, the developers then consider the matter of the course schedule—how long will it last, how often will it meet, and for how many minutes per session.

Assess the Needs of the Learners

The next step is needs assessment; a need is perceived as a gap between a present and a desired state. Thus, the needs-assessment process evaluates the present state of the learners in relation to the general outcomes expected. The data for the needs assessment can come from several sources: achievement scores, surveys, observations, interviews, and measures of performance.

Curriculum Tip

The purpose of data collection is not to judge people's performances or to profile underachieving students.

Data should be regarded as a tool for continuous improvement (Johnson, 2000). In addition, school districts can begin by making better use of existing data, and by choosing a specific area of focus. With clearly defined objectives in place, schools will garner the support and cooperation needed to meet their goals and objectives (Johnson, 2000).

Identify Course Objectives

The curriculum specialist would next take the critical step of identifying the course objectives. This is usually accomplished by first doing a task analysis of the outcome desired. In the case of the career-planning course, the specialist would ask: "Given what is known about how career choices are best made, what specific skills must be mastered?" The results of the task analysis are then checked against the needs-assessment data as a means of determining which of those skills should be stressed for the intended population. The result would be a comprehensive list of course objectives, stated in measurable terms. Exhibit 8.1 shows a list that might be developed for this course in career planning.

Sequence and Cluster Course Objectives

With the objectives determined, the next step is to determine the optimal sequence in which those objectives should be mastered. Curriculum specialists who use the technological process usually opt for a learning-relaxed sequence, determining the optimal sequence by examining the relationships among the objectives and then assessing the entry-level skills, knowledge, and attitudes of the learners. In the case of the career-planning course, the order in which the objectives are listed in Exhibit 8.1 is one that many curriculum specialists would use as the optimal sequence in a course of this sort. The sequence establishes a conceptual basis, moves to the student's awareness of self, and orders the rest of the objectives in what seems chiefly to be a temporal sequence.

Once the specific objectives are sequenced appropriately, the next step is to cluster related objectives into unified learning experiences, such as units of study or instructional modules. The specialist examines the entire list, assesses the constraints of the schedule, reflects on student interest and attention span, and determines which objectives should be placed together in a unified set of learning experiences. Thus, the specialist may determine that objectives 1 and 2 in Exhibit 8.1 might make a good, brief introductory unit, which would establish the conceptual base for what follows.

Identify Learning Activities

The curriculum specialist would identify one or more learning activities for each objective stated that would be specifically shaped to help the learners master the objective. The learning activities are usually seen as an ordered set of learning experiences that move the learner step by step to the objective. Consider, for example, objective 7 in Exhibit 8.1:

In a well-organized essay, explain at least two factors that have influenced your career values.

The following learning activities could be prescribed:

1. Identify several possible factors that might influence career values: culture, ethnic group, family, peers, gender, region in which you were reared, school experiences, physiological factors.

2. By reflecting about yourself and your values, identify two of those having the greatest influence.

Exhibit 8.1   Course Objectives for Career Planning

1. Define these three terms in a way that distinguishes them from each other: *job, career, vocation.*

2. Define these terms correctly: *talent, skill, value.*

3. Describe two career-related talents that you believe you possess to a high degree.

4. List four career-related skills that you possess.

5. Explain three ways in which you might acquire additional career-related skills.

6. Explain the two career values that seem most important to you.

7. In a well-organized essay, explain at least two factors that have influenced your career values.

8. In a well-organized paragraph, explain how you would distinguish between a highly reliable source and a less reliable source of career information.

9. Identify three reliable sources that provide current information about career opportunities and requirements.

10. Using those sources, identify three careers for which you possess the necessary talents and that would adequately respond to your career values.

11. Identify the education and experience you would need for securing an entry-level position in each of those three careers.

12. Describe the processes by which you would obtain the required education and experience.

13. Explain three sources of information you would use in locating an entry-level vacancy in one of the three careers selected.

14. Write a career resume that you could use in applying for one of those positions.

15. Demonstrate that you know how to handle a job interview by role-playing such an interview.

16. In a well-organized essay, explain three factors that might cause you to change careers.

---

3. Check your perceptions and gather supporting information by discussing the question with parents and friends.

4. Develop a plan for your essay; have the preliminary plan reviewed by your teacher and a classmate.

5. Use the revised plan to write the first draft of the essay.

6. Ask a classmate to edit your essay and give you feedback about the essay.

7. Write a revised draft of the essay.

Note that learning activities are chosen primarily on the basis of their fit with the objective; only those activities that move the student step by step to the objective are prescribed.

Select Instructional Materials

With the objectives and activities identified, the next step is to select the instructional materials that will help accomplish the objectives and support the learning activities. A systematic search would be made for texts, computer software, video media, and other instructional media.

Curriculum Tip

Selecting instructional materials that will help accomplish the objectives and support the learning activities is key to the process.

Identify Assessment Methods

The specialist would next determine which assessment methods are needed. Some assessment is done to evaluate readiness for a unit and to diagnose learner needs; some is done to provide the student and teacher with formative feedback to determine whether remediation is needed; and some is done to make summative judgments for grading purposes. In addition to the usual written tests, the specialist might decide to make use of other assessment methods, such as interviews, observations, or performance tests.

The specialist planning the career course, after consultation with measurement specialists, might decide on the following tests: one diagnostic test to determine specific learning needs of each student, one short formative test for each lesson, one longer formative test for each group of five lessons, and one final summative test covering the entire course.

In a more recent approach to assessment, Stiggins (2002) states that we can also use assessments for learning. "If assessments of learning provide evidence of achievement for public reporting, then assessments for learning serve to help students learn more. The crucial distinction is between assessment to determine the status of learning and assessment to promote greater learning" (p. 4).

The term *assessment for learning* was coined by the Assessment Reform Group (1999) in their *Assessment for Learning: Beyond the Black Box*. Whatever assessment teachers decide to use, the following guidelines should be considered:

- Understanding and articulating in advance of teaching, the achievement targets that their students are to reach
- Informing their students about those learning goals, in terms that students understand, from the very beginning of the teaching and learning process
- Becoming assessment literate and thus able to transform their expectations into assessment exercises and scoring procedures that accurately reflect student achievement

- Using classroom assessments to build students' confidence in themselves as learners and help them take responsibility for their own learning, so as to lay a foundation for lifelong learning
- Translating classroom assessment results into frequent descriptive feedback (versus judgmental feedback) for students, providing them with specific insights as to how to improve
- Continuously adjusting instruction based on the results of classroom assessments
- Engaging students in regular self-assessment, with standards held constant so that students can watch themselves grow over time and thus feel in charge of their own success
- Actively involving students in communicating with their teacher and their families about their achievement status and improvement.

(Stiggins, 2002, p. 5)

Curriculum Tip

An important step in developing new courses is to systematize decisions into a curriculum guide.

Develop the Curriculum Guide

While formats vary from district to district, most guides developed from the processes described above include the following components:

1. A rationale for the course or a statement of the philosophy that guided the course planners

2. A list of the objectives, ordered in the desired sequence

3. The recommended learning activities, displayed graphically so that their relationship to the objectives is very clear—in some cases, activities are described under each objective; in some guides, the objectives and activities are arranged in parallel columns

4. A list of recommended instructional materials

5. Copies of tests and suggestions for other assessment activities

The Technological Process Summarized

Observe certain key features of the technological approach. The basic flow of the decision-making process might be described as progressing from specific to general or as "bottom-up." Specific outcomes are identified and then clustered into related sets of learning experiences. Objectives play a central role: They are specified early in the design process and control the selection of learning activities and instructional materials. The process is thus essentially ends-oriented. Methods are determined on the basis of the extent to which they accomplish specified outcomes, and the process is primarily linear.

This technological approach has several advantages when used by an expert or a team of knowledgeable people. It seems orderly and systematic and thus might be more readily mastered by those less skilled in curriculum work.

However, it has several significant limitations. It seems insensitive to the politics of curriculum making. Most curricular decisions in schools are inherently political, because they involve issues of power and "turf." The new course in career planning, for example, might be opposed by any teachers who include career units in the courses they already teach; they would see the new course as dealing with content they believed they owned.

THE NATURALISTIC PROCESS OF CURRICULUM PLANNING

An awareness of the limitations of the technological process and extensive work with curriculum specialists and teachers have led to the development of a special version of the naturalistic process.

Curriculum Tip

The *naturalistic process* attempts to embody the following characteristics:

- attempts to be sensitive to the political aspects of curriculum making
- places greater emphasis on the quality of the learning activities
- attempts to reflect more accurately the way curricula have actually been developed
- takes cognizance of the way teachers really plan for instruction

---

In the following discussion, the steps in the process are described in the order in which courses ordinarily would be taken, although other sequences could just as well be followed. The process has been conceptualized as an interactive and recursive one, in which flexibility is emphasized. To illustrate these steps and to highlight comparisons with the technological approach, the discussion again uses the development of a new course for high school students in career planning. It then shows how an elementary team would use the same process in developing an integrated unit.

Assess the Alternatives

Before developing a new course, the naturalistic process begins with a systematic examination of the alternatives to a new course. Although many of those using a technological approach begin in the same manner, some technological developers seem to move too quickly from the identification of need to the development of the course.

To understand why this assessment of alternatives is important, consider how the initiative for a new course usually develops. Someone with a stake in the outcome, such as a principal, department head, or teacher, assumes that a new course is needed.

Only in rare instances does the conviction emerge from a rational analysis of the data available. Even though most experts urge curriculum supervisors to use such information sources as test scores, parent surveys, and student interviews, such data are often sought to justify a predetermined solution, not to establish the need for a given response.

For this reason it is important for someone in authority—such as the director of curriculum or the principal—to examine the alternatives before allowing the decision to offer a new course to move ahead too quickly. Any new course is costly. It involves what economists call "opportunity cost"—every student who takes the new course loses in the process the opportunity for some other educational experience. It also involves substantial development cost— the time and efforts of those responsible for planning it. Finally, it involves significant implementation costs—the funds needed to staff the course, provide facilities, and secure the necessary equipment and materials.

What are the alternatives to offering a new course? Several alternatives are available for those interested in a new course in career planning:

- Ignore the need, based on the assumption that somehow adolescents will acquire the career-planning skills they need without organizational intervention.
- Ask some other agency to respond to the need. Decide that helping adolescents make wise career choices is the responsibility of the family, the business community, or the YMCA—not the school.
- Provide for the need through the activities program. Arrange for assemblies, career-planning days, or career clubs; develop programs for the homeroom.
- Use noncurricular methods of responding to the need. Put career materials in the library; buy computer software on career planning and make it available in the guidance suite; increase the guidance staff, adding specialists in career planning.
- Integrate the skills into existing courses. In each existing subject, include units in the careers that emphasize career-planning skills.

It is not suggested here that any of these alternatives is necessarily better than offering a new course. The point is simply that the alternatives should be examined before finally deciding that a new course is needed.

Curriculum Tip

The process of staking out territory is very similar to that of identifying course parameters.

Stake Out the Territory

If it still appears that a new course is the most desirable option, then the next step is to stake out the territory. The planning team considers the students for whom the course is intended, makes some initial determinations about the schedule, and tentatively identifies the coverage of the course. Note that the active parties in the naturalistic process are identified as a planning team, in contradistinction to the curriculum specialist, because teams of teachers more typically are involved in using the naturalistic process.

However, there is an important difference between identifying the course parameters and staking out the territory—a difference connoted by the metaphors used. The identification of course parameters tends to be more definitive and final; the staking out of territory is a more tentative and open-ended boundary-setting process.

In order to assist in further development, the course territory should be described in a course prospectus. The course prospectus presents the answers to possible questions—and does so in a manner that will both guide planners and inform others. In the case of the career course, the prospectus might read as follows:

> We're thinking about offering a new course tentatively entitled "Thinking About Careers." As we see the course now, it would be an elective offered to all juniors and seniors, although our hunch is that it would probably appeal most of all to those not presently interested in higher education. It would probably run for one term, and meet three times a week for a total of about 40 classroom hours. As we presently conceptualize the course, it would help students examine their career values, assess career skills, learn how to retrieve career information, and do some systematic career planning. It would probably de-emphasize the study of particular careers and focus on processes instead. Our written materials will include only the mastery component, not enrichment or organic content. All of these notions are very tentative; we need the advice of anyone competent and interested.

Observe that the description is general and the language tentative. The intent is to identify broad boundaries that will be flexible enough to accommodate the ideas of all those who will later be involved in the more detailed planning.

Develop a Constituency

As noted above, all curriculum making has a political aspect. Those developing the new course wield power to advance their own interests. While genuinely concerned with improving the education of students, they are also motivated by personal interests: to enhance their reputations, to make their positions more secure, to win the attention of superiors. For this reason, it is important throughout the naturalistic process for course planners to build a constituency for the new course—to mobilize support and neutralize likely opposition. How much time and energy are devoted to such politicking will depend, of course, upon the likely impact of the proposed change and the extent to which the course seems to have broad-based support.

Win the Support of the Powerful

Early in the process, course planners should try to secure the endorsement of those with power. Several studies (see, e.g., Leithwood & Montgomery's 1982 review) indicate that in most schools the principal plays a key role as the curriculum gatekeeper. If the principal supports a curriculum change, the process moves along well. If the principal opposes the change, major problems develop: meetings are canceled, requisitions are delayed, and space is unavailable.

Central office supervisors who try to impose curricular changes on resistant principals soon discover the folly of such attempts.

Curriculum Tip

Opening up the planning process to all those who want to participate is an important component of the process.

Share the Power and the Glory

It is important to make the new course "our course," not "my course." Make a special effort to involve the undecided. Spread the credit around in all public discussions: "We're making good progress in finding speakers, thanks to the special efforts of Dr. Walker."

If curriculum development is to respond adequately to regional differences, including socio-cultural and ethnic diversity, school districts must allow the stakeholders (the students, parents, and community) the opportunity to participate in the curriculum-development process (Bude, 1999). This decentralization, or school-based curriculum development, provides the advantages of greater teacher involvement in the selection of textbooks, designing of lesson plans, and implementation of teaching practices. However, such involvement also calls for proper in-service training programs for those teachers. In the end, teacher involvement in curriculum development will also provide motivation and ownership to the teaching staff (Bude, 1999).

Be Prepared to Negotiate

The process of getting a new course approved often requires the art of negotiating. Especially when the opposition seems strong, course planners should give themselves room to bargain, by asking publicly for more than they hope to get: asking for four periods, hoping to get three; asking for two classrooms in the expectation of getting one.

All these strategies will require time. For that reason, the process of developing a constituency is not initiated and then dropped; instead, it should continue throughout both the planning and implementation stages.

Curriculum Tip

Course planners should begin with a cursory "needs assessment" of the students.

Build the Knowledge Base

As noted in Chapter 5, another fundamental step that should be initiated early is building the knowledge base—retrieving and systematizing information about the students, assessing faculty readiness, analyzing the relevant research, and identifying available materials and programs. Too often those using the technological process slight this crucial step: Course planners often ignore those who will be teaching the course, slight the research, and act as if nothing else has ever been done in the field before.

The questions listed in Exhibit 8.2 can guide the development of the knowledge base as it relates to course development. Note that the questions here are not as comprehensive as those suggested in Chapter 5; because local course planners usually have limited resources, only the most important questions are listed.

The student questions are designed to help planners understand the constraints imposed by the characteristics of those likely to take the course. In contrast to the usual "needs assessment," which often turns out to be a useless documentation of the obvious ("Students need to reflect about their career values"), this component of the knowledge base reminds developers of the reality they face in implementing the course successfully. Will the course attract less able, unmotivated students? Will many of them have serious reading problems? Will they have trouble understanding abstract concepts?

The teacher questions are intended to guide the developers in deciding how detailed the course planning should be and how much staff development will be required. Comments of the following sort illustrate how the answers might impinge on the planning process:

- We'll have to use teachers not too interested in teaching the course, so we can't expect too much extra time from them.
- This is a new field for most teachers; we'd better be rather explicit as to where to find materials.
- The course will be taught by a few of our most competent people, so we don't need to go into a lot of detail about teaching methods.

The research questions focus on course content and teaching/learning methods. Stated generally here so that they can apply to any new course, they should be rephrased more specifically by the planners so that they can be answered more readily. Thus, those developing the career-planning course might seek answers to these more specific questions:

- What do we know about the career values of adolescents?
- What do we know about general patterns of career choice? How stable are career decisions?
- What do we know about changing occupational trends?
- What do we know about the skills needed for career decision making?
- What instructional methods seem to be most effective in developing decision-making skills?

Finally, the questions on "what's available?" help the planners profit from the experience and work of others. If they locate an excellent program developed by a major curriculum center, they may decide to adopt it with modifications.

Block in the Unit

With the knowledge base developed, the next step that usually should be taken is to block in the units—to determine the number and focus of each unit of study that will make up the

Exhibit 8.2   Questions to Answer in Building the Knowledge Base

---

The Students

Consider the students likely to take the course and find out . . .

1. What is students' IQ range?
2. What levels of cognitive development are represented?
3. What is known about their academic achievement?
4. What are their predominant values and attitudes?
5. What similar learning experiences have they already had?

The Teachers

Consider the teachers likely to be assigned to the course and find out . . .

1. How interested are they in teaching the course?
2. How much do they know about the content likely to be covered by the course?
3. How effective are they as teachers?

The Research

Consider the course territory and find out . . .

1. What research is available that will help planners determine course content?
2. What research is available that will help planners select teaching/learning activities?

What's Available

Consider the course territory and find out . . .

1. Have similar courses been developed by national curriculum centers?
2. Have similar courses been offered by other schools?
3. What materials (texts, video media, computer software) are readily available in the field?

---

new course. Note that while the recommended direction is top-down (from general to specific, from unit to lesson), in some cases it might be desirable to reverse the flow—to identify lessons and then cluster lessons into units.

In blocking in the units, planners make tentative decisions about these issues:

1. How many units of study are planned?

2. How many lessons will there probably be in each unit?

3. What is the general objective of each unit?

4. What is the optimal sequence of the units?

One "unit-blocking process" that seems to work well in most disciplines is the following one. First, identify the probable number of units by reviewing the course territory and assessing the interest span of the learners: "We're planning a one-semester course that will meet three times a week, and many of the learners will probably have a short attention span, so maybe we need about seven to nine units—some two weeks long, some three weeks long."

Then tentatively identify the general objective of each unit. The *unit objective,* as the term is used here, is the one general outcome desired at the end of the unit. How can the tentative unit objectives be produced? One method that seems to work well is to convene the planning team, review with them the course prospectus and the knowledge base, and then ask, "What do we really want the students to learn?"

Here is a list of tentative unit objectives that might be produced by those developing the career course:

- Understanding your career values
- Learning about your skills and aptitudes
- Thinking about the education you need
- Retrieving and using career information
- Career-mobility skills

Once the tentative list of unit objectives has been developed, the planning team should review the list in order to refine it. The refining process attempts to reduce the number of unit objectives to match the number of units previously identified, and to ensure that the final list closely matches the course territory. Questions of the following sort should be asked:

- Which unit objectives might be combined?
- Which unit objectives are of low priority and might be eliminated?
- Which unit objectives are tangential to the central thrust of the course and might be eliminated?

The refining stage is also the best time to make a tentative decision about the number of lessons. In making this decision, the team should reflect on the complexity and importance of the unit and the attention span of the learners, realizing, of course, that the decision is only preliminary.

Thus, the team planning the career course might produce a final list such as the following one, in which both the unit objectives and the probable numbers of lessons are indicated:

- Careers, jobs, and vocations: 6
- Looking at yourself—skills, aptitudes, values: 6
- Changing occupational needs: 6
- Retrieving and using career information: 9

The final step in this stage of blocking out the units is determining the optimal sequence. Again, as with the technological process, course planners would have several types of sequences available to them. However, those using the naturalistic process ordinarily combine several types of sequence, giving considerable weight to student interest and the rhythms of the school year.

Plan Quality Learning Experiences

With the units blocked out, the next stage in the process is planning quality learning experiences—designing a set of learning experiences that together will lead to the unit objective. It is perhaps at this stage that the naturalistic process differs most significantly from the standard model; it therefore might be useful at this point to clarify the distinction.

Curriculum Tip

In the technological model, objectives drive the planning process. In the naturalistic model, objectives are set to produce desirable student experiences or outcomes.

In the technological model, the objectives determine the activities and influence the choice of materials. The intent is to control the learning process to ensure that a predetermined end is achieved. The process is linear and unidirectional, as Exhibit 8.3 suggests.

In the naturalistic process, the planners attempt to design quality learning experiences—stimulating teaching/learning transactions that will produce several desirable outcomes, some of which might occur serendipitously. They think about the learners—their learning styles, their motivations, and their abilities. They keep in mind the unit objective, as the general outcome to be attained, and reflect on the more specific objectives it comprises. They search for excellent materials that will have high interest value and good instructional payoff. They reflect on learning activities that will appeal to the learners, will challenge them to think, and will give them an opportunity to be creative.

Sometimes the specific objectives will dominate their thinking, as in the technological approach. Sometimes, however, planners will begin by thinking about materials, and will derive an objective from a particularly fine text or DVD or video media: "I know of an excellent DVD on career values—let's show it." They will often begin by thinking about a learning activity, something intrinsically worthwhile regardless of its outcome: "I think it would be a good idea for the students to interview their parents about their career values, just as a way of getting to see their parents in a different light."

In the naturalistic model, objectives, materials, and activities are all examined in an interactive and recursive manner as components of a quality learning experience. Exhibit 8.4 illustrates this process.

The intent is to develop plans for quality learning experiences—meaningful learning transactions mediated by the teacher. Some learning requires hard work and, occasionally, drudgery—such as writing a story or solving a math problem. Some learning can be facilitated by a clear and well-organized lecture that derives from the subject content, not the child.

Observe, finally, that this process of identifying quality learning experiences does not preclude objectives-based planning. If, because of the nature of the discipline or their own curricular orientation, planners prefer to start with objectives, they may do so.

Develop the Course Examination

The naturalistic process places less emphasis on assessment. Rather than developing in advance several detailed assessment devices, course planners ensure that teachers are given the staff development needed to make their own ongoing assessments.

Exhibit 8.3   The Technological Process

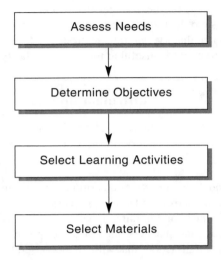

Develop the Learning Scenarios

Instead of using the standard curriculum guide, the naturalistic process culminates in the production and dissemination of *learning scenarios* for each unit of study.

Curriculum Tip

A learning scenario is a more flexible and open-ended guide that assists the teacher in implementing a new course of study.

Learning scenarios usually include these components:

1. A clear and detailed statement of the unit objective

2. A suggested number of lessons

3. A list of recommended quality learning experiences, phrased in a way that integrates objectives, activities, and materials

4. Reprints of articles, maps, and photographs that teachers could use in making lesson plans; observe that resources are not just listed—they are included (the copyright law allows such professional use in a teacher's guide if three conditions are met: proper credit is given; the guide is not sold for profit; and the articles are not reproduced for student use)

An example of a learning scenario is shown in Exhibit 8.5.

Exhibit 8.4   The Naturalistic Model

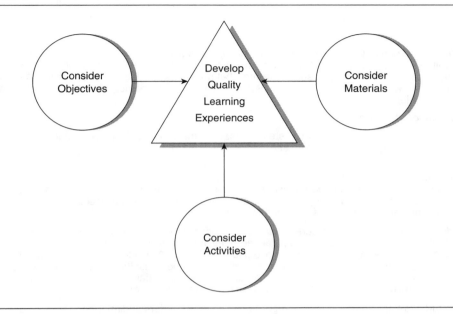

Adapting the Naturalistic Model for Elementary Grades

Curriculum Tip
The naturalistic model can be used effectively, especially at the elementary level.

By making some simple modifications in the naturalistic model, it can become quite effective at lower instructional levels. Assume that a fourth-grade team of teachers, teaching in self-contained classrooms, decides to plan together a unit on "communication," using the naturalistic model. The steps they would take are as follows.

Stake Out the Territory

They begin by defining the boundaries of the unit, considering the pupils, the schedule, the general content of the unit, and the length. They would produce a prospectus for themselves and the principal.

Develop the Knowledge Base

They begin this phase by getting good information about their pupils, reviewing their abilities, and checking with second- and third-grade teachers to determine what was taught in earlier grades about communication in general. They discuss their own expertise and background

Exhibit 8.5   Learning Scenario: Self-Understanding and Career Planning

Course: Career Planning

Unit objective: At the end of the unit it is hoped that the students will have a clearer sense of their talents, skills, and values as they relate to the career-planning process. The goal is to help students become somewhat more realistic as they think about careers—but not to box themselves in or aim too low. Keep reminding them that weak talents can be developed, that new skills can be acquired, that values change with age and experience.

Suggested number of lessons: 6 to 8

Quality learning experiences: (These are listed in what seems to be a desirable sequence, but you should feel free to modify the order as you see fit.)

1. Have students write a paper that they could share with peers, parents, and counselors on "My Ideal Career." Provide some good prewriting discussion and allow time for revision. This is a good initiating activity; the paper will provide you and the student with some baseline data—how the student thinks about self and careers before the unit starts.

2. Conduct a discussion of the nature of talents (the general aptitudes that we possess, such as a talent for music), skills (specific career-related behaviors we have mastered, such as being able to use a word processor), and values (those aspects of life we consider worthwhile, such as liking to be outdoors). Emphasize: People have multiple talents and skills; the strengths of those talents and skills vary for each individual; while all talents and skills have intrinsic worth, our culture accords them varying merit; all of us have different values as they relate to careers.

3. Help students analyze test scores and grades as a way of understanding themselves. If possible, ask the guidance counselor to prepare a test-and-grade profile for each student and to discuss the uses and limitations of test scores and school grades in assessing talents, skills, and values.

4. Have each student develop a talent profile. Identify the range of talents people possess—mechanical, verbal, mathematical, scientific, musical, physical, artistic, interpersonal, managerial. Chart your own highs and lows on the profile to illustrate that talents are differentially strong in one individual.

5. Help each student develop a skills inventory. Most students will probably believe that they have few career-related skills. Help them reflect on their part-time jobs, their school experiences, and their community experiences as sources of skills that can be used in a job.

6. Ask students to interview one or both parents about parental career values. Emphasize that the goal here is not to intrude on parents' privacy (the results will not be shared with classmates or the teacher), but to get a broader understanding of parents and to see whether parent values have influenced student values. Stress that most studies show similarities between core values of parents and of children. Teach students how to conduct a supportive interview, one that helps the interviewee be reflective about self. The students should probably summarize the results of the interviews in their journals, only to systematize what they know—but these summaries need not be shared with the teacher. You may wish to check just to be sure that they were written.

7. Arrange for students to take the values section of the program called SIGI (System of Interactive Guidance and Information). This is a software program produced by Educational Testing Services and available in the guidance office that gives students some useful information on their career values. The results will need some discussion in class.

8. As a culminating activity, ask students to write a final paper on the topic, "Seeing Myself in Relation to Careers." They'll probably need some prewriting help in organizing all the information they have collected. This will also provide a good opportunity for teaching students how to present information in a table or a figure, and how to integrate tables, figures, and text.

9. As an enrichment activity for those with special interest in the subject, discuss how culture shapes career values. Ask them to speculate about the career values of an Eskimo and those of an urban factory worker.

in the field. They review the research on the cognitive development and communication interests of the age group. They take some time to see what is available, checking especially on instructional materials.

Block in the Unit

Now they proceed to block in the unit. They have tentatively considered the general content and think they can spend 3 weeks on the unit before pupil interest wanes. They then move on to consider the general outcomes that they hope to achieve.

Develop Quality Learning Experiences

With those general topics listed and sequenced, they then brainstorm the quality learning experiences they need. Again, as with the career unit, they begin with an activity, with learning materials, or with an objective.

Develop the Unit Test

The team would cooperate in developing the end-of-unit test, assessing all the learnings they considered important.

Develop the Learning Scenarios

As with the career unit, the teachers would systematize and package their work in a learning scenario.

The Naturalistic Model Summarized

The naturalistic model is characterized by several features that set it off from the technological model. It is looser, more flexible, and less rational. It is more responsive to the political realities of curriculum making. It tends to be a "top-down" process, moving from the larger unit to the smaller lesson. It seems to be more in accord with the way teachers actually plan, and it gives equal weight to objectives, activities, and materials, rather than giving primary attention to objectives.

Its advantages seem clear. It should result in curricula that are more likely to be implemented, rather than shelved. Because it addresses the political reality of schools and because it is in accord with teachers' actual planning styles, it should have greater appeal to both principals and teachers. It should also result in more interesting and challenging learning experiences, because it emphasizes the intrinsic quality of the experience.

Its main drawback is its looseness. Especially in the hands of the inexperienced, it can result in a seemingly random collection of entertaining activities that appear unrelated to the intended outcomes.

The Technological Model Summarized

Whatever new course is selected, it is important to note that current technology can empower students as well as teachers to raise their opportunities for inquiry and can increase problem-solving strategies and eagerness to investigate the world around them (Gilbertson, 2003). Students must be successful in employing technological advances to facilitate processing of information in meaningful ways. Teachers planning new courses can now research the Internet to locate current technological equipment available to enable students to better collect and analyze "real-time, real-world" data in the field. For example, teachers could design an action plan for an ecosystem field trip that incorporates current technological equipment for gathering, analyzing, and sharing data.

Many curriculum planners now believe that it is important to get as many people on board as possible when developing new courses via the use of technology. They note that opinions can be dangerous if they are not buttressed by facts and believe that technology should be a learning aid or it will become an educational barrier. The bottom line is that new courses need to be developed on the basis of fact, not fiction. It is therefore crucial to get accurate data before making generalizations as to what is needed in the curriculum and before developing new courses.

According to Conrad Wesley Snyder (2004), advancements in educational technology are helping to transcend both the technological curriculum planning model as well as the naturalistic planning model. Snyder states that there are six objectives for understanding that can also serve as criteria for lesson development using technology:

- Explanation: knowledgeable and justified accounts of events, actions, and ideas
- Interpretation: narratives and translations that provide meaning
- Application: using knowledge effectively in new situations and diverse contexts
- Perspective: critical and insightful points of view
- Empathy: identification with another person's feelings and worldview
- Self-knowledge: wisdom to know one's ignorance and one's patterns of thought and action

These criteria help to assure that understanding is not trained explicitly, but is "awakened more than trained by design, not exhortation." The goal is for students to come to the realization that they are responsible for making meaning of ideas rather than waiting for teacher explanations. The "design" part is similar to a highly structured curriculum approach (sometimes referred to as Instructional Systems Design), and it includes didactic or direct instruction while emphasizing coaching and reflective or facilitative instruction. The latter are fostered by explicit attention to the creation of generative instructional events, created from what can be called an "inverse design" from basic understandings and essential or generative questions.

Inverse Design Process

Inverse design entails three steps: (1) identify the desired results in terms of understandings and questions—that is, develop the essential questions; (2) determine the acceptable evidence to meet the standards specified in the desired results—that is, specify how learning will be assessed; and (3) plan learning experiences and instruction. This includes the following questions:

- What enabling activities will lead to the needed knowledge and skills?
- What needs to be taught and coached, and how should it best be taught, in light of the performance goals?

- What materials and resources are needed?
- Is the overall design coherent and effective?

Each of these steps reflects an important aspect of both the technological and naturalistic approaches. More and more administrators and teachers are currently embodying each of the characteristics listed above. For example, one of Georgia's school superintendents, Beth Kellerhals, believes that when you consider curriculum it is important that you "keep the main thing the main thing" (Shorr, 2003, p. 1). Kellerhals and her staff have been able to negotiate the changing educational environment along with federal mandates such as NCLB (No Child Left Behind Act of 2001). When getting bogged down with political agendas such as NCLB, she believes that it is important to remind individuals that it is all about the needs of students and schools. She says, "By constantly reminding yourself what your priorities are, you're better equipped to make the best decisions for the long term" (p. 1). According to Kenneth Dragseth (as cited in Shorr, 2003), Minnesota Public School Superintendent, "Politics comes and goes, but meeting the needs of your students will stand the test of time" (p. 1). Dr. Milli Pierce (as cited in Shorr, 2003), director of the Principals' Center at the Harvard Graduate School of Education, echoes Dragseth's response by stating that "NCLB and high-stakes tests and the rest all get attended to if administrators are spending time with teachers" (p. 1).

Curriculum Tip

An alternative for addressing NCLB concerns and formulating new courses can be the development of a distance learning component.

Developing Distance Learning Courses as an Alternative

The Internet and related communications technologies, along with political, social, and economic changes in our society, have spawned unprecedented growth of interest in distance education and in the number of courses and programs available through distance learning. Today we have the luxury of selecting from an increasingly diverse range of technology options (Stilborne, 1996).

As a tool for distance learning, the Internet can both deliver content and serve as a multi-purpose communications tool. Increasingly, higher-end technologies, such as videoconferencing, real-time audio, and learning experiences involving animation, are possible, but the most common technologies currently used to deliver distance learning include the following:

- Electronic messaging in the form of listservs, newsgroups, and net-conferencing
- Web applications (most often plain hypertext and visuals, but sometimes incorporating more complex elements, such as audio files, files in portable document format, such as Common Ground or Adobe, database applications, Java applications, or Shockwave files)
- Real-time chats involving software such as Imagiverse at http://www.imagiverse.org/activities/chats/

Developing a Web-Based MUD Object Oriented Curriculum as a Learning Scenario[1]

The following reflect some considerations that should be made before creating and placing courses online. For example, it is important to: answer the what and why; learn how; determine the where; and learn how to distribute your Web site (Saunders, 1999).

Answer the What and Why

Why do you want to put course materials online, and what are the materials you want to include? For example, you may want to have lecture notes or presentation materials accessible to your students. You may want to provide an online resource directory to assist your students' research or information gathering. Or it may be simply to have a course syllabus available for your students. Whatever the reason, you should start small. Online forms, video or animation clips, and many other types of interactive feedback are not something to tackle until you have more experience.

Learn the How

How are you going to take what you have—printed material, computer documents, slides, transparencies, graphics—and get them on the Web? Plus, how do you present them so your students can easily find what they are looking for?

Determine the Where

Where will you publish your course materials? You have more than one choice here as well. There are specialized companies that faculty can use for their Web site: For example, one is the VMS server, on which you can activate your e-mail account for Web publishing, and a second is the UNIX server. You may want to ask your colleagues what server they selected or contact a regional technology center for advice.

Distribute your Web Address

How will your students find your site? You might want to consider posting your Web address (URL) in the classroom, on class handouts, and on a specialized Web site.

Curriculum Tip

Use of WebQuests is one way that the Internet can be meaningfully incorporated into the curriculum.

Using Alternatives to Identify Learning Activities

Locating quality information on the Internet presents a variety of challenges. Users need to be able to sort through the multitude of information to locate the most relevant pieces.

Many teachers avoid using the Web as a resource in their classrooms because students have not acquired the skills needed to use the Internet effectively. Teachers can design a WebQuest to enhance a classroom unit or a particular curriculum area and engage their students in meaningful research (Smith, 2003).

As tempting as it is to develop learning applications that make use of the latest technologies, distance learning and WebQuest educators remind us again and again that learning must be developed around learner needs. While this may be self-evident to many, it is a message that is ignored with surprising frequency. To some extent, this is because our established post-secondary institutions have evolved as teacher- and subject-centered institutions with little emphasis on the students' needs and interests. It is also because—just as anyone can be a publisher on the Internet—on the Internet, anyone can also be a distance educator. Many educators and subject specialists are newly involved in distance education with little or no awareness of some of the important principles that have been developed over the years for developing new online distance courses.

Develop Acceptable Use Policy

With the arrival of Internet connections and distance learning at schools comes the question of safety for children. Educators are rightfully concerned about giving students free rein to "browse" the Web for fear that they might access inappropriate material (Sholten, 2003). At the same time, parents are concerned about the potential of those on the outside gaining access to children. Teachers need to learn how schools guarantee the safe implementation of a technically enriched curriculum through Acceptable Use Policies (AUP) and design a policy for their own schools.

In review, it is important to view curriculum as a way to safely empower students, and to develop creativity and enhance problem solving when developing new courses of study. Teachers using both technological and naturalistic approaches must make sure that the curriculum is relevant and meaningful to all. It is critical that educators of the future be empowered in every way possible to maximize their opportunities and to make the necessary changes needed to deepen and to improve our global understanding of others and of our world.

Our schools today are under the microscope of increased accountability, and a "growing number of U.S. schools have been identified as underperforming on the basis of their low test scores" (Chrisman, 2005, p. 16). Subsequently, the search continues for how schools can improve student achievement and sustain it year after year.

Valerie Chrisman (2005), Director of District and School Support Services at the Ventura County Superintendent of Schools Office, Ventura, California, conducted a study of California's primary and secondary reform programs. Chrisman's study, using "three criteria: analyses of test scores and school characteristics; interview responses from teachers and principals; and questionnaire responses from 356 principals whose schools experienced growth in at least one of the two years of the reform program" (p. 16), revealed the following results for successful schools (see Chrisman, 2005):

- Strong teacher leadership was apparent in each of the four successful sample schools.
- Teachers [at the successful schools] engaged in various forms of informal action research.

- Teachers [at the successful schools] developed their own internal leadership structures—such as team teaching, mentoring new teachers, and collaborating to share lesson designs—support one another's resolve to improve student achievement.
- Teacher leaders at the successful schools also made policy decisions.

Principal Leadership

- The successful schools in the study, as opposed to the unsuccessful ones, more often had the same principal for the last 3 years.
- Principals at the successful schools were more likely to create time for teachers to collaborate and to provide them with structured support.
- Principals [at the successful schools] were comfortable using data and making changes when the data demonstrated that student achievement had not risen.
- Principals from the unsuccessful schools were far less comfortable with data. (Chrisman, 2005, p. 18)

District Office Leadership

- District leaders in successful schools provided more services than their counterparts. The successful schools benefited from focused district-wide professional development on pedagogy.
- At the start of each school term, successful schools more often received assessment data disaggregated by teacher and by individual student than did unsuccessful schools. Teachers and principals also received training on how to use these data to improve instruction and academic achievement.
- New principals were placed in schools in which parent demands and conflicts were expected to be fewer. These schools tended to be in the lowest socioeconomic areas of the district. That assignment . . . was either an entry-level position for new principals or a way of penalizing them for being unable to effectively handle parent conflicts.
- Principals from the successful schools said that their districts scheduled monthly cohort meetings with all the district's state improvement program schools. (Chrisman, 2005, pp. 18–19)

Programs and Practices

- Students who are learning English as a second language and students who are academically below grade level attending the successful schools had quite different experiences from those of comparable students who attended unsuccessful schools.
- At the successful schools, teachers presented instruction that directly reinforced the students' understanding of how the English language works instead of teaching students conversational English.
- Teachers from the successful schools reported that students were grouped by their English language levels.
- In the successful schools, principals and district office personnel were instrumental in supporting all newly adopted district programs. (Chrisman, 2005, pp. 19–20)

The results of the study by Chrisman are supported by researchers such as Mintrop (2003), Darling-Hammond (1997), and Barth (1990). The research unequivocally confirms "that the solutions to improving lie inside the schoolhouse" (Chrisman, 2005, p. 20). The authors of this book believe that school districts can improve student achievement *if* they are willing to examine their practices and to embrace change. In fact, almost all schools can replicate the strategies mentioned and improve education for everyone.

CHAPTER OVERVIEW

This chapter compares and explains how to develop a new course or unit using two contrasting processes: the standard *technological* process, and what is termed here a *naturalistic* process. The chapter also explores how curriculum leaders can develop new courses that involve both the technological as well as naturalistic processes of curriculum planning. How to improve academic achievement and sustain it is covered as well.

CHAPTER TERMS

Technological Process

Naturalistic Process

Curriculum Specialist

Needs Assessment

Learning Scenario

APPLICATIONS

1. Consider this issue: Should the choice of the technological or naturalistic process be influenced by the nature of the educational organization? If so, in what types of organizations should each be used?

2. To test your ability to use the technological model, do the following:

   a. Identify the parameters of a new course you might develop.
   b. Describe the purpose of data in regard to assessing the needs of the learner.
   c. List the learning objectives for the course.
   d. Identify the learning activities you would recommend for one of the objectives.

3. To test your ability to use the naturalistic model, do the following:

   a. Describe the territory of a new course.
   b. Describe the advantages of school-based curriculum development.
   c. List all unit objectives.
   d. Write at least four quality learning experiences for one of the units.

4. Some who have used the naturalistic process have suggested that it is more suitable for elementary grades than for secondary. If you were an elementary principal, would you recommend that your teachers use the naturalistic process? Discuss in detail your rationale for using the naturalistic process rather than a technological process approach.

CASE STUDY

A sixth-grade teacher in Florida discusses with her principal the problem of her students not meeting NCLB standards in the area of reading.

"I'm pleased you were able to drop by my office," says Principal Bill Woodward. "As I recall from a previous conversation, you are interested in individualizing reading instruction and addressing specific skills."

"That is correct, Mr. Woodward," states sixth-grade teacher Nita Caterlin. "I'm looking for ways to identify student strengths and weaknesses in reading as well as determine what strategies I should use to address identified weaknesses."

"How about using an Internet-based data analysis program?" he asks. "We just purchased rights to a program and it has been helping a number of other teachers."

"Is this one of those Internet-based programs that gives you a detailed analysis of student academic strengths and weaknesses?" she asks.

"Yes," says Principal Woodward. "You will have to go through the training online, but that shouldn't be a problem. Mrs. Hall uses it and has found it to be very helpful." The principal can see that Mrs. Caterlin is interested in the possibility of using an Internet-based assessment program.

"How does it work?"

"Well, Mrs. Hall had all of her students go to the lab and go online to take a pretest. The results were immediate in that the students were assessed electronically. She found that her children were having difficulty with the concept of 'main idea,' which is one of the state reading standards."

"That's sounds like a great program!"

"Yes, online assessment programs are becoming quite popular," says the principal. "What is especially important is that the program not only provides pre- and posttests, but also provides teaching strategies and links to other resources."

"I would really like to get started," says Mrs. Caterlin enthusiastically.

"No problem!" notes the principal. "I'll contact the district testing coordinator and have you up and running very soon."

THE CHALLENGE

Analyze the importance of online data analysis as it relates to developing the technological process of curriculum planning and enhancing student achievement. How can Principal Woodward educate and motivate other teachers to use online data analysis strategies to improve test scores and raise student achievement in his school?

Key Issues/Questions

1. What questions should principals ask before incorporating or committing to an online assessment program?

2. What role will politics play and what needs to be done by Principal Woodward to make sure that he develops a constituency of support before embarking on this project?

3. Making sure that an online assessment program is aligned with district, state, and national standards is crucial to the curriculum process. What are some steps that Principal Woodward needs to take to make sure that his online assessment program is aligned with the district's curricula?

4. The expense of online assessment programs can be prohibitive for many school districts. How can superintendents and principals justify such costs to teachers and to the community?

5. Conversion to online assessment programs can be a daunting task. Such changes often affect the development of new courses and units. What measures can be taken to reduce opposition by teachers to such radical curriculum changes?

NOTE

1. MOO stands for MUD Object Oriented, where MUD stands for Multi User Domain.

REFERENCES

Assessment Reform Group. (1999). *Assessment for learning: Beyond the black box* [Electronic version]. Cambridge: Cambridge University School of Education.

Barth, R. S. (1990). *Improving schools from within.* San Francisco: Jossey-Bass.

Bude, U. (1999). The process of curriculum development: Overcoming "panic approaches" and ensuring teacher participation. *ZED Basic Education.* Retrieved July 1, 2004, from Institute for Research on Teaching Web site: http://www.dse.de/zed/texte/process.htmbase

Chrisman, V. (2005). How schools sustain success. *Educational Leadership, 62*(5), 16–20.

Darling-Hammond, L. (1997). *The right to learn.* San Francisco: Jossey-Bass.

Gilbertson, J. (2003). Scientific inquiry and field work: How can I best use technology to collect, analyze and share data in a field setting? *Learning to Teach with Technology Studio.* Course SC201. Retrieved February 26, 2004, from http://ltts.indiana.edu/catalog_main.pl?mod_id=12

Glatthorn, A. A. (1987). *Curriculum leadership.* New York: HarperCollins.

Johnson, J. H. (2000). Data-driven school improvement [Electronic version]. *Journal of School Improvement, 1,* 2–3.

Leithwood, K. A., & Montgomery, D. J. (1982). The role of the elementary principal in program improvement. *Review of Educational Research, 52,* 309–339.

Mager, R. F., & Beach, K. M., Jr. (1967). *Developing vocational instruction.* Palo Alto, CA: Fearon Publishers.

Mintrop, H. (2003). The limits of sanctions in low-performing schools: A study of Maryland and Kentucky schools on probation. *Education Policy Analysis Archives, 11*(3), 32.

Saunders, P. (1999, Winter). *Developing courseware online: Planning course materials on the Web: The process.* Retrieved February 25, 2004, from Western Michigan University, Center for Teaching and Learning Web site: http://www.wmich.edu/teachlearn/winter1999/instruct/placing-process .html

Sholten, C. (2003). *Developing acceptable use policies: How can I develop an acceptable use policy that will work for my school?* Learning to Teach With Technology Studio. Course TE 001. Retrieved February 26, 2004, from Indiana University, School of Education Web site: http://ltts .indiana.edu/

Shorr, P. W. (2003). *12 things top school leaders know (and you should, too)*. Retrieved March 25, 2005, from http://www.scholastic.com/administrator/novdec03/articles.asp?article=secrets

Smith, C. (2003). *Supporting Internet exploration with WebQuests: How do I design a WebQuest to meet my curriculum goals?* Learning to Teach With Technology Studio. Course TE 401. Retrieved February 26, 2004, from Indiana University, School of Education Web site: http://ltts.Indiana.edu/

Snyder, C. W. (2004*). Calendar of activities/itinerary narrative.* An unpublished paper completed for the University of Montana International Studies Program.

Stiggins, R. J. (2002). Assessment crisis: The absence of assessment for learning [Electronic version]. *Phi Delta Kappan, 83,* 4, 5.

Stilborne, L. (1996, April). Meeting the needs of adult learners in developing courses for the Internet. *Ingenia Communications—Lindy Williams and Williams Donaldson Associates.* Retrieved February 26, 2004, from http://www.isoc.org/inet96/proceedings/c4/c4_2.htm

Tyler, R. W. (1949). *Basic principles of curriculum and instruction.* Chicago: University of Chicago Press.

Wulf, K. M., & Schave, B. (1984). *Curriculum design: A handbook for educators.* Glenview, IL: Scott, Foresman.

Part 3

Curriculum Management

Chapter 9

SUPERVISING THE CURRICULUM
Teachers and Materials

Too many curriculum leaders focus unduly on the written curriculum, neglecting the taught curriculum and the supported curriculum. Obviously such neglect is unwise and counterproductive. An excellent written curriculum will have little impact if it is not taught well and supported with appropriate materials. This chapter, therefore, examines the problems and issues in supervision as well as how to improve these two often-slighted aspects of curriculum. The chapter also addresses the following questions:

- Who are some of the major leaders who have been concerned with supervision, and what are some of the current approaches to curriculum supervision?
- What are some of the issues and problems that relate to supervision that are facing curriculum leaders today?
- What are some of the major roles associated with curriculum supervision?
- Why is motivating staff an important component of supervision?
- Why are some of Abraham Maslow's theories on supervision still relevant today?
- What are the elements that make up supportive curriculum, and why is the supportive curriculum important?

Key to Leadership

One of the most important aspects of a quality supervision program is the area of assessment. No program can be significantly improved without assessment of both teacher and instructional programs.

SUPERVISING THE TAUGHT CURRICULUM: CURRENT APPROACHES

According to Cheryl Riggins-Newby (2003), NAESP's Associate Executive Director for Urban Alliances, principals in all schools must be instructional leaders. Curriculum and instruction are at the heart of any school improvement program. Principals need to work with teachers to supervise and coordinate decisions within and between grade levels. Doing so will help align the school's curriculum both horizontally and vertically. A well-aligned and supervised curriculum ensures that students are taught the necessary skills and standards that will be tested on statewide exams.

Curriculum Tip

Leadership is often the key to developing a successful supervision program.

Leaders concerned with supervising the taught curriculum have available to them several current approaches to supervision. The four that seem to have the greatest value are Hunter's (1984) "Knowing, Teaching, and Supervising"; Glickman, Gordon, and Ross-Gordon's (2003) *Supervision and Instructional Leadership: A Developmental Approach;* Costa and Garmston's (1985) *The Art of Cognitive Coaching: Supervision for Intelligent Teaching;* and Glatthorn's (1984) *Differentiated Supervision.* The first three are reviewed in this section; the last is explained more fully in the next section.

Hunter's "Essential Elements"

During the middle of the 1980s, the work of Madeline Hunter seemed to be the dominant mode of supervision: Several state offices of education, in fact, had given the Hunter approach their official blessing and encouraged its adoption through workshops for administrators, supervisors, and teachers. Although Hunter herself advocated a number of "templates" that could be used to analyze and improve teaching, her "elements of lesson design" attracted the most attention. By reviewing the theory of and research on learning, Hunter was able to identify the following elements of good lesson design:

Anticipatory set: Developing in students a mental set that causes them to focus on what will be learned

Objective and purpose: Stating what is to be learned and how it will be useful

Input: Giving students information about the knowledge, skill, or process they are to achieve

Modeling: Demonstrating the process or skill

Guided practice: Directing the student practice of the new process or skill

Independent practice: Assigning independent practice of the process or skill

(as cited in Glatthorn, 1987, p. 222)

What made the Hunter "elements" so popular with practitioners? First, they were based on sound theory, even though the research base seemed thin to some critics. Second, they gave educators a common vocabulary to discuss teaching: Everyone could talk about "anticipatory set" and know what was meant. Finally, they seemed "teacher-friendly": They did not require teachers to adopt new behaviors, but instead helped teachers systematize what they had already been doing.

Hunter's approach, however, was not without its critics, most of whom were university professors, not practitioners. Those critics faulted the model, first of all, because it offered a narrowly constricted view of teaching. Sergiovanni (1985) made the point that she conceived teaching and learning only as an instructional delivery system, a conception that saw teaching as sending information through a pipeline to passive students. Others were unhappy because the elements seemed to be derived from the direct instruction model of teaching and slighted other models, although Hunter argued that the elements could be used flexibly in any model of teaching.

Although many administrators who had adopted the Hunter "elements" approach reported enthusiastic reception on the part of teachers and noted many positive effects, the early research on its impact on achievement indicated that it was not more effective than standard approaches to supervision (see Stallings, 1986.)

Glickman's Developmental Supervision

Carl Glickman, Stephen P. Gordon, and Jovita M. Ross-Gordon's (2003) "developmental supervision" is characterized by two important features that set it off from Hunter's work. First, Glickman argues that the development of teacher thought should be the focus of supervisors' work with teachers—helping teachers increase their conceptual level of development. Glickman posits three levels of development: low abstract (the teacher is confused, lacks ideas, wants to be shown, gives habitual responses to varying decisions); moderate abstract (depends on authority, identifies one dimension of instructional problem, generates one to three ideas about solutions, needs assistance from experts); and high abstract (uses various sources to identify problems, generates multiple ideas, chooses for self the action to be taken).

This "thought-oriented" approach permeates the four ways supervisors can help teachers grow: by offering direct assistance (what is usually called "clinical supervision"); by providing in-service education; by working with teachers in curriculum development; and by helping them carry out action research.

Although Glickman admits that the results on developmental supervision have been "predictably mixed," both features make the model seem very useful for curriculum leaders. He recognizes the fact that teachers are different and require different approaches. He also broadens the prevailing understanding of supervision by emphasizing the importance of in-service, curriculum-development, and action research.

Costa and Garmston's Cognitive Coaching

Like Glickman, Costa and Garmston (1985) emphasize the importance of teacher thinking, though their approach seems quite different. Rather than using all the approaches that Glickman advocates, they give their attention exclusively to direct assistance or clinical supervision. However, it is clinical supervision with a profound difference. They are not concerned initially with skills; they believe it more productive to emphasize teacher thinking. As the supervisor works with teachers in this cognitive coaching mode, the supervisor has these goals: to create and manage a trusting relationship, to facilitate teacher learning by restructuring teacher thinking, and to develop teacher autonomy. Those goals are achieved primarily through in-depth conferences in which the supervisor listens actively, questions insightfully, and responds congruently.

Although the authors indicate that their approach has been based on current theory and sound research on adult development, they do not offer any empirical evidence about its effectiveness. Its emphasis on teacher thinking and its concern for teacher autonomy both seem to be useful from the standpoint of curriculum leaders.

PROBLEMS AND ISSUES IN SUPERVISION

Many unsolved problems are associated with the development of curriculum and the formation of an effective instructional program. Hours can be spent organizing personnel, material resources, and activities of the school.

Curriculum Tip

Three main areas that appear to thread their way through the supervised curriculum include students, classroom climate, and informational resources.

A major problem facing educators is the inability of our instructional programs to reach students and meet their needs (Weeks, 2001). This situation has led to the passage of the No Child Left Behind Act, which is responsible for holding schools more accountable for student learning levels and student achievement. Unfortunately, according to author Tom Allen (2004), there is something wrong with a law that brands good schools with "failing" labels.

Nevertheless, a growing concern over skills and school climate is revolutionizing the way schools are developing curriculum from preschool years through high school. The lack of real understanding in subject areas such as mathematics and reading has led to a series of mandates from the federal government requiring strict proficiency levels and Adequate Yearly Progress (AYP) goals. School leaders are realizing the need for well-written curriculum with quality supportive materials (Gilman & Gilman, 2003).

In the quest to provide well-written curriculum and supportive materials, technology is quickly becoming a major aspect of how classrooms are designed, instruction is planned, and information is delivered. Curriculum planners, administrators, and classroom teachers are finding new and innovative ways to deliver subsequent stages of educational development for students. Schools are learning the importance of becoming part of the communication age as well as becoming a part of a global learning network (Harmon, 2004).

THE ROLE OF THE CURRICULUM SUPERVISOR

Developing ways to get to the heart of curriculum programming and bringing about educationally significant change lies with curriculum leaders as well as school principals.

Curriculum Tip

The role of the principal has grown from that of a manager to that of a change agent, an administrative-organizational specialist.

Principals are having to become aware and knowledgeable about new approaches to curriculum supervision. They have to know how to write and direct curriculum as well as have the ability to find needed supportive materials during a time of declining budgets. Principals and school supervisors are now learning how information is best acquired by children and how it relates to their overall growth and development (Merrow, 2004). A crucial part of that process is providing a quality learning environment based on effective staff development. An important part of this process, therefore, is the development of a quality differentiated professional development program.

DIFFERENTIATED PROFESSIONAL DEVELOPMENT

Differentiated professional development (Glatthorn, 1984) is essentially a reconceptualization of the supervisory function, one that attempts to broaden the practitioner's view of supervision. Glatthorn argues that one of the reasons educational leaders neglect the taught curriculum is that they hold a very narrow view of supervision. Too often it is equated with clinical supervision—the intensive process of observing a teacher, analyzing observational data, and giving the teacher feedback about such data. Such a narrow view is unproductive for several reasons. First, clinical supervision is so time-consuming that principals especially find it impossible to provide it for everyone. Second, clinical supervision is only one of several means of facilitating the professional development of teachers; other processes, as Glickman notes, should be used too. Also, not all teachers need clinical supervision; experienced, competent teachers need some options. Finally, most models of clinical supervision do not give sufficient attention to major aspects of curriculum.

Curriculum Tip

Leaders who wish to improve the taught curriculum need to reconceptualize the supervisory process—to see it more broadly, and to differentiate its use in relation to teacher need.

Such a reconceptualization, Glatthorn notes, can make a modest contribution to what Sergiovanni (1986) calls a "theory of practice for supervision"—a theory that takes account of the complex messiness of classrooms and teaching, that uses the practical language of classroom life, that is sensitive to the way teachers and supervisors construe classroom meanings, and that is explicitly designed to improve teaching and learning. In this attempt to reconceptualize supervision, it seems useful to substitute the term *professional development* for those activities ordinarily subsumed under the heading of *supervision*. The advantage of using new terminology is that it facilitates the task of reconceptualizing the field by distancing users from the restrictive assumptions implicit in the old language. In this reconceptualization, *professional development* is used in this sense: All those systematic processes used by school administrators, supervisors, and teachers to help teachers grow professionally. Those professional development processes are divided into four distinct yet related tasks: staff development, informal observations, rating, and individual development.

Staff Development

The term *staff development* is used here to designate all those district and school sponsored programs, both formal and informal, offered to groups of teachers in response to organizational needs. The importance of staff development has been noted in Chapter 5, as an aspect of the planning process, and in Chapter 7, as a critical ingredient in improving a field of study.

The ability of teachers to develop and guide curriculum requires a sophisticated set of judgments about the content, students, learning, and teaching. Creating a network of educators (colleagues, parents, students, and experts in the community) is one way to increase professional sophistication (Tomlinson et al., 2002). Several issues seem important here in examining staff development as an aspect of broader professional development.

First, staff development can be both formal and informal. Formal staff development programs have a specific agenda, a set schedule, and a structured set of experiences. Typically, such formal programs are skill focused. The research on such skill-focused programs suggests that they will be more effective if they embody the tested practices recommended in Chapter 7.

Even the best formal programs seem to make two major errors, however. Too many seem unduly concerned with the linear transmission and translation of knowledge into practice, using consultants who, in effect, say, "Here is the research on effective teaching; let me explain how you should use it." For example, contributors to the 1983 National Society for the Study of Education yearbook, on staff development, recommend that those planning the content of staff development should begin by examining the results of the Beginning Teacher Evaluation Study, a research project conducted in the late 1970s, in second- and fifth-grade classrooms (see Howey & Vaughan, 1983).

While an obvious need exists for teachers to be informed about such research, much better results could be achieved by using an approach that Buchmann (1985) calls "conversation about teaching," a dialogic encounter of peers. Buchmann describes the tone of such conversation in this fashion:

> In conversation, ideas . . . collide and mingle with one another and are diluted and complicated in the process. The pleasant tone of conversation is inimical to doctrinaire notions. In conversation, one may differ and still not disagree; the defensive, corrective,

and didactic aspects of rhetoric are out of place. People do not insist that partners follow; it is enough that they enter into conversation. Thus, conversation respects great differences and ranges easily over different provinces of meaning: dreams, play, science, and action. (p. 449)

Thus we might imagine a dialogic staff-development session in which a linguist, a district language arts coordinator, an English department chair, a principal, and several English teachers are holding a conversation about the teaching of grammar, discussing the contributions of contemporary grammars, the functions of teaching grammar, the implications of research on the teaching of grammar, and the possibilities of conducting classroom-based research on students' use of language.

The second error reflected in too many district staff-development programs is that they are too individualistic and neglect organizational needs. Here the position taken by Fielding and Schalock (1985) in their review of staff development seems to be a reasonable one:

[Staff] development rarely responds to overall district priorities for improvement. In-service activities are more likely to deal with a series of discrete and unrelated topics or a common theme. It appears that one of the most important responsibilities of central office staff is to anchor plans for staff development to long-term district goals. (p. 56)

So, formal staff-development programs can be effective if they reflect sound research, create a spirit of dialogue, and respond to district goals. However, they should be supplemented with an array of informal staff development approaches. Ineffective principals and supervisors complain that they do not have time for staff development; effective leaders use whatever time is available. They work with small groups of teachers during preparation periods, over lunch, and in faculty meetings in a less systematic and structured fashion, sharing ideas, discussing current educational issues, and engaging in some informal problem solving.

As noted in previous chapters, staff development of both the formal and informal type is essential throughout the curriculum development and improvement process. If staff development has helped teachers change their perceptions of a subject, develop the materials to be used in implementing the new curriculum, and acquire the skills needed to deliver it, then it is quite likely that the written, the taught, the tested, and the learned curricula will be in much closer congruence.

Informal Observations

Informal observations are brief, unannounced classroom visits, lasting from perhaps 5 to 15 minutes. Some term these informal visits "walkthroughs"; some experts in the corporate world call such informal observations "management by walking around."

The process of making numerous brief and informal observations can serve several purposes. It is a useful way of making the principal and the supervisor more visible and less office-bound, thus reducing the isolation that most teachers feel. It provides excellent opportunities for both principal and supervisor to reinforce and praise good teaching—catching teachers doing something right. It can provide useful data about curriculum implementation, and it can alert leaders to curricular and instructional problems before they become critical.

How much value do such informal observations have? Here there is an interesting paradox. While many of the standard texts on supervision disparage such visits and insist that all observations should be for a full period and should be preceded by a conference, the research suggests otherwise. Several reviews of the research on effective schools (see, e.g., Squires, Huitt, & Segars, 1981) conclude that in such schools the educational leader is highly visible, frequently monitors the classroom, stays well informed about daily life in the school, and demonstrates an interest in instruction by spending much time in classrooms. Such visits, however, should be done in the least obtrusive manner possible. An aspect of quality leadership is knowing when visits are an interruption and when they are appropriate. All these functions can be accomplished through informal observations. In every school system where the authors have helped institute a program of informal observations, the teachers have welcomed the process as long as it is not linked to the rating system.

Although there does not seem to be any research available on how to make informal observations most effective, the experience of successful principals and supervisors who use this process suggests that the following guidelines should be useful:

1. At the outset, administrators and supervisors should resolve through discussions with teachers whether the data from informal observations would be used as part of the teacher evaluation or rating process. Teachers will more readily accept the process if it is clear that informal observations are not linked with teacher evaluation, although many administrators would like to use such information in rating teachers.

2. Informal observations should be frequent and numerous. Effective principals and supervisors report that they attempt to make at least ten informal observations each week by reserving time in their weekly schedules. Most find it helpful to make the informal observations on a systematic basis, one week focusing on a particular grade level ("What's our fourth-grade program like?") and the next on a particular field ("How much science is being taught in our intermediate grades?").

3. Immediate feedback is important. If the observer is pleased with what has been observed, then a smile, a gesture of approval, or a brief note may be enough. If some concerns are felt, a brief face-to-face conference is perhaps needed. At such a conference, the concern should be expressed only as a very tentative reaction: "I was there only for five minutes, of course, but I did note that you were discussing a book that I believe is taught in tenth grade—can you clarify this for me?"

4. The informal observations will probably have more value if observers vary their focus. Sometimes it is useful to concentrate on *what* is being taught—its level of difficulty and interest for the learners. At times the *pace* of instruction and curriculum delivery should be noted—how much the teacher has covered so far. At times the *method* should be the center of attention, and at times the *learners* should be the concern.

Rating

In the reconceptualization, the term *rating* is used in this sense: The process of making formative and summative assessments of teacher performance for purposes of administrative decision making. The term is chosen to distinguish this formal assessment function from a more general act of evaluation, which is often construed to mean a judgment about the quality of performance made on any occasion for a variety of purposes. This distinction between rating and evaluation is intended to clarify the conceptual confusion that is so prevalent in our professional discourse. One interesting example of the conceptual confusion is McGreal's (1983) monograph titled *Successful Teacher Evaluation,* which really seems to be a treatise on teacher supervision.

Perhaps some examples of the two concepts would provide more clarity. You make an informal observation of a teacher with a disorderly class. You make a judgment: You do not like what you see. You observe a teacher for the purpose of diagnosing teaching style. You try your best to be objective, but you find yourself smiling in approval. You conduct a staff-development session and ask one of the teachers to demonstrate a particular skill. You are not happy with the demonstration. In each instance you have made an evaluation—a judgment about quality. Despite all attempts to be objective, it is probably impossible to observe the act of teaching without making judgments. Most teachers would not want an observer to pretend that he or she had not made any judgments about their performance. In addition, there is some evidence that supervisors who are candid about their assessments are judged to be more effective than those who do not provide evaluative feedback (see Gersten, Green, & Davis, 1985).

Now consider a contrary example. You visit a teacher's class in September with a rating form in hand, in which very explicit criteria are stated along with the standards of performance. You observe the class and complete the rating form. You confer with the teacher and say, "Your performance in that class was not satisfactory; I hope your supervisor will be able to help you improve before the next rating observation." You have made a formative rating. You make several more formative rating observations throughout the year. Then, in May, you make a summative assessment based upon all your data and say to the teacher, "Your performance this year was unsatisfactory; your contract will not be renewed."

Perhaps one more analogy will help. The gymnast performs a set of exercises at a meet. The coach watches and says, "Your approach was faulty; we'll have to work on that." The coach has made an evaluation. The judges were also watching. They hold up their scorecards with numerical scores on each. The judges have made a rating.

What rating systems are most effective? After studying 32 school districts reported to have effective rating systems, Wise, Darling-Hammond, McLaughlin, and Bernstein (as cited in Glatthorn, 1987) reached five conclusions (their term *teacher evaluation* is used below instead of the narrower term *rating*, because many of the systems included processes that in the reconceptualization are considered primarily developmental):

1. To succeed, the teacher-evaluation system must suit the goals, management style, conception of teaching, and community values of the school district.

2. Top-level commitment to and resources for evaluation are more important than the particular kind of checklist or procedures used.

3. The school district should decide about the main purpose of the rating system and then match the process to the purpose.

4. The evaluation process must be seen to have utility: It is cost effective, fair, valid, and reliable.

5. Teacher involvement in and responsibility for the process improves the quality of teacher evaluation.

(Glatthorn, 1987, p. 229)

Obviously, these conclusions suggest that several types of rating systems can be effective. However, if the purpose is administrative decision making, then a criterion-based system using multiple observations seems preferable. One process that has been used effectively in several districts is described below.

Together, administrators, supervisors, and teachers analyze the job of teaching and the research on effective teaching. From those reviews, they develop a comprehensive set of criteria dealing with the three important aspects of the teacher's role. First, they define the non-instructional aspects of the teacher's role. In most cases, a short list of noninstructional responsibilities is all that is necessary: supervise students in noninstructional settings, communicate with parents, attend faculty meetings and staff-development sessions as required, carry out other assigned duties.

Curriculum Tip

The research-based list of the "essential observables" and the "essential nonobservables" plays a crucial role in both rating teachers and helping them grow professionally.

By reviewing the research, supervisors can identify the essential instructional skills that can be directly observed, such as providing a clear lesson structure. Finally, they identify the essential instructional skills that are probably not always directly observable, such as making valid tests. Therefore, care should be taken to ensure that the list includes only those skills well supported by the research. One formulation of these skills is shown in Exhibit 9.1.

The essential observable skills become the basis of a Rating Observation Form, which identifies each skill and for each one specifies several indicators of performance. A portion of one such form is shown in Exhibit 9.2. That form is then used in making a rating observation. The rater tells the teacher that he or she will be observing the class some time next week in order to rate performance. The teacher is familiar with both the criteria and the indicators and understands clearly that the purpose of the observation is to rate, not to improve instruction. The rater arrives with the rating observation form in hand. The rater observes solely to rate: He or she makes careful notes throughout the lesson about the teacher's performance in relation to each of the criteria and then makes a holistic rating of the entire class. Then the rater holds a rating observation conference, informs the teacher of the general rating, reviews the specific strengths and weaknesses, and in conjunction with the teacher lays out a professional development plan for remedying any perceived deficiencies.

All these formative data are drawn together in a summative rating conference: The rater reviews with the teacher the teacher's performance of the noninstructional responsibilities, summarizes the results of all the rating observations, synthesizes the results of the conferences at which the nonobservable skills were assessed, and provides a final holistic rating of

Exhibit 9.1   Essential Skills of Teaching

The following list of essential skills is intended to provide general guidelines for administrators, supervisors, and teachers. While based on a careful review of the literature and a reflective analysis of shared experience, it is not intended as a definitive prescription of "the best way to teach." Other cautions need to be noted:

1. The list focuses on the instructional role of the teacher; it does not address the important noninstructional responsibilities.
2. The list does not speak directly to the skills of lesson planning and communicating. As will be noted below, effective planning and clear communication lie behind several of the skills listed below.

ESSENTIAL SKILLS OBSERVABLE IN CLASSROOM INSTRUCTION

Skills relating to lesson content and pace might include:

1. Chooses content for the lesson that relates directly to curriculum goals, is at an appropriate level of difficulty, and corresponds with assessment measures
2. Presents content of lesson in a way that demonstrates mastery of subject matter
3. Paces instruction appropriately

Climate

4. Creates a desirable environment that reflects appropriate discipline and supports the instructional function
5. Communicates realistically high expectations for students
6. Uses instructional time efficiently, allocating most of the time to curriculum-related instruction
7. Keeps students on task
8. Provides organizing structure for classroom work: reviews, gives overview, specifies objectives, gives clear directions, summarizes, makes relevant assignments
9. Uses instructional strategies, learning activities, and group structures that are appropriate to objectives, respond to student needs, and reflect sound learning theory
10. Ensures active participation of students in learning activities

Assessment

11. Monitors student learning and uses evaluative data to adjust instruction
12. Questions effectively: asks clear questions; asks questions at appropriate level of difficulty; varies types of questions
13. Responds effectively to student answers: allows sufficient wait time, gives prompt and corrective feedback, praises appropriately

ESSENTIAL SKILLS NOT DIRECTLY OBSERVABLE IN CLASSROOM INSTRUCTION

1. Develops long-term plans that reflect curricular priorities and adequately deal with all aspects of written curriculum
2. Uses tests that are consistent with instructional objectives
3. Grades student learning fairly, objectively, and validly

Note: The above list of skills has been synthesized from several reviews of the research on teaching effectiveness. Three sources have been especially useful:

Berliner, D. C. (1984). The half-full glass: A review of the research on teaching. In P. Hosford (Ed.), *Using what we know about teaching.* Alexandria, VA: Association for Supervision and Curriculum Development.

Brophy, J. E., & Good, T. L. (1986). Teacher behavior and student achievement. In M. C. Wittrock (Ed.), *Handbook of research on teaching* (3rd ed., pp. 328–375). New York: Macmillan.

Rosenshine, B., & Stevens, R. (1986). Teaching functions. In M. C. Wittrock (Ed.). *Handbook of research on teaching* (3rd ed., pp. 376–391). New York: Macmillan.

Exhibit 9.2   Portion of Rating Observation Form

Teacher's Name _____   Rater _____

Class _____   Date and Time _____

Rating Code:

1, unsatisfactory; 2, satisfactory; 3, more than satisfactory; NA, not able to make a judgment.

1. Chooses content that relates directly to curriculum goals and assessment measures, at appropriate level of difficulty

   1 Chooses unrelated content, too difficult or too easy

   2 Chooses related content, with appropriate difficulty

   3 Chooses related content, with appropriate difficulty, relates content to student needs and interests

Rating _____

Observations Supporting Rating

Teacher Comments

Overall Rating for This Class: _____

1. Which essential teaching skill(s) does this teacher seem to use most successfully?

2. Which essential teaching skill(s) does this teacher need to improve?

---

the teacher's performance for that year. The conference ends with a view to the future: How will the teacher build upon strengths and remedy any deficiencies?

Obviously, such a rating system will require a great amount of administrator and supervisor time if it is to be thorough—much more time than is perhaps warranted in relation to the value of the process for teachers who are known to be highly competent. Therefore, the reconceptualized model proposes two rating tracks: standard rating and intensive rating. The standard rating is used for career teachers whose performance is clearly satisfactory; it is a pro forma compliance with the state school code, usually involving one observation and one final conference. An intensive rating is used for all probationary teachers, for any teachers being considered for special promotion, and for teachers whose level of performance is questionable. The intensive rating involves several observations by two or more observers, with a conference following each observation.

Individual Development

In contrast to staff development, individual work is with a single person, not the group; and the needs of the individual, not the needs of the organization, predominate.

> ## Curriculum Tip
>
> Individual development includes all the processes used by and with individual teachers to help them grow professionally.

For two reasons, a differentiated system of professional development is recommended— one that gives teachers some options in the type of developmental processes used (see Glatthorn, 1984). First, as noted above, most principals are too busy to provide clinical supervision to all teachers. Second, teachers vary significantly in their conceptual development, in their learning styles, and in their professional needs; they thus should be provided with different types of developmental services. Accordingly, the differentiated system offers three options for individual development: intensive, cooperative, and self-directed.

Intensive development is what is ordinarily called "clinical supervision," although it is more broadly construed. It is an intensive and systematic process in which a supervisor, an administrator, or an expert teacher works closely with an individual teacher in an attempt to effect significant improvement in the essential skills of teaching. While the intensive development is most needed by inexperienced and struggling teachers, it can be provided for any teacher who wants to work with a skilled educational leader to bring about significant improvement in teaching performance. In providing intensive development, the leader works closely with the teacher in determining which of several processes will be used. Rather than relying solely on planning conferences, observations, and debriefing conferences, they examine together a wide array of common sense processes to determine which ones might be most effectively employed:

1. Planning conferences: conferring with the teacher on yearly planning, semester planning, unit planning, and daily planning

2. Student-assessment conferences: conferring with the teacher about assessing student progress, testing, grading, and record keeping

3. Diagnostic observations and diagnostic feedback: observing all significant transactions in a classroom in order to diagnose priority developmental needs and providing appropriate feedback

4. Focused observations and feedback: observing one particular aspect of teaching and learning (such as classroom management) and providing appropriate feedback

5. Video analysis: making a video of teaching and analyzing it with the teacher in order to complement direct observation

6. Coaching: developing a particular teaching skill by providing a rationale, explaining the steps, demonstrating those steps, providing a supportive environment in which the teacher can use the skill, and giving the teacher feedback

7. Directed observation of a colleague: structuring and guiding an opportunity for the teacher to observe a colleague using a specific skill

Although some administrators would say that certain teachers do not need mentoring, they need firing—intensive development does provide a variety of supportive services; to be most effective, those services should be provided in a systematic manner. First, after an initial orientation session, the supervisor makes a diagnostic observation, one in which all important classroom interactions are recorded and analyzed in order to determine patterns of behavior. The supervisor analyzes those diagnostic data and tentatively identifies which skills can best be developed over the next 2 to 3 months. The supervisor and the teacher then confer about the observation. They review together those observational data and any other information they have and decide together on the skill-development agenda for the months ahead. They formalize this decision in a Professional Development Plan, which lists the skills to be developed, the resources to be used, and the deadlines to be met.

They then begin to work together on the first skill. The supervisor coaches the teacher in the use of that skill. Then the supervisor makes a focused observation of one of the teacher's classes, gathering data on only the skill being developed. They confer again to decide whether more coaching and observing for that skill are needed or whether they should move to the next skill. It is an intensive process of diagnosing, developing a growth plan, coaching, holding a focused observation, and then assessing the next move. Obviously, it takes a great deal of time to implement effectively; the hope is, however, that only a few teachers in each school will be involved in such intensive development.

Cooperative development is an option usually provided only to experienced and competent teachers; it enables small groups of teachers to work together in a collegial relationship for mutual growth. It is intended to be a teacher-centered, teacher-directed process that respects the professionalism of competent teachers. While it requires administrative support, it does not require inordinate amounts of administrator or supervisor time; the expectation is that the cooperative groups can direct their own growth. In doing so, they may decide to use a variety of processes: observing and conferring about each other's classes, exchanging classes, collaborating on action research, and developing curricular and instructional materials.

Self-directed development is an option usually provided to experienced and competent teachers who wish to work on their own, rather than as part of a cooperative team. Teachers who choose this option identify a small number of professional-growth goals for the year and work independently in attempting to accomplish those goals. In a sense, the self-directed model is akin to the management-by-objectives assessment process, except that it is completely nonevaluative. The administrator or supervisor simply acts as a supportive resource for the teacher in the self-directed mode.

Albeit many school districts mandate evaluative policy as dictated by state boards of education or state departments of education, teachers should be able to choose which of these options they prefer, with the understanding that all probationary teachers will be involved in the intensive mode and that the principal will be able to identify tenured teachers who should also be involved in this mode. A form facilitating these choices is shown in Exhibit 9.3. These three individual development options provide teachers with a choice and enable supervisors and administrators to focus their supervisory efforts on those teachers in the intensive mode who most need their skilled services.

MOTIVATING STAFF

As can be seen, staff development, informal observations, rating, and individual development are all crucial parts of the supervision component.

Exhibit 9.3   Options for Professional Development

Teacher's Name _____ School _____ Date _____

Basic Assumptions:

1. All teachers will participate in system-based and school-based staff development.
2. All teachers will be observed informally several times during the year.
3. All teachers will be rated by an administrator.

Teacher's Preferred Option: (Check one)

_____ For this year I prefer not to participate in any special professional development activities other than those outlined above.

_____ For this year I prefer to work cooperatively with colleagues using the processes identified below.

_____ For this year I prefer to work in a self-directed mode using the processes identified below.

Preferred Developmental Processes: (Check all those that at this point seem desirable)

_____ Observe a colleague and confer about observation.

_____ Exchange classes with a colleague and confer about exchange. Develop new course of study.

_____ Develop and try out new instructional materials. Improve an advanced teaching skill.

_____ Conduct action research.

_____ View and analyze videotapes of own teaching.

_____ Plan and implement an independent study program.

_____ Enroll in graduate course or special workshops.

_____ Other _____

Curriculum Tip

A primary factor for curriculum success is motivating teachers to work.

Motivated teachers require less supervision and are willing to accomplish teaching and learning goals. They accept teaching goals as personal goals. They have a sense of confidence, enjoy teaching, are loyal, and are more committed to education as a whole. In contrast, unmotivated teachers are less apt to achieve their curricular goals, have more student discipline problems, and are less interested in change. With strict evaluation strategies, prodding, clear instructions, and close supervision, they often do a satisfactory job at best (Weis & Pasley, 2004).

Effective supervisors, therefore, should focus on the interrelationship of the four processes with an interest in motivating teachers to invest themselves in their work in order to obtain desired returns and rewards. Taking an interest in teachers, helping to build their confidence, assisting in preparing unique lesson plans, and providing new learning programs can make the difference between a good teacher and a great teacher. Greatness in teaching has always been a result of a mentor helping an individual teacher to go the extra mile. The key is to motivate teachers and show them how to exceed normal expectations when developing an interrelationship among the four processes of staff development, informal observations, rating, and individual development.

The Interrelationship of Processes

How do processes for professional development interrelate? Obviously they are closely related.

Curriculum Tip

Data derived from informal observations can be used to supplement the information derived from rating other observations and can play an important part in assessing staff-development needs.

The rating process can help the supervisor or administrator identify those teachers who need intensive development. The activities undertaken in all the options for individual development can be linked with ongoing staff-development programs. In addition, the staff-development program can provide needed support for the individual development. All the processes obviously play a key role in improving the taught curriculum.

Having administrators and supervisors examine these processes separately and analytically has clear advantages, because each requires different skills, provides different kinds of information, and employs different processes. In such an examination, it is most useful to work with individual school districts to assist them in developing their own model, rather than presenting them with a formulaic solution. Thus, some districts link rating and individual development rather closely; others keep them quite distinct. Some emphasize curriculum alignment in the informal observations; others focus on instructional processes. Some offer teachers only the cooperative and intensive options; others provide the full array. Because such matters are much affected by district size, administrative philosophy, and available resources, they are best resolved at the district level.

One particular local option needs to be emphasized here. As each district develops its own model, it determines who will be primarily responsible for each of the four approaches. Some districts limit the informal observations to administrators; others expect supervisors to be involved. Some require that rating be done only by administrators; others expect input from the supervisory staff. Some districts use assistant principals for the intensive development; others use supervisors or expert teachers. Some expect administrators to direct staff development; others see this as a supervisory function. Rather than beginning with a set of foreordained conclusions about these important matters, the professional-development approach suggested here enables local districts to resolve these issues in a way that makes most sense to their administrators, supervisors, and teachers.

Although the differentiated model has been found to be feasible and acceptable to teachers (see Glatthorn, 1984), again no empirical research proves it to be more effective than other approaches. Curriculum leaders, therefore, would be well advised to study all four approaches carefully (as well as any others that seem useful) and choose or develop a model that seems to respond best to their own district's needs.

MASLOW'S THEORY OF HUMAN NEEDS

Any discussion of supervision, staff development, and/or teacher motivation would not be complete without noting the work of Abraham Maslow.

Curriculum Tip

Maslow developed a framework for sorting and categorizing basic human needs such as physiological, security, social, esteem, and self-actualization.

Maslow's need hierarchy is arranged in pyramidal form with physiological needs being at the bottom of the pyramid and self-actualization being at the top. Earlier studies indicated that the esteem level of the need operation is of greatest concern to educators in general. Large deficiencies were reported for autonomy and self-actualization needs, and that the importance of these needs would increase as gains are made in the esteem area. The study showed that security and social needs seemed reasonably met (Sergiovanni & Elliot, 1975).

Maslow's taxonomy specifies that needs at the lower levels of the hierarchy are to be reasonably satisfied before one is interested in needs at the next higher level. For example, teachers who are working at a lower-based need, such as the social-need level, are primarily concerned with obtaining acceptance by administrators, other teachers, and parents. These teachers are less apt to be concerned with self-esteem, autonomy, and/or self-actualization. They could, however, abandon the need for social acceptance if a lower need, such as security or safety, presented itself.

Critics argue as to whether Maslow was practicing a rigorous scientific study of personality and whether it relied too heavily on case studies and not enough on experimental work. Another common criticism is that Maslow's classification of self-actualized individuals related only to highly educated white males. Regardless of these criticisms, it is important for students of curriculum supervision to have some basic understanding of his taxonomy as a historical reference when reviewing curriculum development.

SUPERVISING THE SUPPORTED CURRICULUM

Because time and personnel allocations have been discussed in Chapter 6, this chapter focuses on the commonsense application of instructional materials as a central aspect of the supported curriculum.

Curriculum Tip

Supported curriculum is defined as all the resources provided to ensure the effective implementation of the curriculum: the time allocated to the curriculum, the personnel assigned to plan and implement the curriculum, and the instructional materials required for the curriculum.

The importance of developing an effective system for selecting and using instructional materials cannot be overemphasized. As noted in Chapter 4, the textbook plays a central role in influencing what teachers select to teach and how they teach it. In most classrooms, the use of texts and ancillary materials is the predominant mode of teaching and learning: One study (Durkin, 1978) discovered that students spent as much as 70% of instructional time directly involved with textbooks, workbox copies, and other seatwork activities.

Given that importance, it is especially discouraging to note how little systematic attention is given to the textbook-selection process. One survey by the Educational Products Information Exchange (1978) determined that nearly half the teachers surveyed had no role at all in choosing the instructional materials they were using and that those who were involved reported spending only one hour a year in reviewing and selecting texts. What is needed, obviously, is a sound process for supervising the selection and use of materials—one that recognizes the central importance of the supported curriculum. The procedures outlined below, drawn from a review of the literature on textbook selection, should provide a useful beginning for local leaders who wish to review their current selection and adoption procedures (the discussion that follows uses the term *text* to refer in general to any instructional material that plays a central role in the curriculum; Chapter 14 discusses some current developments in computer software).

Develop a Statement of Board
Policy and Administrative Procedures

The board policy should delineate the functions of instructional materials, specify the roles of the board, school administrators, and teachers in selecting particular materials. That policy should be supplemented with a more specific set of administrative procedures for implementing those policies. The administrative procedures should specify how materials will be selected, how citizens can register complaints, and how administrators should respond to such complaints.

Appoint the Textbook Adoption Committee

The Textbook Adoption Committee should be representative—large enough to include broad representation and small enough to work efficiently. At a minimum, the committee should be composed of one school principal, a supervisor in that field, one teacher from each school who will be using the text, an instructional materials specialist, and a parent. Although Gall (1981) recommends limiting the committee to five or six members in order to increase efficiency, larger districts will probably find it wiser to increase the size in order to ensure adequate representation of all schools involved. The committee should be able to secure the help of a disinterested consultant, if members feel that they need technical assistance. Muther (1985) recommends that the committee be led by an "autocratic manager" who is nonbiased and does not vote.

Textbook Adoption Committee Involving Distance Learning

Distance education is a formal educational process in which the instruction occurs when student and instructor are not in the same place and audio, video, or computer technologies are employed. When distance education is used by a group of schools that receive special services through a central cooperative office, a teacher representing each school needs to be involved in the process. If the cooperative has a curriculum director, he or she needs to be on the committee. If this position does not exist, a school principal needs to be on the committee and in charge of the organization of the committee. Committee membership will be limited to the number of schools involved in the cooperative. Most, if not all, of the meetings could be held over the distance learning video equipment in distance learning conferencing labs of the individual schools.

Prepare the Committee

Because the committee will play such a central role in the adoption process, the committee should be trained in the following skills: understanding board policy and district procedures, maintaining ethical and professional relationships with publishers, understanding current research in the field, assessing district and teacher needs, evaluating instructional materials, and monitoring the implementation and use of instructional materials.

Provide the Committee With Selection Resources

The committee should also have easy access to selection resources. Two types of resources are especially needed. First, the committee should have access to catalogs of available materials and media. Several catalogs of print materials are now available as computerized catalogs, making it possible to conduct sharply focused searches for materials. Second, the committee should have access to objective reviews of materials. The journals published by the several subject-centered professional groups (such as the National Council of Teachers of English) often include such reviews. Two other excellent sources of a more general sort are the journal *Curriculum Review,* which includes reviews of materials and articles about current developments, and the Educational Products Information Exchange (EPIE), which publishes evaluative profiles of textbook materials.

Determine How Teachers Will Probably Use the New Materials

In order to make a wise decision, the adoption committee needs good information about how teachers will probably make use of the materials. Here the committee should survey, interview, and observe teachers to secure answers to these questions:

- For which groups of students will the text be used?
- Will the text be used primarily in class or outside of class?
- Will the text be used chiefly to teach skills and concepts or to provide guided and independent practice?

To understand the importance of this information, contrast two groups of teachers teaching mathematics in elementary school. One team comprises specialists in a departmentalized setting; they have been well trained in modern approaches to mathematics and are highly skilled in explaining concepts. They want a mathematics text to be used primarily as a source of problems for pupils to work on in class and at home. The other teachers are teaching several subjects in a self-contained classroom. They do not have a deep or current understanding of mathematics. They want a mathematics text that can explain concepts clearly and that can reduce their preparation time. Those two contrasting uses of the text require quite different textbooks.

Determine How Teachers Will Allocate Space

How are students and teachers assigned to space in the school in relation to the implementation of new materials? Where will materials be stored? Is it possible to situate instructional teams adjacent to one another? (Teams may actually be created because of space restrictions.) Which classrooms are nearest to the library? (Danielson, 2002). Is there a learning support center and, if so, where is it located? Some of these decisions are essentially arbitrary, but others are more purposeful, and can further the goals of the selection process.

Develop a Sharply Focused and Weighted Set of Criteria for Selection

Muther (1985) notes the dangers involved in using long checklists that include too many criteria. They lead the committee to "select by elimination": The committee spends a great deal of time searching for the perfect text, one that has all the content and qualities specified on the checklist. In the process, they ignore some excellent texts that fall short on just one or two of the less important criteria. She also believes that long checklists exert pressure on publishers to assemble texts that have bits and pieces of many kinds of content, simply to satisfy checklist users. As a result, she recommends that the committee list only three criteria and weigh those criteria in order of importance. One modification has been found to be useful here: The committee also identifies certain basic requirements that all texts should meet, such as being free of racial and sexist stereotyping and being at an appropriate level of difficulty.

District leaders who have the time and the resources needed may also wish to use the Annehurst Curriculum Classification System (ACCS; Frymier, 1977), which uses ten characteristics (experience, intelligence, motivation, creativity, emotion, personality, sociability, verbal expression, auditory expression, and motor perception) to describe both pupils and

Exhibit 9.4   Specifications for Elementary Language Arts Texts

For Which Pupils:

All pupils (except those with limited English proficiency) in Grades 1–6.

How Will Texts Probably Be Used:

Most teachers will use them in class, as the primary source for language arts instruction. Pupils will frequently read the text independently, discuss what they have read, and then do practice exercises.

Basic Requirements:

1. Texts should be free of racial, ethnic, and sexist stereotyping.
2. Texts should be written so that they can be read by all pupils who will use them, but should not be too simple or childish.

Major Selection Criteria: (Listed in order of importance)

1. The texts emphasize a process approach to writing, giving special attention to prewriting and revision.
2. The texts include a number of integrated units that show the interrelationships of writing, speaking, listening, and reading.
3. The texts reflect an informed view of language learning: Good form is stressed as an aid to clarity, not as a set of rigid rules; pupils are encouraged to value their own language and to accept the languages of others; grammar is presented as a system of language structures, not a collection of abstract terms and rules.

Ancillary Materials Required:

1. Testing program.

materials. The objective of the ACCS is to enable educators to match pupils and materials so that achievement and attitudes can be improved. The research on the use of the ACCS has yielded mixed results (see Berneman & Dexter, 1979; Cornbleth, 1979).

One useful way of summarizing all these matters is to record them in a set of specifications similar to those shown in Exhibit 9.4.

Basing Selection on Research

Even though the educational community seems to know much about effective instruction, researchers are concerned that educators have generally not based their selections on research. As a result, the No Child Left Behind Act (NCLB) is requiring school districts to review selections based on scientific research. Other national educational organizations and panels are moving in the same direction as well. For example, in the area of reading, the National Reading Panel concluded that all students must be taught alphabetics (phonemic awareness and phonics), reading fluency, vocabulary, and strategies for reading comprehension. The panel also endorses systematic phonics instruction for all students and one-to-one tutoring for struggling readers. Not everyone agrees, however, in that a number of educators believe that the National Reading Panel and other organizations rule out too many reliable studies before making their decisions. As a result, the debate continues to create controversy. Nevertheless, there is little doubt that more schools are currently selecting their textbook materials based on scientific research ("Perspectives: What Works in Reading?" 2004).

Identify Five Texts That Best Meet the Requirements and the Criteria

The committee should then use the set of specifications to identify five texts or series that meet the criteria and then rank these five in order of merit.

Get Teacher Input on the Top Five Texts

At this point, all teachers who will be using the text should be given an opportunity to review the top five identified by the committee and give their own input. Perhaps the best way to do this is for the committee member representing that school to meet with the teachers from that building, explain the requirements and criteria, and discuss the five texts that have passed the initial screening. The teachers should be encouraged to discuss the merits of each of the texts and then to express their own preferences, with the understanding that the final decision will be made by the committee, not by a majority vote.

Select the Best Text

The committee should then meet, review teacher input, take a fresh look at the five texts, and make their final choice. One of the authors of this book successfully used the following process to select the proper textbook in his school district. The textbook selection committee essentially was formed in a manner similar to the one previously mentioned. However, the final selection of the textbook differed slightly. The major difference in this selection process came in the final stage, and before a service contract was developed with the publisher. The committee selected three (not five) companies whose textbooks most closely matched the requirements and criteria the committee had identified. The companies were asked to send a representative to the school to demonstrate how their company's textbook correlated with the requirements and criteria of the school. The committee members attended the presentation, but only those members who attended all three presentations were allowed to vote on the selection of the final textbook. The presentations served to affirm the committee's confidence in the company's ability to meet the needs of their school and curriculum. The committee used this presentation along with teacher input to make their final choice.

Develop a Service Contract With the Publisher

Muther and other specialists in the field of text adoption recommend that before an order is placed, the district should develop a service contract indicating what services it expects the publisher to provide. Services that can be requested include the following: giving the district the right to photocopy certain portions, training teachers in use of the materials, helping teachers place pupils appropriately in the program, correlating the text with the district curriculum, assisting schools in ordering materials, and providing follow-up assistance when problems develop. Obviously, such services will be costly to the publisher, and the amount of service provided will likely be contingent on the size of the order.

Train the Teachers in the Use of the Textbooks and Provide Materials to Correlate the Texts With the Curriculum

Teachers will need assistance before school begins on how to use the texts most effectively. They also should receive correlation charts showing how the text correlates with the district curriculum. Chapter 11 explains this matter more fully.

Monitor the Use of the Texts

Too many districts purchase expensive textbooks and then consider the matter closed. Experts in the field point out the necessity of monitoring closely the use of the texts to be sure that they are being used appropriately and to identify problems with them. The selection committee can be given this responsibility, although Muther recommends that a separate monitoring committee be established. Once problems have been identified, corrective action should be taken. The loss of books as well as student misuse of texts also needs to be addressed. Replacement copies are expensive. Many districts have policies in place requiring students to pay for damaged or lost texts.

If these steps are taken, it is likely that the supported curriculum will be more effective.

CHAPTER OVERVIEW

This chapter examines problems and issues in supervision as well as how to improve two often-slighted aspects of curriculum: the taught curriculum and the supported curriculum. The chapter addresses major leaders who have been concerned with supervision and some current approaches to curriculum supervision. Major roles associated with curriculum supervision are discussed, including an important component of supervision, motivating staff. It is perhaps important to note that regardless of democracy in the selection process, final decisions are often made based on people's judgments and biases. It is the hope of the authors that educational leaders will make every attempt possible to eliminate arbitrary judgments and biases when selecting and developing supportive curriculum.

CHAPTER TERMS

Elements of Lesson Design	Independent Practice
Anticipatory Set	Professional Development
Objective and Purpose	Rating
Input	Intensive Development
Modeling	Cooperative Development
Guided Practice	Self-Directed Development

APPLICATIONS

1. On the basis of your experience in schools, do you believe that teachers should have some options regarding the types of supervisory services they receive? Give examples and support your position with well-reasoned arguments.

2. Glatthorn recommends that each district develop its own differentiated system of professional development. Sketch out the main components of a system that you think would work well in a district with which you are acquainted. Which components would you emphasize (staff development, rating, informal observations, individual development), which options would you provide to teachers, and who would be responsible for the several components?

3. The list of essential teaching skills presented in this chapter is only one way of describing and analyzing effective teaching. Review the research on teacher effectiveness and develop your own list of essential teaching skills, one that you could use in supervising teachers. Discuss in detail your list of skills and why you chose them.

4. Using a form like the one shown in Exhibit 9.4, develop a set of specifications for textbooks in a subject field you know well. Discuss in detail why you chose those specifications.

5. One of the issues that confront larger districts is whether all the elementary schools in that district should use the same basal reading series. What position would you take on this issue? What reasons would you advance in support of your position?

6. With more and more small schools consolidating, give examples of how distance learning technology can improve your curriculum.

7. What additional problems to supervising the curriculum, teachers, and materials does a school involved in distance learning encounter?

CASE STUDY

An Illinois school district superintendent is looking for ways to make sure that all of his teachers are using the same basal series. He decides to meet with a group of principals for ideas.

"I need to find a way to make sure our staff follows the basal text in each of our curriculum subject areas," says Superintendent Allen Stanford.

Karen Carpenter, principal of a K–5 elementary school, offers an example of what she is doing in her school. "I found that my teachers do best if they receive staff development in smaller bands of time using the same basal series rather than trying to learn everything at once. Whenever I've tried to take a 'one long in-service fits all' approach, I find that the teachers begin to wander away from the text."

"So how do we change our in-service schedule?" asks the superintendent.

"I try to set up in-service by grade level, for only half of a day. I do a substitute rotation plan," says Carpenter. "I also schedule a lot of my Early Outs for in-service relating to the basal text. Whenever I have a series of short in-services spread out over the year, the teachers seem to stick with the text. I find that shorter and more frequent staff development programs keep the basal fresh and the material interesting."

Principal Carpenter continues, "I like to use this format because the teachers don't become so overwhelmed with information. It is also great because it is a better use of their time. My staff has been very happy with the whole process."

"Well, let's take a look at this as an option for our staff-development program," says Superintendent Stanford with a smile. "I'll schedule another meeting to discuss it in more detail."

THE CHALLENGE

Substitute rotation plans proved to be very effective for Principal Karen Carpenter. What are some other supervisory strategies that she can use to support curriculum and free up teachers for staff development?

Key Issues/Questions

1. What are some supervisory steps to consider before adopting any staff-development program?

2. How do you feel about Principal Carpenter's use of a substitute rotation to enhance in-service? Is this something you might use in your school? Why or why not?

3. To what extent could Principal Karen Carpenter's substitution rotation plan lend itself to differentiated professional development?

4. What other innovative supervision strategies can be used to aid the supported curricula?

5. How do you think Principal Carpenter's substitute plan would lend itself to the selection and adoption of textbooks for a school district? What other strategies could be used in the selection and adoption of textbooks as well?

REFERENCES

Allen, T. (2004, January). No school left unscathed. *Phi Delta Kappan, 85,* 396–397.

Berneman, L. P., & Dexter, C. V. (1979, April). *Annehurst Curriculum Classification System: Effect of matching materials and students on achievement, on task behavior, and on interest.* Paper presented at the annual conference of the American Educational Research Association, San Francisco.

Buchmann, M. (1985). Improving education by talking: Argument or conversation? *Teachers College Record, 86,* 441–453.

Cornbleth, C. (1979, April). *Curriculum materials and involvement in learning activities.* Paper presented at the annual conference of the American Educational Research Association, San Francisco.

Costa, A., & Garmston, R. (1985). *The art of cognitive coaching: Supervision for intelligent teaching.* Sacramento: California State University.

Danielson, C. (2002). *Enhancing student achievement: A framework for school improvement* (p. 33). Alexandria, VA: Association for Supervision and Curriculum Development.

Durkin, D. (1978). *What classroom observations reveal about reading comprehension* (Technical Report 106). Urbana: University of Illinois Press.

Educational Products Information Exchange. (1978). National survey and assessment of instructional materials: Two years later. *EPIEgram, 5,* 1–3.

Fielding, G. D., & Schalock, H. D. (1985). *Promoting the professional development of teachers and administrators.* Eugene: University of Oregon, Center for Educational Policy and Management.

Frymier, J. R. (1977). *The Annehurst Curriculum Classification System: A practical way to individualize instruction.* West Lafayette, IN: Kappa Delta Pi.

Gall, M. U. (1981). *Handbook for evaluating and selecting curriculum materials.* Boston: Allyn & Bacon.

Gersten, R., Green, W., & Davis, G. (1985, April). *The realities of instructional leadership: An intensive study of four inner city schools.* Paper presented at the annual meeting of the American Educational Research Association, Chicago.

Gilman, D. A., & Gilman, R. A. (2003, November & December). Standard-based teaching: Overcoming the side effects. *Principal, 83*(2), 44–47.

Glatthorn, A. A. (1984). *Differentiated supervision.* Alexandria, VA: Association for Supervision and Curriculum Development.

Glatthorn, A. A. (1986, March). *Reconceptualizing supervision.* Paper presented at the conference of the National Commission on Supervision, San Francisco.

Glatthorn, A. A. (1987). *Curriculum leadership.* New York: HarperCollins.

Glickman, C. D., Gordon, S. P., & Ross-Gordon, J. M. (2003). *Supervision and instructional leadership: A developmental approach.* Boston: Allyn & Bacon.

Harmon, M. B. (2004, March). Rewriting the book on literacy. *Scholastic Administrator, 3*(5), 18–22.

Howey, K. R., & Vaughan, J. C. (1983). Current patterns of staff development. In G. A. Griffin (Ed.), *Staff development* (Eighty-Second Yearbook of the National Society for the Study of Education, Part II). Chicago: University of Chicago Press.

Hunter, M. (1984). Knowing, teaching, and supervising. In P. L. Hosford (Ed.), *Using what we know about teaching* (pp. 169–193). Alexandria, VA: Association for Supervision and Curriculum Development.

McGreal, T. L. (1983). *Successful teacher evaluation.* Alexandria, VA: Association for Supervision and Curriculum Development.

Merrow, J. (2004, February). Meeting superman. *Phi Delta Kappan, 85,* 455–460.

Muther, C. (1985). *The pitfalls of textbook adoption and how to avoid them* [Video cassette and user's manual]. Alexandria, VA: Association for Supervision and Curriculum Development.

Perspectives: What works in reading? (2004). *Educational Leadership, 61*(6), 5.

Riggins-Newby, C. G. (2003, November/December). Improving curriculum and instruction. *Principal, 83*(2), 8.

Sergiovanni, T. J. (1985). Landscapes, mindscapes, and reflective practice in supervision. *Journal of Curriculum and Supervision, 1,* 5–17.

Sergiovanni, T. J. (1986). A theory of practice for clinical supervision. In J. S. Smyth (Ed.), *Clinical supervision: Theory, research, and practice.* London: Croom-Helm.

Sergiovanni, T. J., & Elliot, D. L. (1975). *Educational and organizational leadership in elementary schools.* Englewood Cliffs, NJ: Prentice Hall.

Squires, D. A., Huitt, W. G., & Segars, J. K. (1981). Improving classrooms and schools: What's important. *Educational Leadership, 39,* 174–179.

Stallings, J. (1986, April). *Report on a three-year study of the Hunter model.* Paper presented at the annual conference of the American Educational Research Association, San Francisco.

Tomlinson, C. A., Kaplan, S. N., Renzulli, J. S., Purcell, J., Leppien, J., & Burns, D. (2002). *The parallel curriculum: A design to develop high potential and challenge high-ability learners.* Thousand Oaks, CA: Corwin.

Weeks, D. J. (2001, Winter). Standards and the impulse for human betterment. *Northwest Teacher, 2*(1), 2–5.

Weis, I. R., & Pasley, J. D. (2004). What is high quality education? *Association for Supervision and Curriculum Development, 61*(5), 24–28.

Wise, A. E., Darling-Hammond, L., McLaughlin, M. W., & Bernstein, H. T. (1984). *Teacher evaluation: A study of effective practices.* Santa Monica, CA: RAND.

Chapter 10

CURRICULUM IMPLEMENTATION

Previous chapters have discussed the processes used in developing new courses and in improving programs and fields of study. Each of these processes represents a type of curriculum change, and the literature on educational change suggests that, to be successful, those new and improved curricula will require careful support throughout several stages. The discussion that follows examines several questions as well as the critical stages. Questions to be addressed in this chapter include the following:

- What is the nature of curricular change?
- What is the role of a curriculum leader as a change agent?
- What is the importance of curriculum leadership and planning?
- What are "learning communities" and how do they affect curriculum change?
- What are the components of the *Planning, Implementation,* and *Institutional Stages* of curriculum development?

Key to Leadership

Today's school administrators face one of the most challenging and exciting times in the educational history of this nation. Setting priorities and formulating curriculum change continues to be an important role of any successful leader.

THE NATURE OF CURRICULAR CHANGE

To understand the nature and importance of the curricular-change process, consider this scenario:

Exhibit 10.1   Elements of Curriculum Implementation

A high level of curriculum implementation can be expected if . . .

1. Teachers perceive the need for the new curriculum.

2. The curriculum changes are not unduly complex and are clearly explained to teachers.

3. Quality materials supporting the new curriculum are made available to teachers.

4. Previous attempts in the district to change curricula have been successful.

5. Principals are strongly encouraged to take responsibility for implementing the new curriculum in their schools and are given the necessary training.

6. Teachers have had substantial input into the new curriculum and are provided with the necessary staff development.

7. There is strong school-board and community support.

8. There is a carefully developed implementation plan that makes specific provisions for monitoring implementation.

9. Administrators take the necessary steps to prevent and respond to the problem of "overload"—when teachers feel overwhelmed and overworked in implementing the new curriculum.

10. Principals play an active role in advocating and supporting the new curriculum.

11. Teachers have an opportunity to share ideas and problems with each other and receive support from supervisors and administrators.

SOURCE: Adapted from Fullan, M., & Park, P. (1981). *Curriculum implementation: A resource booklet.* Toronto, Ontario: Ontario Institute for Studies in Education. Used with permission.

A supervisor and a team of teachers produce a curriculum guide during the summer. With suitable fanfare, they distribute the new guide to the teachers in September and provide one hour of "in-service" about the new curriculum. The teachers give the guide a cursory examination and put it aside. As they plan the first two or three units for that year, they rely on the text they have always used, draw from their knowledge of the subject, and flip through the guide to see if they are generally on target. After the first few units, they file the guide and teach what they have always taught.

How typical is this scenario? As Fullan and Park (1981) note, the answer depends on several key factors. The important elements identified in their review of the research on curriculum implementation are summarized in Exhibit 10.1. When those elements are strongly present, a high level of implementation can be expected; when they are only weakly present or are absent, lower levels can be anticipated.

Are such variations important? The research indicates that they are. In assessing the effects of a second-grade "adaptive education" program, Leonhardt (1974) discovered that the degree of implementation explained 35% of the variance in achievement. Hess and Buckholdt (1974), in evaluating the effects of a "Language and Thinking" program for primary pupils, determined that the mean percentage of mastery for pupils in the classrooms of "high implementors" was 83%, compared with 59% for those in classrooms of "low implementors."

Obviously, it is therefore generally desirable for a new curriculum to be implemented with its main features intact. This is not to suggest, however, that complete fidelity is desired. In challenging the belief that teachers should function as the "faithful implementors" of curricula, Connelly and Elbaz (1980) argue forcefully for a quite different conceptualization—one in which teachers are perceived as partners in developing curricula and as active, deliberating agents in transforming new materials.

In examining this conflict between what some have termed "fidelity" and "mutual adaptation," Huberman (1983) seems to strike a reasonable compromise: "The inference . . . is *not* that one should retreat into improvisation but that one should try actively to deliver as many of the necessary ingredients as possible" (p. 23) [italics in original].

Curriculum Tip

The nature of the school as an organization will immeasurably influence the curriculum change process to be used.

How can curriculum leaders ensure that those necessary ingredients are delivered? The answer, as will be seen below, is complex. Although the suggestions that follow have been drawn from a review of the literature on curricular change, caution should be noted in following these recommendations. In arguing for what they term a "contingency approach" to planned change, Corbett and Dawson (1981) note that eight local factors can affect the implementation of change:

- district priorities
- availability of incentives
- availability of resources
- organizational characteristics
- the political coalitions present
- the success of prior projects
- the local environment
- the complexity of the change itself

The second caution is that the scope of the curriculum project itself needs to be assessed. Large-scale projects will probably require the systematic application of all the recommendations given below. Smaller projects requiring minimal change can be implemented with less attention to change strategies.

CURRICULUM LEADER AS CHANGE AGENT

The roles of a school administrator as an instructional leader and change agent are well documented. Instructional leadership is the raison d'être for the curriculum leader. Having a thorough knowledge of the dynamics of instruction as well as an understanding of the subject matter expertise is often necessary for helping teachers to improve. Developing knowledge of activities or actions, such as successful classroom strategies, is also a major function of any good administrator working in the area of curriculum.

Every school deserves dedicated and talented curriculum leaders. With support and insight from others, individuals can develop a leadership network that is supported by other curriculum specialists. Such a model encourages leaders to take the risks necessary to extend their skills, enhance their effectiveness, and make some positive changes in the curriculum (Donaldson, Bowe, Mackenzie, & Marnik, 2004).

Curriculum Tip

The role of the change agent is to make sure that the educational program is changed in a manner that meets the needs of students to a greater degree.

As effective instructional leaders, administrators also become effective change agents. The role of the change agent is a complex one and includes the following:

1. Developing a "shared vision"

2. Formulating a need assessment

3. Developing or selecting an innovation

4. Targeting group(s) for the proposed change

5. Anticipating problems and resistance to the proposed change

6. Formulating a plan

7. Evaluating the implemented plan and making needed changes (see Gorton, 1976).

Success of a curriculum leader as a change agent largely depends on the extent of formulating a shared vision and developing a strategic plan of implementation. Developing a vision of change and a strategic plan are key components of the process and should include guidelines that help aid the process.

CURRICULUM LEADERSHIP AND PLANNING

Leadership and planning are common threads invariably present in the design of any successful curricula program found in K–12 schools. The changes in curriculum that schools are being asked to accommodate can be both academically threatening and liberating for teachers and administrators. Just the aspect of interfacing technology with the school curriculum can be a daunting task.

In order to exercise the level of leadership required to ensure the successful integration of curriculum, principals and superintendents must reach clear answers to four basic questions:

- What resources are required to make the improvements we wish to see in the student-centered learning environments of our schools?
- Why do we want to commit a great deal of time and money to a curricular initiative for change? Are our motives focused on improving student learning?
- Who is the best person to lead the initiative we are considering?
- Who will be best suited to assess and maintain the quality of curricula programs after the initial stages of implementation are completed?

The ability of the curriculum leader to shift leadership styles can provide a supportive climate for broad-based discussions between administrators and teachers. Such discussions can also build a platform for shared decision making when opportunities are appropriate.

Curriculum Tip

Involving teachers in deliberations may well take a good deal of courage on the part of the administrator, but can produce real benefits for the curriculum.

Researchers are finding many examples of school leaders who are willing to involve parents and community members in the school technology curriculum process. Researchers at the Annenberg Institute for School Reform at Brown University canvassed the country, documenting the practice of public engagement in schools that were large and small, urban and rural, and rich and poor. The researchers found many examples of school leaders who were willing to engage parents and community members in the search for solutions to thorny educational issues (Kimpton & Considine, 1999). For helpful suggestions and a step-by-step example for formulating curriculum committees, see Appendix B.

Quality leadership must prevail at all stages of the project. Planning opens the project to view so participants understand the structure of the curriculum project and what is required of each committee and person. Planning should also address the "who, what, when, where, why, and how" aspects of the program. The traits listed below are adapted from "Technology Standards for School Administrators" (Bosco, 2001). They provide a brief overview of several important factors to consider when a curriculum project is being planned and led.

- Keep students' and teachers' needs at the forefront during the various stages of the curriculum-planning process.
- Consider how students and staff members will be affected by changes and develop appropriate support structures like training, changes in classroom layout, and inclusion into curricula.

- Review school programs to determine how course subjects may be adjusted to make use of changes in the classroom.
- Locate research that both supports and counters the major assumptions upon which the curriculum project is based. Make sure everyone knows both sides of the issue.
- Consider the possibility of having to modify school curricula practices or upgrade regulations.
- Look at the likelihood of having to adjust the school's philosophy and mission statements to align with the initiative you are creating.
- If necessary, create or borrow surveys to probe stakeholder viewpoints.
- Envision what the completed curriculum project will look like and what it will do for teaching and learning. This mental picture can help provide focus for the entire enterprise.

To specifically define project parameters from a curricular perspective, school leaders should refer to standards or guidelines to optimize benefits of change. The notion behind guidelines and standards is the assumption that curriculum reform requires large-scale systemic change. Guidelines and standards can then be used as targets toward which administrators can aim. For a specific example, see Appendix B.

Examples of Curricula Guidelines and Standards

I. **Leadership and Vision:** Educational leaders inspire a shared vision for comprehensive integration of curriculum and foster an environment and culture conducive to the realization of that vision.

II. **Educational Leaders**
   A. facilitate the shared development by all stakeholders of a vision for curricula use and widely communicate that vision
   B. maintain an inclusive and cohesive process to develop, implement, and monitor a dynamic, long-range, and systemic strategic plan to achieve the vision
   C. foster and nurture a culture of responsible risk-taking and advocate policies promoting continuous innovations
   D. use data in making leadership decisions
   E. advocate for research-based effective practices
   F. advocate at the state and national levels for policies, programs, and funding opportunities that support implementation of the district plan

III. **Learning and Teaching:** Educational leaders ensure that curricular design, instructional strategies, and learning environments integrate appropriately to maximize learning and teaching. They
   A. identify, use, evaluate, and promote appropriate resources to enhance and support instruction and standards-based curriculum leading to high levels of student achievement
   B. facilitate and support collaborative-enriched learning environments conducive to innovation for improved learning
   C. provide for learner-centered environments that use resources to meet the individual and diverse needs of learners

D. facilitate the use of resources to support and enhance instructional methods that develop higher-level thinking, decision-making, and problem-solving skills

E. provide for and ensure that faculty and staff take advantage of quality professional learning opportunities for improved learning and teaching with technology

IV. **Productivity and Professional Practice:** Educational leaders apply successful strategies to enhance their professional practice and to increase their own productivity and that of others. They

A. model the routine, intentional, and effective use of new curricula strategies

B. employ technology for communication and collaboration among colleagues, staff, parents, students, and the larger community

C. create and participate in learning communities that stimulate, nurture, and support faculty and staff in using guidelines for improved productivity

D. engage in sustained, job-related professional learning using innovative resources

E. maintain awareness of emerging technologies and their potential uses in education

V. **Support, Management, and Operations:** Educational leaders ensure the integration of curriculum to support productive systems for learning and administration. They

A. develop, implement, and monitor policies and guidelines to ensure compatibility

B. implement and use integrated curriculum-based management and operations systems

C. allocate financial and human resources to ensure complete and sustained implementation of strategic plan

D. integrate strategic plans, technology plans, and other improvement plans and policies to align efforts and leverage resources

E. implement procedures to drive continuous improvement of curricula systems and to support curriculum replacement cycles

LEARNING COMMUNITIES

A major challenge in implementing curriculum change in schools is the focus on the development of learning communities rather than large, whole-school, comprehensive reform plans.

Curriculum Tip

A major concept of learning communities is that "teachers need to teach other teachers."

Large strategic plans are generally elaborate, prescriptive, and systemic in nature. There are times when these types of plans do work, but more schools are finding that the plan's sheer size promotes overload for teachers and staff.

Author Michael Fullan (as cited in Schmoker, 2004) believes comprehensive and elaborate implementation plans are not the solution to better schools. Fullan presumes that large plans promote overloading and fragmentation, and he believes the cumbersome plans outstrip teachers' time and capacity to implement them. The problem appears to be that because teachers have too much to do, the school improvement process often becomes disjointed and incoherent.

Successful schools are now allowing more professional autonomy and are developing more specific goals for student learning. Core teaching teams in the form of "learning communities" are being developed, allowing time for teachers to collaborate and learn together. School improvement is now focusing on teachers teaching teachers and engaging in frequent, continuous, and concrete talk about best practices. This is an old idea that is just now being rediscovered. According to Judith Warren Little and Michael Fullan (as cited in Schmoker, 2004), teachers are currently planning, designing, researching, and preparing teaching materials together. Little (1990) provides a list of salient benefits of teachers teaching teachers:

- Higher quality solutions to instructional problems
- Increased confidence among faculty
- Increased ability to support one another's strengths and to accommodate weaknesses
- Systematic assistance to beginning teachers
- Ability to examine and expand a pool of ideas, methods and materials

(pp. 526–527)

Having teachers work together creates a sense of "communities of teacher researchers." This leads to the forming of small learning communities, allowing for the consensus of expert opinion and a feeling of collaboration when implementing curriculum. Teachers can engage in focused recurring cycles of instruction, formulate strategies, and develop quality assessment. For a specific example, see Appendix C.

EFFECTIVE ACTIONS IN THE STRATEGIC PLANNING STAGE

The first stage in the change process is what Herriott and Gross (1979) call the strategic planning stage. It is the stage that actually antedates the development or improvement of the curriculum. The research on successful educational change in general suggests that the following steps should be taken in the strategic planning stage.

Curriculum Tip

Curriculum leaders need to develop a master plan that indicates year by year which new courses are to be developed, which programs of study are to be improved, and which fields of study are to be strengthened.

Develop an Overall District Plan for Curriculum Development and Improvement. As explained in Chapter 5, a comprehensive plan is needed if problems of overload are to be prevented. A master plan can be created by assessing district needs, by reviewing external requirements from the state or accrediting agencies, and by calculating district resources. Exhibit 10.2 shows one district's master plan; an alternative form can be found in Chapter 5. For a detailed example, see Appendix C.

Exhibit 10.2   A Master Plan for Curriculum Development and Improvement

Year	Curriculum Project	Personnel Primarily Affected
2005–06	Develop new critical-thinking courses for middle school	Middle school principals; supervisors; social studies, science, mathematics, English teachers
2006–07	Improve high school program of studies in preparation for Middle States evaluation	High school administrators, department heads, teachers
2007–08	Improve social studies curriculum, K–12	All elementary teachers, elementary principals, supervisors, secondary social studies teachers
2008–09	No major projects initiated	

NOTE: Plan for a cycle of curriculum planning. For example, subject areas could be planned at a 7-year cycle and technology and vocational could be planned in a 4-year cycle.

Aligning a Master Plan With NCLB and Governmental Mandates

Initiating a table of contents that follows governmental requirements is a helpful guide to the process. The following is an example of a possible table of contents that might be found in any school district comprehensive plan (Reisig, 2004).

Strategic Plan Table of Contents

1. SECTION A

    Student Demographic Data by Subgroups

    Free and Reduced Lunch

    Gender

    IDEA—Individuals with Disabilities Education Act (no accommodations)

    IDEA—Individuals with Disabilities Education Act (with accommodations)

    Ethnicity

    District Climate Data

2. SECTION B

    Beliefs, Values, Mission, and Vision of District

    State of Beliefs and Values

    Vision Statement

Mission Statement

Perspectives on Institutional Change

District Goals

3. SECTION C

Implementing Content, Performance, and Assessment Requirements

4. SECTION D

Process Used to Align Local Curriculum and Assessment

Stakeholder Groups and How Group Worked to Align

Stakeholder Groups and Decision-Making Process

Stakeholder Group Decisions on Professional Development

5. SECTION E

Professional Development Activities (Theoretical Framework)

List Professional Development Activities Provided

Describe Research-Based Strategies

Describe How Technology Is Used as Teaching Tool

The table of contents above gives a rudimentary idea of how a district would outline a 5-year comprehensive plan to be aligned with federal mandates. Formulating a master plan also requires a strategy of systemic incrementalism.

In Developing the Master Plan, Incorporate a Strategy of Systematic Incrementalism

This second guideline speaks to the need for avoiding radical curricular change, which requires major modifications of the organization or significant alterations in the teacher's role; it makes more sense in general to develop or adopt what Loucks and Zacchei (1983) call a "classroom-friendly" innovation. Obviously, there will be times when a new technology will compel more radical changes, but, in general, incremental curriculum change will result in a higher level of implementation.

Develop a Constituency for the Planned Curriculum Change

To be successful, the new project needs to have the support of all those centrally affected. The curriculum leader should move systematically to enlist the support of board members, district administrators, school principals, parent leaders, and teachers. For a detailed discussion of constituency selection and function, see Appendix B. There is a special need, of course, both to inform and to enlist the active support of the teachers who will be affected. Here some research by Loucks and Hall (1979) is especially helpful. Their studies of teachers involved in educational changes indicate that teachers move through various "stages of concern" as the innovation progresses. At the strategic planning stage, the teachers' concerns focus chiefly on information: What change is contemplated—and what are its details? The curriculum leader should hold discussion sessions with teachers to inform them about the general outlines of the project, to solicit their active participation, and to invite their input.

According to author Susan Loucks-Horsley (2004), another framework that has implications for the practices of professional development acknowledges that learning brings change, and supporting people in change is critical for learning to "take hold." One model for change in individuals, the concerns-based adoption model, applies to anyone experiencing change; that is, policymakers, teachers, parents, students. The model (and other developmental models of its type) holds that people considering and experiencing change evolve in the kinds of questions they ask and in their use of whatever the change is. The concerns model identifies and provides ways to assess seven stages of concern.

Curriculum Tip

A task force or project team should be designated to assume primary responsibility for the curricular change.

Appoint the Task Force

Most districts find that a task force team of 12 to 15 is large enough to secure adequate representation from all constituencies, but not so large that it is unwieldy. Typically the task force or team should include one or more representatives from these groups: district administrators, district supervisors, school administrators, school department heads or team leaders, teachers, and parents. In high school curriculum projects, student representation is sometimes desirable as well. For detailed guidance in selecting representation, see Appendix B.

A project leader should also be identified—a key educational leader who knows the curriculum field and is skilled in working with groups of colleagues. Loucks and Hall (1979) call the project leader the "local facilitator," a role that they believe can best be performed by a district curriculum coordinator or staff developer. This local facilitator, they note, should be someone who meets several criteria: has legitimacy; is central in the communication network; and has the time, the skills, the clout, and the resources to do the job. As they see the role, the local facilitator or project leader acts as cheerleader (building commitment through constant encouragement), linker (linking external and internal resources), and troubleshooter (helping teachers solve problems).

Determine the Pace and Scope of Change

One of the initial tasks of the project team should be to determine how rapidly and broadly the curricular change will be introduced into the district. Large-scale changes should probably be introduced the first year on a pilot basis, so that the team can assess and improve the new curriculum.

Secure the Needed Resources

With that determination made, the project team should next secure the resources needed for the successful accomplishment of the project. A detailed project calendar showing the time needed should be developed and disseminated. A realistic project budget indicating the funds needed should be planned and submitted, and personnel and material needs should be calculated and specified. See Appendix C for more detailed resource guidance.

Make Specific Provisions to Secure Continued Input From Teachers

As will be noted throughout this chapter, significant teacher input is needed in every stage of the curricular-change process. Such input is required not only to enlist the support of teachers, but also to improve the quality of the final product and to ensure effective implementation and institutionalization. Connelly and Elbaz (1980) cogently make the point that the teacher's knowledge of the "practical" is essential for curricular quality:

> We are committed to thinking of the teacher as a knower of the practical . . . teachers' thinking is characterized by questions of what ought to be done to encourage the growth that is the purpose of their work, and their thinking takes into account the prescriptive wishes of stakeholders in their intellectual environment. (pp. 110, 111)

Seymour Sarason (1990) notes that teachers must have input in the design process as well as a say in how it is to be planned, implemented, and revised. It is through ownership that teachers' ideas can flourish. Likewise, author Andy Hargreaves (2001), in his book *Learning to Change,* notes that teachers across the world are struggling with educational change and, as a result, continue in their attempt to provide clear images of what successful practices look like.

Michael Fullan (2004) notes in an interview that "people in schools should not take short-cuts in their search for clarity and solutions. They need to engage with all kinds of ideas to improve what they are doing, but not adopt external programs that foster dependency" (p. 3). Fullan goes on to state, "I want schools to constantly sift and integrate the best ideas from the field, not adopt external programs" (p. 3).

Anticipate and Make the Necessary Organizational Changes

The last step in the strategic planning stage is to anticipate and make the necessary organizational changes. A new curriculum or an improved program of studies will often require such organizational modifications as new teaming arrangements, changed time allotments, new role definitions, and alterations in space allocation and utilization. Such changes should be anticipated and the necessary modifications made.

Developing Seven Strategies to Incorporate and Implement Technology

---

Curriculum Tip

Through trial and error, many curriculum leaders are learning about seven major strategies called "Golden Nuggets" that can be used to incorporate technology successfully into their curricula.

"Golden Nuggets" are hard and fast lessons that administrators have experienced during the initial planning and implementation of their technology programs. In most cases, technology should not drive curriculum, but just the opposite—curriculum should drive technology. Technology needs to be transparent and fit the existing curriculum. That is to say, teachers accept and use computers, printers, LCD projectors, scanners, and so forth, much like they would an overhead projector, VCR, or television (Whitehead, 2001). According to Whitehead,

- Leaders need to realize that the key to successful classroom technology is the teacher. Teachers and only teachers can make technology happen effectively in the classroom.
- "Money follows Success." This means that school districts should make technology a major funding priority and have technology as a line item in the budget that represents at least three or more percent of the entire general fund of the district. This provides a stable source of revenue for technology each year and helps to ensure the success of the program.
- Curriculum leaders need to place at least five high-speed networked computers with a printer in each classroom. Schools are finding that this model is one of the most efficient ways to deliver and use technology. This enhances a learning station or cooperative learning environment for each classroom. Students and teachers have equal access to the computers and the Internet all day.
- Curriculum leaders need to formulate strategies on how to "reach the 'reluctants'— those teachers having difficulty fully integrating technology into their classrooms" (Whitehead, 2001, p. 3). Schools are now using "mentor programs" whereby a teacher having difficulty using technology is paired with a master technology teacher. Both, as a team, are sent to conferences and work as partners.
- Curriculum leaders are finding that staff development via "teachers teaching teachers" works very successfully.
- School leaders need to find that it is easy to measure and evaluate success with technology by monitoring such areas as: amount of student writing; quality of student writing; enhancement of cooperative learning; awareness of student learning styles; application of technical cross-age tutoring; and level of e-mail communication among teachers, parents, and administrators.

- Leaders need to realize that formulating an effective public relations program helps develop community awareness. When parents and community leaders understand why classroom technology is so important to the future of their children, they are more often willing to support and fund it.

These seven Golden Nuggets have helped many curriculum leaders bring the effective and successful use of technology to schools all across the country. Both rural and large urban schools have had tremendous success using these strategies to incorporate technology programs into their schools. Nonetheless, any strategy or change in curriculum takes time. How much time will these strategic planning steps require? The answer obviously varies with the scope and complexity of the project. Most districts find that 5 to 8 months is adequate.

EFFECTIVE ACTIONS IN THE INITIATION STAGE

The strategic planning has been completed, and a new curriculum has been developed—or an existing one has been improved. Now the initiation stage begins. The initiation stage is that period of time when the new curriculum is first introduced to the teachers and used in the classroom: It is the lift-off stage of the curriculum project.

Curriculum Tip

If the first year of the new curriculum is seen as a pilot year, then that whole year can be seen as the initiation stage.

If the project is introduced to the entire system in the first year, then the first few months can be viewed as the initiation stage. Like the strategic planning stage, it will be most successful if effective leadership is provided.

Providing required staff development for those who will be initiating the project is important as well. Staff development for curriculum change is an ongoing process that requires attention throughout the project. One of the critical times when staff development is most essential is at the beginning of the initiation stage. According to Loucks and Hall's (1979) "stages of concern" theory, teachers at the initiation stage will typically express both personal and management concerns: "How will the new curriculum affect me?" and "How can I manage all the materials I will need?" Staff development at this stage can deal with these concerns in several ways.

First, the staff-development sessions should give teachers who will be using the new program complete information about the specific changes expected. The importance of such clear understanding is underscored in Herriott and Gross's (1979) research: They found that many innovations were not successfully implemented because teachers never fully understood the nature of the change. In clarifying the specific changes anticipated, the project team might wish to make use of what Loucks and Crandall (1982) term a *practice profile*. The practice profile of any innovation describes the critical components of the change and presents a precise list of implementation requirements. It thus can be used both to communicate the nature

Exhibit 10.3   Excerpt From Practice Profile: Reasoning and Problem-Solving Course

COMPONENT 1: *Instructor Role*		
1	*2*	*3*
Instructor poses some problems; requires students to pose problems; encourages students to develop alternative solutions.	Instructor poses all problems; guides students to one of several "acceptable" solutions.	Instructor poses all problems; directs students to "right" answer.

Code: Variations to the right are unacceptable; variations to the left are acceptable.

of the change and to assess the extent of implementation. A portion of a practice profile is shown in Exhibit 10.3.

During the initiation stage, leaders should communicate these changes and encourage the teachers to follow the new curriculum guides with as much fidelity as possible. Most of those who have researched the process of educational change conclude that teachers should make changes and adaptations only after they have followed the program prescriptions somewhat faithfully for at least a year (see, e.g., Huberman, 1983).

The second focus of the staff development should be to give the users of the new program specific assistance in translating the curriculum documents into instructional plans. A member of the project team who understands both the new curriculum and the world of the teachers should take teachers through the entire instructional planning process. The leader should begin by showing the teachers how to develop a yearly plan with appropriate time allocations. Then the leader should take a typical unit from the new materials and show teachers how to develop unit and daily plans based on the new guide. Teachers can then work in teams in developing additional units under the direction of the leader. In this way, some of their management concerns will be addressed.

Finally, the staff-development sessions should help teachers improve in their use of the instructional skills that the new curriculum requires. If, for example, they will be expected to make frequent use of cooperative learning groups, they will need specific help with organizing such groups, structuring their work, monitoring their progress, and assessing their achievement.

Be Sure All Materials and Equipment Required Are Available and Readily Accessible

This step seems obvious, yet it is one that is too often slighted by busy administrators and supervisors who neglect to place orders in sufficient time. Thus teachers arrive at the beginning of a school year eager to begin the new project and find that texts have not arrived, the computer software was never ordered, and the DVD player does not work.

Secure the Active Support of District Administrators, Supervisors, and School Principals

At the initiation stage, strong administrative support is essential. Obviously, the superintendent should communicate his or her full endorsement of the program. As noted above, the district supervisor must play those roles that Loucks and Hall describe as "cheerleader," "linker," and "troubleshooter." The building principal must also make it clear that he or she is completely behind the new project.

Secure the Active Support of Parents and the Community

A major objective is to foster a sense of community and connection between educators and the community. Another is to increase awareness of current education-curriculum related themes and concerns. Finding common ground for the educational community and parents is critical for the success of any strategic plan. It is difficult to dispute the benefits parent involvement can have upon children's school experiences, and yet parents and teachers often hold each other at arms' length. It is therefore paramount that curriculum leaders examine the community's relationship to the school as well as the current status of parent involvement. The following are some observed outcomes and some keys to success when involving parents and the community in their schools (Northwest Regional Educational Laboratory, 1999):

Observed Outcomes

- Families are less wary of the school, asking more questions and making stronger commitments
- Emphasis on serving families one-to-one can build a strong foundation of family support for the school; there is greater two-way communication between school and home
- The school climate is very friendly and positive
- High expectations from the school, parents, and students have increased accountability among all parties

Keys to Success—A Curriculum Leader . . .

- provides a wide variety of activities for families to participate
- looks beyond the core group of parents who always volunteer
- provides ways the school can serve parents and partner with them
- taps into a variety of outside sources for volunteers, funding, and curricula support
- provides avenues to take school-sponsored curricula out into the community

Monitor the Teachers' Use of the New Curriculum During Its Initiation

Avoid evaluating too early. The initiation stage should be seen as a time when users "debug" the new program, testing its feasibility in real classrooms. Accordingly, principals should be required to work closely with the teachers in noting problems and successes. However, most researchers and practitioners would support Fullan and Pomfret's (1977) recommendation that evaluation during the initiation stage should be concerned with facilitating local system capabilities through feedback, rather than with judging success or failure. It should be more formative and less summative in its emphasis. Seidman (1983) notes that evaluation during the initiation stage should not be unduly concerned with compliance; he cites several studies that indicate that an excessive concern with teacher compliance may actually interfere with successful implementation.

The initiation stage ordinarily is a time of high commitment to and great enthusiasm for the new curriculum. If teachers have been involved in developing it and have been trained in the ways described above, they will usually initiate the project with high expectations for its success. The enthusiasm and commitment of the initiation stage are typically short-lived, however; leaders should be prepared for the predictable problems that will develop during the implementation stage.

EFFECTIVE ACTIONS IN THE IMPLEMENTATION STAGE

Curriculum Tip
The implementation stage occurs when there is widespread adoption of a new curriculum.

During the implementation stage, all teachers should be following the new curriculum guide, which has been revised on the basis of feedback from the initiation stage. And, as Fullan and Pomfret (1977) note, teachers should be encouraged during the implementation stage to experiment systematically in making and adopting their own variations. The following suggestions should be useful in making the implementation stage a successful one.

Continue Providing Staff Development for Teachers

Staff development *continues* to be important during the implementation stage, though it will have a different emphasis at this point. First, some staff-development time should be devoted to an analysis of the effects of the new curriculum. Loucks and Hall's (1979) work suggests that in the implementation stage many teachers will be concerned about the consequences of the new curriculum—"How is the new curriculum affecting my students?" It therefore would be useful to provide opportunities for teachers to share their perceptions about student response to and achievement with the new curriculum. As will be noted below, evaluation during the implementation stage should be more directly concerned with student achievement; and the staff-development sessions should provide a useful forum for analyzing and interpreting these results.

Second, time should be provided for the development and sharing of instructional materials. As noted above, the implementation stage should be a time of some experimentation; therefore, some of the sessions should be devoted to collaborative development of teaching and learning materials.

Finally, staff development should provide an opportunity for peer coaching. Several studies (see, e.g., Showers, 1984) indicate that peers can be effective in coaching their colleagues in the acquisition of new skills. Effective teachers who successfully used the new curriculum in the initiation stage should help first-time users polish the needed technical skills.

Increase Administrative Pressure on Teachers to Use the New Curriculum

While teachers should be encouraged to develop their own variations, they should not be permitted to ignore the new project. As Miles (1983) notes, change projects were most successfully institutionalized when a powerful central office administrator put considerable pressure on users to implement the new program. While this strong pressure initially resulted in some reduced commitment on the part of teachers, that lowered commitment was only temporary. When teachers received the necessary assistance and support, their use and commitment increased.

Make Provisions for Systematic Evaluation

During the implementation stage, the evaluation should emphasize the summative assessment of results. Are students achieving the outcomes intended? Here the use of curriculum-based tests is strongly recommended. The data from such tests should give district and school leaders useful information about the effects of the new curriculum.

This is not to suggest that formative evaluation should be ignored. In fact, the summative data will have validity only if there is good formative data on the extent of use. Here the "practice profile" can play a different role. It now can be used to assess the extent to which teachers are actually implementing key features of the new program.

Solve Emerging Problems

Even if the new curriculum was carefully debugged in the initiation stage, somewhat predictable problems will develop in the implementation stage. Leaders should be alert to the following problems and take the steps needed to deal with them:

- Students have trouble acquiring the skills that the new curriculum requires. If, for example, the new curriculum emphasizes group inquiry, students will need specific training in the new behaviors required in such an approach. Teachers will need specific assistance in providing such training.
- Parents are confused about the new program. Parents familiar with traditional curricula will feel some anxiety and uncertainty about new approaches. Principals should work closely with the parents' organization in developing programs that will answer parents' questions and deal with their doubts.
- Budget cuts threaten the new program. Miles (1983) notes that funding cuts are a frequent manifestation of what he calls "environmental turbulence"—problems within the organization that threaten successful institutionalization. School boards that were eager to provide funds for the new curriculum in the initiation stage too often forget the importance of sustaining the change with adequate fiscal support. Here the superintendent must play a key role in planning for and securing the needed support.

If such problems are anticipated and dealt with, it is more likely that the implementation stage will be successful.

INSTITUTIONALIZATION: THE FINAL STAGE IN THE CHANGE PROCESS

Curriculum Tip

If leaders have worked systematically throughout the strategic planning, the initiation, and the implementation stages, then it is very likely the curriculum change will be institutionalized—it will become a stable part of the district's educational program.

The curriculum change has been successfully implemented. How can it then be institutionalized so that it becomes a somewhat stable part of the district's educational program? Here Miles's (1983) research (summarized in Exhibit 10.4) is illuminating. He notes eight key variables that should be present if the change is to become part of the system. A review of that list will suggest quite clearly that the key actions of the earlier stages—administrative support and pressure, organizational changes, and consistent support and assistance for teachers—are the essential ingredients required for the institutionalization of change.

Exhibit 10.4   Variables Affecting Successful Institutionalization

---

The research suggests that educational changes are more likely to be institutionalized when the following factors are present:

1. There is strong and continuing administrative commitment to the change.

2. Administrators mandate the innovation for all teachers.

3. There is strong administrative pressure on users to implement the solution.

4. Administrators make the necessary organizational changes to support the innovation.

5. There is consistent administrative support for users.

6. Administrators provide continuing assistance to users.

7. There is increased user effort, resulting from administrative pressure and assistance.

8. Increased user effort leads to increased user commitment.

SOURCE: Adapted from Miles, M. B. (1983, November). Unraveling the mystery of institutionalization. *Educational Leadership, 41,* 14–19.

Nevertheless, certain developments requiring continued administrative attention might be noted here. First, evaluation should continue to emphasize summative outcomes. Data from one or 2 years of implementation will not be sufficient to establish long-term effectiveness. Multiyear assessments will yield more valid findings. Principals should continue to monitor the use of the curriculum, but such monitoring may be less frequent and systematic.

Second, staff development should continue, but with less intensity. At the institutionalization stage, teachers are internalizing what they have learned from the once-new curriculum. They need some opportunity to reflect on what they have learned and to share their insights.

Finally, provisions should be made for periodic updating of the curriculum. Several data sources can be used to refine the curriculum still further: student achievement results, information from classroom observations, and surveys of teachers' judgments and perceptions. Change thus becomes a cycle of renewal, not a one-time innovation.

CHAPTER OVERVIEW

This chapter discusses the nature of curricular change and the role of a curriculum leader as a change agent. The importance of curriculum leadership and planning is addressed as well as learning communities and how they affect curriculum change. Finally, the components of the planning, implementation, and institutional stages of curriculum development are reviewed.

CHAPTER TERMS

Change Agent

Learning Communities

Practice Profile

APPLICATIONS

1. Assume that you are the leader of a project team developing a new social studies curriculum for Grades K–12 for your district. Develop a master planning schedule that would show a timeline and the key steps that you and the team would take.

2. The recommendation by Miles that principals should exert strong and continuing pressure on the teachers seems to contradict the advice of those who believe in more democratic leadership. By reflecting on your experience and your knowledge of the literature on leadership, decide whether you follow or reject Miles's recommendation.

3. Some have argued that, in a time of rapid change, the schools should adopt quick-fix approaches to curriculum change, in which the entire cycle is markedly shortened. What is your view on this issue?

CASE STUDY

A group of high school principals from New York are meeting at a National Association of Secondary School Principals' Conference to discuss ways to best implement curriculum.

"I need to explore some quick-fix approaches to changing the curriculum in my school by increasing technology," states high school Principal Phillip Wright. A number of other principals around the table begin shaking their heads as if to indicate that searching for a quick fix is not a good idea.

Principal Bob Kinderwater decides to share some of his ideas. "Well, I have found that it is best to avoid the short quick-fix approach to curriculum. I find that reacting too quickly to challenges in the educational process simply creates more problems. It is important to have a 'shared vision' as well as good planning. The key is to remain flexible—developing an ability to integrate strategy and formulate execution."

"And how do you do that?" asks Principal Wright. Bob Kinderwater pauses and then responds, "It is essential to ask 'What should we do?' instead of 'Why should we do it?' When looking at targets for change as administrators, we need to attack assumptions and assess risks," he says. "Formulating a quick fix approach to educational change simply places us in a reactive mode and allows our subconscious biases to cloud our perceptions. More important, the quick fix to education takes our focus off the most important thing—the students."

"I believe that," says another principal nodding his head approvingly.

All of the high school principals in the group agree that a quick fix approach is not the best way to address the challenges facing secondary education today. They decide to meet again and work out some meaningful solutions.

THE CHALLENGE

Placing groups of high-speed networked computers in classrooms is fast becoming an effective means for teachers to implement and incorporate technology in their curriculum. Analyze this approach and discuss what types of challenges Principal Wright possibly experienced during the planning, initiation, and implementation phase of this program. How do you think he managed to handle resistance at all levels in developing this type of program at his school?

Key Issues/Questions

1. What questions does Principal Wright need to ask before embarking on a *plan* for the implementation of groups of computers in classrooms?

2. If you were to incorporate groups of computers in classrooms (classroom computer centers), what effective actions would you need to take during the *initiation* phase?

3. If you were to incorporate groups of computers in classrooms (classroom computer centers), what effective actions would you need to take during the *implementation* phase?

4. If you were to incorporate groups of computers in classrooms (classroom computer centers), what effective actions would you need to take during the *institutional* phase?

5. Do you believe that a financially challenged school district can manage to develop a high-quality technology program? Defend your position.

REFERENCES

Bosco, J. (2001). *Technology standards for school administrators, TSSA.* Retrieved January 14, 2005, from the Western Michigan University, College of Education Web site: http://cnets.iste.org/tssa/framework.html

Connelly, F. M., & Elbaz, F. (1980). Conceptual bases for curricular thought: A teacher's perspective. In A. Foshay (Ed.), *Considered action for curriculum improvement* (pp. 95–119). Alexandria, VA: Association for Supervision and Curriculum Development.

Corbett, H. D., III, & Dawson, J. A. (1981). *To teach its own: School contingencies in the process of planned change.* Philadelphia: Research for Better Schools.

Donaldson, G. A., Jr., Bowe, L. M., Mackenzie, S. V., & Marnik, G. (2004, March). Learning from leadership work: Maine pioneers a school leadership network. *Phi Delta Kappan, 85,* 539–544.

Fullan, M. (2004). *Interview with Michael Fullan: Change agent.* Retrieved September 12, 2004, from the National Staff Development Council Web site: http://www.nsdc.org/library/publications/jsd/fullan241.cfm

Fullan, M., & Park, P. (1981). *Curriculum implementation: A resource booklet.* Toronto: Ontario Institute for Studies in Education.

Fullan, M., & Pomfret, A. (1977). Research on curriculum and instruction implementation. *Review of Educational Research, 47,* 335–397.

Gorton, R. (1976). *School administration: Challenge and opportunity for leadership.* Dubuque, IA: William C. Brown.

Hargreaves, A. (2001). *Learning to change: Teaching beyond subjects and standards.* San Francisco: Jossey-Bass.

Herriott, R. E., & Gross, N. (1979). *The dynamics of planned educational change: Case studies and analysis.* Berkeley, CA: McCutchan.

Hess, R., & Buckholdt, D. (1974, April). *Degree of implementation as a critical variable in program evaluation.* Paper presented at the meeting of the American Educational Research Association, Chicago.

Huberman, A. M. (1983, November). School improvement strategies that work: Some scenarios. *Educational Leadership, 41,* 23–31.

Kimpton, J., & Considine, J. (1999). The tough sledding of district-level engagement. *School Administrator, 8*(56), 6.

Leonhardt, G. (1974, April). *Evaluation of the implementation of a program of adaptive education at the second grade (1972–73).* Paper presented at the meeting of the American Educational Research Association, Chicago.

Little, J. W. (1990, Summer). The persistence of privacy: Autonomy and initiative in professional relations. *Teacher College Record, 91,* 526–527.

Loucks, S. F., & Crandall, D. P. (1982). *The practice profile: An all purpose tool for program communication, staff development, and improvement.* Andover, MA: The NETWORK.

Loucks, S. F., & Hall, G. E. (1979, April). *Implementing innovation in schools: A concerns-based approach.* Paper presented at the meeting of the American Educational Research Association, San Francisco.

Loucks, S. F., & Zacchei, D. A. (1983, November). Applying our findings to today's innovations. *Educational Leadership, 41,* 28–31.

Loucks-Horsley, S. (2004). *The concerns-based adoption model (CBAM): A model for change in individuals.* Washington, DC: National Academy of the Sciences. Retrieved September 12, 2004, from http://www.nas.edu/rise/backg4a.htm (Originally retrieved September 12, 2004 from http://www.nationalacademies.org/)

Miles, M. B. (1983, November). Unraveling the mystery of institutionalization. *Educational Leadership, 41,* 14–19.

Northwest Regional Educational Laboratory. (1999, March). *Parent partners: Using parents to enhance education.* Portland, OR: Author.

Reisig, D. (2004). *Comprehensive five-year plan.* Plan presented to Missoula School District #4, Missoula, Montana.

Sarason, S. (1990). *The predictable failure of educational reform.* San Francisco: Jossey-Bass.

Schmoker, M. (2004, February). Tipping point: From reckless reform to substantive instructional improvement. *Phi Delta Kappan, 85,* 424–432.

Seidman, W. H. (1983). Goal ambiguity and organizational de-coupling: The failure of "rational systems" program implementation. *Educational Evaluation and Policy Analysis, 2,* 399–413.

Showers, B. (1984). *Peer coaching: A strategy for facilitating transfer of training.* Eugene, OR: Center for Educational Policy and Management.

Whitehead, B. M. (2001, May). Tips for technology success. *Community Update, 87,* 3.

Chapter 11

ALIGNING THE CURRICULUM

Curriculum alignment is a process of ensuring that the written, the taught, and the tested curricula are closely congruent. In too many schools, little correspondence exists between the district curriculum guides, the teacher's instructional plans, and the assessment measures. Curriculum alignment attempts to remedy this situation in order to improve student achievement.

Key to Leadership

It is important that curriculum leaders provide curriculum alignment and teacher professional-development activities that reflect the elements of high-quality instruction with clear, explicit learning goals.

A RATIONALE FOR CURRICULUM ALIGNMENT

The argument for curriculum alignment is clear in that school leaders should begin by asserting the need for a close fit between the written curriculum and the taught curriculum. The written curriculum, it is assumed, represents a district-wide consensus about instructional objectives and their relative importance for a given group of learners. If developed in the manner outlined in previous chapters, it reflects the input of curriculum experts, subject-matter specialists, district administrators and supervisors, and classroom teachers. Because it thus represents an informed consensus, it should be the determining element in what is taught day by day.

If the district does not take reasonable steps to ensure that the guides are followed, the evidence suggests that many teachers will make unwise choices of content. In one study, for example (Fisher et al., 1978), a teacher who taught nothing about fractions over a period of

90 days (even though the topic was mandated by the state for that grade) explained the omission by saying, "I don't like fractions." Her reaction is not too atypical. As Schwille et al. (1981) noted, a teacher's decision about content is influenced by the perceived effort to teach a particular area, the perceived difficulty of that area for the students, and the teacher's feelings of enjoyment while teaching that area. Obviously, then, the district must take reasonable steps to ensure that a teacher's content choices reflect an informed consensus, rather than resulting from such idiosyncratic factors.

School districts can alleviate the problem stated in the preceding paragraph by requiring the following steps when dealing with state standards (Schmoker & Marzano, 1999, pp. 17–21):

1. Start with the standards that are assessed.

2. Beyond state assessments, add judiciously to the list of standards you will teach and assess.

3. Do not add more topics than can be taught and assessed reasonably and effectively.

An obvious need also exists for a close fit between what is taught and what is tested. As Natriello and Dornbusch (1984) note, student effort and achievement will be enhanced if students believe that the evaluation systems are valid and fair. In addition, valid and fair assessment systems require curriculum-based tests that correspond adequately with what was taught. Standardized tests will not suffice, because the content of standardized tests does not correspond closely with what is usually taught in the classroom. In one study (Freeman et al., 1980) it was determined that almost half the items in a standardized mathematics test used in many districts covered content not taught at a particular grade level.

These arguments for curriculum alignment have not totally persuaded the profession. Some educators and researchers are concerned that administrative attempts to align closely the written and the taught curricula will reduce teacher autonomy and creativity. Others have pointed out the dangers of making the test too important: The test becomes the curriculum, and teachers focus all their efforts on preparing students for that test.

Such reservations, it should be noted, support the principles of the mastery curriculum articulated in Chapter 7. As explained there, district curriculum guides should encompass only the mastery curriculum—those aspects of the curriculum that are both essential and structured. District guides should not deal with the organic elements—those that do not require structuring; or the enrichment elements—those not essential for all students. Obviously, then, the alignment process should focus only on the mastery curriculum. Because neither organic nor enrichment components are assessed or monitored, the teacher will thus have an important measure of autonomy.

CURRICULUM DESIGN

Curriculum leaders often formulate a top-down curriculum design model. Curriculum is often designed from an outcome perspective or end-in-mind approach, which is generally inverse in nature. This is usually a standards-based alignment, which often accompanies high-stakes testing. Clearly defined steps are followed, and there is a continual link to content standards. Curriculum work is usually coordinated by a district administrator and enhanced by outside experts, such as a professor from a local university, but the teachers make the essential curriculum decisions. This process usually falls into the categories of goal development, defining courses, dividing courses in units, planning units, and formulating lessons (Danielson, 2002).

Goal-Based Design

Improved public awareness of how alignment and standards can enhance curriculum development is crucial. This often leads to a greater understanding of how curriculum can benefit teachers, students, and citizens. Community appreciation leads to the creation of shared vision and mission statements, joint curriculum committees, appropriate financing programs, infrastructure development, staff development, maintenance and service arrangements, favorable program evaluation, and finally, successful public relations programs.

A key standard for school jurisdictions to consider is the setting of clear and practical goals that will expand the curriculum. Along this line, curriculum leaders need to coordinate school-based services and resources in order to best integrate curriculum for students in their schools. Envision helping participants to become change agents in the teaching-learning process of incorporating new strategies into the classroom curriculum. Questions that might be asked include the following:

- What is the mission of my school?
- What should students be learning?
- What role does activity-based learning play in the curriculum?
- What strategies and tools are we using to achieve our curricular objectives?

Successful guiding principles for curriculum planning might include the following:

- Community involvement in planning and implementing the use of an integrated curriculum should be a high priority for school leaders.
- Developing quality leadership and planning for effective teaching strategies must receive considerable attention.
- Emphasis should be placed on incorporating learning centers into classrooms.
- Curriculum should use technology, but not be driven by it.
- Staff development involving integrated learning should be made highly practical by having "teachers instruct teachers."
- Planning and implementation phases for the inclusion of new instructional strategies should include assessment and evaluation standards.

Successful curriculum mission statements involving technology might include the following:

- To enhance student learning in all curriculum areas from basic skills through higher thinking skills using state and national standards
- To enhance student global understanding
- To stay abreast of new curricula developments
- To assist the staff in completing routine tasks involving curriculum

- To provide staff in-service on curriculum
- To build student competency in using technology to access and process curriculum information

Unit and Lesson Design

An 18-month study titled "Inside the Classroom" reviewed more than 350 lessons that included accurate, significant, and worthwhile content, yet many of the lessons were generally not intellectually rigorous, did not include effective teacher questioning, and did not guide students appropriately (Weiss & Pasley, 2004). One of the purposes of the study was to find high-level lessons that invited students to interact purposefully with content. These types of lessons involve students and try to build on previous knowledge, often using real-world examples or engage students in firsthand experiences.

Developing quality lessons is an important part of curriculum design. As part of a curriculum alignment process, it is important that teachers have a vision of effective instruction to guide the design and implementation of their lessons. Activities should engage students. The classroom curriculum should support and challenge students with appropriate questioning and sense-making strategies. Questioning strategies should enhance the development of students' problem solving, with the teacher emphasizing higher-order thinking skills.

It is important that curriculum leaders provide workshops and other teacher professional development activities that reflect the elements of high-quality instruction with clear, explicit learning goals. It is critical that schools also provide supportive and yet challenging learning environments. The findings of the "Inside the Classroom" study (Weiss & Pasley, 2004) included a number of interventions that will help teachers improve instruction.

Interventions

- Skilled, knowledgeable facilitators who provide teachers with helpful learning opportunities
- Support materials accompanying textbooks and other instructional materials
- Workshops and professional development activities that focus on high-quality instruction
- Policymakers who explore the apparent inequities in quality of instruction and who take steps to resolve them
- Administrators who ensure that teachers receive a coherent set of messages

As can be seen, it is crucial that teachers have assistance in formulating and delivering highly effective lesson plans that relate directly to mastery objectives. This will require the alliance of curriculum leaders who share a vision of quality instruction at district and state school levels.

ORGANIZING THE ALIGNMENT PROJECT

The first important step is to organize the alignment project and to allocate responsibilities. The project is a complex one, involving several critical steps, and it will probably operate most effectively if it systematically involves all those who can contribute. Each district, of course, will develop its own organization and management system for the project; the system outlined below has been derived from an analysis of several successful alignment projects.

One effective way to begin is to appoint a curriculum-alignment task force, a representative group that will be responsible for planning and coordinating the project. The task force should include an appropriate number of representatives from the following constituencies: district administrators, district supervisors, school administrators, teachers, and parents. At the outset, the task force should develop its own planning guide, indicating the steps to be taken, the deadline for each step, and those responsible for each step. A special point should be made here about the allocation of leadership responsibilities. Rather than simply assuming that the principal will play the key leadership role at the school level, the task force should attempt to identify and develop a leadership team at each school, so that the talents of many individuals are utilized and responsibility is shared. Exhibit 11.1 shows a form that can be used to assist in such planning. It lists all the steps in the alignment project and provides space for deadlines and the names of those responsible for each step.

In the discussion that follows, certain assumptions will be made about those providing leadership simply for purposes of illustration; however, each district should develop its own system for allocating leadership responsibilities.

One of the initial decisions the task force should make is the scope of the alignment project: Which subjects at which grade levels will be included? The alignment project of the Los Angeles Unified School District (see Niedermeyer & Yelon, 1981) covers reading, mathematics, and language from K–6; the Monitoring Achievement in Pittsburgh project covers mathematics, reading, grammar/composition, and critical thinking/social studies from K–12 (see Rifugiato & Wilson, 1983). The decision will, of course, be affected by such considerations as the size of the district, the resources available, and administrators' perceptions of needs.

The task force should then make plans to orient all the key groups that will be involved in and affected by the alignment project. The first group to be oriented should probably be the school principals. They should have in-depth preparation to enable them both to discharge their own responsibilities and to explain the project to others. The principals can then, at the school level, orient both their own faculties and parent groups.

ORGANIZATIONAL STRATEGIES

A major focus of the curriculum alignment task force is to determine whether the curriculum will be standards-based or integrated or a blend of both. The task force will then need to determine a sequence, formulate requirements and electives, and eventually coordinate the entire curriculum.

Standards-Based Versus Curriculum Integration

The past decade has witnessed considerable interest in curriculum integration and yet, paradoxically, schools at the same time are being required to move to an "accountability" and "standards-based" subject-centered curriculum. How can curriculum integration survive under such circumstances? One deterrent to curriculum integration is the fact that most state standards and proficiency tests are set up in terms of conventional subject areas, such as reading,

Exhibit 11.1   Alignment Project Planning Guide

Project Step	Deadline	Primarily Responsible	Assists
1. Determine scope of project.			
2. Orient school administrators.			
3. Orient teachers.			
4. Orient students and parents.			
5. Revise curriculum guides.			
6. Identify mastery objectives.			
7. Develop curriculum-based tests.			
8. Correlate mastery objectives with instructional materials.			
9. Develop planning aids.			
10. Help teachers use planning aids.			
11. Monitor teacher use of planning aids.			
12. Develop test-reporting materials.			
13. Help teachers use test reports.			
14. Help school administrators use test reports.			
15. Use test reports in evaluating curriculum.			
16. Provide staff development for school administrators.			
17. Provide staff development for teachers.			
18. Monitor and evaluate the alignment project.			

mathematics, science, or social studies. Another problem is the sheer number of competencies specified in the standards. According to Vars and Beane (n.d.),

It is still too early to obtain reliable data on how students in integrative programs fare on state proficiency tests. However, recent analyses of studies (Arhar, 1997; National Association for Core Curriculum, 2000; Vars, 1996, 1997) point to the same general conclusion: Almost without exception, students in any type of interdisciplinary or integrative curriculum do as well as, and often better than, students in a conventional departmentalized program.

For the most part, these results were obtained using standardized achievement tests designed for a conventional separate subjects program. Most standardized tests are normed—scores of individual students are compared with the mean or average of whatever group is considered "normal." In contrast, current state tests may have arbitrary cut-off scores that all students must meet in order to "pass" or be considered "competent." In other words, the rules of the assessment game have been changed radically. Furthermore, the quality of many statewide assessment measures has been widely criticized, raising serious questions about the morality of using them to determing [*sic*] a student's grade promotion or high school graduation.

It will probably be many years before problems in the assessment of student performance are solved. In the meantime, educators considering curriculum integration will need to proceed carefully and take full advantage of the decades of research and experience with this potentially powerful way of designing and carrying out education (Beane, 1997; Vars, 1993). It also is important to keep all stakeholders—students, teachers, families, and the general public—both informed and involved in continuing efforts to provide every student with meaningful learning experiences. (p. 3)

In support of Vars and Beane, Charlotte Danielson (2002) believes curriculum integration can be done by considering the following design issues: *sequence, required versus elective,* and *coordination and integration* of subject matter.

Sequence

A well-organized curriculum will have goals stated in a clear and concise manner. Complex ideas and skills will follow simpler ones. Student abilities will be considered when determining teaching strategies. Topics are addressed and then covered again in a spiraling curriculum approach with the learning level advancing with each reteaching. Students develop a richer understanding of the subject area, and there is an appreciation of nuances within the material.

Required Versus Elective

Elements of consistency within the curriculum begin to change as students move from elementary to middle to high school levels. The distinction between mandatory and optional is more evident at high school levels. Students at higher levels are able to pick and choose courses as they relate to graduation and college requirements.

Coordination and Integration

Some curriculum specialists consider subjects as distinct bodies of knowledge to be aligned as standards throughout the curriculum. Other curriculum specialists see subject areas as bodies of knowledge that are to be interwoven in a thematic scheme. In the latter, information

Exhibit 11.2   Sample Mastery-Objectives List

GRADE 5. SOCIAL STUDIES: PEOPLE OF AMERICA

Maps, Globes, and Graphics Skills

1. Locate Canada on globe.
2. On an outline map of Canada, identify each province.
3. On an outline map of Canada, with locations of cities indicated, identify: Montreal, Vancouver, Toronto, Winnipeg, Calgary.
4. Use scale on map to estimate distance between two Canadian cities.
5. Identify major ethnic groups and their relative sizes from bar graph.

---

can be covered through methods of inquiry, and topics can be coordinated and integrated across disciplines. Regardless of which approach is used, there is the need for the educational task force to *identify mastery objectives* within the curriculum.

IDENTIFYING THE MASTERY OBJECTIVES

Educational task forces should turn their attention to the critical task of identifying the mastery objectives (as explained in Chapter 1, the mastery objectives are those objectives that are essential for all and require careful structuring). Because that list of mastery objectives will be used in developing both the curriculum-based tests and the teachers' alignment materials, it is essential that the task be done with care and due deliberation. If the district has developed a curriculum that focuses only on mastery objectives, then the task is a very simple one: The objectives have already been identified for each grade level. If the district is basing the alignment project on existing guides that do not embody the mastery approach, then subject-matter committees should be assigned the task of identifying the key objectives.

The subject-matter committees should begin by reviewing and revising the guides, if revision seems indicated. Even the best guides become outdated; it is obviously unwise to base an alignment project on an inadequate curriculum. Once necessary revisions have been made, the committee should identify for each grade the mastery objectives—the key skills, concepts, and information that students are expected to master (a sample list is shown in Exhibit 11.2).

Three types of objectives should probably not be included in the mastery list:

*   Objectives too difficult to assess with district-made tests. Most districts, for example, would probably choose not to assess listening skills, because valid listening tests are very difficult to develop, administer, and score. Similarly, most affective outcomes (such as "appreciating poetry") are difficult to measure validly with objectives.
*   Objectives that are not considered essential for all students. Many district guides include content that has been identified in this text as enrichment material: objectives that are not really basic for all students, but simply broaden the curriculum or challenge the more able.

- Objectives that have been emphasized at some previous grade level or that will be emphasized at some future grade level. While many district guides include objectives that are to be "reviewed" or "introduced," only those objectives to be emphasized at that particular grade level should be identified in the alignment project. It is expected that teachers will review as necessary and will feel free to introduce skills and concepts as the occasion arises.

These preliminary lists of grade-level mastery objectives should then be reviewed by classroom teachers. At the elementary level, the reviews should be made by grade-level teams; third-grade teachers, for example, should have an opportunity to review the mastery lists for all areas for which they are responsible. At the secondary level, the review should be conducted departmentally. This teacher review is essential, because teachers will be expected to teach and test for the objectives on the final list.

The task force should then undertake a final review of the mastery lists. One of the important questions to be raised at this juncture is whether the skills and concepts can be taught for mastery within the time allotted. How much time should be allotted to mastery objectives? The Pittsburgh alignment project suggests a figure of 60% of the total instructional time available; the remaining time is provided for remediation and enrichment.

DEVELOPING CURRICULUM-BASED TESTS

That graded list of mastery objectives should then be used to develop curriculum-based tests. Because these tests play such a key role in the alignment project, they should be developed with the advice of measurement experts who can guide the development of the tests and also assess the tests for reliability and validity. Test development is a highly complex process that requires very specialized technical skills. If districts do not have their own evaluation experts, they may wish to use the services of professional and commercial organizations that will develop such tests on a contractual basis.

Measurement experts usually recommend that a process like the following one be used in developing and assessing the curriculum-based tests (Glatthorn, 1987):

1. Determine test scope and frequency. Will curriculum-based tests be administered at the conclusion of each unit, at the end of each semester, or at the end of the school year? More frequent testing provides administrators and teachers with formative data that can be used to monitor student progress and take corrective actions; however, frequent testing reduces instructional time and seems to increase teacher resistance to the project.

2. Determine how many forms of each test will be required. Larger school systems may require several alternative forms for each test in order to ensure test security. For smaller systems, two forms for each test will probably suffice.

3. For each objective, develop a pool of test items. Be sure that the test items validly assess the objective. Do not use "comprehension" items, for example, to assess "application" objectives.

4. Construct the pilot forms of the tests by selecting a sample of test items, grouping the items in some logical manner, and preparing clear instructions.

5. Develop a scoring system that will provide administrators, teachers, and students with the information they require in order to understand and use test results. Administrators will need information about overall achievement; teachers will need diagnostic information about classes and individual students; and students will want grades.

6. Have content specialists review the tests to ensure that items are valid, that the answers are correct, and that the sampling reflects curricular priorities. Administer the pilot forms of the test to groups of students in order to measure test reliability.

(p. 260)

Those requiring more information about the development of curriculum-based tests should consult one of the standard references: Baron and Boschee's (1995) text provides insightful thoughts on the purposes of evaluation; Bloom, Hastings, and Madaus's (1971) text provides a comprehensive treatment of evaluation; Morris, Fitzgibbons, and Henderson's (1978) kit is also very helpful.

The process outlined above obviously describes the development of objective tests, the type most commonly used in alignment projects. Many districts, however, have seen fit to supplement those objective tests with certain performance tests, especially in the area of written composition. Those performance tests will require quite different methods of development and assessment.

Obviously the process of developing curriculum-referenced tests is a complex and time-consuming one. These tests are so important, however, that such an expenditure of time and effort is fully warranted.

CORRELATING THE MASTERY LIST AND INSTRUCTIONAL MATERIALS

With the tests prepared, the subject-matter committees should turn their attention to the instructional materials. By reviewing texts currently in use and checking their content against the mastery list, the committees should first establish whether new basal texts would be required. Quite often the development of the mastery-objectives list will highlight deficiencies in existing texts—deficiencies that were not apparent when teachers alone determined what they would teach.

The committees should then develop objectives—materials correlation charts for each grade in order to assist teachers in using instructional materials. On the left of the chart are listed the mastery objectives; across the top are the titles of both basal and supplementary texts, including, of course, any new texts that will be ordered. Each mastery objective is then keyed to specific pages in the texts. A sample correlation chart is shown in Exhibit 11.3. Although many publishers make such correlation charts available to districts that have purchased their texts, such publisher-produced charts are not sufficiently reliable for use in the alignment project.

The correlation process thus accomplishes two important goals. It provides a means for the district to ensure that adequate instructional materials are available; and it helps teachers make their instructional plans.

Exhibit 11.3   Sample Objectives: Text Correlation Chart

GRADE 10. SCIENCE: BIOLOGY		
Mastery Objectives	Life Sciences	Modern Biology
1. Define *ecosystem*	pp. 75–78	pp. 14–18
2. Identify three common air pollutants	pp. 78–79	pp. 19–20
3. Explain probable causes of acid rain	pp. 82–83	

DEVELOPING INSTRUCTIONAL PLANNING AIDS

The next important component of the alignment project is the instructional-planning aids. These are materials that will assist teachers in developing and implementing instructional plans. Besides helping teachers plan, they also can facilitate discussions between administrators (or supervisors) and teachers about the planning process. Major types of planning aids that play an important role include: Yearly Planning Matrix, Management and Monitoring Matrix (see Appendix A), and Unit-Planning Guides.

Yearly Planning Matrix

Teachers will first need help in making tentative plans for the school year, to ensure that all mastery objectives are taught and reinforced and that adequate time has been provided. One way of helping them accomplish these goals is by providing a yearly planning matrix, like the one shown in Exhibit 11.4. The teachers first list the mastery objectives, grouped according to subject-matter subdivisions. They then indicate the report or marking period when they plan to teach this objective for mastery and when they expect to reinforce that objective. They then estimate the total number of instructional periods required.

One effective way of using the yearly matrix is as follows:

1. The teacher submits the yearly matrix to an instructional leader. The initial entries reflect the teacher's tentative decisions about yearly planning.

2. The instructional leader and the teacher confer about the yearly plan, discussing issues of sequencing and time allocation and making any changes they both agree are necessary.

3. The yearly matrix is posted in the classroom so that students and classroom visitors can be informed. As the teacher teaches or reinforces a mastery objective, the appropriate entry is marked.

4. The teacher is expected to bring the yearly matrix to any supervisory or evaluation conferences.

Exhibit 11.4   Sample Yearly Planning Guide

	Report Period				
GRADE 8. ENGLISH LANGUAGE ARTS (Literature)					
Mastery Objective	First	Second	Third	Fourth	Total Time Required
1. Define character	T		R		2 periods
2. Identify three means of character	T		R		2 periods
3. Infer character's motivations	T	R	R		4 periods

Code: T = teach for mastery; R = reinforce

Management Planning Matrix

Another design tool is the *Management Planning Matrix* that has been developed to help curriculum leaders plan, implement, and evaluate an effective staff development program (Whitehead, Jensen, & Boschee, 2003). The matrix design encourages planners not only to develop technology staff development goals, but also to formulate measurable indicators of successful in-service. The matrix additionally forces planners to detail activities and leadership roles, and to set implementation and evaluation dates. This has been one of the most successful tools used by school leaders in designing effective staff development programs. A Management and Monitoring Matrix can be found in Appendix A. Both examples of a yearly matrix thus serve several important purposes.

Unit-Planning Guide

Teachers will also need help with their unit planning. Two approaches can be used in deriving unit plans from the yearly matrix. In fields such as mathematics and science, where units are built from closely related objectives, the teacher can begin with the yearly matrix, list related objectives in unit clusters, and check to see that the time allocations seem appropriate for that grade level. In this approach the objectives shape the unit.

In fields such as English and social studies, where several types of objectives are often included in one unit, teachers will need special help in learning how to integrate mastery objectives into thematic units. Most teachers will find it helpful to begin by "roughing in" the unit—identifying the unit theme, determining the approximate length of the unit, specifying

Exhibit 11.5   Sample Unit-Planning Chart

GRADE 10. ENGLISH. Second Report Period

UNIT THEME: The Changing American Family

LENGTH OF UNIT: 10 periods

Thematic Generalizations

1. Understand how American family is changing
2. Understand reasons for changes

Common Readings

1. *My Antonia*
2. *Life With Father*
3. *Kramer vs. Kramer*
4. Selected articles from current magazines

Mastery Objectives to Be Emphasized

1. Write expository essay of causal analysis
2. Identify author's bias in an essay of opinion
3. Identify three means of character portrayal
4. Infer character's motivations

---

the major unit generalizations, and identifying the key resources. Next they turn to the yearly matrix and select appropriate objectives for that unit, checking off each objective as it is included in a particular unit. They then make a final check to be sure that all objectives have been included in at least one unit. Exhibit 11.5 shows one form that can be used in integrating mastery objectives into a thematic unit. In this approach, the unit theme influences the selection of the objectives.

These unit-planning guides should also play an important role in the supervision process. They can assist the supervisor and the teacher in discussing curricular priorities, in reflecting on planning approaches, in determining instructional methods, and in examining issues of individualization and remediation.

In addition to the yearly and unit-planning aids, some school districts expect teachers to indicate in their daily lesson plans which mastery objectives will be covered. Others feel that teachers should have more flexibility and autonomy in daily planning. The research does not provide any clear guidance here. Although well-structured lessons are usually associated with increased achievement (see Berliner, 1984), there is no evidence that the quality of written lesson plans is related to student achievement. Some teachers can write good plans but cannot deliver them effectively; other teachers can deliver well-structured lessons without committing plans to paper (for an excellent review of the research on planning and achievement, see Boschee & Baron, 1993, and Peterson, Marx, & Clark, 1978).

Also, some districts provide pacing charts that indicate when a given set of objectives should be taught and approximately how much time should be devoted to each group of outcomes. While such charts can be helpful to teachers who need assistance with pacing, most teachers seem to view the pacing charts as too controlling. Their use would seem to reduce teacher autonomy in planning, teaching, and providing remediation. The purposes of such pacing charts can perhaps be better realized through discussions between supervisor and teacher about yearly and unit planning and by team or departmental discussions of time allocation and instructional pacing.

The intent of all the instructional-planning aids should be to help teachers plan more effectively, not to control their classroom decision making.

IMPORTANCE OF SCIENTIFIC RESEARCH

Any alignment of reading curriculum at the elementary level should involve understanding of scientific research. This has been especially the case with the No Child Left Behind Act's (NCLB) requirements. According to authors G. Reid Lyon and Vinita Chhabra (2004), current research reveals that a majority of students can learn to read irrespective of their backgrounds, and yet many elementary students are not having success in reading. The problem is that many elementary teachers do not have the background or training in scientific-based reading research. Teachers frequently rely on experience and anecdotal information to guide their teaching. As a result, it is more important that educators have a basic understanding of scientific knowledge as it relates to reading and what needs to be done to guide instruction.

Two major questions that should be asked by curriculum leaders selecting reading programs should be:

1. Does the program comprehensively cover each of the evidence-based skills that students need to read proficiently?

2. Has the program or approach been proven scientifically to work with students?

Asking these types of questions is important for curriculum leaders. Research obtained should include information on appropriate methodologies, peer review, converging evidence, and practical application. For example, Lyon (Lyon & Chhabra, 2004) notes that the National Reading Panel (NRP) found that systematic phonics instruction produced significant benefits for K–6 students and for those having difficulty learning to read. The NRP also found that systematic phonics instruction was most effective when provided within the context of a comprehensive reading program that addressed phonemic awareness, fluency, vocabulary, and comprehension strategies. This is the type of detailed scientific research that curriculum leaders need before selecting, planning, or implementing a reading program.

The U.S. Department of Education is in the process of developing the What Works Clearinghouse as a resource that will provide curriculum leaders with central and independent scientific evidence of what works in class. For more information, contact the clearinghouse (see www.w-w-c.org).

DEVELOPING REPORTING MATERIALS

The task force should also determine, in consultation with administrators, supervisors, and teachers, what reporting materials will be required in the alignment project. The following types of materials have been used in several successful projects:

1. The *planning report* summarizes student performance for each class on the previous year's summative examination. The report is distributed to teachers in workshops that precede the opening of school; teachers use the report to determine which objectives need additional review and which students require special attention.

2. The *class diagnostic summary* is provided to teachers after each test administration. It gives information about the test results of all the students in the class, objective by objective. The teacher uses this report to plan posttest remediation and to make adjustments in the yearly and unit forms.

3. The *individual student report* provides comprehensive information for each student; it also is distributed after each major testing. It gives the student's name and indicates for all objectives the number correct and incorrect. The individual student report is made available to teachers, the student, and the student's parents.

4. *Data analysis reports* are also very helpful. They often provide a practical tool to help educators make better decisions based on information collected over a period of time. School leaders can use data to analyze and utilize information about their curriculum and their school communities. Data reports help curriculum leaders in initializing needed change as well as allowing them to monitor instructional practices successfully (Bernhardt, 1998).

These reports, which provide a great deal of useful information, can be produced at relatively little cost through the use of computers.

PROVIDING STAFF DEVELOPMENT FOR THE ALIGNMENT PROJECT

Once all these decisions have been made and materials have been developed, the school administrators and teachers should be provided with the in-depth training they will need to make the project successful. Part of this staff development should occur, of course, before the project begins, to prepare both groups for the requirements of the alignment project. Much of it, however, should be made available on a continuing basis throughout the year as problems develop. The specific content of the staff development will certainly depend upon local needs. In general, the following topics might be included in staff development for principals:

1. A rationale for curriculum alignment

2. Orienting teachers and parents about alignment

3. Helping teachers use test reports

4. Helping teachers make yearly and unit plans

5. Monitoring teacher planning and instruction

6. Using test reports to evaluate the school's program of studies

7. Using the alignment project to make supervision more effective

8. Evaluating the alignment project

The staff development for teachers will include some similar topics, with a different emphasis. The following topics would probably be helpful:

1. A rationale for curriculum alignment

2. Identifying mastery objectives

3. Using mastery objectives in yearly and unit planning

4. Using test reports to plan instruction and monitor progress

5. Locating and using instructional materials

6. Teaching for mastery objectives

7. Communicating test results to students and parents

The staff-development workshops for both administrators and teachers should also be used to get participants' input about improving the project. Even well-planned projects will need refinement and revision, and the staff-development sessions provide an excellent opportunity for groups to raise problems and suggest solutions.

MONITORING AND EVALUATING THE ALIGNMENT PROJECT

Throughout its operation, the alignment project should be monitored to be sure it is working as planned and then evaluated to assess its overall effectiveness. Two types of monitoring are required. First, district administrators should be responsible for monitoring project management, seeking answers to the following questions:

1. Have all necessary instructional materials been provided, and are correlation charts accurate?

2. Are tests being administered and scored on schedule?

3. Are staff-development sessions being conducted as planned, and are they judged by participants to be helpful?

4. Are principals and supervisors helping teachers plan effectively, teach to mastery objectives, and use test results to modify instruction?

Several methods can be used to answer these questions. First, those responsible for carrying out the steps identified in the planning guide should be expected to submit periodic reports, noting dates when key steps were carried out and identifying any problems that developed. Second, as noted above, some time during each staff-development session should be used to identify problems and assess progress. Regularly scheduled administrative and faculty meetings can also be used, of course, to assess the progress of the project. Finally, a representative sample of administrators and teachers should be interviewed, perhaps once every 2 months, in order to survey their perceptions and probe their concerns.

The second type of monitoring focuses on the teachers' implementation of the project at the classroom level. The intent here is for school administrators to ensure that teachers are carrying out their responsibilities, but to do so in a professional manner that does not create an atmosphere of distrust. This goal can be accomplished if principals present the project as a means of helping teachers, not as a method of controlling them. All of the following activities should therefore be carried out in that spirit. First, of course, the submission of the yearly planning matrix will enable the principal and the teacher to discuss together such essential matters as the organizing of objectives, the optimal sequencing of instruction, and the allocation of instructional time as a reflection of curricular priorities.

Also, the unit plans should facilitate professional discussions between supervisors and teachers. The review of those plans will enable the supervisor and the teacher to discuss issues of unit planning, time allocation, instructional methods, assessment of student learning, and remediation strategies. Because these unit plans are so important, some districts require teachers to submit them for review; others simply expect teachers to develop such plans and review them with colleagues and supervisors, without requiring the plans to be submitted.

Finally, the alignment project can support an objectives-focused supervisory process. Instead of being concerned primarily with instructional methods, supervisors can focus on outcomes. In pre-observation conferences they can help the teacher assess what progress has already been made and determine what mastery objectives should be emphasized in the week ahead. The pre-observation conference should also provide both with an opportunity to reflect on assessment concerns: How will student learning be assessed? What will be an acceptable level of student achievement for a given lesson and a series of lessons? In their observations, they can focus on the clarity of objectives and the evidence of student mastery. In the post-observation conference, they can help the teacher use student-achievement data as a means of diagnosing instruction.

Such outcomes-focused supervision enables the supervisor and the teacher to examine data objectively and to concern themselves with the essential issue of student learning, rather than emphasizing instructional methods. Issues of method are raised only if the data suggest that students did not achieve at the agreed-upon level. As Niedermeyer (1976) notes, "One of the most obvious advantages of using the . . . model is that the interaction between administrators and teachers is referenced to empirical evidence of student accomplishments, rather than to beliefs or opinions about what is 'right' or 'works'" (p. 4).

The summative evaluation of the alignment project can make use of two measures. First, the perceptions of administrators, supervisors, and teachers should be surveyed at the end of each school year. Exhibit 11.6 shows one type of survey form that can be used. The more important measure, of course, is student achievement. School districts should maintain and carefully analyze the results of both curriculum-based and standardized tests, noting trends over a multiple-year period of time. If the project has been designed carefully and implemented professionally, districts should find that student achievement increases. As Niedermeyer and Yelon (1981) note in their report of the Los Angeles project, evaluators who reviewed the project judged it to be

Exhibit 11.6   Survey of Perceptions of Alignment Project

Directions: Listed below are several statements about our alignment project and its components. Circle the symbol that best represents the extent to which you agree or disagree with the statement:

SA = strongly agree   D = disagree

A = agree   SD = strongly disagree

Statement   *Your Perception*

1. The list of mastery objectives helped teachers   SA   A   D   SD
    plan, teach, and assess learning.

2. The objectives-materials correlation charts   SA   A   D   SD
    helped teachers plan and use materials.

3. The yearly planning matrix helped teachers   SA   A   D   SD
    make effective plans for the year.

4. The unit-planning guides helped teachers   SA   A   D   SD
    develop and implement unit plans.

5. The curriculum-based tests provided useful   SA   A   D   SD
    information to administrators and teachers.

6. The alignment project improved the professional   SA   A   D   SD
    climate of the school.

7. The alignment project seemed successful in   SA   A   D   SD
    improving student learning.

Please provide brief responses to the two items below.

8. The main advantage of the alignment project was _____

    _____

9. The alignment project could be improved by _____

    _____

Please check below to indicate your professional role; there is no need to sign your name.

_____ District administrator   _____ District supervisor

_____ School administrator   _____ Team or department leader

_____ Classroom teacher

Exhibit 11.7   School District National Percentile Rank

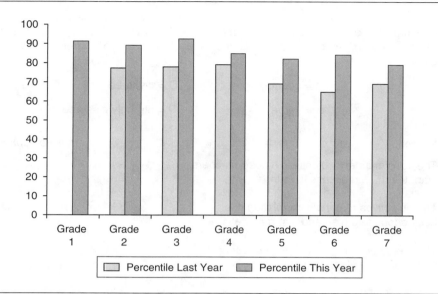

one of the most promising efforts to improve urban schools. One of this text's authors oversaw composite scores in his school district rise more than 10 percentiles for each grade level in one year due to curricular alignment (see Exhibit 11.7).

A summative evaluation of curriculum can also be attained through a reflection on the following questions adapted from Carol Tomlinson et al.'s (2002) *The Parallel Curriculum: A Design to Develop High Potential and Challenge High-Ability Learners.* Does the curriculum

- Guide students in mastering key information, ideas, and the fundamental skills of the disciplines?
- Help students grapple with complex and ambiguous issues and problems?
- Move students from novice toward proficient and expert levels of performance?
- Provide students with opportunities for original work in the disciplines?
- Allow students to encounter, accept, and ultimately embrace challenges in learning?
- Prepare students for a world in which knowledge expands and changes at increasingly rapid rates?
- Allow students to develop a sense of themselves as well as of their possibilities in the world in which they live?
- Provide sufficient challenges to encourage students to develop to the fullest of their capabilities?

UNDERSTANDING THE IMPORTANCE OF CURRICULUM

With the advent of the communication age, a globally shared vision of educational curriculum is not far in the future. Changing societies can change students. Students with knowledge and vision can change societies. Cultural diversity is an important aspect of our world, but cultural understanding is equally as important. While effective curriculum and instruction worldwide contain many diverse elements, curriculum also needs to be responsive to individual students globally. An appreciation of contemporary learners necessitates a need to maximize the capacity of each learner and to guide and align the process through a myriad of opinions and perceptions.

CHAPTER OVERVIEW

This chapter provides a rationale for and a process for curriculum alignment. This process ensures that the written, the taught, and the tested curricula are closely congruent. Curriculum alignment attempts to improve student achievement by remedying the discrepancy that often exists in too many schools between the district curriculum guides, the teacher's instructional plans, and the assessment measures.

CHAPTER TERMS

Curriculum Alignment

Goal-Based Design

Standards-Based Curriculum

Integrated Curriculum

Planning Report

Class Diagnostic Summary

Individual Student Report

Data Analysis Report

APPLICATIONS

1. Be prepared to discuss or write about your views on this statement: Curriculum-alignment projects are unnecessary attempts by administrators to control teachers and damage the climate of trust essential in effective schools.

2. Using the form shown in Exhibit 11.1 (or your own modification of it), develop an alignment-project planning guide that could be used in a school district with which you are acquainted.

3. One of the issues raised in this chapter is the need for pacing charts. Based upon your knowledge of classroom teachers, would you consider such charts helpful or intrusive?

4. What advice would you give this teacher: "Since our competency is being judged by students' test scores, due to No Child Left Behind, do you feel teaching to the test is necessary?"

CASE STUDY

A group of third-grade teachers in Portland, Oregon, meet after school to review student achievement test data. The principal happens to arrive at the door of the classroom as the teachers are reviewing the results.

"I think this whole standards movement and emphasis on tests is a way for administrators to control the faculty," says teacher Melody Taylor, revealing anger in her voice.

Principal Barbara Bevington enters the room. "I understand your frustration, Melody," she says calmly. "Nonetheless, I can assure you that I'm not interested in controlling anyone. I'm interested in our school doing the best it can for our students."

Melody Taylor looks on disapprovingly, as if she is not buying the principal's sincerity.

The principal decides to address the group. "What I don't understand is why our students are falling behind in the area of measurement in mathematics. It can't be because of our teachers—we have some of the best teachers in the state," says Bevington, looking approvingly over at Melody who blushes, embarrassed.

The principal continues, "Math measurement is noted in our district standards as well as being addressed in our textbook, and yet the test data reveal that our students are really struggling in this area." Four of the other teachers are nodding their heads in agreement as they study the data.

Sue Cockrill, another third-grade teacher adds, "I think I know why our students are doing poorly on measurement. The chapter on measurement is one of the last chapters in our math book and we usually never get there."

"You're right!" says Melody Taylor. "Why don't we move the chapter on measurement up on our schedule? That will ensure that we will cover it."

"Great idea!" says another third-grade teacher penciling in the change. Melody Taylor is now smiling.

The principal is beaming. "I am really proud of all of you as a third-grade team. You are really doing some great work in analyzing the test results and adjusting the curriculum accordingly." She then turns and walks back down the hall to her office. Principal Bevington is very impressed that through data analysis, her teachers are able to identify an area in the standards that is not being met by the local curriculum. She is also very proud that Melody Taylor is part of that important team.

THE CHALLENGE

Getting teachers to align curriculum to state and federal standards and regulations is a major challenge for school administrators. Analyze the problems and hurdles that Principal Bevington had to overcome. What other strategies can she use to get her teachers to accept mandated changes and to align her school's curriculum?

Key Issues/Questions

1. What are your impressions of Principal Bevington? Did she adequately handle the issue of data analysis and aligning curriculum? Why or why not?

2. What are your impressions of the third-grade teachers in this elementary school?

3. If the principal has another meeting with the third-grade teachers, what should be discussed?

4. What are some possible reasons that Principal Bevington's third-grade curriculum is out of alignment with state and national standards?

5. What are some other innovative approaches that Principal Bevington might use to increase student achievement scores? Identify the strategies and explain why you think they might be effective.

REFERENCES

Arhar, J. M., (1997). The effects of interdisciplinary teaming on students and teachers. In J. L. Irvin (Ed.), *What current research says to the middle level practitioner* (pp. 49–56). Columbus, OH: National Middle School Association. ED 427 847.

Baron, M. A., & Boschee, F. (1995). *Authentic assessment: The key to unlocking student success.* Lanham, MD: Scarecrow Press, Technomic Books.

Beane, J. A. (1997). *Curriculum integration: Designing the core of democratic education.* New York: Teachers College Press.

Berliner, D. C. (1984). The half-full glass: A review of research on teaching. In P. Hosford (Ed.), *Using what we know about teaching.* Alexandria, VA: Association for Supervision and Curriculum Development.

Bernhardt, V. L. (1998). *Data analysis for comprehensive schoolwide improvement.* New York: Eye on Education.

Bloom, B. S., Hastings, J. T., & Madaus, G. F. (1971). *Handbook on formative and summative evaluation of student learning.* New York: McGraw-Hill.

Boschee, F., & Baron, M. A. (1993). *Outcome-based education: Developing programs through strategic planning.* Lanham, MD: Scarecrow Press, Technomic Books.

Danielson, C. (2002). *Enhancing student achievement: A framework for school improvement.* Alexandria, VA: Association for Supervision and Curriculum Development.

Fisher, C. W., Berliner, D. C., Filby, N. N., Marliave, R. S., Cahen, L. S., & Dishaw, M. M. (1978). *Teaching behaviors, academic learning time, and student achievement.* San Francisco: Far West Laboratory for Educational Research and Development.

Freeman, D., Kuhs, T., Porter, A., Knappen, L., Floden, R., Schmidt, W., & Schwille, J. (1980). *The fourth-grade mathematics curriculum as inferred from textbooks and tests.* East Lansing: Michigan State University, Institute for Research on Teaching.

Glatthorn, A. A. (1987). *Curriculum leadership.* New York: HarperCollins.

Lyon, G. R., & Chhabra, V. (2004). The science of reading research. *Educational Leadership, 61*(6), 12–17.

Morris, L. L., Fitzgibbons, C. T., & Henderson, M. E. (1978). *Program evaluation kit.* Beverly Hills, CA: Sage.

National Association for Core Curriculum. (2000). *A bibliography of research on the effectiveness of block-time, core, and interdisciplinary team teaching programs.* Kent, OH: National Association for Core Curriculum.

Natriello, G., & Dornbusch, S. M. (1984). *Teacher evaluation standards and student effort.* New York: Longman.

Niedermeyer, F. C. (1976). *A basis for improved instructional leadership by school administrators.* Los Alamitos, CA: Southwest Regional Laboratory for Educational Research and Development.

Niedermeyer, F. C., & Yelon, S. (1981). Los Angeles aligns instruction with essential skills. *Educational Leadership, 38,* 618–620.

Peterson, P. L., Marx, R. W., & Clark, C. M. (1978). Teacher planning, teacher behavior, and student achievement. *American Education Research Journal, 15,* 417–432.

Rifugiato, F. J., & Wilson, H. A. (1983). *A guide to the MAP project.* Pittsburgh, PA: School District of Pittsburgh.

Schmoker, M., & Marzano, R. J. (1999). Realizing the promise of standards-based education. *Educational Leadership, 56*(6), 17–21.

Schwille, J., Porter, A., Belli, A., Floden, R., Freeman, D., Knappen, L., Kuhs, T., & Schmidt, W. J. (1981). *Teachers as policy brokers in the content of elementary school mathematics.* East Lansing: Michigan State University, Institute for Research on Teaching.

Tomlinson, C. A., Kaplan, S. N., Renzulli, J., Purcell, J., Leppien, J., & Burns, D. (2002). *The parallel curriculum: A design to develop high potential and challenge high-ability learners.* Thousand Oaks, CA: Corwin.

Vars, G. F. (1996). Effects of interdisciplinary curriculum and instruction. In Peter S. Hlebowitsh & William G. Wraga (Eds.), *Annual review of research for school leaders* (pp. 147–164). Reston, VA: National Association of Secondary School Principals and Scholastic Publishing.

Vars, G. F. (1997). Effects of integrative curriculum and instruction. In Judith L. Irvin (Ed.), *What current research says to the middle level practitioner* (pp. 179–186). Columbus, OH: National Middle School Association. ED 427 847.

Vars, G., & Beane, J. A. (n.d.). Integrative curriculum in a standards-based world. *ERIC Digests.* Retrieved March 27, 2005, from http://www.nmsa.org/research/res_articles_integrated.htm

Weiss, I. R., & Pasley, J. D. (2004). What is high-quality instruction? *Educational Leadership, 61*(5), 24–28.

Whitehead, B. M., Jensen, D. F. N., & Boschee, F. (2003). *Planning for technology: A guide for school administrators, technology coordinators, and curriculum leaders.* Thousand Oaks, CA: Corwin.

Chapter 12

CURRICULUM EVALUATION

Evaluation has a long history. As Guba and Lincoln (1981) point out, a Chinese emperor in 2200 B.C. required that his public officials demonstrate their proficiency in formal competency tests. In the United States, the concern for evaluating schools can be traced at least as far back as the recommendations of the Committee of Ten, which at the end of the 19th century set perhaps the first example of "evaluative standards" for the nation's secondary schools (National Education Association, 1969). In recent years, however, the interest in curriculum evaluation in particular has seemed to increase markedly. The public's insistence on educational accountability, the experts' demands for educational reform, and the educators' concomitant need for evidence of results have all contributed to this current interest in theories and methods of curriculum evaluation. Unfortunately, much of this interest seems to have resulted in an ill-conceived obsession with test results. A broader perspective and more diversified approaches seem necessary.

This desired breadth and diversification have been reflected throughout this work. Chapter 6 described a comprehensive assessment model that can be used in improving a program of studies. Chapter 8 emphasized the importance of evaluating new courses of study. Chapter 10 explicated an approach especially useful during the implementation stage, and Chapter 11 described how evaluation can be used to effect improved alignment. The intent of this chapter is to bring all these approaches into focus and to provide for greater understanding of the evaluation process. To that end, it begins by proposing a broad definition of the term *curriculum evaluation*. It then describes several current evaluation models. It concludes by proposing a comprehensive and eclectic process that can be used to evaluate a field of study, which is perhaps the most difficult curricular element that evaluators face.

Key to Leadership

Successful curriculum leaders realize that evaluation in education is to help the educational process better relate to individual learners.

CURRICULUM EVALUATION DEFINED

That broader perspective mentioned above requires a less constricting view of both the purposes and foci of curriculum evaluation. In acquiring a broader understanding of purpose, two concepts delineated by Guba and Lincoln (1981) seem especially useful: *merit* and *worth.* *Merit,* as they use the term, refers to the intrinsic value of an entity—value that is implicit, inherent, and independent of any applications. Merit is established without reference to a context. *Worth,* on the other hand, is the value of an entity in reference to a particular context or a specific application. It is the "payoff" value for a given institution or group of people. Thus, a given English course may seem to have a great deal of merit in the eyes of experts: It may reflect sound theory, be built upon current research, and embody content that experts deem desirable. The same course, however, may have relatively little worth for a teacher instructing unmotivated working-class youth in an urban school: It may require teaching skills that the teacher has not mastered and learning materials that the students cannot read. In this sense, then, curriculum evaluation should be concerned with assessing both merit and worth.

The foci of curriculum evaluation also need to be expanded. To use the concepts of this present work, curriculum evaluation should be concerned with assessing the value of a *program of studies* (all the planned learning experiences over a multiyear period for a given group of learners), a *field of study* (all the planned learning experiences over a multiyear period in a given discipline or area of study), and a *course of study* (all the planned learning experiences for a period of one year or less in a given field of study). All three levels of curriculum work are important. Substantive differences exist between evaluating a program of studies and a field of study and differences of scope between evaluating a field of study and a course of study.

The foregoing analysis yields this stipulative definition of *curriculum evaluation: The assessment of the merit and worth of a program of studies, a field of study, or a course of study.*

CURRENT EVALUATION MODELS

How can the merit and worth of such aspects of curriculum be determined? Evaluation specialists have proposed an array of models, an examination of which can provide useful background for the process presented in this work.

Tyler's Objectives-Centered Model

One of the earliest evaluation models, which continues to influence many assessment projects, was that proposed by Ralph Tyler (1950) in his monograph, *Basic Principles of Curriculum and Instruction.* As explained in this work and used in numerous large-scale assessment efforts, the Tyler (as cited by Glatthorn, 1987, p. 273) approach moved rationally and systematically through several related steps:

1. Begin with the behavioral objectives that have been previously determined. Those objectives should specify both the content of learning and the student behavior expected: "Demonstrate familiarity with dependable sources of information on questions relating to nutrition."

2. Identify the situations that will give the student the opportunity to express the behavior embodied in the objective and that evoke or encourage this behavior. Thus, if you wish to assess oral language use, identify situations that evoke oral language.

3. Select, modify, or construct suitable evaluation instruments, and check the instruments for objectivity, reliability, and validity.

4. Use the instruments to obtain summarized or appraised results.

5. Compare the results obtained from several instruments before and after given periods in order to estimate the amount of change taking place.

6. Analyze the results in order to determine strengths and weaknesses of the curriculum and to identify possible explanations about the reason for this particular pattern of strengths and weaknesses.

7. Use the results to make the necessary modifications in the curriculum.

(as cited in Glatthorn, 1987, p. 273)

The Tyler model has several advantages. It is relatively easy to understand and apply. It is rational and systematic. It focuses attention on curricular strengths and weaknesses, rather than being concerned solely with the performance of individual students. It also emphasizes the importance of a continuing cycle of assessment, analysis, and improvement. As Guba and Lincoln (1981) point out, however, it suffers from several deficiencies. It does not suggest how the objectives themselves should be evaluated. It does not provide standards or suggest how standards should be developed. Its emphasis on the prior statement of objectives may restrict creativity in curriculum development, and it seems to place undue emphasis on the preassessment and postassessment, ignoring completely the need for formative assessment.

Stufflebeam's Context-Input-Process-Product Model

These obvious weaknesses in the Tyler model led several evaluation experts in the late 1960s and early 1970s to attack the Tyler model and to offer their own alternatives. The alternative that had the greatest impact was that developed by a Phi Delta Kappa committee chaired by Daniel Stufflebeam (1971). This model seemed to appeal to educational leaders because it emphasized the importance of producing evaluative data for decision making; in fact, decision making was the sole justification for evaluation, in the view of the Phi Delta Kappa committee.

To service the needs of decision makers, the Stufflebeam (as cited by Glatthorn, 1987, pp. 273–274) model provides a means for generating data relating to four stages of program operation: context evaluation, which continuously assesses needs and problems in the context in order to help decision makers determine goals and objectives; input evaluation, which assesses alternative means for achieving those goals to help decision makers choose optimal means; process evaluation, which monitors the processes both to ensure that the means are actually being implemented and to make the necessary modifications; and product evaluation, which compares actual ends with intended ends and leads to a series of recycling decisions.

During each of these four stages, specific steps are taken:

1. The kinds of decisions are identified.

2. The kinds of data needed to make those decisions are identified.

3. Those data are collected.

4. The criteria for determining quality are established.

5. The data are analyzed on the basis of those criteria.

6. The needed information is provided to decision makers.

(as cited in Glatthorn, 1987, pp. 273–274)

The context-input-process-product (CIPP) model, as it has come to be called, has several attractive features for those interested in curriculum evaluation. Its emphasis on decision making seems appropriate for administrators concerned with improving curricula. Its concern for the formative aspects of evaluation remedies a serious deficiency in the Tyler model. Finally, the very detailed guidelines and forms provided by the committee provide step-by-step guidance for users.

The CIPP model, however, has some serious drawbacks associated with it. Its main weakness seems to be its failure to recognize the complexity of the decision-making process in organizations. It assumes more rationality than exists in such situations and ignores the political factors that play a large part in these decisions. Also, as Guba and Lincoln (1981) note, it seems very difficult to implement and expensive to maintain.

Scriven's Goal-Free Model

Michael Scriven (1972) was the first to question the assumption that goals or objectives are crucial in the evaluation process. After his involvement in several evaluation projects where so-called side effects seemed more significant than the original objectives, he began to question the seemingly arbitrary distinction between intended and unintended effects. His goal-free model was the outcome of his dissatisfaction.

In conducting a goal-free evaluation, the evaluator functions as an unbiased observer who begins by generating a profile of needs for the group served by a given program (Scriven is somewhat vague as to how this needs profile is to be derived). Then, by using methods that are primarily qualitative in nature, the evaluator assesses the actual effects of the program. If a program has an effect that is responsive to one of the identified needs, then the program is perceived as useful.

Scriven's main contribution, obviously, was to redirect the attention of evaluators and administrators to the importance of unintended effects—a redirection that seems especially useful in education. If a mathematics program achieves its objectives of improving computational skills but has the unintended effect of diminishing interest in mathematics, then it cannot be judged completely successful. Scriven's emphasis on qualitative methods also seemed to come at an opportune moment, when there was increasing dissatisfaction among the research community with the dominance of quantitative methodologies.

As Scriven himself notes, however, goal-free evaluation should be used to complement, not supplant, goal-based assessments. Used alone, it cannot provide sufficient information for the decision maker. Some critics have faulted Scriven for not providing more explicit directions for developing and implementing the goal-free model; as a consequence, it probably can be used only by experts who do not require explicit guidance in assessing needs and detecting effects.

Stake's Responsive Model

Robert Stake (1975) made a major contribution to curriculum evaluation in his development of the responsive model, because the responsive model is based explicitly upon the assumption that the concerns of the stakeholders—those for whom the evaluation is done—should be paramount in determining the evaluation issues. He makes the point this way:

> To emphasize evaluation issues that are important for each particular program, I recommend the responsive evaluation approach. It is an approach that trades off some measurement precision in order to increase the usefulness of the findings to persons in and around the program. . . . An educational evaluation is a responsive evaluation if it orients more directly to program activities than to program intents; responds to audience requirements for information; and if the different value perspectives present are referred to in reporting the success and failure of the program. (p. 14)

Stake (as cited by Glatthorn, 1987, pp. 275–276) recommends an interactive and recursive evaluation process that embodies these steps:

1. The evaluator meets with clients, staff, and audiences, to gain a sense of their perspectives on and intentions regarding the evaluation.

2. The evaluator draws upon such discussions and the analysis of any documents to determine the scope of the evaluation project.

3. The evaluator observes the program closely to get a sense of its operation and to note any unintended deviations from announced intents.

4. The evaluator discovers the stated and real purposes of the project and the concerns that various audiences have about it and the evaluation.

5. The evaluator identifies the issues and problems with which the evaluation should be concerned. For each issue and problem, the evaluator develops an evaluation design, specifying the kinds of data needed.

6. The evaluator selects the means needed to acquire the data desired. Most often the means will be human observers or judges.

7. The evaluator implements the data-collection procedures.

8. The evaluator organizes the information into themes and prepares "portrayals" that communicate in natural ways the thematic reports. The portrayals may involve videotapes, artifacts, case studies, or other "faithful representations."

9. By again being sensitive to the concerns of the stakeholders, the evaluator decides which audiences require which reports and chooses formats most appropriate for given audiences.

Clearly, the chief advantage of the responsive model is its sensitivity to clients. By identifying their concerns and being sensitive to their values, by involving them closely throughout the evaluation, and by adapting the form of reports to meet their needs, the model, if effectively used, should result in evaluations of high utility to clients. The responsive model also has the virtue of flexibility: The evaluator is able to choose from a variety of methodologies once client concerns have been identified. Its chief weakness would seem to be its susceptibility to manipulation by clients, who in expressing their concerns might attempt to draw attention away from weaknesses they did not want exposed.

Eisner's Connoisseurship Model

Elliot Eisner (1979) has drawn from his background in aesthetics and art education in developing his "connoisseurship" model, an approach to evaluation that emphasizes qualitative appreciation. The Eisner model is built upon two closely related constructs: connoisseurship and criticism. Connoisseurship, in Eisner's terms, is the art of appreciation—recognizing and appreciating through perceptual memory, drawing from experience to appreciate what is significant. It is the ability both to perceive the particulars of educational life and to understand how those particulars form part of a classroom structure. Criticism, to Eisner, is the art of disclosing qualities of an entity that connoisseurship perceives. In such a disclosure, the educational critic is more likely to use what Eisner calls "nondiscursive"—a language that is metaphorical, connotative, and symbolic. It uses linguistic forms to present, rather than represent, conception or feeling.

Educational criticism, in Eisner's formulation, has three aspects. The descriptive aspect is an attempt to characterize and portray the relevant qualities of educational life—the rules, the regularities, the underlying architecture. The interpretive aspect uses ideas from the social sciences to explore meanings and to develop alternative explanations—to explicate social phenomena. The evaluative aspect makes judgments in order to improve the educational processes and provides grounds for the value choices made, so that others might better disagree.

The chief contribution of the Eisner model is that it breaks sharply with the traditional scientific models and offers a radically different view of what evaluation might be. In doing so, it broadens the evaluator's perspective and enriches his or her repertoire by drawing from a rich tradition of artistic criticism. Its critics have faulted it for its lack of methodological rigor, although Eisner has attempted to refute such charges. Critics have also argued that use of the model requires a great deal of expertise, noting the seeming elitism implied in the term *connoisseurship*.

DEVELOPING AN ECLECTIC APPROACH

Although the models above seem sharply distinct from each other, some evidence of congruence exists in current theories of evaluation. This congruence is quite evident in the ASCD (Association for Supervision and Curriculum Development) monograph, *Applied Strategies for Curriculum Evaluation* (Brandt, 1981), in which seven experts in evaluation were asked to explain how their "evaluation model" would be used in evaluating a secondary humanities course. While the models proposed by the experts (Stake, Scriven, Eisner, and Worthen) differed in many of their details, several common emphases emerged in the approaches: study

Exhibit 12.1   Criteria for a Curriculum Evaluation Model

An effective curriculum evaluation model . . .

1. Can be implemented without making inordinate demands upon district resources.

2. Can be applied to all levels of curriculum—programs of study, fields of study, courses of study.

3. Makes provisions for assessing all significant aspects of curriculum—the written, the taught, the supported, the tested, and the learned curricula.

4. Makes useful distinctions between merit (intrinsic value) and worth (value for a given context).

5. Is responsive to the special concerns of district stakeholders and is able to provide them with the data they need for decision making.

6. Is goal-oriented, emphasizing objectives and outcomes.

7. Is sensitive to and makes appropriate provisions for assessing unintended effects.

8. Pays due attention to and makes provisions for assessing formative aspects of evaluation.

9. Is sensitive to and makes provisions for assessing the special context for the curriculum.

10. Is sensitive to and makes provisions for assessing the aesthetic or qualitative aspects of the curriculum.

11. Makes provisions for assessing opportunity cost—the opportunities lost by those studying this curriculum.

12. Uses both quantitative and qualitative methods for gathering and analyzing data.

13. Presents findings in reports responsive to the special needs of several audiences.

the context, determine client concerns, use qualitative methods, assess opportunity cost (what other opportunities the student is missing by taking this course), be sensitive to unintended effects, and develop different reports for different audiences.

By using these common emphases along with insights generated from analyzing other models, it is possible to develop a list of criteria that can be used in both assessing and developing evaluation models. Such a list is shown in Exhibit 12.1. Districts with sufficient resources to employ an expert consultant can use the criteria to assess the model proposed by the consultant; districts developing a homegrown process can use the criteria to direct their own work.

The criteria will obviously result in an eclectic approach to evaluation, one that draws from the strengths of several different models. Such an eclectic process has been used successfully in evaluating a field of study; this same process can be used as well to evaluate a course of study with the scope of the evaluation reduced.

Challenges to Program Evaluation

The single largest barrier to effective curriculum implementation continues to be basic awareness of the measurable benefits. Unprecedented assessment of public schools is spurring an investment of billions of dollars, but the lack of research and quality measurement has led to unclear results. The key issues are the establishment of more effective and accurate ways with which we can measure the real benefits of education and measure the true associated costs in money and time spent learning about curriculum and instruction. Sociological acceptance and adoption of new communications technologies continue to represent a challenge as well. Another concern is the lack of leadership in establishing strong evaluation and assessment agendas and programs.

Leadership and Evaluation

Quality leadership is a key component in the success of any evaluation process. One of the most important aspects of that leadership role is for educational planners to understand the process of evaluation and how it should be administered. Understanding the evaluation process means leaders will have to convey knowledge of curriculum as well as instructional strategies. They will also have to convey their expectations of how teaching and learning can be enhanced via the curriculum. There is a special need for leadership and more understanding as to the process of evaluation and how it relates to the development of effective curriculum.

Technology and Evaluation

The rapid changes occurring in computer technology also pose a challenge to establishing effective evaluation programs. Technology capabilities have continued to change faster than educational researchers can sustain. For example, initial evidence on the use of computers in the classroom showed that "drill and practice" activities were successful in reinforcing skills. Now, with continued advances in software and technology, teachers are using computers in classrooms in entirely different ways. It has therefore been difficult for researchers to complete large-scale, controlled studies that lead to solid conclusions because by the time their research is published, new technologies are providing new opportunities for teachers and students. The lack of technology standards and guidelines are other barriers to providing quality assessment. Currently, a limited number of districts in the country have established formal guidelines for evaluating the effectiveness of technology in their schools.

Strong evidence of technology's effectiveness will surely further strengthen public and political support. Richard Mayer (Mayer, Schustack, & Blanton, n.d.), Professor of Psychology at the University of California, stated,

> Our research provides encouraging evidence that appropriate experience with educational technology can promote important cognitive changes in children, including improvements in content knowledge about computing, strategies for comprehending written instruction, strategies for devising problem-solving plans and even in basic academic skills. (p. 6)

As the demand for networked computers in the classroom increases, the need for evaluation also increases. Administrators, teachers, and parents want to know and understand the impact that technology has made on district goals relating to student learning, staff development, and program content.

EVALUATING A FIELD OF STUDY

"How good is our K–12 science curriculum?" The answer to this question comes from evaluating a field of study—a multigrade sequence of learning experiences in one discipline, subject area, or field. Such evaluations are almost always made for a single purpose—to identify strengths and weaknesses in order to plan for improvements. The process of evaluating a field of study includes five important phases: preparing for the evaluation, assessing the context, identifying the evaluation issues, developing the evaluation design, and implementing the evaluation design.

Preparing for the Evaluation

Preparations for the evaluation include three major steps: setting the project parameters, selecting the project director and the evaluation task force, and preparing the evaluation documents.

In setting the project parameters, district administrators in consultation with the school board should determine both the purpose and the limits of the project. They should, first of all, be clear about the central purpose of the review, because purpose will affect both issues to be examined and methods to be used. In identifying the limits of the project, they should develop answers to the following questions:

1. How much time will be allocated and by what date should the evaluation be completed?

2. What human, fiscal, and material resources will be provided?

3. Which fields will be evaluated?

4. What constituencies will be asked for input? Specifically, will parents, community representatives, and students be involved?

With those parameters set, the project director and evaluation task force should be selected. The project director should be a consultant or a member of the district staff who has considerable technical expertise in curriculum evaluation. The task force should function as an advisory and planning group, making recommendations to and monitoring the performance of the project director. It should probably include a total of 10 to 20 individuals, depending upon the size of the district, and have adequate representation from these constituencies: school board, school administrators, teachers and other faculty members, and parents and community organizations. If administrators wish, and if it is felt that their input can be useful, secondary students can be included.

The project director and the task force can then begin to assemble the documents necessary for the program review. The following documents would typically be needed:

1. A statement of the curriculum goals for that field

2. A comprehensive description of the community and the student body

3. A list of all required courses in that field, with time allocations and brief descriptions of each course

4. A list of all elective courses in the field, including time allocations, course descriptions, and most recent enrollment figures

5. A random selection of student schedules

6. Syllabi or course guides for all courses offered

7. Faculty schedules, showing class enrollments

Other materials, of course, will be required as the review gets under way; but the above-listed materials are important at the outset.

Assessing the Context

The next stage in a comprehensive evaluation of a field of study is to assess the context. While this stage is obviously of critical importance for an outside evaluator, it is also essential in district-directed projects. The context assessment stage enables the evaluators to identify both the salient aspects of the educational environment that impinge upon the field of studies and the critical needs of the learners. In assessing the context, the evaluators typically should seek answers to the following questions:

1. What are the prevailing attitudes, values, and expectations of the community?

2. What significant aspects of the school district impinge upon the field of study: size, leadership, organizational structure, fiscal resources?

3. What are the special characteristics of school facilities that impinge upon or constrain this field of study?

4. What are the special characteristics of the student body: scholastic aptitude, achievement, home background, ethnic identity, social and physical development?

5. What are the special characteristics of the faculty: experience, educational values, overall competence, educational background?

6. What is special about the school organization: nature of leadership, organizational structure?

The context assessment should result in a report that calls attention to the salient aspects affecting the field of study and identifies the special needs of the learners.

Identifying the Evaluation Issues

The next step in the process is to identify the evaluation issues, to be sure that the evaluation is sensitive to the special concern of the stakeholders and will provide the information needed. Here the distinctions between the several aspects of the curriculum are essential: the written, the supported, the taught, the tested, and the learned curricula all subsume quite different assessment issues.

Also, each of these five must be assessed if the results are to be at all valid. In too many curriculum evaluations, the team evaluates only the written curriculum (the official course guides) and the learned curriculum (the results on achievement tests). No valid inferences can be drawn from such an assessment, because the other three important components have been ignored. Suppose, for example, that the students in a particular district do not perform well on measures of critical thinking in social studies, even though district guides include such units. District administrators cannot be sure about the causes of the problem. It might well be that teachers have chosen not to teach those units because they lack the training and materials necessary. Only a comprehensive assessment can yield the information needed to make improvements.

As shown in Exhibit 12.2, those five components subsume more than 50 different issues. Obviously, not all these issues will be used in every evaluation. Here it is essential for the evaluation team to identify the issues by surveying and interviewing stakeholders. That list of issues can be used to survey such constituencies as board members, school administrators, faculty, and parents, using a form similar to the one shown in Exhibit 12.3. The responses can then be analyzed to determine which issues should be evaluated, given the constraints previously identified. The surveys, of course, should be supplemented with interviews of key individuals to provide supplementary data.

Developing the Evaluation Design

With the evaluation issues identified, the project director and the task force should cooperatively develop the evaluation design. One useful framework for such a design has been proposed by Worthen (1981). For each evaluative question (or evaluation issue, to use the terminology employed here), identify the information required, the sources of information, and the methods for collecting that information. Thus, in an example used by Worthen, if the evaluation proposes to answer the question, "Do student attitudes demonstrate that the curriculum is producing the desired results?" the attitudes of students with regard to the values and concepts taught constitute the information required. Students are the source of information; and the methods employed might include a comparative design using attitude scales and simulated situations requiring an attitudinal response.

In identifying the methods for collecting information, evaluators should be certain to include qualitative approaches. As noted above, current evaluation theory gives strong emphasis to such qualitative methods as interviews and observations in assessing curriculum impact.

Those decisions—about the issues, the information required, the sources of information, and the methods for collecting information—should form the basis of a detailed evaluation plan, which would include as well the specific tasks to be undertaken, the names of those responsible for each task, and the deadline for accomplishing the task.

Focusing on Student Performance

Thomas Guskey (1994) believes that technology and assessment should be important factors of the evaluation process. He states, "If a performance-based assessment program is to evoke more stimulating, intellectually challenging tasks for students, extensive professional development opportunities for teachers will need to accompany the assessment program" (p. 4). It is therefore essential that the direction for the technology initiative remain focused on student

Exhibit 12.2   Evaluation Issues: Field of Study

THE WRITTEN CURRICULUM

Goals

1. Are the goals of this subject clearly and explicitly stated and readily accessible to those who need to refer to them?
2. Are those goals congruent with relevant curricular goals of the school district?
3. Are the goals in accord with the recommendations of experts in the field?
4. Are the goals understood and supported by parents?
5. Are the goals understood and supported by school administrators?
6. Are the goals understood and supported by classroom teachers?
7. Are the goals understood and supported by students?

Scope and Sequence of Level Objectives

1. Have the goals of this field been analyzed into a set of grade-level (or achievement level) objectives that identify the important concepts, skills, and attitudes to be attained?
2. Are those level objectives sufficiently comprehensive so that they adequately reflect the goals of this field?
3. Are those level objectives clearly displayed in some form (such as a scope-and-sequence chart) that facilitates understanding and use?
4. Are the level objectives in accord with and do they reflect the recommendations of experts in the field?
5. Does the grade placement of objectives reflect the best current knowledge of child development?
6. Does the grade placement of objectives provide for sufficient reinforcement without undue repetition?
7. Is the grade placement of objectives appropriate in relation to their difficulty for learners at that level?
8. Are the objectives appropriately distributed over the grades so that there is balance between the grades?

Written Course Guides

1. Are there written course guides for this field covering all grade levels?
2. Are those guides readily available to administrators, teachers, and parents?
3. Does the format of the guides facilitate revision and amplification?
4. Do the guides clearly specify grade-level objectives in a format and manner that facilitate use?
5. Do the guides make appropriate distinctions between mastery, organic, and enrichment outcomes and focus primarily on the mastery outcomes?
6. Do the guides indicate clearly the relative importance of the mastery outcomes and suggest time allocations that reflect their importance?
7. Do the guides suggest ways of organizing the objectives into learning units, without requiring a particular type of unit organization?
8. Do the guides recommend (but not mandate) teaching/learning activities that seem likely to lead to the attainment of the relevant objectives?
9. Do the teaching and learning activities recommended reflect the best current knowledge about teaching and learning and are they qualitatively excellent?
10. Do the guides suggest appropriate evaluation processes and instruments?
11. Do the guides recommend appropriate instructional materials and other resources?

THE SUPPORTED CURRICULUM

Time

1. Has the school district clearly specified time to be allocated to this field of study at each level of schooling?
2. Does the time allocated to this field seem appropriate in relation to the district's goals, the goals of the field of study, and the recommendations of experts?
3. Do school master schedules and administrative guidelines on time allocation appropriately reflect district allocations?

Materials

1. Is the quantity of instructional materials adequate in relation to student enrollments?
2. Are the learning objectives of the instructional materials consonant with the objectives of the written course guides?
3. Do the instructional materials reflect the best current knowledge in this field of study?
4. Are the instructional materials free of gender bias and ethnic stereotyping?
5. Are the instructional materials written at an appropriate level of difficulty?
6. Are the instructional materials designed and organized in a manner that facilitates teacher use?
7. Do the instructional materials reflect sound learning principles, providing adequately for motivation, explanation, application, reinforcement, and enrichment?

Staff Development

1. Does the district provide on-going staff-development programs that help the teachers use the curriculum guides effectively and involve teachers in improving the guides?

THE TAUGHT CURRICULUM

1. Do the teachers allocate time to this field of study in accordance with district and school guidelines?
2. Do the teachers allocate time to the several components of this field of study in a way that reflects curricular priorities?
3. Do the teachers teach for the objectives specified for that grade?
4. Do the instructional methods used by the teachers reflect the best current knowledge about teaching that field of study and are they qualitatively excellent?
5. What unintended effects does this curriculum have on teaching?

THE TESTED CURRICULUM

1. Does the district provide curriculum-based tests that adequately reflect and correspond with the objectives stated in the course guides?
2. Are such tests valid and reliable measures of performance?
3. Does the district make use of standardized tests that provide norm-referenced data on achievement in this field of study?
4. Do any standardized tests used by the district adequately reflect and correspond with the objectives stated in the course guides

THE LEARNED CURRICULUM

1. Do pupils believe that what they are learning is useful and meaningful?
2. Do pupils achieve the specified objectives at a satisfactory level?
3. What unintended learning outcomes are evidenced?
4. What are the opportunity costs for pupils involved in this field of study?

FORMATIVE ASPECTS

1. By what processes was this field of study developed, and did those processes provide for appropriate input from all constituencies?
2. What specific provisions are there for continuing input from those constituencies?
3. What specific provisions are there for revising and modifying the program of studies?

Exhibit 12.3   Survey Form—Evaluation Issues: Mathematics

Directions: As you probably are aware, our school district will soon begin to evaluate the mathematics curriculum in our district. Listed below are the questions we might ask in such an evaluation. Tell us how important you think each question is. Read each question and then circle one of the following symbols:

VI: I think this question is *very important.*

 I: I think this question is *important.*

LI: I think this question is *less important.*

Your responses will help us decide which questions to study.

Question   *Your Response*

1. Are the goals of this subject clearly and explicitly   VI   I   LI
   stated and readily accessible to those who need to
   refer to them?

---

performance. The key behind computer assessment is to create a more symbiotic relationship between technology and the curriculum. In doing so, correlations between student performance and the use of technology in the classrooms will become more evident. Thus, appropriate mechanisms and administrative structures will need to be made so that student performance can be measured and assessed in relevant ways. The key here is that teachers, students, administrators, and the external community see that technology is having a positive effect on student achievement and that students are performing better because of the technological changes enacted within your school.

Electronic Testing

According to Allan Olson (2004), president and executive director of Northwest Evaluation Association (NWEA), schools in the future will not be grouped by age, but be grouped by instructional needs and it will be done electronically. Students will not be assigned one teacher and will not be in a closed-door classroom, but will have multiple teachers and be in a more open and collaborative environment. Students will be matched with teachers who have the skills and proficiency to best instruct them. To arrive at this future, schools must use cutting-edge evaluation tools such as adaptive electronic testing that provides a comprehensive assessment of a student's needs.

The ultimate indicator of an effective school is the measure of academic growth of its students. Without sufficient data, schools cannot fine-tune programs or respond to students' individual needs quickly enough to meet local, state, or federal guidelines. This is a major problem with the states and the federal government mandating that schools attain a high proficiency rate of student achievement.

New developments in technology are allowing schools to use Internet-enabled assessment tools that adjust in difficulty to the individual students' ability. Because electronic tests are customized on demand, each student is engaged and the results are more accurate. Electronic results are also instantaneous. This allows teachers to see quickly whether students are succeeding or falling behind. Curriculum and instruction can then be modified to address the results. Electronic adaptive tests can be given any time: fall, winter, or spring. Tests can be tailored to meet federal, state, and district mandates.

Unlike conventional evaluative tests, computerized adaptive tests measure achievement status and academic growth for every child. Schools and curriculum leaders can assess a program's effectiveness for children with different instructional needs. Timely, accurate data provide school leaders with information to adjust instruction and/or programs as needed during the school year to ensure individual learning and to improve program effectiveness. Using up-to-date Internet-enabled assessments, curriculum leaders and teachers will have a chance to shape tomorrow's schools, today.

Value-Added Assessment

Value-added assessment is a technique of using test data to determine the value that teachers add to the learning of each student. It focuses on how test data can help each child academically. This type of assessment makes it possible to isolate the impact of the individual teacher and to respond with appropriate rewards or corrective training. Former University of Tennessee statistician William Sanders, who helped pioneer value-added research, notes that this method offers a way to ensure that as few children as possible suffer a disadvantage in learning. Sanders (as cited in Holland, 2001) believed that "under effective teachers, students could make gains no matter what their ability or achievement levels were when they started" (p. 3).

Value-Added Assessment Format

- Each spring, students take a norm-referenced state test in five core subjects (math, science, reading, language, and social studies). Nonredundant test items are added each year in an attempt to discourage blatant "teaching to the test."
- Each fall, districts receive a report card broken down by school and grade showing progress in each subject in the context of 3-year averages. The system records student achievement gains in scale score points and in the form of comparisons to local, state, and national averages. School and district reports are reported to the public.
- Each teacher receives a report card—one that is not released to the general public—showing the year-to-year progress of his or her students. Supervisors also receive these reports. It is this application of these data that holds the greatest promise for building a better teacher.

Evaluation of the Curriculum Using Student Achievement and Effective Instruction

The increased involvement of the state and federal government in education and curriculum has had a definite impact on the development of curriculum. With the implementation of the No Child Left Behind Act, states have increasingly become involved in setting standards for course curricula. These standards are the basis for state testing and for meeting the regulations set forth by the NCLB Act. Therefore, the written curriculum of schools very much follows the state standards. With this in mind, the evaluation of the written curriculum and its effectiveness is ever more dependent on the taught curriculum. To be effective, the written curriculum needs to be the "taught curriculum."

In a recent study by Pam Homan (2003), in the Sioux Falls, South Dakota, school district, the importance of teaching and testing the "written curriculum" was reinforced. Dr. Homan looked at all fifth-grade teachers in the district. By studying three consecutive years of test results and by using a multiple regression analysis, Dr. Homan was able to identify the fifth-grade teachers whose children always scored higher on the standardized tests administered by the school district. She also identified the teachers whose students performed below expectations on the same tests. Through a process of observations, Dr. Homan and other district administrators were able to identify effective instruction as the major contributing factor in student achievement.

Results

The observational analysis found a difference in the presence of 12 of the 14 categories of effective teaching between teachers with high student achievement and teachers with low student achievement. No difference existed in the presence of Re-teaches and Positive Self-Concept. The greatest differences between the two groups were in Instructional Planning, Instructional Techniques, Provides Feedback, Communicates Expectations, Manages Behavior, and Maximizes Instructional Time. Table A shows the difference in percentages of the indicator traits demonstrated between the two groups. Table B lists the specific indicators within each category of effective teaching.

Summary

The results indicate that specific indicators of effective teaching do exist to a greater degree in classrooms with high overall student achievement versus classrooms with low overall student achievement. Given the implications of the No Child Left Behind Act and the expectation that all students be proficient by the year 2013–2014, it is very important that effective teaching be maximized for each student. The findings of this study confirm the need for both identification and follow-up of targeted interventions to help classroom teachers maximize effective teaching.

The district will develop a training model to assist building principals in observing and providing specific feedback to teachers regarding the presence or lack of indicators of effective teaching in their classrooms. In addition, this model will provide principals a vehicle for training teachers within their building to self-assess the presence or lack of indicators of effective teaching in relationship to student achievement.

Evaluation Checklist

Evaluation checklists are helpful to educational planners trying to gauge the success of their classroom curricular program. The checklist below is easy to administer and provides a quick assessment of program components.

- Does the curriculum provide evidence of administrative and school board support?
- Does the curriculum plan incorporate a mission statement?
- Does the curriculum plan establish a task force or advisory committee?
- Does the curriculum plan facilitate the involvement of parents and the community?

Table A contains the categories for effective teaching and the percent of indicator traits demonstrated by teachers:

Categories of Effective Teaching	Teachers With Low Student Achievement	Teachers With High Student Achievement
	Percentage of Indicator Traits Demonstrated	
Instructional Planning	46	100
District Curriculum	93	100
Effective Lesson	83	100
Instructional Techniques	68	97
Enhances Self-Concept	92	96
Assesses Students	80	100
Provides Feedback	77	100
Communicates Expectations	60	100
Re-Teaches	100	100
Checks Understanding	80	100
Organizes Classroom	92	95
Manages Behavior	75	100
Maximizes Instructional Time	70	100
Positive Self-Concept	100	100

SOURCE: Homan, P. (2003). *Sioux Falls School District 2002–2003 value added analysis of student achievement and effective instruction.* Unpublished manuscript.

- Does the curriculum design allow for research development?
- Does the curriculum plan utilize student learner outcomes as a measure?
- Does the curriculum plan have an evaluation tool that provides for the collection of qualitative data?

Evaluation tools such as the checklist do not have to be complicated. These instruments help determine whether key components are present in the classroom program.

Evaluation Strategies

The following are strategies that successful administrators use in developing assessment and evaluation programs.

Setting Goals and Indicators

The evaluation and assessment process must be linked back to the original mission statement and objectives of the district. Indicators of successful curriculum integration for the purposes of evaluation should be established during the early planning stages of the program.

Table B contains additional observation summaries made by central office administrators as a result of the classroom observations they conducted:

Teachers With High Student Achievement	Teachers With Low Student Achievement
• Strong instructional focus—knew the curriculum and where he/she was headed	• Low expectations not directly related to grade appropriate curriculum • Lacked clear, purposeful instruction
• Smooth and quick transitions	• Spent excessive time telling students what they would be doing • Transitions were chaotic
• Maximized time on purposeful instructional tasks—all aspects of the lesson were clearly connected to a district learning standard	• Lost time on task with noninstructional tasks—parts of the lesson included activities not related to grade-appropriate learning standards
• Naturally and positively redirected students without disrupting instruction for others	• Redirection disrupted learning for others and did not maintain dignity of students
• Naturally and immediately included students returning from pull-outs	• Did not attend to students returning from pull-outs
• Established routines known by all students	• Constant low-key commotion in the room

SOURCE: Homan, P. (2003). *Sioux Falls School District 2002–2003 value added analysis of student achievement and effective instruction.* Unpublished manuscript.

Identifying Target Populations

Successful evaluation and assessment procedures should focus on targeting specific external and internal population groups. Parents and community represent external groups. Trustees, administrators, teachers, and students represent internal target groups. Data collection needs to focus specifically on these target areas and how they relate to school and curriculum.

Evaluation Centers

The National Study for School Evaluation located in Schaumburg, Illinois, provides a wealth of information on technology evaluation and assessment. *Technology: Indicators of Quality Information Technology Systems in K–12 Schools* by Fitzpatrick and Pershing (1996) is considered to be one of the nation's best publications on assessment and evaluation.

Regional Technology Training Centers

The Northwest Regional Educational Laboratory and other regional technology centers across the United States provide a plethora of information on best practices involving assessment and evaluation. They also provide conferences and workshops on evaluation strategies. Regardless of the process used to evaluate a program, planners need to be willing to utilize data and to make changes and adjustments where necessary. They must understand that curriculum improvement and instructional improvement are interconnected and that a change in one area will probably elicit a change in another area. Problems and concerns can cloud issues at hand, making evaluation an important tool. With higher quality and more detailed information at our disposal, curriculum leaders will be able to focus more on how technology can help teachers with student achievement in the future.

Implementing the Evaluation Design

With the design developed, the evaluation team can move expeditiously to implement the design and report the results. Two matters should be stressed here. First, the implementation process should be flexible: If new issues develop or if additional data sources become apparent, they should be built into a revised design and incorporated into the implementation process. Second, the results should be reported in ways that will accommodate the special needs of the several audiences. Thus, several reports might be envisioned: a summary written in plain language for the public, an action plan presented to the board and school administrators, a detailed technical report for the broader educational community.

Once people know, firsthand, and are able to measure the benefits of effective curriculum planning and evaluation, the public support for funding will become viable. Indicators of success used to measure the impact of student achievement in schools will be a determining factor. It is hoped that future research will be based on these indicators to give educational planners a more complete picture as to the impact of technology on teaching and learning in our nation's classrooms. A key to the success of any curricular program in the future is the ability of school leaders to develop awareness and understanding through the implementation of an effective evaluation program. Throughout the entire evaluation process, the focus for administrators should be on combining appropriate strategies with measurable results indicating positive correlations on teaching and learning.

CHAPTER OVERVIEW

This chapter brings approaches of curriculum leadership into a global focus and provides for greater understanding of the evaluation process. To that end, it proposes a broad definition of the term *curriculum evaluation*. It also describes several current evaluation models. The chapter proposes a comprehensive and eclectic process that can be used to evaluate a field of study as well as technological applications. In addition, challenges to curriculum leadership are addressed.

CHAPTER TERMS

Curriculum Evaluation	Course of Study
Merit	Context Evaluation
Worth	Input Evaluation
Program of Studies	Process Evaluation
Field of Study	Product Evaluation

APPLICATIONS

1. Choose one of the issues identified for the field of study evaluation. Use the Worthen framework in developing a design for that issue.

2. Select one of the models described and write a detailed explication and critique of that model.

3. Suppose a classroom teacher posed this question to you: "I want to evaluate my own course. I don't know much about statistics. Can you tell me how to evaluate it in a way that won't take too much time?" Write the answer you would give that teacher.

4. Examine Dr. Homan's study on effective teaching and its importance in relationship to student success. Develop an in-service presentation for teachers in your school district in which you could effectively use this study to enhance teaching and improve student performance.

5. Given the implications of NCLB and the expectation that all students are proficient by the year 2013–2014, how can teachers maximize their effectiveness to make sure students meet these requirements?

CASE STUDY

A school trustee shares with Kathy Peterson, District Superintendent, that one of the school district teachers is teaching to the test.

"I understand that one of our sixth-grade teachers is teaching to the test in Principal Ron Harris's building," says Board Trustee Ron Dawson.

Superintendent Peterson smiles, "It would be a problem if we are talking about a norm-referenced standardized test as the evaluative tool. Fortunately, it is my understanding that the sixth-grade teacher is referring to our criterion-referenced test that is currently based on state standards. In this case, we want the teachers to analyze the items and adjust their curriculum to benchmarks on the test—so in effect, she is teaching to the test."

Trustee Dawson looks as if he is slightly confused.

Peterson continues, "Not only is she teaching to the test, but she has also developed a computerized grading system that has the capability of providing e-mail reports to parents. This way, the parents can also help address the acquisition of certain basic skills. The result is that we have basically hard-wired the testing process into our curriculum evaluation process."

"And how is that?" Trustee Dawson asks.

"Well, at a push of a button, your sixth-grade teacher can average and total any student's grade at any time. If parents walk through the door, she can tell them exactly how their child is doing. She also has an electronic portfolio of every student as part of the evaluative process."

Trustee Dawson likes the idea of having the district's teachers addressing basic skills that are on the state test. "This concept of teaching to the test—a criterion-referenced test—is what we should have been doing all along," he says enthusiastically.

THE CHALLENGE

Using electronic testing and setting benchmarks is proving to be a very successful evaluation strategy for Principal Ron Harris. What are some other novel or innovative ways that Principal Harris can use to evaluate and assess student achievement as well as his overall school curricula?

Key Issues/Questions

1. What are some major differences between electronic testing and regular testing? Do you feel that electronic online testing is worth the cost? Why or why not?

2. How might Principal Harris deal with resistance from teachers who oppose the use of electronic testing and data analysis?

3. If the principal meets with other teachers about using a data analysis approach, what should be discussed?

4. What future role will online electronic testing have in evaluating a field of study?

5. What are some other technological approaches that Principal Harris might use to assess student achievement? Identify the strategies and explain why you think they might be effective.

REFERENCES

Brandt, R. S. (Ed.). (1981). *Applied strategies for curriculum evaluation.* Alexandria, VA: Association for Supervision and Curriculum Development.

Eisner, E. W. (1979). *The educational imagination: On the design and evaluation of school programs.* New York: Macmillan.

Fitzpatrick, K., & Pershing, J. A. (1996). *Indicators of quality information technology systems in K–12 schools.* Schaumburg, IL: National Study of School Evaluation.

Glatthorn, A. A. (1987). *Curriculum leadership.* New York: HarperCollins.

Guba, E., & Lincoln, Y. (1981). *Effective evaluation.* San Francisco: Jossey-Bass.

Guskey, T. (1994). *What you assess may not be what you get.* North Central Association: Commission on Accreditation and School Improvement. Retrieved March 28, 2005, from the North Central Association Web site: http://www.ncacasi.org/documents/other/what_you_assess (Originally published in the March 1994 issue of *Educational Leadership*)

Holland, R. (2001, December). *Indispensable tests: How a value-added approach to school testing could identify and bolster exceptional teaching.* Retrieved March 17, 2004, from the Lexington Institute Web site: http://www.lexingtoninstitute.org/education/schooltesting.htm

Homan, P. (2003). *Sioux Falls School District 2002–2003 value added analysis of student achievement and effective instruction.* Unpublished manuscript. Available from Sioux Falls School District, South Dakota.

Mayer, R., Schustack, M. W., & Blanton, W. E. (n.d.). *What do children learn from using computers in an informal collaborative setting?* Retrieved March 28, 2005, from http://129.171.53.1/blantonw/5dClhse/publications/tech/mayer_schustak_blanton.html

National Educational Association. (1969). *Report of the Committee of Ten on secondary school studies.* New York: Arno Press and the *New York Times.* (Originally published in 1893 by the Government Printing Office)

Olson, A. (2004, March). Tailor tests for every student. *Scholastic Administrator.* Retrieved March 28, 2005, from http://www.scholastic.com/administrator/march04/articles.asp?article=opinion

Scriven, M. (1972). Prose and cons about goal-free evaluation. *Evaluation Comment, 3*(4), 1–4.

Stake, R. E. (Ed.). (1975). *Evaluating the arts in education: A responsive approach.* Columbus, OH: Bobbs Merrill.

Stufflebeam, D. L. (1971). *Educational evaluation and decision-making.* Itasca, IL: Peacock.

Tyler, R. W. (1950). *Basic principles of curriculum and instruction: Syllabus for Education 305.* Chicago: University of Chicago Press.

Worthen, B. R. (1981). Journal entries of an eclectic evaluator. In R. S. Brandt (Ed.), *Applied strategies for curriculum evaluation* (pp. 58–90). Alexandria, VA: Association for Supervision and Curriculum Development.

Part 4

Current Trends in the Curriculum

Chapter 13

CURRENT DEVELOPMENTS IN THE SUBJECT FIELDS

One of the best ways to understand general developments in the curriculum is to examine trends in the specific subject areas. While certain innovations transcend the discipline, most of the important changes take place and are worked out in the subject areas themselves. Recently, with the passing of the No Child Left Behind legislation, standards (state and national) have driven curriculum to look first at the standards, and then mold curriculum decisions around those standards. Many developments and trends in K–12 education are altering the landscape for curriculum work. Although history shows that it is often hard to predict which changes will have a substantial impact on schools and which will turn out to be nothing more than fads, it is worthwhile to assess current trends as part of curriculum renewal. This chapter will examine those developments in the subject areas that ordinarily constitute the common curriculum: English/language arts/reading; social studies; mathematics; science; foreign language; physical education and health; technology, vocational education, and the arts. In each case, the discussion begins with a review of the recent history of that field, starting with the curricular reform movement of the post-Sputnik era, and concludes with a description of current trends along with standards.

Questions addressed in this chapter include the following:

- What are some of the trends and issues involved in the subject area of English?
- What are some of the trends and issues involved in the subject area of language arts?
- What are some of the trends and issues involved in the subject area of reading?
- What are some of the trends and issues involved in the subject area of mathematics?
- What are some of the trends and issues involved in the subject area of social studies?
- What are some of the trends and issues involved in the subject area of science?
- What are some of the trends and issues involved in the subject area of foreign language?
- What are some of the trends and issues involved in the subject area of arts education?
- What is the current role of brain research in curriculum planning for subject areas?
- How is technology impacting the delivery and implementation of curriculum in subject areas?

Key to Leadership

Successful curriculum leaders are finding that a multitiered approach involving high-quality classroom instruction combined with targeted, small-group interventions enhances learning.

DEVELOPMENTS IN ENGLISH/LANGUAGE ARTS/READING

All across the United States, literacy has become a high priority. With the onset of a new millennium, public attention has been sharply focused on education and particularly on language arts instruction. Policymakers and parents see direct evidence that our country's future depends upon the education of its workforce, and they worry that schools are not as effective as they need to be. With the global economy increasingly demanding high levels of literacy from both workers and managers, a series of questions has become part of a national conversation: How can we break the cycle of failure? What will it take to help all children achieve academically? What kinds of changes in curriculum and instruction will increase student achievement? How can schools ensure that every child learns to read and write well?

As Linda Darling-Hammond explains in *What Matters Most: Teaching for America's Future* (1996),

> In this knowledge-based society, the United States urgently needs to reaffirm a consensus about the role and purposes of public education in a democracy—and the prime importance of learning in meeting those purposes. The challenge extends far beyond preparing students for the world of work. It includes building an American future that is just and humane as well as productive, that is as socially vibrant and civil in its pluralism as it is competitive. (p. 11)

The National Institute of Child Health and Human Development (2000) published the *Report of the National Reading Panel, Teaching Children to Read: An Evidence-Based Assessment of the Scientific Research Literature on Reading and Its Implications for Reading Instruction.* Taking into account the foundational work of the National Research Council Committee, *Preventing Reading Difficulties in Young Children* (Snow, Burns, & Griffin, 1998), the report has identified and summarized research literature relevant to the acquisition of beginning reading skills. The report highlights the importance of teacher preparation and emphasizes both phonics and comprehension as critical skills for young readers. These reports illustrate that consensus is emerging on the components of a successful reading program.

Curriculum Tip

Successful reading programs depend upon knowledgeable teachers.

Excellent Reading Teachers, a position statement issued in 2000 by the International Reading Association (IRA; 2004), urges that "every child deserves excellent reading teachers because teachers make a difference in children's reading achievement and motivation to read" (p. 15). According to the IRA (2000), excellent reading teachers share several critical qualities of knowledge and practice:

- They understand reading and writing development and believe all children can learn to read and write.
- They continually assess children's individual progress and relate reading instruction to children's previous experiences.
- They know a variety of ways to teach reading, when to use each method, and how to combine the methods into an effective instructional program.
- They offer a variety of materials and texts for children to read.
- They use flexible grouping strategies to tailor instruction to individual students.
- They are good *reading* "coaches" (that is, they provide help strategically).

(International Reading Association, 2000, p. 235)

In addition, the IRA statement says, excellent reading teachers share many of the characteristics of good teachers in general. They have strong content and pedagogical knowledge, manage classrooms so that there is a high rate of engagement, use strong motivation strategies that encourage independent learning, have high expectations for children's achievement, and help children who are having difficulty.

Issues Facing K–12 English Language Arts

As we move into the 21st century, many issues confront K–12 English language arts teachers, administrators, and curriculum specialists. Some of the most pressing issues include the following:

- The ongoing debate over best practices in the teaching of reading
- The influence of standards on curriculum and instruction
- The increasing attention being paid to assessment and student results

International comparisons of student achievement have persuaded the public that education in general, and literacy in particular, is the key to personal happiness and financial security. Every politician has a stand on the subject and a plan for "fixing" schools. The American public wants more say in what happens in its schools, as well as clear evidence that schools are producing measurable results.

The standards movement continues to drive curriculum and instruction. Every state but Iowa has established standards in language arts, and most are in the process of developing standards-based assessment instruments, many with high-stakes consequences for students. There is a growing commitment to the idea that clear and shared goals for students are the foundational pieces upon which effective teaching and powerful learning occur. Standards provide direction for curricular improvement. As James W. Stigler and James Hiebert (1999) explain in *The Teaching Gap: Best Ideas From the World's Teachers for Improving Education in the Classroom,* "Standards set the course, and assessments provide the benchmarks, but it is teaching that must be improved to push us along the path to success" (p. 2). The impetus to hold students, teachers, schools, and districts accountable for results gains momentum daily.

Standards for English Language Arts

The vision guiding these standards is that all students must have the opportunities and resources to develop the language skills they need to pursue life's goals and to participate fully as informed, productive members of society. These standards assume that literacy growth begins before children enter school as they experience and experiment with literacy activities—reading and writing, and associating spoken words with their graphic representations. Recognizing this fact, these standards encourage the development of curriculum and instruction that make productive use of the emerging literacy abilities that children bring to school. Furthermore, the standards provide ample room for the innovation and creativity essential to teaching and learning. They are not prescriptions for particular curriculum or instruction. Although we present these standards as a list, we want to emphasize that they are not distinct and separable; they are, in fact, interrelated and should be considered as a whole.

- Students read a wide range of print and nonprint texts to build an understanding of texts, of themselves, and of the cultures of the United States and the world; to acquire new information; to respond to the needs and demands of society and the workplace; and for personal fulfillment. Among these texts are fiction and nonfiction, classic and contemporary works.
- Students read a wide range of literature from many periods in many genres to build an understanding of the many dimensions (e.g., philosophical, ethical, aesthetic) of human experience.
- Students apply a wide range of strategies to comprehend, interpret, evaluate, and appreciate texts. They draw on their prior experience, their interactions with other readers and writers, their knowledge of word meaning and of other texts, their word identification strategies, and their understanding of textual features (e.g., sound-letter correspondence, sentence structure, context, graphics).
- Students adjust their use of spoken, written, and visual language (e.g., conventions, style, vocabulary) to communicate effectively with a variety of audiences and for different purposes.
- Students employ a wide range of strategies as they write and use different writing process elements appropriately to communicate with different audiences for a variety of purposes.
- Students apply knowledge of language structure, language conventions (e.g., spelling and punctuation), media techniques, figurative language, and genre to create, critique, and discuss print and nonprint texts.
- Students conduct research on issues and interests by generating ideas and questions, and by posing problems. They gather, evaluate, and synthesize data from a variety of sources (e.g., print and nonprint texts, artifacts, people) to communicate their discoveries in ways that suit their purpose and audience.
- Students use a variety of technological and information resources (e.g., libraries, databases, computer networks, video) to gather and synthesize information and to create and communicate knowledge.

- Students develop an understanding of and respect for diversity in language use, patterns, and dialects across cultures, ethnic groups, geographic regions, and social roles.
- Students whose first language is not English make use of their first language to develop competency in the English language arts and to develop understanding of content across the curriculum.
- Students participate as knowledgeable, reflective, creative, and critical members of a variety of literacy communities.
- Students use spoken, written, and visual language to accomplish their own purposes (e.g., for learning, enjoyment, persuasion, and the exchange of information).

ENGLISH/LANGUAGE ARTS

The discussion that follows focuses on all the language arts except reading; reading is considered so important that it is given special attention in the subsequent section.

Trends in English and Language Arts

Four developments in English curricula seem to be significant. The first is a widespread interest in the composing process and a concomitant attention to diverse types of writing. Motivated primarily by the widely disseminated National Writing Project, the developers of English curriculum guides are stressing the importance of an inclusive writing process that gives due attention to prewriting and revision, rather than focusing solely on the final product, and are emphasizing varied forms of writing for real audiences and purposes, rather than limiting writing to standard school essays written to satisfy the demands of a teacher.

The second development is a more comprehensive and diversified view of the student's response to literature. While previous curriculum guides stressed the interpretive and evaluative responses, more enlightened approaches encourage students to respond personally and creatively to the work studied. The intent is to help students find personal meaning in literature, not to develop young literary critics.

The third gives specific attention to the teaching of critical thinking in English. As part of a general nationwide interest in teaching thinking (see Chapter 14), curriculum leaders and experts such as Staton (1984) have been urging English teachers to see thinking as central to all classroom uses of language.

Finally, there is renewed interest in integrating the English language arts. While such interest can be traced back at least to *English for Social Living* by Roberts, Kaulfers, and Kefaurer (1943), the present emphasis on *IRA/NCTE Standards for the English Language Arts: The 12 Standards,* by the National Council of Teachers of English (2005), seems to have resulted in the development of measures to "develop the language skills [students] need to pursue life's goals and to participate fully as informed, productive members of society" (n.p.). The "standards assume that literacy growth begins before children enter school as they experience and experiment with literacy activities—reading and writing, and associating spoken words with their graphic representations" (n.p.).

How are these developments to be translated into effective curricula? Three publications seem to offer guidance to curriculum workers. The first, *Three Language-Arts Curriculum Models: Pre-Kindergarten Through College* (Mandel, 1980), is a collection of essays that describe the *competencies,* the *heritage,* and the *process* models of curricula.

The second, *A Guide for Developing an English Curriculum for the Eighties* (Glatthorn, 1980), emphasizes a process for developing an English curriculum, rather than prescribing specific content.

The third publication is the *IRA/NCTE Standards for the English Language Arts: The 12 Standards* referred to above (National Council of Teachers of English, 2005). Exhibit 13.1 summarizes the outcomes recommended by the council. As is apparent, the goals are broad based and comprehensive and would provide a useful beginning point for curriculum leaders.

These volumes together should provide sufficient guidance for local curriculum workers interested in both substantive and process guidelines for the English curriculum.

Differentiating Curriculum

Teachers of English are currently focusing on differentiated instruction to help energize and expand learning. Dialectical journals, expository writing, critical analysis, analytical writing skills, and evaluation are some current topics. Students are writing stories about single authors, about alienation and hardship, and about adulthood.

Curriculum Tip

Students should research and write from a multitude of perspectives and approaches.

Teachers of English are using the Backward Curriculum Design Process developed by Grant Wiggins as well as an Understanding by Design Process by Jay McTighe (Schneider, 2000). A form of Socratic seminar is in effect throughout our nation's language arts classrooms. Teachers are beginning and ending the year with discussion and writing prompts. Think-and-write sessions are providing challenging activities. A form of cognitive coaching and student mentorship is becoming commonplace. According to Evelyn Schneider (2000), Director of Educational Associates, English teachers are now using strategies such as Circle Writing, Sketch to Stretch, Literature Roles, as well as Literature Circles as new ways to teach language arts.

Circle Writing

Students in groups of three review photos from a multitude of aspects, including historical background, prediction, five senses, comparison, classification, and evaluation. The group creates a template for designing opening questions for discussion. The opening question becomes a starting point for circle writing. Each student adds his or her perspective as the paper is shared around the classroom.

Sketch to Stretch

Using a novel with controversial themes such as racism, homelessness, or literacy, students develop questions relating to community and humanity. A paper is folded into four sections

Exhibit 13.1   The Twelve Essential Goals of English

1. Students read a wide range of print and nonprint texts to build an understanding of texts, of themselves, and of the cultures of the United States and the world; to acquire new information; to respond to the needs and demands of society and the workplace; and for personal fulfillment. Among these texts are fiction and nonfiction, classic and contemporary works.

2. Students read a wide range of literature from many periods in many genres to build an understanding of the many dimensions (e.g., philosophical, ethical, aesthetic) of human experience.

3. Students apply a wide range of strategies to comprehend, interpret, evaluate, and appreciate texts. They draw on their prior experience, their interactions with other readers and writers, their knowledge of word meaning and of other texts, their word identification strategies, and their understanding of textual features (e.g., sound-letter correspondence, sentence structure, context, graphics).

4. Students adjust their use of spoken, written, and visual language (e.g., conventions, style, vocabulary) to communicate effectively with a variety of audiences and for different purposes.

5. Students employ a wide range of strategies as they write and use different writing process elements appropriately to communicate with different audiences for a variety of purposes.

6. Students apply knowledge of language structure, language conventions (e.g., spelling and punctuation), media techniques, figurative language, and genre to create, critique, and discuss print and nonprint texts.

7. Students conduct research on issues and interests by generating ideas and questions, and by posing problems. They gather, evaluate, and synthesize data from a variety of sources (e.g., print and nonprint texts, artifacts, people) to communicate their discoveries in ways that suit their purpose and audience.

8. Students use a variety of technological and information resources (e.g., libraries, databases, computer networks, video) to gather and synthesize information and to create and communicate knowledge.

9. Students develop an understanding of and respect for diversity in language use, patterns, and dialects across cultures, ethnic groups, geographic regions, and social roles.

10. Students whose first language is not English make use of their first language to develop competency in the English language arts and to develop understanding of content across the curriculum.

11. Students participate as knowledgeable, reflective, creative, and critical members of a variety of literacy communities.

12. Students use spoken, written, and visual language to accomplish their own purposes (e.g., for learning, enjoyment, persuasion, and the exchange of information).

so that students can sketch the most important theme from each reading segment. Ideas emerge about varied choices, visual representations, titles, or sentence summaries.

Differentiated Roles

Students develop short biographies using strips of paper containing information about an important person. The strips of paper are passed around the classroom. Students classify the strips into reader-friendly labels, patterns of the subject's life, or metaphors, and then compare these aspects to other well-known individuals.

Literature Circles

Students review literature as part of a group of four individuals. One student is the reader while another finds quotable quotes. The other two students become either the illustrator or the "vocabulary enricher," who looks for unfamiliar words.

These are just a few strategies being used by English teachers to revitalize their classrooms. In actuality, there is a plethora of ways that teachers can change their language arts curriculum. One of the fastest growing and most popular approaches is the incorporation of a critical literacy component.

Critical Literacy

There is a strong trend toward the implementation of a critical literacy component in classrooms today. Language arts teachers are looking for ways to capture children's imaginations in and out of the classroom. This is being done by immersing students in rich, provocative literature—a literature that has the potential to challenge, arouse interest, and awaken in students a passion for reading, writing, and imaging (Long & Gove, 2004).

Critical literacy is questioning the stance and possibility of change in the teaching of language arts. This trend is rooted in the work of Paulo Freire (1921–1997), the Brazilian educationalist, who left a significant mark on thinking about progressive practice (McDaniel, 2004). Critical literacy has developed into a way to encourage English teachers and their students to adopt a questioning stance and to work toward changing themselves and their worlds. The approach goes beyond critical thinking skills. It promotes a certain version of reality for both teacher and student.

READING

Although reading in the strictest sense is one of the language arts (usually construed to cover reading, writing, speaking, and listening), it has so much importance, especially in the early grades, that it is given separate consideration as a curriculum field.

Trends in Reading

Research studies on reading have generated much controversy and confusion among educators. A current trend is that teachers need to be more and more creative in order to interest students in reading and in books (Glendening, 2004). The focus is now on a statistical procedure called meta-analysis that synthesizes data from a number of studies as to "what works" in classrooms (Camilli & Wolfe, 2004). Evidence from many successful schools and from multiple research studies seems to show that a multitiered approach involving high-quality classroom instruction and in combination with targeted, small-group interventions can substantially reduce the proportion of students who struggle to read (Lyon, Fletcher, Torgeson, Shaywitz, & Chhabra, 2004). According to Reid Lyon, a recent classroom Title I study reveals that effective instruction alone can reduce reading failure to approximately 6%. Other studies noted by Lyon et al. seem to substantiate that a combination of effective classroom instruction and targeted small-group instruction can reduce the number of students having a problem in reading.

Curriculum Tip

Regardless of expert tutoring or the use of small-group instruction, most reading researchers seem to be agreeing that a strong exposure of teachers to a variety of approaches and different types of instruction is highly beneficial.

No one secret formula emerges for reading, albeit most studies seem to concur that a balance of methods that incorporate both direct instruction and means-based approaches appear to be prevalent in successful schools (Camilli & Wolfe, 2004, p. 28). According to noted researcher and author Richard Allington (2001), the goal of all students reading on grade level will be achieved only with an expansion of expert tutoring, which has repeatedly been shown to be the most effective intervention. Allington says, however, that this will require much more funding than anyone has imagined. Recent classroom studies are underscoring the importance and cost-effectiveness of allocating resources to improving teacher knowledge.

Brain Research

A major trend in the study of reading continues to be a renewed interest in brain research and how the brain functions. Some scientists are concerned about an emphasis on brain research and how it is related to the field of reading. Others, such as author Patricia Wolfe (2001), say that it would be foolish not to discuss the implications and applications of this field. Wolfe believes that it is like saying that physicians need not understand the body in order to treat it. Wolfe believes that the more we understand the brain, the better we will be able to design instruction to match how it learns best.

Author Marge Scherer (2004) notes that brain research using MRI technology has yielded fascinating information about how the brain works—especially how brain images of struggling readers and proficient readers differ. According to Scherer, studies show that intensive, expert tutoring changes the signature of dyslexia and helps struggling readers.

Professors of Pediatrics at Yale University, Sally and Bennett Shaywitz (2004), share Scherer's views on brain research. They conclude that all children must be taught alphabetics, comprising phonemic awareness and phonics; reading fluency; vocabulary; and strategies for reading comprehension. In addition, according to Professors Sally and Bennett Shaywitz, these elements must be taught systematically, comprehensively, and explicitly. It is inadequate to present the foundational skills of phonemic awareness and phonics incidentally, casually, or fragmentally.

But not everyone agrees with recent events in brain research. Psychologist Gerald Coles (2004) is concerned about "brain glitch" research and how it might be misinterpreted. He feels that it is crucial that any such research address the following questions:

- Will alternative teaching approaches configure brain activity in alternative ways?
- Will children's differing assumptions about what it means to "read" correspond to differing brain activity and organization?
- How do different aspects of reading, such as comprehension, syntax, and word analysis, interact in certain reading tasks, and what kinds of brain activity do the interactions produce?
- How does the knowledge children bring to literacy learning affect brain activity?

Technology and Reading Improvement

Electronic classroom networks can enhance student participation and achievement in reading. Classroom networks facilitate learner-centered environments because they require every student to think actively during class (Roschelle, Penuel, & Abrahamson, 2004). The rapid accumulation of student feedback enables the teacher to adjust instruction as needed. The integration and success of classroom technology is attracting the attention of professional researchers.

For more information on the reading research community, browse through a few of the following Internet sites (Perkins-Gough, 2004):

- **The International Reading Association (IRA).** This is a professional membership organization with members and affiliates in 99 countries. The organization's mission is to promote high levels of literacy by improving the quality of reading instruction, disseminating research and information about reading, and encouraging the lifetime reading habit. At the IRA Web site (www.reading.org) you can find sample archives of selected articles from *The Reading Teacher, Journal of Adolescent & Adult Literacy,* and *Reading Research Quarterly* as well as IRA's peer-reviewed online journal, *Reading Online.*
- **Education Commission of the States.** See Reading/Literacy section at (www.ecs.org/html/issue.asp?issueid=97). This site includes links to *Common Strategies to Improve Student Reading; A Consumer's Guide to Evaluating a Core Reading Program;* and *Preventing Reading Difficulties in Young Children.*
- **Council for Learning Disabilities (CLD).** This organization's Web site contains a collection of InfoSheets designed to support the translation of research into practice. Go to www.cldinternational.org.

Recommendations for Curriculum Leaders

According to noted researcher Marie Carbo (2003), founder and executive director of the National Reading Styles Institute in Syosset, New York, curriculum leaders and principals should refer to the following recommendations to improve reading in their schools.

1. *Help students become familiar with rich, well-written language.* Have teachers read a variety of literature aloud to their classes.

2. *Help students associate reading with pleasure.* Encourage teachers and parent-support groups to provide cozy reading areas with lots of high-interest books.

3. *Support the development of a library of specially recorded books* (slow paced, special phrasing). Encourage struggling readers to listen to an audiotape and follow along with the text a few times before reading aloud.

4. *Provide recorded textbooks and a tape dubber in the media center.* This tactic enables struggling readers to become familiar with the content and can raise reading levels substantially.

5. *Become familiar with a variety of reading methods.* When one method isn't working, teachers need to try an alternate method.

6. *Encourage teachers to allow students choices.* Allow students to decide with whom they wish to read.

7. *Make skill practice fun.* Allow students to work with peers, and provide some skill practice in the form of hands-on games.

The role of the school library is also important in improving reading scores. Curry Lance Keith (2004) notes that researchers are showing more and more evidence that a well-stocked and well-staffed library plays a key role in student achievement. This is largely due to school libraries' offering students resources for both conducting research and for reading for fun. Well-stocked school libraries can therefore do much to help nonproficient readers.

Predominant reading styles of nonproficient readers are global, tactile, and kinesthetic. The gap between our poor and excellent readers is widening. It is therefore important for school administrators and curriculum leaders to provide as many intervention strategies as possible. The International Reading Association's (IRA) Exemplary Reading Program Award Committee found three common characteristics necessary for developing quality reading programs: a focus on reading throughout the curriculum, strong administrative leadership, and an emphasis on encouraging students to read for pleasure (International Reading Association, 2004). Whether it be a focus on reading throughout the curriculum, small-group instruction, expert tutoring, a multitiered approach, staff development, or just an awareness of the problem, leaders need to address the issue of improving reading.

SOCIAL STUDIES

In many ways, the history of the social studies curriculum is similar to that of English. As the following discussion will reveal, early attempts at reform resulted in seemingly little change, and the current period seems marked by some confusion of aims.

The post-Sputnik curriculum reform movement, which first affected science, mathematics, and foreign languages, seemed initially to make a major impact on the field of social studies as well. More than 40 curriculum development projects of national scope were initiated under the aegis of the U.S. Office of Education's (USOE) Project Social Studies and the National Science Foundation. All the USOE project centers were located at universities, and the curriculum efforts clearly reflected an academic orientation.

Exhibit 13.2   Dominant Organizational Patterns for Social Studies

K—Self, school, community, home

1—Families

2—Neighborhoods

3—Communities

4—State history, geographic regions

5—American history

6—World cultures, Western hemisphere

7—World geography or history

8—American history

9—Civics or world cultures

10—World history

11—American history

12—American government

The period following the curriculum-reform era has been characterized by Jarolimek (1981) as a time when social studies was in disarray. The projects had run their courses, and there were no funds available in significant amounts for new projects.

The backlash was perhaps predictable. In what seemed to many to be a well-orchestrated response, several conservative organizations and local parent groups attacked any course that raised questions of values and morality. *Man: A Course of Study,* a course that attempted to involve fifth graders in an examination of values from an anthropological point of view, seemed to be a favorite target; the furor even resulted in Congressional hearings, because federal funds had been used to produce that particular curriculum package.

Several studies of the status of the field suggested a somewhat discouraging picture at the time of the present work (the following synthesis is drawn from Ponder, 1979; Shaver, Davis, & Helburn, 1979; Superka, Hawke, & Morrissett, 1980). First, the discipline-centered projects of the post-Sputnik era do not seem to have made a lasting impact; even generous estimates suggest that they were being used in only 20% of the school districts of the nation. Second, despite a widely held belief that there was little uniformity in the social studies, a standard organizational pattern had firmly taken hold. Exhibit 13.2 shows the sequence of what Superka and colleagues call "a virtual nationwide curriculum held rather firmly in place by state laws, district requirements, textbook offerings, and tradition" (p. 365).

Despite improvements in texts, the taught curriculum had changed very little. The whole-class lecture-recitation method dominated, and students were tested primarily on their ability to remember and reproduce information. Experience-based curricula and inquiry learning were rare. Teachers were the final arbiters of the curriculum actually delivered, and those teachers tended to support a somewhat traditional view of the field.

While the National Council for the Social Studies (1984) recommended a scope and sequence that very closely resembles the dominant patterns noted in Exhibit 13.2, they also sketched in three optional structures for Grades 6 to 12 that they believed would afford local districts greater flexibility. Thus, in Grade 8, these optional frameworks were offered:

Option 1—U.S. History with emphasis on social history and economic developments

Option 2—Economics and law-related studies

Option 3—Interdisciplinary study of the local region

Trends in Social Studies

New trends in teaching social studies appear to be focusing on a technique that engages students. The new century is bringing a broadening scope to the teaching and learning of history. For example, concept mapping, clustering, brainstorming, mind maps, and other types of graphic organizers are all being used in social studies classes today. These visual learning symbols, pictures, and other representational techniques allow students to go deeper into ideas and concepts (Chandler, 2003). New perspectives are causing social studies and history teachers to rethink their approach to teaching. Teachers are now finding that achieving a high standard in the learning of history goes well beyond the basics. Students are no longer just focusing on "learned facts," but are learning how to think in a different and deeper way. An important influence on social studies curriculum and teaching has to do with the differences between traditional and restructured schools as they have emerged over the last decade (Crocco & Thornton, 2002). There is now an interest in not just giving dates, places, and names, but giving students an opportunity to question, to investigate, and to make a personal connection to the lives of people they are studying. Students are now using historical thinking skills to examine rich content. "Inspired history" is allowing students to make a connection to the past as well as to open ideas and thinking about how to address the future.

Curriculum Tip

Social studies and history need to come alive for students. Finding ways to engage students appears to be the key to successful curriculum planning.

According to Alan Stoskopf (2001), Associate Program Director for Professional Development at Facing History and Ourselves, a national nonprofit educational foundation in Brookline, Massachusetts, a set of historical thinking skills helps students learn about history. These skills include: point of view, credibility of evidence, historical context, causality, and multiple perspectives.

Point of View: Relates to how an author's personal background and status influence what is written. How is the point of view of the author being interpreted?

Credibility of Evidence: Is the source reliable? Where did it originate and for what purpose was it used at the time?

Historical Context: How does one see the past on its own terms? Are current values obscuring what really happened?

Causality: How does one avoid seeing past events as caused by one factor? Complex history should not be reduced to a single driving force.

Multiple Perspectives: How does one weigh different interpretations of the same event? There is a need to search for the ideas and opinions of different historical individuals to gain a more sophisticated understanding of the past.

Building understanding is a major factor in revolutionizing how social studies and history is taught. For example, students learn that they can view texts as "just someone's ideas written down"—ideas that may not always be clear or complete (Beck & McKeown, 2002). They can ask questions such as, "What is the author trying to say?" or "What did the author say to make you think that?" As students read a text or material, the teacher can intervene at selected points and pose queries to prompt students to consider new information. Student queries can drive discussion and keep it focused on meaning. This helps build understanding as the students read.

The skills noted above are being integrated into social studies and history units all across the United States. The role of technology is also important. For example,

WETP (Worker Education and Training Program) advocates using geographical, mapping, and history-based software applications, as well as age-appropriate simulations with elementary students who are expanding their understanding of the world beyond themselves and their families. Simulations offer students the opportunity to participate in historical events or major decision-making events by virtue of role playing. Whether studying the 50 states or debating the pros and cons of declaring American's independence from England, students will find a wealth of excellent technology-based applications to make exploring social studies themes exciting. (North Central Educational Regional Laboratory, n.d.)

Students are now turning in their presentations in the form of WebQuests (Chandler, 2003). A WebQuest is an inquiry-oriented activity in which most or all of the information used by learners is drawn from the Web. WebQuests allow students to use selected Internet resources to find specific information about their topic. Resources are previously organized by either a student or a teacher into subject-based Web sites.

These new ways of addressing social studies and history are forcing teachers to rethink how they should teach. They are forcing a rethinking of dominant assumptions of how history is written and how it is taught. Pedagogy is broadening and expanding to include narratives relating to such fields as social, economic, and cultural histories.

MATHEMATICS

The question on everyone's mind is, "Can this generation U.S. students add, subtract, multiply, and divide better than previous generations?" According to authors Tom Loveless and John

Coughlan (2004), researchers have pointed to causes for optimism. Scores on the main math test of the National Assessment of Educational Progress (NAEP) have risen steadily over the past decade. From the 1990s to 2003, eighth graders picked up 15 scale score points and fourth graders increased their results by a whopping 22 scale score points, which is equal to almost 2 years of knowledge. These data suggest that the Untied States' future in math achievement looks bright.

Except for the short-lived reform movement of the post-Sputnik era, the mathematics curriculum has perhaps undergone less change than other disciplines. However, as the discussion below will note, greater change seems likely to occur during the coming decades.

Trends in Mathematics

If trends in the subject areas are strongly influenced by the widely disseminated pronouncements of professional associations, then trends in mathematics are relatively easy to identify. Here, the National Council of Teachers of Mathematics (NCTM) has played a very active role. First, the NCTM published a very useful set of guidelines for the teaching of mathematics titled *An Agenda for Action: Recommendations for School Mathematics of the 1980s* (National Council of Teachers of Mathematics, 1980). Then, with support from the National Science Foundation, their Priorities in School Mathematics Project (PRISM) surveyed several thousand classroom teachers, college instructors and mathematics-teacher educators, supervisors of mathematics, principals, and school-board and parent-organization presidents about most of the issues covered in the agenda's recommendations. The general recommendations and a summary of the survey results are shown in Exhibit 13.3; details of the survey results are reported in the publication *Priorities in School Mathematics: Executive Summary of the PRISM Project* (National Council of Teachers of Mathematics, 1981).

Exhibit 13.3   Recommendations for School Mathematics

---

1. Problem solving must be the focus of school mathematics.

2. The concept of basic skills in mathematics must encompass more than computational facility.

3. Mathematics programs must take full advantage of the power of calculators and computers at all grade levels.

4. Stringent standards of both effectiveness and efficiency must be applied to the teaching of mathematics.

5. The success of mathematics programs and student learning must be evaluated by a wider range of measures than conventional testing.

6. More mathematics study must be required for all students, and a flexible curriculum with a greater range of options should be designed to accommodate the diverse needs of the student population.

7. Mathematics teachers must demand of themselves and their colleagues a high level of professionalism.

8. Public support for mathematics instruction must be raised to a level commensurate with the importance of mathematical understanding to individual and society.

The College Board's (1983) recommendations for college preparatory mathematics seem quite similar to those of the NCTM. The board recommends several goals for all college-bound students in each of the following areas: computing, statistics, algebra, geometry, and functions.

Implementing these recommendations in a comprehensive K–12 program is a much more difficult matter than simply making recommendations about goals and the placement of subjects. The NCTM publications, along with the other resources listed, provide at least a framework for a contemporary mathematics curriculum.

The teaching of mathematics is a cultural activity: learned implicitly, hard to see from within the culture, and hard to change. The key to change will be teachers and students working on problems as lessons unfold (Stigler & Hiebert, 2004). New lesson study will not be about just improving a single lesson—it will be about building pathways for ongoing improvement of instruction. Observers may focus on one student who struggles with math concepts, one who quickly finds the correct answer and becomes bored, or one who is an English language learner. Information about what students are actually learning is essential to instructional improvement (Lewis, Perry, & Hurd, 2004). The result will be a common, coherent, and challenging curriculum that can transform mathematics education in the United States (Schmidt, 2004). Teachers will be changing the way they teach mathematics. The National Council of Teachers of Mathematics (NCTM) is now emphasizing the important role of communication in helping children construct understanding of mathematical concepts and develop connections between their informal knowledge and the abstract symbolism of mathematical concepts (Hunsader, 2004). Teachers are becoming more guided about learning as well as developing a common continuum of goals that relates to mathematics standards (Boss, 2001). As a result, the learning process is becoming more seamless from grade to grade. The focus is now on developing a rich math curriculum, built on a deep understanding.

Curriculum Tip

Mathematics teachers are now asking the questions: What do my students understand? How do I know they understand?

We live in a mathematical world. Whenever we decide on a purchase, choose an insurance or health plan, or use a spreadsheet, we rely on mathematical understanding. The Web, CD-ROMs, and other media disseminate vast quantities of quantitative information. The level of mathematical thinking and problem solving needed in the workplace has increased dramatically.

In such a world, those who understand and can do mathematics will have opportunities that others do not. Mathematical competence opens doors to productive futures. A lack of mathematical competence closes those doors. For example, the choice of textbook often determines what teachers will teach, how they will teach it, and how their math students will learn (Reys, Reys, & Chavez, 2004).

Students have different abilities, needs, and interests. Yet everyone needs to be able to use mathematics in his or her personal life, in the workplace, and in further study. All students deserve an opportunity to understand the power and beauty of mathematics. Students need to learn a new set of mathematics basics that enables them to compute fluently and to solve problems creatively and resourcefully. According to authors Strong, Thomas, Perini, and Silver (2004), recognizing different mathematical learning styles and adapting differentiated teaching strategies can facilitate student learning.

The Standards 2000 Project

With the release of *Curriculum and Evaluation Standards for School Mathematics* in 1989, the National Council of Teachers of Mathematics (NCTM) moved to the forefront of efforts to improve mathematics education in the United States and Canada. The document marked a historically important first step by a professional organization to articulate extensive goals for teachers and policymakers in a school discipline. Since its release, the *Curriculum and Evaluation Standards* has provided focus, coherence, and new ideas to mathematics education.

In 1991 the NCTM, which is an international organization of teachers and others committed to excellence in mathematics teaching and learning for all students, published *Professional Standards for Teaching Mathematics,* which described the elements of effective mathematics teaching. *Assessment Standards for School Mathematics,* which appeared in 1995, established objectives against which assessment practices can be measured. Together, these three documents have given focus, coherence, and new ideas to efforts to improve mathematics education.

Educational decisions made by teachers, school administrators, and other professionals have important consequences for students and for society. The principles for school mathematics provide guidance in making these decisions.

The Equity Principle

Excellence in mathematics education requires equity—high expectations and strong support for all students.

All students, regardless of their personal characteristics, backgrounds, or physical challenges, must have opportunities to study—and support to learn—mathematics. This does not mean that every student should be treated the same, but all students need access each year they are in school to a coherent, challenging mathematics curriculum that is taught by competent and well-supported mathematics teachers.

Too many students, especially students who are poor, not native speakers of English, disabled, female, or members of minority groups, are victims of low expectations in mathematics. For example, tracking has consistently consigned disadvantaged groups of students to mathematics classes that concentrate on remediation or do not offer significant mathematical substance. The Equity Principle demands that high expectations for mathematics learning be communicated in words and deeds to all students.

Some students may need more than an ambitious curriculum and excellent teaching to meet high expectations. Students who are having difficulty may benefit from such resources as after-school programs, peer mentoring, or cross-age tutoring. Students with special learning needs in mathematics should be supported by both their classroom teachers and special education staff. An excellent resource for understanding mathematical standards can be found at the Internet site titled "Principles and Standards for School Mathematics" (National Council of Teachers of Mathematics, 2004).

SCIENCE

The recent history of science curricula perhaps provides a paradigmatic example of federal influence in curricular matters and therefore deserves a close examination.

Trends in Science

In analyzing trends in science, three sources are especially useful for the curriculum leader. First, the National Science Teachers Association (NSTA) has adopted and promulgated a position statement that, while somewhat general in nature, does indicate some important curricular emphases. As the summary in Exhibit 13.4 indicates, this professional association places strong emphasis on laboratory and field experiences, on inquiry and problem solving, on a comprehensive concept-based curriculum, and on science-related societal issues.

How such a curriculum might be achieved is the focus of a second valuable study. The NSTA's "Search for Excellence in Science Education" project identified 54 exemplary science programs throughout the nation and examined their common characteristics (see Yager, Aldridge, & Penick, 1983).

The curricular order of high school science is also currently being examined. Since the recommendation by the 1893 Committee of Ten education task force, high school science curriculum has been traditionally taught in the sequence of biology first, then chemistry, followed by physics. Only the top 25% of high school students continued taking science classes through physics (Allen, 2004). The National Science Education Standards endorses students' taking physics first, then chemistry and biology, reversing the traditional order of physics and biology. Changing the order holds many curricular implications. The aim of this curricular reversal is to allow students a more in-depth understanding of the concepts and connections across the three science disciplines. A different curriculum approach will require major pedagogical adjustment as physics has been taught to older students, who have a strong grounding in abstract math. In lieu of math skills, students will need to be taught physics from a hands-on and inquiry approach (Allen, 2004). However, students who have studied physics build a stronger understanding of atoms and molecules, which will enable them to better understand the complexities and interrelationship with chemistry and biology. In addition, proponents of the curricular order change advocate that by students' taking physics first, they will be motivated to take more advanced science courses. Nobel Prize–winning physicist Leon Lederman states, "I'm mostly interested in improving science literacy. By the end of high school, a student should be ready for all possible futures, whether at work, in the military, in engineering school, college, or family life. A good science and math education prepares students for life" (Allen, 2004, p. 8).

According to authors Ingrid Chalufour, Cindy Hoisington, Robin Moriarty, Jeff Winokur, and Karen Worth (2004), more teachers are now engaging science students in the rich process of inquiry. There can be seen a strong focus in current reform documents on increasing student understanding in the area of science processes and the nature of science, in addition to gains in content knowledge (Melber, 2003). For example, the two most current trends in science education are constructivism and inquiry-based learning. Studies by Piaget and others since the 1970s have led to the constructivist philosophy, which focuses on the framework that students carry into learning situations. Constructivism says that learners bring their personal experiences into the classroom, and these experiences have a tremendous impact on their views of

Exhibit 13.4   National Science Standards

Physical Science

Levels K–4

Properties of objects and
  materials
Position and motion of
  objects
Light, heat, electricity, and
  magnetism

Levels 5–8

Changes of properties
  in matter
Motions and forces
Transfer of energy

Levels 9–12

Structure of atoms and
  properties of matter
Chemical reactions
Structure of atoms
Motions and forces
Conservation of energy and
  increase in disorder
Interactions of energy and
  matter

Life Science

Levels K–4

Characteristics of
  organisms
Life cycles of organisms
Organisms and environments

Levels 5–8

Structure and function in
  living systems
Reproduction and heredity
Regulation and behavior
Populations and ecosystems
Diversity and adaptations of
  organisms

Levels 9–12

The cell
Molecular basis of heredity
Behavior of organisms
Interdependence of
  organisms
Matter, energy, and
  organization of organisms
Biological evolution

Earth and Space Science

Levels K–4

Properties of earth materials
Objects in the sky
Changes in Earth and sky

Levels 5–8

Structure of the Earth system
Earth's history
Earth in the solar system

Levels 9–12

Energy in the Earth system
Origin and evolution of the
  Earth system
Origin and evolution of the
  universe
Geochemical cycles

Science and Technology

Levels K–4

Abilities of technological
  design
Understanding about science
  and technology
Abilities to distinguish
  between natural objects
  and objects made by
  humans

Levels 5–8

Abilities of technological
  design
Understanding about science
  and technology

Levels 9–12

Abilities of technological
  design
Understanding about science
  and technology

how the world works. Students come to learning situations with a variety of knowledge, feelings, and skills, and this is where learning should begin. This knowledge exists within the student and is developed as individuals interact with their peers, teachers, and the environment. For example, hands-on activities help students understand the concepts and reveal differences in understanding levels (Robertson, Gallagher, & Miller, 2004). Learners construct understanding or meaning by making sense of their experiences and fitting their own ideas into reality. Children construct thoughts, expectations, and explanations about natural phenomena to make sense of their everyday experiences. Constructivists believe that actual learning takes place through accommodation, which occurs when students change their existing ideas in response to new information (Schulte, 1996). Constructivism allows students to learn by asking questions and forming their own opinions.

Inquiry-based learning is not a new technique—in fact, it goes back to John Dewey—but it does stand in contrast to the more structured, traditional framework of today's school. Asking questions is at the heart of inquiry-based learning. The goal is not to ask just any questions, but ones that children honestly care about. The role of the educator is to guide the children in finding the answers themselves and encourage them to ask new questions along the way (Morino Institute, 2001). Students are not only becoming interested in science, but they are also learning how to develop a repertoire of strategies for dealing with science (Topping & McManus, 2002). Inquiry-based learning also allows students to retain information and become more scientifically literate. Finding new and improved ways of teaching science is important, but what is equally important is making a connection between the science curriculum and standards.

Standards help provide students with meaningful and engaging science learning (Stepanek, 2001). They not only outline content that students study, but also define high expectations for students. Standards can be an effective tool for selecting specific areas from the textbook. They also help teachers focus on the information that students really need and standards make the content much more manageable.

Curriculum Tip

Perhaps the most powerful role that standards can take is as a guideline for the curriculum.

FOREIGN LANGUAGE

There seems to be a growing realization that we live in a "global village" where the price of oil from the Middle East affects employment levels in Texas. In such a global village, competence in a foreign language would seem to be a vital necessity. Such was the obvious conclusion of several of the reform reports of the 1980s. Recent studies indicate, however, that only about one fourth of the nation's students were studying a foreign language. The discussion that follows examines some current trends in language study.

Trends in Foreign-Language Education

Trends in foreign-language education can perhaps best be analyzed by dividing them into curricular approaches and instructional approaches, although such a division is in some ways misleading, especially with respect to foreign language.

Curricular Approaches

Several new approaches to the design and development of curricula have appeared in recent years. One is termed *problem-posing education,* a foreign-language curriculum with an existentialist emphasis.

The second curricular approach gaining attention, at least from leaders in the profession, is the functional-notional syllabus. Influenced greatly by the theories of psycho- and sociolinguistics, the functional-notional syllabus is predicated on the importance of two closely related aspects of language: the functions of language (such as requesting information, giving instructions, clarifying the order of events); and the notions or semantic meanings (concepts such as time, quantification, possession, modality). Thus, the functional-notional syllabus stresses the purposes for which learners need the language and the notions or concepts involved with those purposes.

A third approach to curriculum development might be termed the *proficiency approach.* These are curricula developed around the proficiencies identified by the American Council of Teachers of Foreign Languages (ACTFL; 1982). The ACTFL guidelines describe in very specific terms six proficiency levels in speaking, reading, listening, and writing: Level 0, no functional ability; Level 1, elementary survival-level proficiency; Level 2, limited working proficiency; Level 3, professional working proficiency; Level 4, full professional proficiency; Level 5, the proficiency of a native speaker.

Instructional Approaches

Two quite different instructional approaches have attracted the attention of foreign-language specialists: immersion programs and "Suggestopedia."

Immersion programs were first developed in Canada in response to the concerns of English-speaking parents in Quebec. Teachers use the target language to teach regular school subjects: The second language is not another subject, but is instead the medium of instruction. In early total-immersion programs, all instruction for the first three or four grades is presented in the target language; the native language is not introduced until second or third grade. By the end of elementary school, each language is used to teach about half of the curriculum.

Suggestopedia, first developed by Lozanov (1978), is an instructional method that attempts to involve both conscious and unconscious faculties by using intensive time periods (3- or 4-hour sessions for 5 days a week), a secure group atmosphere (ideally, six males and six females with a highly skilled teacher), rhythmic breathing exercises, and baroque music. Its instructional procedure consists of three parts: a review of the previous day's work through conversation, games, and skits; new material introduced using dialogue in familiar situations; and a "seance" that aims at unconscious memorization using yogic breathing and baroque music.

Students in U.S. classrooms are culturally, linguistically, ethnically, and socioeconomically diverse (Hammerberg, 2004). It is important that educators understand the current methods of comprehension instruction taught to students from diverse backgrounds. Professionals need to deepen their understanding of the impact of culture and language on the instructional and assessment process (Santos, 2004). In any educational field, a close relationship exists between assessment and instruction. In the current educational climate, policymakers and national organizations often initiate new trends in standards and assessment to bring about changes in instructional objectives and approaches at the classroom level. As these instructional objectives and approaches change, updated assessment practices are needed to reflect the changes. This interactive relationship between assessment and instruction, in which each influences the other, has characterized the foreign language field during the past decade. Since the early 1980s, the focus of foreign language instruction has moved away from the mastery of discrete language skills, such as grammar, vocabulary, and pronunciation, to the development of communicative proficiency—that is, the ability to communicate about real-world topics with native speakers of the target language. Widely termed the "proficiency movement," this change has developed in tandem with changes in how students' foreign-language skills are assessed.

The traditional assessment tools of earlier decades—usually discrete-point tests that focused on individual skills, such as knowledge of vocabulary and grammatical accuracy—evaluated students' knowledge *about* the language, not what they could *do with* the language. Although discrete-point tests are still used in many circumstances, particularly for large-scale standardized assessments, many of the newer assessment measures and techniques are performance based; that is, they require students to demonstrate knowledge and skills by carrying out challenging tasks. This enables teachers to measure what the students can actually do in various communicative contexts using the target language.

Changes in foreign-language assessment in recent years can be divided into two main categories based on their catalysts. National assessment initiatives have widely influenced classroom instruction in a top-down approach; local assessment initiatives, which have appeared in response to curricular and instructional changes, may be seen as bottom-up initiatives. Top-down and bottom-up influences on foreign language assessment will undoubtedly continue. The publication of the national foreign language standards (National Standards in Foreign Language Education Project, 1996) means that attainment of these standards will need to be assessed (see Exhibit 13.5).

It will take time before the real extent of the impact of the enforceable curriculum standards on multicultural education and/or foreign language is known (Bohn & Sleeter, 2000). To many curriculum leaders, standards make visible the expectations for learning that otherwise might be implicit. At the same time, teachers of foreign language or multicultural education are not looking for a quick fix.

Curriculum Tip

Teachers must be given time to examine their own views on foreign language and multicultural education as well as be able to relate those views to standards that are adopted.

Exhibit 13.5   Standards in Foreign Language Education

Statement of Philosophy

Language and communication are at the heart of the human experience. The United States must educate students who are linguistically and culturally equipped to communicate successfully in a pluralistic American society and abroad. This imperative envisions a future in which ALL students will develop and maintain proficiency in English and at least one other language, modern or classical. Children who come to school from non-English backgrounds should also have opportunities to develop further proficiencies in their first language.

Standards for Foreign Language Learning

COMMUNICATION

Communicate in Languages Other Than English

Standard 1.1: Students engage in conversations, provide and obtain information, express feelings and emotions, and exchange opinions

Standard 1.2: Students understand and interpret written and spoken language on a variety of topics

Standard 1.3: Students present information, concepts, and ideas to an audience of listeners or readers on a variety of topics

CULTURES

Gain Knowledge and Understanding of Other Cultures

Standard 2.1: Students demonstrate an understanding of the relationship between the practices and perspectives of the culture studied

Standard 2.2: Students demonstrate an understanding of the relationship between the products and perspectives of the culture studied

CONNECTIONS

Connect with Other Disciplines and Acquire Information

Standard 3.1: Students reinforce and further their knowledge of other disciplines through the foreign language

Standard 3.2: Students acquire information and recognize the distinctive viewpoints that are only available through the foreign language and its cultures

COMPARISONS

Develop Insight into the Nature of Language and Culture

Standard 4.1: Students demonstrate understanding of the nature of language through comparisons of the language studied and their own

Standard 4.2: Students demonstrate understanding of the concept of culture through comparisons of the cultures studied and their own

COMMUNITIES

Participate in Multilingual Communities at Home and Around the World

Standard 5.1: Students use the language both within and beyond the school setting

Standard 5.2: Students show evidence of becoming life-long learners by using the language for personal enjoyment and enrichment

---

SOURCE: Reprinted with the permission of the American Council on the Teaching of Foreign Languages (ACTFL), 700 S. Washington St., Suite 210, Alexandria, VA 22314.

The best way to face the challenge of assessing attainment of national goals may be by using alternative assessments that are developed in specific instructional contexts. Yet educators must remember, as Genesee and Upshur (1996) stress, that there is "no right way" to assess second-language proficiency in a given context. Given the wide variation among foreign-language students, teachers, courses, and contexts, an assessment tool or procedure that works well in one situation may be totally inappropriate in another. To evaluate students' progress and proficiency effectively, teachers need to learn about and gain competence in the use of a variety of assessment measures and procedures to discover what works best for them in each of the changing contexts in which they teach and with the full range of students in their classes.

The Internet can also be a valuable tool in aiding assessment and instruction of foreign languages in U.S. classrooms. Diane Vitaska, a French teacher, uses the Internet to research cultural aspects of France in her classroom (Vitaska, 2002). Students can create a PowerPoint presentation, a brochure, or a newsletter as a Web page. LCD projectors are used to help students view computer images on a screen. Digital cameras can be used to help students develop personalized notebooks or practice language skills. Some teachers of foreign languages are using mobile video-conferencing labs with a webcam and speaker microphone to connect U.S. classrooms to classrooms in Europe. As can be seen, technology can be used in a plethora of ways to aid the teaching and assessing of students in foreign-language classes.

EDUCATION IN THE ARTS

Over the years, the arts have had to struggle for a place in the school's curriculum. Ever since the Committee of Fifteen's report (National Education Association, 1895/1969), the arts have usually been defined as "minor" subjects taught only an hour or two a week up to Grade 8 and then offered as electives at the high school level. As the survey below notes, this situation seems unlikely to change in the near future.

Trends in Art Education

During the 1950s and 1960s, art education was conceived rather narrowly as including only the visual arts and music. Children in the elementary grades were assisted by art and music specialists who emphasized performance (drawing and singing, primarily) as a way of making those subjects interesting. At the junior high level, units and courses in art appreciation and music appreciation were introduced, usually emphasizing the study of the great masters as a means of teaching students some elementary aesthetic principles. At the high school level, students majoring in art spent five or more periods a week in art studies. The emphasis on performance continued: Many suburban high schools offered courses called band, orchestra, and chorus, in which students spent most of their time preparing for public performances.

This patchwork arts curriculum, which seemed to lack any organizing principle or governing theory, was the target of two major reform efforts during the 1970s, both supported with the federal funds that seemed so abundant in that decade. When federal funds were no longer available, the local districts found it possible to support these exemplary projects for only a few more years.

The lack of continued federal funding for projects in the past decade has not deterred leaders in the field from their continued efforts to strengthen education in the arts and to reassert the importance of the arts at a time when the rest of the profession seems obsessed with the academic curriculum.

Those efforts seemed to have found expression in three related developments. The first is an attempt to broaden the field. Rather than limiting the arts to the visual arts and music, current thinking stresses the multiple nature of aesthetic expression. While such an expanded understanding of the nature of the arts seems theoretically desirable, practitioners have expressed reservations about the difficulties of finding the time, the money, and the staff to support such a diversified and comprehensive program.

The second development is an attempt to formulate and promulgate a new rationale for the arts. In previous years, those advocating the arts tended to speak in terms that connoted a subtle elitism: The arts refine the aesthetic sensibilities and help people appreciate the finer things in life. The tendency in the current period is to defend the arts as an essential and unique way of knowing—one that is basic for all students.

Finally, there seems to be a resurgence of interest in interdisciplinary humanities courses in which the arts play a central role. Such courses enjoyed a period of brief popularity in the early 1960s; during that period, these courses tended to emphasize literature and history and gave only scant attention to the fine arts. After this, there seemed to be a concerted effort to position the arts more centrally in such interdisciplinary courses.

According to Donovan Walling (2001), Director of Publications and Research at Phi Delta Kappa, the changing priorities of schools, coupled with high standards, high-stakes testing, and the ascendancy of math and science is pushing art education back to the heart of education.

Curriculum Tip

Curriculum leaders are urging the approach to the teaching of art along three broad avenues: universals, the community, and the individual.

The arts have had a long struggle finding an appropriate place in the school curriculum. The arts did not figure in the America 2000 program, but were included in President Clinton's 2000 bill. The published standards were discipline specific to dance, music, theater, and the visual arts. The five general standards for the visual arts illustrate their placement.

1. The student understands and applies media, techniques, and processes related to the visual arts.

2. The student knows how to use the structures—sensory qualities, organizational principles, expressive features—as a function of art.

3. The student knows a range of subject matter, symbols, and potential ideas in the visual arts.

4. The student understands the visual arts in relation to history and cultures.

5. The student understands the characteristics and merits of one's own artwork and the artwork of others.

These standards primarily addressed general principles and are open to interpretation. Discipline Based Art Education (DBAE) follows these standards and is often found in school curriculum today. One of the originators of Discipline Based Art was Dwaine Greer, whose aim was to develop mature students who are both comfortable and familiar with major aspects of the disciplines of art (Walling, 2001, p. 628).

New trends in educational art are favoring aesthetics, art history, and art criticism. Complementary interest in extending art education through interdisciplinary studies—across all disciplines—appears to be currently driving the process. Walling (2001) notes several questions that pertain to this movement:

- How should we define "universals," and who should have a say in the definition?
- What traditions characterize "the community," and how can they be incorporated into the art curriculum?
- How will "the individual" be recognized, and how will individual differences be accommodated, validated, and valued?

No matter how art educators address the questions noted above, a move continues today to incorporate technology into the art curriculum. Two themes appear here. The first incorporates creating art by using the computer to create and manipulate images, and the second is using the computer to investigate the visual arts. Teachers and students are finding a plethora of ways to use the computer and Internet in the field of visual arts. So many Web sites about art exist that it takes a considerable amount of time to review them. There is little doubt that technology is fast becoming a major factor in how art is both viewed and integrated into the local school curriculum.

PHYSICAL EDUCATION AND HEALTH

To complete the education of the child, virtually every state, district, and school in the United States requires physical education (Pate et al., 1995). Quality physical education programs increase physical competence, health-related fitness, self-esteem, and enjoyment of physical activity, and they better equip students for lifetime physical fitness (Seefeldt & Vogel, 1996).

Trends in Physical Education

Physical education teaches students to add physical activity to their daily lives and exposes students to content and learning experiences that develop the skills and desire to be active for life (see Exhibit 13.6, National Standards of Physical Education). In addition to physical activity's improving muscular strength and endurance, flexibility, and cardiovascular endurance, physical activity helps children establish self-esteem and set and achieve goals. The American Heart Association (Department of Health and Human Services, 1995) recommended that all children aged 5 years and older should engage in at least 30 minutes of daily physical activity at a moderate intensity and in vigorous activity for 30 minutes at least 3 days per week.

The Centers for Disease Control and Prevention (CDC) finds that most major health problems in the United States today are caused by six categories of behavior: behaviors that lead to intentional and unintentional injuries; smoking; alcohol and other drug use; sexual

Exhibit 13.6   Physical Education Standards

A physically educated person:

Standard 1:   Demonstrates competency in motor skills and movement patterns needed to perform a variety of physical activities.

Standard 2:   Demonstrates understanding of movement concepts, principles, strategies, and tactics as they apply to the learning and performance of physical activities.

Standard 3:   Participates regularly in physical activity.

Standard 4:   Achieves and maintains a health-enhancing level of physical fitness.

Standard 5:   Exhibits responsible personal and social behavior that respects self and others in physical activity settings.

Standard 6:   Values physical activity for health, enjoyment, challenge, self-expression, and/or social interaction.

SOURCE: Standards for Physical Education by the National Association for Sport & Physical Education, 1900 Association Drive, Reston, VA 20191. Reprinted with permission.

behaviors leading to sexually transmitted diseases, HIV infection, and unintended pregnancy; poor nutrition; and lack of physical activity (Kolbe, 1993b). According to Kolbe (1993b), behaviors and attitudes about health that are initiated during childhood are responsible for most of the leading causes of death, illness, and disability in the United States today.

Comprehensive school health education programs represent one effective way of providing students with the knowledge and skills to prevent health-impairing behaviors.

Health education works. Hundreds of studies have evaluated health education and concluded that education effectively reduces the number of teenage pregnancies, decreases smoking rates among young people, and prevents many high-risk behaviors. Nevertheless, its effectiveness depends on factors such as teacher training, comprehensiveness of the health program, time available for instruction, family involvement, and community support (Gold, 1994; Seffrin, 1990). Sequential school health education programs for K–12 students have been found to be more effective in changing health behaviors than occasional programs on single health topics (Kolbe, 1993a).

The Louis Harris survey of more than 4,700 students in Grades 3 through 12 who were attending 199 public schools found that health knowledge, attitudes, and behaviors improved with increasing years of health instruction (Harris & Associates, 1989). The School Health Education Evaluation (Connell, Turner, & Mason, 1985), which looked at four different health curricula for 30,000 fourth through seventh graders in 20 states, found the following:

- Students receiving health instruction had higher knowledge scores than students with no health instruction, with the greatest differences seen in knowledge of substance use and abuse.
- Knowledge, attitudes, and skills improved even with minimal instruction, but gains were most apparent when students received at least 50 hours of health instruction per school year.
- More hours were needed to improve attitudes than to enhance health knowledge and practices.

CHAPTER OVERVIEW

This chapter examines general developments in the curriculum by examining trends in specific subject areas, because even though innovations transcend the discipline, most of the important changes take place and are worked out in the subject areas themselves. Many current developments and trends in K–12 education are altering the landscape for curriculum work, and it is worthwhile to assess current trends as part of curriculum renewal. This chapter includes some of the trends and issues involved in the subject areas of English, language arts, reading, mathematics, social studies, science, foreign language, arts education, and physical education. This chapter also addresses the current role of brain research in curriculum planning for subject areas. Finally, the chapter includes some ways that technology is impacting the delivery and implementation of curriculum in subject areas.

Other areas in education that are currently developing standards are vocational studies and technology/computers. Vocational studies such as shop, family and consumer science, and mechanics are important to career opportunities for today's students. Technology and computers are constantly changing. Curriculum should be developed for these areas and updated on a regular basis. Computer curriculum and education is discussed in greater depth in the next chapter.

CHAPTER TERMS

IRA, International Reading Association	Equity Principle
Back to the Heart of Education	Mentorship
Benchmarks	Proficiency Movement
Circle Writing	Worker Education and Training Program (WETP)
Critical Thinking Skills	

APPLICATIONS

1. An analysis of the curriculum trends suggests quite clearly that the ideal curriculum proposed by national commissions is always far ahead of the taught curriculum delivered in the classroom. In a well-organized essay that draws from your own experience and your knowledge of the research, explain why it seems to be difficult to change the taught curriculum.

2. Select one of the fields discussed. By analyzing how it has changed and is changing now, project the major changes that might occur during the next 10 years. Write a summary of your projections.

3. Based upon a close reading of this chapter and your own observations, determine which of the fields seems to have experienced the greatest changes. Write a brief essay in which you explain why this particular field seems to have changed more than the others.

4. Knowing that constructivism is linked to the higher achievement of students in science, how can this strategy be implemented into other areas of the curriculum?

CASE STUDY

When planning and developing curriculum, it sometimes happens that what is taught in the classroom is not always what is proposed as the district's curriculum. As an example, a south-western school principal has been having differences with several teachers who do not want to follow the district's proposed curriculum, which matches national recommendations. This situation is a major concern for Superintendent Dave Anon, who has Principal Bob Huerta on the phone.

"Bob, I asked for curriculum surveys from your teachers and I found that what they are teaching in their classrooms does not follow our district's curriculum scope and sequence," says Dave Anon, the superintendent in charge of a number of small southwestern rural schools. "For example, I noted on the surveys that the teachers are not covering Geometry in the fourth grade. Our district math curriculum is based on national recommendations and specifically requires that Geometry be taught at that level."

"Yes, I know," states Principal Huerta. "I have several fourth-grade teachers who have taught for a number of years and just do not like to change." There is silence on the phone. Bob Huerta can tell that the superintendent is upset.

"Bob, I e-mailed you a month ago that our math scores are down and we need to align our elementary curriculum with state standards. I specifically noted that your fourth-grade students are not doing well on math test items related to Geometry."

"It is a concern," says Principal Huerta. "I am trying my best to get this resolved."

"Well, you need to get this situation under control. It is crucial that our teachers follow the curriculum that we have outlined and that the national commission recommends," notes the superintendent. "How do you plan to address this problem?"

THE CHALLENGE

Good communication and an understanding of curriculum applications between the district office and a local school is a critical issue. What else can Superintendent Anon do to improve communication with his principals . . . as well as with his teachers and with local parents?

Key Issues/Questions

1. What are your impressions of Superintendent Anon and Principal Huerta? Do you think the issue of communication will be resolved? Why or why not?

2. How do you feel about technology and its impact on communication in schools?

3. What are some areas in language arts and reading that have changed dramatically with the advent of technology? Explain your answer.

4. What are some areas in mathematics and science that have changed dramatically with the advent of technology? Explain your answer.

5. What are some areas in social studies and art that have changed dramatically with the advent of technology? Explain your answer.

REFERENCES

Allen, R. (2004, Summer). Shaking up science: Putting physics first changes more than sequence. *Curriculum Update,* 1–2, 6, 8.

Allington, R. L. (2001). *What really matters for struggling readers: Designing research-based programs.* New York: Addison-Wesley Educational.

American Council of Teachers of Foreign Languages. (1982). *ACTFL provisional proficiency guidelines.* Hastings-on-Hudson, NY: Author.

Beck, I. L., & McKeown, M. C. (2002). Questioning the author: Making sense of social studies. *Educational Leadership, 60*(3), 44–47.

Bohn, A. P., & Sleeter, C. E. (2000, October). Multicultural education and the standards movement: A report from the field. *Phi Delta Kappan, 82*(2), 156–159.

Boss, S. (2001, Winter). Teachers taking charge of change. *Northwest Teacher, 2*(1), 6–9.

Camilli, G., & Wolfe, P. (2004). Research on reading: A cautionary tale. *Educational Leadership, 61*(6), 26–29.

Carbo, M. (2003, November/December). Achieving with struggling readers. *Principal, 83*(2), 20–24.

Chalufour, I., Hoisington, C., Moriarty, R., Winokur, J., & Worth, K. (2004). The science and mathematics of building structures. *Science and Children, 41*(4), 30–34.

Chandler, H. (2003, January). Concept mapping & WebQuests in social studies. *Media and Methods, 39*(3), 38–39.

Coles, G. (2004). Danger in the classroom: "Brain glitch" research and learning to read. *Phi Delta Kappan, 85*(5), 344–351.

College Board. (1983). *Academic preparation for college: What students need to know and be able to do.* New York: Author.

Connell, D. R., Turner, R. R., & Mason, E. F. (1985). Summary of findings of the School Health Education Evaluation: Health promotion effectiveness, implementation, and costs. *Journal of School Health, 55,* 316–321.

Crocco, M. S., & Thornton, S. J. (2002, Spring). Social studies in the New York City public schools: A descriptive study. *Journal of Curriculum and Supervision, 17*(3), 206.

Darling-Hammond, L. (1996). *What matters most: Teaching for America's future.* New York: National Commission on Teaching and America's Future.

Department of Health and Human Services. (1995). *Strategic plan for promoting physical activity.* Dallas, TX: Centers for Disease Control and Prevention; American Heart Association.

Genesee, F., & Upshur, J. A. (1996). *Classroom-based evaluation in second language education.* Port Chester, NY: Cambridge University Press.

Glatthorn, A. A. (1980). *A guide for developing an English curriculum for the eighties.* Urbana, IL: National Council of Teachers of English.

Glendening, M. (2004, February/March). Learning through literature connections. *Reading Today, 21*(4), 10.

Gold, R. S. (1994). The science base for comprehensive school health education. In P. Cortese & K. Middleton (Eds.), *The comprehensive school health challenge: Promoting health through education* (pp. 545–573). Santa Cruz, CA: ETR Associates.

Hammerberg, D. D. (2004). Comprehension instruction for socioculturally diverse classrooms: A review of what we know. *Reading Teacher, 57*(7), 648–661.

Harris, L., & Associates. (1989). *Health—You've got to be taught: An evaluation of comprehensive health education in American public schools.* New York: Metropolitan Life Foundation.

Hunsader, P. D. (2004, April). Mathematics trade books: Establishing their value and assessing their quality. *Reading Teacher, 57,* 618–629.

International Reading Association. (2000, October). Excellent reading teachers. *Reading Teacher, 54*(2), 235.

International Reading Association. (2004, April/May). Setting an example. *Reading Today, 21*(5), 15.

Jarolimek, J. (1981). The social studies: An overview. In H. D. Mehlinger & O. L. Davis, Jr. (Eds.), *The social studies* (pp. 3–18). Chicago: University of Chicago Press.

Keith, C. L. (2004, February/March). Libraries called key. *Reading Today, 21*(4), 1–4.

Kolbe, L. J. (1993a). Developing a plan of action to institutionalize comprehensive school health education programs in the United States. *Journal of School Health, 63*(1), 12–13.

Kolbe, L. J. (1993b). An essential strategy to improve the health and education of Americans. *Preventive Medicine, 22*(4), 1–17.

Lewis, C., Perry, R., & Hurd, J. (2004). A deeper look at lesson study. *Educational Leadership, 61*(5), 18–22.

Long, T. W., & Gove, M. K. (2004). How engagement strategies and literature circles promote critical response in a fourth-grade, urban classroom. *Reading Teacher, 57*(4), 350–361.

Loveless, T., & Coughlan, J. (2004). The arithmetic gap. *Educational Leadership, 61*(5), 55–59.

Lozanov, G. (1978). *Suggestology and outlines of Suggestopedia.* New York: Gordon and Breach.

Lyon, G. R., Fletcher, J. M., Torgeson, J. K., Shaywitz, S. E., & Chhabra, V. (2004). Preventing and remediating reading failure: A response to Allington. *Educational Leadership, 61*(6).

Mandel, B. J. (Ed.). (1980). *Three language-arts curriculum models: Pre-kindergarten through college.* Urbana, IL: National Council of Teachers of English.

McDaniel, C. (2004). Critical literacy: A questioning stance and the possibility for change. *Reading Teacher, 57*(5), 472–473.

Melber, L. M. (2003, Fall). Partnerships in science learning: Museum outreach and elementary gifted education. *Gifted Child Quarterly, 47*(4), 251–258.

Morino Institute. (2001). *From access to outcomes: Raising the aspirations for technology initiatives in low-income communities.* Retrieved March 28, 2005, from http://www.morino.org/divides/report2.htm

National Council for the Social Studies. (1984). In search of a scope and sequence for social studies. *Social Education, 48,* 249–262.

National Council of Teachers of English. (2005). *IRA/NCTE standards for the English language arts: The 12 standards.* Retrieved on March 28, 2005, from http://www.ncte.org/about/over/standards/110846.htm

National Council of Teachers of Mathematics. (1980). *An agenda for action: Recommendations for school mathematics of the 1980s.* Reston, VA: Author.

National Council of Teachers of Mathematics. (1981). *Priorities in school mathematics: Executive summary of the PRISM project.* Reston, VA: Author.

National Council of Teachers of Mathematics. (1989). *Curriculum and evaluation standards for school mathematics.* Reston, VA: Author.

National Council of Teachers of Mathematics. (1991). *Professional standards for teaching mathematics.* Reston, VA: Author.

National Council of Teachers of Mathematics. (1995). *Assessment standards for school mathematics.* Reston, VA: Author.

National Council of Teachers of Mathematics. (2004). *Principles and standards for school mathematics.* Reston, VA: Retrieved April 22, 2004, from http://standards.nctm.org/document/

National Education Association. (1969). *Report of the Committee of Fifteen.* New York: Arno Press. (Original work published in 1895 by New England Publishing)

National Institute of Child Health and Human Development. (2000). *Report of the National Reading Panel: Teaching children to read: An evidence-based assessment of the scientific research literature on reading and its implications for reading instruction.* Washington, DC: U.S. Department of Health and Human Services.

National Standards in Foreign Language Education Project. (1996). *Standards for foreign language learning: Preparing for the 21st century.* Yonkers, NY: Author. (ERIC Document Reproduction Service No. ED 394 279)

North Central Educational Regional Laboratory. (n.d.). *Integrating technology into the curriculum: Technology in social studies.* Retrieved March 28, 2005, from http://www.ncrel.org/tplan/guide/int7.htm

Pate, R. R., Small, M. L., Ross, J. G., Young, J. C., Flint, K. H., & Warren, C. W. (1995, October). School physical education. *Journal of School Health, 65*(8), 312.

Perkins-Gough, D. (2004). Web wonders. *Educational Leadership, 61*(6), 91–92.

Ponder, G. (1979). The more things change: The status of social studies. *Educational Leadership, 36,* 515–518.

Reys, B. J., Reys, R. E., & Chavez, O. (2004). Why mathematics textbooks matter. *Educational Leadership, 61*(5), 61–66.

Roberts, H. D., Kaulfers, W. V., & Kefaurer, G. N. (Eds.). (1943). *English for social living.* New York: McGraw-Hill.

Robertson, W. C., Gallagher, J., & Miller, W. (2004, March). Newton's first law: Not so simple after all. *Science & Children, 41*(6), 25–29.

Roschelle, J., Penuel, W. R., & Abrahamson, L. (2004). The networked classroom. *Educational Leadership, 61*(5), 50–53.

Santos, R. M. (2004, January). Ensuring culturally and linguistically appropriate assessment of young children. *Young Children, 59*(1), 48–50.

Scherer, M. (2004). Perspectives: What works in reading? *Educational Leadership, 61*(6), 5.

Schmidt, W. H. (2004). A vision for mathematics. *Educational Leadership, 61*(4), 6–11.

Schneider, E. (2000). Shifting into high gear. *Educational Leadership, 58*(1), 57–60.

Schulte, P. L. (1996, November/December). A definition of constructivism. *Science Scope, 20*(6), 25–27.

Seefeldt, V., & Vogel, P. (1996). *The value of physical activity.* Reston, VA: AAHPERD & NASPE.

Seffrin, J. R. (1990). The comprehensive school health curriculum: Closing the gap between state-of-the-art and state-of-the-practice. *Journal of School Health, 60*(4), 151–156.

Shaver, J. P., Davis, O. L., Jr., & Helburn, S. W. (1979). The status of social studies education: Impressions from three NSF studies. *Social Education, 43,* 150–163.

Shaywitz, S. E., & Shaywitz, B. A. (2004). Reading disability and the brain. *Educational Leadership, 61*(6), 7–11.

Snow, C. E., Burns, M. S., & Griffin, P. (Eds.). (1998). *Preventing reading difficulties in young children.* Washington, DC: National Academy Press.

Staton, J. (1984). Thinking together: Interaction in children's reasoning. In C. J. Thaiss & C. Suhor (Eds.), *Speaking and writing K–12* (pp. 144–187). Urbana, IL: National Council of Teachers of English.

Stepanek, J. (2001, Winter). Using standards to illuminate big ideas in science. *Northwest Teacher, 2*(1), 10–13.

Stigler, J. W., & Hiebert, J. (1999). *The teaching gap: Best ideas from the world's teachers for improving education in the classroom.* New York: Free Press.

Stigler, J. W., & Hiebert, J. (2004). Improving mathematics teaching. *Educational Leadership, 61*(5), 12–17.

Stoskopf, A. (2001). Reviving Clio: Inspired history teaching and learning (without high stakes testing). *Phi Delta Kappan, 82,* 468–473.

Strong, R., Thomas, E., Perini, M., & Silver, H. (2004, February). Creating a differentiated mathematics classroom. *Educational Leadership, 61*(5), 73–78.

Superka, D. P., Hawke, S., & Morrissett, I. (1980). The current and future status of the social studies. *Social Education, 44,* 362–369.

Topping, D. H., & McManus R. A. (2002). A culture of literacy in science. *Educational Leadership, 60*(3), 30–33.

Vitaska, D. (2002, September/October). The new language classroom. *Media & Methods, 39*(1), 10–13.

Walling, D. R. (2001). Rethinking visual arts education: A convergence of influences. *Phi Delta Kappan, 82,* 626–631.

Wolfe, P. (2001). *Brain matters: Translating research into classroom practice.* Alexandria, VA: Association of Supervision and Curriculum Development.

Yager, R. E., Aldridge, B. G., & Penick, J. E. (1983). Current practice: School science today. In F. K. Brown & D. P. Butts (Eds.), *Science teaching: A profession speaks.* Washington, DC: National Science Teachers Association.

Chapter 14

CURRENT DEVELOPMENTS ACROSS THE CURRICULUM

Ordinarily, most curricular change takes place within a given discipline, because the discipline tends to be the beginning point of curriculum work. In recent years, however, curriculum workers have become concerned with changes that transcend a single discipline, such as using writing to learn, improving thinking skills, speaking, listening, and the placing of the computer in the curriculum. Such changes require both a different perspective on curriculum change and different processes for planning and implementation. Questions addressed in this chapter include the following:

- What are some of the curriculum changes that are improving *writing skills*?
- What are some of the curriculum changes that are improving *thinking skills*?
- What are some of the curriculum changes that are improving *speaking skills*?
- What are some of the curriculum changes that are improving *listening skills*?

Key to Leadership

Successful curriculum leaders realize that the writing process is itself made up of a number of processes. As an act of making meaning, it assumes recursive movement through five major processes: prewriting, drafting, revising, editing, and publishing.

USING WRITING TO LEARN

State academic standards broadly support the writing process, including the planning (prewriting), drafting, revising, editing, and publishing (sharing) stages. There is also widespread recognition that a valuable part of the writing process is conferencing, either between teacher and student, student and student (often referred to as peer feedback), or both (Schuster, 2004). The interest in using writing as a way of learning, sometimes called "writing across the curriculum," stemmed initially from two intersecting research thrusts. One thrust was research into the composing process, derived from several detailed studies of how skilled and unskilled students write. Building upon a seminal study by Janet Emig (1971), numerous researchers have determined that skilled writers in general work through a process that includes several interactive and recursive stages:

1. Prewriting: the writer searches for a subject, gathers information, considers audience, reflects on purpose, and makes a tentative plan.

2. Drafting: the writer begins to write, using a word processor, typewriter, pen, or pencil.

3. Revising: almost as soon as the drafting process has started, the writer begins to evaluate what has been written and makes changes in the larger elements of content, order, paragraphing, and sentence structure.

4. Editing: at the end of a generally successful draft, the writer polishes, paying close attention to matters of form.

5. Publishing: the writer shares what has been written with the intended audience.

Students often use multiple writing strategies that differ across developmental stages (Dahl et al., 2003–2004). It is important that students use writing as a way of learning. The 6+1 Trait Writing Program was developed 20 years ago and has been consistently refined by teachers. The six-trait analytical model is centered on these six traits of writing: Ideas, Organization, Voice, Word Choice, Sentence Fluency, and Conventions. A study conducted in Portland, Oregon, by Northwest Regional Educational Laboratory indicated that using the six-trait writing process resulted in considerable gains in students' writing ability. This process is used in every state in the Union (Northwest Regional Educational Laboratory, 2001).

Regardless of the perspective and processes of writing, concern continues over plagiarism. This has been a major problem with the development and accessibility to the Internet. According to Doug Johnson (2004), the director of media and technology for Mankato Area Public Schools, educators are expending much effort trying to "catch" plagiarism in student work. Teachers and library media specialists use various Web services and Internet search techniques to detect student work that is lifted from online sources. Hopefully, educators will find effective ways to curb the problem of plagiarism.

Curriculum Tip

Skilled writing requires facility with a wide range of genres and accompanying purposes. Helping students acquire these multifaceted writing competencies is an important job for any curriculum leader.

Encouraging and developing quality student writing that is not plagiarized is the goal. To communicate effectively, student writers must achieve focus, clarity, and coherence using a suitable style, a meaningful organizational plan, and appropriate conventions (Henk, Marinak, Moore, & Mallette, 2003–2004). Writers must be reflective and regularly call upon their powers of analysis, synthesis, and evaluation.

According to Henk and colleagues, (2003–2004), curriculum leaders have seen a major shift in the basic way writing is taught within the past three decades. The focus has changed from evaluating students' written product to examining the processes that writers employ during writing.

Given cogent theoretical reasons, what response should local curriculum leaders make? According to educational consultants David and Meredith Liben (2004), students need to be aware not only of how to write, but also of how they learned to write. Glatthorn (1984) recommends a teacher-centered process that he has found useful in several staff-development workshops. This process asks teachers in each department to develop their own writing-to-learn framework. Teachers need first to identify what Glatthorn calls the "continuing" uses of writing in their discipline. These continuing uses are ways that teachers use writing in an ongoing manner, without making special assignments or giving special instructions; they include such uses as taking notes from lectures, taking notes from the text, writing essay answers, doing written exercises at home or in class, keeping a journal for that subject, and writing responses in class to clarify and fix learning.

Glatthorn next turns to what he calls *special* uses—writing tasks in that discipline that require special assignments and focused instruction. These special uses include the following: writing a report citing several sources, reporting on one's own investigations, describing one's problem-solving processes, translating from one symbol system to another, writing a creative paper based on that subject, writing about one's response to a work, explaining how that subject relates to one's personal life, explaining to other students how to do some process related to that subject, persuading students about some issue relating to that subject, and doing an exercise that teaches a thinking skill important in that subject.

Through discussion and analysis, therefore, each department identifies the special and continuing uses of writing that teachers consider appropriate for that subject. The final task in developing the framework is for the teachers in each department to identify the essential qualities they want evidenced in all longer pieces of writing in that discipline. Thus, science teachers might note the importance of objectivity and accuracy in reporting experiments, social studies teachers might recognize the careful use of historical evidence in supporting conclusions, English teachers might ascertain the value of creative personal responses in interpreting literature, and mathematics teachers might determine the need for precision in writing verbal translations of mathematical equations.

A sample framework summarizing all three types of information is shown in Exhibit 14.1.

With that framework established, each department would then develop instructional materials to support both the special and continuing uses. These instructional materials would typically include the following resources:

- A description of the composing process and a summary of the pertinent research
- A reproduction of the framework
- Suggestions for implementing the "continuing uses" proficiently
- Suggestions for making the "special-uses" assignments more productive

Exhibit 14.1   Framework for Writing to Learn Project

Department: Family and Consumer Science

The following *continuing uses* of writing are important in family and consumer science:

1. Taking notes from lectures and class discussions
2. Taking notes from texts and other resources
3. Keeping a home economics journal

The following *special uses* of writing are important in home economics:

1. Writing recipes
2. Writing directions for craft and decorating projects

The following qualities are considered essential to writing in home economics:

1. Precision in measurements and quantities
2. Clarity in giving directions

- Sample assignment sheets for the "special-uses" assignments
- Suggestions to the teachers on responding to and grading student writing
- Handouts for the students, clarifying matters of format and style and explaining the special qualities desired

Obviously, all this curriculum work would be supported by continuing staff development. Each set of departmental writing-to-learn materials would then be reviewed by curriculum leaders.

According to Gibbons (2004), research shows that with a shift in perspective, teachers can have students naturally connect new content to their personal knowledge and experience. This can be worked into various frameworks of instruction. The instructional leaders of the school would then examine all the frameworks together, to be sure that the total school writing-to-learn program seemed comprehensive, balanced, and likely to be effective.

The writing process is made up of a number of processes. As an act of making meaning, it assumes recursive movement through five major processes: prewriting, drafting, revising, editing, and publishing. Students need consistent experience with all five processes if they are to develop writing strategies, learn to consider alternatives, and mature in the writing process. Teachers need to model the process by writing with their students, demonstrating writing strategies, and sharing their finished products with students.

Because writing is primarily learned rather than taught, the role of the teacher shifts from instructor to facilitator. Instead of telling students what and how to write, teachers help students find their own topics and voices, model the processes and strategies, and foster an accepting and dynamic communication environment.

Thinking

The second major movement to effect improvements across the curriculum is the concerted effort to improve thinking. A major focus area for improving thinking is the engagement of students with content (Weiss & Pasley, 2004). High-quality lessons involving thinking skills generally invite students to interact purposefully with the content. Various strategies are used to involve students and to build on their previous knowledge using real-world examples or engaging students in firsthand experiences. This is one of the best ways to get students to think.

Another major strategy that involves the integration of thinking skills is the concept of metacognition, or, thinking about thinking. This is the process of becoming aware of and gaining control over our thoughts (Gibbons, 2004). Studies in metacognition have led to a number of applications in teacher-directed learning. Some of these focus on teaching students to relate academic success to personal effort rather than to chance. Other applications emphasize the teaching of self-regulation. Students learn the efficient management of their own participation, studies, and assignments. Other applications emphasize teaching students learning strategies, processes, and systems that they can apply to a range of tasks and situations—in other words, teaching students how to think and learn. Some individual teachers believe engaging students is not enough—they must be involved in a critical thinking process as well.

Bruce Smith (2004), editor of the *Phi Delta Kappan,* notes in his editorial that it is important for students to exchange ideas. Smith states that "there will be no give and take, no working out of differences, as long as 'memorize and test' is the dominant pedagogy and as long as test scores are the sole legal tender." He believes that "it is important for young people to be introduced to the marketplace of ideas and made to feel comfortable and competent there."

Many educators ask, "Can students learn to think critically if they are not asked to engage with critical issues?" According to Nel Noddings (2004), Lee Jacks Professor of Education Emerita, Stanford University, fostering critical thinking is frequently stated as a fundamental aim of education. Nevertheless, many teachers report that they have been forbidden to discuss such critical issues as wars, religion, or cultural differences in styles of parenting.

A second question that seems to divide the profession is whether thinking skills are more usefully perceived as a set of general processes that transcend the disciplines or as content-specific skills that should be anchored in a discipline. If thinking is a set of general processes, then these processes can best be taught in separate thinking courses. If thinking is subject-specific, then it is best taught within the context of a discipline.

Researchers are now finding that it is crucial to engage students in the process. Research results indicate that student success depends on three qualities of teaching: Teachers' content knowledge, pedagogy, and strong relationships with students (Lewis, 2004). Studies, reports, and initiatives affirm that engagement in learning, environments that value trust, and integrity in relationships between teachers and students and their families work together to make a critical difference in learning as it relates to subject-centered curriculum.

Both the general approaches and the subject-anchored materials suffer from perhaps the same weakness: They attempt to change the curriculum through a top-down process, asking teachers to use materials developed by central office staff. Others in the field are placing more emphasis on staff-development programs that teach teachers how to think critically and how to use their own curriculum as a means for improving student thinking.

Glatthorn (1985) has had some success in using such an approach. After reviewing current theory and research on thinking, teachers in each secondary department are first asked to select one of the following units of study as being most appropriate for each grade level they teach: controlled problem solving (using algorithms and heuristic strategies for solving convergent problems with one right answer); open-ended problem solving (using systematic strategies to find the optimal solution to an open-ended problem); information processing (storing, retrieving, and evaluating information); reasoning (the systematic application of logic); evaluating (using critical thinking processes to evaluate products and individuals); analyzing persuasive messages (including critical analysis of the mass media); mastering disciplinary inquiry (learning the special inquiry processes and truth tests used in a discipline); making moral choices (making ethical judgments); and using thinking in making other life choices (especially college and careers). These particular unit topics, focusing as they do on more general processes that are relatively simple to link to a given discipline, seem to appeal to most teachers as both important and subject-relevant. After each departmental team reaches a consensus on the units to be developed, the team works together to develop discipline-based instructional materials focusing on the general processes identified. They are thus able to produce a graded series of units that, while lacking professional sophistication, are likely to be used.

With that phase of the project accomplished, they turn their attention to specific thinking skills that were not incorporated into the units. They review a comprehensive list of such specific skills as classifying and making inferences and identify those that they think should be taught. In teams, they decide whether each skill so identified would be better taught in an "integrated" or a "focused" lesson (see Exhibit 14.2 for a form that can be used to assist teachers in making these decisions). In an *integrated* lesson, as the term is used here, a content objective (such as being able to describe Cortez's first meeting with Native Americans) is the focus of the lesson; the thinking skill (in this case, perhaps, contrasting) is taught as part of that lesson. In a "focused" lesson, a thinking skill, such as evaluating sources for bias, is the focus of the lesson. Subject content is merely the carrier.

Also worth noting are the Six Correlates of Effective Schools developed by Ronald Edmonds and John Frederickson (Taylor, 2002). The Six Correlates of Effective Schools are listed below:

- Clearly stated and focused school mission
- Safe and orderly climate for learning
- High expectations for students, teachers, and administrators
- Opportunity to learn and student time-on-task
- Instructional leadership by all administrators and staff members
- Positive home-school relations

The Effective Schools Process is considered by many a tried and true process of school change that can create schools in which all children make progress and are ready for study at the next grade level. To complement the Effective Schools Process, a number of schools are developing and using instructional design as well (March & Peters, 2002). The instructional design process can help schools to restructure the delivery and assessment of classroom instruction and to integrate thinking skills into the curriculum. If school leaders are to formulate an instructional design process to enhance the use of thinking skills, it is also important to involve three thinking skills strategies: Independent Thinking, Self-Managed Learning, and Self-Directed Learning (Gibbons, 2004, p. 466).

Independent Thinking requires students to address subsets of related questions and to develop essential skills outlined in the curriculum. Requirements include inquiry into essential questions that students pose for themselves. These pursuits are supported by a number of excellent instruments, practices, and services.

Self-Managed Learning requires that students have outcomes to achieve. Students make their own timetables; work alone; work with others; attend seminars, workshops, and labs; work online; and use other resources to help them in their self-regulated efforts.

Exhibit 14.2   Identifying Specific Thinking Skills

The following critical thinking skills are often taught in school subjects. Consider that skill and its importance in the subject and grade level you teach. Indicate your preference for teaching that subject by putting an (X) in the appropriate column. A *focused lesson* is one in which the thinking skill represents the main objective of that lesson. An *integrated lesson* is one in which a subject-matter concept or skill represents the main objective; the thinking skill is taught in the process of teaching that concept or skill. *Not Appropriate* means that you do not think that particular skill is appropriate for your subject or grade level.

Skill	Focused	Integrated	Not Appropriate
1. Finding and defining problems	_____	_____	_____
2. Representing problems in an appropriate symbol system	_____	_____	_____
3. Organizing facts and concepts in a systematic way	_____	_____	_____
4. Inferring a conclusion from what is stated	_____	_____	_____
5. Locating and evaluating sources	_____	_____	_____
6. Synthesizing information to reach a conclusion	_____	_____	_____
7. Distinguishing between observations, assumptions, and inferences	_____	_____	_____
8. Classifying logically	_____	_____	_____
9. Making predictions	_____	_____	_____
10. Interpreting nonliteral material	_____	_____	_____
11. Identifying persuasive messages and techniques	_____	_____	_____
12. Applying logical operations of negation, disjunction, and conjunction	_____	_____	_____
13. Making and using analogies	_____	_____	_____
14. Determining likely causes	_____	_____	_____
15. Explaining cause-and-effect relationships	_____	_____	_____
16. Avoiding misleading use of language	_____	_____	_____
17. Avoiding statistical fallacies	_____	_____	_____
18. Other:	_____	_____	_____

Self-Directed Learning requires that each day of the week is set aside for independent activities, regular education, trips, or challenging exercises. This may include the Walkabout program, logical inquiry, creativity, practical applications, or community activities. Students present their accomplishments to their peers, teachers, parents, and other adults at graduation. Individual work is supported by an adviser. According to Dave Brown (2002), Professor of Education at West Chester University, Pennsylvania, educational researchers dream about such a classroom, write about the possibilities, and encourage teachers and administrators to use such approaches as student choice, curriculum integration, differentiated learning, and self-assessment to engage students deeply into learning.

When focusing on the classroom restructuring process, it is important to place an emphasis on the integration of thinking skills. As part of this process, we find the development of activities in processing information, inventing and expanding upon ideas, and examining and evaluating facts and processes to be an essential part of every discipline. Similarly, thinking skills should be deeply embedded in all strands of the communication arts. Students must think to respond to literature, to write, to speak, to use media, to listen, and to read. In short, thinking skills provide students with the means to make the most effective use of all areas of their education.

It is important, in planning curricular strategies, to introduce thinking skills, to reinforce them throughout the content levels, and to build more complex processes on the foundation of skills introduced earlier. Students should be encouraged to "think about their thinking," examining the thinking skills and strategies they apply to interpret literature and media, to choose language, to make an appeal in advertising, or to follow directions.

Speaking

Children enter school with some basic competence in speaking, but without social contact and modeling, speech may not develop as it should. A child's self-concept is largely formed through interaction with significant people in the child's environment. The role of the teacher is to help students improve and refine their speaking skills in a variety of situations. Good speaking skills are important to students for their success in school and in the workplace. Employers frequently identify oral communication skills as the most important skills considered for initial employment, retention, and promotion. An average of 30% of our communication is spoken, and speech is second only to listening in frequency of use in everyday life. Speech has an important place in the curriculum.

Speaking is developmental. Instruction should be direct, frequent, and sequenced as the individual grows in proficiency. However, districts often see speech as limited to public speaking rather than intrapersonal, interpersonal, group, and mass communication. While speech instruction at the secondary level is often relegated to a speech elective, at other grade levels students often give speeches without receiving instruction on how to become better oral communicators.

Given the importance of speech and the position it has often had in the curriculum, districts developing speaking curricula should keep in mind the following statements. Instruction in speaking should (a) address the communication needs of students that arise from everyday situations; (b) provide direct instruction, supervised practice, constructive feedback, and more practice in a variety of situations rather than offering only opportunities to speak; (c) include all communication contexts, (e.g., intrapersonal, interpersonal, group, public, and mass communication); (d) be integrated with the teaching of all of the other communication arts strands;

(e) be interdisciplinary and across the curriculum; (f) offer opportunities for cocurricular programs that aid students in refining their speaking skills; and (g) be sensitive to the diversity of culturally appropriate speaking behaviors.

Listening

Listening is the first source of communication. By developing competent listening skills, one expands vocabulary, develops sentence structures, and begins to discriminate what is heard. Speaking, reading, and writing are built upon this foundation. Students come to school with some degree of competence in listening, acquired "naturally" in the developmental process. Consequently, often the most neglected area of instruction in the communication arts curriculum is listening. Many educators have assumed that listening skills can be developed by telling the students to listen and periodically reminding them they are not listening. Also, teacher education programs, textbooks, communication research, and assessments give little assistance in listening instruction. In spite of this neglect, the importance of listening in everyday life has long been documented. Listening is a skill that can be improved through direct instruction and practice. Students learn to hear accurately and evaluate what is said so they may respond in conversation and discussion.

Instruction in listening should

1. address communication needs of students that arise from real-life situations

2. involve direct teaching of listening strategies and practice of those strategies in a variety of listening situations

3. include listening in all communication contexts including interpersonal, small group, public communication, and mass communication

4. integrate with the teaching of all of the other communication arts strands

5. be interdisciplinary and across the curriculum

6. be incorporated in cocurricular programs that aid students in refining their listening skills

7. be sensitive to the diversity of culturally appropriate listening behaviors

THE COMPUTER AND THE CURRICULUM

After several decades of having computers in public education, it is amazing that questions still abound regarding their usefulness and purpose in the classrooms of the nation (Whitehead, Jensen, & Boschee, 2003). It is also interesting that governments, public businesses, and private enterprise are not asking these questions regarding implementing technology in their sectors. Schools have access to the same hardware that the external community does. They also have access to a plethora of software programs designed specifically to meet educational needs. For example, the Internet allows students to access real-world research in a variety of fields. Students can then help solve real-world issues using technology (Allen, 2004). Unlike the external community, most school districts have the ability to access a variety of means of financial support to implement technology in the classrooms. So why has business succeeded, and in what areas has education failed?

Changing Contexts

Layton (2000), in an article on digital learning, noted that administrative leaders have misdirected planning efforts by envisioning technological direction around where educators are and how to move forward. Instead, he suggested that we envision where we want to be and then work backward to design the appropriate frameworks to get us there. The important realization in this process is that students in the 21st century are different and do require different learning styles. This is especially true when applying new developments in distance learning. When examining the qualities of targeted distance learner groups, host institutions can develop electronic support tools to address a variety of needs effectively (Halpin, Scheer, & Lockee, 2003). Attempts to apply outdated models of technology use to current realities highlight why we are having a hard time realizing the full potential that technology can offer to learning environments of today.

The dilemma is that when implementing technology in the schools of America, we have not connected technology to the changing learning contexts needed by students. For example, there is the unwritten rule that schools should not buy technology unless they are certain they have the expertise to manage it (Van Horn, 2004). Under the existing structures, various entities concerned with technology and education have spent significant dollars in establishing school computer labs, but no one is managing them or assisting students. The problem with this approach is that computer labs counter the notions of time, relationships, flexibility, and learning style upon which students rely. As the President's Panel on Educational Technology stated, "One of the enduring difficulties about technology and education is that a lot of people think about the technology first and the education later, if at all" (Panel on Educational Technology, 1997). It is in response to this changing student context that educational administrators should consider adding technology classroom designs to their existing school infrastructures.

Technology can make a difference. As Lowell Milken of the Milken Foundation notes,

It is our experience and belief that technology—properly managed and applied—provides the opportunity to restore rigor to children's learning, to rebuild public confidence in American education, and to help ensure that the equality of opportunity in which we pride ourselves as a nation has meaning. (Peck, Cuban, & Kirkpatrick, 2002)

With an increase in interest in how technology can change schools, a continuing widespread introduction of computers into the schools has taken place in recent years. In 2000, the average public school contained 110 computers. One important technological advance that has come to schools following the introduction of computers has been connections to the Internet. The proportion of instructional rooms with Internet access increased from 51% in 1998 to 77% in 2000. About 98% of schools had access to the Internet in 2000 (see Exhibit 14.3 for the percentage of public schools having Internet access).

As can be seen, moving technology into our nation's classrooms has the capability of significantly reshaping education in America. Today's schools are exploding with new technological innovations and a host of educational changes. Satellite dishes are popping up on school roofs all over the nation, and fiber optic cables are being dropped through classroom ceilings. Two of the newest educational buzzwords are "video conferencing" and "virtual reality." Interested and knowledgeable teachers and administrators are becoming media specialists, and students are stepping into a learning environment that was unimaginable only a decade or two ago.

Exhibit 14.3   Percentage of All Public Schools and Instructional Rooms Having Internet Access: Fall 1994 to Fall 2000

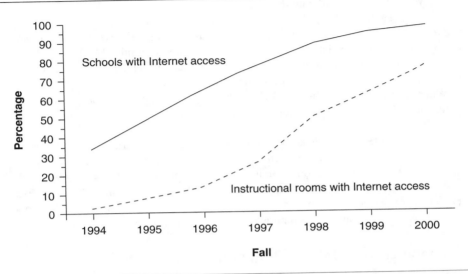

SOURCE: U.S. Department of Education, National Center for Education Statistics, Fast Response Survey System, Internet Access in Public Schools and Classrooms (1994–2000).

School Technology Realities

A careful look around the country reveals that some schools are making giant steps in their use of computer technology while a vast majority of schools and teachers remain tied to past educational strategies. As a result of limited funding for technology, most schools locate the majority of their computers not within the individual classrooms, but in specialized computer labs that are shared by all classes. This makes student computer use with small groups impractical in most classrooms. Knowledgeable school principals and superintendents are beginning to express concern over this state of affairs. These administrators feel a strong need to refocus district and state efforts to continue challenging school technology infrastructures so that they more appropriately address students' academic and social needs. With their help, a movement is now underway to bring the benefits of electronic information gathering and other technological advances to classrooms across America.

When school administrators and teachers begin to analyze the academic and social needs of their students carefully, they quickly see the value of putting technology into the hands of teachers and students. Researchers and educators are now discovering that a bank of four to six computers in a classroom is one of the most pedagogically sound ways to create connections between the curriculum and technology.

The success of state-of-the-art classroom technology centers is causing school administrators, board members or trustees, and teachers to shift their ideas of how technology best works in schools. Within this alternative structure, school administrators are compelled to ask several penetrating questions:

- Does the new technology enhance academic achievement?
- Can technology be integrated into our existing classroom arrangement and educational programs without significant disruption?
- Will the new technological approach have the impact we expect?
- Is changing our technological program worth the financial expenditures required to upgrade or replace existing facilities, equipment, and programs?
- Are new technological advances on the horizon that will render our intended equipment purchases obsolete in the not-too-distant future?
- Where can we go as a school (or school district) to get the best advice about serving our technological needs for upgrading or staying current?

At present, limited research is available that shows a correlation between increases in student achievement and the use of technology in schools. As a result, some people question technological changes in education when it is not clear to them that such resources are directly tied to student achievement. The reality is that new developments in technology, changing societal and career needs, and new learning strategies are challenging schools to accommodate a symbiotic relationship among technology, curriculum, and the learning environment.

The Computer as an Integral Tool in the Curriculum

Technology is not about how much hardware or software your school has, but rather what tools your teachers and students need (Sweeney, 2004). Computer-based instruction (CBI) is a broad term and refers to general use of the computer in an educational setting. Some of these uses include drill and practice, tutorials, simulations, instructional management, supplementary exercises, programming, database development, word processing, and networking. These may be stand-alone or enrichment activities.

Schools continue to offer courses and develop and adopt new class offerings as rapidly as technology changes in today's society. Programming classes are offered and updated as new hardware makes the classes more user friendly. Networking classes have taken shape as the Internet has become an expected tool in schools and classrooms rather than a luxury. More than 70% of teachers with high-speed Internet connections in their classrooms utilize this form of information technology for research (Becker, as cited in Means, 2000/2001).

Some examples of the Internet's usefulness as a tool in schools are cited by Means and Coleman (as cited in Means, 2000/2001). According to Elizabeth Anne Viau (2004), the World Wide Web can provide a number of avenues to learning. She notes that her students use the Internet as an information-rich playground of learning. According to Viau, her Web sites have clearly delineated major concepts, focused assignments, plenty of choices, and opportunities to exercise creativity. Almost any science department can benefit from using The Global Learning and Observations to Benefit the Environment (GLOBE) Web site, which allows students to participate in real science projects. Data from students are entered in the site's database and analyzed by scientists who depend on students for the information and interact with students in Web chats. Hands-On Universe from the University of California, Berkeley's Lawrence Hall of Science uses students to analyze images from space and search for supernovas and asteroids, while sharpening their research and astronomy skills. Some of these students have made discoveries that have been published in a scientific journal.

Elementary students have been able to find many uses for computer technology, such as art programs to make scientific drawings of penguins and newspaper publishing to culminate a unit on the Great Depression. Fourth- and fifth-grade students are trained in some districts to assist with younger students and teachers' computer instruction. These students also work with some senior citizens who come to school to learn about technology. High school students have produced portfolios demonstrating district computer technology competencies (O'Donnell, 2000). While computers and technology are tremendous assets to the learning community of any school, the integration of these machines and skills across the curriculum is where the real value is found.

Technology in schools is also benefiting the process of managing assessment. Data analysis is yielding immediate and easy-to-analyze results that appear to be improving learning (Roschelle, Penuel, & Abrahamson, 2004). As can be seen, classroom networks are able to overcome one of the greatest hurdles to improving classroom assessment: the collecting, management, and analysis of data. The networks make it easier for teachers to provide frequent formative assessment to all students.

One of the exciting, new technology tools to be integrated into the classroom is the digital whiteboard (Solvie, 2003). The digital whiteboard is an electronic version of a dry-erase board. The board can be written on with dry-erase markers or can be used with electronic or "virtual" markers. It has proven to be a useful organizational tool for both lesson preparation and instruction. The electronic whiteboard is only one of the many new technology devices being used extensively in the classroom. When looking for the right technology tool, budgetary issues and handheld computer uses are important (McAnear, 2004). A good source for finding out what is new and useful in the way of networking advances and new technology tools is to contact products@iste.org ("What's New," 2004).

The Computer as the Curriculum

With new developments in technology and communications, the computer has become a tool with which to deliver a total curriculum or course of study. For example, the Internet can yield rich resources for curriculum development. Teachers can use Web sites to see how others have created powerful learning around standards (Pearl, 2001). In addition, educators utilize a number of technology programs to deliver curriculum for a variety of uses in schools today. Some of these uses are, but are not limited to, offering dual college and high school credit for upper-level students in high schools; credit recovery; discussions; and collaborations among students from various locations in the state, country, or world; virtual schools; alternative virtual schools; and home-school uses.

Curriculum design can be greatly assisted by technology. Kristen Lee Howard (2004) notes how technology can be used in a Universal Design for Learning or UDL. Universal Design for Learning focuses on educators' using flexible curricula that provide students with multiple ways of accessing content, multiple means for expressing themselves, and multiple pathways for engaging their interest and motivation (see Exhibit 14.4 for an example of using the computer to manage curriculum). Howard advocates asking the following questions when planning curriculum:

- What is the basic idea that the students need to learn?
- What are different ways to learn this idea: Demonstration? Games? Shared experience?
- If reading is involved, do they have to read independently or can they use other tools and strategies to get the information?

Exhibit 14.4   The Computer as Manager of the Curriculum

Developing the Curriculum

1. Store and provide data on student achievement and interests
2. Locate and retrieve exemplary scope-and-sequence charts
3. Locate and retrieve objectives from objectives banks
4. Locate and retrieve exemplary learning activities
5. Locate and retrieve appropriate learning materials

Facilitating and Monitoring the Learned Curriculum

1. Using student achievement and interest data to identify appropriate objectives
2. Recording and storing student performance with individual learning objectives
3. Using performance data to suggest remediation, further exploration, or next new objective

Aligning the Curriculum

1. Storing written curriculum in retrievable form
2. Storing teacher reports of objectives taught; matching written and taught
3. Storing test items; matching test items with written and taught
4. Storing test scores; providing achievement data in usable form to teachers and administrators
5. Analyzing congruencies and discrepancies between two or more of the above

Evaluating the Curriculum

1. Storing, analyzing data on student and teacher perceptions
2. Storing, analyzing achievement data relevant to specific units, objectives

---

This type of curriculum planning greatly enhances the use of technology, computer networks, and the Internet.

Computer networks also use software designed to enhance communication between teacher and students. The computer network makes it easier for teachers to engage in best practices, facilitate group discussions, and provide timely feedback. There are some limitations in that some software and courseware packages are more reliable than others (Roschelle et al., 2004).

Curriculum Tip

Technology and data analysis help indicate what students are doing as well as what they are thinking, thus enabling teachers to enhance the natural communication flow in the classroom.

Student Achievement and Technology

Placing wide-area computer networks and other forms of advanced technology in schools has been taking place for a number of years. This implementation process has been expensive for school districts and, at times, a source of controversy and frustration for school boards, upper- and mid-level administrators, and teachers. This is mainly because technology has not yielded the expected curricular and student learner achievements once thought possible. On the other hand, a growing body of evidence now substantiates the notion that, when implemented appropriately, technology does have a relevant impact on student achievement.

Several beneficial outcomes have been noticed when a symbiotic relationship is established among technology, curriculum, and the learning environment. Some academic benefits of technology include the following:

- improving problem-solving skills significantly
- enhancing the quality and quantity of writing processes and content
- facilitating independent work, teamwork, and collaborative inquiry
- increasing performance in basic skills learning, especially in math and reading
- widening the scope of instructional opportunities
- increasing mastery of vocational and workplace skills
- promoting higher student retention rates
- encouraging higher-order thinking skills (organizing, analyzing, and communicating complex information)
- serving students with special needs effectively and efficiently (Chambers, 1999)

According to the available research on the effectiveness of technology in the student-learning environment, a variety of conclusions and opinions are offered. At one end of the continuum, supporters allude to research studies showing the positive impact of technology on student learning. At the other end of the spectrum, critics present little argument, if any, from the research to support the claim that the use of technology in classrooms is worthy of the resources it requires. The supporters of technology point out that, in addition to student achievement, creating a technology culture that is more indicative of student needs has made a significant impact in at least ten areas.

1. Increased student writing. Simply measuring the degree to which students are using computers to write reveals one positive impact of technology. Students are writing more compositions and doing so more often. Many teachers now find that students are producing three times the amount of written documents than they did before word processors were made available to them. Teachers who carefully watch students find that it often appears to be easier for their pupils to use a keyboard rather than a pen or pencil to write. The direct result is that students are writing more often and with seemingly greater ease. This trend is likely to become even more pronounced with the advent of voice recognition programs and other technological applications.

2. Higher-quality student writing. Analysis of student writing by numerous researchers has shown that word processing helps students become more effective writers. This is not surprising to anyone who uses word processing to any degree because today's user-friendly computers and powerful programs allow students to check grammar, spelling, and revise all or part of their work as often as they wish.

3. Enhanced cooperative learning. Schools whose teachers are using wide-area networked computers and a printer in classrooms are finding that this format enhances and supports cooperative learning strategies. By using classroom computer centers as learning stations, many teachers are finding it easier to have students engage in collaborative efforts. When collaborative learning is linked with technology, it is known to have a strong positive influence on student achievement.

4. Enhanced integration of curriculum. Teachers whose classrooms have access to the Internet and electronic scanning devices are finding that using computers can make it easier to integrate social studies, literature, math, and science into a more coordinated series of learning experiences for students. A practical example of this type of learning opportunity would occur when students use the Internet and scanner to create content-integrated presentations utilizing material from several disciplines. In addition, maps, graphs, tables, and illustrations from a variety of subject areas can be incorporated into student projects and visual presentations by means of computers.

5. Greater application of learning style strategies. A significant correlation exists between the use of technology and the ability to accommodate different student learning styles in the classroom. Rita Dunn (1995) pointed out in her research that multimedia computer technology is structured to enhance the visual, auditory, and kinesthetic components of student learning.

6. Increased applications of cross-age tutoring. Students having access to high-speed wide-area networked systems are now able to use computers at any site in the school district. As a result, teachers are finding that older students can work with younger students on cooperative or tutorial projects over the network.

7. Increased teacher communication. An analysis of message logs across school districts indicates an interesting trend. Teachers with access to e-mail and Internet services at their schools are communicating more with their administrators as well as with other teachers at the same grade level. Today's new wave of technological advances is allowing teachers to exchange information more easily with other educators on local, state, national, and international levels. A very positive consequence of this increased use of electronic communication is the improvement of communication among school staffs at all levels.

8. Greater parent communication. Voice mail as well as e-mail capabilities have provided a promising new link between home and school. Many teachers can now have parents contact the school via computer and receive updated reports on homework assignments and upcoming school activities. Looking at schools' message logs also demonstrates the impact and effectiveness of computers in helping to bridge the information and understanding gaps that can occur between school and home.

9. Enhanced community relations. Bringing the school and community together provides another compelling reason for implementing technology in schools. In many school districts, community residents and local business members are regularly invited to take part in on-campus training programs using classroom facilities and computer labs. As a result, adult education classes using technical instructors and school computer facilities are on the rise. In addition, students and teachers across the country are helping civic groups and small businesses develop Web pages, formulate listservs, and use e-mail.

10. Enhanced global learners. Never before have educators and students been able to develop a better understanding of other cultures and people than is possible today. Many schools are now using computers to access information from all parts of the globe. New advances in voice translation and voice recognition will improve this capability even more in the future. As one considers this phenomenon, it becomes increasingly evident that technology in schools is paving the way for students, teachers, and citizens to enter a new community of global learners.

Classroom Technology

New understandings of systemic leadership and management frameworks are melding with technological advancements to revitalize concepts and designs for the computer-aided classroom of the future. These new designs direct educational technology away from using it merely as a tool, to something that addresses the academic needs of a new generation of learners. The concentration of the melded leadership framework makes the implementation and regular use of technology student centered. The philosophy is to build awareness as well as a vision of how technology can advance education, enhance student opportunities for exploration, and provide a transition between present and future forms of learning.

This educational vision creates a suitable climate for the use of technological advances in both computer labs and classrooms. For those schools with access to computer labs, advances in technology are providing opportunities for teachers and students to use high-speed and high-memory machines to access the Internet as well as to assist with curricula programs. For the first time in our educational history, teachers and students will have the hardware, courseware, and service support to truly enhance curriculum and instruction in a lab setting. Some educators are deciding to make technology even more accessible by placing clusters of computers in their classrooms. Such opportunity is due to recent advances in technology that allow administrators to place a minimum of five high-quality networked computers and a printer in every classroom. Developing a cluster of classroom computers promotes collaboration and cooperative learning activities among students and creates an environment for school improvement.

In addition, computer networks now link classrooms with centralized file servers and provide powerful information-gathering tools for students and teachers. Many teachers are now finding that they are learning to use technology effectively in their classrooms because they have open access to the appropriate equipment and software programs. Ruth Wishengrad (1999), educational editor and former teacher, offered three reasons for making computers part of a student's regular classroom education:

1. Computers can make learning all subjects easier and are especially valuable in developing students' language and problem-solving skills.

2. Students can use computers to reach hundreds of telecommunication networks, and these sources provide a huge amount of information students cannot get from textbooks and more traditional learning tools.

3. Computer literacy (understanding computer technology) is necessary for many high-paying and interesting careers in a computer-dependent economy.

Innovative teachers now access and use information from a wide array of multimedia formats. Technologically integrated classrooms provide opportunities for using automated libraries, interactive video, voice recognition software, electronic whiteboards, flex cams, hypertext presentations, Internet access, CD-ROMs, cellular phones, and down-linked feeds to improve learning opportunities for students. As a result, teachers in technologically advanced schools are discovering that the classroom of tomorrow is here today. Nevertheless, no technology program or curriculum can be truly successful without quality staff development.

A key to quality staff development and curriculum delivery via technology is the formation of a teacher-to-teacher mentoring program. One of the first steps in developing a mentoring program is to assess and increase the teachers' comfort levels. Once the teachers are committed to a plan, they should follow steps as noted by authors Kathleen Gora, Janice Hinson, and Don Hall (2003–2004).

- Identify three or four topics or concepts to explore based on school goals.
- Submit a work plan with specific goals.
- Meet quarterly at designated times.
- Use expert teachers to learn new applications and techniques.
- Provide feedback on progress through group member surveys and mid- and end-of-year evaluations.

The development of a quality mentoring program to help integrate technology into the curriculum is an important aspect of the curriculum-planning process. To be effective, the mentoring process must be continually adjusted to enable every teacher to exhibit stronger technology-integration skills. With a quality mentoring program in place, teachers begin to see the real value of using technology in their classroom.

It has been said that we are living in the information age, but some theorists have suggested that we are now entering the learning age. The reality is that many people are also living and working in an age of increasing interconnectedness. There seems to be little doubt that new advances in technology are capable of providing America's classrooms and citizens with a new and long-awaited window to the world. Because students thrive on creating and being a part of a community, this technology design is beginning to make a difference in teaching and learning, as it is in society.

Developing Local Community Awareness

Michael Lowe (Lowe & Vespestad, 1999), a school principal in Lawrence, Kansas, declared that the overarching theme to be developed throughout new millennium schools involves the nature and significance of community. Increased community awareness of the uses of educational technology is directly impacting the role of technology in the classroom. According to author and psychologist Fredrick Bennett, educators, politicians, parents, and concerned citizens must understand how schools can use computers more effectively to improve education and to benefit students and teachers (Bennett, 2002). In many districts, parents and community members are now communicating with teachers in their classrooms via electronic mail, school hotlines, and interactive Web pages. In addition, some progressive schools are providing students and parents with portable laptop computers that can be used for homework or class projects.

Public involvement is growing in many schools as advances in educational technology occur and, as a result, community members are beginning to revise their views about education. Increasingly, business leaders are recognizing the connection between students' technological skills and their ability to be successful in the world of work. This consciousness has led to the formation of school-to-work programs funded by state money and local taxpayers. In addition, school/business partnerships are on the rise. Students and teachers routinely help business people by doing such things as creating Web pages for them. In return, local businesses often donate equipment to schools in an effort to capitalize on a new market for educational products. An important byproduct of these various forms of contact between schools and citizens is that community members are often more willing to support tax levies for education when they understand where their tax dollars are going. The resulting interaction between schools and community members is being seen more and more as a positive outcome for both groups.

School Technology Goals

A key standard for school jurisdictions to consider is the provision of four clear and practical technological goals that will expand the boundaries of traditional schooling and help children reach new levels of learning development. First, school administrators should coordinate school-based services and resources in order to heighten access to interactive technology for students in their schools. Statewide telecommunication infrastructures are usually most capable of providing the necessary level of linkage and delivery for schools.

Second, guidelines for equipment use and programs designed to enhance communication and technological awareness within communities need to be developed. A study in Ohio found that 77% of the school superintendents indicated they had a strategic plan in place, but only 28% had shared that vision or its accomplishments with their stakeholders; and 53% of the parents surveyed indicated that they had never received information about technology goals at their schools (Ohio SchoolNet Commission, 1999). Improved public awareness of the technology that is available often leads to a greater understanding of how technology can benefit students and citizens. Community appreciation also leads to the creation of shared vision and mission statements, joint technology committees, appropriate financing programs, infrastructure development, staff development, maintenance and service arrangements, favorable program evaluation, and finally, successful public relations programs. Education leaders must expand traditional school boundaries to involve the community in planning, financing, implementing, and evaluating technology.

Third, school leaders would be wise to share school success stories with their communities. Data obtained from student assessments can add substantial credibility to the positive things happening in schools when effectively presented to the public. This information can be easily retrieved and presented with the aid of computers.

Fourth, data from student assessments can provide school administrators and teachers with a valuable mechanism for checking exam results to ensure that student performance meets or exceeds local, state, and national standards. If required, a statewide data retrieval system for student performance could assist school leaders in determining aggregate achievement levels for all schools. As well, an accompanying item analysis of standardized test questions would provide administrators and teachers with a means of making a sound appraisal of strengths and weaknesses in the school or district curriculum.

It is through the development of clear public information programs that state legislators and citizens will best understand how technology is impacting student achievement. As community support increases, school leaders are better able to provide the administrative support necessary to accommodate the needs of teachers and students. Community support also breaks down classroom walls by making the positive activities in schools more visible and educators more accessible to parents. Computers and other technologies provide a practical avenue to connect teachers and students with learning opportunities that await them as they begin to make contact with the rest of the world. There is little doubt that leading-edge technology holds the promise of many positive elements for American education. A few of these positive outcomes would be the fostering of exploratory learning, the empowering of teachers, and the equipping of school leaders with advanced resources needed to manage schools. In reality, the task of illuminating the role of technology in our nation's classrooms is a complex and important one. It is only through an effective public information campaign that policymakers, practitioners, and citizens can be equipped with the facts needed to make wise decisions about the new electronic advancements available to their schools.

State and National Levels of Awareness

State and national organizations are now working to develop a shared vision that will establish a workable frame of reference for school technology programs. It is crucial that education leaders at state and national levels develop a coordinated plan directed at helping schools use technology. It is unfortunate that, at present, state and federal agencies often confound this process by duplicating each other's efforts. While numerous government agencies are capable of providing financial and technical support to schools, they are often unable to offer this aid efficiently. As a result, many schools are trying to work with a mishmash of networks, database providers, hardware and courseware applications, and all of the difficulties associated with such a technological conglomeration. In practice, this uncoordinated array of appliances and applications creates confusion for educators. Fortunately, a concerted effort is under way to eradicate this problem. In an effort to improve the situation, savvy school leaders are spearheading a movement to develop new frameworks for including influential noneducators into the brainstorming and implementation process before bringing new technologies into their districts.

The creation of national and state standards for the use of computers and other electronic resources is a major factor in the development of an overall plan to deal with the complexity of today's hi-tech educational landscape. The National Council for the Accreditation of Teacher Education (NCATE), for example, requires schools of education to meet verifiable technology standards for program accreditation. This accreditation body recognizes the importance of advanced technology in schools and supports this stance by stating that technology needs to move from the periphery to the center of teacher education.

Many local and state educational leaders are considering a proposal to collaborate closely with the U.S. Department of Education on matters related to computers in schools. The results of these coordinated efforts would be specifically directed at better understanding of Internet use, the integration of curriculum via technology, software and courseware development, and course content for technology classes. This national organization will be composed of a consortium of capable people from the ranks of higher education, business, research institutes, and governmental agencies. The intention will be to share research information and data from many sources to develop a national technology initiative. The outcome of subsequent proposals made by the national and state technology task forces will be to place a greater emphasis on technology in classrooms by fostering close cooperation among teachers, administrators, parents, experts from higher education, and business. Individual states are also moving forward with initiatives designed to capitalize on the benefits of technology for schools and students. Some perceptive state lawmakers are advancing legislation to provide teachers with computer skills to allow for a wider use of technology in classrooms, while legislators in other states are establishing statewide standards to regulate the use of desktop computers in schools and classrooms.

STRATEGIES FOR SUCCESS

To be successful in our increasingly technological world, all learners and educators must be skilled in the use of computers. Also, to bring about change and establish equity, factors such as proper training programs, technical support, and time for learning must be provided simultaneously for educators. Goals to be successful with technology include the following:

- Community involvement in planning and implementing the use of computers and other technology in schools should be a high priority for school leaders.
- Developing quality technological leadership and planning for effective computer use within the jurisdiction must receive considerable attention.
- Finances for computers and other forms of school technology should come from the district's general budget.
- Emphasis should be placed on incorporating computer learning centers into classrooms.
- Curriculum should use technology, but not be driven by it.
- Staff development involving technology should be made highly practical by having "teachers instruct teachers."
- Planning and implementation phases for the inclusion of new technology should include assessment and evaluation standards.
- A well-planned public relations program should be used to share the benchmarks of a successful program with the community.

In our rapidly changing world, the economic vitality of communities and individuals will depend more and more on the ability to access information, build knowledge, solve problems, and share success. Because technology will increasingly play a key role in this process, students must develop the necessary skills to use computers capably while they are in school (see Exhibit 14.5 for an example of proposed scope and sequence for information technology education). This means that today's students must be prepared now for the technological world that will be a very real part of their lives in the future.

Exhibit 14.5   Proposed Scope and Sequence: Information Technology Education

Grade	Subjects		
	English	Social Studies	Science
5	Talking with computers		How it works: broadcast and video
6		Computers in our community	How it works: lasers; sound and sight
7		Doing what's right with computers and video	How it works: the computer
8	Using, not being used by, the new technology		Scientific discovery in the new technology
9	The computer as a communications medium	The new technology and politics	
10	The new technology as art		
11	Careers in the new technology	The new technology shapes our society	
12	The new technology and the future	Ethical choices and the new technology	

FUTURE CHALLENGES

One might say that "technology is here to stay." The 88 million children of baby-boomer adults find using digital technologies no more intimidating than using a VCR or a toaster. These children are often referred to as the Net Generation because they are media literate and watch much less television than their parents did at the same age. Two thirds of the children today use a personal computer either at home or at school, which implies that they want to be active participants, not just viewers or listeners. In fact, television to many in the current generation is somewhat old-fashioned. A survey by Teenage Research Unlimited in which more than 80% of the teenagers polled said it is "in" to be online, and puts being online on a par with dating and partying (Tapscott, 1998). To meet the challenge for the future, the following questions beg for answers:

- How do we engage youth in our schools to be active participants in all of our class-rooms with online activities?
- If only 20% of the 2.5 million teachers who work in our public schools feel comfort-able using technology in their classrooms, what must a school district do to make 100% feel comfortable with technology?

The Claremont Unified School District in California answers the question, "What must a school district do to make 100% feel comfortable with technology?" The school district developed a district-wide Educational Technology Master Plan. The document includes the following language:

Preparing the Claremont Community; students, faculty and parents to function successfully in the world today and tomorrow is one of the primary aims of education. As we have changed from an industrial society to an information society, the projected impact of technology on our lives makes the development of technology literate students an increasingly necessary goal of education. The students of the Claremont Unified School District will be continuously educated in the effective use of technology at each grade level K–12.

Technology in the form of telecommunication networks, microcomputers, and audio/video equipment is becoming an increasingly important resource for instruction as well as an integral part of the worlds of work and home. We believe this document will insure [sic] the delivery of a common core technology curriculum to all students and assist sites in their development of individual school technology plans. Furthermore, this document provides the guidelines for the integration of such technology into the instructional programs for the students in the Claremont Unified School District. (See Education Technology Master Plan at http://www.cusd.Claremont.edu/tech/plan/intro.html for the complete document.)

Today, with the heightened national interest in improved student performance, high-stakes testing, and school accountability, the school administrator's role must change. Traditionally, principals have been seen as managers responsible for implementing district policies. Until the arrival of the information age, the mentality of school administrators was, "If it ain't broke, don't fix it." At present, because investments in equipment have not always been accompanied by changes in teaching, school administrators must take on the role of leadership. Teachers need help to overcome obstacles and integrate technology into their instructional practice. The overriding question is, "What must school administrators do?" Also, if computer technology is to help create a more egalitarian society, disparities in the quality of home and school access across different socioeconomic groups must be addressed.

As educators give further thought to the impact of technology in our present world, and as they consider the nature of the world our children will inherit from us, it becomes readily apparent that we must carefully meld computers and other technologies into the current structure of individual classrooms. The potential for creating schools and school districts of high quality is possible only through the timely and adroit application of existing knowledge. In order to benefit from this knowledge, it is important that a comprehensive blueprint be adopted and followed. It is generally recommended that educators and community leaders carefully consider and adhere to suggestions in this book as they explore unique ways on how to integrate technology into the curriculum to enhance student learning.

MEDIA TECHNOLOGY

As our society continues to advance in the information and learning age, the importance of media within the school's overall curriculum increases. In today's technological world, the communication of information and ideas is channeled through a variety of computers and media; each is appropriate for a particular type of message. Information and ideas thus received can be assimilated, organized, and communicated to others using computers and media.

Instructional programs must effectively integrate media throughout the curriculum. The basis of this integration is a media skills program that offers students the opportunity (a) to become fluent users and producers of media, (b) to use media resources effectively in everyday learning process, and (c) to demonstrate awareness of the manipulative power of the media.

Students need the tools to efficiently search through and make use of the ever-growing numbers of information source levels. Teaching should support continuous, natural, and increasingly sophisticated use of media and should include regular use of the library/media center. To the extent possible, assistive technology should be used to help learning-impaired children achieve their educational goals. Media literacy must take a vital place in our national school curricula.

CHAPTER OVERVIEW

This chapter addresses curricular changes that transcend a single discipline. The major curricula changes include using writing to learn, improving thinking skills, speaking, listening, and the placing of the computer in the curriculum. Transcending the discipline to address these skills requires both a different perspective on curriculum change and different processes for planning and implementation.

CHAPTER TERMS

Writing Across the Curriculum	Metacognition
Writing Process	Effective Schools Process
Six-Trait Analytical Model	Universal Design for Learning
Writing to Learn	

APPLICATIONS

1. Develop the outlines of a writing-to-learn project that could be used in a subject or discipline you know well. Use the framework suggested in Exhibit 14.1 to describe the major components of the program.

2. If you were charged with the responsibility of developing a district curriculum in critical thinking, would you recommend developing separate courses, integrating critical thinking into existing courses, or using both approaches? Provide a rationale for your recommendation.

3. Consider the four uses of the computer in relation to the curriculum: the computer as developer, the computer as deliverer, the computer as a tool, and the computer as the curriculum. As you assess the needs of a school system with which you are familiar, how would you prioritize these four approaches? What systematic processes would you use in making such a determination?

4. As reported in Chapter 2, the reform report *A Nation at Risk* identified "computer literacy" as one of the "Five New Basics" and recommended that a one-semester course in computer literacy be required for each high school student. What is your assessment of the wisdom of such a suggestion?

5. One of the issues dividing specialists in early childhood education is how much use should be made of the computer as an instructional tool for the early elementary grades. Based upon your knowledge and your values, explain the position you would take on this issue and the reasons you would advance in support of your position.

CASE STUDY

This case study provides an example of how a principal solves the problem of a fifth-grade teacher who is not using the Writing to Learn Project—a district-mandated curriculum program.

"I've noticed that our fifth-grade students are not using the school district's Writing to Learn Project," states Principal Drucker. "Is there a reason that we are not using this program?"

Fifth-grade teacher Pam Hollenbeck looks up from her desk. "That is correct. I just don't have the time to work this program into my schedule. There are so many other subjects during the day that I cannot get to it."

"I realize that time is a concern," says Principal Drucker. "Nevertheless, according to our curriculum and district policy in regards to that curriculum, we will have to find a way to incorporate the 'Write to Learn Project.' This is a mandatory project."

Mrs. Hollenbeck realizes that the principal is very concerned and quickly comprehends the seriousness of the situation. "Well, I don't know. I suppose that I can incorporate my social studies, science, and art into a language arts block," says Hollenbeck as she reflects on the problem. "It will mean, however, that I will have to cut back on individual subject areas. Is that okay with you?"

"Yes," says the principal. "We can look at parallel curriculum, compacting, as well as other curriculum strategies to gain more instructional time in your classroom. The Writing to Learn Project should go nicely with this type of approach. What do you need in the way of some staff development training or time to get this up and running?"

"Well, one of my students is using a word processing program to write a great story on Seaman, Captain Lewis's dog, the Newfoundland dog that accompanied the men throughout the Lewis and Clark expedition. Students also made a PowerPoint presentation of the story and sent it by e-mail attachment to all of the fourth-grade teachers in the district. The fourth grade is trying to develop a new course on Montana history."

"Yes, I received a nice note from the fourth-grade teachers," says the principal. "The teachers loved it! It is really great that we have secondary students providing new course materials via technology for our elementary grades. Would it be possible for your high school students to come over to the elementary grades to put on a presentation?" he asks.

"Sure!" says the teacher. "They would like that very much!"

THE CHALLENGE

Teacher Pam Hollenbeck uses technology successfully to improve student writing and thinking skills. What specific steps can Principal Drucker take to get his other teachers to use these ideas and strategies? What kind of resistance might he encounter from teachers and staff?

Key Issues/Questions

1. Is it possible to bring a school facing the problem of unsatisfactory student writing levels up to national standards with the use of technology? Why or why not?

2. What are your impressions of Pam Hollenbeck's program in this Montana high school. Can this program be replicated in other states using their own history as a guideline?

3. What are some of the problems that educators face as they begin using the computer as a deliverer of the curriculum?

4. What other innovative technology strategies can be used to improve student writing and thinking skills? How can a high school principal best initiate these strategies?

5. How does computer technology use in a middle and high school differ from how it is used in an elementary classroom setting?

REFERENCES

Allen, R. (2004, February). Web wonders. *Educational Leadership*, *61*(5), 92.

Bennett, F. (2002). The future of computer technology in K–12 education. *Phi Delta Kappan, 83*(8), 621–623.

Brown, D. (2002). Self-directed learning in an 8th grade classroom. *Educational Leadership, 60*(1), 54–59.

Chambers, L. (1999). Does technology improve student learning? *Changing Schools, 1–2*, 8.

CUSD Instructional Center. (2005). *Educational technology master plan.* Retrieved March 29, 2005, from: http://www.cusd.claremont.edu/tech/plan/intro.html

Dahl, K., Bart, A., Bonfils, A., Carasello, M., Christopher, J., Davis, R., Erkkila, N., Glander, S., Jacobs, B., Kendra, V., Koski, L., Majeski, D., McConnell, E., Petrie, P., Siegel, D., Slaby, B., Waldbauer, J., & Williams, J. (2003–2004). Connecting developmental word study with classroom writing: Children's descriptions of spelling strategies. *Reading Teacher, 57*(4), 310–321.

Dunn, R. (1995). Analysis of learning research. *Educational Research Newsletter, 8*(5), 6.

Emig, J. (1971). *The composing processes of twelfth graders.* Urbana, IL: National Council of Teachers of English.

Gibbons, M. (2004). Pardon me, didn't I just hear a paradigm shift? *Phi Delta Kappan, 85*(6), 461–467.

Glatthorn, A. A. (1984). *Writing to learn.* Unpublished manuscript, University of Pennsylvania, Philadelphia.

Glatthorn, A. A. (1985). *Teaching critical thinking: A teacher-centered process.* Unpublished manuscript, University of Pennsylvania, Philadelphia.

Gora, K., Hinson, J., & Hall, D. (2003–2004, December/January). Teacher-to-teacher mentoring. *Learning & Leading With Technology,* pp. 36–39.

Halpin, D. M., Scheer, S. B., & Lockee, B. B. (2003). Supporting distance learners: The IT studio model. *Instructional Journal of Instructional Media, 30*(4), 343.

Henk, W. A., Marinak, B. A., Moore, J. C., & Mallette, M. H. (2003–2004). The writing observation framework: A guide for refining and validating writing instruction. *Reading Teacher, 57*(4), 322–333.

Howard, K. L. (2004, February). Multidisciplinary universal design: Meeting the needs of all students. *Learning & Leading With Technology,* p. 26.

Johnson, D. (2004). Plagiarism-proofing assignments. *Phi Delta Kappan, 85,* 549–552.

Layton, T. (2000, September). Digital learning. Why tomorrow's schools must learn to let go of the past. *Electronic School.Com,* p. 6.

Lewis, A. C. (2004). Schools that engage children. *Phi Delta Kappan, 85*(7), 483–484.

Liben, D. M., & Liben, M. (2004). Our journey to reading success. *Educational Leadership, 61*(6), 58–61.

Lowe, M. J., & Vespestad, K. (1999). Using technology as a tool to enhance learning. *NASSP Bulletin, 83*(607), 30–35.

March, J., & Peters, K. (2002). Curriculum development and instructional design in the effective school process. *Phi Delta Kappan, 83,* 379–381.

McAnear, A. (2004, February). Finding just the right tool. *Learning & Leading With Technology,* p. 4.

Means, B. (2000/2001, December/January). Technology use in tomorrow's schools. *Educational Leadership, 58*(4).

Noddings, N. (2004). War, critical thinking, and self-understanding. *Phi Delta Kappan, 85,* 489–495.

Northwest Regional Educational Laboratory. (2001, March/April). *6+1 Trait Writing research: Study findings on the integration of writing assessment & instruction.* Retrieved April 10, 2005, from the Northwest Regional Educational Laboratory Web site on http://www.nwrel.org/assessment/department.php?d=1

O'Donnell, J. (2000, October). What students want to learn about computers. *Educational Leadership, 58*(2).

Ohio SchoolNet Commission. (1999). Data from the Ohio SchoolNet Commission survey results. Washington, DC: KPMG Economic Consulting Service.

Panel on Educational Technology. (1997, March). *Report to the President on the use of technology to strengthen K–12 education in the United States.* Washington, DC: President's Committee of Advisors on Science and Technology.

Pearl, A. (2001, Winter). Technology and standards: Connecting to curriculum. *Northwest Teacher, 2*(1), 14.

Peck, C., Cuban, L., & Kirkpatrick, H. (2002). Techno-promoter dreams, student realities. *Phi Delta Kappan, 83,* 472–479.

Roschelle, J., Penuel, W. R., & Abrahamson, L. (2004). The networked classroom. *Educational Leadership, 61*(5), 50–53.

Schuster, E. H. (2004, January). National and state writing tests: The writing process betrayed. *Phi Delta Kappan, 85,* 375–378.

Smith, B. M. (2004). No time for thinking [Editorial]. *Phi Delta Kappan, 85,* 482.

Solvie, P. A. (2003). The digital whiteboard: A tool in early literacy instruction. *Reading Teacher, 57*(5), 484–487.

Sweeney, J. P. (2004, March/April). Does your school need high-tech? *Principal, 83*(4), 65.

Tapscott, D. (1998). The Net generation and the school. *The Milken Exchange on Education and Technology.* Retrieved April 14, 2005, from: http://www.mff.org/edtech/article.taf?_function=detail&Content_uid1=109

Taylor, B. O. (2002). The effective schools process: Alive and well. *Phi Delta Kappan, 83*(5), 375–378.

Van Horn, R. (2004). Technology and common sense. *Phi Delta Kappan, 85*(7), 553.

Viau, E. A. (2004, February). Building a world. *Learning & Leading With Technology*, pp. 18–19.

Weiss, I. R., & Pasley, J. D., (2004). What is high-quality instruction? *Educational Leadership, 61*(5), 24–28.

What's new. (2004, February). *Learning & Leading With Technology,* p. 42.

Whitehead, B. M., Jensen, D. F. N., & Boschee, F. (2003). *Planning for technology: A guide for school administrators, technology coordinators, and curriculum leaders.* Thousand Oaks, CA: Corwin.

Wishengrad, R. (1999). Are paper textbooks ready to fold? *Education Digest, 64*(6), 57.

Chapter 15

INDIVIDUALIZING THE CURRICULUM

Plato may have been one of the first writers to recommend individualization through tracking. In his *Republic,* Plato made clear his belief that children should be directed toward roles of philosopher, guardian, or artisan based upon their talents. While contemporary educators reject such a deterministic differentiation, the search for curricula that respond to individual differences continues. The search is one that involves curricula promoting student choice, curriculum integration, differentiated learning, and self-assessment that engage students deeply in learning (Brown, 2002). This chapter analyzes the types of individualized programs, reviews previous attempts to respond to individual differences, and assesses current models. The chapter concludes by examining the challenging problems inherent in providing for very special student populations. Questions addressed in this chapter include the following:

- What early attempts were made to individualize curriculum?
- What are some examples of current individualized programs, and why are they considered to be successful?
- What individualized adaptive approaches are being used in gifted education, and are they considered successful?
- What are some examples of specialized curriculum, and how are they enhancing the concept of individualization?
- What role does bilingual education play in individualizing curriculum?

Key to Leadership

Successful curriculum leaders know that an important aspect of any curriculum change is that it relates to standards and that it can be translated into individual academic performance indicators.

TYPES OF INDIVIDUALIZED PROGRAMS

It would be useful to begin the analysis by clarifying the concept. Here it seems wise to substitute the clearer term *adaptive* for the more ambiguous *individualized.* Largely because of the vague and conflicting connotations associated with the latter term, specialists in the field often refer to *adaptive* curricula and *adaptive* instructional practices.

Curriculum Tip

Adaptive curricula and instructional practices are educational processes that arrange the conditions and materials of learning so that they fit individual learner differences.

According to Dave Brown (2002), Professor of Education at West Chester University Pennsylvania, adaptive and instructional practices involve students in developing their own curriculum; study methods and assessments are built around questions that are important to the students. Involving students in curriculum development encourages them to explore the topics they study deeply and allows them a voice of their own as well as opportunities to share their learning with the community. Students and teachers in this type of program are generally revitalized and refreshed as they experience the benefits of the processes' self-directed, integrated curriculum (Brown, 2002).

The National Association for the Education of Young Children (NAEYC & NAECS/SDE, 2004) has drafted a series of indicators that best reflect the design of this type of curriculum. These indicators include the following:

- Children are active and engaged.
- Goals are clear and shared by all.
- Curriculum is evidence-based.
- Valued content is learned through investigation, play, and focused, intentional teaching.
- Curriculum builds on prior learning and experiences.
- Curriculum is comprehensive.
- Professional standards validate the curriculum's subject-matter content.
- The curriculum benefits children.

As noted by the National Association for the Education of Young Children, it is important to realize the overarching need to create an individualized and integrated curriculum that addresses the needs of all children. Such a curriculum has the capacity to support learning and development for children living in poverty, children with disabilities, children whose home language is not English, and children who need to be academically challenged. The focus needs to be on believing that students with the interest, motivation, and capacity for learning should be challenged in every classroom, each and every day (Page, 2000).

PREVIOUS ATTEMPTS TO INDIVIDUALIZE

A major challenge facing our schools today is the diversity of students. Consider the range of abilities present in most classrooms in U.S. education during its long history. Visualize that both extremes of the learning curve are equally far removed from the norm (Winebrenner, 2000). As Grinder and Nelsen (1985) note, attempts to individualize education in the United States go back to Colonial times, a period they characterize as individualized instruction by default. One hundred youngsters would be seated in a large ungraded classroom, working on exercises, while one teacher monitored their work. The need to educate large numbers of children in a more systematic manner led 19th-century educational reformers to institute graded classrooms, each with a teacher in charge, presenting a standard program. While this self-contained graded classroom has persisted as the norm for at least 100 years, during this time numerous attempts have been made to break out of the constraints imposed by standardized education. Rather than presenting a comprehensive historical review of such attempts, the discussion that follows concentrates on those approaches that persist to the present (for a fuller discussion of the history of individualized instruction, consult the Grinder and Nelsen work).

Providing Elective Courses

During the first century of American education, educators seemed concerned solely with identifying the common curriculum for all students; electives as such were not even considered. Even though Charles Eliot was chairman of the Committee of Ten, he was not able to persuade the committee that electives were desirable; the only option provided in their recommendations was that bookkeeping and commercial arithmetic could be substituted for algebra (see Committee of Ten, 1893). The first official statement recommending elective courses was the *Cardinal Principles of Secondary Education,* published by the Commission on the Reorganization of Secondary Education in 1918. In their formulation of the ideal program, the commission recommended a balance between the constants (those courses to help all students achieve essential goals), curriculum variables (special courses determined by the student's specific educational and career goals), and free electives (courses chosen in response to special interests).

For the past 70 years, the debate over what constitutes the best balance of these three components has continued unabated. The debate has not been informed by rational analysis and too often has produced prescriptions that reflect only the participants' biases about the need to control the education of the young.

Curriculum Tracking

Tracking of students should also be an area of discussion. According to Janet Atkins and Judy Ellsesser (2003), conversations with an online teachers' network reveal different experiences with tracking and reflections on its implications for students. Curriculum tracking, sorting students into somewhat rigid tracks based upon career and educational goals, was probably first formally recognized as a desirable practice by the Committee of Ten. Their report recommended four tracks, differentiated chiefly by the language studied: Classical,

Latin Scientific, Modern Languages, and English. The committee was quite explicit about the relative qualities of those four: "The programs called respectively Modern Languages and English must in practice be distinctly inferior to the other two" (p. 48). Thus, the practice of tracking and the status accorded to certain tracks have continued for almost 100 years; all that changes are the number of tracks and their names. Most high schools now provide for three tracks, determined primarily by educational and career goals: college preparatory, general, and vocational/technical.

Curriculum Tip

Research suggests rather clearly that curriculum tracking is not a useful way of responding to individual differences.

Janet Atkins and Judy Ellsesser (2003) quote a teacher from Alaska as stating,

> Whenever we start leveling and tracking our students we send a loud, personal message to each student. It is important to never forget that these students will be next to voice opinions about what is right or wrong about their own children's education. (p. 46)

As a result, many schools have eliminated tracked classes and have adopted a universal accelerated program and instituted heterogeneous grouping, with dramatic results. Using this type of curriculum reform, high achievers seem to be doing better and more students are becoming high achievers (Burris, Heubert, & Levin, 2004).

Offering "Mini-Courses"

As noted in Chapter 2, many school districts attempted to give students content options within a field of study by developing mini-courses lasting from 6 to 18 weeks. Rather than taking English II, students could choose from an array of offerings with titles such as *Women in Literature, The Mass Media,* and *The Search for Wisdom.* While such mini-courses were more often developed in the fields of English and social studies, they could also be found in science and mathematics; in fact, many schools prided themselves on offering more than 200 mini-courses.

The mini-course approach was highly popular with teachers, because it enabled them to develop and teach courses relating to their special interests and knowledge. Most schools using a mini-course curriculum reported high levels of student satisfaction. Most of these courses seemed poorly designed, however. They seemed not to have been produced with some overall conceptualization of that field and gave scant attention to important skills and concepts. Thus, the claim that this *smorgasbord curriculum* contributed to the decline in academic achievement seems warranted, even though no persuasive empirical evidence was evident on this point.

Open Classrooms

The open classroom popular during the late 1960s and early 1970s attempted to respond to individual differences in several ways. First, open classroom teachers felt less constrained by district curriculum guides and fashioned curricula that they believed responded to the special needs and interests of their pupils. While elementary teachers in open classrooms all taught language arts, social studies, mathematics, and science, they chose content that they believed would be most meaningful to their pupils, and that content typically involved the integration of several subject fields. Second, pupils had some options about their use of time: They could work in special learning centers any time during the day, unlimited by bells and artificial distinctions between subjects; and they could spend as much time as they needed. They also had some choice about activities and materials; the learning centers were usually provisioned with a rich assortment of materials for learning. Finally, there was an atmosphere of informality, which advocates believed was truly individualized: Pupils could talk together and move about the room as necessary.

The open classroom movement was short-lived, succumbing to conservative pressures for more teacher control and higher achievement in the basics. Its rapid demise was probably unfortunate.

Self-Paced Instruction

During the 1960s and 1970s, there was also much interest in several varieties of self-paced instruction, usually called *individualized learning*. While these programs varied in their details, they shared several common elements:

- The curriculum is analyzed into several components, arranged in a tightly controlled sequence.
- The learner is assessed and placed appropriately along that sequence.
- The learner works on self-instructional packets or lessons, usually in isolation, in order to achieve clearly specified objectives.
- The learner gets feedback about progress and remediates where necessary.

In most such programs, only the pace of learning (and, concomitantly, the time spent on learning a particular set of objectives) is adapted to learner needs; every other important element is controlled and standardized.

An important aspect of self-paced programs is the emphasis on using a multitude of textbooks and packaged materials. According to Valerie Chapman, University of Texas, El Paso, and Diane Sopko, Tarleton State University, Fort Worth, Texas (2003), having students reading combined textbooks is much like peeling an onion. When students use textbooks, they read in layers. The layers include illustrations, informational text, and narrative text, as well as additional details such as directions and borders. Learning how to read a variety of texts helps develop a sense of organization for self-paced learners.

CURRENT ADAPTIVE APPROACHES

An important aspect of any adaptive approach is that it relates to curriculum standards and that it is able to be translated into academic performance indicators with well-organized unit plans and congruent unit objectives (March & Peters, 2002). Educational consultants Judith March and Karen Peters note nine important factors for developing a new curriculum design or approach:

- Greater attention to problem solving
- Focus by the entire staff on the most important parts of curriculum
- Alignment of expected outcomes
- Connections between subject areas through curriculum mapping
- Inclusion of a variety of methods (inquiry, guided discussion, action research)
- Authentic performance assessments
- Multiple opportunities for teachers to collaborate
- High-quality materials
- Consistency in preparation of students for following grade

Curriculum Tip

Awareness and a willingness to actually restructure and realign the classroom curriculum is the key to developing successful adaptive change.

To assist in the curriculum design process, five major adaptive approaches will be addressed: the adaptive learning environments model (ALEM), cooperative learning models, learning-styles models, mastery learning models, and computer-based models. Because computer-based models were reviewed in the previous chapter, this section examines the other four models. In each case, the discussion below describes the model and reviews the research on its effectiveness.

Adaptive Learning Environments Model

The adaptive learning environments model (ALEM) was developed at the Learning Research and Development Center of the University of Pittsburgh. It is, in the views of its developers, an attempt to combine prescriptive or direct instruction with those aspects of open education that have been found to be effective. ALEM is a rather ambitious model that attempts to restructure the school environment, not simply alter the instructional system.

Cooperative Learning Models

Dedicated teachers are always looking for better ideas for meeting the many challenges they face in school, especially as diversity increases in the student population. Cooperative learning methods provide teachers with effective ways to respond to diverse students by promoting academic achievement and cross-cultural understanding (California Department of Education, 2004).

The Team-Assisted Individualized program (TAI) combines group and individual work for the teaching of mathematics. Students are assigned to four- and five-member heterogeneous teams and are given a placement test to determine placement. During the individualized portion of the program, they work on prepared curriculum materials that include an instruction sheet, several problem sheets, a practice test, and a final test. Students work on their units in teams, helping each other and assisting with the practice tests. The teams receive scores, with special recognition for high performance. The teacher works each day with groups of students who are at about the same point in the curriculum.

Learning-Styles Models

"Even the slowest and most reluctant readers can learn to read well when taught according to their individual learning styles," says Marie Carbo (2003), founder and executive director of the National Reading Styles Institute in Syosset, New York. Learning-styles models are built upon the assumptions that learners differ significantly in their styles of learning, that those styles can be assessed, and that knowledge of styles can help both teachers and learners.

What should educators do once a student's learning style has been identified?

Many learning-style advocates recommend a matching strategy: Find the student's preferred learning style and then provide learning experiences that match that style.

What does the research say about the usefulness of the learning-styles models? First, a considerable body of evidence supports the aspects of cognitive style, especially, playing an important role in learning. Here the dimension of field independence/field dependence is perhaps the most studied. The field-dependent person in perceiving phenomena is less able than the field-independent person to keep an item separate from its context.

For additional information on learning styles see the Web resources at the following:

- The National Reading Styles Institute Program titled Research Update; see www .nrsi.com
- The Northwest Regional Educational Laboratory and the National Clearinghouse for Comprehensive School Reform provide a downloadable PDF version of The Catalog of School Reform Models, including reading and language arts models at http:// www.nwrel.org/scpd/catalog/index.shtml/

(Carbo, 2003, p. 24)

Mastery Learning Models

As explained in Chapter 2, mastery learning principles were first enunciated by Benjamin Bloom; they have since been adapted in several different approaches. Anderson (1985) analyzed all these mastery learning approaches and found they have six features in common: clearly specified learning objectives; short, valid assessment procedures; current mastery standards; a sequence of learning units; provision of feedback on learning progress to students; and provision of additional time and help to correct specified errors of students' failing to meet the mastery standard. In his review of all the research on mastery learning, Anderson concludes that learning-for-mastery students have outperformed students in conventional classrooms on measures of achievement, retention, learning rate, attitudes, and self-esteem.

He also calls attention to some important findings about the application of the mastery model. First, the research evidence suggests that standards between 85% and 95% correct are most appropriate; setting lower performance standards seems to result in no substantial improvement. Second, the effective use of corrective procedures is critical; in fact, he concludes that corrective instruction targeted to the needs of particular learners and their learning problems is more important than the clarity of the original instruction.

ADAPTIVE PROGRAMS FOR THE GIFTED

Most researchers agree that special educational programming is advisable for academically gifted students, although the best type of programming is a matter of controversy (Swiatek & Lupkowski-Shoplik, 2003). The field of gifted education, like the fields of special education and child psychiatry, is experiencing rapid change. These changes are influenced by dramatic ideological, political, economic, and cultural shifts and by recent technological advances. For example, a shift in the intellectual and cultural zeitgeist has made gifted education more vulnerable to challenges from regular education and the inclusion movement and has raised troubling questions about the need for special programs (Pfeiffer, 2003). Focusing on gifted traits that are not solely cognitive provides educators with a way to understand how we can create conditions that will stimulate more people to use their gifts in socially constructive ways (Renzulli, 2002).

Curriculum Tip

Most adaptive models can be used in educating the gifted and talented.

Several programs have been especially designed to adapt to the special needs of this population. Before reviewing specific adaptive programs, however, it would be useful to identify some general guidelines for developing and evaluating programs for the gifted. Those that seem to be most widely used by educators in the field are the ones proposed by the Leadership Training Institute (as cited in VanTassel-Baska, 1985):

- The content of curricula for the gifted and talented (G/T) should focus on and be organized to include more elaborate, complex, and in-depth study of major ideas, problems, and themes that integrate knowledge within and across systems of thought.
- Curricula for the G/T should allow for the development and application of productive thinking skills to enable students to reconceptualize existing knowledge and/or generate new knowledge.
- Curricula for the G/T should enable students to explore constantly changing knowledge and information and develop the attitude that knowledge is worth pursuing in an open world.
- Curricula for the G/T should encourage exposure to, selection of, and use of specialized and appropriate resources.
- Curricula for the G/T should promote self-initiated and self-directed learning and growth.
- Curricula for the G/T should provide for the development of self-understanding and the understanding of one's relationship to persons, societal institutions, nature, and culture.
- Evaluations of curricula for the G/T should be conducted in accordance with prior stated principles, stressing higher-level thinking skills, creativity, and excellence in performance and products.

Parallel Curriculum for the Gifted

An inescapable truth is that gifted learners vary. Their abilities may be strong in one area and weak in another. Their capabilities may appear easy to some and difficult to others. A gifted student may find easy what a talented student finds difficult.

The concept of a parallel curriculum takes its basic definition from paralleling other forms of curriculum. For example, the overall or umbrella curriculum spans and parallels four different curriculum approaches for the gifted learner. They include: *Core Curriculum, Curriculum Connections, Curriculum of Practice,* and a *Curriculum of Identity* (Tomlinson et al., 2002). The *Core Curriculum* parallels a discipline while the *Connective Curriculum* makes connections within and across times, cultures, places, and disciplines. The *Curriculum of Practice* guides gifted learners in understanding and applying the facts, concepts, principles, and methodologies of the discipline. The *Curriculum of Identity* guides gifted students to understand their own strengths, preferences, values, and commitment. Teachers who use a parallel curriculum approach do so by creating a challenging and overarching curriculum as well as a framework for thinking.

Compacting

Curriculum compacting was first developed by Joe Renzulli at the University of Connecticut. It is designed to help advanced or gifted learners maximize their use of time for learning. According to noted author Carol Tomlinson (2001), compacting has three stages.

Stage 1: The teacher identifies gifted and talented students who are candidates for compacting and assesses what they do and do not know. Students who are compacting are exempt from whole-class instruction and activities in content areas they have already mastered.

Stage 2: The teacher notes any skills or understandings covered in the study in which the student did not demonstrate mastery. The teacher then lays out a plan to make certain the student achieves those goals and meets those objectives. The plan may require the student to work with other individuals in the classroom.

Stage 3: The teacher and student design an investigation or study for the student to engage in while others are working with the general lessons. Project parameters, goals, timelines, procedures for completing tasks, and criteria for evaluation are determined at that time.

Compacting helps gifted or accelerated learners to avoid having to go over mastered material while offering them a chance to challenge themselves in the classroom. This provides for invigorating and productive learning in school.

Discovery Method

Discovery, occasionally referred to as the Socratic method, is often used by teachers when working with gifted and talented students, but can certainly apply to all students. The perception is that it is often better to "discover" how to perform a skill or tactic than to be directly taught the skill or tactic (Marzano, Pickering, & Pollock, 2001). Through a process of inductive and deductive reasoning, students can become better able to "discover" a deep understanding of a problem, hopefully leading to greater motivation or different levels of learning.

There is little research to substantiate the discovery method, according to Marzano and colleagues (2001). They state that some skills are not amenable to discovery learning. In mathematics, for example, students often are required or need to follow a series of specific steps to reach the solution to a problem. It is better to demonstrate those steps and then provide opportunities for the students than to alter the steps or change them in some way. The key to the success of the discovery-oriented approach probably lies with the teacher and with the student. Both the teacher's and student's awareness and interest in the problem will lead to a point of understanding or to a point of discovery.

Brain-Based Learning

The teacher's ability to give sufficient examples relating to the students' experiences and to involve gifted and talented students in experiences makes the abstract concepts of brain-based learning understandable. According to Patricia Wolfe (2001), many of our strongest neural networks are formed by actual experience. It is often possible to take advantage of this natural proclivity by involving students in solving authentic problems in their school or community. In addition to the obvious benefits of engaging in authentic problem solving, teachers report that it also immeasurably enhances students' motivation, sense of efficacy, and self-esteem. The key is to make curriculum meaningful through brain-engaging problems, projects, and simulations that challenge the student.

Special Pace: Acceleration

Acceleration as an adaptive strategy helps gifted students advance through the grades and master advanced academic content at a rapidly accelerated rate. Thus, a highly gifted 10-year-old might be placed in a ninth-grade science class, or a very intelligent elementary school pupil might be studying the mathematics normally taught in high school. Also, high school students preparing for and taking the Advanced Placement (AP) examinations of the College Entrance Examination Board are experiencing a type of acceleration.

Classroom technology and the Internet can provide an alternative to advancing students into another grade level. Accessing the Internet to build Web sites or to obtain information globally allows gifted and talented students a way to enhance and accelerate learning and still remain in their classrooms. Adaptive hypermedia is a good example of how just one type of program can be used to keep gifted students in a classroom and yet move them into more advanced material.

According to Peter Brusilovsky (2004) of the Carnegie Technology Education Institute, Adaptive hypermedia systems can build a model of the goals, preferences, and knowledge of each individual user. For example, a student in an adaptive educational hypermedia system might be given a presentation that is adapted specifically to his or her knowledge of the subject. Suggested sets of most relevant links are also given to the student to proceed further. An adaptive electronic encyclopedia helps personalize the content of an article to augment the user's existing knowledge and interests. A virtual museum can be adapted for the presentation, noting each visited object or path taken by the student. Hypermedia is just one example among hundreds of ways teachers can use technology to build an accelerated program for gifted and talented learners.

Special Curricula

It is crucial when formulating special curricula for the gifted and talented that teachers develop materials that clarify specific learning goals that are implicit in the standards

(Hamilton & Stecher, 2004). It is sometimes necessary to supplement state standards with more detailed descriptions of goals and objectives so that teachers and administrators understand what students are expected to know and what they are expected to do. Curricular modifications for the gifted have in general taken two forms: offering special subjects and providing for enrichment activities. In many school districts, gifted students can study subjects ordinarily not included in the curriculum by following independent study programs or by receiving group instruction in a special program. The *Philosophy for Children* program has been used by many school districts for such purposes, with generally successful results.

Several enrichment models have been used in programs for the gifted. Two of those that seem in widest use are Renzulli's (1977; Renzulli, Reis, & Smith, 1981) triad/RDIM model and Meeker's (1985) SOI model.

Triad/RDIM Model

The triad/RDIM model combines the enrichment triad model originally proposed by Renzulli (1977) with a relatively recent approach to selection, the revolving door identification model (Renzulli et al., 1981). The enrichment triad model is based upon three types of enrichment activities for the gifted. Type I activities are *general exploratory activities*, in which learners explore areas of personal interest. Type II activities are *group-training activities*, consisting of materials and instructional techniques designed to develop critical and creative thinking skills. Type III activities are *individual or small-group investigations*, in which students have an opportunity to investigate real problems through research and inquiry.

The revolving door identification model begins by identifying a pool of the top 15% to 20% of the student population. All these students are exposed to Type I and Type II activities on a regular basis. As these students work on these enriching activities, teachers remain alert for students who demonstrate signs of interest, creativity, task commitment, and advanced ability. As a student is so identified, the teacher encourages the student to move into a Type III activity, using either the resources of the regular classroom or attending the special "resource room" until the project is completed.

On the basis of implementation studies in 30 Connecticut schools, Reis and Renzulli (1984) have been able to identify several key features that account for successful programs: thorough orientation of teachers, parents, and administrators; extensive planning by the local school team; in-service and administrative support; schoolwide enrichment teams composed of the principal, the resource teacher, classroom teachers, parents, and in some cases a student; developing in the entire staff a sense of ownership of the program; detailed orientation of the students; communication with prime interest groups; program flexibility; and evaluation and program monitoring.

The triad/RDIM model seems to be a very productive means for providing interesting learning experiences. The obvious question arises again, however: Why for only the top 20%?

Meeker's Structure of the Intellect Model

Over the course of several decades, J. P. Guilford (1977) has been conducting research on and refining his structure of the intellect (SOI) model of intelligence, represented by a three-dimensional cube. The three dimensions are the five operations of the intellect, the four contents of the intellect, and the six classes. Of the 120 possible intellectual abilities that result from the intersection of these three dimensions, 96 have been substantiated through testing.

Mary Meeker and her associates (Meeker, Meeker, & Roid, 1985) have been able to validate 26 of those factored abilities as necessary for successful learning. Those 26 intellectual abilities have been used to develop several tests that have been very useful in identifying potentially gifted students, especially minority students. Meeker has found in her own work that Blacks, Hispanics, and Native Americans score higher on some SOI measures than do white students. The SOI model has also been useful in diagnosing and prescribing for the developmental needs of the gifted.

Special Resources

The third general approach is to provide special resources—that is, special schools (such as the Bronx High School of Science), special summer programs, or special mentors for the gifted. Of these, mentoring deserves perhaps a more detailed examination here. The mentoring approach involves associating a gifted student with an adult mentor who can serve as a role model, provide support and encouragement, and give the necessary direction on a one-to-one basis. As VanTassel-Baska (1985) notes, some mentoring programs are more highly structured, requiring a contract between mentor and student that stipulates the tasks to be accomplished, the types of supports provided, and a schedule for completion.

Staffing for Gifted and Talented Students

Teachers around the country are entrusted with the task of fostering the academic and intellectual development of the students they teach. The conundrum is that each teacher is a unique individual just as each student is a unique individual. The challenge that arises is that some teachers who are particularly effective in teaching one group of students may not be equally effective in teaching other students.

The expertise, certain personality traits, and cognitive style preferences of teachers may be critical as to how they teach. Carol Mills, PhD, of Johns Hopkins University, recommends that we expose gifted students to many different styles of teaching and to teachers with many different cognitive preferences. In a study, Dr. Mills (2003) found that the personality types of teachers are similar to the personality types of the gifted students. This suggests that teachers who are judged to be highly effective in working with gifted students prefer abstract themes and concepts, are open and flexible, and value logical analysis and objectivity. Results suggest that a teacher's personality and cognitive style may play a role in his or her effectiveness in teaching gifted students. According to Dr. Mills, students need to understand styles other than their own.

PROVIDING FOR MILDLY HANDICAPPED LEARNERS

Conceptions of how best to educate students with disabilities have shifted toward one of two extremes: denying that disabilities exist or accommodating them to the extent that there is no expectation of student progress toward realistic goals. The authors contend that both attitudes defeat the primary educational aim of helping all students achieve their highest potential. James Kauffman (Kauffman, McGee, & Brigham, 2004), a professor of education at the University of Virginia, notes that many successful adults with disabilities express common themes when asked about their ability to succeed in the face of a disability. Tom Cray, a

Rhodes Scholar who has a severe learning disability, claimed that having to deal with the hardest experiences gave him the greatest strength.

As explained in Chapter 4, Public Law 94-142 was landmark legislation that radically changed how the schools were to provide for these special students. Four basic rights and protections are specified in PL 94-142, According to Macmillan's (1982) analysis of the law, the right to due process in the classification and placement of learners, protection against discriminatory testing during assessment, placement in the least restrictive educational setting, and Individualized Educational Programs (IEPs).

Curriculum Tip

Programmatic responses to PL 94-142 in general have been of three types: early intervention programs, mainstreaming, and special curricula.

Early Intervention

A combination of school and teacher factors was found by researcher Barbara Taylor, EdD (2001), to be the most important factors in beating the odds in teaching all children how to read. Factors to use in early intervention include the following:

- Schools with strong links to parents
- Collaboration of teaching staff
- Shared system for assessing oral reading fluency, accuracy, and text level
- Extensive professional development on instructional practices

An emphasis on one-on-one instruction is also an important factor. Taylor (2001) notes some great strategies used in early intervention by teachers:

- Small-group instruction
- Time for independent reading
- Communication and reading with parents
- Applying word identification
- Asking higher-level questions

These are all excellent early intervention strategies used by accomplished primary grade teachers in effective schools. According to Barbara Taylor, they have been especially effective in large urban poverty environments.

Since the relationships between poverty environments and developmental learning problems have been clearly established, most early intervention programs have focused on the children of the poor. Increasingly, such programs have attempted to reach infant children and their parents, on the theory that *the earlier, the better*.

Early Intervention Programs

Reading Recovery®, Reading for Success, and many other phonemic-based programs are now being used extensively in schools. Reading Recovery is perhaps the most widely known of these early intervention programs and is a highly effective short-term one-on-one tutoring program for low-achieving first graders. The intervention is most effective when it is available to all students who need it and is used as a supplement to good classroom teaching. In Reading Recovery, individual students receive a half-hour lesson each school day for 12 to 20 weeks with a specially trained Reading Recovery teacher. As soon as students can read within the average range of their class and demonstrate that they can continue to achieve, their lessons are discontinued, and new students begin individual instruction.

How effective is Reading Recovery? During the 2000–2001 school year, 149,009 Reading Recovery students were served nationally. In the program, 112,814 students received a full program (a full series of lessons). Seventy-eight percent of the students who received a full program met the criteria to discontinue Reading Recovery. These students were at or above their classroom average for reading and writing ability after a full series of Reading Recovery lessons (Gomez-Bellenge, 2002). Since the inception of Reading Recovery in North America, the average success rate for Reading Recovery children receiving a full series of lessons is 81% (Reading Recovery Council of North America, 2002).

Success in Reading Recovery means a student has demonstrated independent reading and writing strategies—allowing that student to show continued achievement subsequent to participation in Reading Recovery. The student has been assessed and can read within the average performance range for his or her class without special assistance. This is important because the Reading Recovery Program serves the lowest-achieving students first. Before these students are included in the program, they have demonstrated that they are not able to profit from regular classroom literacy instruction in the same way as their peer group (Zalud, 2002).

Reading Recovery meets the requirement of the No Child Left Behind Act that reauthorizes the Elementary and Secondary Education Act of 2001 (ESEA; Reading Recovery Council of North America, 2002). According to this act, reading programs must meet research criteria that apply rigorous systematic and objective procedures utilizing empirical methods that draw on observation or experiments to meet ESEA criteria (Zalud, 2002).

Reading Recovery is a one-to-one teaching program specifically designed to meet the needs of low-progress first-grade children. It is a program designed to be part of a school's literacy initiative. It is an intensive, short-term intervention aimed at quickly returning the child to the classroom, positioned to profit from regular classroom instruction. It is data-driven and validated as being effective in schools that implement the program according to its established standards and guidelines (Zalud, 2002).

Mainstreaming/Inclusion Process

Mainstreaming, or what is often called the inclusion process, is the educational practice of integrating mildly handicapped learners into regular classrooms; one commonly used standard is that such integration should account for at least half of the learner's program if it is to count as mainstreaming. In addition to such integration, mainstreaming is often accompanied by the specification of Individualized Educational Programs (IEP) and the support of a multidisciplinary team.

More schools are now embracing the concept of inclusion of special education students. As a result, fewer mildly handicapped students are being pulled out of their classrooms. Professors James McLeskey and Nancy Waldron (2002) of the University of Florida, Gainesville, note that students with disabilities are making at least as much progress as, if not more than, they did in separate educational classes. McLeskey and Waldron also point out ten lessons that they learned about how some schools changed their practices and became more inclusive.

1. Change must be supported from both the top and the bottom.

2. Schools must be empowered to manage their own change.

3. To develop a successful inclusive school requires major changes in the entire school.

4. Substantive change should transform current school practices and is not simply an "add-on."

5. Change should seek to make differences ordinary in the general education classroom.

6. Change has a ripple effect. It is systemic.

7. Change must be tailored to each school.

8. Professional development must be provided as needed.

9. Resistance should be expected.

10. The work of developing an inclusive school is never done.

Developing the concept of mainstreaming or "inclusion" in schools can be challenging. It can be a very complex issue. It is therefore critical that teachers, administrators, and community members work together to develop an awareness of the benefits of inclusion and how it may have a positive impact on mildly handicapped learners.

Students With Disabilities at Secondary Level

Working with mildly handicapped and students with disabilities at the secondary level can be an even more demanding process. According to Robert Stodden, L. Galloway, and Norma Jean Stodden (2003), using a rigorous standards-based curriculum to teach secondary students with disabilities is complex and difficult. Curriculum leaders addressing this issue need to consider the following:

- The complex needs of students with disabilities in learning standards-based curricula
- The needs of educators to effectively teach this population standards-based curricula in secondary schools
- Contextual factors that impact teaching and learning standards-based curricula in secondary schools

Curriculum leaders at the secondary level need to address these complicated and challenging issues through improved staff development. Administrators must also provide support in the way of parent-volunteers or para-educators in helping to work with students one-on-one where necessary.

According to Ken Jones (2004), director of teacher education, University of Southern Maine, secondary teachers need to apply a "balanced approach" when working with mildly handicapped learners. A balanced approach exhibits the following characteristics:

- Intended primarily to improve student learning
- Aligns with local curricula
- Emphasizes applied learning and thinking skills, not just declarative knowledge and basic skills
- Embodies the principle of multiple measures, including a variety of formats such as writing, open-response questions, and performance-based tasks
- Is accessible to students with diverse learning styles, intelligence profiles, and cultural backgrounds

Secondary schoolteachers and administrators are continuing to make great strides in addressing the issue of mildly handicapped students and students with disabilities in general. Viewing the process from a standpoint of finding out what works and how to balance the curriculum to accommodate these students is the key.

Special Curricula

The hope is that curricular modifications will make an impact. In general, most curricula for the mildly handicapped have emphasized the development of the basic skills, along with expressing a broader concern for improving social skills, helping handicapped learners manage their own behavior, and improving their cognitive skills. It is important, however, to avoid a "scattershot type of curriculum" when planning units and lessons for mildly handicapped learners. Scattershot approaches have insufficient planning, the objectives are not tied to goals, and goals are not tied to the school mission statement or vision. This form of curriculum planning is often unreliable and is hit or miss at best. It is a hodgepodge of instructional aims and subject matter whose content and expectations vary sharply from classroom to classroom (Jerald, 2003). It is important to have a focused and well-planned curriculum when developing and implementing cognitive skills for mildly handicapped learners.

The emphasis on the cognitive skills of the mildly handicapped seems especially promising, because recent research has provided some productive insights into the special learning problems of the learning handicapped. A review of such research suggests that the following specific cognitive deficiencies are prevalent among this group: they are deficient in attention; have poor short-term memory; make inadequate use of memory strategies; have slower perceptual speed; are less efficient at categorizing incoming data into chunks; fail to organize input efficiently; use memory rehearsal strategies inefficiently; and cannot plan, select, sequence, and evaluate the use of such strategies.

BILINGUAL EDUCATION

According to Janette Klingner and Alfredo Artiles (2003), the percentage of students from diverse cultures is growing in schools across the United States. In recent years, schools have made some progress in meeting the needs of culturally and linguistically diverse students, especially bilingual students with special education needs. Nonetheless, this area is fraught with controversy. Perhaps there is no area of the school's curriculum that has been the subject of such vehement controversy as bilingual education.

Curriculum Tip

Controversy regarding bilingual education has normally revolved around four issues: What is bilingual education? How extensive is the need for special education for those with limited English proficiency (LEP)? To what extent should local districts have flexibility in responding to those needs? Is bilingual education effective for such students?

As indicated in Chapter 4, bilingual educational programs were institutionalized in the law primarily as a result of political forces. The political controversies surrounding bilingual education continue, with partisans unable to agree on several issues.

What Is Bilingual Education?

Central to understanding all the controversy is having some clear understanding of several complex and somewhat ambiguous terms. As noted below, much of the controversy focuses on matters of definition. In order to be as objective as possible, the following definitions have been drawn from a current review of the literature (chiefly from Fillmore & Valadez, 1986).

- **Submersion programs**. These are sink-or-swim approaches—essentially nonprograms that make no effort to accommodate the special needs of LEP students.
- **English as a Second Language (ESL) programs**. These are formal courses that teach English as a foreign language to nonnative speakers. In the strictest sense of the term, such courses should not be categorized as *bilingual education*.

Bilingual Education

The two significant characteristics of bilingual education, as Fillmore and Valadez (1986) define the term, are these: instruction is given in two languages—English (in the United States) and the home language of the LEP student; and instruction in English is given in a way that permits students to learn it as a second language. As will be noted below, the definition of the term has become a matter of much controversy.

Bilingual Transition Programs

There are several types of transitional programs that have the chief goal of enabling LEP students to move as quickly as possible into an all-English program of studies; dual language in instruction is offered only until LEP students have acquired enough English to deal with instruction in English.

Bilingual Maintenance Programs

In maintenance programs, the goal is to develop proficiency in both languages; students remain in these programs even after they have achieved proficiency in English.

How Extensive Is the Need?

Partisans in the debate about bilingual education cannot agree on even the extent of the need. Most states refer to federal guidelines involving ESL. For example, in Montana (Montana Office of Public Instruction, 2004), limited English proficiency (LEP) refers to the following:

- Individuals who were not born in the United States or whose native language is a language other than English
- Individuals who come from an environment where a language other than English is dominant
- Individuals who are American Indian and/or Alaskan Natives who come from environments where a language other than English has had significant impact on their level of language proficiency

Is Bilingual Education Effective?

The challenge is the increasing number of bilingual students who need special education help. Educators are becoming concerned about the overrepresentation of culturally and linguistically diverse students in certain special education categories—learning disabilities, mental retardation, and emotional disturbance—and their underrepresentation in programs for the gifted and talented (Klingner & Artiles, 2003). One of the major problems has been the assessment of culturally and linguistically diverse students. This situation is being addressed through the No Child Left Behind Act (NCLB) and through the testing of subgroups. Nonetheless, it still continues to be fraught with theoretical misunderstandings and flawed practices (Klingner & Artiles, 2003).

Several possible solutions to this problem emerge. First, professional development needs to be provided to enhance professionals' understanding of culturally and linguistically challenged students. Second, administrators need to make sure that professionals with expertise in English-language acquisition should be present during meetings relating to the Student Assistant Team (SAT), Child Study Team (CST), and the Individualized Educational Program (IEP). Incorporating these strategies will help develop a better understanding and awareness for our bilingual program as well as provide needed help to some of our culturally diverse and linguistically challenged students.

CONCLUSION

In review, we can say that the important ingredients for creating successful curriculum reform include a culturally and linguistically responsive staff as well as a thoughtfully planned and developmentally appropriate curriculum that is likely to promote positive outcomes for all children—including both gifted students and students with disabilities. As part of that process, we are learning how to formulate innovative ways of teaching; we are learning how to reform local, state, and national policy for schools; and we are learning how to help those interested in producing a high-quality education for all children through effective administration, curriculum planning, and development. What is important is that we must act and we must act now: Curriculum leadership is the key.

CHAPTER OVERVIEW

This chapter analyzes the types of individualized programs that promote student choice, curriculum integration, differentiated learning, and self-assessment that engage students deeply in learning. The chapter reviews previous attempts to respond to individual differences, and it assesses current models. The chapter concludes by examining the challenging problems inherent in providing for very special student populations. Chapter topics include early attempts that were made to individualize curriculum and current successful examples of individualized programs. The chapter also includes individualized adaptive approaches that are being used in gifted education as well as examples of other specialized curriculum and how they are enhancing concepts of individualization. Finally, the role of bilingual education in individualizing curriculum is addressed.

CHAPTER TERMS

Adaptive Versus Individualized

Adaptive Learning Environments Model

Cooperative Learning Models

Learning-Styles Models

Mastery Learning Models

Core Curriculum

Curriculum Connections

Curriculum of Practice

Curriculum of Identity

Compacting

Discovery Method

Brain-Based Learning

Acceleration

Triad/RDIM Model

SOI Model

Mildly Handicapped Learners

Early Intervention

Mainstreaming/Inclusion Process

ESL Programs

Bilingual Programs

APPLICATIONS

1. Some have argued that all learning is individualized: The learner makes individual meaning out of what is learned. They continue by disparaging the need for any type of individualized or adaptive instruction, contending that group-paced learning can be just as effective. How would you respond to such an argument?

2. Identify a subject or grade level you know well. Which of the adaptive approaches do you think would work best? Explain your choice and the reasons supporting it.

3. Some have suggested that knowledge about learning styles will produce an "educational revolution." Others are much less sanguine about the possibilities, pointing out that the research so far has not yielded significant gains for learning styles adaptations. As you review the models described and analyze the research findings, what position do you take regarding this issue?

4. Several in the field have criticized the Dunns' (Dunn, Dunn, & Price, 1978) Learning Style Inventory and other similar instruments that place too much emphasis on environmental considerations. They argue that such matters are trivial. As you analyze your own learning style, do you find that such considerations are important? Do you think it would be useful for educators to assess these matters?

5. Suppose you were not limited by laws, such as PL 94-142, that mandate mainstreaming. As an educational leader, would you use mainstreaming in your school? On what grounds would you justify your position?

6. How would you justify and present adding a Reading Recovery or similar program to the board of education?

CASE STUDY

Involving the special education students in the regular classroom can be rewarding, but it can also pose some difficulties for the student with special needs. The following is an example of how one Colorado school principal handled a problem that involved homework assignments for special needs students.

Mrs. Rusk, a special education teacher, meets with Middle School Principal Susan Thomas.

"I want to visit with you about one of my students being mainstreamed in Mrs. Trent's sixth-grade classroom," she says, entering the principal's office. She appears to be angry. "I'm upset that Mrs. Trent continues to give too much homework and that the homework is far too difficult for the special needs student," she says in a huff.

Principal Susan Thomas meets the woman at the door and welcomes her into her office. "Well, I'm glad you were able to come down to the office so that we can talk about this," says the principal. "Mrs. Trent and I have been talking about homework and the difficulties that some of our special needs students are having when they are mainstreamed in the regular classroom."

"And what are we going to do about this?" asks Mrs. Rusk, still sounding agitated.

"Well, it is an interesting problem," says the principal, smiling. "Mainstreaming is a major focus of our special education program. Mainstreaming means that we want our special needs students to be in the regular classroom as much as possible. I was at the IEP meeting that we had when we discussed the issue of homework last year. I have already visited with Mrs. Trent and explained that by federal law she has to follow the student's IEP that she agreed to last spring. She didn't realize the homework was such a problem and has agreed to work with you as to what the student can do and what the student cannot do."

"That sounds reasonable," says Mrs. Rusk, starting to relax for the first time.

The principal continues, "Yes, I think both you and Mrs. Trent can come to some type of agreement on homework. Otherwise, we will have to call for a new IEP meeting and change the student's program."

"I sure don't need another meeting," Mrs. Rusk says looking around the room. "I'm sure that the teacher and I can agree on some type of arrangement that follows the present IEP."

"It will be great to have you both working together in a positive manner in regards to mainstreaming," says Principal Thomas. "Let me check around and ask some other teachers how they are handling their mainstreaming. I'll make some phone calls and get back to you as soon as possible."

THE CHALLENGE

Making sure that curriculum is individualized and addresses the needs of all students is a critical component of any school district across the country. Analyze how Principal Thomas used mainstreaming to enrich curriculum in her school. How can she best share this idea as well as other innovative programs with principals and administrators from other schools?

Key Issues/Questions

1. What are your impressions of Principal Thomas and how she dealt with the issue of homework? Did the principal adequately address the parent's needs? Why or why not?

2. What are your beliefs on giving a great deal of homework to students? How much time should an elementary student spend on homework versus a student in middle school or high school?

3. If the principal meets with parents about a teacher, what should be discussed? When should the teacher be involved in the discussion?

4. What are your feelings on curriculum tracking? Do you feel that curriculum tracking is a viable option?

5. What are some innovative approaches that principals might use to individualize their school's curriculum? Identify specific strategies and explain why you think they might be effective.

REFERENCES

Anderson, L. W. (1985). A retrospective and prospective view of Bloom's "Learning for Mastery." In M. C. Wang & H. J. Walberg (Eds.), *Adapting instruction to individual differences* (pp. 254–268). Berkeley, CA: McCutchan.

Atkins, J. T., & Ellsesser, J. (2003). Tracking: The good, the bad, and the questions. *Educational Leadership, 61*(2), 44–49.

Brown, D. F. (2002). Self-directed learning. *Educational Leadership, 60*(1), 54–59.

Brusilovsky, P. (2004). Adaptive hypermedia: From intelligent tutoring systems to Web-based education. *Carnegie Technology Education and HCI Institute*. Retrieved April 24, 2004, from http://www .sis.pitt.edu/~peterb/papers/ITS00inv.html

Burris, C. C., Heubert, J. P., & Levin, H. M. (2004, February). Math acceleration for all. *Educational Leadership, 61*(5), 68–72.

California Department of Education. (2004). Cooperative learning: Response to diversity. *California Department of Education-Curriculum Instruction Web Team*. Retrieved April 25, 2004, from http://www.cde.ca.gov/iasa/cooplrng2.html

Carbo, M. (2003). Achieving with struggling readers. *Principal, 83*(2), 20–24.

Chapman, V. G., & Sopko, D. (2003). Developing strategic use of combined-text trade books. *Reading Teacher, 57*(3), 236–241.

Commission on the Reorganization of Secondary Education. (1918). *Cardinal principles of secondary education.* Washington, DC: Government Printing Office.

Committee of Ten. (1893). *Report of the Committee of Ten on secondary school students.* Washington, DC: National Education Association.

Dunn, R., Dunn, K., & Price, G. E. (1978). *Learning style inventory.* Lawrence, KA: Price Systems.

Fillmore, L. W., & Valadez, C. (1986). Teaching bilingual learners. In M. C. Wittrock (Ed.), *Handbook of research on teaching* (3rd ed., pp. 648–685). New York: Macmillan.

Gomez-Bellenge, F. X. (2002). Reading recovery and Descubriendo la Lecura (National Report 2000–2001). Columbus: The Ohio State University College of Education, National Data Evaluation Center.

Grinder, R. E., & Nelsen, E. A. (1985). Individualized instruction in American pedagogy. In M. C. Wang & H. J. Walberg (Eds.), *Adapting instruction to individual differences* (pp. 24–43). Berkeley, CA: McCutchan.

Guilford, J. P. (1977). *Way beyond the IQ.* Great Neck, NY: Creative Synergetic Associates.

Hamilton, L., & Stecher, B. (2004). Responding effectively to test-based accountability. *Phi Delta Kappan, 85*(8), 578–583.

Jerald, C. (2003). Beyond the rock and the hard place. *Educational Leadership, 61*(3), 12–16.

Jones, K. (2004, April). A balanced school accountability model: An alternative to high-stakes testing. *Phi Delta Kappan, 85,* 584–590.

Kauffman, J. M., McGee, K., & Brigham, M. (2004). Enabling or disabling? Observations on changes in special education. *Phi Delta Kappan, 85,* 613–620.

Klingner, J. K., & Artiles, A. J. (2003). When should bilingual students be in special education? *Educational Leadership, 61*(2), 66–71.

Macmillan, D. L. (1982). *Mental retardation in school and society* (2nd ed.). Boston: Little, Brown.

March, J. K., & Peters, K. H. (2002). Curriculum development and instructional design in the effective schools process. *Phi Delta Kappan, 83,* 379–381.

Marzano, R. J., Pickering, D. J., & Pollock, J. E. (2001). *Classroom instruction that works: Research-based strategies for increasing student achievement.* Alexandria, VA: Association for Supervision and Curriculum Development.

McLeskey, J., & Waldron, N. L. (2002). School change and inclusive schools: Lessons learned from practice. *Phi Delta Kappan, 84*(1), 65–72.

Meeker, M. N. (1985). SOI. In A. L. Costa (Ed.), *Developing minds: A resource book for teaching thinking* (pp. 187–192). Alexandria, VA: Association for Supervision and Curriculum Development.

Meeker, M. N., Meeker, R., & Roid, G. (1985). *The basic SOI manual.* Los Angeles: WPS.

Mills, C. J. (2003, Fall). Characteristics of effective teachers of gifted students: Teacher background and personality styles of students. *Gifted Child Quarterly, 47*(4), 272–281.

Montana Office of Public Instruction. (2004). *Montana comprehensive assessment: Limited English proficiency.* Helena: Montana Office of Public Instruction.

NAEYC & NAECS/SDE. (2004, January). Where we stand on curriculum assessment and program evaluation. *National Association for the Education of Young Children, 59*(1), 51–63.

Page, S. W. (2000). When changes for the gifted spur differentiation for all. *Educational Leadership, 58*(1), 62–65.

Pfeiffer, S. I. (2003, Spring). Challenges and opportunities for students who are gifted: What the experts say. *Gifted Child Quarterly, 47*(2), 161–169.

Reading Recovery® Council of North America. (2002). *More than one million children served: Results 2000–2001.* Columbus: The Ohio State University College of Education, National Data Evaluation Center. Retrieved April 20, 2005, from http://www.readingrecovery.org/pdfs/FinalARlayout.pdf

Reis, S. M., & Renzulli, J. S. (1984). Key features of successful programs for the gifted and talented. *Educational Leadership, 41,* 28–34.

Renzulli, J. S. (1977). *The enrichment triad model: A guide for developing defensible programs for the gifted.* Mansfield Center, CT: Creative Learning.

Renzulli, J. S. (2002). Expanding the conception of giftedness to include co-cognitive traits and to promote social capital. *Phi Delta Kappan, 84*(1), 33–58.

Renzulli, J. S., Reis, S. M., & Smith, L. H. (1981). *The revolving door identification model.* Mansfield Center, CT: Creative Learning.

Stodden, R. A., Galloway, L. M., & Stodden, N. J. (2003, Fall). Secondary school curricula issues: Impact on postsecondary students with disabilities. *Exceptional Child, 70*(1), 9–28.

Swiatek, M. A., & Lupkowski-Shoplik, A. (2003, Spring). Elementary and middle school student participation in gifted programs: Are gifted students underserved? *Gifted Child Quarterly, 47*(2), 118–120.

Taylor, B. M. (2001, Spring). Beating the odds in teaching all children to read. *Of Primary Interest. National Association of Early Childhood Specialists, 8*(2), 1–2.

Tomlinson, C. A. (2001). *How to differentiate instruction in mixed-ability classrooms* (2nd. ed.). Alexandria, VA: Association for Supervision and Curriculum Development.

Tomlinson, C. A., Kaplan, S. N., Renzulli, J. S., Purcell, J., Leppien, J., & Burns, D. (2002). *The parallel curriculum: A design to develop high potential and challenge high-ability learners.* Thousand Oaks, CA: Corwin.

VanTassel-Baska, J. (1985). Appropriate curriculum for the gifted. In J. Feldhusen (Ed.), *Toward excellence in gifted education* (pp. 45–67). Denver, CO: Lows Publishing.

Winebrenner. S. (2000). Gifted students need an education, too. *Educational Leadership, 58*(1), 52–56.

Wolfe, P. (2001). *Brain matters: Translating research into classroom practice.* Alexandria, VA: Association for Supervision and Curriculum Development.

Zalud, G. (2002). *Reading Recovery executive summary 1997–2002.* Vermillion: The University of South Dakota, Regional Reading Recovery Training Center.

Epilogue

Curriculum leaders must adopt a dramatically new global perspective if they are to be prepared for the educational challenges facing today's culturally diverse world. Charting the way forward will involve creating a compelling and credible shared vision as it relates to curriculum planning. To capture the interest of teachers and students during this age of unprecedented change, educational leaders will need commitment, clarity, and focus.

The purpose of this book is to provide a guide for educational leaders as they work through the myriad processes involving curriculum history, theory, planning, implementation, and evaluation. It is the belief of the authors that curriculum leaders must create a connection between a school's organizational vision and its actions—whether individual or collective in nature. Knowledgeable curriculum planning and quality leadership are primary keys to building successful schools. Against a backdrop of change, there continues to be the development of new technologies, new organizational structures, and an emphasis on the alignment of standards at local, state, and national levels.

All of these new ideas and changes are currently testing school hierarchies and pushing the boundaries of traditional leadership in education. As noted in this book, there is a new focus on administrative strategies needed to address these challenges. Future curriculum leaders, therefore, need to be knowledgeable as well as flexible—and they must be able to build upon relationships as well as evoke a sense of ownership and trust in their schools.

As noted throughout this text, new advances in digital technologies appear to be moving education to a pivotal point—a critical juncture in history. Curriculum must move forward. The ability of curriculum leaders to "map" and "plan" curriculum will be crucial. Both traditional and contemporary considerations are in the offing. For those who share a common vision and who have a willingness to explore and test solutions, there will be a sense of pride, commitment, and spirit in curriculum planning and development.

Today's curriculum leaders are now setting the stage for exploring and testing new ways to individualize curriculum, and it is our curriculum leaders who are developing the vision and skills needed to meet tomorrow's challenges. Successful leadership practices often result in the development of strong character, and it is strong character that often leads to destiny. It is these futuristic curriculum leaders who are—as well as continue to be—the visionaries and determiners of the nature, scope, and character of curriculum for the coming age.

APPENDIX A

Management and Monitoring Matrix

Target Area _____

1. GOAL _____

Product _____

End Point _____

3. STATUS TODAY What is the situation today?	4. ACTIVITIES What must be done to get from 4 to 3?	5. LEADERSHIP Who is responsible to initiate/follow through with activities?	6. SCHEDULE What is the timeframe for accomplishing each activity being monitored?	2. INDICATORS If the goal were attained, what would really be happening? What would the target area look or be like? List 8 to 10 indicators
A.				A.
B.				B.
C.				C.
D.				D.

Appendix B

Developing a Program Philosophy and Rationale Statement[1]

The philosophy and rationale statement for a school program, also known as a subject area curriculum or discipline, must augment a school district's philosophy, vision, mission, and exit (graduation) outcomes. The school administrator in charge of curriculum holds the responsibility to provide the destination and/or direction for the development and implementation of a comprehensive school curriculum. Curriculum development for all disciplines necessitates the establishment of a district-wide curriculum council that meets on a monthly basis during the school year.

The curriculum council should consist of professional staff in leadership positions, that is, the curriculum director, building principals, department heads, team leaders, and others in leadership positions. Council members should be cognizant of the school district's mission, vision, philosophy, exit outcomes, program philosophies and rationale statements, program goals, program objectives, learning outcomes, learning activities, assessment, textbooks used (including publication year, edition, and condition), and so on.

A major function of the curriculum council is to develop a sequence and review cycle for district-wide curriculum development. For example, a typical 5-year cycle is illustrated in the following table.

The curriculum council should also select teacher representation for curriculum development. The representatives should be chosen using one of five methods: voluntary, rotation, evolvement, peer selection, or administrative selection.

The procedure for developing a district-wide language arts English program philosophy and rationale statement and examples of the declarations follow.

PROCEDURE

To develop a sound philosophy for a language arts English program (or any school program), a language arts English program committee (also known as a subject area committee) must

Typical 5-Year Curriculum Development Cycle

2005–2006	Language Arts-English	2010–2011
2006–2007	Science and Social Studies	2011–2012
2007–2008	Fine Arts	2012–2013
2008–2009	Mathematics and Health	2013–2014
2009–2010	All Others	2014–2015

NOTE: Technology and business/vocational subjects may need a shorter development cycle.

be established for the initial phase. The steps for structuring, along with responsibilities for the committee, are as follows:

Step 1

- The school district superintendent and board of education must approve the process for district-wide curriculum development.

- The curriculum council should form a language arts English program committee composed of language arts English teachers representing all grade levels (K–12), preferably two teachers from each grade level. In smaller districts, however, one teacher per three grade/course levels is satisfactory (with feedback from those teaching the other grade/course levels). In smaller districts, a curriculum director could be hired by their cooperative (if such a co-op exists) to lead this process (a cooperative is a consortium of school districts cooperatively working together toward common goals). Co-op superintendents would need to support this approach to curriculum development. The superintendents, building principals, and content-area teachers would need to see the value of receiving input from other teachers in the cooperative, and embrace the idea of a similar curriculum in cooperative schools. Although there may be resistance to adopting a first-grade curriculum throughout the co-op, there would be some classes that would benefit from a standard curriculum. Distance learning classes (e.g., foreign languages) would benefit from having a co-op curriculum coordinator help the schools set up a common curriculum. This common curriculum (including the textbook) would give the co-op schools much more flexibility in creating a schedule. Schools would not be tied to one school in the co-op. If school A could not fit its students into the schedule of the school that usually offered the class, the students could receive the same class from another school in the cooperative and be confident that the materials and content would be the same. In this process, the curriculum coordinator could use the distance learning equipment to facilitate meetings. Each school could have staff sit in their own distance learning rooms and share with the other members of the co-op. This would eliminate travel and make the possibility of having meetings more often realistic.

- Building principals (or designees) from the elementary, middle level or junior high school, and senior high school must be members of the committee as well (preferably with one principal or designee from each level).

- The school district curriculum director (or designee) should serve as chairperson and be responsible for organizing and directing the activities of the language arts English program committee.

- The school district's board of education should be informed by the board curriculum committee about the process used for program (curriculum) development.

- All language arts English program committee members must have a thorough understanding of the school district's philosophy, vision, mission, and exit (graduation) outcomes to enable committee members to blend them into the language arts English program philosophy and rational statement.

- The Dialogue Technique, the Delphi Technique, the Fishbowl Technique, the Telstar Technique, or the Nominal Group Technique could be used to guide the language arts English program committee in developing a program philosophy.

- The number of meetings to complete the task of writing a program philosophy by the language arts English program committee should be limited to three or four during the school year.

- The curriculum meetings should be held in a comfortable environment; in other words, comfortable work seats, circular seating arrangement, tables with room for participants to spread their papers out, and good acoustics. Name tents for the participants should be made by folding a piece of paper so it will stand on its own.

Step 2

- Immediately after completion of the language arts English program philosophy, disseminate it to the language arts English staff and building administrators throughout the school district for their input. Grade- and department-level meetings should be organized by the building principals to peruse the program philosophy developed by the committee.

- A timeline for return of the program philosophy with additions, corrections, or deletions from noncommittee language arts English staff and administrators is one week.

Step 3

- After the language arts English program philosophy is returned to the curriculum director, the original language arts English program committee should reassemble to consider the additions, corrections, and/or deletions that are suggested by noncommittee language arts English staff and administrators.

Step 4

- The completed language arts English program philosophy is now ready to be given to the school superintendent and board of education for approval.

- After approval by the school superintendent and board of education, the language arts English program philosophy is given to the language arts English writing committee responsible for writing the language arts English program scope and sequence, program goals, objectives, learning outcomes, and authentic tasks.

The step-by-step process should be used to develop a program philosophy, followed by the same procedure to develop a program rationale statement (see the following illustration of the Process for Developing a Program Philosophy and Rationale Statement, which represents this top-down as well as bottom-up process).

Process for Developing a Program Philosophy and Rationale Statement

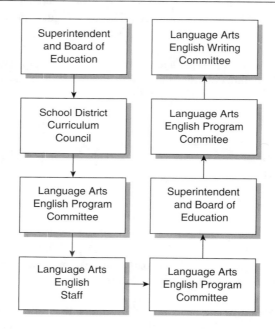

The process heightens commitment by the district language arts English staff, building administrators, central administration, and the board of education to the language arts English program.

SAMPLE LANGUAGE ARTS ENGLISH PROGRAM PHILOSOPHY[2]

Learning is a complex process of discovery, cooperation, and inquiry, and is facilitated by the language arts English program. The language processes of listening, speaking, reading, writing, viewing, and representing are interrelated and interdependent. Language is not only systematic and rule-governed, but also dynamic and evolving, facilitating communication with others and flexibility of meaning. Through interaction with the social, cultural, intellectual, emotional, and physical components of the environment, the learner acquires language developmentally along a continuum.

Language learning thrives when learners are engaged in meaningful use of language. The process of constructing meaning is influenced by the learners' previous knowledge, attitudes, experiences, and abilities. All forms of communication, oral and written, expressive and receptive, are equally valuable. The language arts English program utilizes an integrated approach that treats skills as part of all subject areas. Through the study of language, literature, and media, students broaden their experience, weigh personal values against those of others, become appreciative of the past, sensitive to the present, and inquisitive about the future.

The language arts English program accommodates each learner's abilities, interests, and background by allowing for a range of learning styles, teaching styles, instructional strategies, and resources. The program supports a classroom environment that encourages mutual respect, risk taking, and experimentation. Effective evaluation is an integral part of the learning process. Continual evaluation that encompasses both process and product and both cognitive and affective domains allows each learner to take ownership of and responsibility for learning. The learner is already processing information and constructing meaning when formal schooling begins and continues to refine the processes of communication throughout the years of formal education and beyond.

SAMPLE LANGUAGE ARTS ENGLISH PROGRAM RATIONALE STATEMENT[3]

The language skills and processes developed through the language arts English program are central to successful achievement in all subject areas and equip students with skills necessary to pursue learning throughout life. Students who read, write, speak, represent, view, and listen with intelligence, empathy, respect, and discrimination will develop the skills in thinking and communication, as well as the attitudes and knowledge that will prepare them for active participation in a complex society.

The language arts English program allows students to better understand themselves and others. The reading and study of literature enhance the aesthetic, imaginative, creative, and affective aspects of a person's development. Literature preserves and extends the imaginative power of individuals. It allows young people to explore imaginatively the places where they live and provides them with an understanding of cultural heritage and a historical perspective, exposing them to points of view other than the present and personal.

- Through fiction, the reader has the power to be transported in time and place, to experience vicariously places, people, and events otherwise unavailable.
- Through poems, the reader may achieve heightened perceptions of the world, sharpened senses, clarified thoughts, and broadened emotions.
- Through drama, the participant continually renews a sense of the vitality and complexity of human actions.
- Through nonfiction, the reader accesses a wide range of possibilities, opinions, and interpretations.

The electronic media provide a similar range of possibilities and furnish material for experience and study. In addition, the study of literature and of media provides models of effective and varied language use for students to draw upon in their own compositions.

The language arts English program encourages students to develop meaning, both through active response to others' work and through their own speaking and writing. Through speaking and writing, students learn to clarify thought, emotion, and experience, and to share these ideas, emotions, and experiences with others. Like reading, writing is a source or pleasure, enjoyment, and knowledge. It is a way to experience the delight and wonder of everyday life.

Writing proves the opportunity for careful organization of one's picture of reality and stimulates development of the precision, clarity, and imagination required for effective communication. In this way, writing is socially valuable, one of the ways individuals engage in and contribute to the activities and knowledge of society. Writing is personally valuable, and is also an important means of learning within this program and all other subject areas. It allows students to create personal meaning out of the information offered in and out of school.

Education today increasingly emphasizes evaluation and analysis skills, critical thinking, problem-solving strategies, organizing and reference skills, synthesis, application of ideas, creativity, decision making, and communication skills through a variety of modes. All these skills and processes are based in language use; all are the material of a language program; all are developed through the language arts English program at Anytown School District, U.S.A.

METHODS FOR CHOOSING TEACHER REPRESENTATION

The five methods for choosing teacher representation for curriculum development have advantages and disadvantages. Discussion of each method of selection and recommendations as to when it should be used follow.

Voluntary

The advantages of the voluntary method are that

- people who volunteer are interested in the program
- the use of volunteers is an open, democratic process

The disadvantages of this method are that

- incompetents may volunteer
- calling for volunteers may indicate unimportance of the task

Recommended use:

- when everyone is acceptable

Rotation

The advantages of the rotation method are that

- all possible participants can eventually be involved in curriculum development
- rotating eliminates the need for selection

The disadvantages of this method are that

- there is little or no continuity
- there is an assumption that all eligible participants have equal ability

Recommended use:

- when the rotating membership will not hinder the development of an acceptable process or product

Evolvement

The advantages of the evolvement method are that

- it produces leadership from the group
- cooperation from committee members is high because they choose the leader or representative through their own process

Disadvantages of this method are that

- the evolvement process is feasible only in a long-term situation
- emerged leaders exist without being recognized as authority

Recommended use:

- when determining who the most competent teachers are in curriculum development

Peer Selection

The advantages of the peer selection method are that

- committee members feel that they have control over their own destiny
- cooperation is more likely

The disadvantages of this method are that

- committee representatives may be chosen for the wrong reasons
- groups do not always know the kind of leadership or representation they need

Recommended use:

- when the group has maturity and experience

Administrative Selection

The advantages of the administrative selection method are that

- it tends to legitimize a committee member's position
- administrators generally know who the best qualified people are

The disadvantages of this method are that

- administrators may not know who the best qualified people are for curriculum development
- it could have negative implications if the selections were based on politics rather than reason

Recommended use:

- when peer selection is not practical

The main characteristic of the Dialogue Technique is that participants in the process are expected to rely more on dialogue to make decisions and less on individual preparation.

- Participants do not deal with content decision making until they are in the actual development process with other participants.
- The dialogue approach gives participants the opportunity to listen to other views that will either contradict or support their positions.
- The dialogue approach gives participants the opportunity to acquire ownership of a group product.

The Delphi Technique is a method for reaching consensus without the need for face-to-face meetings of all participants.

- Each member of the program committee writes a philosophy statement that they submit to the curriculum director.
- The philosophy statement written by each committee member is copied and distributed to all members on the program committee.
- Each committee member reviews the written philosophy statements and indicates which ones are germane.
- The curriculum director places the philosophy statements into two columns, one for those that are mostly agreed upon and one for those for which general agreement was not found.
- The most-agreed-upon philosophy statements are resubmitted to committee members and the process repeated until consensus is reached.

The Fishbowl Technique is one where representatives from each of a large number of subgroups meet to reach consensus on a list of philosophy statements.

- Subgroups of six to eight participants meet and develop a philosophy statement.
- One elected representative from each subgroup meets with representatives from the other groups, who will bring their own group's philosophy statement.
- The representatives sit in a circle facing each other while all others remain seated outside the circle.
- Representatives within the circle discuss each of the subgroup's philosophy statements until consensus is reached.

The Telstar Technique is similar to the Fishbowl Technique but differs in the method of involving all committee members and their degree of involvement.

- The large group is divided into subgroups with each group representing specific grade level groupings (e.g., primary grades, intermediate grades, middle level or junior high school, and senior high school).
- Two representatives are elected from each group to represent that group and bring their respective group's completed philosophy statement to the group of all representatives.
- Each two-member delegation may be joined by a small advisory committee from its constituency.
- Any member of an advisory committee can stop the discussion at any time to meet with his or her representatives regarding the issue at hand.
- This procedure continues until a general consensus among all representatives is reached.

The Nominal Group Technique is a process that encourages divergence by individuals.

- A small group convenes to focus on a program philosophy. Members of the group work on an identified task, which is to develop a program philosophy, in the presence of each other but without any immediate interaction.
- Once the task of developing a program philosophy is explained by the curriculum director, group members are given time (20 to 30 minutes), during which each individual will write a program philosophy.
- After the time has expired, the committee members present the program philosophies one at a time. The program philosophies are posted. No discussion of alternative philosophies takes place until all program philosophies have been disclosed.
- Following disclosure, committee members rank the program philosophies presented and start the process over, considering the top three program philosophies.
- After individual committee members have chosen and modified one of the three program philosophies, one is selected by the committee to be adopted as the program philosophy.
- A disadvantage of the process is that during the initial brainstorming no interaction exists for one's idea to inspire another. However, because committee members know that each member is developing a program philosophy and that everyone's philosophy will be displayed, the competitive pressure establishes impetus.

NOTES

1. Excerpts from *Outcome-Based Education*: *Developing Programs Through Strategic Planning* (1993) by Floyd Boschee and Mark Baron (pp. 49–79) were used for most of the content in Appendix B. Permission granted by Rowman & Littlefield Education, Lanham, Maryland.

2. The language arts English program philosophy statement was excerpted from the *Language Arts English Primary-Graduation Curriculum Guide*. (1992). Victoria, BC: Canada, Ministry of Education, p. 12.

3. The language arts English rationale statement was excerpted from the *Language Arts English Primary-Graduation Curriculum Guide*. (1992). Victoria, BC: Canada, Ministry of Education, p. 13.

APPENDIX C

*Developing a Scope and Sequence,
Program Goals, Objectives, Learning
Outcomes, and Authentic Tasks*[1]

To make a scope and sequence for a program, program goals, objectives for the program goals, learning outcomes for the objectives, and authentic tasks for the learning outcomes (practical and results-centered) for students, they must be correlated with the district's philosophy, vision, mission, exit (graduation) outcomes, and the program's philosophy and rationale statement.

The following presents procedures for developing these program elements.

THE COMMITTEE STRUCTURE

To develop a scope and sequence, program goals, objectives, learning outcomes, and authentic tasks for any school program, a subject area writing committee must be established. The steps for structuring the committee, along with responsibilities, follow.

Step 1

- The writing committee is selected by and from the program committee members. It must be made up of teachers representing all grade levels (K–12) and preferably two staff members from each grade grouping: primary, intermediate, middle level or junior high school, and high school. In smaller school districts, one teacher per three-grade/course level is satisfactory as long as there is feedback from those teaching the other grade/course levels.

- A building principal or designee from the elementary, middle level or junior high school, and senior high school must be represented on the committee.

- The school district curriculum director or designee should serve as chairperson and be responsible for organizing and directing the activities of the writing committee.

- The school district's board of education must be apprised by the board curriculum committee about the process used to write curricula.

- The writing committee work space must be in a comfortable environment: comfortable work seats, tables to spread their papers out on, good acoustics, access to the district's curriculum lab containing sample courses of study and program textbooks, and clerical assistance.

- The ideal time to develop and write the program scope and sequence, program goals, objectives, learning outcomes, and authentic tasks is after the school year is completed. One week to ten days is a normal timeline for a writing committee to complete the writing exercise for a program or subject area.

- Reasonable stipends or an extended contract should be given to members of the writing committee.

- All writing committee members must understand and be able to write meaningful program goals and objectives.

- The writing committee must be informed that the process for developing a course of study—the language arts program, for example—entails the following sequential tasks.

   1. Review and use the school district's philosophy, vision, mission, and exit (graduation) outcomes for developing a course of study for the specified program.

   2. Review and use the specified program philosophy and rationale statement developed by the language arts English program committee for developing a course of study for the language arts English program.

   3. Develop a language arts English program scope-and-sequence matrix for the K–12 grade levels (for an example, see "Sample Scope-and-Sequence Matrix for the Objectives of a Language Arts English Program" ["Matrix"]).

   4. Develop language arts English program goals (usually seven to nine) that are driven by the exit (graduation) outcomes (see Matrix).

   5. Develop language arts English program objectives (usually six to nine) for each program goal (see Matrix).

   6. Develop language arts English program learning outcomes for the objectives (i.e., primary, elementary intermediate, middle level or junior high, and high school (see Matrix).

   7. Develop language arts English program authentic tasks for the learning outcomes (see Matrix).

   8. Develop criterion-referenced test items for the developed program (curriculum). If this is not possible, an item analysis of the standardized tests used should be made.

9. Correlate the program scope and sequence, program goals, objectives, learning outcomes, and authentic tasks with textbooks and learning materials.

10. Include learning materials for each learning outcome and authentic task.

The Dialogue Technique (see Appendix B) should be used to guide the language arts English writing committee. Also, a taxonomy-of-thinking guide is useful in developing new programs (see "Taxonomy of Thinking" for categories and cue words).

Step 2

• After the program scope and sequence, program goals, objectives, learning outcomes, and authentic tasks have been written, they must be distributed to all language arts English teachers and building administrators throughout the school district for additions, corrections, and/or deletions during the school year. Teachers and administrators should be given four to six weeks to return the document to the curriculum director or designee.

• During the four- to six-week district-wide review period for the program scope and sequence, program goals, objectives, learning outcomes, and authentic tasks, grade-level and department meetings at the building level must be utilized to peruse the document. Members of the writing committee should be used as consultants (to provide clarification) at the grade-level and department meetings.

Step 3

• After receiving the corrected program documents from district-wide noncommittee language arts English grade- and course-level teachers and administrators, the curriculum director (or designee) must reassemble the writing committee to consider the additions, corrections, and/or deletions suggested.

Step 4

• After the language arts English program course of study (curriculum resource guide) is completed with suitable additions, corrections, and/or deletions suggested, the document should be given to the school superintendent and the school board curriculum committee for presentation to the board of education for district-wide adoption and implementation.

Step 5

• Once the language arts English program course of study (curriculum resource guide) is adopted, a textbook review committee, encompassing members from the language arts English writing committee, is selected by that committee. Membership must include one person representing each grade and course level.

• Members of the textbook review committee must evaluate and rank each language arts English series using a similar textbook selection guide from the various publishing companies for their grade level.

TAXONOMY OF THINKING

CATEGORIES	CUE WORDS	
KNOWLEDGE		
Recall Remembering previously learned information	Cluster Define Label List Match Memorize Name Observe	Outline Recall Recognize Record Recount State
COMPREHENSION		
Translate Grasping the meaning	Cite Describe Document Explain Express Give examples Identify	Locate Paraphrase Recognize Report Review Summarize Tell
APPLICATION		
Generalize Using learning in new and concrete situations	Analyze Dramatize Frame How to Illustrate Imagine Imitate	Manipulate Organize Sequence Show/Demonstrate Solve Use
ANALYSIS		
Break Down/Discover Breaking down an idea into component parts so that it may be more easily understood	Analyze Characterize Classify/Categories Compare/Contrast Dissect Distinguish/Differentiate Examine	Infer Map Outline/No format given Relates to Select Survey
SYNTHESIS		
Compose Putting together to form a new whole	Combine Compose Construct Design Develop Emulate Formulate Hypothesize	Imagine/Speculate Invent Plan Produce Propose Revise
EVALUATION		
Judge Judging value for a given purpose	Appraise Argue Assess Compare/Pros/Cons Consider Criticize Evaluate	Justify Judge Prioritize/Rank Recommend Support Value

ANY SCHOOL DISTRICT NO. 3
Any Town, USA

LANGUAGE ARTS ENGLISH TEXTBOOK SELECTION GUIDE

_____	_____	_____
(Textbook)	(Publishing Company)	(Grade Level)

Rate each characteristic listed for the textbook on a scale of 1 to 5. Circle your choice and total your ratings to obtain a single overall measure for each textbook reviewed.

Content   Low   High

1. Matches the program objective   1   2   3   4   5
2. Presents up-to-date, accurate information   1   2   3   4   5
3. Avoids stereotyping by race, ethnicity,   1   2   3   4   5
    and gender
4. Stimulates student interest   1   2   3   4   5

Organization and Style

1. Is clearly written   1   2   3   4   5
2. Uses language and style appropriate for   1   2   3   4   5
    students
3. Develops a logical sequence   1   2   3   4   5
4. Contains useful practical exercises   1   2   3   4   5
5. Provides thorough reviews and summaries   1   2   3   4   5
6. Includes clearly outlined table of   1   2   3   4   5
    contents and index
7. Includes helpful student aids such as   1   2   3   4   5
    illustrations, charts, etc.
8. Provides practical teacher aids such as   1   2   3   4   5
    lesson plans, test questions, etc.

Physical Features

1. Has attractive cover   1   2   3   4   5
2. Presents up-to-date, interesting   1   2   3   4   5
    illustrations and photographs
3. Has well-designed page layout   1   2   3   4   5
4. Uses clear type appropriate for students   1   2   3   4   5
5. Has durable binding   1   2   3   4   5

Readability Level _____

Sub Totals = _____

Total = _____

Evaluator _____   Grade Level/Subject _____

• The entire language arts English staff should consider for review the three highest-ranked textbook series selected by the textbook review committee.

• The language arts English program scope and sequence, program goals, objectives, learning outcomes, and authentic tasks should be submitted to the three highest-ranked publishing companies selected by the textbook review committee for their review and presentation to the district-wide language arts English staff.

• The presentations by the three selected publishing company representatives should be scheduled during the school year, preferably with no more than one presentation each day.

• All language arts English staff and school principals must be invited to attend. Voting rights are granted to only those who attend all three presentations by the publishing company representatives.

• The textbook series preferred by a majority of staff for the language arts English program must be submitted, with rationale for the selection and cost to the district, to the school superintendent and the school board curriculum committee for presentation to the school board for adoption.

Step 6

• Appropriate in-service activities must be planned for the language arts English staff to accommodate the newly developed language arts English course of study (curriculum resource guide). Some in-service activities may need to take place before the program is implemented and some should take place after teachers have implemented the program.

Step 7

• Evaluation of the language arts English program must be an ongoing process and in-flight corrections should be made until the next 5-year cycle. The curriculum director should have expertise in program (curriculum) evaluation.

The step-by-step process should be used to develop a course of study (curriculum resource guide) for all programs in the public schools. As illustrated in "A Process for Developing a Course of Study for the Language Arts English Program," this top-down, bottom-up model will engage the process of planning, implementing, and evaluating in such a way that the work of content experts—the teachers—is facilitated.

The process described will consolidate the efforts of staff, district administrators, and the board of education. Teachers, especially, will be advocates of a program if the process permits them to be the decision makers.

A Process for Developing a Course of Study for the Language Arts English Program

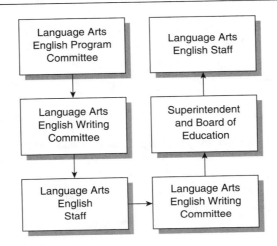

SAMPLES OF PROGRAM SCOPE AND SEQUENCE, PROGRAM GOAL, EXIT OUTCOMES MET, OBJECTIVES, LEARNING OUTCOMES, AND AUTHENTIC TASKS[2]

The following are examples of a scope-and-sequence matrix, a program goal, objectives for the program goal, learning outcomes for the objectives, and authentic tasks for the learning outcomes of a language arts English curriculum. The program goal is driven by exit (graduation) outcomes, and the objectives, which constitute the program goal illustrated, are given specific implementation direction (scope and sequence) at the proposed groupings of primary, elementary intermediate, middle level or junior high, and high school.

Continue on to the program goal and outcomes that follow.

Program Goal 1[3]

To develop the knowledge, skills, and processes needed to communicate effectively by listening, speaking, reading, writing, viewing, and representing.

Exit Outcomes Met

1. A purposeful thinker who
   - uses strategies to form concepts, make decisions, and solve problems
   - applies a variety of integrated processes including critical and creative thinking to accomplish complex tasks

Sample Scope-and-Sequence Matrix for the Objectives of a Language Arts English Program

P EI ML/JH HS	These indicate the proposed groupings, which are primary, elementary intermediate, middle level/junior high, and high school.
O	Indicates an orientation stage. Preparatory activities are undertaken prior to the explicit teaching and learning activities suggested in the learning outcomes related to the objective. Refer to learning outcomes at the next stage if appropriate.
E	Indicates an emphasis stage. Learning outcomes are suggestions in this course of study (curriculum resource guide) as examples of appropriate authentic tasks (activities) and observable behaviors. Explicit teaching and learning activities are expected.
M	Indicates a maintenance stage. Provisions are made to reinforce learning outcomes and authentic tasks related to the objective.

- evaluates the effectiveness of mental strategies through meaningful reflection
- demonstrates flexibility, persistence, and a sense of ethical considerations

2. A self-directed learner who
    - directs own learning
    - sets well-defined goals and manages the process of achieving them
    - acquires, organizes, and uses information
    - initiates learning activities in the pursuit of individual interests
    - applies technology to specific tasks
    - applies realistic self-appraisal in selecting the content, method, and pace for learning
    - integrates knowledge and skills in both familiar and new situations

3. An effective communicator who
    - conveys messages through a variety of methods and materials
    - adapts messages to various audiences and purposes
    - engages the intended audience to understand and respond
    - receives and interprets the communication of others

4. A responsible citizen who
    - understands diversity and the interdependence of people in local and global communities
    - demonstrates a respect for human differences
    - makes informed decisions
    - exercises leadership on behalf of the common good

Continue with the objectives that follow.

Objectives	P	EI	ML/JH	SH
Students will be able to				
1.1 Identify reasons for communicating	E	E	E	E
1.2 Communicate ideas with clarity and precision	E	E	E	E
1.3 Experience satisfaction and confidence in the communication skills and processes	E	E	E	E
1.4 Produce, explore, and extend ideas and information	E	E	E	E
1.5 Read and examine independently, by choosing appropriate strategies and processes	O	E	E	E
1.6 Comprehend that the communication skills and processes are interrelated avenues for constructing meaning	E	E	M	M

Continue with the learning outcomes and authentic tasks that follow.

Learning Outcomes and Authentic Tasks for a Language Arts English Program

Objective 1.1: Students will be able to identify reasons for communicating.

Primary Grades

Students will be able to

1.1.1 Recognize why they are communicating

Authentic task: Students will express feelings, solve problems, or confirm the meaning of a message.

1.1.2 Discuss the purposes of communicating

Authentic task: Students will make a classroom chart on "Why We Read."

1.1.3 Plan and lead classroom activities

Authentic task: Students will chair news time, act as spokesperson for a small group, or introduce a visitor.

1.1.4 Listen to and follow directions to perform a new activity

Authentic task: Students will playact a new game.

1.1.5 Choose to read for a variety of purposes

Authentic task: Students will read for enjoyment, to find new ideas, or to confirm ideas.

1.1.6 Choose to write for a variety of purposes

Authentic task: Students will write to request information, to express gratitude, or for entertainment.

1.1.7 Compose notes and lists to themselves

Authentic task: Students will write a list of telephone numbers or a reminder note to return library books.

1.1.8 Engage in prewriting discussion

Authentic task: Students will choose a topic, focus ideas, or clarify purpose.

1.1.9 Use a grid, chart, graph, cluster, or web to organize information

Authentic task: Students will organize collected facts from researching an animal.

Elementary Intermediate Grades

Students will be able to

1.1.10 Describe the broad purposes that are common to communication skills and processes

Authentic task: Students will advise, command, direct, entertain, inform, persuade, or socialize.

1.1.11 Arrange their own specific purposes that identify the desired result and focus attention

Authentic task: Students will tune in to the radio news to get information on a specific item.

1.1.12 Arrange their own purposes for listening

Authentic task: Students will listen attentively to a poem to form sensory images.

1.1.13 Organize their own purposes for speaking

Authentic task: Students will make a speech to express a personal point of view.

1.1.14 Determine their own purposes for reading

Authentic task: Students will read a selection to answer specific questions.

1.1.15 Determine their own purposes for writing

Authentic task: Students will record observations to write a science report.

1.1.16 Arrange their own purposes for viewing

Authentic task: Students will analyze TV commercials to identify persuasive techniques.

1.1.17 Determine their own purposes for representing

Authentic task: Students will develop a diagram to organize similarities when comparing two opinions.

1.1.18 Identify the purposes of other people's communication

Authentic task: Students will recognize propaganda and the desire to convince in a biased presentation.

1.1.19 Recognize the purposes of various media

Authentic task: Students will infer that television aims to entertain, to inform, and to persuade.

Middle Level/Junior High

Students will be able to

1.1.20 Recognize the broad purposes that are common to communication skills and processes

Authentic task: Students will do controlling, imaging, informing, and socializing.

1.1.21 Identify the audience to which communication is addressed

Authentic task: Students will communicate with adults, friends, or relatives.

1.1.22 Recognize and focus attention on the desired result of communication

Authentic task: Students will write a letter of complaint or speak to a group in order to raise funds for a project.

1.1.23 Engage in preparatory activities for listening, speaking, and viewing

Authentic task: Students will recall prior knowledge of the topic or predict what could be learned about a topic.

1.1.24 Establish a purpose for speaking

Authentic task: Students will give a formal speech to persuade a group to accept a personal point of view.

1.1.25 Create a purpose for representing

Authentic task: Students will use a chart to show similarities of themes in American literature.

1.1.26 Recognize persuasive techniques

Authentic task: Students will recognize bias, propaganda, use of connotation, and use of emotive language.

High School

Students will be able to

1.1.27 Employ language strategies and processes that are most likely to elicit the desired results

Authentic task: Students will choose between a telephone call and a letter to deal with business.

1.1.28 Identify the audience to which a communication is to be directed

Authentic task: Students will choose peers, adults, or special interest groups as the appropriate audience.

1.1.29 Select the desired result of a communication

Authentic task: Students will write a letter of application or a student council letter of request to the principal.

1.1.30 Appraise the difference between active and passive listening by discussing which activities require no effort on the part of the listener and which will demand full attention

Authentic task: Students will decide that background music is passive listening, and listening for a main idea is active listening.

1.1.31 Develop and apply criteria to evaluate what is heard

Authentic task: Students will utilize criteria agreed to by the class, such as the main idea, details, and examples to be applied to class speeches.

1.1.32 Identify main ideas

Authentic task: Students will write down the main ideas after hearing a passage read or will paraphrase a speaker's message orally or in written form.

1.1.33 Distinguish fact from opinion

Authentic task: Students will, after listening to a reading, list orally or in writing what is fact and what is opinion.

1.1.34 Recognize the influence of the listener's bias or perception

Authentic task: Students will examine possible preconceived ideas on a topic before the class hears a speech.

1.1.35 Recognize a speaker's purpose and bias

Authentic task: Students will peruse differences between speeches from the opposing sides on an issue such as capital punishment.

Each program goal should also list a wide variety of resources, accessible to the staff, to help students accomplish the exit outcomes. Examples of resources include textbooks, textbook activities, novels, nonfiction books, anthologies, collections, handbooks, dramas, selected readings from reserved material in the library or classroom, printed handouts, kits, periodicals, transparency sets, video recordings, audio recordings, and computer software. The language arts English staff should have an updated inventory of materials available that lists where each is located, such as in the classroom, departmental media center, school media center, district media center, regional media center, or state media center.

The program (curriculum) development process described is a design-down, deliver-up model (see "Design-Down, Deliver-Up Model"). Samples of scope and sequence, program goal, objectives for the program goal, learning outcomes, and authentic tasks provided should enable a school district to develop a performance-based education program. Once a program is developed, teachers can easily develop unit plans and daily lesson plans for their students.

INDICATORS OF EFFECTIVE CURRICULUM DEVELOPMENT[4]

How can a developed and implemented curriculum be measured for effectiveness? The ten indicators that follow should be considered when measuring curriculum effectiveness.

Design-Down, Deliver-Up Model

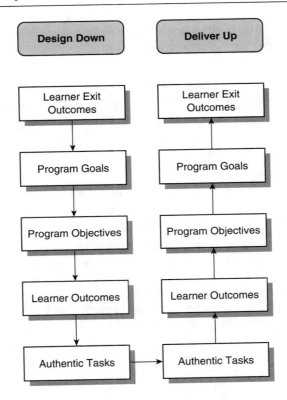

1. *Vertical curriculum continuity:* The course of study reflects a K–12 format that enables teachers to have quick and constant access to what is being taught in the grade levels below and above them. Also, upward spiraling prevents undue or useless curricular repetition.

2. *Horizontal curriculum continuity:* The course of study developed provides content and objectives that are common to all classrooms of the same grade level. Also, daily lesson plans reflect a commonality for the same grade level.

3. *Instruction based on curriculum:* Lesson plans are derived from the course of study, and curriculum materials used are correlated with the content, objectives, and authentic tasks developed.

4. *Curriculum priority:* Philosophical and financial commitments are evident. Clerical assistance is provided and reasonable stipends are paid to teachers for work during the summer months. In addition, curriculum topics appear on school board agendas, administrative meeting agendas, and building-staff meeting agendas.

5. *Broad involvement:* Buildings in the district have teacher representatives on the curricular committees; elementary, middle level or junior high, and high school principals (or

designees) are represented; and school board members are apprised of and approve the course of study.

6. *Long-range planning:* Each program in the district is included in the 5-year sequence and review cycle. Also, a philosophy of education and theory of curriculum permeate the entire school district.

7. *Decision-making clarity:* Controversies that occur during the development of a program center on the nature of the decision, and not on who makes the decision.

8. *Positive human relations:* All participating members are willing to risk disagreeing with anyone else; however, communication lines are not allowed to break down. Also, the initial thoughts about the curriculum come from teachers, principals, and the curriculum leader.

9. *Theory-into-practice approach:* The district philosophy, vision, mission, exit (graduation) outcomes, program philosophy, rationale statement, program goals, program objectives, learning outcomes, and authentic tasks are consistent and recognizable.

10. *Planned change:* Tangible evidence shows that the internal and external publics accept the developed program course of study for the school district. The process of developing a course of study for each program or discipline in a school district is no longer one of determining how to do it, but one of determining how to do it better. Developing a program's course of study assures continuity of instruction across grade levels and, subsequently, allows a smoother transition from one grade level to the next. It is a road map for staff and students in a district.

NOTES

1. Excerpts from *Outcome-Based Education: Developing Programs Through Strategic Planning* (1993; pp. 49–79) by Floyd Boschee and Mark Baron were used for most of the content in Appendix C. Permission was granted by Rowman & Littlefield Education, Lanham, Maryland.

2. The language arts English program scope and sequence, program goal, objectives, and learning outcomes were excerpted from the *Language Arts English Primary-Graduation Curriculum Guide.* (1992). Victoria, BC: Canada, Ministry of Education, pp. 18–30.

3. The program goal listed was excerpted from the *Language Arts English Primary-Graduation Curriculum Guide.* (1992). Victoria, BC: Canada, Ministry of Education, pp. 19–27. The nine goals for the language arts English program are as follows:

- Program Goal 1 develops the knowledge, skills, and processes needed to communicate effectively by listening, speaking, reading, writing, and representing.
- Program Goal 2 develops knowledge, understanding, and appreciation of language and how it is used.
- Program Goal 3 develops knowledge, understanding, and appreciation of a wide variety of literary genres and media forms.
- Program Goal 4 develops knowledge, understanding, and appreciation of American and other world literature.
- Program Goal 5 develops and extends knowledge of self, the world, and our multicultural heritage through language, literature, and media.

- Program Goal 6 extends capacity for creative thought and expression within the context of language, literature, and media.
- Program Goal 7 extends capacity for critical thought and expression within the context of language, literature, and media.
- Program Goal 8 develops the wide variety of strategies for learning.
- Program Goal 9 develops attributes of wonder, curiosity, independence, and interdependence necessary for lifelong learning.

4. The ten indicators of effective curriculum development were excerpted from Bradley, L. H. (1985). *Curriculum leadership and development handbook.* Englewood Cliffs, NJ: Prentice Hall.

Author Index

Subject Index

ABOUT THE AUTHORS

Allan A. Glatthorn is Distinguished Research Professor of Education (Emeritus) at East Carolina University, Greenville, North Carolina. He formerly was a member of the faculty at the University of Pennsylvania Graduate School of Education. During his 55 years of working in education, he has served as a teacher, principal, supervisor, and professor. He is the author of more than 20 books in the fields of curriculum and supervision. He has consulted with more than 200 school districts, assisting them in developing and implementing their curricula.

Floyd Boschee has an extensive background in teaching and educational leadership. He has served as a teacher, coach, and school administrator in the public schools in North Dakota, and as professor and chairman of departments of education at the collegiate level. He is a Professor Emeritus in the Division of Educational Administration, School of Education, at The University of South Dakota and a former school board member of the Vermillion School District, Vermillion, South Dakota.

He has published many articles in major educational journals and previously authored or coauthored seven textbooks: *Grouping Equals Growth*; *Effective Reading Programs: The Administrator's Role*; *Outcome-Based Education: Developing Programs Through Strategic Planning*; *Authentic Assessment: The Key to Unlocking Student Success*; *Special and Compensatory Programs: The Administrator's Role*; *School Bond Success: A Strategy for Building America's Schools*; and *Planning for Technology: A Guide for School Administrators, Technology Coordinators, and Curriculum Directors*.

Bruce M. Whitehead is an author and international consultant in the areas of educational curriculum, technology, and administration. He also serves as an elementary principal for School District 4 in Missoula, Montana, as well as a Governmental Relations Specialist for the International Reading Association. In addition, he is an Adjunct Professor for the University of Montana and a member of the university's School of Education Advisory Board.

His career includes appointments to numerous national and international committees as well as serving as president of the Montana State Reading Association and president of the Montana Association of Elementary School Principals. He also served as chairman of the Montana Governor's Task Force on Technology.

As an author of six books and numerous articles in the field of education, he is a recipient of the University of Montana's highest honor, the Montana Distinguished Alumni Award. Additional honors include the International Reading Association's Presidential Service Award, NAESP's National Distinguished Principal Award, Milken Family Foundation's National Outstanding Educator Award, the John F. Kennedy Center's Award for Arts in Education, and Japan's International Mathematics Soroban Institute Award.